FRONT VIEW OF MAIN BUILDING, UNITED STATES SIGNAL STATION,
POINT BARROW, ALASKA.

Illustration painted by John Murdoch

Ethnological Results of the
POINT BARROW EXPEDITION

John Murdoch

Introduction by William W. Fitzhugh

SMITHSONIAN INSTITUTION PRESS
WASHINGTON, D.C.

© Smithsonian Institution Press 1988
Introduction

Originally published 1892
Reprinted 1988
New material for reprint edition edited by Jan Danis

Library of Congress Cataloging in Publication Data
Murdoch, John, 1852–
    Ethnological results of the Point Barrow Expedition.
    "And other documents related to the International
Polar Expedition to Point Barrow, Alaska, 1881–83."
    Reprint of works originally published 1884–1895.
    1. Eskimos—Alaska—Barrow, Point, Region.
I. International Polar Expedition to Point Barrow,
Alaska (1881–1883) II. Title. III. Title: Point
Barrow Expedition.
E99.E7M9 1987 917.98'7 87-9503

Reprinted from the Ninth Annual Report of the Bureau of Ethnology
1887-88

Cover
Scene in Ŭglaamie. Tent with natives at work.
Summer Camp. From Ray, *Report of the International Polar Expedition to Point Barrow, Alaska* (1885), facing page 38.

Frontispiece
Front view of main building, United States Signal Station, Point Barrow, Alaska, painted by John Murdoch. From Ray, *Report of the International Polar Expedition to Point Barrow, Alaska* (1885), frontispiece.

⊗ The paper in this book meets the guidelines for permanence and durability of the Committee on Production Guidelines for Book Longevity of the Council on Library Resources.

CONTENTS

PUBLISHER'S NOTE

John Murdoch's monograph, with line drawings, appearing in this volume is a photographic reprint of the first edition, which was published as pages 3–441 in the Ninth Annual Report of the Bureau of [American] Ethnology (Washington: Government Printing Office, 1892). The original pagination has been kept. Appendix 1 and Appendix 2 are field reports reset typographically from Appendix 62, "Arctic Research," pages 622–34 of volume 4, Report of the Chief Signal Officer, in Annual Report of the Secretary of War for the Year 1883 (Washington: Government Printing Office, 1884). Appendix 3 is reset typographically from pages 14–16 of "Report of the Secretary" in the Annual Report of the Smithsonian Institution for the Year 1883 (Washington: Government Printing Office, 1895). Appendix 4 through Appendix 10 are photographic reprints of pages 7–9 and 21–49 and unpaginated photographs, plates, and tables from *Report of the International Polar Expedition to Point Barrow, Alaska*, House Ex. Doc. 44, 48th Cong., 2d sess. (Washington: Government Printing Office, 1885); the original pagination has not been kept.

No attempt has been made to conform biological species names or native linguistic text material to modern usage. No errata were included in either Ray's or Murdoch's volumes, and none are noted here. However, for Appendix 2, Joseph S. Powell's relief expedition to Point Barrow occurred in 1882, not in 1883 as given in the original report title.

FOREWORD

The North Slope Borough's Inupiat Commission on History, Language, and Culture was founded to preserve and protect Inupiat culture as it has lived and changed in the northermost part of Alaska. Toward that end, we have worked to gather the data stored in the minds of our elders and to turn it into teaching materials for our schools and reference books for scholars outside our communities. We want our elders' works and deeds to have a positive influence on young Inupiat. We feel the elders' knowledge can also be used by scholars in their interpretations of Inupiat culture.

Locating and acquiring photographs, manuscripts, and printed materials dealing with the Arctic and Arctic peoples has also been a goal of the commission. While our elders' knowledge spans a broad panorama of information and skills, we recognize the need for printed works written by competent researchers outside the Inupiat culture. Perhaps the most valuable of the descriptive printed works on Barrow is John Murdoch's report.

Murdoch also collected items that have become rarities, either through inherent fragility or because they fell from normal or ceremonial use. Barrow is a particularly appropriate example here, since flu and measles epidemics had so decimated the coastal population after the turn of the century that Stefansson and Jenness both estimated a large proportion of the population of Cape Smythe by 1913 or 1914 was not native to the area but was recently resettled from interior villages. If the change in population was rapid, and if many of the knowledgable people fell to disease, coastal customs and ceremonies may well have been lost. If that is true, Murdoch's report assumes an even more significant role, one of providing a thread of continuity from the early contact period to a later historical era.

The Inupiat people of today are fortunate in being able to draw on Murdoch's work to complement the vivid and valuable memory culture of the elders. By reprinting the Murdoch report, the Smithsonian Institution is providing greater access to this unique and very important study.

The Inupiat Commission on History, Language, and Culture
North Slope Borough
P.O. Box 69
Barrow, Alaska 99723

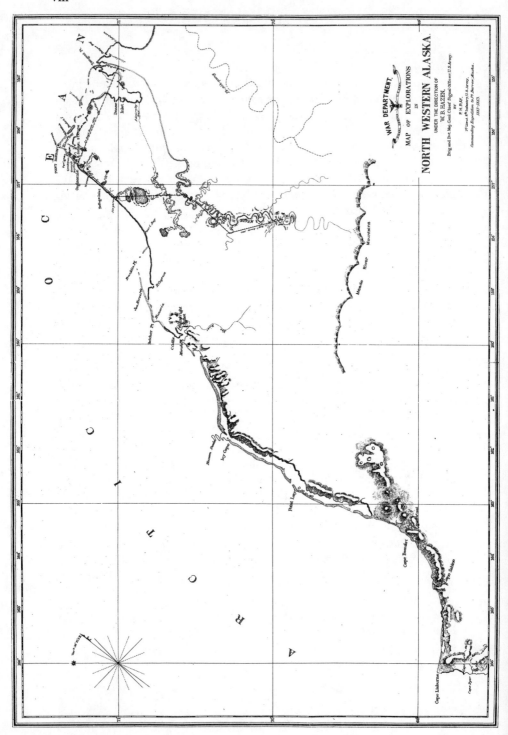

PREFACE TO THE 1987 EDITION

More than a century has passed since the International Polar Expedition to Point Barrow, Alaska, provided the world with its first comprehensive scientific account of natural history and human life at the northernmost point of mainland North America. Under the direction of Lt. Patrick Henry Ray, the expedition was probably one of the earliest interdisciplinary scientific enterprises initiated in the United States. In addition to gathering meteorological data, during their two-year residence on the shore of the Arctic Ocean members of the expedition recorded information on such diverse subjects as tidal amplitude, auroral display, earth magnetism, minerals, plants, insects, invertebrates, fish, mammals, birds, ethnology, and linguistics. The breadth of study was the direct result of a collaborative effort by the United States Signal Corps (forerunner of the Weather Bureau), an agency of the U.S. Army, and the Smithsonian Institution. The former organization was primarily interested in the weather and magnetic data, while the Smithsonian was most interested in obtaining natural history and anthropological collections from the little-known Arctic coast.

These goals were largely realized with the publication of Ray's report to Congress in 1885. In 695 pages of narrative and description, this report presents voluminous records on atmospherics and proportionally less data on natural history and anthropology. Partly this imbalance reflects the weather bias of the Signal Corps, which selected the personnel and controlled the field work. Nevertheless, the report contains important information on the history of the project, interaction with native groups, and descriptions of natural history. Ray's ethnographic sketch (Appendix 6) is a useful document, as is Murdoch's listing of artifact types. However, it was clear that a more detailed description of ethnographic collections was needed. This task fell to John Murdoch, one of the two naturalists on the expedition. With the combined assistance of his Army salary and facilities offered by the Smithsonian, Murdoch completed this task in 1887. His publication appeared in 1892 in the Ninth Annual Report of the Bureau of American Ethnology as *Ethnological Results of the Point Barrow Expedition*.

Murdoch's monograph is the only major ethnography of nineteenth-century Inupiat Eskimo culture in the Western Arctic. Strongest in its description of technology and material culture, the volume provides a relatively comprehensive view of a North Alaskan Eskimo culture at a time when many traditional features of this culture were being replaced by those of Western origin. In terms of its importance in Eskimo ethnological literature the monograph takes its place comfortably beside other nineteenth-century Smithsonian classics such as *The Central Eskimo* (Boas 1888), *The Eskimos About Bering Strait* (Nelson 1899), and *Ethnology of the Ungava District* (Turner 1894). For these reasons it has been selected for reprinting in Classics of Smithsonian Anthropology.

Murdoch's monograph can best be used as a research tool when seen in the context of the larger Point Barrow expedition of which he was a part. Consequently, the Introduction contains his personal letters from the field, other unpublished material, and photographs made by the expedition, which are now preserved at the National Archives and the Smithsonian's National Anthropological Archives. In addition, this volume contains several appendixes. The first three are interim field reports: Ray's (1884) account of the first year's work, the report of the Army's relief expedition (Powell 1884), and the Smithsonian's perspective. Also reprinted, as appendixes 4 through 10, are significant parts of the final report of the Point Barrow expedition, which, owing to its limited circulation, is relatively inaccessible today. These parts are the Chief Signal Officer's instructions, Ray's narrative, his ethnographic sketch, a census of the village of Utkiavik (Appendix 7), data on stature, weight, and craniometry (Appendix 8), vocabularies (Appendix 9), and artifact plates (Appendix 10). These documents amplify and augment Murdoch's monograph, producing a nearly complete compendium of nineteenth-century ethnology of the Point Barrow Eskimo culture, lacking only Simpson's report from 1852–54 (Simpson 1875).

Now in the late twentieth century, it has become increasingly important that such a compendium be more widely available. During the past two decades, the people of Point Barrow have experienced a revolutionary change in their situation with respect to the outside world. This is the second such revolution that they have encountered, the first being the appearance of whaling vessels in the 1850s carrying white men eager to trade with the Point Barrow people and equally eager to hunt the great whales that passed close to their village each spring. Like their first encounter with white men, the mid–twentieth-century establishment of the Naval Arctic Research Laboratory and later the oil boom were not initiated by Eskimo request. While these encounters have been successively more disrupting to traditional culture, even to the point of raising questions about the right of native North Alaskans to take whales, which has been an integral part of their culture for more than one thousand years, these interactions have had both positive and negative effects.

Speaking here only to the positive effects, bodies that include native representatives now provide legal authority over certain territories and resources and deal with political, social, and economic issues. Barrow people are no longer in the position of waiting each year to see what the southerners are going to do when they show up for the summer season. In addition, new forums link North Slope people to other Alaskan Eskimos, to Canadian Inuit, and to Greenlanders. Some of them, such as the Inuit Circumpolar Conference, now have powerful voices. In cultural affairs, efforts are being made to protect Eskimo lifeways, language, traditions, and resources for future generations. Notable among these efforts are the work of the Elders Conferences, publications in native language, and art, film, and museum displays. Perhaps we are entering a phase of history in which stable growth can occur that does not threaten the lives and cultures of northern peoples. At least we may hope that Point Barrow need not experience upheavals such as occurred in the late nineteenth century when nearly the entire population of the region fell to the invasions of introduced microbes and viruses.

With the establishment of local schools and new cultural programs the people of Point Barrow and the larger North Slope have sought to provide both modern and traditional education. In like fashion, generating, preserving, and disseminating information has long been a tradition of the Smithsonian Institution. Smithsonian scientists pioneered the study of Alaskan natural history and anthropology in the decades following the purchase of Alaska in 1867. Today we enter a new era in which native Alaskans are no longer simply informants and bystanders used by outsiders intent on gaining knowledge about their land and its resources. Better educated and skilled, native peoples are increasingly judges of history and planners for their own future.

The Smithsonian holds large amounts of information on nineteenth- and twentieth-century Alaska, as do many other institutions. In collections and archives, many of these resources are yet to be rediscovered, developed, and used. As seen by the success of the recent exhibits and publications using Edward Nelson's ethnographic materials from the Bering Sea region, these resources can expand awareness of cultural and historical conditions and guide approaches and attitudes about the present and the future.

The relationship between the Smithsonian and Point Barrow created by the Ray expedition is now in its second century. During the first century the Smithsonian's role has been to gather, publish, and preserve data. We may hope that the second century will bring more active collaboration in which people from this northernmost village on the North American mainland will use museum collections and staff expertise to further their own goals. I am pleased, therefore, to begin this second century by making available a new, improved version of the monograph that was the most important result of all to come from the International Polar Expedition to Point Barrow of 1881–83 and to dedicate it to present and future generations of Point Barrow people.

Many institutions and individuals have contributed materials and assistance for this reprint. For assistance in obtaining photographs and archival materials I wish to thank staff at the National Archives, Rasmuson Library of the University of Alaska at Fairbanks, the National Anthropological Archives, and the Smithsonian Institution Archives, especially Alison Wilson, Paula Fleming, and Harry Heiss. Allison Young tracked down most of the Ray photographs in these institutions and made it possible for me to assemble the inventory. At various stages in the work I have benefited from suggestions and information provided by Susan Kaplan, Glenn Sheehan, Gregory Reinhardt, William Sturtevant, and Jean-Loup Rousselot. Information on the current status of the Ray collection was gathered under the direction of Joe Brown. Important library services were provided by Gloria Atkinson and Janette Saquet. Laurice Stewart assisted in getting the manuscript into final form for the press. To Daniel Goodwin and others at the Smithsonian Press I express gratitude for publication assistance.

William W. Fitzhugh

Top right, John Murdoch at Point Barrow, winter 1882 (National Archives 111-SC-91069); *center*, Group of Ooglamie natives at Signal Station (University of Alaska 76-857); *bottom*, Scene in Ooglamie, Alaska, June 7, 1882 (University of Alaska 76-858).

Apidow, wife, and child at Ooglamie, Alaska. (University of Alaska 76-840)

John Murdoch as librarian of the Smithsonian Institution ca. 1890. (SI 3666)

INTRODUCTION TO THE 1987 EDITION

Background to the Expedition

In early summer of 1881 a group of ten men under the command of
Lt. Patrick Henry Ray left San Francisco by boat bound for the northernmost point on the North American mainland. Their destination was
Point Barrow, Alaska, and their primary task was to make a three-
year unbroken series of weather and magnetic observations as part of
an international effort to understand weather patterns, to learn about
the causes of magnetic anomalies that plagued earlier Arctic expeditions, and to study Arctic Ocean tides, currents, and ice. Because of
the multinational control of Arctic lands, such a study had to be done
by many governments acting in coordinated fashion. Although a semblance of such coordination had existed during the Franklin search
years, when many of these anomalies were first discovered, the res-
olution of these questions called for detailed logistical and scientific
planning.

Following some years of discussion among scientists and government
officials, a course of action began to emerge at the polar conference
held in Hamburg, Germany, in October 1879. Among the matters discussed was the ideal location of observation stations, the kinds of data
to be gathered, and the equipment and standards necessary to insure
comparability of records over time and across the entire Arctic region
(see Hazen's orders and instructions in Appendix 4). The United States
agreed to establish two observation stations, one in the Eastern Arctic
and another in the Western Arctic. Both were to be located as far
north as possible to improve the value of the observations. The location
of the eastern station was to be at Lady Franklin Bay, northern Elles-
mere Island, at 81 degrees north latitude; the western station was to
be at Point Barrow, at 72 degrees north. Adolphus Greely was asked
to lead the eastern expedition. After successfully maintaining his station for two years, Greely's expedition was struck by disaster when
relief vessels failed to deliver food and supplies. Greely evacuated his
base during the third summer and found some caches to the south, but
he was forced to winter over and lost several men to starvation and
frost before being rescued by relief vessels the next summer (Greely
1886). Providentially, the scientific records survived, and the results
of the expedition were eventually published (Greely 1888).

The western station had a different history. This region of the Arctic,
previously Russian, was poorly known by comparison with the eastern
areas that had been extensively searched in the mid–nineteenth-cen-

tury decades after Franklin. The need for studies in Alaska had a large constituency in commercial, governmental, and scientific circles. These subjects were of practical interest to the whaling industry, which had lost many vessels in the dangerous ice-filled waters off Point Barrow since 1854, while government required climate, magnetic, and geographic information on its newly acquired territory. These interests dovetailed closely with the purposes of the Hamburg convention. Finally, natural scientists were interested in expanding knowledge and collections from the little-known Arctic coast.

Consequently, through the intercession of Spencer F. Baird, assistant secretary of the Smithsonian, arrangements were made for natural history work to be done as a second priority after weather and magnetic observations. Funds and equipment were to be provided by the Smithsonian for this purpose, and naturalists were to be appointed in the positions of two of the observers. Similar arrangements had been made beween the Signal Corps and the Smithsonian for studies at Lady Franklin Bay, at Kodiak Island, in the Aleutian Islands, in Bristol Bay, and at St. Michael near the mouth of the Yukon River. Although no work had been done on the Arctic coast of Alaska, some familiarity had been derived from a pioneering expedition in 1881 by a research team including Edward W. Nelson, John Muir, and Irving Rosse on board the U.S. Revenue Cutter *Corwin* (Hooper 1884). This multidiscipline penetration achieved important results in ornithology, geography, and oceanography, but natural history and ethnological studies had been restricted by the scientists' inability to spend more than brief periods on shore in several places in Siberia.

As a result of the congruence of these interests, the opportunity for long-term, land-based research by the Point Barrow expedition were ideal, and a workable organization and means of supporting the research were implemented by the various government agencies. Control of the expedition was vested in the United States Signal Corps. To insure adherence to discipline in the systematic gathering of weather and magnetic records needed for international comparison, an Army officer, Lt. Patrick Henry Ray, was given command. Ray, who later regretted his lack of prior training and experience for scientific work in the Arctic, assisted in planning the expedition under the direction of Gen. W.B. Hazen, Chief Signal Officer, obtained supplies and equipment, and took charge of hiring those personnel not already committed to the expedition by his superiors, whose judgment in this matter he grew to question (Ray [1885] 1987:lxix).

By agreement with Baird, the Smithsonian's interests were to be met by appointing one of two naturalists to the team. The Smithsonian's man was John Murdoch. Born in New Orleans on 9 July 1852, Murdoch had received his B.A. degree from Harvard University in 1873 and his M.A. degree, studying zoology at the Museum of Comparative Zoology, in 1876. At the time the Point Barrow expedition was being organized in the spring of 1881, Murdoch held a temporary appointment teaching zoology at the University of Wisconsin. Hearing of an opening for a naturalist, Murdoch applied to Baird for the position. Murdoch already had prior acquaintance with members of the Smithsonian's curatorial staff, notably zoologist Richard Rathbun. Murdoch also received favorable endorsements from one of his Wisconsin colleagues. W.A. Henry noted on 27 April 1881 in a letter to a Smithsonian friend that the expedition to be sent "to Point Barrow or some place in Alaska" required "a person of peculiar disposition and habits for such a place and my acquaintance with him leads me to think that he is the man for the place" (#15997 Secretarial Files, Smithsonian Institution Archives). In fact, Murdoch proved to be one of the most productive and dedicated members of the scientific team, and he was highly credited in Ray's final report. Certainly, Murdoch's energy, knowledge, and skills and his published reports are what distinguishes the Point Barrow expedition.

Conduct of Field Studies

Once assembled, the expedition departed from San Francisco on board the schooner *Golden Fleece* on 18 July 1881. One of the interesting features of the voyage was the brief layover at Plover Bay, Siberia, where Ray had been instructed to calibrate his solar instruments. As the vessel was about to depart Plover Bay, the *Corwin* hove into the bay, returning from its historic cruise deep into the Arctic Ocean where it had been the first vessel to land on Wrangel Island. *Corwin* personnel reported that the unusual ice-free condition of the Arctic Ocean should allow Ray's party to reach Barrow without difficulty. In addition members of the two scientific teams exchanged notes and advice. Murdoch met Nelson and Muir for the first time, and Ray acquired reindeer skin clothing purchased from Plover Bay natives and canvas tents from the *Corwin*'s emergency stores. Nelson's Eskimo sled was also transferred to Ray's party.

Upon arriving at Point Barrow a site was selected for the location of the signal station at Ooglaamie, midway between the native villages of Utkiavik (meaning "place for hunting owls" [Okakok and Kean 1981:156]) six miles to the southwest and Nuwuk at Point Barrow, eight miles to the northeast. The station needed to be as far north as possible to make suitable observations, but Ray thought it should not be too near the villages for security reasons. A further complication was that much of the coast along the west side of Elson Bay, and further south, was so low that it was periodically overridden by storm waves and ice.

Lumber and supplies were landed, and in short time a suitable building was erected. Scientific observations began 15 October. Ray noted the bewilderment of the natives upon discovering that the white men actually planned to move ashore, but soon their reserve passed and they provided boats and men that were instrumental in getting the equipment and supplies safely ashore and established in their quarters. Ray named the station "Ooglaamie," his tin-eared approximation of Utkiavik. He insisted that "Ooglaamie" appear on all official records and on all artifacts and specimens collected, even after he learned his error, a tribute to a consistent military mind. Ray demonstrated considerably more skill in the construction of the station building, which was ready for occupation in less than a month despite the onset of fall storms. The building was cramped, but it was fully satisfactory and even had an elevated observation tower and a Parrot windvane identical to the one installed on the Smithsonian tower in 1880. Murdoch's watercolor painting of the station appeared as the frontispiece to Ray's 1885 report.

Upon arrival at Point Barrow Murdoch sent a letter to his Smithsonian friend, Richard Rathbun, by way of the return voyage of the *Golden Fleece*. The letter, and Murdoch's other correspondence from the field, are preserved at the Smithsonian Institution Archives (Record Unit 7078, Richard Rathbun Papers, 1870–1918 and undated, Box 5, Folder 17). The first letter provides an interesting personal account of the voyage and Murdoch's new surroundings, including his fellow expedition members. His frustration at not being able to make collections is already apparent, a result, partly, of the rigid structure of Ray's command.

> Pacific Ocean
> lat. 58 N., long. 150 W.
>
> Monday, August 8th, 1881

My Dear Dick,

I may as well wish your fortune now as you shall have a chance to send letters back before the vessel returns, for we are to stop at St. Paul's, and should be there in a few days now. We are still out of sight of land, and have been for three weeks. With anything like good luck, we should be at Chimmak Pass by this time, but with the exception of a few hours the other day we haven't had a fair wind since we left San Francisco. Headwinds sometimes blowing hard but more often light and baffling have been our continual luck. Early in the voyage we had a good deal of clear weather but lately it has been continually foggy. We are pretty well crowded. The hold and the deck are filled with our stuff, while we are so

crowded in the cabin that we are only able to keep out the simple necessary articles and a few books. All our collecting outfit is so packed up in
cases that it will be impossible to get at any of it till we get to Pt. Barrow. I had hoped to have things so that I might do some work on the
voyage up, but the vessel is so small and we have so much material that
it is entirely out of the question. I have my shotgun out and some arsenic
and cotton, so that perhaps at Plover Bay I might be able to get hold of
some birds, perhaps the Eurynorhynchus, who knows. I have seen very
little in the way of marine life except Velellas?, and some enormous solitary Salpae? four or five inches long. A few birds, albatrosses, shear-
waters too, have followed us. We shall probably see a great many more
now in a few days as we come up to the land. Apart from the crowding
we are comfortably enough fixed. They feed us very well and by reading,
writing, eating and sleeping we manage to fill up the time. The party as a
whole is not exactly a jolly one, but we get on very well together. Smith
is the chief wet blanket–fussy old woman ready to take offense, besides
being stupid. I can't imagine how he ever came to join the party as Naturalist, for he seems to be most utterly ignorant of zoology and in fact of
everything else, except a few things Librarian in Washington. The rest of
us are pretty well informed men. Everybody has had about enough of the
sea. I don't know what our chances are of getting to Point Barrow. We
started pretty late—there's no question about that. Still the whaler who
came in just before we started, reports an unusually open season in the
Arctic. So we hope for the best. We shall stop at St. Paul only long
enough to send our letters ashore. We have already had a chance to send
home letters having spoken to a large english ship when we were about
ten days out from San Francisco. I suppose by the time this letter
reaches you, you will all be back in Washington, and I hope settled in
your new house. I hope you will write me next spring and give me all the
Washington and Eastport news. I enclose a letter for Mrs. Porter which I
wish you would please deliver for me. I have never got her post-office
address, and used to find my way up there without thinking of street or
number. Please give my kindest regards to Lena, and remember me to all
the Smithsonian people and all my Washington friends. Please tell Prof.
Baird that I shall write to him from Point Barrow, if we get there, or at
[?] from where the vessel leaves us. Please extend my congratulations
to Clark. I hope Captain Collins did get down to Gloucester finally.

> Sincerely yours
> Jack Murdoch

> Aug. 31st.
> Off Cape Lisburne Alaska—

We never went to St. Paul after all! The [?] us after we left Chimmak
Pass and we kept right on for Plover Bay. Caught a bit of fair wind, and
arrived on the 21st and stayed through the 25th before we got our observations. The day before we left, the "Corwin" came in from the Arctic
having landed on Wrangel Land. I met Nelson. He had seen 3 or 4 "spoon

bills." They say that the "Rogers" was coaling at St. Michael's. We can't find out what has become of those Germans, who went up on the "Legal Tender." There was a report that they were landed at St. Lawrence Bay, but nobody knows. The "Corwin" found the ice unusually far off the shore, so that we stand a good chance of getting to Point Barrow in a few days now. I wish I could have dredged a few days back in the Straits. The codline brought up the biggest [?] and Asadias I ever saw—a regular Eastport bottom. I got a few birds at Plover Bay, but nothing of any value. We are fairly in the Arctic, but have seen no ice—an unusually favorable season—no drawbacks, except [?] and thick weather which we continue to have.

Sept. 11th

We are discharging our supplies just beyond Cape Smyth, six miles this side of Pt. Barrow. This is a better place for the station than the point which is too low. Got here the 8th. Rough cold weather and hard time landing cargo.

Murdoch also sent an optimistic letter to his mentor, Spencer Baird, at the Smithsonian:

Cape Smyth, Alaska,
Sept. 15th 1881

Professor S.F. Baird,
Dear Sir:
We have arrived at this place and established our station here instead of Point Barrow itself, which is only six miles distant, as it is a mere sandspit, and this is the last high land. We had a long and tedious passage up from San Francisco, and were so crowded in a small vessel that it was impossible to do any collecting on the way up. The supplies were packed up in such a way that it was impossible to get out the dredge or any of our collecting implements. I have made careful notes all the way up, but that is all I have been able to do. Since our arrival we have been exceedingly busy landing our cargo, and shall probably be unable to do any zoological work before winter sets in as we have our house to build. The prospects for next year are excellent. There are still a great many birds here, chiefly water birds and the water seems to swarm with invertebrate life, especially acalephs. I have also found a large number of lamellibranch shells and gasteropod eggs on the beach. The party is in good health and spirits.

Respectfully Yours
John Murdoch

As the ten-man team settled in, the organization and duties of the expedition began to have a bearing on scientific matters. Ray served as commanding officer over both military and nonmilitary members. The latter included a cook, a carpenter, and a laborer, all hired in San Francisco, and A.C. Dark, who served as the astronomer and magnetic observer. The Army members included George Scott Oldmixon as surgeon, E.P. Herendeen as interpreter and storekeeper, James Cassidy as observer, and Middleton Smith and John Murdoch as observer-naturalists. The three observers were required to serve two four-hour watches each day, during which time they recorded general weather conditions and took hourly meteorological readings following the Hamburg conference protocols. In addition, on "term days," the first and fifteenth of each month, readings were taken for twenty-four hours at five-minute intervals. Because the nonobservers showed little interest in sharing these duties and Ray, in good military fashion, did not encourage them to do so, Murdoch and Smith found themselves tied to the confines of the station, and their natural history work suffered greatly. This difficulty was a major frustration to Murdoch, who complained frequently about it in his letters and official reports. Only Herendeen and Ray, who designated themselves responsible for ethnographic work in the absence of a specialist in this field, had the freedom to travel, and they and Oldmixon, principally, were responsible for making decisions on most of the ethnographic specimens collected. Unfortunately, none of these men were particularly scientifically inclined nor interested in keeping detailed records of their observations.

Ethnological collecting suffered considerably under these circumstances, especially in the early period of the work. Furthermore, no member of the team had any familiarity with Inupiat Eskimo language, so that during the first year few data were collected except the specimens and artifacts themselves and their native names. During the second year linguistic ability improved, but it still was not adequate for detailed inquiry.

In addition, the amicable spirit displayed by the Eskimos in unloading Ray's freight and helping in the construction of the station was not universally held. Nuwuk people, in particular, tended to be aggressive, even to the point that Ray feared open conflict in the first six months. Disgruntlement developed because the Eskimos had not been able to acquire their usual supply of liquor, guns, and ammunition from the whalers during the 1881 season, and they held Ray responsible. Trading these materials was illegal, and Ray's presence as a government official certainly depressed this under-the-counter activity. Nevertheless, the trade continued, as did Ray's frequent appeals to General Hazen to send a revenue cutter to police the whaler trade. Ray noted that the same rebellious Eskimos who occasionally threatened the station were those most involved. To reduce the chance of incident, Ray discouraged visits to Nuwuk and Utkiavik.

In fact, the direct experiences of the team beyond the confines of the signal station were few. The most important event, the "great winter festival" of 1881–82, was missed because of poor relations between the station and Utkiavik at that time. Later, however, Ray and Herendeen were able to attend ceremonies in Utkiavik, but Murdoch found the notes they took so fragmentary as to make a description impossible (Murdoch [1892] 1987:373–4; but see Ray [1885] 1987:xciii). During the second year there were no major social events due to widespread starvation and many deaths in the villages.

Specimens therefore had to be obtained from Eskimos who came to the station for the express purpose of selling them. The order would go out as to what kinds of things were "collectible." Generally it seems that Ray made this decision, and he also insisted that he personally approve all purchases. Smithsonian funds were used for this purpose. Eskimos who needed money, who could speak some English, and who were on good terms with station personnel would periodically bring materials in for sale. If the items were not considered typical of traditional culture according to Ray's definition, like a pair of sealskin dance gauntlets whose puffin beak rattles had been replaced by cartridge shells, they were refused (Murdoch [1892] 1987:366). Because few women visited the station, few articles of female ornamentation or use were collected, in striking contrast with Edward Nelson's many articles of this type from the Bering Sea Eskimos. For these and other reasons one cannot rely on the representativeness of the Ray collection, except in the area of general technology and hunting equipment.

In fact, conditions for gathering data on artifacts was poor, and the expedition's procedures tended to promote bias, commercialism, and fakery. No Eskimos were permitted indoors at the station during the first year for fear of theft or damage to the scientific instruments. Where possible, the function, manufacturing, and native terms for implements were noted, and Eskimos sometimes gave demonstrations. Notes on these observations were used by Murdoch in preparing his monograph. Murdoch kept the log of these and other specimens collected, but inspection of this document in the Smithsonian Institution Archives shows it to be a simple inventory listing of what each item was, its native name, and the collector's name. Contextual information is minimal, and observation of artifact use in native social settings was rarely available. This again biased the collection heavily against materials having social or religious significance.

Although geographical exploration was not a priority, Ray made a few dogsled trips each winter to obtain fresh caribou meat for the station and to take sightings. His experiences on these excursions are related in his reports and did not include important ethnological results. They did however, familiarize him with Eskimo methods of winter travel and survival, and this led him to a conclusion reached fifteen years earlier by Charles Francis Hall (1865) in Baffin Island. Ray noted it prominently in his transmittal letter to Congress: "The work of exploration in the Arctic can be carried on, at any season of the year, with the assistance of the natives, with comparative safety and but very little suffering, and I trust that our experience will tend to remove some of the prejudices now existing in the public mind against Arctic explorations" (Ray 1885:3). Another winter activity of note occurred when a recent-style pair of wooden Eskimo snow goggles was found in frozen gravel twenty-three feet below ground surface in a vertical shaft dug into the permafrost below the station. Rather than indicating antiquity of the goggles, their location was correctly interpreted as evidence of rapid beach accretion.

By the end of the first winter, the team had settled into its routine with all systems operating well, except for some personality complaints. As spring approached, the arrival of birds and general stirring of life brought new collecting opportunities close to the station. While Ray experimented with making photographs of Eskimos at the station and at Utkiavik village, Murdoch's catalogue entries shifted from dribs and drabs of ethnographic artifacts, on the order of a few every few days, to large numbers of birdskins and other creatures, both purchased and caught. When the pack ice broke up, the first whaling vessel of the year, *North Star*, arrived. But she had hardly reached the station when she became beset by ice and was "nipped," sinking rapidly. Ray rescued the crew and installed them in tents until they could be evacuated by other, more fortunate whaling vessels.

The relief steamer *Leo* arrived on 2 August, bearing letters from home, new scientific equipment, fresh supplies, three new observers, and official communications. Some crew members were relieved and sent home, and the round of reports and letters that were dispatched south provide an opportunity to gauge the year's results from both official and personal standpoints. Ray's interim report (Appendix 1) gives a brief account of the year which, from his position, was nearly flawless. The report of Lt. Joseph S. Powell, in command of the *Leo*, contains additional information, partly derived from Ray and partly from Sergeant Cassidy, who accompanied Powell south on the *Leo*, and also from Powell's own subjective observations, expressed in florid prose (Appendix 2). Especially noteworthy are his descriptions of the "song of the icy sea" (p. lix) and his overwrought farewell from Point Barrow: "[P]reparations were made to leave this dreary region—a region which seems to me to be one in which the bright sunshine of hope enters with a light so subdued that it is but the gleam from a far distant planet penetrating the cavern of ceaseless solitude and woe" (p. lxii). Cassidy, having been relieved from duty "by reason of the severity of the climate," probably agreed.

In addition to the reports, Ray sent off the first year's collections to the Smithsonian, including a box of exposed photographic plates. Not having had previous experience with cameras, he expressed some trepidation about the outcome and requested advice as to how he could improve his technique.

The letters from the field from Murdoch to Rathbun and Baird cast a rather different light on the expedition, that of the naturalist at once awed by his surroundings and frustrated by his inability to work. Alternatively, Murdoch was buoyed by optimism at gathering specimens and depressed by the relative impoverishment of animals and plants. Apparently, Murdoch had good reason to be concerned by the lack of official sanction for his studies from Ray and those above him. With such a large crew available, and with Smithsonian funds to support collecting, better use of Murdoch's services could have been made. Murdoch had greater hopes for the second year.

Ooglaamie, Cape Smyth, Alaska
March 18th, 1882

My dear Dick:

We are so near the end of our winter that I may as well begin my letter to you now. When the decent weather begins I hope I shall be so busy with zoological work that I shan't have time to write. There has been practically no chance to do any work so far, and you wouldn't be surprised had you seen what we had to do last fall. In the first place, the vessel was simply crowded as full as she could hold with freight, over one hundred tons, including lumber enough to build a house and all our stores. Of course, I couldn't get at any of my collecting material on the way up, nor indeed until quite lately, when I have been able to put up a few specimens of Lycodes turneri? (I can't make much out of Bean's description—lacking descriptions of other species) and Cottus verrucosus (I think) which the natives are catching through the ice, along with plenty of polar cod, which we are eating at present, as they are brought in frozen and much battered. Well we had to get our stuff, ashore on an open beach with frequently a heavy sea breaking on it, and there were only ten in our party, with six or seven on board the vessel. If it hadn't been for the natives from the Cape Smyth village about three quarters of a mile off, we should have had rather a hard time of it. However with the help of their oomiaks we managed to get our supplies landed in about a week, and the vessel left us. Then the house had to be built. Ray is very energetic about such work, though exceedingly arbitrary and disagreeable in his manner. Bullying and cursing is his idea of discipline, which of course made it very pleasant for all hands. However, since he got the house built, and the work started he has been more reasonable and better-tempered. He is unfortunately one of these self-made men who because they know a few things well fancy they know everything. He is an excellent quartermaster, and knows how to do all sorts of carpenter work and that sort of thing, but gets decidedly beyond his depth when he tries to talk science, though of course as commanding officer—a fact he never loses sight of—he can say anything he pleases without contradiction. He has treated me personally quite well but he isn't a very agreeable person to be housed up with for three years. In fact there isn't very much sympathy in the party, though we are working well together and have accomplished a great deal more than was, I know, expected of us. The "boss" insists on carrying out the printed instructions to the letter, and the result is that with four observers, for the commanding officer will do no scientific work, and will not order the doctor or Herendeen to work, we are making hourly meteorological and magnetic observations, with magnetic term days twice a month of five-minute readings for twenty-four hours. Dark does all the astronomical work, in addition to this. You see I had to learn all the magnetic business, which I never looked at before, and which nobody knew anything of except Smith and he mighty little for he is very stupid and learns slowly. However, we are all in good running order now, and the work goes on pretty smoothly, though it is terribly monotonous. I have to give six hours a day to this work, and have the rest of my time to myself [3 lines of text scratched out by Murdoch], and was sick for three weeks which made it very hard for us as Cassidy, Dark and I had to do all his work and our own too. Otherwise, the health of the party has been pretty good considering where we are—not a sign of scurvy. We got our house built enough to move in about two weeks, and commenced our meteorological work in the middle of October, and the magnetic on December 1st. The house is a very good house, and keeps warm and comfortable, though we have had some very cold weather—54 below zero—and 30 below has been very common. Of course we are a little crowded for room as we have to do all our work in a room 16 × 18. Each man has a little stateroom to himself, to sleep and keep his private traps in. I have got a good deal of the collecting material stored in my room. By the way all the collecting apparatus that came from Washington was all right, but on the list that Ray had purchased in San Francisco, they made every mistake they possibly could. For instance, I have no specimen forceps, only a sort of clumsy magnified common pair, no dissecting scissors, except my own, a dozen "reamers" instead of egg-drills, two <u>dozen</u> instead of two <u>oz.</u> of cover glasses and so on. Ray rushed off and bought everything instead of waiting for me to help him as Craig expected but apparently didn't tell him to do, and this is the result. However, I think I shall manage to make out. The arctic winter has not been so terribly hard to bear, though the monotony combined with the monotony of the work was pretty tough. We have been kept in the house a great deal, partly by the weather and partly by our work, and those who had no work have stayed in from sheer laziness. We had no absolute all day darkness, though the sun set Nov. 16 and didn't rise again till Jan 23rd. He was so near the horizon that even on the shortest day we had considerable twilight for a couple of hours in the middle of the day. Of course we had to burn lamps all day for a long time. Day light is increasing very rapidly now.

We have had very little snow, though it drifts a great deal and is piled up around the house level with the roof. During the <u>night</u>, we had a good deal of clear weather, but before and since it has been more cloudy and blustering. We have some high winds here now and then—up to a hundred miles an hour once. This gale picked up not only snow, but sand and even pebbles and acted like a regular sand blast on our anemometers. One glass was so completely "ground" by the sand, that the dial couldn't be read through it. The weather has generally been just cold enough to make it very disagreeable out doors, and this with the scarcity of game has prevented much hunting. We haven't seen a single bear, but few foxes, and until lately no reindeer. We saw seven deer a week ago, but couldn't get near them on the open tundra. The ice has been pretty bad, very much "nipped" and piled in hummocks so that open water has been scarce, and seals consequently hard to get. About Christmas time there was good ice three miles off shore, and they caught a good many seals in nets set under the ice. This is very cold work, especially as the darkest nights are the best time for netting. We weren't able to get off on the ice for some time after the fishing began, and unluckily the day we did get out, the ice had just closed and stopped the fishing. However we saw larger numbers of freshly-caught seals. We have eaten a good deal of seal meat and are learning to like it very well. We had fresh venison up to Christmas time.

Time has been very dull here because we have so few amusements. Nothing at all has been done in the way of systematic amusement. Ray doesn't even consider it necessary to try make things pleasant for people, in fact goes out of his way to be disagreeable to Dark and Cassidy, to whom he has taken a dislike. Consequently we are all thrown on books, especially light-reading as almost our only relaxation. The work is so arranged that there is no chance even to play cards. Nobody plays except the "boss" and Herendeen. I think the winter has been made harder to get through with than was necessary. However, it has not been very bad after all. The prospect for work in the spring is pretty good unless Ray interferes with some of his thousand and one plans—By the way he had special orders from Gen. Hazen <u>to postpone the zoological work to everything else.</u> The birds appear to be very plenty, fish scarcer but in good numbers, while the sea must be very rich in invertebrates, especially Gephyrian worms, judging from what washed up last fall. Jelly fish were very thick here last fall and stayed very late. Cyanaia arctica was seen several times under the ice, and one was actually caught and brought up to the house from the hole where we took the temperature of the sea, on Feb. 6th! Pretty late record, isn't it? I never heard of their living so late in temperate climates. By the way, if you know of any convenient book for identifying sea anemones, down to genera at least, I wish you'd have it sent up to me in '83. They are very plenty here but of forms strange to me. I tried to dry some starfish last fall, but the weather was too damp and they became gruesome instead. The little pools on the tundra swarm with Apus and Cladocera—(I didn't find this out till they were frozen and we went to cut ice for our winter's water supply. A living Daphnia? appeared in my tumbler of water at table one day. He must have been in the ice several days at least.) The blackish lagoon near the house is full of gammari which will be convenient for making skeletons. Well, when I come to get this ready for the mail, next August or September I hope I shall have a good deal to tell you.

<u>Aug. 23rd.</u> I have got a great deal to tell you, and next to no time to tell it you in. Your letter with Lena's arrived by the *Leo*, and I was very glad to get it. My dear fellow, I am heartily sorry for the loss of your boy, both for your sake and Lena's. I hope Lena has wholly recovered her health and strength. When this winter comes on and I have the time, I will write you each a good long letter, and talk everything over. Now I must confine myself to a few necessary things for the *Leo* will be off on the 25th if she is lucky. She got here on the 20th. I have been working very hard this spring, with small results. Everything is very scarce here, though we have had great flights of eiders. These all passed on to the northeast and east and comparatively few birds stopped here to breed making egg collecting difficult and unremunerative. There are very few fish here, though they are known to be plenty not far off. Still, I can't go after them, and "them as can," won't go. A man who has to be on duty every day observing from quarter of six to quarter past eleven P.M. is considerably hampered in his zoological work. Besides cold and rough weather has interfered considerably with collecting water animals. There has been very little fit for towing and very little obtained by the towing net except a few small amphipods and pteropods. I have been all ready to go dredging ever since the ice left us in the middle of July, but have been obliged to wait for the "power that be," so we have only been once, and then after making a few hauls and finding a muddy bottom Ray got sick of it and ordered us home. I haven't sent in any of the material that we got as we didn't go until by his orders, we had packed up everything and closed the list for this year. He wishes to order and supervise everything even to the number the bird skins of each species that shall be collected. Speaking of birdskins, our collection though small contains examples of nearly every species we have seen, and I have sent in eggs of nearly every bird known to breed here. Most of the birds go some distance off to breed. I mean to find out where if I can. I made nearly all the birdskins myself as Smith though he makes good skins works very slowly, and this of course took off lots of my time from other work. Insects have been very scarce, as the summer, has been, I think, unusually cold. There aren't any mammals here at all, practically speaking. I mean to do better next year, if it's a possible thing. I find I am going to have a little more meteorological work this year as Cassidy goes home, leaving me Senior Sergeant! (Such nonsense!) However there will be five of us so we shall divide up the time a little better. I'm going to give Cassidy a letter of introduction to you. He is a very nice fellow in his way and will tell you the truth about the way things have gone on here. I can't help feeling as if the meagreness of our collections required some explanation. However, I have worked hard and been pretty well helped. Laboratory facilities, of course, are very poor, but I have hope that we may be better off next year. Speaking of laboratory facilities, I want you to buy me some things, which I don't care to apply to the government for but wish to own. I want a set of good egg-drills, some assorted watch-glasses, like yours, and a supply of cover-glasses not too many. My people will pay the bills

for them if you send them, or I'll pay you when I come home. If you want any particular thing collected, if Ridgway wants larger series of any birds, or anything in the way of more duplicates, than I have sent in, I wish you'd get the Professor to send in a regular formal request through the Signal Office to Lieut. Ray, not to me. The ethnological work is supposed to be done by the Doctor and Ray himself—and done badly (this is between ourselves)—and he rather doesn't want me to meddle with it. However, I am doing a little all by myself, which Ray won't let me publish, at any rate in his report. We've sent in a heap of stone hammers, doing pretty well on stone implements altogether. I shall write to Professor Baird, though unofficially of course. Officially I can't report to him. Well, I shall have to end up my letter now, old man. Give my kindest regards to Lena, and tell her I shall be sure to write in the course of the winter. Remember me to Mrs. Porter and tell her that I have received her last kind letter and will answer it in winter when I have some time. Goodby till next year. Give me all the information you can when you write—and by the way, send me all the directions you can for preserving acalephs—as detailed as possible. Remember me to Earll and Clark and all at the Smithsonian.

Sincerely yours,
John Murdoch

P.S.

I enclose my letter to Professor Baird in this to avoid making him pay ship letter postage. I want you, please, if you can, to make him understand that if the work isn't satisfactory, it's not because I haven't tried to do my best. By the way, I have used on my labels the official name of the Station which is Ray's version of the name of the native village, and which is near *ŭt-kĭ-ā'-mĭ* or *Uglá-mi*, as I hear the natives pronounce it. They call themselves *Ŭt-kĭ-ā'-mĭng-me-ŭn*. These words are spelled according to Major Powell's rules. I have used the same method of spelling in giving the native names of birds. Well goodby again. By the way, Cassidy will probably come to Washington and, I shall give him a letter of introduction to you. He is a good fellow and will tell you all about. Please do all you can for him.

U.S. Signal Station
Ooglaamie, Alaska
Aug. 24th, 1882.

Professor S. F. Baird;
Dear Sir:

We were so much occupied with building our house, and preparing for the meteorological and magnetic work, last fall, that it was impossible to do any zoölogical work before winter had set in. During the winter, our situation was such as to prevent my collecting anything more than a few fishes. The zoological work has been hindered or at least limited by the fact that both Mr. Smith and myself have had to perform daily six hours of meteorological and magnetic work, with magnetic term days—double

duty—semi-monthly. This, of course, has prevented us from extending
our collecting any distance from the station, and the immediate vicinity is
comparatively bare of animal life in spring and early summer especially.
There are practically no land mammals, and seals are not plenty. I am
pleased to be able to send in even a mutilated skin of Histriophoca fasciata, which was killed by a native close to the station. The collection of
birdskins comprises specimens of all the species seen here except about a
dozen, which have been seen but seldom. There are but few fishes in the
ocean excepting Boreogadus Saida of which I have sent in a series of
specimens. The natives have brought in several species of freshwater
fishes, but none in fit state for preservation, and so far none of the party
have been able to go to the waters they came from. The ponds and lakes
in the immediate neighborhood of the station are absolutely barren,
though the pools on the tundra have been rather productive of small crus-
tacea. Lt. Ray has been unable to dredge excepting once, too late to send
in the material obtained, and the weather since the sea opened has been
rough and particularly unfavorable to surface work with the towing net.
The beach has also been singularly unproductive owing to the prevalence
of easterly winds. The ethnological specimens have been obtained almost
entirely by purchase, and represent most of the implements in common
use. More stone implements could I think be obtained if desired.

   We have this year had an addition into our force of observers, and hope
to be able to do more satisfactory zoölogical work. I am happy to say that
the whole party has got through the first year without hardship and in
good health.

Very respectfully Yours
John Murdoch

The expedition's second year was relatively uneventful. There were
no serious storms, and the only relief from the boredom of the daily
schedule was the arrival of natives, who began to spend more time at
the station as the two groups grew accustomed to each other. Although
it cannot be documented, a considerable amount of ethnographic data
seems to have been recovered from Eskimo informants during the
second year. This was accomplished both by discussions with Eskimos
who were selling artifacts at the station and by increasing contacts in
Utkiavik. Consequently, the collections and documentation gathered
in 1882–83 were considerably better than the previous year. There
seem to have been no conflicts over illegal trade. On the other hand,
the failure of the 1882 whaling season brought severe distress to the
villages, as has been noted.

   In April, using Nelson's sled and native guides, Ray and Dark made
a ten-day exploration into the interior south of Point Barrow following
the course of the Meade River toward its headwaters. A number of
discoveries were made on this trip, including finding an abandoned sod
house village in country that had formerly been occupied year-round
for three generations by a group related to the Point Barrow people.

According to tradition, the village had been abandoned due to starvation. Ray noted considerable numbers of caribou and other game, and found fossil ivory in stream beds. He continued his education in Eskimo survival and travel techniques, learning how to shoe sleds, build snow houses, use snow goggles, and do other tasks. As a result, he felt confident winter exploration in the interior was feasible by white men if accompanied by Eskimo guides. Near the foothills of what he called the "Meade River Mountains" at 70 degrees north latitude, Ray's guide refused to proceed further because he was beyond his familiar territory and feared enemies, presumably Indians (Ray [1885]1987:lxxviii).

Natural history collecting took front stage again in May and June with the arrival of birds and sea life. This season the Eskimos succeeded in capturing a bowhead whale, the only one taken during the expedition's stay. It was thought that the failure of the previous season resulted from using iron-tipped harpoons rather than traditionally prescribed stone-bladed ones. In 1882 the elders declared that only stone-bladed weapons could be used for the initial thrust, after which iron weapons would be permitted.

The summer season again brought whalers, and with them mail indicating a decision had been reached to evacuate the signal station a year earlier than had been planned. Possibly this decision was made after reviewing weather data collected the previous year, but it may also have been a reaction to the failure of relief ships to reach Greely's party in Lady Franklin Bay. Stores and equipment were sold to the whalers, and collections were prepared for shipment. However, the season wore on and the *Leo* did not appear. Finally, word reached the station that she was lying off the edge of the ice pack near Wainwright, reluctant to proceed to Barrow for fear of being swept north by the northeasterly current into the arctic pack, where she would surely be crushed. Traveling south in their launch, Ray, Murdoch, and Herendeen eventually located the *Leo* and succeeded in guiding her to the station. Considerable difficulty ensued as gales and ice jams threatened to abort the evacuation, but it was eventually completed, and a homeward course was set. At St. Michael, the party met Lt. Frederick Schwatka, who had recently completed a raft trip down the entire length of the Yukon River, and both groups proceeded on the *Leo* to San Francisco. From there members of the Ray party traveled to Washington with the expedition records. Later, in his final report, Ray recounted the termination of the work and its notable results:

The object for which the expedition was organized being accomplished, it was formally disbanded October 15 [1883]; its work having extended through a period of over twenty-seven months, during which time the expedition had sailed over 7,500 miles, had established and maintained itself at the northern extremity of this continent in latitude 71° 16′

north, and successfully carried out the instructions received from the
Chief Signal Officer, and brought back the record of an unbroken series
of hourly observations in meteorology, magnetism, tides, and earth
temperatures, besides a large collection in natural history and ethnology, and penetrated into the interior to a point never before visited by
civilized man. (Ray [1885] 1987:lxxxvi)

Murdoch also prepared a brief summary (Appendix 3) of the work
at the request of Spencer Baird, who promised Murdoch that his au-
thorship would remain anonymous. This was necessary because all
publications were officially under Ray's control, and Murdoch was still
officially under the supervision of Ray and the Signal Corps.

Report to Congress

Upon the expedition's return to Washington, responsibilities were determined for preparing a final report. Meteorological records were to
be prepared by the Signal Corps, and the Coast and Geodetic Survey
took charge of presenting the magnetic, astronomical, and auroral
descriptions. Ray was assigned the task of assembling the publication,
for which he would also write the narrative and ethnographic sections.
Murdoch would, in addition to preparing the natural history notes,
submit a catalogue of the ethnographic objects. Congress formerly
authorized the report and appropriated funds in December 1884 for
publication the following year.

The collections arrived at the Smithsonian safely and were accessioned in November 1883. The shipment included boxes, tanks (of
"alcoholic fishes"), kegs (of salted skins), and bales (of long weapons),
depending on the shipping and preservation requirements of different
classes of objects. Included, in addition to the 1,722 specimens catalogued into the ethnology collections, were eggs, birdskins, mammal
pelts, vertebrate skeletons and skulls, invertebrates, fish, insects,
plants, fungi, mosses, minerals, a census, linguistic data, and photographs. All were turned over to various museum departments for
processing. Murdoch was given access to the material and to library
and comparative collections, and he obtained valuable assistance from
various museum curators and external specialists in identifying those
specimens unknown to him. Many needed new species descriptions.

The final product of little more than a year's analysis and writing
appeared in 1885. This report may well be the first integrated, multi-
disciplinary scientific study ever produced on an Arctic location; certainly it was first in North America. Greely's expedition was planned

for scientific work in a similar fashion but produced much less natural history and ethnological field data, and the final report (Greely 1888) did not appear until three years later. Ray's report opened with General Hazen's orders and instructions (Appendix 4), followed by Ray's narrative (Appendix 5) and ethnographic sketch (Appendix 6). While the narrative is informative, it is but a skeleton account. Ray was a man of action, not a writer. The absence of an extended account from him is a considerable loss to science for of the expedition team he was most free to travel and make observations (Appendix 1). Nevertheless, Ray's report is useful to compare with John Simpson's 1852–53 (1875) and Murdoch's (1892) accounts. In particular, Ray provides useful observations on festivals, religious beliefs, and cultural change, but at other times he paraphrases Simpson. Ray also includes a census, Eskimo physical measurements, and linguistic data (Appendix 7, 8, and 9).

While Murdoch considered himself better qualified to write the ethnographic descriptions, his lack of mobility and his other duties clearly had limited his ability to gather field data. More importantly, his first publication obligations were to the natural history descriptions. Having been in charge of the ethnographic specimen inventory, however, he prepared a classification of the objects for publication using Otis T. Mason's typology and organization. The catalogue, not reprinted here, is little more than a key to the collection, but it does provide a complete list of artifacts, field and museum numbers, brief descriptions, and native names. Murdoch realized, as did others at the Smithsonian, that this did not constitute a final report and that more would have to be done. However, Murdoch's descriptions of the twenty-seven mammal species collected at Point Barrow contain large doses of ethnological data. Though less eloquent than Edward Nelson's (1887), these descriptions have information on native names, hunting methods, customs and superstitions regarding particular animals, uses to which the animals were put, including ceremonial uses, and, in the case of species collected at but not native to Point Barrow, information on where they originated and how they were acquired, whether by trade or travel.

A final point to note is the difference in attitude toward Eskimo people evidenced in the Ray volume when compared with Joseph Powell's 1882 field report. Powell, with his purple prose and his view that those he met "are quite respectable people for savages" ([1884] 1987:lxi), typified white attitudes of the day in which "savage filthiness" dominated discussion and restricted objective understanding of Eskimo social values. By contrast, Ray's report is relatively free of subjective comment, providing a more factual account of Point Barrow people and culture.

The Collections

The ethnological collections returned from Point Barrow included 1,722 specimens, accessioned under no. 13,712 in three groups of catalogue numbers: 56,489–56,774; 72,754–77,251; and 89,233–89,914. Virtually all specimens were described, individually or by type, in Murdoch's monograph, and a great many were illustrated in it or in Ray's 1885 monograph. This comprehensive treatment makes the Point Barrow collection the most completely published of any of the Smithsonian's large Eskimo collections. Like Lucien Turner's materials from Ungava Bay (Fort Chimo), the Barrow collection represents materials from a single localized area, whereas Nelson's collection is important for its broad geographic coverage.

The Point Barrow collection is notable for its excellent collection of manufacturing and hunting equipment. Because rifles had virtually replaced bows and arrows, the expedition obtained a large number of the older weapons. Similarly, stone-bladed knives, scrapers, and harpoons were both available for sale and preferred by the collectors because of their traditional form. Less interest was expressed by Ray for items of contemporary manufacture or those made mainly from European materials, hence the refusal of the cartridge-case dance gauntlets. These preferences had been established, probably, by the curators at the Smithsonian, whose main interest was in traditional culture rather than changes in material culture. At this stage in its development, museum anthropology was heavily influenced by geographical theory, so that representative "culture types" were seen somewhat akin to species, and artifact forms were studied in terms of their geographic variation. To undertake such studies required, it was thought, collections free of external (i.e., European) influence. In this regard, Point Barrow presented the collectors with a problem, because thirty years of contact with whalers had drastically changed Eskimo material culture and was rapidly making inroads in religious and social practices. Partly for this reason the Ray collection has relatively few specimens of ceremonial life, especially of festival gear and accoutrements, and only a small collection of amulets, charms, and fetishes. While the latter were formerly in greater use, the presence of Europeans and European materials, both from trade and from salvaged ice-crushed vessels, were resulting in secularization of religious views. Relaxed prohibitions in hunting ritual, in particular, were becoming common. The same may be said for ceremonial and social events. In addition, the introduction of European diseases, occasionally accompanied by periodic bouts of alcoholic intoxication, compounded by natural fluctuations in faunal cycles had resulted in major demographic changes at Point Barrow and Northwest Alaska in general. For instance, Simpson (1875:237) reported 309 individuals living at Nuwuk in 1852–53, a figure that according to native account was considerably lower than previous years as a result of influenza. A similar population decline occurred at Utkiavik. In 1881–83 the total population of these villages had dropped to 150 and 130, respectively (Ray [1885] 1987:xcix). These factors must be weighed together with the collection methods when comparing the Ray material with other collections from Arctic regions.

The intent of the collectors was to acquire a representative sample of as many different kinds of objects as possible. Excepting some relatively inexpensive items, of which larger numbers were purchased (for instance, twenty-eight stone mauls), most of the Barrow collections consist of only one or a few of each of the 196 specimen types listed by Murdoch in his published catalogue. This is a very different kind of collection than Nelson made among the Bering Sea Eskimos, where large series of similar items were collected from many different villages. For this reason the Nelson materials can be used for studies of cultural variation both within and between villages, as well as across Inupiat, Yupik, and Indian boundaries. The Ray collection has less potential in this regard since only a few pieces came from outside the Point Barrow area.

Because the Ray collection was purchased by men who neither spoke Inupiat nor had the advantage of observing their culture from the inside, other factors restrict its usefulness. First, of course, it was impossible to learn much about the manufacturing processes and materials used to make the artifacts. Generally, the information gathered about a piece was limited to its primary function. Secondary levels of data, for instance those involving form, symbolism, religious or social significance, art, object history, and other nontechnological aspects, were rarely documented. Only in a few cases, as in the magical properties of various materials used in projectiles, was this type of data evinced. Second, artifacts made or used by women are not as well represented as those made or used by men. Nor, of course, was data collected for women's artifacts as thorough as that for men's. Third, acquisitions were frequently requested by the expedition to fill perceived gaps in the series. Since it is likely that certain Eskimos had more favored status with Ray's team, they quite likely acted as middlemen in acquiring materials from other members of the community; having no personal involvement with these pieces, the intermediaries probably conveyed even less of their meanings and histories to the record. Fourth, as already mentioned, items made with European materials, or items of Eskimo manufacture based on European artifacts or concepts, were generally not acquired, resulting in a strong traditional filter being exerted throughout the collection. Despite the relatively pure look of the Ray collection, Eskimos who were selling these old pieces or even heirlooms were sometimes living in sod houses with oak-panelled walls taken from the officer's quarters of crushed whaling vessels. Most Point Barrow people were thoroughly acquainted with most other features of European technology found in the whaling fleet. The only impediment in their use of those materials was short supply and social or religious convention.

Finally, and perhaps most obviously, in order to make a sale and to cater to the desire for traditional items, some of the specimens were faked or composites were assembled by fitting, for instance, an old stone blade to a modern bone handle. Numbers of knives, arrows, and scrapers were given this treatment, often with mixing modern and archeological specimens. While the expedition refused to purchase some items of this sort, and it usually refused materials that seemed to be made explicitly for sale, many slipped by, leaving one uncertain as to the authenticity of some pieces and even confused about whether a particular specimen was archeological, traditional, or market-oriented. For this reason, primarily, the Ray collection is often compared unfavorably to Nelson's, although some of the latter's St. Michael pieces are similarly flawed.

The Murdoch Monograph

Upon completion of the Ray report the Signal Service and the Smithsonian Institution entered into an agreement to support John Murdoch for another two years to finish writing up the ethnological collections. Murdoch, who by this time had become familiar with the Smithsonian's ethnologists, especially Otis T. Mason, assembled the expedition's ethnological notes, laid out the collections, and began extensive reading in Arctic ethnology. Without having been a "participant observer" in Eskimo society, and without linguistic fluency, Murdoch could not base his work on firsthand experience in Eskimo culture. Because of the confining nature of signal station duties, even his experience with the Arctic environment was limited to the immediate environs of the station.

Murdoch's raw materials were a disparate set of field notes, assembled without standard formats by different crew members, a set of artifacts, general familiarity with Eskimo culture, and a strong knowledge of Arctic natural history. Murdoch set about his task, therefore, in a different way than Edward Nelson, whose ethnography was being written at about the same time. One difference was that Nelson was writing in the Southwest, where he was convalescing from illness acquired in Alaska, while his artifacts were in Washington. Nelson's ethnography drew heavily on his observations of living and traveling with Eskimos, in which artifacts were but a component of social life. For this reason and because Nelson was a gifted writer, his writings have special freshness and vibrancy. Murdoch described Point Barrow Eskimo culture using artifacts rather than direct observation as the primary source of data. While both men were experienced naturalists and neither was trained in ethnology, and both organized their writings around descriptions of material culture, Nelson's was far the richer in contextual data. Where Nelson's work is a compendium on Bering Sea Eskimo culture, Murdoch's is primarily a monograph on Point Barrow material culture. A further, and fundamental, difference between the two works, of course, is that there is a major difference between these two cultures; while many artifact types, beliefs, ways of life, and social phenomena were shared between them, the two actually represented distinctly different cultures and linguistic stocks.

Murdoch's monograph therefore took a technological path in which artifacts themselves were the primary object of study. He had at his fingertips Nelson's extensive Bering Sea Eskimo collections, in addition to Eskimo collections from Bristol Bay, Kodiak Island, Greenland, Baffin Island, and Labrador–Ungava. He also had at arm's reach all the pertinent literature on Eskimo culture from a half-century of research and exploration in Greenland and the Eastern Arctic. Using both data types Murdoch produced a detailed study of Point Barrow material culture set into a broad North American Eskimo perspective. Murdoch described the objects carefully and illustrated minute details: knots, lashing systems, clothing patterns, parka trim designs, describing them correctly as carrick bends, beckets, martindales, slices, gussets and gores (pp. 128, 223, 229, 302). Methods for stitching waterproof seams (p. 134), for looping up a bolas cord (p. 245), and many other techniques are shown. Fully 428 line drawings were produced for this volume by artists of the Bureau of American Ethnology, making it one of the most heavily illustrated of Arctic monographs. For this reason the report is a priceless manual of technological description (see, for example, his bird dart description, p. 211). One quickly realizes how much has been lost from today's vocabulary when confronted with a good nineteenth-century descriptive scholar.

Murdoch, moreover, rises above the description when he compares, as he frequently does, Point Barrow artifacts and the systems of which they are a part with those of other areas. These comparisons are especially strong with Eastern Arctic Eskimo materials for several reasons. First, Point Barrow Eskimos share the Inupiat language and culture with the eastern Eskimo to which they are closely linked by virtue of the latter's origins from prehistoric groups that formerly occupied Northwestern Alaska but not the regions south of Bering Strait. Cultural, linguistic, and biological links are especially close between these groups. Links to the Yupik-speaking Bering Sea Eskimos are much weaker (Fitzhugh 1983:17–19; 1984:31). One example of this regional division is seen by the fact that the Ray collection contains only twelve quite unelaborate dance masks, while Nelson's collections contain scores of complicated ones. This difference signifies major differences in ceremonial and religious concepts between the two areas. Secondly, because Murdoch and Nelson were writing up their collections at the same time, Murdoch seems to have been reluctant to make more than passing reference to Nelson's materials so as not to preempt him, as happened with Hoffman's (1897) analysis of Nelson's pictographic drillbows. In addition, of course, there was very little literature available on Bering Sea, St. Lawrence Island, and Siberian Eskimo, or Chukchi ethnology for Murdoch to consult.

The detail and thoroughness of Murdoch's descriptions and comparative studies resulted in his monograph's becoming the major western anchor for later interpretations of a relatively unified ethnography and culture history for the entire Arctic coast of North America from Bering Strait to Greenland and Labrador. Although many collections came to other museums, especially to the Field Museum of Natural History, the American Museum of Natural History, and the University Museum of Philadelphia, in the two decades after the early 1880s, few of these Alaskan Eskimo collections were published. As a result, the realization that the Inupiat and Yupik linguistic boundary was also an important cultural boundary has only recently been recognized.

A further point needs to be made about the importance of Murdoch's work as the first comparative study of Eskimo material culture. This relates to his use of sociocultural details from other Eskimo societies to illuminate Point Barrow material culture. Where Murdoch lacked these critical data in his artifact collections and field notes, he made use of data from other groups and regions to extend its significance or to imply further dimensions. Careful citation of sources prevented this practice from becoming blurred with his own observations. Through his use of Eskimo data drawn from a wide geographic area, Murdoch successfully compiled the first synthetic ethnology of Eskimo cultures of Arctic North America.

While Murdoch's monograph is not very illustrative of Point Barrow Eskimo religious and ceremonial life, it does provide insight into aspects of these symbolic systems. Murdoch learned that men's tattoo marks on their chins or chests were whale tallies. He discovered that Point Barrow Eskimos had strong religious views about compatible and incompatible juxtapositions that linked human actions, animals, and physical raw materials in the real world with supernatural beliefs. For instance, he noted the above-mentioned practice of using stone rather than iron points for killing and processing large sea mammals (p. 240), caribou antler for making caribou arrow points, and stone-tipped arrows for killing wolves (and men) (p. 264). He was aware of the spiritual dichotomy between land and sea evidenced in strictures against allowing a woman who had recently been working on caribou skin clothing to touch either a seal that had just been caught at its breathing hole or the sled on which it was being drawn home. This prohibition lasted until the seal had been drawn onto the land and had been given a mouthful of fresh water (p. 207). Murdoch referred to similar practices among Eskimo groups as distant as Siberia and Baffin Island. The concepts behind these land–sea oppositions (not reported from Bering Sea Eskimos) were not to be clarified until Rasmussen's 1921–24 traverse across the Arctic.

Murdoch represented data on trade and economic exchange largely through descriptions of artifacts or materials having exotic origins, rather than by discussion of the general topic. He noted that chert and bent-wood buckets were obtained from the interior-dwelling Nunamiut (p. 60, 86) and soapstone and hammerstones from the east (p. 60); that jade and jade whetstones came from the Kobuk region (p. 60); that Siberian reindeer fur used for piece-work in Point Barrow garments were identifiable by their red-tanned color, whereas Alaska hides were tanned white (p. 109); that dentalium shells were imported into Barrow from the Northwest Coast (p. 149). In an interesting comment on iron, Murdoch notes that Point Barrow Eskimos use the term *savik*, which also means 'iron,' to mean 'knife,' although the term *iron* itself was only recently coming into use through contact with the whalers. *Savik* is also used by Greenland Eskimos to mean 'knife.' "If, then, there was a time, as these people say, when their ancestors were totally ignorant of the use of iron—and the large number of stone implements still found among them is strongly corroborative of this—their use of this name indicates that the first iron was obtained from the east, along with the soapstone lamps, instead of from Siberia. Had it first come from Siberia, as tobacco did, we should expect to find it, like the latter, called by a Russian or Siberian name" (p. 157). This provocative statement has been overlooked by those interested in eastern, and possibly Norse, origins of iron among Western Arctic groups and its potential impact on the eastern spread of Thule culture one thousand years ago (cf. McGhee 1984). Another prophetic note relates to the presence of a "lake" of tar one day's sail east of Point Barrow.

A number of specimens in the collection came from archeological contexts—old house mounds and middens—in which Point Barrow people occasionally dug to find things they could sell. While Ray did not seem to encourage this activity, his collection has interest in terms of the development of ideas about Eskimo prehistory. Murdoch described these specimens, noting their considerable age. He also recognized in the series of harpoon heads "a number of steps in the development of the modern pattern of harpoon head from an ancient form" (p. 219). He proceeded in several pages of detailed discussion to present a developmental sequence based on stylistic changes that closely approximates today's ideas of harpoon changes for the past fifteen hundred years based on stratigraphic excavations. Murdoch seems to have been the first to discover the importance of harpoon-head typology for chronological studies. He also had observations to make on the recent loss of certain kinds of hunting technology at Point Barrow, like the bladder dart, whose former presence was attested to by float nozzles from old house sites (p. 215).

As a final point it is interesting to note Murdoch's attitude about linguistic terms and Eskimos as individuals. In addition to recording in his field catalogue the names of objects and their Eskimo donors, Murdoch in many cases published this information in his final report. Giving credit to individuals has not been common in ethnographic collecting. This information has research value when questions are raised, as they frequently are in modern studies, about object variation within cultures and about the origins and histories of objects and the families that produced them.

In sum, Murdoch's monograph is a highly professional account of a collection important not only in documenting the material culture of the Point Barrow people but also in placing this culture in context with other Eskimo cultures in the Western and Eastern Arctic. In Murdoch's words, "it contains, it is believed, all that is known at the present day of the ethnography of this interesting people" (p. 20). In fact, it may be the only major Eskimo collection from an early date for which there is a description of nearly every artifact, illustrations of every type of implement, and multiples of many.

John Wesley Powell, director of the Bureau of American Ethnology, agreed to publish Murdoch's paper and introduced it in the Ninth Annual Report with these words:

> In this report Mr. Murdoch has presented a simple and exhaustive account of the Eskimos of Alaska with a commendable absence of theory. At the same time he makes judicious comparisons between the people observed and the eastern division of the same race, including the Eskimo of Greenland, and also between all the American divisions and those of Siberia. These comparisons were made possible by his extensive reading and by his study of former collections deposited in the United States National Museum.
>
> The ample illustrations of the text, 428 in number, are nearly all sketched or photographed from the articles brought to Washington by the expedition, and show in connection with them the numbers attached to those articles as now deposited and displayed in the National Museum. Thus the opportunity for verification and for further examination is proffered. The topics discussed are so many and varied that they can not be recapitulated here with advantage. An examination of the table

of contents will be more satisfactory and useful. Such examination will invite the study of the paper, which will prove to be a compendium of all that is noteworthy about a body of peculiar people who have lately been included among the inhabitants of the United States. (Powell 1892:xlii–xliii)

Aftermath

Having completed his assigned tasks resulting from the Point Barrow work, Murdoch's association with the Signal Corps terminated. Undoubtedly, he had hoped, as had other productive naturalists working for Baird, eventually to land a permanent position on the Smithsonian staff. Unfortunately, this rarely happened, perhaps because they were primarily protegés of Baird rather than of Powell or of the staff of the U.S. National Museum. As early as October 1884 Murdoch had approached Baird for a recommendation for a position at the Smithsoninan, but Baird had been unable to comply. However, later Baird was instrumental in Murdoch's receiving an appointment as the Smithsonian's librarian, a post which he assumed in April 1887 and held until 1892. Then he returned to live in Boston and after 1896 served as an assistant in the catalogue department of the Boston Public Library. One night not long after arriving in Boston, his dog overturned a lamp and his house and possessions (and probably his Alaska notes) burned to the ground.

During this period when Murdoch served as Smithsonian librarian he continued his interest in ethnology, apparently having been lured away from biological studies while he was preparing his Eskimo report. In addition to editing Lucien Turner's Ungava study (Turner 1894) for the Bureau of American Ethnology, Murdoch wrote many papers on Eskimo ethnography. Some of these he considered important enough to publish while in the midst of his Point Barrow work, such as his description of the retrieving harpoon, previously undescribed, and his distributional study of Eskimo bows in the U.S. National Museum collections. He also published a paper on Siberian relationships of the Alaskan Eskimos (1888). These and his many other articles on Eskimo ethnography, mythology, and linguistics are listed on page xlvii. He was a frequent contributor to the *American Anthropologist* in the 1880s and early 1890s, and his subject matter expanded from Eskimos to other cultures of the world, with topics as diverse as Mayan manuscripts, metal-working in New Guinea, modesty and clothing in Africa, teeth mutilation among the Wanyamurzi, Polynesian languages, and primitive games. Many of these papers were based on research done with Smithsonian collections during his tenure as librarian.

Photographs Taken by the Expedition

The following inventory of photographs taken during the International Polar Expedition to Point Barrow is based on records held in the Still Pictures Branch of the National Archives and Records Administration (NA), the National Anthropological Archives of the Smithsonian Institution (NAA), and the Archives of the Rasmuson Library at the University of Alaska at Fairbanks (UAF). The National Archives seems to hold the largest body of material, more than three dozen captioned prints located in the Records of Office of the Chief Signal Officer (RG111). Although the captions are not written in Ray's or Murdoch's hand, at least some of them were taken from a list of photographic negatives that Ray sent from Point Barrow to General Hazen, Chief Signal Officer, at the end of the first year of the expedition, entitled "Catalogue of Photographic Negatives" (Table 1). These photographs seem to have been taken by Ray between March and July 1882. National Archives negative numbers are given in the table, but a few of the attributions are uncertain because Ray used the title "Scene in Ooglaamie" for several photographs. Two additional photographs were found at the Center for Polar Archives in Records of the U.S. Weather Bureau (RG27).

Despite holding Ray's list the National Archives Still Pictures Branch does not have the original negatives, which, presumably, were glass plates. The large majority of negatives in this collection are four-by-five-inch copy negatives prepared from their print file in 1960 and 1982. A few large-format negatives exist, but they also are not originals.

In addition to the twenty, the National Archives holds seventeen other prints from the expedition taken during its final year. No information is available on the accession date of these photographs, nor on the disposition of the original negatives. However, twenty prints (overlapping Ray's list and with multiple copies) were catalogued by the Bureau of American Ethnology and are now held in the Smithsonian's National Anthropological Archives. These prints date from the 1880s because a few have notes made by Murdoch to the artist who produced the line drawings for his monograph. Copy negatives were made from these prints in 1976. It is possible that the original negatives exist in the Smithsonian's large uncatalogued collection, but attempts to locate them have not been successful. The University of Alaska's Rasmuson Library also has a set of copy negatives made in 1983. Table 2 has been compiled to coordinate information about the prints and negatives from various collections. Notes on or attached to negatives or prints are given. The source of the caption or note follows in brackets.

The photographs taken by Ray at Point Barrow are probably the first ever taken at this location; they are certainly the first to portray

Point Barrow people. Ray apparently did not have much prior experience in photography before these images were made. When he sent his first shipment of negatives back on the *Leo* in 1882 he asked advice as to how his technique might be improved. We assume that his request would have been taken up had the expedition remained at Barrow for the full three years as planned. The images used in the introduction to this reprint are among the best that Ray took. Even so they are of rather poor quality, especially compared to the photographs taken by Edward Nelson in Western Alaska several years earlier. Ray's field situation, with a permanent headquarters to work at and a minimum of overland transportation of equipment and fragile plates involved, was more favorable to taking photographs.

Ray seems to have taken his photographs in only two locations. One was in the vicinity of the signal station and the other was in the village of Utkiavik (Ooglaamie). A large number of plates were taken of houses in this village, but few are very clear, and few show people. Nevertheless they do give an impression of the village and its sod houses, its elevated storage racks, umiaks, and other equipment. Ray also took a number of shots of Eskimos against a wall of the signal station. These shots appear to have been done according to the style used by anthropologists, to give full and profile views. Less attention seems to have been given to photographs as a means of documenting details of clothing or ornament, and no close-up views were taken. The group shots of Eskimos at the station are the most interesting photographs, but they are of rather poor quality. Since the original negative plates have not been found, it is unlikely that these images can ever be improved upon. Nevertheless, they are useful as research documents and were used to advantage in Murdoch's monograph.

Ray used a number of his photographs (listed in Table 3) to illustrate his 1885 congressional report. All of these images were heavily retouched, even to the extent of having been re-drawn. This was done to enhance detail in the prints that would not have survived the printing process. Appendix 5 and 6 in this edition reprint the images from Ray's report.

In illustrating his monograph on Point Barrow, Murdoch utilized a variety of the expedition photographs. Because the quality of these photographs was not good enough to illustrate features of dress, or in some cases even of people themselves, the photographs were used as the bases for engravings and line drawings. Most of the artwork was used to illustrate the physical type, hair styles, and clothing of the people from Point Barrow. Details from photographic images were also drawn for use in other sections of the report to illustrate specific activities, practices, and details of dress. Table 4 identifies the Murdoch figures based on photographs.

Table 1. Ray's "Catalogue of Photographic Negatives"

Ray	NA neg.	subject	date
1	91070	Front of main building, U.S. Station	March 1882
2	91071	(same)	March 1882
3	91106	Head of cow walrus, front view	[not given]
4	91107	Head of cow walrus, side view	[not given]
6	91082	Group of Ooglaamie natives	April 1882
7	91102?	Cape Smythe from S. Station	April 1882
8	91099	Ice pack looking west from Station	April 1882
9	91075	Native hut built of turf. Ooglaamie	June 1882
10	91077	Angaroo's house, Ooglaamie	June 1882
11	91076	Scene in Ooglaamie	June 1882
12	91078	Scene in Ooglaamie	June 1882
13	91087	Group of Ooglaamie natives	June 1882
14	?	Duplicate	June 1882
15	91080	Scene in Ooglaamie	June 1882
16	91081	Scene in Ooglaamie. Tent with natives at work	June 1882
17	91079	Scene in Ooglaamie	June 1882
18	?	Scene in Ooglaamie	June 1882
19	91101	Steam whaler *North Star* in the ice	July 6, 1882
20	91100?	Steam whaler *North Star* in the ice, crushed July 8.	July 7, 1882

? uncertain attribution

Table 2. Photographs of the International Polar Expedition to Point Barrow

Ray	NA neg.	NAA	SI spec.	UAF	captions, notes on negatives or prints
	91069				"Sgt. John Murdoch"
1	91070			83-162-8	"Front of Main Building, USS Station" [Ray]; "*North Star* crew ashore after the wreck, July 1882" [NA]; "Front view, Main Building. U.S. Signal Station" [UAF]

Ray	NA neg.	NAA	SI spec.	UAF	captions, notes on negatives or prints
2	91071				"Main Building, winter view, U.S. Signal Corps Station" [NA]; "Front of Main Building. U.S. Signal Station [UAF, Ray]
	91072			83-162-10	"Crew of wrecked whaler *North Star*, in camp at U.S. Signal Station, Ooglaamie, after wreck, July 1882" [NA, UAF]
	91073				"Eskimo grave. Ooglaamie, Alaska" [NA]
	91074				"Native Igloo, Ooglaamie, Alaska, June 25, 1882" [NA]
9	91075				"Duplicate" [of 91074 and poorer quality]
11	91076	76-850	75983	83-162-11	"Native Igloo and boat. Ooglaamie, Alaska, June 25, 1882" [NA]; "At Ooglaamie—skin boat" [UAF]
10	91077	76-852	75987	83-162-12	"Angaroo's Igloo, Ooglaamie, Alaska, June 7, 1882" [NA]
12	91078				"Scene in Ooglaamie, Alaska, June 7, 1882" [NA]
17	91079	76-853	75984		"Native Igloo, Ooglaamie, Alaska, June 7, 1882" [NA]
15	91080	76-858	75986	83-162-7	"Scene in Ooglaamie, Alaska, June 7, 1882" [UAF]
16	91081	76-839	75985	83-162-6	"Scene in Ooglaamie. Tent with Natives at Work" [UAF]
6	91082	76-857	75982	83-162-9	"Group of Ooglaamie Natives" [NA, possibly Ray no. 13, as no snow is visible]
	91083	76-854	75980	83-162-4	"Angwah and wife, natives of Ooglaamie, Alaska" [NA]; "Draw woman for costume. Walrus skin. Woman only" [Murdoch note on NAA print]

Ray	NA neg.	NAA	SI spec.	UAF	captions, notes on negatives or prints
	91084	76-844	75979		"Yuksingah and family, Noowmook, Alaska" [NA]
	91085		75978		"Utiaklovwin", "Native woman and her two boys" [NAA]
	91086	76-840	75977		"Apidow, wife and native child, Ooglaamie, Alaska" [NA]
13	91087	76-847	75981		"Group of Ooglaamie Natives" [NA]; "Natives of Utkiavwin" [NAA]
	91088	76-849	75975		"Pinkerton, a native of Nuwuk, Point Barrow" [NA]
	91089	76-845	75974		"Anatanah, Ooglaamie native" [NAA]; "A native of Nuwuk, Point Barrow" [Ray (1885) 1987:ci]
	91090	76-843	75970		"Punikpu, a woman of Nuwuk" [NAA]
	91091		75973		"Akibiena, native of Ooglaamie, Alaska" [NA]; "Akabiana, a youth of Utkiavwin" [Murdoch (1892) 1987:fig. 3]
	91092	76-846	75972		"Poobah, native of Ooglaamie, Alaska" [NA]; "Puka, a young man of Utkiavwin" [Murdoch (1892) 1987:fig. 4]
	91093		75971.5		"Unalina—Prince of Nuwuk, Alaska" [Ray (1885) 1987:xcviii]; "Unalina, a man of Nuwuk" [Murdoch (1892) 1987:fig. 1]
	91094	76-855	75971		"Mum-in-ne-nah, wife of Unalenah, Noowook, Alaska" [NA]; "Mumunina, a woman of Nuwuk" [Murdoch (1892) 1987:fig. 2]; 'Mummunina, Princess of Nuwuk" [Ray (1885) 1987:lxxxviii]

Ray	NA neg.	NAA	SI spec.	UAF	captions, notes on negatives or prints
	91095				"Steam whaler *Bowhead*, off Station, Sept 1882, boiling out" [NA]
	91096				"Ice floe on the beach near Station, Sept 1, 1882" [NA]
	91097				"Ice along shore, looking seaward, Aug 24, 1883" [NA]
	91098				"Ice arch ¾ mile off shore, near Station" [NA]
8	91099				"Ice pack from the Station, west, June 7, 1882" [NA]
20?	91100				"Ice barrier, off Station, ¾ mile" [NA]
19	91101				"Steam Whaler *North Star* in ice pack off station, 2.5 miles, July 1882" [NA]
7	91102				"Cape Smythe and Ooglaamie, from U.S. Signal Station" [NA]
	91103				"Ground ice, off Station, Aug 10, 1883" [NA]
	91104				"Eskimo grave, Ooglaamie, Alaska" [NA]
	91105				"Walrus head, Ooglaamie, Alaska" [NA, ¾ view]
3	91106				"Walrus head, Ooglaamie, Alaska" [NA, front view]
4	91107				"Walrus head, Ooglaamie, Alaska" [NA, side view]
	91108				"Port of Oonalaska Village, Oonalaska" [NA]
	91109				"Port of Ooalaska Village, Oonalaska" [NA]; "Unalaska" [Ray (1885) 1987:civ]
	91122				"Musk Oxon. Mt. Carpmael. Photographed at midnight, August 1881" [NA]
				83-162-5	"Summer outlook at Cape Smythe, Alaska" [UAF]

Ray	NA neg.	NAA	SI spec.	UAF	captions, notes on negatives or prints
			75976		"Abakkana of Utkliavwin" [NAA; same shot/subject as 75973?]
18		76-851	75988		"Scene in Ooglaamie" [NAA]
20					"Whaler *North Star* in the ice. Crushed July 8."
					"Taipava, from Point Barrow" [NA RG27]
					"Oodlamau, a lad from Point Barrow" [NA RG27]

Table 3. Illustrations in Ray's 1885 Report

NA neg.	location in 1885 report	location in 1987 reprint	subject
91070	Frontispiece	Frontispiece	Front view of the Main Building, United States Signal Service Station, Point Barrow, Alaska.
91098	facing page 22	lxxi	Ice-arch, June 1883.
91072	facing page 24	lxxiv	View of the Station from the west, with the crew of the *North Star* in camp.
91096	facing page 30	lxxxi	Floeberg on the beach, August 1883.
91101	facing page 30a	lxxxiv	Arctic Ocean from the Station, August 1883.
91094	facing page 37	lxxxviii	Mummunina. "Princess of Nuwuk."
91081	facing page 38	xc	Scene in Uglaamie. Tent with natives at work.
91076	facing page 42	xcv	Scene in Uglaamie.
91093	facing page 44	xcviii	Unalina. "Prince of Nuwuk."
91089	facing page 47	ci	A native of Nuwuk, Point Barrow.
91109	facing page 48	civ	Unalaska.
	Plates I–V	cxx–cxxiv	[Selected artifacts]

Table 4. Murdoch Illustrations Based on Photographs

illustration	subject	NA neg.
Figure 1	Unalina, man of Nuwuk	91093
Figure 2	Mumunina, a woman of Nuwuk	91094
Figure 3	Akabiana, a youth of Utkiavwin	91091
Figure 4	Puka, a young man of Utkiavwin	91092
Figure 12	House in Utkiavwin	91092 [detail]
Figure 15	Tent on beach at Utkiavwin	91081 [detail]
Figure 51	Man in ordinary deerskin clothes	91086 [detail of man on right]
Figure 52	Woman's hood	91081 [detail of woman on right]
Figure 56	Man wearing plain, heavy frock	91089 [detail]
Figure 86	Woman with ordinary tattooing	91084 [probable]
Figure 335	Old "Chief" with staffs	91084 [detail]

Murdoch's Publications on Eskimo Studies

1885a Catalogue of Ethnological Specimens Collected by the Point Barrow Expedition. In *Report of the International Polar Expedition to Point Barrow, Alaska*, edited by P.H. Ray, 61–87. Washington: Government Printing Office.

1885b The Retrieving Harpoon; an Undescribed Type of Eskimo Weapon. *American Naturalist* 19:423–425.

1885c A Study of the Eskimo Bows in the U.S. National Museum. In Annual Report of the Smithsonian Institution, part 2:307–316. Washington: Government Printing Office.

1885d Seal-catching at Point Barrow. *Transactions of the Anthropological Society of Washington* 3:102–108.

1885e The Sinew-backed Bow of the Eskimo. *Transactions of the Anthropological Society of Washington* 3:168–180.

1886 A Few Legendary Fragments from the Point Barrow Eskimo. *American Naturalist Extra*, July 1886, 593–599.

1888a Dr. Rink's "Eskimo Tribes." *American Anthropologist* 1:125–133.

1888b On the Siberian Origin of Some Customs of the Western Eskimos. *American Anthropologist* 1:325–336.

1888c A Remarkable Eskimo Harpoon from East Greenland. *Proceedings of the United States National Museum*, 169–171.

1890a The History of the "Throwing Stick" which Drifted from Alaska to Greenland. *American Anthropologist* 3:233–240.

1890b Notes on Counting and Measuring among the Eskimo of Point Barrow, Alaska. *American Anthropologist* 3:37–43.

1890c Notes on Names of the Heavenly Bodies and the Points of the Compass among the Point Barrow Eskimo. *American Anthropologist* 3:136.

1891 Photograph of the South Greenlanders. *American Anthropologist* 4:160.

1892 *Ethnological Results of the Point Barrow Expedition*. In Ninth Annual Report of the Bureau of American Ethnology, 1–441. Washington: Government Printing Office. Reprint, with introduction by William W. Fitzhugh. Washington: Smithsonian Institution Press, 1987.

1898a Further Notes on Eskimo Boot-strings. *American Anthropologist* 11:122.

1898b The Name of the Dog-ancestor in Eskimo Folk-lore. *American Anthropologist* 11:223.

REFERENCES

Boas, Franz
  1888   *The Central Eskimo.* In Sixth Annual Report of the Bureau of
          American Ethnology for the Years 1884–1885, 399–669. Washing-
          ton: Government Printing Office.

Fitzhugh, William W.
  1983   Introduction to the 1983 Edition. *The Eskimo About Bering Strait*
          by Edward William Nelson, 5–51. Classics of Smithsonian An-
          thropology. Washington: Smithsonian Institution Press.
  1984   Images from the Past. *Expedition* 26(2):24–39.

Greely, Adolphus W.
  1886   *Three Years of Arctic Service: An Account of the Lady Franklin
          Bay Expedition of 1881–1884 and the Attainment of the Farthest
          North.* 2 vols. New York: Charles Scribner's Sons.
  1888   *Report on the Proceedings of the United States Expedition to Lady
          Franklin Bay, Grinnell Land by Adolphus Greely . . . Com-
          manding the Expedition.* 2 vols. Washington: Government Printing
          Office.

Hall, Charles Francis
  1865   *Arctic Researches and Life Among the Esquimaux: Being the Nar-
          rative of an Expedition in Search of Sir John Franklin, in the
          Years 1860, 1861, and 1862.* New York: Harper.

Hoffman, Walter J.
  1897   *The Graphic Arts of the Eskimos: Based Upon the Collections in
          the National Museum.* In Annual Report of the United States
          National Museum for 1895, 739–968. Washington: Government
          Printing Office.

Hooper, Captain Calvin L.
  1884   *Report of the Cruise of the U.S. Revenue Steamer* Thomas Corwin
          in the Arctic Ocean, 1881. Washington: Government Printing Office.

McGhee, Robert
  1984   Contact Between Native North Americans and the Medieval Norse:
          A Review of the Evidence. *American Antiquity* 49(1):4–26.

Nelson, Edward William
  1887   *Report Upon Natural History Collections Made in Alaska Between
          the Years 1877–1881.* U.S. Army Signal Service, Arctic Series of
          Publications, III. Washington: Government Printing Office.
  1899   *The Eskimo About Bering Strait.* In Eighteenth Annual Report of
          the Bureau of American Ethnology, 3–518. Washington: Govern-
          ment Printing Office. Reprint, with introduction by William W.
          Fitzhugh. Washington: Smithsonian Institution Press, 1983.

Okakok, Kisautiq-Leona, and Gary Kean
1981   *Puiguitkaat. The 1978 Elders Conference.* Point Barrow, Alaska: North Slope Borough Commission on History and Culture.

Powell, Joseph S.
1884   Report of the Relief Expedition of 1883. Appendix 62: Arctic Research. Report of Progress in Connection with Point Barrow Station. In Annual Report of the Secretary of War for the Year 1883. Vol. 4: Report of the Chief Signal Officer, 622–630. Washington: Government Printing Office. Reprint, Appendix 2 in *Ethnological Results of the Point Barrow Expedition,* by John Murdoch. Washington: Smithsonian Institution Press, 1987.

Ray, Patrick Henry
1884   Work at Point Barrow, Alaska, from September 16, 1881, to August 25, 1882. Annual Report of the Secretary of War for the Year 1883. Vol. 4: Report of the Chief Signal Officer, 630–634. Washington: Government Printing Office. Reprint, Appendix 1 in *Ethnological Results of the Point Barrow Expedition,* by John Murdoch. Washington: Smithsonian Institution Press, 1987.
1885   *Report of the International Polar Expedition to Point Barrow, Alaska.* Washington: Government Printing Office. Reprint, Narrative as Appendix 5, Ethnographic Sketch as Appendix 6 in *Ethnological Results of the Point Barrow Expedition,* by John Murdoch. Washington: Smithsonian Institution Press, 1987.

Simpson, John
1875   Observations on the Western Eskimo, and the Country They Inhabit; from Notes Taken during Two Years at Point Barrow. In *A Selection of Papers on Arctic Geography and Ethnology,* 233–275. London: John Murray. Originally published in *Further Papers Relative to the Recent Arctic Expeditions in Search of Sir John Franklin.* Parliamentary Reports. London, 1855.

Turner, Lucien
1894   *Ethnology of the Ungava District, Hudson Bay Territory.* John Murdoch, editor. In Eleventh Annual Report of the Bureau of American Ethnology for the Years 1889–1890, 159–350. Washington: Government Printing Office.

APPENDIX 1

Work at Point Barrow, Alaska, from September 16, 1881, to August 25, 1882

Lt. P.H. Ray

UNITED STATES SIGNAL STATION,
Ooglaamie, Alaska, August 25, 1882.

SIR: I have the honor to report that after the sailing of the Golden Fleece on the 16th of September, 1881, the whole energies of the party were devoted to securing the stores and instruments and erection of the buildings. The weather continued very stormy and inclement all during the month of September, so our lumber and material was wet and coated with ice, adding great discomfort to the labor of building, but the rapidly forming ice on the lakes and inlets showed we had no time to lose. By the 22d of September the building was so far advanced that we moved in all the stores that were likely to become damaged by the weather, and on October 3 it was so far completed that the whole party was enabled to move in. More or less snow had fallen during this time, and the ice was 5 inches thick on the inlet; the sea still remained open, with no heavy ice in sight. A strong current, setting continuously to the northeast along this shore, kept the young ice from becoming solid, but the sea was covered with loose pancakes of ice as far as the eye could reach. Storms of snow and sleet continued up to late in October; during that time we had several severe westerly gales, sending in a heavy sea on this shore. One on September 17 raised the water 4¼ feet above mean low tide, and running clear over the long sand spit between us and Point Barrow, making the little patch of dry land on which the village of Noowook stands virtually an island, and showing us that there was not a single place between the station and the extreme point where it would have been safe to build the observatory, without carrying our stores a long distance back from the beach, which it was impossible to do with my small party. There was never a time after the Golden Fleece sailed, and before the sea was closed by ice, that it would have been possible for us to have landed with our stores. As it was, there was not a pound of stores lost or damaged, or an instrument injured. I send a map of the country in the immediate vicinity of the station, with plan of buildings.

The inside work on the main building was completed after the party moved in, and at the same time the meteorological instruments were placed, and hourly observations in that department were commenced October 17. The three magnetic instruments were mounted on wooden piers, the season being too far advanced to place masonry. Posts 12 inches square were set into the frozen earth to a depth of 1 foot, and cemented into their place by pouring water around them and allowing it to freeze. These piers answered every purpose, were perfectly solid, and did not change their position in the slightest degree; and when the observatory was taken down this summer, I found the ice around their base unmelted. As soon as the weather was warm enough, brick piers capped with stone were placed, and the instruments are now all in position on permanent piers.

On December 1, 1881, hourly observations, were commenced in the three elements of magnetism, and were kept up uninterruptedly until July 22, 1882, when the work was suspended for seven days, while moving the observatory and placing the instruments on new piers, so as to be fully prepared for the year commencing August 1, 1882. The galvanometer was placed the latter part of July, and observations commenced August 11. The location of the observatory is such, that but one ground, the east, is on land, the south being in the lagoon, and the north and west in the sea (see map.) The east ground is in oil; all the others are held by a box of gravel strapped with iron, to which the plates are attached. It was impossible to place this instrument earlier, as the earth was frozen so hard the wires could not be laid, and there were no poles to be had to string the wires in the air.

There have been no tidal observations, owing to the fact that no gauge was furnished the expedition, and it would be almost impossible to make any ordinary gauge, such as I might construct here, remain in place at this station. The inlet near the station is not affected by the tide, except when it is open to the sea, which is only about two months during the year. A gauge placed on the beach could not be made to stand when the sea is open, owing to the heavy sea during westerly gales, and in the early winter it would be disarranged by the ice. I believe, though, I will be able to get observations for one term in each year, between the months of March and June, and I shall build a gauge if none is sent this year.

NATURAL HISTORY

In this department every effort has been made to make the collection as perfect as possible. All of the spare time of every member of the party has been devoted to this work, and to Dr. Oldmixon, especially, the department of botany and ethnology. All collections made during the past year, I send by return vessel. In the ethnological department we have had many difficulties to contend with, as not a single member of the party could speak a word of the language of these people when we landed, but as several of the party are acquiring it rapidly, I am in hopes to be able to make a satisfactory report upon our return.

The supply of fresh meat is limited, but sufficient can always be obtained for a party of this size. Reindeer and seal only can be depended upon. We have seen but one or two walrus. During the summer a few reindeer come as far north as the station, but cannot be found in any number this side of Dease Inlet, or north of Refuge Inlet, and during the winter they cannot be found north of latitude 70°. Seal can be taken all through the winter after the sea closes, by means of nets set after the manner of the natives, at their breathing holes. The meat of the white whale I find to be excellent for food; have killed one this summer, and am in hopes to be able to take more, and also to get to the eastward and kill deer enough to last us through the winter, should the supply vessel reach us in time to permit me to make the trip after her departure. Last fall I purchased about 500 pounds from the natives before the winter set in.

There is no fuel to be obtained in this vicinity, except drift; that which is indigenous to this country and comes ashore is a very inferior quality, being mostly of a species of cottonwood or balm. Even the natives cannot make it burn without pouring oil over it. A few remnants of old wrecks are lying along the coast, but none of any importance near the station, and even where I have tried to get at them they are so buried in the sand that the labor was very great; what little timber I obtained would be of no consequence as fuel. I have utilized all I got in building a bastion 10 feet square and two stories high, on the corner of the main building, where I have mounted the Gatling gun and stored the ammunition.

The natives have, as a rule, behaved in a friendly manner, and those belonging to Ooglaamie especially rendered valuable assistance at the time we landed, both in landing stores from the ship in their canoes and in carrying them from the beach to the site of the station. Some of the leading men from Noowook came down last winter and demanded presents, which I refused to give. At the same time they made threats to come down and clean out the station, which they have not done. I have no fears of a general open attack: first, because no native has enough followers to be able to do anything serious; second, their struggle for existence keeps them too busy to make war upon any one. The spite of the disaffected ones is aimed at me, principally, owing to the fact that they have been unable to obtain their usual supply of whisky, arms, and ammunition from the whaling fleet this year. They think I am the cause of it, and I understand have made some threats in the matter; but I shall use every precaution against surprise. So far I have kept them at a distance; have never allowed any but a very few headmen to come inside of the house, and do not permit my people to go into their village or to meddle with them in any respect.

The safety of the station would be very much increased if the law relating to the sale of contraband goods by whalemen and traders on this coast could be enforced. In the past there has been no check upon it in any way whatsoever, as we found them abundantly supplied with breech-loading arms and ammunition when we landed. The sending of the revenue-cutter into this sea a month or two after the fleet has entered is simply a farce, and, from all I can learn, unless her course in the future should be different from that of the past, she had better stay away entirely. I believe the offenders in the fleet this year are confined to two or three ships. I met nearly all the masters when they first came up, and they all promised a strict compliance with the law. But in spite of all that, the natives here have been drunk three different times during the last month.

I have made but two expeditions from the post during the past year. The first was made during the month of March, for the purpose of obtaining fresh meat. On the 23d of that month I left the post with a sled drawn by a team of eight dogs, accompanied by two natives with their families. We traveled along the coast on the ice southwest to the entrance of Woody inlet. We there left the sea and struck inland in a southerly direction, and camped in a snow-hut, without fire, 27 miles from the station, on the shore of what the natives told me was a large lake with an outlet leading into Woody inlet.

March 24th. Broke camp at 5 a.m.; weather cloudy, with light snow; wind southwest, very cold; traveled nearly due south; crossed during the day several large lakes and two streams flowing northeast, it being almost impossible to define their banks, as the whole country is nearly a dead level and covered with snow. I only knew when I passed from ice to land, as the natives told me. Traveled 18 miles and went into camp at 1 p.m. Built a snow hut to sleep in. The dry snow drifting with the wind made traveling very difficult, and it was hard work to make the dogs face the sharp wind. Camped on the left bank of a small stream flowing northeast; country along it more rolling and broken than that traveled over earlier in the day.

March 25th. Broke camp at 6:30 a.m.; weather still stormy, with light snow; wind southwest; traveled in a southerly direction. Very difficult to keep the course by the compass, as the guide and dogs were constantly getting out of their direction by the force of the wind, and the drifting snow hiding every landmark left us nothing to travel by, it being impossible to see but a few yards ahead of the team. After traveling about 15 miles came to a large river with high banks; as they were swept clean by the wind, the river was well defined. It was 200 yards wide at the point where I crossed it, and, where the ice was exposed, seemed very winding. Its general course is northeast true. Named it Meade River, in honor of the late Maj. Gen. George G. Meade, U.S. Army. A low growth of stunted willows, about 4 feet high, fringes its banks, it being the first growth of anything like timber seen since leaving the station. We traveled up the right bank 3 miles and came to the camp of a native deer-hunter named Mung-y-a-loo, who belongs at Ooglaamie. These natives, while hunting deer in the winter, never remain long in one place and live exclusively in snow huts, which they construct very quickly whenever they wish to camp. They are simply oblong holes dug into the hard snow where it has drifted deeply, and covered with slabs of the same material, cut out with a large knife they carry for that purpose. I have never seen any of them build a circular hut, and they do not seem to know how. Camped with Mung-y-a-loo. Traveled 18 miles.

March 26th. Broke camp at 5 a.m.; traveled in a southwesterly direction along the right bank of Meade River 7½ miles, and crossed over to the left bank; channel 250 yards wide at this point. At this place the trail left the river. I could see a large fork coming from the southeast, and the land was higher to the south, so I am of opinion it breaks into several forks a short distance above where I left it. Found several specimens of lignite coal among the drift on a sand-bar. Natives told me that there is a large vein a few miles higher up the river. If so, it is the nearest to the station of any yet discovered. Continued to travel in about the same direction all day; saw several bands of reindeer for the first time. At 6:30 p.m. came into the camp of an Ooglaamie native named Nick-a-y-a-loo, on a small stream that, from what the natives told me, I judge flows into Wainright's inlet. Weather clear, but very cold, with strong southwest wind, the sun and the snow affecting the eyes of the whole party very much. Marched 32 miles.

March 27th. Laid over in camp. Purchased four reindeer, also a number of white fish. Natives tell me they caught them in Meade River. Weather very cold.

March 28th. Broke camp at 5:30 a.m. for return trip, having obtained all the venison I could haul. As the wind remained in the southwest, was enabled to use a sail on the sled, and made excellent time, reaching Mung-y-a-loo's camp at 4 p.m. Hired one native boy to return with me.

March 29th. Wind blowing a gale from the west. Native refused to travel; obliged to lay over; weather very cold.

March 30th. Wind fell during the night, but still blowing fresh from the west. Broke camp at 5 a.m., following my outward-bound trail; marched 27 miles, and camped in an abandoned snow-hut.

March 31st. Broke camp at 5 a.m.; traveled on trail; wind fair for sailing; weather very much moderated; reached the station at 6 p.m.; traveled 36 miles.

On this trip I did not carry any instrument but a compass and pocket chronometer, as the sun was too low to make observations of any value. The trip was made solely to obtain fresh meat, as I dared not allow the party to go any longer without it. I wished to test the question if I was able to travel with safety alone with these natives, and they treated me with the utmost kindness throughout the whole trip; was obliged to travel most of the time on foot to keep from freezing.

On the 28th of April I left the station with one native and a dog-team to locate the mouth of Meade River; traveled east 23° south, 45 miles; found that it emptied into the Arctic Ocean by five mouths, in latitude 70° 59′ north, longitude 154° 32′ west; returned to the station April 30th. The wind being fair, I made the trip from the mouth of the river to the station in 13 hours. Since then I have been too busy with the more important work at the station to be able to leave.

The sea, after the night of November 21, was closed, without any sign of open water until the 23d of April, when a small lead was reported 4 miles out, northwest from Noowook. Whales were also reported, and the natives reported seeing them nearly every day during the month of May and up until the 10th of June. In January we saw what is commonly known as a water sky, extending along the horizon to the northwest. As it was very black and heavy, and seemed very near, I started out to it. After traveling between 6 and 7 miles over the ice, the heavy cloud faded away from in front of me and was just as visible between me and the land. It was simply the moisture rising through cracks in the ice. This I found to be the case in every instance where a *water* sky was seen. There is a strong current setting along the coast to the northeast, except during a strong northeast gale, which will sometimes make a surface current to the southwest, but such a current is not of any duration, for invariably upon a change of wind to any other quarter the current returns again to its old northeast course. I tested it a number of times through the ice, when the sea was entirely closed, and always found it set to the northeast.

On June 25, the steamer North Star hove in sight, working up through a small lead of open water, about 9 miles from the station. When she got nearly abreast of the station, she became fast in the ice, the pack closing down upon her. Captain Herendeen and myself went off to her, and received our first mail since sailing. The ship at the time was suffering from a severe nip, and was considerably raised up. She remained in this position until July 7, when the pressure slacked up, and she worked her way in to within 3 miles of the station, and again the ice closed upon her. She did not seem to suffer any until about 2 p.m. on the 8th, when suddenly we heard a great shout raised by the crew, and we could also hear her timbers breaking. In twenty minutes she was out of sight. I went off to their assistance at once with Captain Herendeen, taking our small boat to ferry across the open holes, and the crew, forty-seven, all told, were all safely ashore and in camp at the station at noon on the 9th.

As they saved only a little flour and hard bread, I ordered an issue of such articles of the ration as was necessary for their subsistence. I was unable to communicate with the fleet, as the ice had forced them away to the south, but succeeded in getting the most of them on board the "Bowhead," which worked up near here on the 15th, and we sent off the last of them on the 25th.

To Captains Campbell, Cogan, Smith, Heppinstone, and Knowles, we feel we owe a special debt of gratitude in sending us fresh vegetables as soon as they could reach us, and to all of the captains of the fleet we are indebted for many acts of kindness.

During the winter a shaft was put down 13 feet for earth temperatures (see table), and at that point a room was excavated of sufficient capacity to store 2,000 pounds of fresh meat. As the temperature is below freezing, winter and summer, there is no limit to the time we can preserve it. Shall carry on the work in the coming winter.

I ship one box (twenty-four) negatives of scenes and natives in this vicinity. My short course of instruction, and want of experience, I hope, will be sufficient excuse for the quality of the work, but hope they will be of some service. Would like to have some prints returned to me with an expert's advice as to the course to pursue where I have failed to make a good negative.

There are some parts of the work which I will be unable to carry out with a party so small as this; for instance, observations of the aurora from different points, also sketches of the same, as the display is never the same for two consecutive seconds.

Measurements of the ice formation taken each month on the inlet adjacent to the station are entered on the meteorological reports; 6 feet 2½ inches was the greatest thickness attained. The heaviest ice seen was that which came down from the north with the pack in November. Eight feet was the maximum. I am of the opinion that ice never forms beyond that depth in this sea, as we could not find that it increased in thickness perceptibly, even after the temperature of the sea fell below the freezing point for sea-water. The ice accumulates in great masses under the pressure caused by the currents and gales, so that it often grounds in 30 fathoms of water. These masses become so firmly cemented by frost in the winter that they do not break up until July.

There has been no sickness of any consequence in the party during the year, and all have performed their duties with commendable zeal and fidelity, and as the full work has been carried on so far with four observers, the work for the ensuing year will be lighter than that of the past.

The carpenter and cook began to show signs of breaking down, and as I was able to replace them by two excellent men from the whaling fleet, I have discharged them at their own request.

The Leo, with Lieutenant Powell, reached here on the 20th of this month, and she was discharged by the 25th. Lieutenant Powell brought but one magnetic hut, and it is designed for pendulum observations. I shall put it up and use it for the new magnetic instruments, but I cannot be responsible for the results, as it is nailed with iron nails throughout. It is a disappointment to me that the vessel did not arrive earlier, so as to enable me to have the instruments in position for international work. It was a mistake in allowing her to stop at intermediate places with private freight. Had she not done so, she would in all probability have reached here in time. As it is, the ground is now covered with snow, and winter is upon us, rendering the work of putting up brick piers very difficult. If a vessel cannot be chartered for this service alone, it would be better to ship by the tender of the whaling fleet, which sails from San Francisco in June, and generally returns early in September. I have retained all the men I have quarters for. Should more be sent next year, additional lumber should be sent to construct quarters, of which I have furnished Lieutenant Powell a memorandum. I send estimates of stores for the year ending 1884. For the errors which may be found in my work for the past year, I hope the Chief Signal Officer will take into consideration my want of previous knowledge and instruction in scientific work. I return Sergeant Cassidy by the Leo.

I am, sir, very respectfully, your obedient servant,

P.H. RAY,
First Lieutenant, Eighth Infantry,
A.S.O.,
Commanding Post.

The CHIEF SIGNAL OFFICER, U.S.A.,
Washington, D.C.

From Annual Report of the Secretary of War for the Year 1883, Vol. 4, Appendix 62 (1884).

APPENDIX 2

Report of the Relief Expedition of 1882

Lt. Joseph S. Powell

WASHINGTON, D.C., *December 5, 1882.*

SIR: I have the honor to submit herewith the following report, relative to the relief expedition to Point Barrow, Alaska, placed under my charge:

The schooner Leo, of 150 tons burden, having been chartered by the Government for the purpose, sailed from San Francisco, California, at 8:30 a.m., June 24. We encountered head-winds and half gales during the passage over the Pacific. No incident of importance occurred until July 14, when land was sighted, which proved to be the Shumagin Islands, bearing NE. from Unimak Pass, in longitude 160° W., latitude 55° N. After sighting these islands, the ship was tacked to the southwest, and on the 19th of July we reached the pass, but were prevented from clearing it by head-winds until the 20th. Our position in the pass on the night of the 19th was rather dangerous. A heavy fog settled down toward night, turning into rain, with a heavy sea, rendering it impossible to see land, and the only course left us was to beat forward and backward within the narrow limits of the pass, by the clock, until morning. The distance between the islands is but 7 miles, and the land rises almost perpendicularly on each side. After clearing the pass on the 20th, the wind hauled to the southeast and blew a gale.

The cook having been taken seriously ill after the first ten days out, it became necessary to secure some one in his place, and with that end in view the master of the vessel endeavored to make Saint Paul's Island, but we were not successful, owing to the gale before mentioned. I then directed that we proceed to Saint Michael's, a station of the Alaska Fur Company, with the hope of securing a native. We reached Saint Michael's July 26, and, after considerable persuasion, shipped a native named Kan-u-ark as cabin-boy. One of the principal objects I had in view in selecting this native was, in case we found it impossible on account of ice to reach Point Barrow, to have him act as interpreter and messenger.

Judging from the name, one would suppose that some sort of a colony was located at Saint Michael's, but such is not the case. The only whites at this place are the agent of the Alaska Fur Company, his wife, and one assistant, together with the United States weather observer. As the vessel sailed into the harbor we were greeted with a salute by mountain-howitzers.

As before stated, considerable difficulty was experienced in securing a native. The news of the loss of the Jeannette had already reached the people, and consequently they seemed loth to venture abroad in the white man's ships, which were thus liable to sail away and never return. The savage man all the world over is extremely prone to superstitious fears, and it is not at all to be wondered at that the simple native of these shores should be considerably impressed when he sees the mighty "oomiaks" of the white man go away in the gloom of the mysterious north and return no more.

A jealous spirit seems to the poor native to reign over these gloomy solitudes, who will not permit the secrets of his realm to be explored with impunity, and when the mighty "Tungah" seizes upon the large vessels of the white man and dashes them to pieces in his anger, terror thrills through the poor savage, and he refuses to venture within the reach of the baleful power of the icy north, so potent for evil.

Kan-u-ark understood a few words of English, and proved tolerably handy in waiting on the table, &c., although such employment must have been a new experience to him. We left Saint Michael's on the morning of the 27th and sailed for Golovin Bay, directly opposite, where we took in a supply of water. Owing to heavy gales on the outside, we lay in this harbor two days and then sailed for Point Barrow. On reaching Behring Sea we encountered a heavy gale from the north, with weather so thick as to prevent making any headway toward the straits. Finding it impossible to make northing, and the gale increasing, I directed that the vessel proceed to Plover Bay, having by this time become aware that with a sailing vessel we might be unable to make this point on our return. Weather still continued thick, and having proceeded in the direction of Plover Bay as far as it should lie, as registered by log, the vessel was hove to, waiting for the fog to lift, that bearings could be taken. We laid there two days, without a sight of land or of the sun, but on the morning of the third day it cleared sufficiently to distinguish the land, and we found ourselves about 4 miles from the entrance of the bay. On this morning the wind, which had been blowing steadily from the north ever since we left Norton Sound, lulled almost to a calm.

A steamer was sighted in the morning bearing down on us, and made out to be the United States revenue-cutter Corwin; to the captain, J.T. Healy, I am much indebted for courtesies. She came alongside and towed our vessel up the bay. Anchor was dropped at 1 p.m. At this hour the sky was clear, but the time too early for taking observations for rating chronometers in this latitude. At 2:30 p.m. I found the sky becoming overcast, with every appearance of another gale, and made all haste for taking such observations as could be had. It became foggy and cloudy in a short time, and but two observations of any value could be secured. The captain of the Corwin informed me that he would leave at 6 p.m. and would tow our vessel out if we were ready, and also that I could consider myself fortunate in securing the observations I had, as at this season of the year it was liable to be foggy or cloudy for a week at a time.

After considering the advantages of his offer, and there being every evidence of a long duration to the cloudiness, I accepted it. In order to check the observations taken on shore, I had comparisons made with the chronometer on board the Corwin, believing that good results could be obtained, as this steamer was only three weeks out from San Francisco, and her chronometer properly rated.

The observations taken at Plover Bay, though the number is small, are considered as very good, and are contained in an appendix to this report.

It became evident, after leaving Plover Bay, that the opinion formed as to a lengthy continuance of cloudy weather was correct. Outside of the bay we laid in a calm until 8 p.m., August 7. All this time the fog grew denser, to such an extent that we could not see a ship's length ahead. At the above-named hour a breeze sprang up from the south, and gradually worked itself into a gale. All day it continued, and increased in violence during the night, with no appearance of the fog lifting. The next morning land could be distinguished through the fog, dead ahead, and not distant over 2 miles, and seemed to extend to the east and west. The master of the vessel imagined he was still on the Siberian coast, and the bluff we saw was the south head of Saint Lawrence Bay, and that our position was due to a strong current moving to the northwest. The gale had so increased that it became necessary to close-reef the sails. Then it became apparent that we were drifting ashore, and our only hope was to weather the point of land lying to the east, believing, if this could be done, we would find refuge in Saint Lawrence Bay. It seemed an almost hopeless attempt, as we kept drifting nearer and nearer, but at last were successful in weathering it, though our distance from shore was less than one-half mile.

Our disappointment was great when we discovered that the land on the other side of the bluff trended toward the northeast instead of to the northwest, as we expected it would. We kept on a course about southeast until near dark, when low land was discovered right ahead. The chart and log-book were consulted, and it was clear to my mind that, owing to the foggy weather and a sailor's natural timidity of land, we had made more casting than should have been done, and the land we saw in the first instance was a small bight between Cape Prince of Wales and Cape York, on the Alaska side, and the low land a portion of the spit at the entrance of Port Clarence.

It being considered impossible to again weather the bluff we had been working around all day, I instructed the master to endeavor to make the harbor of Port Clarence, which was accomplished at 10 p.m., and anchor dropped. The making of this harbor I consider quite fortunate, for the gale increased in fury, and had we still been exposed to it, off a lee-shore, as we were earlier in the day, I am afraid the Leo would have ended her voyage then and there, and all on board gone to the bottom. The wind was estimated as blowing 70 miles an hour, and the sea running so high that had the ship struck she would been dashed to pieces in a few minutes, and no one could have reached the shore alive. The storm was a very extensive one, and continued till the 11th, the barometer in the mean time going down to 29.20. We remained at anchor three days and then started on our way to Point Barrow. We passed through Behring Strait on the morning of the 13th, and crossed the arctic circle at 12 m., same day.

Cape Lisburne, the northwestern point of America, was sighted on the 14th, and the next day a heavy gale struck us from the east, in the face of which we were unable to make more than 10 miles in the next two days. At 12 m. August 18, we were in a calm, in longitude 158° 50′ W., latitude 71° 21′ N. At 8 p.m. a breeze sprang up from the southeast and we headed for the station, only one point out of our course. At this time, we were only 48 miles from Point Barrow, and in nearly the same latitude, and supposed, with the four-knot breeze blowing, we would be able to see the point about 6 a.m. next day. At that hour next morning a sight was had of the sun and latitude approximated, and found, to our surprise, we were considerably to the northeastward of Point Barrow in longitude 155° or less (dependent upon latitude), and latitude assumed to be 71° 30′, though afterward it was determined it should have been much more. We were surrounded by ice-floes, and to the eastward, could see the old ice-pack. Our position was determined to be the result of the action of a strong northeast current. This was verified by Lieutenant Ray, with whom I conversed about the matter, and who stated that there is a strong current moving past the station to the northeast at a velocity of from two to three knots an hour, and that our vessel was in rather a dangerous position, for should it have become calm, we should have drifted to the northeast, beset with and crushed by ice; that vessels caught in this current move off to the northeast and not a piece of timber ever returns.

We came to anchor Sunday, August 20, at 8 p.m., off the station at Ooglaamie. On the 21st the wind blew so strongly and the surf was so high that the landing of supplies, or even boats, was out of the question.

During the time we were landing supplies all station instruments were compared with the standards I carried with me for this purpose.

Lying, as we were, in an open harbor, with every probability of a gale, which would have caused our weighing anchor and standing out to sea, and not knowing when we could ever return, I believed it to be my first duty to land all supplies. Officers, enlisted men, and natives performed their share of labor, and I believe it was owing to the energy displayed by the party at the station that we were saved from a gale which commenced the morning after we sailed, and would undoubtedly have beached us or blown us so far to sea that the chances of returning would have been small. We began the work of unloading Tuesday, though the surf was still high. Wednesday and Thursday this work was continued.

On Thursday the ice, in extensive fields, began moving rapidly to the southwest quite close to the vessel. Thursday night ice came into contact with the vessel, but no damage resulted. Friday opened with a half gale, accompanied by snow. Saturday same condition as on Friday. All work was suspended on these days. Heavy ice closing around vessel and sharp lookout kept for the old pack, the approach of which the fields and small bergs were sure indications. Sunday the landing of supplies was finished, and after receiving mail on board, &c., we weighed anchor, homeward bound, at 2 p.m.

By reason of certain facts, which I have explained to the Chief Signal-Officer, an official inspection of records of station was not made, so that a report relative thereto is not possible. From personal observation, and from conversations with Lieutenant Ray, I feel safe in asserting that the work is conducted in a highly creditable manner, and more accomplished than was considered could be, taking into consideration all the difficulties which had to be encountered and overcome. The success of this expedition is due solely to the energy, intelligence, and indefatigable labor of Lieutenant Ray.

The magnetic instruments in present use are the unifilar (declinometer) dip-circle and bifilar, and all are properly adjusted. The dip-circle has been used for absolute determinations, I presume, on "term" days, and weighted and used as a differential instrument the remainder of the month. The value of the weight, Lieutenant Ray informed me, is known. He also informed me that all readjustments have been computed and preserved.

All buildings about the station are substantial, and the dwelling-house is very comfortable. No sickness occurred during the winter; this, I believe, was due to the stringent rules enforced by Lieutenant Ray relative to exercise.

During my stay at the station I had comparisons made daily, whenever landing could be made, with chronometers on shore. For this purpose number 1692 was used as a "hack." This instrument was handled carefully, and but small variations occurred by transporting it. There was but one day on which the sun shone sufficiently to make observations. On this day twelve sights were secured at different intervals. All observations and comparisons of chronometers going from and returning to San Francisco are embodied in a separate report.

But little time was afforded me for familiarizing myself with the country or the customs and habits of the natives, and to Lieutenant Ray and Sergeant Cassidy I am indebted for valuable information, not only in this connection, but of the work performed during past year.

The winter had been long and severe, but hardly so much as had been expected. After the expedition arrived, in September, 1881, a dwelling-house and observatories were at once erected, and on the 17th of October, hourly meteorological observations began, and hourly magnetic on the 1st of December, and from that time no interruptions in the work have occurred. The magnetic work was especially trying during the very cold weather, for delicate instruments had to be manipulated and read in temperature sometimes as low as −45°. At such times it was almost impossible to touch brass or other metals with the ungloved hand. From the 1st of December, 1881, to the 1st of August, 1882, over 90,000 readings of the magnetic instruments alone were taken and recorded. A corresponding amount of meteorological work was carried on at the same time.

The station is located on Cape Smyth, on a low ridge, about fifteen feet above water-level and about one hundred and fifty yards from the water's edge. The native village of Ooglaamie, containing about thirty "igloos" and one hundred and fifty inhabitants, is situated about half a mile distant to the southwest. Point Barrow is ten miles distant to the northeast. Cape Smyth is only a cape by courtesy, for there is scarcely a break in the coast-line, which runs uniformly in a northeast and southwest direction from Point Barrow to Wainright Inlet.

The prospect from the station, even in summer, when it is at its best, is monotonous and uninviting, and in winter it must be dreary indeed. The tundra spreads away level and brown, relieved here and there by patches of sickly green, guttered in all directions by shallow water-courses, and covered with small shallow pools, while at no point within view does it reach an elevation of fifty feet above the level of the sea. Vegetation is very scanty, consisting chiefly of moss and lichens and other cryptogamous growths, with occasional patches of hard, wiry grass and a few simple flowers. The only shrub to be found is the dwarf willow, which, instead of growing in an erect position, creeps along under the moss as if trying to hide from the inclement blasts, and in summer it shoots forth its pretty rose-colored catkins and green leaves through its mossy covering in a timid and hesitating manner, as if aware of the uncongenial character of its surroundings.

During eight months of the year the earth is frozen, and during the remaining four it thaws to the depth of a foot from the surface, but below that depth it is permanently frozen to an unknown depth, probably 150 to 200 feet. It is a desolate land, interesting no doubt, but destitute of beauty, one in which the struggle for existence, both by animal and vegetable life, is of the hardest, where the aspects of nature are harsh without grandeur and desolate without being picturesque, and where the dead level of monotony everywhere prevails, the greatest variety being in the length of days and nights, which vary from seventy-two days to about as many minutes. The year is divided into seasons— a winter eight months long and a rather uncertain summer of four months. The latter season, if summer it can be called, is only such by contrast with the preceding winter, for the temperature rarely reaches 60°, at any time a snow-storm may occur. Snow fell on every day we were at station. The lowest temperature experienced at station was 60° below zero. Luckily at such low temperatures the air is mostly still, and consequently people do not suffer so much as they do when the wind is blowing strongly with the temperature considerably higher. Only two remarkable gales occurred, both in January— one continuing from the 11th to the 14th, and the other from the 21st to the 23d.

A description of the latter was given me. The wind reached a velocity of 104 miles an hour, while for twenty-four hours the average velocity was over 50 miles. It is said the force of this gale was tremendous. Before its force the snow became impalpable powder and disappeared as if a sudden thaw had occurred. Sand and even coarse gravel were carried along in clouds, and acted on exposed surfaces much the same as a sand-blast would. Wood and iron looked as if they had been subjected to a strong scouring process, and glass was ground so as to be almost opaque. One of the anemometers at station was broken long before the wind reached its high velocity—the end of the spindle on which the cups revolve being twisted off—but another stood the storm through without further damage than the blowing away of the wires which connect it with the self-register. The ice at sea, that previously seemed as immovable as the land, was broken up into fragments, as close in shore as half a mile, and when the storm abated was rushing away to the northeast with the velocity of a mill-race.

The sea at Point Barrow does not freeze to a greater depth than 6 or 7 feet; the ice with which it is filled comes from a distance, and is generally a mixture of new and old worn ice. There is nothing in this sea approaching an iceberg, but still some very respectable masses are formed, especially near the coast, where the pressure of the moving floes from without is met by the resistance of the land, and huge fields of ice are driven over each other until they become grounded in water from 15 to 20 fathoms deep and are piled up some 40 or 50 feet. No doubt the grandeur and sublimity given to arctic scenery by the immensity of icebergs are here wanting, but the immensity of power displayed by the chaotic jumble of these enormous ice masses is more calculated to impress the mind than the mere bulk of lofty bergs that stud the seas on the eastern side of this continent. The broken floes are thrown together in every conceivable position, and at every possible inclination of surface, in a profusion of irregularity, of which no language can convey an adequate idea, and which must needs be seen to be appreciated.

Traveling over such a surface as this is next to impossible, and men without incumbrances could possibly advance 8 or 10 miles in a day, but if laden with food, or otherwise, their progress would be far less than this with heavy ice-sleds would be almost impossible. Wherever there is land there is always an ice-foot—a narrow strip of level ice along the coast, over which sled-travel can be easily carried on, or in narrow channels without currents, when the ice may be comparatively smooth, but in the open sea, at a distance from land, such travel must never be attempted by any means now at our command, for nothing but failure will attend such attempts. The fringe of grounded ice along the Point Barrow coast follows an irregular line, more or less distant from the shore, depending on the depth of the water, and varies from 3 to 5 miles in width.

Beyond the grounded line the surface of the hummocks and floes is just as rough and uneven as it is anywhere else, but there is always more or less change going on—sometimes slowly, and sometimes rapidly. Although to the eye the broad expanse of jumbled ice-hummocks seems as stable as the solid land, the stability is only apparent; a kind of vibratory motion takes place from time to time; the pressure increases and decreases alternatively; currents set in, and the whole body of the ice seems to oscillate to and fro, so that it is seldom that the peculiar noises occasioned by the grinding and crushing together of the slowly moving masses cannot be heard. This song of the icy sea is a very peculiar one, and can scarcely be described so as to convey any clear idea of its nature. It is not loud, yet it can be heard to a great distance; it is neither a surge nor a wash, but a kind of slow, crashing, groaning, shrieking sound, in which sharp, silvery tinklings mingle with the low, thunderous undertone of a rushing tempest. It impresses one with the idea of nearness and distance at the same time, and also that of immense forces in conflict. When this confused fantasia is heard from afar through the stillness of this Arctic zone, the effect is strangely weird and solemn—as if it were the distant hum of an active, living, world breaking across the boundaries of silence, solitude, and death.

The sun set on the 16th of November and did not rise again until the 22d of January, remaining below the horizon for seventy-two days, but there was no day during this long, dreary period that there was not two to three hours of twilight—twilight sufficient to hide the stars. On the 16th of May the sun ceased to set, and from that day until the 29th of July there was continual day.

During the latter part of winter and early part of summer the ice-drift at Point Barrow is almost always from the southwest to the northeast, but about October it begins to move in an opposite direction, and continues in November and December drifting in the same way.

A description of auroral displays, furnished me by members of the party, would lead me to suppose that no known portion of the globe surpasses Point Barrow and few equal it in the intensity and brilliancy of these displays. The brilliancy of the displays bears no proportion to their number. It was only occasionally that great splendor and magnificence were reached, and the duration of the greatest brilliancy was only brief, compared with that of the display of which it formed a part. Individual auroras often lasted ten or twelve hours or more, but the great bursts of splendor and motion seldom lasted more than thirty minutes, and often did not continue even so long; but while they lasted they were magnificent indeed. On such occasions the sky became a gorgeous canopy of flames, all splendor, color, and motion; arch, column, and banner flashed and faded; silvery rays, with rosy bases and fringed with gold or emerald green, danced and whirled around the zenith, and broad curtains of light flung across the sky in every form of graceful curve and convolution, shook rainbow tints from every fold, until the beholder became bewildered and lost in the dazzling brilliancy.

In lower latitudes the aurora is mostly seen as a luminous arch extending across the northern sky. At Point Barrow the arch form, though common, was not the prevalent one, and the arches that appeared were seldom perfect, or if so, only for a few moments at a time, and the changes of form were so incessant that it was hard to decide which was the prevailing type. The curtain form, mostly broken, but always convoluted and folded on itself like an immense scroll, was a common form, but whatever the form, the phenomena passed over the sky in a succession of waves, sometimes from north to south, and *vice versa*. Intimately connected with the aurora was the disturbance of the magnetic needles—in fact, during the prevalence of the aurora the magnets were in a state of chronic perturbation, especially during the great displays, when they were often so disturbed that some of them could not be read.

Lieutenant Ray informed me that upon one occasion he saw what he considered to be land, apparently elevated by mirage, directly north of the station. It seemed quite extensive, and appeared like the rounded hill-tops of a large island rising above the horizon. Because of the existence of the strong current, moving to the northeast at Point Barrow, which runs like a mill-race, it would seem probable that land should exist to the north, and the current between these two lands should be considerably increased according to well-known scientific principles, or, possibly, no current, save that created by winds, would be found along Point Barrow coast unless there was land to the north. If the problem of the pole is ever solved, I venture to assert that land will be found at or near it, extending as a continuation of Greenland.

Lieutenant Ray also informed me that while making a trip to the southward in March last he discovered a large river, flowing in a northeasterly direction, and emptying itself into Dease Inlet, about 40 miles to the eastward of the station. This river he named the Meade River, after the late General Meade. It is over 100 yards wide in some places, and is deep enough to allow plenty of large fish to live in it during winter.

The Esquimaux race, to which the natives of Point Barrow and other places on the American side at which the vessel stopped belong, have already been pretty fully described by Arctic explorers; but the description of the Point Barrow Esquimaux, as given me by Lieutenant Ray and Sergeant Cassidy, is very valuable. Very little has been written about the natives. They are called Innuits, from the word "Innuit," which means man in their language, the plural of which is "Innuine," meaning men or people. Although there is great general resemblance between all the subdivisions of the Esquimaux race, yet there is considerable disparity existing between the various families, both in language and manners, depending, no doubt, on the accidental circumstances of locality, surroundings, &c.

The language of the eastern Esquimaux would be entirely unintelligible to the natives of the western coast; and even the native of our side of Behring Strait speaks a dialect differing considerably from that of the Siberian side. There are, in fact, many more points of similarity between all the natives of the eastern side of Behring Sea than there are between them and the natives of the opposite side; thus the natives of the Diomedes Islands, in the middle of Behring Straits, differ more in language and dress from the natives of East Cape, Asia, only 20 miles away, than the natives of Point Barrow do from those of Norton Sound, nearly 700 miles to the southward. The natives on the American side are, on the whole, superior to those on the Asiatic—better looking, more intelligent and cleanly, where cleanliness, of course, only means a less degree of filthiness—and the natives of Point Barrow are a trifle superior to any of the natives I saw at any other point of the American side.

It seems to be the universal law that the savage deteriorates when he comes in contact with civilization, and the longer the contact the more abject he becomes; no one passing along the coasts of Behring Sea and of the Arctic Ocean to Point Barrow can fail to be struck by the clear exemplification of this law. There seems to be a strong tendency in savage man everywhere to acquire the bad habits of the civilized rather than the good, whenever the two races come into contact, and the Esquimaux is no exception to this rule. Thus the natives of Point Barrow, having had but little intercourse with the white man, have deteriorated less than the tribes to the southward, and are quite respectable people for savages. They are rather good-looking people, with interesting but not handsome faces. In general their noses are too flat and the complexions too coppery for beauty. Their bodies are well formed and of average stature; their hands and feet are smaller and better formed than those of the average white man, and, if they would lay aside one or two rather nasty habits and learn to wash themselves occasionally, they might be considered tolerably handsome. The women are more intelligent and better-looking than the men, and are treatd with more consideration than among most savages. Still the man is the lord and master, and his wife or his daughters have no rights he is bound to respect by any code of law or morals existing among them. A woman cannot choose her husband, but is given away much the same as a cow or horse, and her husband can beat her, or put her away, or sell her, at pleasure, except she may happen to have more friends than he has, and then it may not be altogether safe for him to exercise his lordly prerogatives too freely. Self-interest, however, and the indolent, easy-going habits of these people prevent the existence of much harshness between man and wife. The females of a marriageable age are seldom in excess of the males, and consequently there is but little choice allowed; besides it is imperative that every man shall have a wife if possible, because an Innuit without one is about as forlorn and helpless an individual as can be well imagined. Without a woman to cook his food, mend his boots and clothing, and attend to various other matters, the performance of which is considered to be beneath the dignity of the masculine nature, the man soon becomes ragged and out at the elbows, unless some sisterly relative takes him under her care. There is no such thing as marriage ceremony. The whole affair is a bargain, and of no more importance than any other bargain. No morality, in the proper sense of the term, exists, nothing intrinsically right or wrong. Individuals have rights if they are able to maintain them, so that really might is the great arbiter of right, except in such cases where superstition steps in and exerts a regulating influence over conduct.

Not withstanding all this, the social relations are carried on as smoothly and with as little injustice as among civilized people. There are leading men whose influence depends on their wealth and the number of their relatives and friends, but no chiefs, hereditary or otherwise, whose behests any one is bound to obey. There are shamans or medicine-men who talk to the spirits of good or evil and whose interference is required in almost every relation in life. Before a man goes hunting, fishing, or on a journey, when any mishap befalls him, sickness, ill-luck, or adversity of any kind, the shaman is called upon to deal with the spirit, which means to howl in the most discordant way imaginable, with an accompaniment played on skin drums or tom-toms. This office of shaman belongs to no one in particular, as any one who can howl with the proper amount of discordance can fill it, but if any one turns out more fortunate than the rest in bringing good weather, in effecting cures, and in bringing success in hunting or fishing, he will be most in demand for the time being. Every one seems to believe in spirits, and plenty of them, some of them evil and some good, which may be conciliated or driven away by the shaman. There seems to be no belief in any other state of existence than the earthly one, and death is the end of all things to each and every one; when a man dies that is the end. It would seem that the poor savage treats life more philosophically than we do. To him there is neither reward nor punishment in the hereafter, and when the end approaches he passes away from this world as peacefully as an infant, with none of the terrors which possess many civilized persons when brought face to face with death.

Still, some trace in a belief of a future state that formerly did exist, and probably in some dim way exists still, is to be found in the habit of sometimes burying with the dead his bow and arrows, his knife, pipe, and other articles which he used while living, but curiously enough, nearly all of them are previously broken, and thus it might be considered as a mournful observance rather than an evidence of spiritual belief. Burial, of course, with the Innuit means simply exposure. The dead body is rolled up in a deer skin or walrus hide and laid between the runners of a broken sled on some convenient knoll, where the winter winds and summer suns, aided by the wild foxes of the tundra, soon accomplish the work of disintegration.

The social habits of these people, although no worse than the rest of their race, are very repugnant to an ordinary civilized man. Squalor and filth are everywhere; dirt prevails in their food, in their living, and in all their personal surroundings. Indeed, some of their habits are unmentionably repulsive; and, I believe, there are no words in their language corresponding to our words dirt and cleanliness. I will, however, do them justice to say that they are entirely unconscious of their condition, and that they are simply dirty by the prescriptive right of ages of antecedent conditions, moving always in the conservative grooves of savage life. It seems that, if a savage man makes any progress toward civilization, cleanliness is about the last line in which he makes any advance.

As is well known, the food of the Innuit consists, mainly, of the flesh of the seal, the walrus, and the reindeer, with occasional variations of birds and fish. The mode of cooking is by boiling, which is done over a wood fire, in open air, during summer, and over their oil lamps in winter. The blood and intestines of bird and beast are carefully preserved and boiled with the rest of the animal, and anyone who has seen the process in operation, must needs feel the stings of hunger pretty sharply before he can bring himself to partake of the resulting dish. The seal and the reindeer furnish by far the greater portion of their food, and should the supply of either of these animals fail, but more especially the former, starvation would ensue. Seals are caught during the winter in large numbers through their breathing holes in the ice, either by spearing or netting. The reindeer are killed during the months of March, April, October, and November. During the winter months, food is often very scarce, and many families have to depend for weeks on the little polar-cod, a fish about 6 inches long. No doubt since the advent of civilized man, there has been considerable change in the Innuit modes of living and obtaining food. The arrow and the sling, though still in use, have given place to the rifle and the shot-gun; flint and ivory have been somewhat superseded by iron and lead, and their summer tents are now seldom made of anything but canvas, while cooking is done in iron pots and kettles instead of in the stone basins formerly in use.

Having turned over all supplies to Lieutenant Ray, Sunday, August 27, and relieved from duty under my charge Sergeant Joseph E. Maxfield and Privates Charles Ancor and John A. Guzman, and receiving all mail destined for the United States, preparations were made to leave this dreary region—a region which seems to me to be one in which the bright sunshine of hope enters with a light so subdued that it is but the gleam from a far distant planet penetrating the cavern of ceaseless solitude and woe.

By reason of the severity of the climate, Sergeant James Cassidy was relieved by Lieutenant Ray from duty at Ooglaamie, and returned with me to San Francisco.

Anchor was weighed at 2 p.m. Sunday, and our homeward voyage begun in a snow-storm. Heavy drift-ice was moving rapidly to the southwest. This ice was of very peculiar construction and of varied tints, with height from 3 to 30 feet. Before the gale began, which was previously mentioned as occurring on the 24th, the ice began drifting from the northeast, in a contrary direction to its usual course, and I judged from the movement on Sunday, being identically the same, we would have another gale from the same quarter. My judgment was correct; for, on Monday, the gale commenced in earnest. We passed Point Belcher at 9 a.m., August 28, and Icy Cape at 11 p.m.

During the day the temperature of the water changed in one hour from 36° to 31.5°, showing that there existed a warm current, which we crossed. We passed Cape Lisburne at 12 m., August 29.

By the terms of the contract, the owner of the vessel was allowed to engage in any private enterprises he saw fit, after delivering supplies at Ooglaamie. Consequently, when we left station, I turned the vessel over to the master and ceased to direct its movements, but stipulated that we would return to Plover Bay in order to obtain more observations.

We reached East Cape, Asia, Saturday, September 20, and lay there Sunday and Monday. There is quite a large village located at East Cape, and the natives have a regularly installed chief—the only place we visited where we found a chief. We sailed from East Cape to the Diomedes Islands, reaching there at 8 a.m. in a gale from the east. Left the Diomedes at 12 midnight, bound for Saint Lawrence Bay, and anchored inside the harbor at 3 p.m. next day. This bay is full of historic reminiscences connected with the burning of the United States steamer Rodgers, of the Jeannette Relief Expedition. The natives came on board clothed in some of the apparel left them by the officers and crew of this ill-fated vessel. Several had recommendations from the Rodgers party, and in compliance with requests made therein, each one was supplied with tobacco, bread, and molasses. One of the natives described to me the accident which befell Master Putnam of the Navy, and stated that some time after the ice-floe bearing Putnam drifted out to sea, a southeasterly wind brought the floe back to shore, and he saw the remains of Putnam on it, his face and hands much discolored and the body swollen. The ice did not remain long, but floated out again, moving toward the Arctic.

We left Saint Lawrence Bay on September 8, and reached Plover Bay on the 11th, at 2 p.m. Owing to cloudiness, I failed to get an observation of the sun on that day. On Tuesday, the 9th, I left the vessel for shore at 7:30 a.m., but had to wait an hour for the fog to rise. Succeeded in getting two sights, but had to suspend operations, as rain began to fall. It cleared up sufficiently by the afternoon to secure six sights through the clouds—three upper and three lower limb.

We sailed from Plover Bay September 13 for Fort Saint Michael's to return the native, Kan-u-ark, who shipped with us at that place. Shortly after leaving Plover Bay a gale sprang up, which compelled us to alter our course and run to the south of Saint Lawrence Island. At 5 p.m. of the 14th, the ship struck a reef of hidden rocks, not marked on chart, about 6 miles south of the island. For a while it looked as if we would winter in this region, or else go to the bottom. The heavy sea favored the vessel in getting off. The pumps were manned, and, to our satisfaction, we found but little water was making. Made Saint Michael's September 17. While at this place I made an informal inspection of the signal office. Left Saint Michael's on the 20th, and touched at Golovin Bay same date. On the 28th September, in Behring Sea, the barometer commenced falling rapidly, and a fierce gale sprang up from the east, which soon blew with so much violence that we were obliged to take in all our canvas and heave to under a double-reefed mainsail and foresail. We expected by the next day that it would have blown itself out and the worst be over, but it only increased in fury, and for the next day, and the next, and for full five, we were tossed to and fro, at the mercy of such a storm as I hope I shall never again experience. By the time the storm was over, the entire party were worn out, and the patience exhibited under such circumstances certainly became a virtue. We passed through Unimak Pass on the 5th of October. Our voyage from thence across the Pacific to San Francisco was, on the whole, favorable, and we reached the latter place October 2. It was three days before the vessel could be docked, and mail and freight forwarded to Washington.

I turned over to the United States Coast and Geodetic Survey the chronometers for the purpose of rating. As the rates of the several chronometers have been determined, it would appear, from a careful examination of the record, that I was justified in using number 1683 (the standard) at Point Barrow without correction for rate, as the rate changed from losing to gaining during the voyage.

I regret that I am so pressed for time that I cannot embrace in this report any results deduced from the meteorological observations made during the voyage. Hourly meteorological observations were made without a single interruption. In this connection I desire to refer, with pleasure, to the great assistance given me by Sergeant James Cassidy and Private Frederic H. Clarke. These two men, on the return voyage, took all meteorological observations. These had to be made at all times, and the bravery shown by Sergeant Cassidy and Private Clarke in venturing on the deck of the vessel during storms, when heavy seas were pouring over her, is praiseworthy, and I earnestly commend them to the favorable consideration of the Chief Signal Officer.

Strong currents were found in Behring Sea and in the Arctic. At some near date I hope to be able to make an additional report relating to these, and also submit certain theories relative to the movements of areas of low barometer across Behring Sea. I am of the opinion that the theory of the ocean being the birthplace of storms is erroneous. But these matters will be investigated as soon as an opportunity presents itself.

Very respectfully, your obedient servant,

JOSEPH S. POWELL,
Second Lieutenant, Signal Corps, U.S. Army, Assistant.
To the CHIEF SIGNAL OFFICER, *U.S.A.*

From Annual Report of the Secretary of War for the Year 1883, Vol. 4, Appendix 62 (1884).

APPENDIX 3

Arctic Coast

John Murdoch

The most important exploration that has ever been prosecuted directly on the Arctic coast of the United States is that of the Point Barrow party, under Lieutenant Ray, sent up in 1881 by the Chief Signal Officer for the purpose of taking part in the international system of certain polar meteorological stations. Lieutenant Ray was accompanied by Messrs. J. E. Murdoch and Middleton Smith, as civilian assistants in meteorology and magnetism, and also as collectors and observers in natural history.

The expedition was organized in San Francisco, the last member of the original party of ten reporting for duty on July 5, 1881, and it sailed from that city on the 18th of the same month, in the schooner *Golden Fleece.*

On September 8 the vessel arrived at Cape Smyth, 10 miles from Point Barrow, to the southwest, and it was decided to establish the station here, as the ground at Point Barrow itself was unsuitable for this purpose. The supplies of the party were accordingly landed with all possible speed, on account of the lateness of the season, and on September 16 the schooner returned.

The house was finished and occupied October 3, and the regular work of the station commenced October 17. The station received its official name, "Ooglaamie," from an Eskimo village of the same name, about half a mile distant. The expedition succeeded in obtaining a continuous series of hourly meteorological observations from October 17, 1881, to August 27, 1883, when the party was recalled and the station abandoned. Hourly magnetic observations began on December 1, 1881, and continued till the station was closed. The 1st and 15th of each month were observed as magnetic-term days, the observations being made every five minutes on these days. Numerous observations were also obtained of auroras, tides, temperature of the sea and earth, &c.

The zoölogical work was carried on assiduously when the season permitted, and resulted in the securing of 497 bird-skins, comprising about 50 species, and 177 sets of eggs, mostly of wading birds; a small collection of skins, skulls, and skeletons of mammals; 11 or 12 species of fishes, not yet identified; a very few insects; and some marine and fresh water invertebrates. The plants of the region were carefully collected.

A considerable number of Eskimo vocabularies were obtained, together with a large collection of implements, clothing, &c.

The commanding officer made two expeditions into the interior, which resulted in the discovery and partial exploration of a large river flowing into the Arctic Ocean.

The Arctic whaling fleet visited the station, bringing mail, in the summers of 1882 and 1883; and in 1882 a relief expedition in the schooner *Leo* brought supplies and reënforcements.

The steam-whaler *North Star*, of New Bedford, was crushed in the ice near the station, July 8, 1882, and her crew were received at the station and cared for till they could be placed on board the other vessels.

The station was closed and abandoned August 27, 1883, and the expedition proceeded on the schooner *Leo* to San Francisco, where it was disbanded October 15, 1883.

Due report will be made by Lieutenant Ray to the Chief Signal Officer of the meteorological and physical researches of the party. The collections in natural history and ethnology just referred to are of the very greatest interest and value, including large numbers of birds, some plants, but principally rich in ethnological matter.

The National Museum has heretofore been much favored by ample illustrations of the life of the Eskimo of Greenland, of the Mackenzie River region, and of Northwestern River from Kotzbue Sound around to Cook's Inlet. The acquisition of very large collections from Northern Labrador, made by Mr. Turner, and from Point Barrow and its vicinity, by Lieutenant Ray and his party, nearly completes the series, and enables the Institution to claim for the National Museum the possession of by far the finest series in existence of illustrations of Eskimo life.

Among the choice ornithological treasures of the Point Barrow Expedition are over 50 skins of Ross's gull, a bird of which only a few specimens are elsewhere known.

APPENDIX 4

Orders and Instructions

Gen. W.B. Hazen

[Special Orders No. 102.]

WAR DEPARTMENT, OFFICE OF THE CHIEF SIGNAL OFFICER,
Washington, D. C., June 24, 1881.

[Extract.]

*　　○　　❋　　＊　　❋　　○　　＊

IV. By direction of the Secretary of War, the following-named officers, civilians, and enlisted men are assigned to duty as the expeditionary force to Point Barrow, Alaska Territory, viz: First Lieut. P. Henry Ray, Eighth Infantry, Acting Signal Officer; Acting Assistant Surgeon, George Scott Oldmixon, U. S. Army,; Sergt. James Cassidy, Signal Corps, U. S. Army, observer; Sergt. John Murdoch, Signal Corps, U. S. Army (A. M., Harvard), naturalist and observer; Sergt. Middleton Smith, Signal Corps, U. S. Army, naturalist and observer; Capt. E. P. Herendeen, interpreter, storekeeper, &c.; Mr. A. C. Dark, astronomer and magnetic observer (Coast Survey); one carpenter; one cook; one laborer.

V. First Lieut. P. H. Ray, Eighth Infantry, Acting Signal Officer, is hereby assigned to the command of the expedition, and is charged with the execution of the orders and instructions given below. He will forward all reports and observations to the Chief Signal Officer, who is charged with the control and supervision of the expedition.

VI. As soon as practicable, Lieutenant Ray will sail with his party from San Francisco for Point Barrow, latitude 71° 27′ north, longtitude 156° 15′ West (Beechey), and establish there a *permanent* station of observation, to be occupied until the summer of 1884, when he will return here, unless other orders reach him. On the way out and back, a stoppage of a few days only will be made at Plover Bay (latitude 64° 22′ 0″ north, longtitude 173° 21′ 32″ west), for the purpose of determining the error and sea rate of his chronometers. The vessel conveying him to his destination will not be detained at the *permanent* station longer than is necessary to unload the stores.

W. B. HAZEN,
Brigadier and Brevet Major-General, Chief Signal Officer, U. S. Army.

Official:
LOUIS V. CAZIARC,
First Lieutenant, Second Artillery, Acting Signal Officer.

———

[Instructions No. 76.]

WAR DEPARTMENT, OFFICE OF THE CHIEF SIGNAL OFFICER,
Washington, D. C., June 24, 1881.

The following general and detailed instructions will govern in the establishment and management of the expedition organized under Special Orders No. 102, War Department, Office of the Chief Signal Officer, Washington, D. C., dated June 24, 1881.

The *permanent* station will be established at the most suitable point in the vicinity, and, if practicable, at or in the immediate neighborhood of Point Barrow, Alaska Territory, (latitude 71° 27′ north; longitude 156° 15′ west, as determined by Beechey).

The chronometers will be rated at San Francisco, and will have their sea rates determined by an observation of time at the United States Coast and Geodetic Survey station at Plover Bay (latitude 64° 22' 0" north; longitude 173° 21' 32" west).

The vessel should, on arrival at the permanent station, discharge her cargo with the utmost dispatch, and at once be ordered to return to San Francisco, Cal. Before permitting the vessel to leave, a careful examination of the vicinity will be made and the exact site chosen for the permanent station will be located in latitude and longitude, chronometrically, both by Lieutenant Ray and by the navigator of the vessel independently, and a report in writing will be sent by the returning vessel. By the same means will be sent a transcript of all meteorological and other observations made during the voyage, and also a list of apparatus and stores known to be broken, missing and needed, to be supplied next year.

After the departure of the vessel, the energies of the party should first be devoted to the erection of the houses required for dwellings, stores, and observatories.

Special instructions regarding the meteorological, magnetic, tidal, pendulum, and such other observations as were recommended by the Hamburg International Polar Conference, are transmitted herewith.

Careful attention will be given to the collection of specimens of the animal, mineral, and vegetable kingdoms. These collections are to be made as complete as possible, and are to be considered the property of the Government of the United States, and are to be at its disposal. The collections in natural history and ethnology are made for, and will be transferred to, the National Museum.

It is contemplated that the *permanent* station will be visited in 1882, 1883, and 1884 by a steam or sailing vessel, by which supplies for, and such additions to, the present party as are deemed needful will be sent. Lists of stores required to be sent by the next season's vessel will be forwarded by each returning boat.

The subject of fuel and native food-supply, its procurement and preservation, will receive full and careful attention, as soon after the establishment of the post as practicable. Full reports upon this subject will be expected.

A special copy of all reports will be made each day, which will be sent home each year by the returning vessel.

The full narrative of the several branches will be prepared with accuracy, leaving the least possible amount of work afterwards to prepare them for publication.

In case of any fatal accident or permanent disability happening to Lieutenant Ray, the command will devolve on the officer next in seniority, who will be governed by these instructions.

W. B. HAZEN,
Brigadier and Brevet Major-General, Chief Signal Officer, U. S. Army.

Official:

LOUIS V. CAZIARC,
First Lieutenant, Second Artillery, Acting Signal Officer.

INSTRUCTIONS FOR THE COMMANDING OFFICERS OF THE INTERNATIONAL POLAR STATIONS OCCUPIED BY THE SIGNAL SERVICE.

I. GENERAL.

1. Regular meteorological and other observations will be maintained uninterruptedly, both at sea and at the *permanent* station, in accordance with instructions issued to Signal Service observers and those contained in the accompanying extract from the proceedings of the Hamburg conference, to which special notes are appended where needed.

2. The original record of these observations will be kept in the blank books supplied for this purpose, and a fair copy of the corrected and reduced results will be made upon Signal Service and special forms, as supplied in bound volumes.

3. At sea a daily record will be kept, by dead reckoning and astronomical observations, of the latitude and longitude of the vessel, by which the positions at the times of meteorological observations will be deduced, and on arriving at the *permanent* station the local time and longitude will be immediately determined, whence the Washington and Göttingen times will be found by applying the correction for longitude.

4. All meteorological and tidal observations will be made at exact hours of Washington civil time. (The longitude of Washington Observatory is 5^h 8^m $12^s.09$ west of Greenwich.) The regular magnetic observations will be made at even hours and minutes of Göttingen mean time. (Göttingen is 0^h 39^m $46^s.24$ east of Greenwich, or 5^h 47^m $58^s.33$ east of Washington; whence 12 noon Washington time is simultaneous with 5^h 47^m $58^s.33$ p. m. Göttingen time, or 6^h 12^m $1^s.67$ a. m. Washington time is simultaneous with 12 noon at Göttingen.)

If hourly meteorological observations of all these phenomena cannot be taken, then, if possible, take bi-hourly observations at the hours 1, 3, 5, 7, 9, 11 a. m. and p. m., or *at least* six observations at 3, 7, and 11 a. m. and p. m. On no account will the meteorological observation at 7 a. m., Washington time, be omitted.

5. Upon arrival at the permanent station the local time and longitude will be determined at once, without waiting for the erection of permanent shelters which will be built for the meteorological, magnetic, and astronomical instruments, according to the plans and material as specified.

The meteorological and astronomical observatories will be located conveniently near to the dwelling of the observers, but that of the magnetic observatory will be determined by the consideration that these instruments must be removed from all danger of being affected by the presence of steel or iron, including galvanized and tinned iron. If needed to keep off intruders, a guard or fence should surround the magnetic observatory.

6. The observation of tides will be made as complete as possible in summer by a gauge on the shore, and in winter through an opening in the ice, according to the instructions furnished by the Superintendent of the United States Coast and Geodetic Survey. The necessity for observing the tides will suggest that the dwelling-house should be located as near the sea as is safe and convenient.

7. In addition to the ship's log and the official journal of the party, to be kept by the commanding officer, and the official record of observations, to be kept by the meteorological, magnetic, tidal, and astronomical observers, each member of the party will be furnished with a diary, in which he will record all such incidents as specially interest him. This diary will not be open to inspection until delivered to the Chief Signal Officer for his sole use in compiling the full record of the expedition.

8. Accurate representations, either by the photographic process or sketching, will be made of all phenomena of an unusual character, or of whatever is characteristic of the country.

9. Carefully prepared topographical maps will be made of as much of the surrounding country as is practicable.

APPENDIX 5

Narrative

Lt. P.H. Ray

On the 18th day of July, 1881, at ten o'clock in the forenoon, we sailed from San Francisco, Cal., on board the schooner Golden Fleece, a staunch little schooner of one hundred and fifty tons burden, and, being towed outside the heads, we began our voyage in the teeth of a strong northwest gale; and it was three days before the reefs were shaken out of our sails.

The expedition, on the day of sailing, was organized as follows: First Lieut. P. H. Ray, Eighth Infantry, commanding; Act. Asst. Surg. George S. Oldmixon, U. S. Army, surgeon; E. P. Herendeen, interpreter; Sergt. James Cassidy, Signal Corps, U. S. Army, observer; Sergt. John Murdoch, Signal Corps, U. S. Army, observer; Sergt. Middleton Smith, U. S. Army., observer; Mr. A. C. Dark, astronomer; Vincent Randit, carpenter; Albert Wright, cook; Frank Peterson, laborer. With one exception, all were strangers to me, and I subsequently had occasion to regret that more time was not given and care exercised in selecting the *personnel*, especially those intended for the scientific work. For even with experienced observers it is very difficult to do accurate work in this high latitude.

The voyage was uneventful. Owing to adverse winds and calms, it was not until August 9 that we raised the high lands of the Aleutian peninsula to the eastward of Ounimak Pass. A succession of calm days left us at the mercy of the currents, which here are strong to the eastward, and carried us in sight of Kadiak, before a breeze sprung up that would enable us to bear up for the pass. We entered it on the afternoon of the 15th, when the wind fell, but the tide serving, we drifted through during the night. After entering Behring Sea we had stronger winds, and after clearing the pass we were enabled to stand on our course, which carried us about sixty miles to the eastward of the Pribyloff Islands.

On the morning of the 19th we sighted the island of Saint Mathews, passing three miles to the eastward of it, its highest peaks only showing above the fog. We were favored with fair, strong winds from this time on until we arrived at Plover Bay, Siberia, where we anchored at 6 p. m. August 21. The weather being stormy, we were unable to get a sight of the sun until the 24th, when a series of excellent observations were obtained. This delay proved fortunate for us, for on the 22d the U. S. revenue steamer Corwin came into the harbor for coal. Her master, Captain Hooper, reported the ice very light in the lower latitudes of the Arctic Ocean; so much so that he had been enabled to reach Wrangel Land, a point never heretofore attained. To him we became indebted for a fine supply of reindeer clothing and tents, which he had collected in view of a possibility of his wintering in the Arctic. The supply came very opportunely, as we had been unable to obtain any deer-skins at San Francisco and were depending upon sheep-skins for our winter clothing.

We found that our chronometers were running steadily and well, and, after laying in a supply of fresh water, were towed outside the harbor by the Corwin on the morning of the 25th. The wind dying away suddenly, left us at the mercy of the current, which was setting strong to the northward, and during the night we drifted through the straits, getting only a glimpse of the Diomede Islands and East Cape as we passed, as we were enveloped in a dense fog the most of the time. While at Plover Bay we obtained from the natives a quantity of most excellent trout, which proved an agreeable addition to our sea fare.

After passing the straits we encountered strong northeasterly winds, which retarded our progress very much. We sighted Cape Lisburne on the afternoon of August 31, and soon after it came on to blow so heavily that the vessel was hove to, and in that position rode out the gale. For over forty-eight hours we were unable to have fires on board for any purpose whatever. The force of the gale having abated on the 3d of September, we stood to the southeast, the weather remaining so thick that we were unable to obtain a sight of the sun to determine our position. On the 7th we sighted Icy Cape, and then stood along shore to the northeast, keeping the land aboard until we sighted the point on the afternoon of September 8, and came to anchor about one mile to the northeast of Cape Smythe, thus successfully accomplishing the first and most important stage of our work.

The voyage, though long and tedious, had been remarkably free from any accidents, and the meager comforts of our little schooner grew wonderfully luxurious when compared with the low desolate shore, which we could occasionally catch a glimpse of through the drifting snow.

/ Point Barrow, situated in latitude 71° 23′ north, longitude 156° 40′ west, the destination of the expedition, was first discovered by Mr. Elson, master in H. M. S. Blossom, commanded by Captain Beechey, in August, 1826; and is graphically described by him in his report of his memorable voyage, made to the Pacific and Arctic Sea, during the years 1825, 1826, 1827, and 1828. /

In the lapse of sixty years but few changes have taken place on this coast. The people of the generation that Captain Beechey met have all passed away, and the story of the coming of the first white man is one of the legends of the band of Nuwŭkmeun. The next visit made by white men was that of Captains Dease and Simpson, of the Hudson's Bay service, who, in July, 1837, started from Fort Good Hope, and by boat passed down the Mackenzie to the sea, and along the northern shore as far as Return Reef, the point where Franklin was turned back by meeting with impassable ice, in 1826. They here found the ice fast on the land, and further progress by boats being impossible, Captain Simpson accomplished the remaining distance on foot, and thus succeeded in determining the coast line of the northern shore from Behring Straits to the mouth of the Mackenzie. H. M. S. Plover, Captain Maguire, wintered at Point Barrow the winters of 1852, 1853, and 1854, since which time the coast has been frequently visited by vessels of the American whaling fleet.

Upon arriving at the point we at once set about finding a suitable location for the observatory. At the extremity of the point is the village of Nuwŭk, which occupies all the land that is free from inundation by the sea. To locate the observatory among their huts would entail endless trouble and annoyance. Between the village and the mainland, three miles away, is a low, barren sandbank, from forty to one hundred yards wide, across which, during a westerly gale, the sea breaks when open. To the south and west of this the land gradually rises, until at Cape Smythe it is fully thirty feet above the sea; but here again we found the most suitable ground occupied by the village of Ŭglaamie, a cluster of about twenty-three winter huts. We were unable to go any distance back from the beach, as we had no means of transporting our stores by land, and the marshy condition of the country would have prevented us from going any distance back from the beach even if we had the facilities. /A point about twelve feet above the sea level, lying between the sea and a small lagoon three-fourths of a mile northeast from Ŭglaamie, was finally selected. The soil was firm and as dry as any unoccupied place in that vicinity, and, as it was marked by mounds of an ancient village, would be free from inundation. / The lateness of the season gave us but little time for deliberation. The young ice was already forming, and the migration of the birds about over. It was on the morning of the 9th of September that the work of debarkation was commenced in a driving storm of snow and a northeast gale.

The lumber for the house and observatories was rafted alongside the vessel and warped ashore. This work was difficult and arduous, owing to the heavy surf on the beach, and the ice being some distance off shore, the strong northeast wind blowing at the time got up considerable sea, the spray froze wherever it struck, so the lumber was coated with ice as soon as it was taken out of the water. There was too much surf to use our boats, and it was not until the 13th, when the wind fell, that we were able to commence putting the stores ashore. A temporary wharf was constructed, so the boats could be discharged without putting them on the beach. The natives, who at first appeared bewildered at the idea of our coming to stay, showed every disposition to be friendly now, and rendered us valuable assistance with their large skin boats (umiaks), and also

From *Report of the International Polar Expedition to Point Barrow, Alaska* (1885)

ICE-ARCH, JUNE, 1883.

in carrying stores up from the beach. After one or two attempts at petty thieving had been firmly and quietly checked, they showed no disposition to commit any depredations upon our property. Though it was snowing heavily, the work of landing stores was pushed with the utmost vigor, as the wind was very light from the southwest and the sea was quiet, and we could land the umiaks on the beach without the fear of staving them, so that on the morning of the 15th the party was moved on shore into tents. We landed the last of the cargo during that afternoon, and the Golden Fleece was cleared the following morning, and sailed at 12 o'clock. She was the last link that bound us to civilization, and we knew that nearly a year must roll around before we could hope to hear from the civilized world again; but I did not see a single despondent face among the little party as they turned from watching the gallant little vessel out of sight to their work.

At the same time the stores were being landed the foundation of the house was laid. This was made safe and solid by excavating down to the frost, a distance of a little over one foot, and the sills and floor timbers firmly shored with blocks cut from pieces of drift-wood. Plates 1 and 2 give a ground plan and elevation of house. The bastion on the northwest corner was constructed from pieces of wreckage and drift-wood, and was pierced for musketry below and for the Gatling gun above. As soon as the house was inclosed and roofed the stores were all moved in, except a supply for about six months, which was placed in a tent as a reserve in event of the loss of the main building by fire. The party moved in on the 22d, to put up the ceiling and partitions. We were obliged to bring the lumber in and pile it around the stove, so as to melt off the ice before we could work it.

Winter came on rapidly; the lagoon, near the station, was closed entirely on the 26th; the weather continued stormy and thick until the sea closed toward the last of November. The work of carrying the stores and coal from the beach up to the site of the station (a distance of about one hundred yards) was very laborious, there being over one hundred tons of it besides the lumber, and we never for one moment caught sight of the sun from the time we landed until the 28th of September, and then only for a few moments. As soon as the house was made inhabitable we turned our attention to getting the instruments into position. We commenced taking hourly observations in meteorology on October 15, and in magnetism on December 1.

The transit and magnetic instruments were temporarily mounted on wooden piers, which were constructed in the following manner: Timbers sixteen inches square were cut to the proper length and placed on end in position in the observatories, the earth being removed so that the lower end rested on the perpetually frozen earth; they were cemented in their place by pouring water around them and allowing it to freeze. They remained firm and never altered their position in the slightest degree. The ice was found to be intact when the piers were taken down the following July, to be replaced by brick.

Every clear night the sky was illuminated by the most beautiful displays of aurora it has ever been my fortune to witness; they always commenced in the northeast and northwest, and seemed to spring from a dark low bank of clouds. The lights were never stationary for a single second, neither did they ever take the form of bows or arches so often seen in other latitudes, but great curtains of light flashing with all the prismatic colors seemed to be drawn across the heavens, ever rising and changing and often culminating in a corona at the zenith, falling like a shower of meteoric fire. As the winter advanced these displays were more brilliant, and were always of a character that defies description, either by pen or pencil, as they were never for two seconds alike. They were unaccompanied by any sound so far as we were able to observe, and the deadly stillness that always prevails in this region when the sea was closed gave us an excellent opportunity to detect any sound had there been any.

During the last days of September, when the ice on the fresh-water ponds and lakes was from ten inches to one foot thick a sufficient quantity was cut, hauled to the house and conveniently piled, for winter use.

In December, as soon as the drifted snow was sufficiently hard to cut into cakes, covered ways were constructed leading to the observatories, and the ice piled so that during severe weather no person was obliged to go into the open air to carry on the regular work of the station.

Life at the station now settled down into the dull monotony of the routine work; hourly observations in meteorology and the three elements of magnetism were carried on without interruption. To insure the health of the party each member was required to take exercise daily in the open air.

In January, 1882, work was commenced on a shaft for the purpose of getting the temperature of the earth, the results of which are given in Part V. The formation for the whole distance was sand and gravel, mingled with a deposit of drift-wood and marine shells, showing that each stratum represented the successive lines of ancient sea-shores. The earth was saturated with water. At a depth of thirty-five feet a deposit was found of clear water, unmixed with earth, too salt to be congealed at a temperature of + 12, which was the unvarying temperature of the earth at this depth. At a depth of twenty feet a tunnel was run to the east a distance of ten feet, and at the end of it a room ten by twelve was excavated out of the hard frozen ground. In this the temperature never rose above 22°. The walls were always dry and free from moisture, and the accumulation of hoar frost was very light. Here we stored whatever fresh meat, in the way of ducks, reindeer, walrus, or seal, that we were able to accumulate beyond our daily consumption. Our main supply was eider-ducks, which, during the spring flight in May, were easily killed. We took four hundred in 1882, and five hundred in 1883; we found them excellent food, and when stored in the subterranean store-house they were at once frozen solid, and would keep for any length of time.

Fresh meat is the great safeguard against scurvy in this region; I never saw a trace of it among the natives, and meat is their only food. The immunity of my party from all disease or sickness of any kind I deemed was owing to the fact that through our own exertions, and with some assistance from the natives, we were seldom without it.

In March, 1882, I made a trip into the interior, an account of which I submitted in my report of last year. Some narrow leads opened in the ice to the north and west of the point on the 20th of April, and the natives reported seeing whales passing to the northeast on the 23d of the same month, and they were seen passing in the same direction every day from that time until June 15; that seemed to terminate their northern migration, as we saw no more of them until August 15, when they were seen going to the southwest along the edge of the pack. It is at this season that most of the whales are taken, as it is impossible for the vessels to follow them into the ice during their northern migration.

In the spring of 1882 eider-ducks were first seen on the 27th of April flying to the northeast, far out over the ice, and a few straggling flocks were seen from time to time until May 12, when they appeared in immense numbers flying low along the shore ice to the northeast. This migration continued until about June 1, and then almost entirely ceased.

About the time the first flights along shore were seen a number of male king eider were found on the land, apparently exhausted from long flight and want of food. Some were caught and brought in alive, but they were generally dead when found, and always in an extremely emanciated condition. All species were represented in this flight, the king, Pacific, spectacled, and stellers. The Canada goose was never seen; but a few brent, white-fronted, and snow or arctic geese came at this season and stopped with us through the hatching season, bringing forth their young on the mainland. The eider duck, with but few exceptions, continued their flight to the north and east: During July and August large numbers of the males were constantly flying to the westward over Perigniak, a point about four miles to the southwest of Point Barrow. The fact that they came from the breeding-grounds was shown in the naked condition of the breast of some of those taken, the down having been plucked away to construct their nests. Those killed at this season were poor and unpalatable compared to those killed in the spring. But the natives take great numbers of them at this point at this season of the year; one often sees half a dozen families here in camp for that express purpose. Their methods of taking them will be found fully described in the chapter devoted to ethnology.

By the last of June the tundra was nearly free from snow, and narrow leads of water were open along shore. The few hardy flowers indigenous to this high latitude were in bloom, and conspicuous among them were the buttercup and dandelion. There was also a small yellow poppy, named by the natives "tûkälûkäd jaksûn," which is also the name given by them to a small

VIEW OF THE STATION FROM THE WEST, WITH THE CREW OF THE "NORTH STAR" IN CAMP.

butterfly that appears at this season. The butterfly appears as the poppy fades, and they believe that the poppy is transformed, takes wings, and flies away.

On the afternoon of the 25th of June a vessel hove in sight to the southwest. She appeared to be in the solid pack, as there was no water in sight, but we soon discovered she was working her way along a narrow lead, about six miles from shore, which was not visible to us. At about 8 o'clock that night she was bearing about west true from the station, when she came to a halt; I at once dispatched interpreter Herendeen off to her. He returned the next day at 11 a. m., and reported that it was the steam-whaler North Star, (Captain Owen), on her first voyage from New Bedford. He brought a few letters and a file of New York papers, giving us news from the outer world. It was the first information we had of the death of President Garfield and loss of the Rogers. On the 27th I went out to her; found her fast in the ice, with no sign of open water in sight from her mast-head. Captain Owen reported she had suffered a severe nip the night before, and she was raised up bodily about four feet while I was on board of her. I visited her again on the 4th of July and she was still uninjured. During the night of the 6th the wind hauled around to the eastward, causing the pressure to slacken up, and several large cracks opened in the ice, one of them in close proximity to the ice-bound ship. Early on the morning of the 7th we saw she was afloat and working through the broken ice toward shore; when about two and a half miles from the station she again became fast, and lay there all night. The following day (July 8) the pressure again slacked and a lead opened along shore past where she was laying; she got under way and steamed slowly along the lead to the southwest. After proceeding a couple of miles she again became fast; the ice closing in from the west, she was now caught between the ground-ice and the great pack which was setting bodily to the northeast. She remained immovable from about noon until 4 p. m., when our attention was suddenly attracted to her by a great outcry raised by her crew, and we could distinctly hear the cracking of her timbers as her sides were crushed in by the ice; her masts fell a few moments after, and her crew escaped to the ground-ice. I at once set off to their assistance with what men could be spared from the station; we found they had saved nothing but their clothing, a cask of bread, and three boats; the few remaining fragments of the wreck were fast disappearing in the distance, being carried away by the moving pack. The crew all safely reached the land that night, being ferried across the open leads by the boats from the station; tents were pitched to shelter them, and every care given to their comfort. Captain Owen subsequently went out with his crew and brought in the bread, and boats to be used in moving to the southward along the shore-lead, in the event that no other vessel should be able to reach the station. On July 14 other ships fortunately hove in sight, and the wrecked people were distributed through the fleet, between that time and August 2, the last going on board the bark Thomas Pope, bound for San Francisco. Different vessels of the fleet remained in sight of the station off and on until September 23, the steamer Bowhead being the last to visit the station. We sent by her our last mail to the United States.

On August 2 a small schooner was seen coming around the point to the north and east, which proved to be the relief vessel Leo, Lieutenant Powell in charge. She had been carried out of her course to the northeast by the current, in a thick fog; her master, being ignorant of the dangers attending navigation along this shore, having allowed her to drift into a position where, but for the providential springing up of a light breeze, she would certainly have been lost. By her we received three additional observers, Sergt. J. E. Maxfield and Privates Charles Ancor, and John Guzman, of the Signal Corps, U. S. Army; a year's additional supply of provisions and coal; also the new magnetic instruments. With the help of the natives, she was discharged on the 26th, and sailed the following day. I relieved and sent back by her Sergt. James Cassidy, Signal Corps, U. S. Army.

The new magnetic observatory was at once put up and the instruments mounted upon permanent brick piers, and observations with them commenced September 12.

Now that the ships were gone and all connection severed with the outside world, we had nothing to break the old routine of our duty at the station but the occasional visit of a native from some distant village. The faces of those living at Nuwŭk and Ŭglaamie had become as familiar to us as those of our own people; they had ceased to be intrusive, but visited us almost daily with some curio or game for barter; and as the season advanced and water became scarce we were daily besieged by the seal-hunters coming in from the sea and begging for a drink of water, of which there is a great scarcity after the frost has sealed up all sources of supply. The scarcity of fuel, together with their inadequate means for melting ice and snow, causes them to suffer under a constant water famine from October to July, and they seemed to think that our supply was never failing.

During the fall of 1882 we experienced none of the heavy westerly gales so common in 1881, and the main pack, though always in sight, did not come close in, and the sea along shore froze over comparatively smooth save for the small floes that were always drifting to and fro with the current. This remained unbroken until January, when a heavy westerly gale drove in the old ice to the three-fathom bar, which here lies parallel with the coast and about one and one-half miles from it. Inside this bar the ice formed to a thickness of five and one twenty-fourth feet, and a vessel might have wintered with perfect safety at the anchorage off the station in four fathoms of water. Both the winters we were there, about two and one-half miles to the southwest and three miles to the northeast, the old ice came in on the land with great force. In November and December the snow galleries were again constructed to the observatories, and the winter's work went on uninterruptedly. Observations of temperature in sea-water ice were carried on, and a series of tidal observations were made extending through a period of one hundred and twelve days. These observations were taken on the open coast, and go to show that the open Arctic Sea is practically tideless, the mean rise and fall being only about two-tenths of a foot. (Report on tides.)

A peculiar disturbance was observed frequently during these observations. There would be a sudden rise and fall of from three to five hundredths of a foot, like a sudden wave. These occurred when the sea was entirely closed, with not a trace of open water in sight, and apparently in no way connected with the regular action of the tide. There would also be a variation in the height of the water of from four to five feet, often extending through a period of from seven to ten days, but in no manner affecting the normal rise and fall.

During the winter of 1882-'83 temperature of the sea-ice was taken in the following manner: The thermometer was secured in a wooden box 6 by 6 by 15 inches, with a sliding door; this was placed in the ice one hundred yards from the beach, where the sea was smoothly frozen over, one foot below the surface, and frozen in so that the bulb was frozen solid in the ice.

The temperature of the sea-water was taken top and bottom through the hole at the tide-gauge in three fathoms of water. The results are given in the meteorological tables submitted with this report. I found that the second winter with its long night was much more trying upon the spirits and strength of the party than the first; the novelty had now worn off; there was no longer anything new or strange to interest them and there was no relief from the monotony of the routine of the regular work, and there is none so wearisome and wearing as this, without any change and without hope, for we had positive knowledge that there could be no change for us until our work was finished; so the slow time dragged on; days into weeks, months into years; so that exploration, or any work that required action, would have been hailed with joy. After the return of the sun I made preparations for a trip into the interior, to locate geographically some of the discoveries made last year. I had by this time secured one excellent team of eight native dogs, and the sled made at Saint Michael's, given me by Sergeant Nelson in 1881, still being strong and serviceable, I was well equipped for inland work.

Everything being ready, I left the station at 5.30 a. m., March 28, with Mr. A. C. Dark, assistant, a native guide Apaidyao, and his wife. A team of eight dogs and one sled was our only means of transportation; and on it we carried our instruments, arms and ammunition, camp equipage, twenty days' supply of coffee, sugar, hard bread, and pemmican, a small kerosene stove, and one gallon of oil. The sled was rigged with a small lug sail, which was a great help with a fair wind. We traveled along the smooth shore ice to the southwest about eight miles after leaving the station, when we came to where the pack had come in onto the land, and the ice on the sea was too rough and broken for our sled. We here took to the tundra and traveled parallel to the shore until we reached the mouth of a small stream about ten yards wide, coming in from the southeast, called Siñaru, which has its source in a lake seven miles inland. We here left the coast, our general course being south, crossing the lake at the head of Siñaru, which I found to be seven miles across, and camped at 6 p. m. on a small stream flowing to the northeast; marched thirty-seven miles. The country after leaving the coast was flat, and in the summer must be almost entirely covered with water, as we traveled the whole afternoon over a series of small lakes without seeing a single elevation of land that was over five feet above the surrounding country. Saw but few signs of reindeer and no natives, but saw where a hunting party had been in camp a few days before. Our dogs hauled their load with ease, though there was over seven hundred pounds weight on the sled. Weather clear, with light northeast wind.

March 29.—Snowing heavily this morning when we broke camp at 6 a. m. After traveling four miles we struck a stream about thirty yards wide, within a narrow valley, flowing to northeast. Natives gave it the name of Iuáru. The storm broke at ten o'clock and the sun came out by eleven. The country grew more rolling and broken, and at 12 m. we came in sight of Meade River, which here flows through a valley about one and one-half miles wide, with bold bluffs on either bank from forty to sixty feet high ; obtained a meridian sight of the sun at noon for latitude and a fair sight for time during p. m. Traveled up the river on the ice six miles and then left it on our right; crossed a neck of land eight miles wide and struck it again at a point where a large stream called Usûuktu comes in from the eastward, with a channel about forty yards wide and high, bold banks. Here we again traveled on the ice to a point four miles above the mouth of Usûktu, and camped at 4.30 p. m. on the left bank of the river; marched fifty-three miles. I found an Ûglaamie native here in camp ; he was engaged in fishing, and told us his nets were set just opposite to the camp. We obtained from him some fine whitefish ; having no rifle he had been unable to take any deer. I ascended the bluffs on the right bank, which were here fifty feet high. On them found the ruins of several winter huts, built entirely of turf ; the natives say that three generations ago all this region was inhabited by a people that lived by fishing and hunting reindeer, and did not come to the coast, but that the deer and fish grew scarce and there came a very cold season and the people nearly all died from cold and starvation ; the few that survived went away to the Colville or joined the little bands on the coast, so that now this whole region is not inhabited and is never visited except by the hunters from Nuwŭk and Ûglaamie, who come here for deer during the months of February and March ; each year a few fish are also taken with gill-nets in the deep holes along Meade River, the fish being here confined by the river freezing solid on the bars ; all movement of water on this water-shed is suspended during the winter, there being no rainfall or melting of snow from October to May, and springs are unknown.

March 29.—Broke camp at 6 a. m. ; weather clear and moderate. Continued the march in a southerly direction along the river-bed four miles, when we left it, climbing some high bluffs on the left bank to get on the level plain above and avoid the windings of the river ; traveled parallel with its general course all day, crossing it twice, and camped at 5 p. m. on a small tributary of Meade River, and about six miles from the main stream. Marched twenty-five miles ; during the afternoon passed a high bluff which is a noted landmark among the natives and known as Nŭa-suk-nan ; it is in latitude 70° 37′ N., longitude 157° 11′ W., and rises from fifty to seventy-five feet above the surrounding country and is visible for many miles around. Camped to-night with Mŭ′ñialu, a native whom I had furnished with a rifle and ammunition to kill deer for the station. Found he had a fine supply on hand, and he very proudly showed us ten as our share. Got excellent sights of the sun during the day for latitude and longitude. Saw several large bands of reindeer and our guide succeeded in killing two. Temperature last night $+ 16°$; during day rose to 29°.2.

March 31.—Weather cold and stormy, and as we are in a very comfortable snow-house we conclude to lie over for the day. My guide has never been beyond this camp, and I can see he has no desire to add to his knowledge of the geography of this region, so I have made arrangements with Mŭ′ñialu to go on with me. They were busy at work to-day preparing their sleds to haul in their venison to the settlement on the coast; their manner of doing it I have never before seen noted. The sleds which they use for this purpose are made from drift-wood fastened with whale-bone and raw-hide lashing ; they are about ten feet long, two feet wide, and the runners eight inches wide and one and one-half inches thick, straight on top and no rail ; they are shod for ordinary use with strips of bone cut from the whale's jaw-bone, and sometimes with walrus ivory, but this would not do in hauling a heavy load over the snow where there is no beaten trail, so they are shod with ice in the following manner : From the ice on a pond that is free from fracture they cut the pieces the length of a sled runner, eight inches thick and ten inches wide ; into these they cut a groove deep enough to receive the sled-runner up to the beam; the sled is carefully fitted into the groove, and secured by pouring in water, a little at a time, and allowing it to freeze. Great care is taken in this part of the operation, for should the workmen apply more than a few drops at a time, the slab of ice would be split and the work all to do over again; after the ice is firmly secured the sled is turned bottom up and the ice-shoe is carefully rounded with a knife, and then smoothed by wetting the naked hand and passing it over the surface until it becomes perfectly glazed; the sled when ready for use will weigh over three hundred pounds, and they load them with the carcasses of from seven to nine deer, weighing over one hundred pounds each. **Men,** women, and children harness themselves in with the dogs to haul these loads to the coast, often the distance of one hundred miles and over, seldom making more than eight or ten miles each day.

April 1.—The weather being clear, we improved the opportunity to determine accurately our position. Observations were made for time, latitude, and declination.

April 2.—Broke camp at 8 a. m. with Mû′ñïalu for guide; traveled south thirteen miles parallel with Meade River, which we struck at the confluence of a small stream coming in from the westward. For the last six miles the country had become much more rolling and broken, and at the point where we struck the river to-day the bluffs were over one hundred feet high and showed successive layers of turf and sand, where the action of the river had cut them away during the freshets in the summer. I noticed one stratum of turf five feet thick fifty feet below the surface. There was not sufficient moisture in the sand between the strata of turf to cause it to solidify under the action of the frost. On the bars in the river we found a few fragments of fossil ivory; a fringe of scrub arctic willow skirted the bank of the stream, but no drift-wood of any size was seen. Traveling now became quite difficult, as the river was too winding for us to follow its course by traveling on the ice, so we kept a southerly course, climbing the bluffs, where practicable, to cut off the bends. The dogs became tired out early in the afternoon, and we were finally obliged to go into camp on the ice under the lee of a high bluff on the right bank of the river. Marched twenty-three miles. Before dark I climbed to the summit of the bluff, which was one hundred and seventy-five feet above the river, and could see a low range of mountains, running nearly east and west, about fifty miles away. From the break of the country, I have no doubt Meade River has its source in that range, so I named them Meade River Mountains. The native guide notified me upon my return to camp that he did not wish to go further south; that he was unacquainted with the country, never having been so far in the interior before. Beyond this he peopled the country with imaginary enemies. Nothing I could offer would induce him to go further. As I could not well get along without their help in dragging the sled up the hills, I was obliged to make this my turning point, much against my will. We saw no signs of deer, wolves, or any game after we struck the foot-hills; the range of the reindeer seems to be the flat country we had crossed to the north.

April 3.—Broke camp at 8 a. m. and returned to Mû′ñïalu's camp, reaching there at 4 p. m. Weather clear. The sun on the snow fields affected our eyes very seriously in spite of the shaded glasses we wore, and the natives were affected equally as bad as ourselves.

April 4.—Lay over in camp, having our boots dried and repaired and getting ready for the return journey. Weather clear and cold.

April 5.—Broke camp at 5.30 a. m. Traveled on our outward trail to camp No. 2 and slept in the hut we used on our way out. Weather clear and cold, with very little wind.

April 6.—Broke camp at 6 a. m. Followed old trail back to camp No. 1. Weather bright and clear; suffered intensely all day from my eyes, becoming so inflamed I could scarcely see. Mr. Dark does not seem to be so seriously affected. Temperature fell last night to — 13°.4; during the day, — 24°.

April 7.—Broke camp at 5.30 a. m., and reached the station at 5 p. m. Was obliged to travel with my eyes bandaged; Apaidyao was also nearly blind. No person can be exempt from this terrible suffering who travels in this region at this season of the year; the blinding glare of the sun upon the snow affects the strongest eyes, and we found no preventive. We had several varieties of shaded glasses and goggles, but found as much protection in the wooden shades made and worn by the natives as we did in our own improved glasses, and they were much more comfortable, as the moisture from the face did not congeal upon them so readily as upon the wire gauze and frames of the goggles. Other than this, there are but few hardships attending travel to a small party properly equipped in this region at this season of the year, and the nearer one conforms to the habits of the natives the less liable he is to meet with disaster, and the less he will be burdened with unnecessary camp equipage and blankets.

The snow hut (iglu) of these people is very quickly and easily constructed, and ordinarily does not consume more time than is required to pitch a wall tent, and is constructed in the following manner : A place where the snow is about four feet deep is selected for camp and a space 5 by 9 feet is laid off ; the upper surface is cut into blocks two feet square and eight inches thick and set on edge around the excavation for side walls ; at one end three feet of the space is dug down to the ground or ice ; in the balance about eighteen inches of snow is left for a couch ; sides and ends are built up tight and the whole is roofed with broad slabs of snow six feet thick, cut in proper dimensions to form a flat gable roof, loose snow thrown over all to chink it, and at the end which is dug down to the ground a hole is now cut just large enough to admit a man crawling on his hands and knees ; the hut is now finished, sleeping-bags, provisions, and lamp are passed inside, dogs are fed and turned loose after everything they would be liable to eat or destroy is secured by caching them in the dry snow. Arms, instruments, and ammunition should never be taken into the hut ; it is always best to leave them on the sled in the open air. After all outside work is done everybody goes into the hut and the hole is stopped from the inside with a plug of snow which has been carefully fitted, and no one is expected to go out until it is time to break camp the next morning. The combined heat from the bodies of the inmates, together with the lamp, soon raises the temperature up to the freezing point, and a degree of comfort is obtained that is not attainable in any other manner of camping in this region. The more permanent snow huts of the deer hunters, which they often occupy for a month or more, are much more elaborate. They are usually built where the snow is six or eight feet deep, so the room is high, and is approached by a covered way and an ante-room, in which the heavy outside clothing is stored, and when fuel is obtainable a kitchen is added to the structure, with a fire-place cut out of the solid walls of snow, with jambs and chimneys of the same perishable material. I saw fire-places in use that had had a fire in them for at least one hour each day for a month or more and were still intact ; the parts that were exposed had softened a little under the effects of the first fire and at once hardened into ice, and remained unchanged so long as the temperature in the open air remained below zero.

By the latter part of April or the first part of May snow houses are no longer tenable and natives take to their tents (túpeks). Their winter huts at this time are also vacated, as they become too damp for comfort. After the snow began to soften so it was no longer practicable to build a snow hut I camped very comfortably by digging a hole in the snow 6 by 8 feet, building up side walls three to four feet high, and stretching over it a deer-skin blanket or the sled sail, using the sled mast for a ridge-pole and our showshoes for rafters. The natives in their excursions usually carry a small stone lamp and a supply of seal blubber for illuminating purposes ; they use no blankets or sleeping bags when traveling, but carry a deer-skin or a piece of walrus hide to lay on the snow underneath them ; on this they huddle together without any covering other than the clothing they travel in. At such times their food (meat or fish) is eaten raw, except where they have provided themselves with a kind of pemmican, which is made by mixing chewed deer meat with deer tallow and seal oil. This food is not agreeable to the taste, probably owing to the fact that the masticators are inveterate tobacco chewers.

The sled we used on all our journeys was made by a native at Saint Michael's, and presented to the expedition by Sergeant Nelson when at Plover Bay ; it was twelve feet long and twenty inches between the runners ; had side rails, with a steering handle at the rear end, and was fastened throughout with rawhide lashings ; the runners were shod with steel, and it was far superior to any sled I ever saw on the northern coast ; it was still in excellent condition after two years' service ; its carrying capacity was about 800 pounds, and I think it was the best pattern of a sled I ever saw for Arctic work ; it was light (weighing only about fifty pounds), strong, and durable, and could always be repaired with the material at hand among the natives, should it at any time become damaged.

Early in May the hunters began to come in, and altogether I succeeded in getting from them eighteen deer, which together with five hundred eider-ducks killed by the party during the spring flight, gave us a large reserve supply of fresh meat, which was carefully stored in the cellar.

Sergeants Murdoch and Smith were indefatigable in their work, completing the collection so far as practicable in natural history, and many valuable specimens were obtained. Cracks opened in the ice to the north and west of the point, and whales were reported seen by the natives April 12; the leads were narrow, often closing entirely, with no water in sight for days, and the natives reported hearing or seeing whales nearly every day up to June 12.

The spring was very backward and we experienced a great deal of cold, disagreeable weather; the shore leads opened slowly. In Elson Bay and along shore to the eastward of Point Barrow the ice held on until late in August, and this prevented my getting along shore to the eastward with the whale-boat before the arrival of the relief vessel, as I had intended. It was my desire to explore the coast as far as the boundary at least, and had the season been as favorable as that of 1882 I could have left the station by June 12.

On June 9 the natives succeeded in killing a large whale, the first they had taken since we had been on the coast, and was the cause of considerable excitement among them for several days; they came in from all points to join the general feast on the carcass, which was free to all who cared to come and partake.

By the first of August we were becoming extremely anxious about a vessel reaching us this season, as the ground ice was still intact from Point Barrow to the Sea Horse Islands, and it was impracticable to work a small boat along shore. The whale-boat was fitted and provisioned for a voyage and held in readiness for a move as soon as the ice would let us out; outside the bar there was one narrow open lead extending as far as the eye could reach to the southwest, but there was no break in the ground ice to let us into it; besides, it closed under a westerly wind or when the prevailing northeast wind slacked up. On the morning of August 1 a thick fog hung over the ocean, and when it lifted, about 7 o'clock, our eyes were gladdened by the sight of three steamers six miles away, working slowly up the lead from the southwest. With Captain Herendeen I at once crossed the ground ice and went on board the nearest ship, reaching her about 11 a. m. Found it to be the Orca, Captain Colson, from San Francisco, a new vessel on her first voyage. From her we received our first mail, and from private letters learned that the station was to be abandoned as soon as a vessel could reach us. Captain Colson reported the balance of the whaling fleet lying at anchor along the coast between Point Hope and Cape Belcher; not being so well fitted as the new vessels, they would not venture into the pack. The Orca tied up to the ground floe off the station until along in the afternoon, when, in company with the Bowhead, Balæna, and Narwhal (all steamers that had now come up), she proceeded on up to the Point; the lead here was closed and the pack was solid to the north and east, and fast on the land to the eastward of Point Barrow; they tied up under the lee of a large floe berg that had grounded in four fathoms of water.

The following day the steamers Belvidere, Lucretia, and Mary and Helen, came up bringing considerable mail, but no orders, except one from the Chief Signal Officer directing me to dispose of such stores as could be sold to advantage. I sold what I could to the fleet, packed everything not required for immediate use, and as far as possible, without discontinuing the work of observation, made everything ready to embark, so that when the vessel sent to our relief should arrive she would be delayed as short a time as possible.

By August 15 several sailing-vessels had worked up to the station, and all were at anchor behind the ground ice which had now broken away in several places; there was also an open lead along shore. On the 16th the bark Sea Breeze (Captain McDonald) anchored off the station and reported that he had spoken the schooner Leo at anchor off Point Belcher, eighty or ninety miles to the southwest, with orders for the station. He also reported the ice close in off Sea Horse Islands, and that he thought the master of the Leo did not care to venture into the ice, as he had been lying there over a week. I at once prepared to go to her in the whale-boat by working along shore, but a heavy gale springing up from the northeast on the 17th prevented our sailing. In the mean time Capt. L. C. Owen, of the bark Rainbow (who was master of the North Star when she was wrecked in 1882), came to the station and tendered me the services of his steam whale-boat for the trip, which was very gratefully accepted. He sent it down to me on the 19th, with Mr. Rogers, his first mate, in charge, and a crew of three men. I left the station at 6.40 p. m. the same day, with Sergeant Murdoch and Interpreter Herendeen. The weather was clear and warm,

FLOEBERG ON THE BEACH, AUGUST, 1883.

with little or no wind when we started, so we steamed along shore about one-fourth mile from it, keeping inside the ground ice. At 8 p. m. a strong breeze came out from the northeast, when all sail was set, and we made great speed, so that by midnight we were off Sea Horse Islands; by this time there was a heavy sea running, and the wind had increased to a gale, and we were running before it under close-reefed mainsail and all steam, to avoid being pooped and swamped, as the sea was breaking heavily on the shoals off Point Franklin. The heavy pack was aground on the outer bar, but there was room for a vessel to pass between it and the shoals.

After rounding Point Franklin we headed for Point Belcher, and at 2 a. m. sighted several vessels at anchor off the point, apparently making very bad weather of it, as there was no shelter here from the wind and sea. As we neared them we were able in the dim twilight to make out the Leo by her peculiar rig, she being a topsail schooner, and we bore up to her and succeeded in getting a line on board as we swept past, and with considerable difficulty were taken on board. The gale increased in fury, and before we could hoist in the launch the Leo dragged her anchor and drifted rapidly to the leeward. The captain ordered the cable to be slipped, and the vessel got under way, and I requested him to keep her on a northwest course until he came up with the ice. While the vessel was being got under way, Mr. Rogers, who saw his launch was in danger of being swamped, sprang into her with his crew, cut the painter, and they disappeared from our sight in the storm. We were extremely anxious for his safety, and we had seen that all of the whalers had been obliged to put to sea at the same time we did, and that it would be impossible for him to land north of Wainwright's Inlet without losing the boat, and it was doubtful if he could keep her afloat until he reached that point. At 4 a. m. we came up with the main pack, and the vessel was hove to under the lee of a large field of ice that seemed to be nearly stationary. Here she safely rode out the gale, which abated during the night, so that on the morning of the 21st we were able to stand in toward the land, which we sighted at 7 a. m., and stood in in search of the launch and the anchor which had been slipped and buoyed the day before. At 10 a. m. the captain recovered his anchor, and we stood to the southwest along shore in search of the launch, but were unable to find any trace of her that day.

The next morning, when off Wainright's Inlet, we spoke the bark Helen Mar, and found she had the boat and party safe on board, having picked them up that morning. We then learned that Mr. Rogers had succeeded in making Wainright's Inlet after he went adrift from the Leo, and had ridden out the gale at anchor there, and, sighting the Helen Mar before he did the Leo, had gone on board of her. The wind being southwest, strong and favorable, I directed Captain Jacobson to put the Leo on her course for Úglaamie, which he did, and we came to anchorage off the station at 7 p. m., on the 22d, passing through and past considerable pack on our way. I at once landed Mr. Marr, an assistant of the United States Coast and Geodetic Survey who had been sent up to make a series of pendulum observations, with a part of his instruments; gave them all the assistance I could. At the same time I pushed the preparations for embarking, as the ice was liable to close in at any moment. We suspended work at 10 p. m. It came on to blow heavily from the southwest during the night, sending the pack in. The Leo slipped her cable, and escaped around the Point to avoid being crushed or forced ashore. We could see her spars above the ice to the eastward of the Point when we got out in the morning. Private Clarke, of the Signal Corps, and Mr. Schindler (Mr. Marr's assistant), who remained on the Leo, came down to the station overland during the day, and reported the Leo uninjured. During the night of the 23d the wind came out from the northeast and blew heavily, setting the ice about one and one-half miles off the western shore, allowing the Leo to work around to the westward of the Point during the following day, where she came to anchor at 10 p. m., the wind being too light for her to stem the strong northeast current that was setting along the shore. The wind hauled to the southeast and freshened during the night of the 24th, so that she was enabled to get under way and reach the station, anchoring there at 7 a. m. I at once caused the balance of Mr. Marr's instruments and material to be landed, but was unable to embark any stores, as Captain Jacobson in his efforts to recover his cable and anchor which he had slipped on the 23d, had gotten so far off shore that we were unable to run a line to the vessel for the purpose of warping our boats to and fro. This was necessary, as I had not sufficient men to fully man the boats and handle the stores, and the natives' boats could not be with safety used in the sharp ice that was running with the current and piled high on the beach. We worked all day trying to kedge the schooner in, but the wind blowing a gale off-shore rendered all our efforts futile. I placed Interpreter Herendeen on board that night, so that Captain Jacobson could have the benefit of his experience and advice should she again be driven away from her anchorage, as Captain Jacobson was totally inexperienced in Arctic navigation.

Just before dark five whaling barks came around the Point and anchored one and a half miles above the station. We all spent an anxious night for, the wind increased to a gale and hauled to the southwest and we could hear in the darkness the grinding of the pack as it came in, and were not surprised in getting up the next morning to find that the Leo was gone again, and that the sea was closed as far as the eye could reach. The Leo had escaped again around the Point, but three of the whaling barks had not been so fortunate; they were all fast in the pack, the crews were passing and repassing from the ship to the land over the ice. Two of the vessels had gotten foul of each other, and one, the Abraham Barker, had lost her rudder. With a glass from the lookout we could make out the Leo to the eastward of the Point, looking like a speck among the great ice fields. During the day the gale abated, the pressure slackened up, and toward night several small leads were visible. The wind came out from the southeast during the night, and early the next morning the Leo was seen to be under way slowly working her way back to the station through a narrow shore lead that opened during the night; she came to anchor off the station two hundred yards from the beach. Upon going on board I found her considerably damaged; she had been nipped, her stem partly knocked off, her rudder post split, and she was leaking badly.

In view of these facts, and orders having been received for the return of the party to the United States, I determined to abandon the station at once. During the past two days I had caused all the subsistence and quartermaster stores worth saving to be carried down from the house to the beach; a whale-line was run from the shore to the vessel, so one man could haul the boats to and fro, and the embarking was commenced at once, the first boat-load going on board at 8 a. m. Mr. Marr discontinued work on the pendulum, and took down the parts he had placed; the work went on rapidly with the two whale-boats belonging to the station. It was still impossible to use the native boats with safety, as there were great masses of loose pack-ice running with the current, and the beach was piled high with broken ice; at 2 a. m. the instruments were taken down and packed, and observations on shore ceased; the last boat-load was sent off at 10 p. m., and at 12 midnight the party went on board, leaving one man on shore, to see that the natives did not carry off anything that might have been accidentally left.

The ice was too heavy and compact the next morning to enable us to get under way, so the captain improved the time in grappling for the anchor and cable he had slipped the night of the 25th; he succeeded in recovering it, which was extremely fortunate for it was his best, the remaining one being very light. I took a party on shore and brought off the few remaining articles of any value that I did not intend to give to the natives. I left them the house and furniture intact with the stoves, and about 12 tons of coal, a grindstone, some old canvas, and a few worn-out tools, were about all that was left; but these were of great value to the natives, and after giving them a feast of hard bread and molasses we bade them good bye, amid many expressions of regret at our departure. I placed the buildings in charge of some of the most influential men, who promised they would not allow them to be torn to pieces, but be kept as a place of refuge for any shipwrecked people who may chance to be cast ashore on this barren coast. A whale-boat passed up during the day with Captain McKenna, of the bark Cyanne. He reported that his vessel was driven ashore off Point Belcher, in the gale of the 25th, and would prove a total loss. He came up to get assistance from vessels at the Point in saving her valuable cargo of whalebone.

On the morning of the 29th, the lead to the southwest being open and the wind being favorable, the captain took his anchor and got under way at 6 a. m., and we commenced our homeward voyage. The familiar shore and village and the house that had been so good and comfortable a home to us for two long years soon faded in the distance. After sailing two miles we got clear of the loose ice that was running with the current and into clear water, with the old pack close in to the northwest, arriving off Point Franklin at 9.30 p. m., when the wind fell, and we came to anchor in company with eleven ships of the whaling fleet that had worked out and had come down

ARCTIC OCEAN FROM THE STATION, AUGUST, 1883.

the same time we did. The wind came out from the westward during the night, and the captain got under way; stood off and came up with the pack about six miles from the land, when he tacked and stood in towards land; but again the current was setting so strong to the northeast that we could not make any headway on our course, and we were very glad to get back to our our anchorage under the lee of Point Franklin, where we lay until the next day, when we again got under way with a light southeast breeze, which let go after we had gotten around the Point, and we were again obliged to anchor at 10 a. m., to prevent being carried off to the northeast by the strong current setting along shore here.

Sailing-vessels navigating this sea should never allow themselves to get off soundings north of Point Belcher, except in a strong, steady wind, nor allow the vessel to drift during thick, calm weather, if it is possible to get an anchor down. The needle is useless here; the land or lead line is the only safe guide, for, should a sailing-vessel be carried off soundings off Point Barrow with light winds or calm, she runs great danger of being lost; this has been the fate of nearly all vessels so caught, especially late in the season.

At 4 p. m., the breeze freshening, we got under way again and stood on our course along the coast and about four miles from it. We experienced light, baffling winds, making but little headway from that time until the afternoon of September 2, when the wind came out strong and steady from the northeast. We sighted and passed Cape Lisburne that day and sighted the Diomede Islands at noon on the 3d. During the day the wind increased to a gale and the weather grew thick and cold, with considerable snow; sail was shortened, and at 3 p. m. we passed Cape Prince of Wales, running at great speed before the wind; after passing through the straits the vessel was headed for Norton Sound, it being necessary that I should go to Saint Michael's to land Private E. Clarke, of the Signal Corps, who had been sent out to relieve Sergeant Leavitt, an observer on that station. As soon as we hauled under the high land to the south and east of Cape Prince of Wales we ran out of the wind, and our progress was slow.

On the 4th of September the fog lifted and we sighted Kings Island and Cape York, and on the 6th passed close to the southward of Sledge Island, but, owing to a head wind, did not sight the high land near Saint Michael's until the 8th. We stood in towards it and came to anchor off the fort at noon on that day, where we were received by a salute fired from a couple of old ship guns. Soon after a boat came off to us bringing, very much to our surprise, Lieut. Frederick Schwatka, Third Cavalry, who reported that he had made the passage of the Yukon on a raft, exploring its course from its source to its mouth, making one of the most remarkable raft voyages on record. He had been at Saint Michael's since the last of August, and was extremely anxious to get away with his party. Though we were very much crowded on the Leo I did not think it would be right to refuse him passage, as there would be no opportunity for him to return to the United States before another year, this station being visited only by vessels of the Alaska Commercial Company, and there would be none due before the following June. So I directed him to hold his party in readiness to come on board as soon as we were ready to sail. We were short of fresh water and had to lay in a supply before again putting to sea. For the first two days we were in port it blew a gale from the southeast, so it was impossible to get any water off to the ship; on the afternoon of the 16th the captain reported he had succeeded in getting enough on board to last us until we could reach Únalaska or Plover Bay, whichever place I should conclude to go to, so at daylight on the 11th Lieutenant Schwatka and his party were taken on board and we put to sea at 10 a. m. Found it was blowing a gale from the northwest when we got outside, and after making a few tacks under close-reefed sails, found we were making no headway, so we were glad to run back into the harbor, where we came to anchor at 3 p. m.

The following morning, the wind having hauled more to the north, we again put to sea, and the next morning sighted Cape Darby, a high headland on the northern shore of Norton Sound. We were obliged to make this northing to avoid a dangerous shoal that makes out from the mouth of the Yukon; in running out of Norton Sound it is not safe to run west, south of 64 Lat. During the afternoon of the 13th the wind settled in the northwest and blew hard and steadily all that night, and we found it would be slow work beating up to Plover Bay. The ship was leaking so badly that the pumps were kept going one-third of the time and the slightest accident to them would soon send her to the bottom; and as I knew that the meridian of Únalaska had been as well, if not better, determined than that of Plover Bay, I decided not to go to the latter place, but to proceed direct to Unalaska and there make an effort to repair the vessel, as I was told that there was sufficient tide at that place to enable us to get at her bottom by discharging her cargo and placing her on the beach at high tide and working on her during low water; so as soon as we were clear of the Yukon flats she was put on her course for that place. The wind increased to a heavy gale from the northwest on the 15th, and we made excellent time as we were running nearly before it. During the night of the 16th, the vessel was hove to to wait for daylight, as we knew we were near land, and on the morning of the 17th we sighted the island of Unalaska to the south and about twenty miles away; the wind had fallen so light during the night we were able to make but little headway and did not get into the harbor and at anchor until 10 o'clock that night.

We found the United States steamer Corwin and the Alaska Commercial Company's steamer Dora at anchor here, the former on her return from Kotzebue Sound and the latter on her annual voyage to the Aleutian Island stations. The wind not being favorable to sail into the inner harbor, which was the only place where the vessel could be safely beached, I made application to Captain Healy, commanding the Corwin, for the assistance of the cutter to tow the Leo in, he very readily complied with the request, and at once got up steam, and at 11 a. m. placed the Leo at the company's wharf, where the bulk of her cargo was discharged; owing to a severe wind storm prevailing at this time we were unable to haul her up until the afternoon of the 20th, when she was beached at high tide; we improved the time in getting observations of the sun, and determining the declination of the needle. We were unable to get at the leak on the first ebb, but on the 21st the water fell sufficiently low to enable the workmen to repair the damage, which was found to be about four feet below her water line, where a butt had been started, and the water was so clear that we could see that she had sustained no damage below that point, and we were pleased to find upon floating her off on the next high tide that the leak was entirely stopped.

Such stores as had not been disposed of were re-embarked on the 22d and the vessel warped out to her anchorage ready for sailing. The 23d was too stormy to admit of our going to sea, but the wind having abated slightly toward night, I directed the captain to get under way on the morning of the 24th, which was done at 8 a. m., being towed outside the heads by the Corwin, whose services had again been kindly placed at our disposal by Captain Healy. We found the wind blowing strong from the northwest when we got outside, and a very heavy sea running; we parted company with the Corwin as soon as we passed the capes by the breaking of our tow-line, and the Leo was at once headed for the pass of Akoutan, through which we passed out into the Pacific at 12 m. From this time the wind continued fair during the whole of the voyage across the North Pacific. We followed nearly in the track of the great circle route, and made such remarkably good time that the Farallones were sighted at 3 p. m.

On October 6 the wind fell as we ran in toward land, and we drifted through the Golden Gate in a dead calm that night at 12 o'clock, coming to anchor off the Presidio at 2 a. m. October 7, and reporting to the Chief Signal Officer by telegraph the same day.

The object for which the expedition was organized being accomplished, it was formally disbanded October 15; its work having extended through a period of over twenty-seven months, during which time the expedition had sailed over 7,500 miles, had established and maintained itself at the northern extremity of this continent in latitude 71° 16′ north, and successfully carried out the instructions received from the Chief Signal Officer, and brought back the record of an unbroken series of hourly observations in meteorology, magnetism, tides, and earth temperatures, besides a large collection in natural history and ethnology, and penetrated into the interior to a point never before visited by civilized man.

During the whole period all the members of the expedition enjoyed excellent health, not having a single man on the sick report for two years.

To the individual members of the expedition who returned with it to the United States great credit is due for their obedience to orders, faithfulness, and intelligence in performance of their duties, and for their patient endurance of the many trials they were called upon to suffer; for the work of scientific observations in these high latitudes is one of patient endurance on the part of the observer, confined, as he is, within narrow limits, without the excitement incident to travel. The unvarying monotony of the work is necessarily very wearing, but during the whole time no murmur or complaint was ever heard.

APPENDIX 6

Ethnographic Sketch of the Natives of Point Barrow

Lt. P.H. Ray

During our stay we improved each opportunity to add to our knowledge of the peculiar people inhabiting this coast. A want of sufficient knowledge of their language at first made the work difficult, as we had no interpreter. So our first energies were devoted to learning their language sufficiently well to communicate with them, as none of them could speak a word of English, neither did they show any disposition to learn.

Of their origin and descent we could get no trace, there being no record of events kept among them. Even the sign record of prominent events in individual life, so common among some of the natives in the lower latitudes, is almost unknown among them. Their language abounds in legends, but none of these gave any data by which we could judge how long these desolate shores have been inhabited.

That the ancestors of those people have made it their home for ages is conclusively shown by the ruins of ancient villages and winter huts along the sea-shore and in the interior. On the point where the station was established were mounds marking the site of three huts dating back to the time when they had no iron and men "talked like dogs"; also at Perigniak a group of mounds mark the site of an ancient village. It stands in the midst of a marsh; a sinking of the land causing it to be flooded and consequently abandoned, as it is their custom to select the high and dry points of land along the sea-shore for their permanent villages. The fact of our finding a pair of wooden goggles twenty-six feet below the surface of the earth, in the shaft sunk for earth temperatures, points conclusively to the great lapse of time since these shores were first peopled by the race of man. That they have followed the receding line of ice, which at one time capped the northern part of this continent, along the easiest lines of travel is shown in the general distribution of a similar people, speaking a similar tongue, from Greenland to Behring Straits; in so doing they followed the easiest natural lines of travel along the water-courses and the sea-shore, and the distribution of the race to-day marks the routes traveled. The sea-shore led them along the Labrador and Greenland coasts; Hudson's Bay and its tributary waters carried its quota towards Boothia Land; helped by Back's Great Fish River, the Mackenzie carried them to the northwestern coast; and down the Yukon they came to people the shores of Norton Sound and along the coast to Cape Prince of Wales. They occupied some of the coast to the south of the mouth of the Yukon, and a few drifted across Behring Straits on the ice, and their natural traits are still in marked contrast with their neighbors, the Chuckchee. They use dogs instead of deer, the natives of North America having never domesticated the reindeer, take their living from the sea, and speak a different tongue. Had the the migration come from Asia it does not stand to reason that they would have abandoned the deer upon crossing the straits.

The following table will show that physically the Inyu of North America coast does not conform to the typical idea of the Eskimo. They are robust, healthy people, fairer than the North American Indian, with brown eyes and straight black hair. The men are beardless until they attain the age of from twenty to twenty-five years, and even then it is very light and scattering, and is always clipped close in the winter; at this season they also cut off their eyebrows and tonsure their crown like a priest, with bangs over their forehead. Their hands and feet are

MÛMMÛÑĬÑÄ, "PRINCESS OF NUWŬK."

extremely small and symmetrical; they are graceful in their movements when unincumbered by heavy clothing; they are kind and gentle in disposition and extremely hospitable to strangers; though they may rob a stranger of every means of obtaining a subsistence one moment, they will divide with him their last piece of meat the next. They have no form of government, but live in a condition of anarchy; they make no combinations, either for offensive or defensive purposes, having no common enemies to guard against, nor have they any punishment for crimes. I never knew one to attempt to reclaim stolen property, though they might see it in the hands of the thief or left on his cache; though given to petty pilfering they rarely, if ever, break into a cache (except into one of meat when driven to it by hunger) or enter a tent or hut for that purpose. During the first winter we had stores, of which they were in great need, in a Sibley tent, and they all knew they were there; and although the tent was only tied, with no regular guard over it, nothing was ever disturbed, though if anything was carelessly left out it would be stolen at once. They never made the slightest resistance to our reclaiming property when discovered, and would laugh about it as though it were a good joke. They are very social in their habits and kind to each other; we never witnessed a quarrel between men during the whole time we were on the coast, neither did we ever see a child struck or punished; and a more obedient or better lot of children cannot be found in all Christendom. I never saw one of any age do a vicious or mean act, and while they were always around the station during the fall and winter, they did no mischief, but, on the contrary, would busy themselves in shoveling the snow out of the tunnels and running on errands and doing any work they could for a little food each day. The children would wait around the door for members of the party to come out to take their daily exercise, and, even more, would accompany each member, and every few moments they would say "naumi-tanity" (now let me see), and would scan the traveler's face for frost-bites, and were ever ready with a handful of snow to be applied should they detect the slightest sign of freezing; for when the temperature gets below −45°, and there is a light breeze, it cuts every exposed part of the body as though white hot metal were applied, causing no pain. Their games were very alike what we see played among children of our own race, and in imitating the pursuits of the elders, we often saw them with snow play-houses cut into the hard snow, with snow images set up, and the little fur-clad mites of humanity bustling around, playing at keeping house and making calls, with the temperature at − 40°.

All the people on that coast from Wainwright Inlet around to the mouth of the Colville are comprised in the following villages whose population comprise all the inhabitants of this coast:

Name of village.	Location.	No. of families.	Total population.
Kuñmeun	Wainwright Inlet...............	10	80
Sidáru	Southwest Point Belcher.......	8	50
Ŭglaamie	Cape Smythe	23	130
Nuwŭk	Point Barrow.	31	150
Total....		....	410

Between Point Barrow and the Colville the country is uninhabited in the winter. The resources of this region are so limited that in the struggle for existence, these people are obliged to devote all their energies and time to procuring necessary food and clothing to maintain life, never being able to get a sufficient supply of meat ahead to lay in a reserve; famine always stares them in the face should they relax their efforts.

With the return of the sun each year their active life commences. Those that have arms and dogs go into the interior about the 1st of February to hunt reindeer; those belonging to the villages of Nuwŭk and Ŭglaamie go to the south and hunt along the Meade and Ĭk-pĭk-pŭñ; those from the vicinity of Wainwright Inlet hunt along the Ku; the others scatter along the western shore for the purpose of taking seal, and ducks as the season advances. Their tents, one or two in a place, seen by summer voyagers in this sea, has given rise to the belief that this coast is much more densely populated than it is in fact. For when the tents are out the villages are empty.

SCENE IN ÜGLAAMIE. TENT WITH NATIVES AT WORK. SUMMER CAMP.

The hunters return to the winter huts between the 1st and 10th of May, and the omélĭks or boat-headers make up their crews for the whaling season. A boat-header (omélĭk) is one who is noted for his success in taking whales, and of course is a man of experience and considerable influence. The crews are made up of men and women, generally ten to each boat; some crews are paid by the omélĭk, who feeds them and pays them in deer skins or other articles of native traffic; others ship on a lay, each member furnishing his own supplies and they all share alike in the catch, the boat-header furnishing the gear. The women who are tabooed and the children cook and carry food out to the crews, who come in to the land as seldom as possible, and never go into a house, if it can be avoided. At this season, too, no work is done that will necessitate pounding or hewing or in fact any noise, neither shall there be work of any kind carried on in the tent (tupĕk) of any member of a crew. Should their garments be accidentally torn, the woman must take them far back on the *tundra* out of sight of the sea and mend them; they have little tents, in which just one person can sit, in which this work is done. During the spring of 1882 they came to me and asked that I stop the work on the shaft, saying that it would offend the whales at this season. Early in March all hands turn to and build a road through the pack over which the boats can be hauled out to the lead; this often necessitates a great deal of labor, especially when the lead opens far off shore, as it did in 1882.

The village and camps are in a constant state of bustle and excitement at this season of the year; boat covers are being renewed or repaired; harpoons and lances are gotten out and every part of the woodwork carefully scraped; seal-skin pokes are lying about, looking like bloated seals, and the skulls of wolves, raven skins, or eagle skins are in great demand, for no no boat would be considered equipped without some such talisman. Daily the old men, especially those who are successful in curing the sick, meet on the sea-shore and (abawa) talk for an east wind, so the ice will be driven off shore and a lead, favorable for whales, opened; and their faith remains unshaken through repeated failures, and when questioned as to the reason why their supplications remained unanswered they always attributed it to some offense they had given to the spirit. When the lead opens there is great rejoicing, and for a few days they display the utmost vigilance; but should the whales fail to appear in a few days, they soon grow careless and cease cruising, haul their boats up on the ice and patiently wait for a whale to come to them, taking turns in standing watch while the others sleep or shoot seal and duck, which abound in the open leads at this season.

As the season advances the boat crews are gradually broken up, and by the middle of June all boats are brought to the land, when parties are made up to go to Nĭgalĕk, a place at the mouth of the Colville, where the people from Nuwŭk and Ŭglaamie go to meet a band called Nu-na-tá′ñ-meun (inland people), where they barter oil and blubber for deer, fox, and wolverine skins. They sometimes meet here the Kŭñ-mŭ′d′-lĭñs and It-kŭ′d′-lĭñs, bands that live along the coast between the Colville and Mackenzie. This meeting breaks up about the 15th of August, when they slowly return along the coast, hunting by the way, and reach their winter villages from the 15th of September to the 1st of October, about the same time the traders go to the eastward.

A few of the leading families from both villages pitch their tents at Perigniak, a point on the sand spit, about five miles from Nuwŭk, where the eider ducks fly over, and spend the summer there, living entirely upon ducks and whitefish. The ducks they take with slings and guns and the fish with gill-nets made from sinews of the reindeer. Those who are too poor to own a gun or to have oil for trade scatter through the interior, carrying their kaiaks on their heads to cross the numerous lakes and rivers, and gain a precarious livelihood by catching the young reindeer, the young and moulting ducks which are found in great numbers in the lakes and along Meade River, where they also take a few whitefish with gill-nets. The ducks are taken with a light ivory-headed spear, which has a shaft seven feet long, one-half inch in diameter, with three long ivory barbs in the middle. It is thrown with a hand-board from a kaiak, the barbs catching the birds by the neck when missed by the lariat stroke.

Their usual mode of travel along the shore in summer is by the umiak, the large skin boat; with a fair wind they hoist a small lug-sail, but the boats being flat bottom will not sail on the wind, so with a head wind or calm weather the boats are towed by dogs, using the walrus harpoon line for a towing line; they never resort to the labor of paddling except when in pursuit of game or in some emergency. When a landing is made the boat is hauled up above high water, and turned over and serves temporarily for a tent. By the 1st of October all have returned to their winter huts, and are busy getting them in order for the winter; all the inside timbers and floors are carefully scraped, the passages which have become filled with ice during the summer are picked out, windows of walrus intestines are stretched over the openings, and by the 15th all are housed for the winter. And the seal-nets and spears are repaired and made ready, and, as soon as the ocean is frozen over, parties are constantly out on the ice, hunting for air-holes where the seal come to get air. As soon as one is discovered a number of families go off to it in the following manner: the nets are twenty-five feet long and fourteen feet deep, with meshes large enough to admit a seal's head, and are rigged with stone sinkers along the bottom, and at the two upper corners are attached two rawhide thongs about forty feet long, one of which has a light weight attached to the end. Holes twelve inches in diameter, about thirty-five feet apart, are drilled through the ice about sixty feet back from the air-holes; the weighted line is dropped through one hole, and hauled up through the other by a long pole with a hook attached; this pole is made from small pieces of drift-wood carefully spliced together with lashings of whalebone; by this line the net is hauled underneath the ice, hanging down like a curtain between one of the holes and held in its place by the lines being attached to a wooden pin. In this manner the air-hole is surrounded by nets as far as practicable; one man or boy is left to attend to each net, and the strictest silence enjoined; no word is spoken; the watcher, wrapped in his heaviest coat, patiently awaits through the long hours; he occasionally scratches the surface of the ice with a scratcher, which is made of a set of seal claws attached to a piece of wood. The seal, in coming to the hole for air, strikes into the net; the strain loosens the lines from the peg and he entangles himself and soon drowns, when he is hauled out through one of the sealing holes and the net reset. Over one hundred seal are sometimes taken at a single air-hole within twenty-four hours, but they can be taken in this manner only during the dark of the moon—any light will betray the presence of the net. During May quite a number are taken at their breathing-holes, which have become enlarged, and through which they haul out on the surface of the ice at that season, by removing the weights from the nets and setting it across the hole with four lines on the under side of the ice.

At this season, also, many seals are taken with the hand spear, at the "adlu," the breathing-hole of a single seal. It is usually detected by an excessive deposit of hoar-frost on the surface of the snow over the hole; the snow is cleared away down to the solid ice, and in the hole, which is about one inch in diameter at the surface, is placed an ivory needle about one foot long and one-eighth of an inch in diameter; to the upper end a small cross-bar is attached, to prevent it dropping through, and a small feather, and the hunter takes his stand on a three-legged stool, which is always a part of his regular equipment, and patiently awaits the coming of the seal, of which the feathered needle gives warning; after the stroke is delivered, if he succeeds in fastening to the seal, he proceeds to enlarge the hole until it will admit hauling him to the surface; this is usually done with an ivory pick attached to the shaft of his spear; as soon as a seal is taken its mouth is fastened open with a piece of ice, and a slot cut through the lower jaw before it becomes frozen. Should he be far out in the pack, where the ice is too rough for a sled to be used, the seal is dragged home by a hand drag, which is a strong loop about two feet long, made of walrus hide thong, fitted with an ivory toggle or handle, generally carved in imitation of two seals fastened together; this loop is passed through the slot in the seal's jaw and over the toggle; each hunter must be supplied with at least one of these drags, as it is not considered proper to fasten to a seal with a line that is used for any other purpose; when they get near shore the drag is removed and a few drops of fresh water is poured into the mouth of each seal before it is taken from the ice to the land; they generally go through with the same ceremony with ducks that have been killed at sea, but never with those that have been killed over the land, and the bones of seals are carefully preserved unbroken and returned to the sea, if possible, either by being left in a crack in the ice, far out from the land, or dropped through some open hole in the ice. By so doing they believe that good fortune will follow them in pursuit of seal, which is their main dependence, for from its skin they make their summer boots and soles for their winter boots; its blubber supplies the oil for their lamps during the long night, and with any surplus they may have they purchase deer-skins for clothing from the natives from the interior, and its flesh when cooked is an excellent article of food. The few reindeer and water fowl they take are looked upon more as a luxury than a necessity, and the flesh of the reindeer is the greatest luxury of all; those who have it carefully hoard it, and when they knew that we had some in store they would often come and beg for a small piece to be used as medicine for some sick person.

Immediately after the departure of the sun, when food is plentiful, it is customary for each village to hold a kind of high carnival for three days; friends are invited from the neighboring villages, and the time is passed in dancing, singing, and feasting; the "kûdyïgïn" (council-house) is fitted up with a new roof of ice, and crowded day and night, fresh dancers taking the places of those tired out, and the dull tum-tum of the drum, mingled with snatches of song and shouts of laughter can be heard coming from almost every iglu.

It is customary at this season to exchange presents, especially among the more wealthy and influential ones; but the giver expects value received in return, and should he fail to receive a satisfactory present he does not fail to let his wants be known, and he often announces beforehand what articles would be most desirable in case he should make a present. In 1883 I was invited to attend one of these gatherings at Numŭk, and the old omélïk who was sent as bearer of the invitation brought a statement of what they were going to give me; after waiting around the station for an hour or two he called me to one side and called over a long list of articles that they expected me to give in return, but as rum (tûñ-a), rifles, and ammunition were leading items in the list, the visit was never made. A trade is made a matter of grave debate, and frequent discussions asking for a little more, no matter how much has been offered, and when an offer has been made they will go away and send the article by another person; and often when a trade has been completed they will come and demand their goods back, often leaving the articles they had received on the door-step, and when asked what they will take have great difficulty in making up their minds; and in making boots and clothing they will slight their work in every imaginable way unless carefully watched. I had occasion to purchase seal-oil, and they commenced bringing it to me in old tin cans that they had picked up at the station, and after a few honest deliveries they commenced bringing us cans filled with two-thirds ice and a little oil on top, and betrayed themselves by being over-anxious to get their pay before we emptied the cans.

My first invitation to one of their ceremonies came in December, 1881, through old Nïkawáalu, of Ûglaamie, who came over to the station with a small delegation and in a grave, dignified manner said that the people of Ûglaamie would be made glad if Captain Herendeen and myself would come with him and see the dance. We at once started over, and as we approached the village we found a crowd upwards of 200 people collected around the council house; besides the Ûglaamie people, there were delegations from Nuwŭk and Sidaru. They were silently watching a pantomime that was being enacted by five men and two women who were standing in a row with the women on the right and left, facing the south, with the council-house behind them, and the crowd in front. They were attired in new suits of deer-skin worn with the flesh side out, dressed perfectly white; the men wore tall conical hats of seal-skin, ornamented with dentalium shells and tufts of ermine and Arctic fox fur. The women were bareheaded, with their hair neatly plaited. Behind the dancers sat a drummer and two singers, to whose doleful chant the dancers kept time with their feet, at the same time swaying their bodies from right to left with spasmodic jerks, the women occasionally joining in the song, while the men one at a time would spring a few paces to the front and in wild gestures portray how they had taken seal, bear, or deer, being cheered by the crowd as they finished and took their place in the line. The day was clear, and their grotesque figures showed in sharp relief against the southern sky that glowed with the twilight of a winter noon; their wild surroundings, backed by a frozen ocean, made up a picture peculiar only to the Arctic, and, once seen, not soon to be forgotten. After each had danced in turn, and it seemed a long time to us standing waiting in the snow in a temperature of 18°, they adjourned to the council-house, where as many crowded in as could find standing room, in a room 16 by 20; the air was redolent with odors from the lamp and the unwashed crowd, and, as the frost had hermetically sealed the roof and walls, there was no ventilation and the heat and stench soon became almost unbearable to us who were unaccustomed to such life. Two large stone lamps lit up the low room with a hazy light; across the side opposite to the entrance a space 6 by 8 feet was curtained off with deer-skins, and in front of it was a model of a tree suspended from the ceiling, and, as the knowledge of the native who designed it was confined to the few pieces of drift-wood found on the beach and some pieces of timber cast ashore from wrecks, the specimen was unique; it consisted of two oblong boxes open at both ends loosely attached together endwise with seal thong; the part representing the body was 2 feet long, 8 inches square, and that representing the top 18 inches long and 6 inches square, and was suspended by a thong with the lower end two feet from the floor. On the right and left of the tree hung the skull of a wolf and the dried carcass of a raven; two of the singers sat flat upon the floor with their legs extended, one close behind the other, the foremost one with his nose just touching the tree. As soon as all were in position the drummers, accompanied by the women, struck up a doleful chant to which the man at the tree kept time in his supplications to (Tuña) the Great Spirit to give them success in pursuit of whales, deer, seal, &c., and to send white men with plenty of rum and tobacco; and he particularly dwelt upon certain articles he knew we had at the station; at the same time he beat the body of the tree with a wand. As he completed his schedule of wants the lower edge of the curtain was raised and five natives crawled forth on their hands and knees. They were dressed in the skins of the bear, wolf, lynx, fox, and the dog,t he heads being dressed complete, showing the grinning teeth. On their hands were large mittens of dried seal-skin, with shells and small pieces of copper attached with pieces of thong, so that they swung and rattled as they moved their heads. They crawled slowly forward, swinging their heads in unison, keeping time to the music in hoarse growls, and by shaking their huge mittens until their heads touched the singers by the tree, when they all sprang to their feet with a loud shout, and the performance was brought to a close by all joining in a wild shout accompanied by spasmodic gestures that seemed to threaten a dislocation of their joints.

As we came out in the open air we found another party just commencing the out-door dance, and so they kept it up night and day. Each party as they completed their dance were feasted by friends in different iglus. The invisible spirit (Tuña) peoples the earth, sea, and air; we never could find that they gave it any place of fixed abode; visible at times, as many of the old men insisted that they had seen him, and described him as resembling the upper part of a man, but very wide, with an extremely large head and long fangs: he is the creator of all things, and also the destroyer, is ever to be feared, especially in the night, and men and women, when out at such a time, usually carry a large knife to defend themselves should they meet him. That they believe in ghosts was apparent in the case of a woman who had been doing some work for our party. Coming to the station one day and being asked to mend a pair of gloves, said she dare not, as there was a dead man in the village, and his body had not yet been carried out; that he would see her and some evil would befall her. Upon being urged, she first obtained her husband's permission, and then seating herself in the middle of the floor, she drew a circle around her with a bone snow-knife she carried, and remarked that now he could not see her; she was very careful to keep her work all inside the circle, and would not leave it until all was completed.

They dislike to go out on a dark night, but if obliged to, they generally carry a bone or ivory snow-knife or a long bladed steel knife, to keep off Tuña and Kíolya (Aurora), which they believe to be equally evil; but Tuña especially is concerned in producing all the evils of life. Should the whales fail to put in an early appearance, the birds fly high or far out over the pack, the shore lead open late, a gale blow down their caches and break their gear and boats, the old and wise would meet in solemn conclave to devise some means whereby the works of Tuña shall be exorcised and he shall be driven forth from the village. Various means are resorted to; the most common one is for the principal men to meet and (abawa) talk, chanting together in a loud tone, accompanied by beating of drums; they call for the east wind (nigyû) to blow on the ice (siko) to open it. Individual wants are by personal supplication, and to them, earth and air are full of spirits. The one drags men into the earth by the feet, from which they never emerge; the other strikes men dead, leaving no mark, and the air is full of voices; often while traveling they would stop and ask me to listen, and say that Tuña of the wind was passing by. With the return of the sun he is hunted out of each iglu by incantations that would daunt the boldest spirit. A fire is built in front of the council-house, and at the entrance to each iglu is posted an old woman wise in ghost lore; the men gather around the council-house while the young women and girls drive the spirits out of the iglu with their knives, thrusting them under the bunk and deer skins in a vicious manner, calling upon Tuña to leave the iglu; after they think he has been driven out of every nook and corner,

SCENE IN ÜGLAAMIE.

they drive him down through the hole in the floor and chase him out into the open air with loud shouts and frantic gestures. While this was going on the old woman at the entrance, who was armed with a long knife used for cutting snow, made passes over the air with it to keep him from returning. Each party drove the spirit towards the fire and invoked him to go into it; all were by this time drawn up in a half circle around the fire, when several of the leading men made specific charges against the spirit; and each, after his speech, brushed his clothing violently, calling upon the spirit to leave him and go into the fire; two men now stepped forward with rifles loaded with blank charges while a third came with a vessel of urine, which was thrown upon the fire; at the same time one fired a shot into it; and, as the cloud of steam rose, it received the shot, which was supposed to have finished him for the time being. While they were ever threatening or supplicating Tuña we never knew them to offer thanks or be grateful for any benefits he was supposed to bestow; everything they received was taken as a matter of course, and as the result of some particular incantation.

I saw a very ingenious contrivance an old man had rigged up to keep Tuña from entering his iglu. He had his seal drag, which was fitted with a carved ivory handle, suspended over the entrance inside his hut; the thong was fastened by his hunting knife being driven through it into the roof; he explained to me that Tuña in coming in would catch hold of the handle of the seal drag to help himself through the hole and would pull the knife down upon his head and be frightened away. He contemplated his contrivance with a great deal of satisfaction, and assured me that Tuña was very much afraid of his iglu.

Their dead are carried out and laid on the tundra without any ceremony other than the near relatives following the body to its last resting place; it is usually wrapped in deer skins, and if a man, his sled and hunting gear are broken and laid over the body; if a woman, her sewing kit and some few household utensils are placed at her head, but everything so left is broken and rendered useless. With but few exceptions I never knew them to pay any attention to their dead after they were carried out, and all showed great reluctance about speaking of them. The bodies are usually eaten by the dogs, especially in the winter, and it is no uncommon sight to see them gnawing the bones on the roofs of the iglus. The sled used to carry the body out on the tundra is not brought back to the village at once, but left out on the tundra not less than two moons, and while they all claim that it is bad to use anything that belonged to the dead, I noticed that no matter how good an outfit he had while living his was the most worthless sled and gun that could be found, and I knew of a number of cases where there was a general division of a dead man's effects on a basis of first come first served. As a rule the dead (Nu'nami-sinĭk, on the ground asleep) are soon forgotten, and the names of the noted whalemen or hunters only live in legend.

There is no marriage ceremony among them, but children are often betrothed by their parents at an early age, and this promise is very faithfully kept, and they enter upon their marriage relations at the age of twelve to fifteen years; where there has been no childhood engagement the mother makes a selection of the wife for her son, and the girl selected is invited to the house, where she takes the place of a servant for a short time, doing the housework and cooking, generally returning to her father's iglu to sleep. They usually avail themselves of the summer trip along the coast or into the interior, and take upon themselves the full obligations of marriage. They often have family disagreements, the husband resorting to blows when the wife is sulky and disobedient, sometimes with the result of her running away; and we knew of one instance where, owing to a slight mistake the husband had made in his estimate of his wife's character, he obtained results not anticipated, for while out on a deer hunt he attempted to chastise her for some fancied neglect of duty when she retaliated, and, being the stronger of the two, she gave him a severe thrashing, and then taking with her an adopted child she fled to a village seventy-five miles away. She subsequently gave up the child, but would not return to him, and soon after became the wife of another man. At the time we landed at Úglaamie this same woman carried on her back a box of lead weighing two hundred and eighty pounds a distance of over two hundred yards.

The women as a rule seem to have an equal voice in the direction of affairs, when once admitted to the position of wife, and in each village there are a number of old women who are treated with the greatest consideration by all, they being credited with wonderful powers of divination, and are consulted in all important affairs. And the wives are treated with more consideration by their husbands than they are by savages of the lower latitudes, though to her falls the drudgery of housekeeping, dressing skins, and making boots and clothing; his task is equally hard, as he is exposed to the dangers of the ice and storms in the pursuit of seal and deer, often returning to his iglu completely exhausted. She aids and assists him by following his trail with the dogs and sleds to bring in the game which the hunter catches in the snow where he kills it, setting up a cake of snow or ice with his mark upon it, to mark the place. The wife is invariably consulted when any trade is to be made, and the husband never thinks of closing a bargain of any importance without her consent. When traveling they take turn about in leading out ahead of the team, and all assist in building the snow hut when camp is made. The wife also has the care of the dogs, with whom she often shares her food, giving as much care to the puppies as she would to a child, carrying them in the back of her ahtega or wrapped in skin on the sled when traveling, until they are old enough to be harnessed into the team, when by their faithfulness and endurance they make full return for all kindness shown them in their childhood (puppyhood), and although a dog team would try the patience of a saint, they never use a whip and rarely strike them; they coax and encourage them along by the voice; and often toward the end of a journey they hasten their pace by dragging a piece of fresh meat by a string in front of the team, being careful to keep it just beyond their reach. They give the most careful attention to their foot-gear, especially when traveling during the winter; and here a woman's services are invaluable, as she is very expert in the use of her needle, and she dries and repairs the boots of the party before she sleeps; this is necessary owing to the frail character of the skins used in making their winter boots. Men do such work when alone, but not so well as the women. She also carries a seal-skin water-bottle on her back under her "alige," which is replenished with snow after each draught, and is their sole dependence for water on long, rapid journeys during the winter.

Large families are very rare, and children are born at intervals of from two to four years; they do not often bear children before twenty, and a couple is very seldom met with that has a family of more than three, though upon inquiry they may have some that "nuna-mi-sinĭk, "sleep on the ground," and where the people are poor it is not unusual for a mother to give away all but the first-born to some couple that have no children; boys are in greater demand than girls for adoption, and the adopted mother gives it all the care she would a child of her own, and will rarely if ever tell who the real mother is. So it is very difficult to trace the antecedents of any one man, for during his childhood he may have passed into two or three different families by adoption, and many of them do not know who their mother is, much less their father, and matters are still further complicated by a custom of exchanging wives. This is often done when a man is obliged to make a long trip, and his wife from any cause is unable to accompany him. He will exchange with some friend who has an able-bodied wife, each entering upon their new relations with the greatest cheerfulness.

Polygamy is not common, being confined to the leading influential men; even then, they are taken into the family more as assistants for the first wife, as she rules over them, treating them as servants; the system is not popular among the women, and we knew instances where the first wife abandoned the iglu in a rage when a second was brought home.

When a man of matured years loses his wife, either by death or from incompatibility of temper, he selects one for himself, and that they sometimes use force to coerce them, when they have no near relations to protect them, I am well satisfied from an incident that occurred at the station. A native from a village to the westward, whose wife had left him, came up to Ŭglaamie to obtain another; one day we were attracted by loud outcries from a woman who had been waiting around the station for food, and upon going out to see what the difficulty was, we found our friend from Sidàru vigorously cuffing her ears, and it was some time before we could make him desist; as soon as she got free from him she ran off, and he explained that he wanted her for a wife, but that she was not willing to go with him, and he was persuading her. His courtship was certainly unique, and I never heard that he succeeded in winning the affections of an Ŭglaamie maiden, and it is but just to add that he was very unpopular among both men and women.

The tie of relationship binds them to deeds of kindness that they would not show to people outside of the family; if a brother dies the survivor takes the family to his iglu until he can find another husband for the widow, and we know of an instance where a man lost his wife, and his

UNALINĂ, "PRINCE OF NUWŬK."

brother who had two (who were sisters) gave him one. Their efforts to get husbands for the widows of dead relatives were often very amusing. Mŭ′ñialu, a hunter employed at the station, was supporting his widowed mother, who was a great scold; he brought to his iglu several candidates for her hand, who had been induced to take the step by Mŭ′ñialu offering to make them presents provided they would take her, but a few days or weeks was about all the most patient could bear; after several trials and failures among the men of Nuwŭk and Ŭglaamie, he finally gave it up, but on one of his trips to the eastward he brought back with him a Nunatáñ-meuñ from Colville; as he was quite deaf and could not understand the Ŭglaamie language very well, her shrewishness had no effect upon him, and Mŭñi was happy; he would laugh immoderately when talking about it; but never, through it all, was he disloyal to his mother; she always had a place in his iglu, plenty to eat, and was always treated with the greatest respect.

In the treatment of their aged and infirm parents, the example set by these people could well be followed by many of the more civilized nations to their advantage; they never forget the tender care they received in their childhood, and as their parents grow old and are unable to maintain themselves the children display the greatest devotion. The first fruits of the chase is freely given up to them, and no project undertaken without their approval; and in all things the son remains obedient to the father so long as he lives, and speaks of him with the greatest respect after his death. In their summer journeyings, should they wish to remain at home they fit them up a tent (tupĕk) in some pleasant locality, and leave them an abundant supply of provisions, but more often accompany them in their wanderings, being comfortably transported by sled or boat; but the old people are rarely idle, for while the father busies himself making new seal spears and nets the mother assists in providing clothing and boots and dressing skins. We often had our day's journey brought to a sudden termination by some old woman in the party announcing that it was time to go into camp because she was tired or cold, and nothing we could say would overrule her decision.

Owing to the exposure and hardships they are obliged to undergo in the struggle for existence they very rarely attain a very great age, and the majority by far die under the age of forty years, and a man at sixty becomes very decrepit. They have no means of keeping a record of their age, and it is generally calculated from some event connected with their history, as the coming of some ship, or a time of famine or pestilence. There was one man at Ŭglaamie, on board H. M. S. Plover, Captain Maguire, in 1853 and 1854, who, Captain Hull (who was master under Maguire) informs me, was about thirty years of age when the Plover passed her winters there; at the time of our visit he was very decrepit, was bent nearly double, and crawled rather than walked, with a staff in each hand; his shriveled skin, toothless gums, and shrunken limbs gave him the appearance of great age, but he could have seen but little more than sixty years, if that. I met several who said they were children in Maguire's time, and they had every appearance of men of forty-five or fifty.

That the race is rapidly decreasing is shown by the fact that during the two years we were on the coast, in the village of Ŭglaamie alone, there were eighteen deaths and only two births in a population of one hundred and thirty souls; and Dr. Simpson states that in 1854 the village had a population of over two hundred. He also reports forty iglus, while we found only twenty-six. At Nuwŭk, he reports forty-eight iglus, and two hundred and eighty-six people. We found this village had dwindled to thirty iglus, and less than one hundred and fifty people; and the freshly-cached bodies and numerous half-ruined iglus bore silent testimony to the fact that famine and disease had quite recently been at work. This is undoubtedly owing to the fact that the food-supply is rapidly growing less, and that the great number of whales taken off the coast by the American whaling fleet during the last twenty years has nearly exterminated that valuable animal. That they are decreasing in numbers is well known among the whalemen, and the fact that Dr. Simpson reports that during the time the Plover was at Point Barrow there were twenty-four whales taken by the natives, while only two were taken during our stay, one of which was a calf, goes to prove that they will soon be classed among the extinct mammals, and with them will soon pass away many of the people inhabiting this shore; they are slow to take up with an innovation, and they do not really adapt themselves to the new condition of affairs which the loss of this great food-supply has brought about. The seal are not numerous, and often leave this coast entirely for a season. When this occurs, famine with all its horrors is upon them, and they have no place to flee to for help. During the first winter at the station, food became very scarce, and scarcely a day passed but some poor native, with starvation written in every line of his face, hung around our doors begging for a mouthful of food. We gave them all we could spare with safety to ourselves, and undoubtedly saved many lives. Walrus hide and pieces of old boat-covers were considered delicacies, but we never knew them to resort to violence to obtain food, and cannibalism is looked upon by them with horror, and I could not find that a case had ever occurred. They will not even eat their dogs. Some seasons a few white whales (Beluga) are taken. The skins of this animal are in great demand for soles to water-proof boots, and often bring a high price.

Dr. Simpson reports that quite a number of narwhal were taken on the coast during the stay of the Plover, but I could find but one Indian that had ever seen one, and they are not common in this ocean at the present time.

Physically, both sexes are very strong, and they possess great powers of endurance; are capable of making long journeys on foot, with a very small allowance of food; in fact, when food is at all scarce, or while traveling, they never eat but once each day, and it was a surprise to us to see them when on a journey get out before daybreak, and, without taking a mouthful of food, make a journey of thirty or forty miles before breaking their fast; and they treated their dogs in the same manner, saying that they traveled better when fed only at the end of the day's journey; sometimes they would give them a mouthful apiece toward the middle of the day, but the practice was looked upon as bad.

The flint and steel is the most common method of procuring fire, using for tinder the down from the seeds of plants, impregnated with mealed powder or charcoal. Sometimes two pieces of iron pyrites are used, and we found the ancient fire drill still in use among some of the old, conservative men; the drill was a shaft of spruce eighteen inches long and three-fourths inch in diameter, the lower end terminating in the frustum of a cone, the upper end made to fit the socket of a stone rest that is held between the teeth; a block of hard wood with a small cavity in the center is used as a friction block; a small quantity of tinder is placed in the bottom of the cavity and the drill pressed down by the mouth-rest and turned rapidly with a small bow like a jeweler's bow. They are anxious to obtain matches, but they are not considered a necessity, and will not buy them as a rule. Flints are an article of traffic, and are brought from Cape Lisburne and the Romanzoff Mountains, there being none indigenous to this part of the coast. They believe that the pyrites come down from heaven in the form of meteors, and they call it fire-stone for that reason.

The children receive the tenderest care, and we never saw one punished by its parents. It is no unusual sight to see a child nourished at the breast until it is four or five years of age; this is especially the case with boys, who, as a rule, receive more care than girls. His food is carefully selected by his mother, and he is enjoined from eating certain articles that have been tabooed by some old woman, usually a relative; and this prohibition extends through life. With each individual there is always one or more article of food from which they carefully abstain, though the pangs of hunger may be upon them, and, as an old man expressed it, when declining a piece of bear meat, "It may be good for all men but me," shows the individuality of the custom.

To us the treatment the women receive during confinement seems harsh in the extreme, and it is a matter of surprise that either mother or child ever survives the ordeal. Several days before her confinement the mother is placed in a small snow hut, if in the winter, and in a small tent, if in the summer; no one is allowed to go near her, except her husband, who brings her food and passes it in to her without entering the hut. Here she remains entirely alone until the child is one moon old. Should the child die, then she can return to her husband and iglu after eight or ten days. No person will knowingly drink from the same cup or eat from the same dish that a woman has used during her confinement until it has been purified by certain incantations. And any woman who has suffered from premature childbirth, or given birth to a child during the winter, is allowed to go into a canoe or out into the pack during the spring. Premature childbirth is of frequent occurrence among them, and we frequently noticed the greatest solicitude on the part of the husband to guard the wife from any accident during pregnancy.

A NATIVE OF NUWŮK, POINT BARROW.

During the long winter night, when food is plenty, they delight to meet at the council-house, or at different iglus, and over their work recount, recall, different events of their lives, and repeat the legends of their race, which have been handed down from father to son, to which the young people listen with rapt attention. These legends go back to the origin of man, and they tell with care full detail of a time when there were no men in all the land, but that a spirit called "á-sĕ-lu" dwelt here alone, and that he made the image of a man in clay, set it up by the shore of the sea to dry, and after it was dry he breathed upon it and gave it life and sent it out into the world. And he called the dog from a long way off to go with man, that he might have help in traveling. After a time the spirit made the Tuk-tu (reindeer) and sent him out into the land, and the teeth of the deer were like the teeth of the dog. After many days man came to the spirit and said, "The deer is bad, he devours man." Whereupon the spirit called in all the deer and removed all the front teeth from their upper jaws, since which time men have lived on deer, and the deer have lived on moss and grass. Then the man asked the spirit that there might be fish in the rivers and sea. And the spirit took a piece of pine and a piece of balsam and sat by the river where it emptied into the sea, and he whittled long shavings from the pieces of wood, and the shavings fell into the water, and the shavings from the yellow wood became salmon, and those from the white wood became whitefish and swam away.

Their faith in these legends is very strong, and they are extremely opposed to any expressions of doubt or ridicule, and it is only by gaining their confidence and abstaining from any expressions of doubt in their presence that they can be induced to talk about their people or repeat their legends. We heard but one legend that referred in any way to the regions to the northward. It was said that many generations ago a man from Nuwŭk was caught in the moving pack that was setting to the northward so rapidly that he was unable to return to the land. After a great many days, more than he could count, he came to a land where dwelt a strange people; they spoke a strange language, and dressed in deer skins like the inyu. He remained with them a long time, but, wishing to return to his people, he left them one winter and started south over the ice, living upon the seal he caught by the way, and renewing his boots with their skins. The journey was so long that he wore out fifteen pairs of boots in returning to Nuwŭk. Dr. Simpson reports a similar legend told him during his stay.

They all have a natural craving for rum and tobacco; it is always the first thing they ask for when they come to trade, and they are never satisfied unless they can get sufficient rum to make them dead drunk. The old men deprecate its use, and will tell how bad it is, and how certain men were killed in drunken fights, and will be very strong in their denunciations of its use so long as they cannot get it, but generally fail to resist the temptation when it is offered to them, or an opportunity occurs for them to get it. Fortunately there is but little to tempt the trader in this region, and the little they get from the whale ships is consumed on the spot, so there is no drunkenness after the sea is closed. Their tobacco they hoard carefully, and it is used by old and young in quantities only limited by the supply; they prefer a black-leaf Russian tobacco, but this is hard to get, as only small quantities of it reach this coast by the way of Behring Straits and the Diomede Islands. Next to this they prefer the black navy-plug of the commonest kind. Men and women both smoke and chew, and the children are given tobacco in their earliest infancy. It is no uncommon sight to see a child not old enough to walk lying asleep with its cheek distended with a huge chew, or to see a woman with an old quid behind each ear which has been thoroughly masticated, and put up to dry, for the future use of her lord and master. Chewing does not seem to have the slightest deleterious effect upon the children, while smoking affects the men very seriously. Their pipes are made of either stone, wood, or ivory, and consist of a flanged bowl, from one and one-half to two inches in length, with a bore one-fourth of an inch in diameter, attached to a curved wooden stem made from two pieces of wood grooved and lashed together with seal thong; the bottom of the bowl they fill with deer hair and place on top of it a piece of tobacco about the size of a pea. It is all consumed at one whiff, and they hold the smoke in their lungs until they become nearly suffocated; a violent fit of coughing follows each smoke, and with the old men it frequently so prostrates them that they are quite unable to walk for some little time after each indulgence. From what the old men told us, and from some ancient stone pipes found in the ruins of ancient iglus, it would seem that they smoked before tobacco was known among them, and they used a kilikinick made from the catkins and bark of the arctic willow, which they now use to adulterate their tobacco. They all seem to have a natural appetite for this weed in any form. The men would often beg the privilege of cleaning the deposit from the stem and bowls of our pipes, which they ate with great relish, and, strange to say, without being nauseated in the slightest.

That these people have not yet made the transition from the stone to the iron age is shown by the large number of stone and bone implements still in use among them at the present time. Many of the old conservative men still cling to the habits of their fathers, and believe that stone arrow and lance heads possess virtues that makes them superior to those made of iron. They still teach the young men the art of chipping flint, and over their work tell them of the happy days before the white men came to drive away the whales and walrus, and when food was always plenty. An old man, when asked what he would do without the things the white men brought them, answered it would be very hard, and then to show us what he could do he showed a pair of boots he had on, and told us with great pride how, when his boots gave out while hunting, he killed a deer, made a needle from a piece of his bone, thread from the sinew, and made himself a new pair of boots from the skin, and asked, Could a white man do that ? In the spring of 1883, when they came to prepare their boats for whaling, they decided after many grave debates that the bad luck of the previous year was owing entirely to their having equipped their boats with white man's gear, of which they had abundance, obtained from wrecked whalers; so it was decided that they would go back to the implements of their fathers, and the old ivory and stone harpoon and lance heads were brought forth and repaired, and that they took one whale was attributed entirely to this change; the fact that the whale was killed by a shot from a bomb gun we loaned them to the contrary notwithstanding.

From the head of Kotzebue to the mouth of the Mackenzie there is not found any timber of any size indigenous to that region, and the Colville, Ĭk-pĭk-pûñ, and Meade River bring down no drift of any size, only the arctic willow. The drift cast up by the sea consists chiefly of spruce, birch, and poplar; it often comes ashore with the bark and roots intact and but slightly water-worn. That this drift comes principally from the Mackenzie is shown by the fact that it is found in great abundance to the eastward of Point Barrow, while to the west of it not so abundant. We occasionally saw large trunks of trees, from two to three feet in diameter, stripped of roots and branches, generally of cottonwood, which seemed to have been a very long time at sea. What little drift we saw coming from the westward was always old.

The streams that have their source in Meade River Mountains bring down no drift larger than the arctic willow, and we saw no drift along the arctic shore that resembled that from the Yukon, found along the shore of Norton Sound. The natives in the vicinity of Point Barrow are always on the lookout for pieces of drift wood, and every piece that can be utilized in building hut or boat is at once marked and placed above high water. At leisure they work them down to the size required, stick them up so as to show above the snow in winter, when they are hauled to the iglu and placed on the cache. It is often a work of from three to five years to accumulate enough timber to construct a boat or iglu. Every cache shows a store of neatly dressed sticks, that are highly prized, and that have a commercial value.

In the small inlets along the coast drift wood was found from ten to fifteen feet above the high-water mark of the sea, and at first we were led to believe that such drift represented an unusually high tide, but we subsequently learned that it was caused by the heavy ice pack, which, in the winter, is forced in on the land by the violent gales, and makes a dam across the entrance to the inlets. The water from the melting snows in the spring fill up the inlets and finds no outlet until it overflows this barrier, when, running down rapidly, it leaves the drift high above the sea level.

These openings, seen in the early summer, have often been mistaken for the mouths of rivers by people passing on ships. It is very doubtful if this vast stretch of country contains anything that will ever render it of any commercial value to the world. But on our voyage south we were struck with the fertile appearance of the Aleutian Islands where we halted for a few days to repair our vessel. On the island we visited, though late in September, we found a luxuriant growth of grass still untouched by frost. All the islands we saw were high and rolling, intersected by beau-

UNALASKA.

tiful valleys, watered by streams that abound in excellent trout. They were destitute of timber, but we could see no reason why they should not be valuable as grazing lands. The climate is similar to that of Ireland, and in about the same latitude; the lowest recorded temperature in seven years is —6° F., and the annual mean is.

The great Japan current gives to these islands a climate peculiarly mild and equitable for so high a latitude, and I think a careful geological and geographical survey would develop valuable resources.

From *Report of the International Polar Expedition to Point Barrow, Alaska* (1885)

APPENDIX 7

Approximate Census of Eskimos at the Cape Smythe Village

[Each brace includes one household. A dash indicates that the person's name was not obtained.]

Man.	Wife.	Male children.	Female children.
{ Nĭk-a-wá-a-lu.	At-kak-sá.		Nĕt-tû-pûñ.
O-we-ĭ-nä.	———	Ä-lĭ-brú-ra.	
Pú-kä.	Nĕ't-û-lu.	———	
A-ka-bĭ-ä-nä.	Ä-lĭ-bru-nä.		
(Ĭ't-ù-ma-lu, deceased.)	Mû-mûñ-ĭ'n-ä.		Yu-kû'l-ya-lu.
Tá-gaⁿ. }		Seak-a-bwû'n-ä.	
{ Äm-ai-yú-nä.	Seak-a-bwñu-ä.		
	(Iä-kûg-ĭ-cá, mother-in-law.)		
Kai-yá-nä. }	Säg-wa-dyû-ä.	I-gû-cû.	
Túñ-a-zu.	Ak-sĭ-gû't-tä.	Añ-nû'bw'-gä.	
Añ-nû'k-sä.	Pû'-si-myñ.		Mûl-i-gi-á-ra.
{ A-bä'k-ka-ná.	Mû't-u-mi-ä.	Mûn-ĭ'k-sä.	
Aí'-bwûk. }	Paû-sĕn-ä.		
Taú-yu'-ä.			
{ I-ga-lá.	Añ-nû'bw'-gä.		
Kû-ma-sia. }	I-dro.		
Äk-qlá-nä.	Al-á-li.	Kút-yĕ.	———
A'ñ-o-ru.	Ni-äk-sá-rä.		
Tú-kû.		Kĕ-pĭ'ñ-a-su.	I'd-ĭĭ-gû ti-ä.
Tcuñ-aú-rä.			I'g-nĭ-bĭn-ä.
{ U-já-lu.	Ĭa-xo-xû'n-ä.		
Yû'k-sa. }	Añ-nlg-ä-la.	Ĭ-tá-qlu.	
{ I-ga-la-ti-ä.			
Ir-ĭ-ti-ä-la.			
Mû'ñ-ĭ-a-lu.	Ka-ka-gû-nä.		Pĕ-gá+-lu.
A-pai-dyá-o.	Ku-ná-nä.		
I-lû'bw'-gä. }	A-kĕ'b-û-xû.		
Añ-o-ai-já.			Tĕr-ĭ'g'-lu.
{ Nû'g-ĕ-ru.		I'n-yu-ti-ä.	Pĕ-gá+-lu.
Tû'k-a-lûñ.	Súk-sa-nä.		Nú-ta.
U-já-lu. }	Túok-qlûñ.		
			Kĭ'ñ-a-lu-ku-ná.
{ Yú-wai-á-lu.	Al-á-li.	Ku-ná-lu.	
Yu-wai-a-lú. }	A'l-a-lu.		
Ni-a-yu.		Kiñ-ia.	Ad-wû'n-ä (adult).
Äd-yu-ĭn'-ä.		I'n-yu-ti-ä.	
Sí-sa-nä.	Ku-sĭ-brû-nä.		
Áñ-o-a.	Taĭ-pa-nä.	I't-tû.	Kúd-lä-lu.
	(———— mother-in-law.)		
Áb-wûm-lñ.		Kók'-la.	
Äd-yĭ-gi-ä.	Ú-su.		Kĭb-vä.
Kúg-rau-tä.		Ko-ko-lĕ'n-ä.	
Käx-yo-h'n-ä.		Pûn-Ĭ-yú-nä-yu.	
(Näga-waú-rä, deceased.)	Mû't-u-mi-ä (wife's sister).		
Nĕ't-ú-na.		———	
A-bä'k-ka-ná.	Á-no-u.	———	
A-múp-ka-ná.			
Kä'k-äk-pa.	Nĭ'p-plü.		
Ad-ĭĭ-gaud'-lo.		———	
Pau-yú-nä.	Kú-pĭ-dro.		
(Ne-cä'g-a-lo, deceased.)	A-tûñ-û'n-ä.	Is-Ĭ-gai-û'.	
	Ni-yu-Ĭ-sû'n-ä.		
	Tuek-qlûñ.		
	Nu-syûñ-ĭ'n-ä.		

Totals: 45 men, 52 women, 27 boys, 14 girls; in all, 137 souls.

From *Report of the International Polar Expedition to Point Barrow, Alaska* (1885)

APPENDIX 8

Measurements and Weights of Some Eskimos from Cape Smythe and Point Barrow

[Collected by George Scott Oldmixon, acting assistant surgeon, United States Army.]

No.	Name.	Age.*	Height. Ft.	Height. In.	Weight. Lbs.	Occipito-frontal circumference. Inch.
	MALES.					
1	O-re-ī-nä	30	5	6	161	23
2	Añ-o-rú, "Big"	45	5	7½	182	23¼
3	Áñ-nûk-sä	35	4	11	126	22
4	U-já'-lu	26	5	2	142	22½
5	U-na-lí-nä	32	5	7¾	171	23
6	A'ñ-o-â	50	5	7½	186	23½
7	Su-pĭn-yá-o	30	5	7¼	146	22½
8	Tá-gaⁿ, "Shadow"	30	5	0½	145	22
9	Yû'k-sĭñ-a	65	5	2	147	23¼
10	Nĕt-tû-ná	33	5	7	156	22
11	Nû'g-ĕ-ru, "Antlers"	40	5	5	150	22¼
12	Tu-kû, "Walrus-harpoon head"	40	5	0¾	146	22
13	Yö'k-sa, "cheek"	20	5	3	143	20¼
14	Näg-a-waú-rä, "Little Näg-a-wû'n-ä"	35	5	3½	149	20½
15	Ab-wúm-ĭñ	40	5	0	135	19
16	A-bă'k-ka-ná	23	5	5½	159	23
17	A-múp-ka-ná	33	5	8	165	22¼
18	Ī-tú-ma-lú	40	5	2	137	20¾
19	A-bă'k-ka-ná	20	5	5½	156	22½
20	U-já-ra	50	5	5½	154	22¼
21	Nu-cûñ-ĭ'n-ä	45	5	3	170	23
22	At-ká-nä	20	5	3¼	137	20¼
23	Nĭk-a-wá-a-lu, "Big Näg-a-wû'n-ä"	45	5	6½	161	22
24	Mû'ñ-ī-a-lu	28	5	6	148	22
25	Sí-na, "Beach"	40	5	5	149	22¼
26	Nä's-su-ä	35	5	4½	144	21
27	U-já-lu	30	5	7¼	161	22
28	Yö'k-sa, "Check"	30	5	7¼	174	22½
29	I-gä-la-tí-ä, "Little Igalá"	35	5	6¼	138	20½
30	Ám-ai-yú-nä	40	5	4	163	20¼
31	Nĭk-a-wá-a-lu, "Big Näg-a-wû'n-ä"	45	5	8¼	173	22
32	Áx-lo, "Grampus"	55	5	7½	204	22
33	Añ-na-ti-na	55	5	7	147	21¼
34	Túñ-a-zu	35	5	6	155	19
35	Pú-kä	23	5	2	131	19½
36	At-ká-nä	22	4	11½	132	19
37	Tcuñ-aú-rä, "Beads"	60	5	2¼	132½	19½
38	I-ga-lá, "Window"	40	5	5¼	147	22½
39	Paú-yu-nä, "Sooty"	35	5	4	169	21
40	Näg-á-wû'n-nä	48	5	6½	151½	22
41	A-pai-dyá-o	22	5	3½	136	21½
42	Nau-já-li	23	5	5¾	165	22

No.	Name.	Age.*	Height. Ft.	Height. In.	Weight. Lbs.	Occipito-frontal circumference. Inch.
	MALES.					
43	I-péak-sĭ-na	45	5	8¾	188	23½
44	A-tûñ-aú-rä	30	5	0	130	21¼
45	A-pai-dyá-o	45	5	3½	160	21½
46	Nud'-lûñ	36	5	4	156	21
47	A-bă'k-ka-ná	27	5	3	147	21¾
48	Áñ-a	19	5	3½	144	22
49	Säg-ä-bwaú-tyä	38	5	4	137	20¾
50	Yû'k-sĭñ	25	5	4¾	166	21¾
51	An-ät-ká-nä	20	5	4	149	21
	FEMALES.					
1	Ni-ăk-sá-rä	35	5	3	148	22½
2	Pû'-si-myû	26	4	10	124	22½
3	Mù-mûñ-ĭ'n-ä	30	5	1½	131	21¼
4	Taí-pa-nä	26	5	1	139	20½
5	A-sĭ-saú-nä	25	5	2	128	20
6	A-lá-li	30	5	3	172	22½
7	U-nĭ-rí-ma	40	4	10	130	21¾
8	Á-no-u	35	4	0½	100	18¼
9	Á-lä-ri-ä	35	4	8½	120	20
10	Sŭ'k-sa-nä	25	4	9	124	19
11	A-na-rĭ't-tĭ	30	5	2	152	21½
12	Ak-sĭ-gû't-ä	33	5	3	156	20½
13	Nu-ta, "Young"	40	4	9	144	19½
14	Ni-yu-ĭ-sû'n-ä	28	4	10½	142	21
15	Mû't-u-mi-ä	18	5	0	127½	21¼
16	Túd-wi-a-lu	27	5	1¾	148	20½
17	Sur-wĕ'n-a	35	5	0	132	18¾
18	At-kak-sá	28	5	2¾	146	19
19	Nĕ't-û-lu	23	4	1½	150	18½
20	Ku-mĭ-yĕ'-nä	30	5	1¼	143	19
21	At-ká-nä	20	5	2	127	19¼
22	Sĕ-mí-ya	40	5	0½	122	20¼
23	Ku-ná-nä	18	4	11	117	21
24	Säg-wä-dyú-ä	20	4	11½	106	22
25	Kak-a-gú-nä	22	5	1	135	21
26	Tai-pĕ-rú-nä	38	5	0½	139	20½
27	A-tûñ-û'n-ä	20	4	9	128	20¼
28	Tuok-qlúñ	28	5	3	153	20¾
29	Pû'n-ĭk-pûñ	22	5	2½	148	22
30	Ăk-pa-lú	23	5	2	141	22

*Estimated.

Average height .... 5 ft. 2[illegible] in.
Average weight .... 146[illegible] lbs.
Average height of males .... 5 ft. 3[illegible] in.
Average height of females .... 4 ft. 11[illegible] in.
Average weight of males .... 153[illegible] lbs.
Average weight of females .... 135[illegible] lbs.
Tallest male .... 5 ft. 8¾ in.
Tallest female .... 5 ft. 3 in.
Shortest male .... 4 ft. 11 in.
Shortest female .... 4 ft. 0½ in.

From *Report of the International Polar Expedition to Point Barrow, Alaska* (1885)

APPENDIX 9

Vocabulary Collected among the Eskimos of Point Barrow and Cape Smythe

[This vocabulary is arranged according to the schedules given in the second edition of the "Introduction to the Study of Indian Languages," by Maj. J. W. Powell. The alphabet (which will be found on page 87) used in writing the words is that given in the same work, with the addition of the character ö for the sound of the French *eu*. A sound indistinctly or occasionally heard is put in parentheses.]

English.	Eskimo.	English.	Eskimo.
Persons.		*Parts of the body—Continued.*	
1. Man.	áñ-un.	39. Shoulder blade.	ki-a-si-a.
2. Woman.	áñ-na.	40. Back.	tu-nú-a.
3. Old man.	añ-aid-yo-kwák-to, -sä.	41. Breast of a man.	i-bi-ñ'ñ-ni-ä, sñ't-ka.
4. Old woman.	a-ko-ák-sa.	42. Breast of a woman (mamma).	mî'l-u.
5. Young man.	nu-kü't-pi-ä.[1]		
6. Young woman.	ni-vi-û'k-si-a.	43. Nipples.	múdr'-ga.
7. Boy.	nu-kút-pi-á-ru.[2]	44. Hips.	múk-i-sá.
8. Girl.	ni-vi-úk-sá-ru.[3]	45. Belly.	nád-dra.
9. Child, able to walk.	múk-qlú'k-to.	46. Navel.	kúl-a-si-a.
10. Child, creeping.	pá-mòk-tu-ä.	47. Arm.	túd-lî-a.
11. Infant, nursing.	múk-qlúk-to-a-yá.	48. Armpits.	úñ-a.
12. Male infant.	añ-u-tí'k-sa.	49. Arm above elbow.	ák-sút-kwa.
13. Female infant.	añ-nú'k-sa.	50. Elbow.	i-ku-si-a.
14. Twins.	mád-i-ví-ríñ, mád-re-ru ä, a-no-kú't-i-gé.	51. Wrist.	ï'n-ui-brún, nûb-gu-ñ'ñ-a.
		52. Hand.	á-drï-gai.
15. Married man.	í'íñ-a.	53. Right hand.	túl-ñ'k-pi-ä.
16. Married woman.	nu-li û'ñ-ñ.	54. Left hand.	saú-mi-ä.
17. Widower.	nu-lí-fí'k-so.	55. Palm of hand.	ł t-u-ma.
18. Widow.	nu-lí-ü'k-súñ, u-i-dî-fí'k-to.	56. Back of hand.	a-drí-gau-tu-nú-a.
19. Bachelor (old).	nu-lí-gë't-to.	57. Fingers.	ï'n-yu-gai.
20. Maid (old).	u-wí-gë't-to.	58. Thumb.	kúb'-lu.
21. A mother.	öñ-ñ'a-rä.	59. First finger.	tîk-ï-rá,-tï'k-a(l).
22. The young people.	u-nu-nu t'á'-kun.	60. Second finger.	ka-tú'k-qluñ.
23. A great talker.	u-ka-lú-tu-ru.	61. Third finger.	mîk-ï'l-yë-rá.
24. A silent person.	i-mûñ-i-á'k-to, ma-kî-ma't-tu-a.	62. Small finger.	yíñ-kut-ko.
25. Thief.	tîg-a-lí-a-yú'k-tu-o.	63. Finger-nail.	kú-kin.
26. An active person.	yúk-i't-yu-ä.	64. Knuckle.	núb-vu-dïn.
27. A lazy person.	yúk-i-a-su-ru-ä.	65. Space between knuckles.	ná-lîk-kï.
28. A fair Eskimo.	mi-su ë't-yu-ä.	66. Finger-tips.	nú-bu-ä.
29. A name.	át-ka.	67. Rump.	núd'l-u.
		68. Leg.	nî-úñ-ñ.
		69. Leg above knee.	kók-pa.
		70. Knee.	sit-kwuñ-a.
Parts of the body.		71. Knee-pan.	sit-kwa.
		72. Leg below knee.	kíu-a-gá.
1. Head.	ni-á'k-o-ä.	73. Calf of the leg.	na-ka-súñ-nä.
2. Hair.	nu't-yë, mî't-ko.	74. Shin.	kîñ-a.[4]
3. Crown of the head.	na-yü'g-i-a.	75. Ankle.	si-sï'ñ-ue-ríñ, síñ-ni-ñ'ñ-në-ríñ.
4. Scalp.	ki-si-á.	76. Ankle-bone.	kû'm-a.
5. Face.	ki-na.	77. Instep.	kö-ni.
6. Forehead.	kau.	78. Foot.	ï's-i-gai.
7. Eye.	i-dîn.	79. Sole of foot.	al-ñ-a, al-ñ-na.
8. Pupil of the eye.	tû'k-u-vi-ä.	80. Heel.	kï'ñ-mi-ä.
9. Eyelash.	kîm-mêr-îd-yë'n.	81. Toe.	pu-tu-gñ-a.[5]
10. Eyebrow.	ká'b'-lun, ká'b'-lu-ł.	82. Large toe.	pu-tu-gú-a, tud-lî-á.
11. Upper eyelid.	káñ-a, ir-ríp-kód-lä.	83. Second toe.	tïk-l-rá.[6]
12. Lower eyelid.	ír-rí-bñ't-a.	84. Third toe.	mî-k ï'l-yö-rá.[6]
13. Ear-lobe.	a-ki-á-go-a, pú-wa.	85. Fourth toe.	yíuk-ut-ko.[6]
14. Ear.	si-u, pl. si-u-tín.	86. Toe-nail.	kú-kin.
15. Perforation in ear.	pu-tú-ä.	87. Blood.	au.
16. External opening of ear.	cub'-lú-a.	88. Vein or artery.	tú'k-kúñ.
17. Nose.	kî'ñ-a.	89. Brain.	káx-za.
18. Ridge of nose.	núñ-a.	90. Bladder.	nä'-ka-su(n).
19. Nostril.	kîñ-un.	91. Caul.	ká-pis-i-yúñ-ä.
20. Septum of nose.	pi-tú-ta, ká'k-i-vi-a.	92. Heart.	ú-ma-ta.
21. Perforation of septum of nose.	pu-tu-gá.	93. Kidney.	ták-tu.
22. Alae nose.	at-kát-yu.	94. Lung.	pú-wi.
23. Cheek.	yíők-sa.	95. Liver.	tï'ñ-u.
24. Beard.	kñ-kug-lú-č-tín.	96. Stomach.	a-ké-a-xo.
25. Moustache.	úm-ñyîn.	97. Rib.	túd-lî-múd-rín.
26. Mouth.	káñ-a.	98. Vertebræ.	pî'k-kwïn.
27. Upper lip.	u-mí-drú-ín, úm-ni.	99. Spine.	ku-ya-pî'k-kún.
28. Lower lip.	kák-qluñ.	100. Sternum.	sñ'k ï-úñ-ïñ.
29. Tooth.	kî'g-u, kî'g-u-tai.	101. Clavicle.	kú-tú-ä.
30. Tongue.	ó-ka.	102. Humerus.	ák-sat-ko-(a).
31. Saliva.	nú-wa, mî'-wûñ.	103. Femur.	kúk-tu-ä.
32. Palate.	kî'l-ta, u-kaú-ra.	104. Radius and fibula.	a-mî'l-ya-rúñ.
33. Throat.	tûák-qlu-ra.	105. Ulna.	súk-ï'b-ru-ta.
34. Chin.	táb'-lu-a.	106. Foot-print.	tú-mîn ? pl. tú-mai.
35. Neck.	kuñ-a-sí-na, kák-éa-lu.	107. Skin.	á-mia.
36. Adam's apple.	tup-kú-ra.	108. Bone.	saú-ná.
37. Body.	ká-ti-gai.	109. Intestines.	i-na-lu-úñ-a.
38. Shoulder.	tu-ín-yä, twi-twí'n-yä, nîg-ä-blñ-ä.	110. Penis.	ú-an, u-sú-ä.
		111. Vulva.	út-yu.
		112. Fist.	yá-kït-kai.

[1] "Youth."
[2] Dim. of "youth."
[3] Dim. of "young woman."
[4] Same as nose.
[5] ï'n-yu-gai toes, =fingers.
[6] All natives do not give names for these toes. These correspond to the names for the fingers.

English.	Eskimo.	English.	Eskimo.
Dress and ornaments.		*Implements and Utensils.*	
1. Cap attached to frock.	nĕ's-û.	1. Bow of wood.	pi-zĭ'k-sĭ.
2. Tunic.	a-tī-gĕ.[1]	2. Bowstring.	nu-kă'k-ta.
3. Outer tunic.	ka-lŭ-rú-a.	3. Sinew on back of bow.	kă'k-u-tai, kám-ni-gai.
4. Inner tunic.	ĭ-lu-pá.	4. Arrow.	kă'k-a-ru.
5. Knee-breeches.	kă'k-ā-lĭx.	5. Notch in end of arrow for bowstring.	ăg-glu-a.
6. Fur socks.	á-lŭk-sĭn.		
7. Pair of moccasins, reaching to knee.	kû'm-mûñ.	6. Notch in end of arrow for arrow-head.	ĭ't-cr-o.
8. Pair of moccasins, reaching to knee, water-proof.	yu-kă'k-qlĭñ.[2]	7. Arrow-head of stone.	kú-kĭn.
9. Shoes.	kĭ'b-lu-a-tyi-ă.[3]	8. Arrow-head chipper (made of horn, &c.).	kĭ'g-li(x).
10. Woman's moccasins.	kû'm-mûñ.[4]	9. Point of arrow-head.	ĭ'g-ni-ă.
11. Girdle.	táp-se.	10. Arrow-shaft of wood.	ĭ-pû-a.[8]
12. Rain-frock, of walrus-gut.	sĭ-lŭ'ñ-a.[5]	11. Arrow-feathers.	su-lû-ĭn.
13. Mittens, deerskin.	ait-kăt-ĭ.	12. Quiver.	pi-zĭ'k-si-zaq.
14. Mittens of bearskin.	pú-a-lu[6].	13. Quiver strap.	mû'n-nau-ta.
15. Gloves.	aŭ-ri-gŭd-rĭ'n.	14. Wrist-guard.	mû'n-gĭd-zĭñ.
16. Blanket.	ŭ-lĭg-ru-a.	15. War club, small.	tĭ'g-a-lun.
17. Robe of deerskin.	ŭ-li-ga.	16. Sling-shot.	tŭ'b-lu-kûñ.
18. Buckskin.	yéa-kĭ-vĭ'k-sa.	17. Fish spear.	kăk-ĭ-bu-a.
19. Fringe of skin.	nĭ-gra-ka.	18. Bird dart.	nu-yă'k-pai.
20. Sinew.	nú-kĭñ-a.	19. Deer lance.	kă'p-un.
21. Thread (of sinew).	ĭ-val-u.	20. Bear lance.	pû'n-nû.
22. Paint, black lead.	mĭ'ñ-un.	21. Seal harpoon (stabbing).	û-nû.
23. Tattoo marks.	tab-lu-rá-tĭn.	22. Head of same.	naû-lû.
24. Pouch.	pûk-sak.	23. Line of same.	tŭ-kăk-tĭn.
25. A ring.	ka-tŭ'k-qlĕ-rûñ.	24. "Loose-shaft" of same.	ĭ'-gi-mû.
26. An earring.	no-go-lu.	25. Fore shaft of same.	kú-tû.
27. Labret.	tû-tú.	26. Wooden shaft of same.	ĭ-pû-ă.
28. Barehead.	nĕs-á-su.	27. Line on the same.	să-bro-mi-a.
29. Barefoot.	u-sĕa-su, u-sĭ-lák-to.	28. Ivory ice-pick of same.	tû-u.
30. Naked.	mût-:ák-to.	29. Seal harpoon, darting.	naû-lĭ-gû.
		30. Head of same.	naû-lû.
Dwellings.		31. Short "loose-shaft" of same.	ĭ'-gi-mû.
		32. Heavy fore shaft of same.	u-ku-mai-lu-ta.[9]
1. Village.	ĭn-yu-gĭ-û'k-to, ĭ'g-a-lon.	33. Short line to "loose-shaft" of same.	ĭp-ĭ'-u-ta.
2. Wigwam (permanent dwelling).	ĭ'g-lu.	34. Long wooden shaft of same.	ĭ-pû-ă.
3. Doorway.	pañ, pa.	35. Lashing of same.	nĭm-xa.
4. Wooden trap-doorway.	kú't-tû.	36. Ivory ice-pick of same.	tú-u.
5. Smoke-hole.	pu-yu'k-o-vi-a, i-gát-ĭk-la.	37. Ivory finger-rest of same.	tĭ'-ka.
6. Fire-place.	ĭ-ga, á-ga-run.	38. Ivory peg for line of same.	kĭ'-ler-bwĭñ.
7. Fire.	ĭ'g-ni-ă.	39. Bone seal-spear head.	ă'k-qlĭ-gûk.
8. Fire-wood.	kun-na-tá-kĭn.	40. Head of walrus harpoon.	tú-kĭn.
9. Blaze.	ka-mûñ-ĭ-su-a.	41. Whale harpoon.	áj-yûñ.
10. A light.	mûñ-a-ru-a.	42. Head of same.	kĭ'-a-gron.
11. Living coals.	ki-rúk-tn-ga.	43. "Poke" for same.	a-po-tû'k-pûñ.
12. Dead coals.	ki-rû-ĕ-to.	44. Line or rope.	ă'k-qlu-na.
13. Ashes.	kăm-nĭ-û'm-na-rĭñ.	45. Knife of stone.	û-yûm-ĭ-ga.
14. Smoke.	ĭ-súk.	46. Knife-handle.	ĭ-pûñ-a, să-vĭk-i-pû-ă.
15. Soot.	pau.	47. Woman's round knife.	u-lú-ra.
16. Poker.	ĭ'g-nia-kun.	48. Sling.	ĭ'd'-lu.
17. Bench or bed-place.	ĭg-la-ré, ĭ'g-li-sĭn.	49. Bird bolas.	kĕl-au-wĭ-tat-tĭn.
18. A post.	ĭt-kéa-rûñ.	50. Canoe, single.	kaĭ'-a (k).
19. Ridge-pole or joist.	tu-rûn.	51. Large skin-boat.	u-mi-ă (k).
20. Roof.	kĭ'l-ĭ-sĭñ.	52. Paddle.	áñ-un.
21. Wall.	kût-yĕ.	53. Mast.	na-pák-sä.
22. Short beams below window.	ĭn-ĭt-kaú-rĕn.	54. Sail.	tĭñ-ĭ-draû-tä.
		55. Harpoon rest.	kû'n-nû.
23. Opening for window.	i-ga-lá.	56. Canteen made of seal skin.	ĭ'-mu-tĭn.
24. Window-frame.	kĭ'ñ-ĭñ.	57. Fish-line.	ĭp-ĭ'-u-ta.
25. Window-stretchers.	ĭ't-kûñ.	58. Fish or seal net.	kû-brä.
26. Window-skin.	ĭ'n-a-lu.	59. Fish-hook.	nĭ'k-sĭu, ĭ'ñk-qlûñ.
27. Floor.	pûn-ĭ'k-sä, nát-kylñ.	60. Net for catching fish.	sä'p-o-tĭn.[10]
28. Pole hung up for drying clothes.	ĭ-máv-wĭñ.	61. Pipe.	ku-ĭ-n-yä.
29. Frame for same.	ĭ-nĭ-tûn.	62. Pipe of stone.	nĭ'-a, sĭ-u-na.
30. Lower frame for same.	ĭ-nĭ-sat-yăⁿ.	63. Pipe-stem of wood.	ĭ-pû-ä.
31. Lodge (temporary dwelling) tent.	tû-pĕk.	64. Sledge.	kă'm-o-tĭn.
32. Bed.	si-nĭ'g-wi.	65. Flat sledge.	û-ni-ä.
33. Snow house.	a-pú-yä.[7]	66. Dog-harness.	á-nun.
34. Little house.	ĭ'g-lo-yu, ĭg-lú-rä.	67. Seal-dart.	kú-ki-gû.
35. Little tent.	tu-pĕ'k-o-yu, aû-rûk-tû, ka-lox-wĭñ.	68. Snow-shovel.	pĭ'k-sun.
		69. Walrus harpoon.	û-nak-pûk.
36. Sewing-tent.	sûd-lĭ-vwĭñ.		
37. A ladder.	tu-mai-kûn.	*Wooden-ware.*	
38. A stone.	u-já-rûñ.		
39. Spring.	ĭm-éak-su-ĭn.	1. Cup or dipper.	ĭ'-mo-syû.
40. Water.	ĭ-méak, ĭ-mûk.	2. Meat tray.	ĭ'-li-bi-ä, nû'l-u-ĭn.
41. Passage-way.	ap-ko-át-tä, kaĭ-nĭt-tĭn.	3. Bowl.	pĭ't-tûñ-o.
42. Trail or path.	áp-ko-tĭn.	4. Fire-drill.	nĭ'-o-o-tĭn.
43. Seat, chair.	ĭt-sĭ-bán-tĭn.	5. Bucket.	kût-aû-ä.

[1] "parka," Russian territory.
[2] Lit. "sealskins."
[3] Deer, or sealskin.
[4] Trousers and shoes in one piece.
[5] f. silä, "weather."
[6] Also of dogskin for children.
[7] apun == "snow."
[8] "Shaft" in general.
[9] "Weight."
[10] Set-net.

VOCABULARY COLLECTED AMONG THE ESKIMOS, &c.—Continued.

English.	Eskimo.	English.	Eskimo.

Wooden-ware—Continued.

6. Tub (large).	Il-u-lĭ'k-pŭñ."		
7. Tub.	kád-lĭ-vwĭñ.		
8. Tub.	kăk-ĭ-tá.		
9. Tub (urinal).	kŭ-o-vwĭñ.		
10. Oil tub.	ŭ'k-si-vwĭñ.		
11. Deep dish for cooked meat.	u-ré-nea-vwĭñ.		

Stone implements.

1. Adze.	úd-lĭ-man.
2. Knife-point.	ĭ'g-ni-ä.
3. Knife-edge.	kĭ'-na.
4. Scraper.	ĭ'-kun.
5. Borer.	ĭ'-taun, ĭ'-tŭg-et-san.
6. Curved knife for wood.	mĭ'd-lĭñ.
7. Curved knife for ivory.	sa-vĭx-rón.
8. Whalebone tool.	sá-vĭx-ŭ.
9. Lamp.	kód-lö.
10. Bridge or partition in lamp.	sá-po-tĭñ.
11. Blubber stick for lamp.	ĭ'-pĕk-tŭn.
12. Kettle. [1]	út-ku-zĭn.

Utensils of shell, horn, bone, &c.

1. Horn cup.	ĭ'-mo-syŭ.
2. Horn ladle.	kĭl-ĭ-yŭ-tŭ.
3. Fossil-ivory dipper.	kĭl-ĭg-wŭ'g-a-ro. [2]
4. Ivory oil-cup.	ó-ho-vwĭñ.
5. Ivory needle case.	ŭ-ya-mi.
6. Bow-drill of bone.	nĭ-ä'k-tun.
7. Drill-bow.	pi-zĭk-su-á.
8. Drill mouth-piece.	kĭ'ñ-mĭ-ä. [3]

Food.

1. Food, meat.	n'ĭa-kĕ.
2. Soup.	n-ĭ't-yu-a n'ĭa-kĕ.
3. Milk.	ĭ'-muñ.
4. Juice of meat.	ŭk-lē-ru.
5. Whale skin.	mŭ'k-tŭk.
6. Juice of meat cooked.	ŭ-rún.
7. Whale's gum.	mŭ'm-a.
8. Dish of deer-tallow.	a-kŭ'-to.

Colors.

1. Black.	măñ-ä'k-tu-ä.
2. Blue.	u-mu-drák-tu-ä, kaŭ-ma-ru-ä.
3. Green.	u-mu-drák-tu-ä.
4. Red.	ka-bĕ'k-su-ä, ka-nä'k-tu-ä, i-pi-sá.
5. White.	ka-tŭ'k-tu-ä.
6. Yellow.	ka-pŭñ-ea-su-ĭ't-yu-ä.
7. Spotted.	ăg-lŭ'k-tu-ä.

Numerals—Cardinal numbers.

	SUBSTANTIVE.	ADJECTIVE.
1. One.	a-taŭ-zi-ä.	a-taŭ-zĭk.
2. Two.	aĭ'-pa.	mád-ro.
3. Three.	pĭñ-ä-yŭ-ä.	pĭ'ñ-a-sun.
4. Four.	sĕ-sa-má.	sĕ-sa-mán..
5. Five.	tŭ'd-li-ma.	tŭ'd-li-man, tŭ'd-li-mŭt.
6. Six.	a-taŭ-tcim-ĭñ a-ka-bĭn-ĭ'd-i-gĭn, tŭd-li-ma. [4]	
7. Seven.	mad-ró-nĭñ, &c.	
8. Eight.	pĭñ-a-sŭn-ĭñ, &c.	
9. Nine.	kod-lĭn-o-o-tai-la. [5]	
10. Ten.	kód'-lĭn.	

Numerals—Cardinal numbers—Continued.

11. Fourteen.	a-kĭ-miar-ot-aĭ't-yŭñ-ä. [6]
12. Fifteen.	a-kĭ-mĭ'-ä.
13. Twenty.	ĭ'n-yu-ĭ'n-ä.
14. Twenty-five.	ĭ'n-yu-ĭ'n-a tŭd-li-mŭ'n-ĭñ a-ka-bĭn-ĭ'd-ĭ-gĭn.
15. Thirty.	ĭ'n-yu-ĭ'n-a kod'-lĭ'n-ĭñ, a-ka-bĭn-ĭ'd-ĭ-gĭn.
16. Thirty-five.	ĭ'n-yu-ĭ'n-a ak-ĭ-mia-mĭñ aĭ'-pŭ-lĭñ.
17. Forty.	măd-ro ĭn-yu-ĭ'n-ä.
18. One hundred.	tŭd-li-mŭ'b-i-pi-ä.
19. One-half.	nŭ'b-va.
20. All.	mŭ'k-wä.

Numerals (answering the question, "How many?")

1. One.	a-taŭtch-m-ĭñ. [7]
2. Two.	mad-ró-nĭñ.
3. Three.	pĭñ-a-sŭn-lĭñ.
4. Four.	sĕ-sá-ma-nĭñ.
5. Five.	tŭd-li-mŭ'n-lĭñ.
6. Ten.	kod'-lĭ'n-lĭñ.
7. Fifteen.	a-kĭ-mia-mĭñ.
8. How many?	kap-si-nĭñ?
9. A great many.	a-ma-drák-tŭ(k). [8]

Division of time.

1. A moon.	tŭ't-kŭñ a-taŭ-zĭk.
2. Fourth quarter of moon.	nĭp-ta-kák-tu-ä.
3. Winter.	u-kĭ-o.
4. Summer.	u-pĭñ-ák-sa.
5. One winter ago.	u-kĭ-o.
6. Two winters ago.	u-kĭ-o-si-bwŭ-a-ni.
7. Night.	ta. [5]
8. Dawn.	úg'-lu.
9. Sunrise.	sŭk-ŭn-yŭk-paŭñ-a.
10. Dusk.	nĭ'p-ĭ-ru.
11. Day before day before yesterday.	ĭ's-fa. [10]
12. Day before yesterday.	ĭk-pŭ'k-sa.
13. Yesterday.	u-nŭñ-mŭn, uñ-a-li-a-nä.
14. To-day.	kŭñ-mŭ'm-ĭ.
15. To-morrow.	u-blá-xo.
16. Day after to-morrow.	ĭk-pŭ'k-sa.
17. Day after day after to-morrow.	ĭ's-fa. [11]
18. Now (adverb).	tŭ'd-wä.
19. Past time (adverb).	ai-pá-ni. [12]
20. Future time (adverb).	ná-ná-ko. [12]
21. Anciently.	a-drä-ni.
22. When? (in past).	kŭ'ñ-ä?
23. When? (in future).	ká-ko-go?
24. Autumn moons, when the women work on deerskins in the sew-ing-tent.	sŭd-li-vwĭñ.
25.	sŭd-li-vwĭñ kĭñ-ó-li-ä, s.-aĭ'-pa.
26. Dark winter moon.	i-dás-u-gä-ru.
27. Moon when sun returns.	kai-bwĭ'd-a-wĭ.
28. Moon to start deer-hunt-ing.	aud-lák-to-bwĭ.
29. Next moon.	sŭk-ŭn-yá-su-ga-wi.
30. Whaling moon.	u-mi-sŭ'r'-bwĭñ, sŭk-sĭ-lá-bwi.
31. Duck moon.	kaŭ-ker'-bwĭñ.
32. Egg moon.	yö'g-ni-a-bwĭñ.

The rest of the year—"No moon, sun only."

Animals—Mammals.

1. Bear, polar.	nä'-nu.
2. Bear, cinnamon (barren ground).	ä'k-qlak.
3. Caribou (barren ground).	tŭ'k-tu.
4. Caribou fawn.	nó-xa.
5. Caribou young buck.	nŭ-ka. [14]
6. Caribou, old hornless doe.	ai-nŭñ.

---

[1] Stone or iron.
[2] Kĭñgwĭ, fossil ivory.
[3] "Heel."
[4] 1 added to 5.
[5] "10 reduced." (?)
[6] "I don't get to fifteen."
[7] "One in number," "to the number of one."
[8] The common reply for any number over five.
[9] Lit. "darkness."
[10] And preceding days.
[11] And succeeding days.
[12] More than four years ago.
[13] Lit. "by and by."
[14] Under five years.

VOCABULARY COLLECTED AMONG THE ESKIMOS, &c.—Continued.

English.	Eskimo.	English.	Eskimo.

Animals—Mammals—Continued.

Birds—Continued.

English	Eskimo	English	Eskimo
7. Dog.	kĭ′m-mer, kĭ′ñ-mŭk.	17. Goose (white).	kŭ′ñ-o.
8. Dog puppy which can walk.	kĭm-mĭ-á-ru.	18. Goose (brant).	nŭg′-lŭ′g-nŭ.
9. Dog puppy, blind.	kĭ′m-mĭ-yu.	19. Grouse (white), Ptarmigan.	a-kŭ′d-a-gĭn.
10. Ermine.	tër-ĭ′-ä.	20. Gull.	naú-yä.
11. Fox.	kai-ä′k-tŭk.	21. Gull, Sabine's.	yŭk-kŭd-rĭ-gŭg-ĭ′-ä.
12. Fox (red).	ka-ná′k-tu-ä.	22. Gull, Ross' Rosy.	kä′ñ-max-ä-lu.
13. Fox (black).	kai-áñ-a, kai-ä′k-tŭk mäñ-ä′k-tu-ä.	23. Ivory gull.	naú-ya-bwúñ.
		24. Gerfalcon.	kĭ′d-rĭ-gúm-ĭñ.
14. Fox, Arctic.	tër-ĭ′g-ún-i-ä.	25. Loon (white-billed).	tŭd′-lĭñ.
15. Lemming.	áv-wĭñ-ŭ.	26. Loon (red or black throated).	kä′k-sau.
16. Marmot (Parry's).	sĭ′k-sĭñ.		
17. Moose.	tŭ′k-tu-wŭñ.	27. Owl (white snowy).	úk-pĭ(k).
18. Narwhal.	tu-gä-lĭñ.	28. Phalarope, red.	sä-braⁿ.
19. Ox, musk.	ú-mĭñ-mau.	29. Phalarope, northern.	sa-bráñ-na.
20. Sable.	kä′b-we-a-ti-a.	30. Pigeon (sea).	scák-bwŭk.
21. Seal, ringed.	nё′t-yĭ.	31. Plover (black-bellied).	kĭ-rai-ŏu.
22. Seal, ringed, young.	nёt-yĭ-á-ru.	32. Plover (golden).	tŭd′-lĭñ.
23. Seal, harbor.	ka-sĭ-gĭ-ä.	33. Raven.	tu-lŭ-ä.
24. Seal, ribbon.	kai-xó-lĭñ.	34. Sandpiper (pectoral).	ai-bwŭk-i-ä.
25. Seal, bearded.	úg′-ru.	35. Sandpiper (Bonaparte's).	kaiñ-i-a-lu.
26. Sheep, mountain.	ĭ′m-nea.	36. Sandpiper (red-backed).	méa-ka-pĭñ.
27. Wolf.	a-má-xo.	37. Sandpiper (semi-palmated).	nĭ-wĭl-ĭ-wĭ′l-ŭk.
28. Walrus.	aĭ′-bwŭk.		
29. Whale.	ák′-bwŭk.	38. Sandpiper (buff-breasted.)	núd-lu-a-yu.
30. Whale, killer.	áx-lo.	39. Snipe, robin.	tŭ-a-wi-a.
31. Whale, white.	kĭl-ё′l-yu-ä.	40. Swan.	kúg′-ru.
32. Wolverine.	káb-wĭñ.	41. Skua.	ĭ-suñ-ŭ.
33. Mammoth (fossil).	kĭl-ĭ′g′-wä.	42. Tern.	ut-yu-tá-kĭu.
34. Fœtus.	ĭ′-blau.	43. Turnstone.	tŭl-ĭ′g-u-ä.

Parts of the body, &c., of mammals.

Parts of the body, &c., of birds.

English	Eskimo	English	Eskimo
1. Antlers.	nú′g-ё-ru.	1. Beak, or bill.	sĭ-go.
2. Bone.	sañ-nä.	2. Mouth.	káñ-a.
3. Brain.	káx-za.	3. Eye.	ĭ′d-drúñ.
4. Claw.	kú-kiu.	4. Neck.	kó-mo-zĭn.
5. Dung.	ún-na.	5. Feathers.	tu-lú-gä.
6. Entrails.	i-na-lu-úñ-a.	6. Wings.	ĭ′s-a-xo, ĭ′s-a-xu-lu.
7. Fat.	úk-suk.	7. Wing-feathers.	sú-lu.
8. Hair.	mĭ′t-ko.	8. Tail.	púp-kĭn-éa-ko-ko.
9. Heart.	ú-ma-ta.	9. Tail-feathers.	pú′p-kĭ.
10. Meat.	nĭa-kё.	10. Legs.	mĭ′p-kwo.
11. Milk.	ĭ′-muñ.	11. Toes.	ĭs-ĭ-gai.
12. Paw.	ĭs-ĭ-gai′.	12. Claws.	kú-kiu.
13. Penis.	u-sŭ-a, ú-su.	13. Gizzard.	a-ké-a-xo.
14. Stomach.	a-ké-a-xo.	14. Vent.	ĭ′t-ka.
15. Skin.	á-mia.	15. Egg.	mú′n-nĭ.
16. Tail.	púm-ĭ-ú-nä.	16. Shell (of egg).	sañ-nañ-a.
17. Tendon or leader.	ĭ′-va-lu.	17. Yolk (of egg).	kú-nuñ-ra.
18. Teeth.	kĭ′g-u-tá.	18. White (of egg).	ĭ′k-tĭ-a.
19. Walrus-tusk or ivory.	tú-ga.	19. Bird's nest.	ú-glu(n).
20. Tongue.	ó-ka.	20. He flies.	tĭñ-i-ru-ä.
21. Testicles.	ĭ′g-gru.		
22. Whale-bone (a "slab").	cú-kŭk, cú-kai (pl.).		
23. Seal's breathing-hole (in ice).	a(d)-lu.		

Birds.

Fish.

English	Eskimo	English	Eskimo
1. Bird.	{ kaú-we.[1] tĭ′ñ-mia.[2]	1. A fish.	yú-ka-lu.
		2. Burbot.	tĭ-tá-lä.
2. Auk.	át-pa.	3. Cockle.	sĭ-ú-tĭ-go.[4]
3. Bunting (Lapland).	nёs-aúd-lĭ-gä, ♀ nёs-aúd-lĭ-ga-bĭ-ä.	4. Crab.	ki-naú-ra.[5]
		5. Lycodes.	kŭx-rau-nä.
4. Bunting (snow).	a-maú-lĭ-ga, ♀ a-maú-lĭ-ga-bĭ-ä.	6. Sculpin.	kú′l-ai-o, kú′n-ai-o.
5. Crane (little sandhill).	tŭt-ĭ′d-rĭ-gú.	7. Smelt.	ĭt-ho-á-nĭñ.
6. Curlew (Eskimo).	tu-rá-tu-rá.	8. Whitefish.	a-nák-qlŭñ.
7. Duck.	kaú-we.[3]		
8. Duck (pintail).	ĭ′v-wŭ-gŭ.		
9. Duck (king).	♂ kĭ′n-a-lĭñ, ♀ añ-na-bĭ-ä.	*Parts of the body, &c., of fish.*	
10. Duck (Pacific eider).	♂ a-maú-lĭñ, ♀ cu-gä-lŭ′k-tun.		
11. Duck (Steller's).	ĭg-nĭ-kaúk-to.	1. Mouth.	káñ-a.
12. Duck (Spectacled eider).	ká-wa-so, ♂ tú-tŭ-lu, ♀ yú′k-qlu-lu.	2. Eye.	id-rúñ.
		3. Gills.	más-sĭ.
13. Duck (long-tailed).	á-bád-lĭñ, úd-yĭ-gĭ-ä.	4. Breast-fin.	añ-u-tañ.[6]
14. Eagle (golden).	tĭ′ñ-miak-púk.	5. Back-fin.	sĭt-ka.
15. Finch or any little passerine bird.	sú′k-sa-xĭ-ä.	6. Tail-fin.	púm-i-ú-nä.
		7. Scales.	káp-ĭ-sĭ.
16. Goose (white-fronted).	nú′g′-lúg′-ru-ä.	8. He swims.	añ-o-ák-tu-ä.
		9. Claw of a crab.	pú-dju-tĭn.

[1] "Fowl."
[2] "Small bird."
[3] Lit. "fowl."
[4] Siu-"ear."
[5] *Hyas latifrons.*
[6] From añun "paddle."

VOCABULARY COLLECTED AMONG THE ESKIMOS, &c.—Continued.

English.	Eskimo.	English.	Eskimo.
Insects.		**Geographical names—Continued.**	
1. Bee (humble).	í-gu-tyai.	5. Land below village, south-west.	A-múñ-ná.
2. Butterfly.	túk-ä-lú′k-ĭ-ca, túk-ä-!úk-ĭ-dják-sûn.[1]	6. Next piece of land.	Kĭ′k-ku.
3. Fly.	ni-bra-ru-ä.	7. Land at double lagoon.	Nu-na-vá.
4. Horse-fly.	í-gyu-ta (?).	8. First camp below.	Séak-qlu-ka.
5. Louse.	kú-múk.	9. Second camp below.	Na-ké′d-rĭ-xo.
6. Mosquito.	kĭ′k-to-ri-ä.	10. Third camp below.	Ku-o-sug′-ru.
7. Spider.	pi-drai-ru-ra.[2]	11. Fourth camp below.	Nu-nä′k-tu-au.
8. Worm.	kú-pĭ-dro.	12. Fifth camp below.	Ĭ′p-per-su-a.
9. Branchipus (aquatic).	í-rĭ-túñ-a.	13. Sixth camp below.	Wä′l-äk-pa.
		14. Seventh camp below.	Ér-ni-vwiñ.
		15. Eighth camp below.	Sĭ′ñ-a-ru.
Plants.		16. Ninth camp below.	Sá-kám-na.
1. Leaf.	kĭñ-mö-ré.	17. Wainwright's Inlet.	Nu-ná-ri-ä.[10]
2. Willow catkins.	kĭ′m-mi-u-ru.[3]	18. Wainwright's Inlet.	Si-dá-ru.[11]
3. Limb.	kwa-ré.	19. Wainwright's Inlet.	Á-tûn-ö.[12]
4. Body or trunk.	núñ-a.	20. Village, southwest of the inlet.(?)	Kĭl-an-ĕ-tá-wĭñ.
5. Root.	kĭ′l-yĕn-ĕ-ra.	21. Point Hope.	Tĭk-ĕ-rá.[13]
6. Tree, willow.	ĭ′k-pĭ(k).	22. Elson Bay.	Tä′s-yúk.[14]
7. Wood.	kĕ′-ru.	23. Little pond at Pern-yú.	Kĭk-yúk-tú′k-tu-ro.[15]
8. Small wood.	na-kĭ′t-yu-ä kĕ-rú.	24. First beach lagoon (salt).	I-meak-pú′n-ĭg-lu.[16]
9. Large wood (timber).	na-pák-tn.[4]	25. Second beach lagoon (fresh).	I-méak-púñ.[17]
10. A flower, yellow poppy or buttercup.	túk-a-lú′k-ĭ-ca, &c.[5]	26. Third beach lagoon (fresh).	Sĭ′n-ñyú.[18]
11. Flowers.	naú-ru-un.	27. Fourth beach lagoon (salt).	Ĭ′k-pĭ-lĭñ.[19]
		28. Fifth beach lagoon (goose-pond).	I-sú′t-kwa.
Geographic terms.		29. Sixth beach lagoon (at station).	I-sú′t-kwa.
1. North.	ú-na-ni.	30. Little village-ponds.	Tûs-ĕ-rá-ru.
2. Northeast.	a-kĭl-yúñ-ná-mĭ.	31. Little stream east of Point Barrow.	Ku-á-ru ai-pa.[20]
3. East.	ká-ba-ni.	32. First large river east of Point Barrow.	Ku-á-ru.
4. Southeast.	ka-wa-ni-kú′n-nä.	33. Second large river east of Point Barrow (Meade).	Ku lú-gru-ä.
5. South.	pá-ni.	34. Third large river east of Point Barrow.	Ĭ′k-pĭk-púñ.[21]
6. West.	á-wa-ni.	35. Great Lake connected with this.	Tä′s-yúk-púñ.[22]
7. Southwest.	a-wa-ni-kú′n-nä.	36. Mackenzie River.	Kú′-púñ.[23]
8. Northwest.	wäl-úñ-ná-nĭ.	37. The Colville River was always spoken of as "Nĕg-a-lĕñ-mĭ-ku," "the river at Negalek," and we did not obtain the name.	
9. Northward.	u-núñ-ä.		
10. Northeastward.	a-kĭl-yúñ-ná-mun.		
11. Eastward.	ka-wú′ñ-ä.		
12. Southeastward.	ka-wú′ñ-ä-kú′n-nä.	38. River at Wainwright's Inlet.	Ku.[24]
13. Southward.	paúñ-ä.	39. River of the Nunatañ-nĕm.	Nú-(n)a-tŏk.[25]
14. Westward.	a-wú′ñ-ä.	40. Locality for gypsum, one day's journey east.	Tú′t-yŏ.
15. Southwestward.	a-wú′ñ-ä-kú′n-nä.	41. "Fair-ground" at mouth of Colville River.	Nĕ′g-a-lŏk.[26]
16. Northwestward.	wäl-úñ-ná-nun.		
17. Here.	má-ni.		
18. Hither.	maúñ-ä.	**The Firmament.**—Meteorological and other physical phenomena and objects.	
19. Where. (?)	cú-mĭ. (?)		
20. Whither?	cú-mun. (?)		
21. Sea.	táx-ai-o.	1. A cloud.	a-no-wi-ĕ′k-sa-xo.
22. Bay.	tú′ñ-úk-qlúñ.	2. The clouds.	nu-bú-yä.
23. Strait.	tĕ′d-at-kŏñ.	3. Clear sky.	a-lú′k-tu-ä.
24. Lake.	i-meak.[6]	4. Sky, weather, "all out-doors."	sí′-lä.
25. Island.	kik-yĕ′k-tú.	5. Sun.	sú′k-ún-yú(k).
26. Point.	nú-wúk.	6. Moon.	tú′t-kúñ.
27. River, stream.	ku.	7. Full-moon.	ím-íg-lúk-tu-ä.
28. River mouth.	púñ-a.	8. Half-moon.	náx-äk-to.
29. Cape.	ú-lúk-to.	9. Crescent-moon.	a-nĭ′t-yu-ä.[27]
30. Sandspit.	teu-äk-á-ru.	10. Stars.	u-glú-ri-ä.
31. Sandy island.	tú′p-kún.	11. Meteor.	u-glú-ri-ä a-ná′k-tu-ä.
32. Beach, shore.	sĭ-ua.		
33. Peninsula.	í-su.		
34. Cliff.	ĭ′k-pĭk.		
Geographical names.			
1. Point Barrow and village.	Nú-wúk.[7]		
2. Summer camp, Elson Bay.	Pérn-yú.		
3. U. S. signal station.	I-sú′t-kwa.[8]		
4. Village at Cape Smythe.	Út-k(l)i-áv-wĭñ.[9]		

[1] Cf. túk-ú-ya, "flag."
[2] "Little braider."
[3] "Puppies."(?)
[4] Cf. na-pák-sä, "mast."
[5] Same as "butterfly."
[6] "Water."
[7] "The Point."
[8] Also name of lagoon.
[9] "The Cliffs."
[10] Deserted village.
[11] New village.
[12] A few houses.
[13] "The Forefinger."
[14] "Enclosed water."

[15] "Island Pond."
[16] "Big water, too."
[17] "Big water."
[18] "Shoestring." (?)
[19] "With high banks."
[20] "The Second Kuáru."
[21] "The Great Cliffs."
[22] "Great enclosed water."‡
[23] "The Great River."
[24] "The River."
[25] "Inland."
[26] "Goosetown."‡
[27] Lit., "thin."

VOCABULARY COLLECTED FROM THE ESKIMOS, &c.—Continued.

English.	Eskimo.	English.	Eskimo.
The Firmament—Continued.		**Social organization.**	
12. Aurora.	ki-ó(l).yä.	1. Eskimo.	Ĭ'n-yu.[9]
13. Rainbow.	ni'-gñ.	2. White man.	ka-blú-na, tŭ'n-ñyĭn.
14. Fog.	tŭ'k-tu.	3. Negro.	ták-si-pŭñ.
15. Hoar-frost.	sĭ'-ko nûg-ĕ-rŭ'k-to.	The following are local designations, signifying "men of such and such a place."	
16. Snow.	á-pun.		
17. Falling snow.	ka-nĭn.		
18. Drifting snow.	pĕ'q-su.	1. Point Barrow.	Nu-wŭ'ñ-mĕ-un.
19. Hail.	tĕg-mĭt-ko-sák-to.	2. Cape Smythe.	Ut-ki-av-wĭ'ñ-mĕ-un.
20. Ice.	si-ko.	3. Wainwright's Inlet.	Si-dá-rŭñ-mĕun.
21. Icicle.	ku-sŭ-gñ, ko-ko-lu-tĭn-yä.	4. River "Ku."	Kúñ-mĕ-un.
22. Water.	i'-meak, i'-mŭk.	5. Kĭl-au-l-tá-wĭñ.	Kĭl-au-l-ta-wĭ'ñ-mĕ-un.
23. Deep water.	i'ti-ra.	6. Point Hope.	Tĭk-ĕ-ráñ-mĕ-un.
24. Shallow water.	i'-ka-to.	7. Hotham Inlet.	Si-la-wĭ'ñ-mĕ-un.
25. Image reflected by water.	tá-ga*.	8. Hotham Inlet.	Ku-wŭ'ñ-mĕ-un.
26. Foam.	ká-pak-qlu.	9. Nú-a-tàk and Colville Rivers.	Nu-na-táñ-mĕ-un.[10]
27. Wave.	mŭ'l-lĭñ, mŭ'l-lŭk-so.		
28. Current.	séak'-bwñ.	10. Mouth of Mackenzie River.	Ku-pŭ'ñ-mĕ-un.
29. Northeast current.	kai-jáñ-nä.		
30. Southwest current.	pi-ro-à'ñ-nä.	*Tribal names.*	
31. North current.	ait-táñ-nä.		
32. South current.	tŭk-sŭ'ñ-nä.	11. Between Colville and Mackenzie.	Kŭñ-mŭ'd'-lĭñ.[11]
33. Eddy.	ki'd-lä.[1]		
34. Whirlpool.	i'-cúk-a-ru-ä.	12. Inland beyond Colville.	Ĭt-kŭ'd'-lĭñ.[12]
35. Overflow of river.	cu-pĭ-rú-a.	13. Inland beyond Colville (?).	Ĕn-a-ko-ti-na.[13]
36. Flood tide.	u-lŭ'k-tu-a.		
37. Ebb tide.	kĭn-l'k-tu-a.		
38. Rain.	si'-la-lu.	*Government.*	
39. Thunder.	kŭ'd-lu.		
40. Lightning.	ĭ'g-ni-ä.[2]	1. Captain of a boat.	u-mi'a-lĭk.
41. Wind.	á-no-ĕ.		
42. Strong wind.	a-nŭk-lŭ'k-so.	*Religion.*	
43. North to east wind.	lk-ŭ'ñ-nä.		
44. Southeast wind.	ni'-gyñ.		
45. South wind.	kĭl-u-ñ'ñ-nä.	1. A demon or hobgoblin.	tŭ'ñ-a.
46. Southwest wind.	ûñ-a-lŭ.		
47. Northwest wind.	kûn-ŭ'ñ-nä.	*Mortuary customs.*	
48. Whirlwind.	u-ya-lŭ-nä.		
49. The ground.	nŭ-nä.		
50. Dust or sand flying.	pi-yŭ'k-so.	1. Dead body.	í-lu-wŭñ.
51. Mud.	a-kŭtc-l-ni-a.	2. Dead, he is.	{ tu-kŭ-ru-ä.
52. Sand.	si'na.		{ nú-na-mĭ si-nĭ'k-to.[14]
53. Salt.	táx-ai-o.[3]		
54. Rock.	uj-yá-rŭñ, á-lĭ-go.	*Medicine.*	
55. Stone (jadeite, pectolite).	kañd'-lo.		
56. Coal.	al-lŭ-ä.	1. Headache.	a-nûñ-náq-tu-ä.
57. Soapstone.	tu-nä'k-tŭ.	2. Toothache.	ki-o-sñ'k-l-ru-ä.
58. Pitch.	à'dn-grŭn.	3. A cold.	nŭ-wûk.
59. Amber.	aŭ-mä.	4. Syphilis.	u-su-lŭ'k-l-ro.
60. Eclipse of sun or moon.	pŭd-la-ru.	5. A boil.	á-yu-á.
61. Earthquake.	i-bwa-rú-a.	6. A cut.	pí-lŭk-á.
62. Storm.	n-ma-lä'k-pŭk.	7. A lame man, woman, or girl.	tu-si-ĕ't-to.
63. Surf.	ĭ'n-i-u-lĭñ.	8. A lame boy.	nu-pi-á-du.
64. Bubbles.	pŭb'-lûn.	9. A blind man.	ad-rĭ-gaŭd'-lo.
65. Ursa major (tail).	tä'k-tu-o-ru-ĭn.	10. A blind woman.	a-yañ-a-rú-ä.
66. Pleiades.	pa-tŭ'k-ta-rĭn.	11. A deaf man.	tu-sĭl-ák-to.
67. Arcturus.	si-bwŭd'-li.	12. Breath.	an-ea-sák-tu-ä.
68. Altair.	á-gru.	13. Sweat.	uk-nák-tu-ä.
69. Vega.	a-grú-lu-bwŭk.	14. Blood.	au.
70. Cassiopea.	i'-bro-si.	15. Urine.	ku, kú-i-ru-ä.
71. Orion's belt.	tŭ-at-san.	16. Dung.	kók'-la, án-na.
72. Ice-hummock.	mŏ-ni'l-ya.	17. A medicine man.	a-nŭk-sá.
		18. A medicine woman.	pûn-lĭñ-ŭ-nä.
Kinship.		*Amusements.*	
1. My child!	á-pa!⁴	1. Song.	a-tŏ'k-tu-ä.[15]
2. My daughter!	pŭ'n-i-ò, pŭ'n-i-gŭ.⁵	2. Dance.	ŭ-a-mi.
3. My father.	áñ-o-ta.	3. Mask.	ki-nau.
4. My father's father.	a-dá-ta.	4. Gorget.	sñ'k-l-mûñ.
5. My mother's father.	á-na.	5. Dance-cap.	kä'b-rñ.
6. My grandfather!	a-ta'-ti-gŭ.⁵	6. Drum.	kĕ'l-yau.
7. My elder brother.	á-nĭñ-a.	7. Whizzing-stick.	ĭm-ĭg-lŭk-tu-ä.
8. My sister.	ni'-ya-ga.	8. Teetotum or top.	kaĭp-sa.
9. My younger brother.	nŭ-ka.⁶	9. "Bean-snapper."	mĭ-tĭ'g-l-gaun.
10. My uncle.	ák-ka-ka.	10. Playing-sticks.	ka-pŭ-tä.
11. My father's sister.	áñ-na-ru-ä.		
12. My mother's sister.	á-ta-ga.		
13. My mother's brother.	áñ-a-gä.⁷		
14. My mother's sister.	áñ-na-ru-ä.		
15. My father's brother's wife, male speaking.	a-sañ-ä.		
16. My wife.	nu-lĭ-ŭ'ñ-ä.		
17. A step-brother.	kŭt-ûñ-ŭ-tä.⁸		
18. Orphan.	ĭl-l-á-ru.		

¹ Lit. "hole."
² "Fire."
³ "Sea."
⁴ Address; also child to parent.
⁵ Address.
⁶ Nu-ka-rŭñ, "brothers."
⁷ Female speaking.
⁸ Of a different nation.
⁹ Lit. "a human being."
¹⁰ Come to Point Barrow every summer.
¹¹ Eskimos.
¹² Red Indians—"Tinné."
¹³ Red Indians.
¹⁴ Lit. "sleeps on the ground."
¹⁵ "He sings."

VOCABULARY COLLECTED AMONG THE ESKIMOS, &c.—Continued.

English.	Eskimo.	English.	Eskimo.
New words.		*Number and gender of nouns—pronouns—Continued.*	
1. Barrel.	i-mo-si-á-ru.	14. One boy.	nu-kŭt-pī-á-ru a-taú-zīk.
2. Large barrel, cask.	i-mo-si-á-ru-ru-ä.	15. Two boys.	nu-kŭt-pī-á-ru mad-ró.
3. Small barrel.	i-mo-si-á-ru-a-yu.	16. Three boys.	nu-kŭt-pī-a-rū-īn pī'ñ-a-sun.
4. Whip.	i-pi-raŭ-tä, a-naŭ-tä (without lash).	17. Many boys and girls.	mŭk-qlŭk-tu-a-rū-īn.
		18. One dog.	kī'm-mea a-taú-zīk.
5. Axe.	a-naŭ-tä, tu-kī'n-ga-ru-ä.	19. Two dogs.	kī'm-mīñ mad-ró.
6. Iron-headed arrow.	sáv-íd-līñ.	20. Three dogs.	kī'm-mīñ pī'ñ-a-sun.
7. Nails of metal.	ki-ki-ĕñ.	21. Few dogs.	kīm-mér-l-rūñ-ä.
8. Beads.	tcuñ-aú-rä.	22. Many dogs.	kīm-mi-u-mä-ru.
9. Broom.	tī'l-ax-a-zi.	23. All the dogs.	mŭ'k-wä kī'ñ-mŭk.
10. Button.	tu-taŭ-rä.[1]	24. One arrow.	kä'k-a-ru a-taŭ-zīk.
11. Cloth.	u-kī-trá, á-tīk-qluñ.	25. Two arrows.	kä'k-a-ru mad-ró.
12. Cloth, sail.	tīñ-ī-draŭ-tä.	26. Three arrows.	pīñ-a-sun-kák-a-rú-līñ.
13. Comb.	ī(d)-laí-u-tīn.	27. Few arrows. (I have?)	kák-a-ru-kĕ't-tŭñ-ä.
14. Clock.	sŭk-ŭn-yaŭ-ra.[2]	28. Many arrows.	kák-a-ru-rúñ-ä.
15. Knife, pocket.	pīñ-á'k-tŭ.	29. One stone.	uj-yá-rúñ a-taŭ-zīk.
16. Hammer.	kaŭ-tŭ.	30. Two stones.	uj-yák-kúñ.
17. Iron kettle.	ŭt-ku-zīn.	31. Three stones.	pī'ñ-a-sun uj-yá-rúñ.
18. Tin can or pannikin.	ŭt-ku-zī-aú-rä.[3]	32. Many stones.	uj-yá-ga-rīn.
19. Tin fish-horn.	ni-pák-qlŭk-taun.	33. All the stones.	uj-yá-ga rīn, uj-yá-ra-rīn (mŭ'k-wä).
20. File.	á-gī-nn.		
21. Saw.	u-lu-á'k-tun.	34. Male dog.	añ-u-sĕ'l-u.
22. Glover's needle.	ko-ág-ru-līñ.	35. Female dog.	añ-na-sĕ'l-u.
23. Scissors.	sú'd lī-sīñ, pl.; sing. one blade, sá'd-līñ.	36. Male seal.	ti'x-gŭñ.[15]
		37. Female seal.	nŭ-nŭq.[18]
24. Watch chain.	kŭ'l-mi-nñ.	38. Male bearded seal.	kád-:1-gŭñ.
25. Pistol.	cu-pŭñ-aŭ-ra.[4]	39. Male reindeer.	pŭ'ñ mŭñ.
26. Gun.	cú-pŭñ.[5]	40. Female reindeer.	kŭ-lau-ŭñ.
27. Rifle, Winchester.	a-ki-mia-līñ.[6]	41. This man.	ī'n-yu ŭ-na.
28. Rifle, Sharps'.	sa-vīx-ró-līñ.	42. I.	wŭñ-ä.
29. Rifle, Spencer.	kaí'p-sua-līñ.	43. To me.	u-ñ'n-nun.
30. Rifle cartridge.	kaí'p-s!.	44. Thou.	ī'lu-īt.
31. Cartridge shell.	īt-ŭ'g-ĕ-ru.	45. To thee.	īl-ī'ñ-nun.
32. Bullet.	kä'k-a-ru.[7]	46. He or she.	ŭ-na.
33. Cap, percussion.	kä'b'-lu.	47. You two.	īl-īp-tīk.
34. Powder.	áx-ĕ-rä.[8]	48. At your "place," household, &c.	īl-īp-tīñ-īnī.[16]
35. Shot.	kák-a-rú-rä.[9]		
36. Iron.	sá-vīk.	49. To your "place," &c.	īl-ī'p-tīñ-nun.
37. Lead.	ó-xa.	50. We.	u-ŭ'g-un.
38. Bullet-mold.	kák-a-rī'-bwīñ.	51. At our "place," &c.	u-á'p-tīñ-nī.
39. Target.	nĕ'k-sa-ra.	52. To our "place," &c.	u-á'p-tīñ-nun.
40. Cap or hat.	nĕs-a-rä.	53. Ye.	ī-lī'p-sī.
41. Coat.	a-tī'-gĕ.	54. At your "place," &c.	ī-lī'p-sīñ-nī.[17]
42. Pants or drawers.	kŭ'm-mŭñ.	55. To your "place," &c.	ī-līp-sīñ-nun.
43. Bread (hard).	kák-o-lá.	56. This, that.	ŭ-na, ó-kwa.
44. Flour.	"pŭ-ladä."	57. This here.	u-na-hĕ, mŭ'n-na, mŭn-na-hĕ.
45. Match, friction.	kīl-ī-á'k-sa-gau.	58. All this.	mŭ'k-wä-he.
46. Candle or white man's lamp.	nĕ'-nĕx-ron	59. Who?	ki-nä. /
		60. What, what is it?	sŭ-nä.
47. Sugar.	"sŭú-rä."		
48. Molasses.	túñ-.,'k-qlu.		
49. Soap.	i'a-kák-kŭn.	*Personal and article pronouns—transitive verbs.*	
50. Tobacco.	taŭ-wak, tau-wák-o, "tī'-ba."		
51. Spirits.	tŭ'ñ ä.		
52. Finger-ring.	ka-tŭ'k-qlē-rŭñ.	1. I am striking him (now) with closed hand.	ka-ka-ta-rŭ'ñ-ä ú-nä.
53. Mirror.	kī'/na-raun, ta-gák-tu-en.		
54. House (our station).	īg-lŭ-kpŭk.[10]	2. He is striking with closed hand.	tī'g-lu-ka.
55. Door.	i-ka-rä, ŭp-kwa.		
56. Pencil.	mīñ-a ä'k-tun.[11]	3. I am kicking (him).	wŭ'ñ-ä a-ki-gá.
57. Paper, book, newspaper.	mŭk-pa-rá.	4. He is kicking him.	ak-sŭñ-ear-ñ-nä.
58. Steamboat.	ī'g-nī-līñ.[12]	5. Ittŭ killed one duck with the sling.	Ittŭ ataŭtcīmīñ kĕlauītaŭtīnī kauwŭksīmero.
59. Ship.	u-mi-ä'k-pŭk[13].	6. He kills deer.	tŭ'k-tu-tu-ä.
60. Ship, "three-master."	u-mi-ä'k-pŭk pīñ-a-sun-īñ-na-pák-sa-līñ.	7. He kills ducks.	kau-wŭ'k-tu-ä.
		8. He has killed no ducks.	kau-wŭñ-ait-yo.
		9. Who killed the crane?	ki'-ä tŭt-īd-ñ-gaú-tä?
Number and gender of nouns—pronouns.		10. They kill walruses.	aí'-bwŭk-twŭn.
		11. He kills seals.	nĕ't-yī(l)-su-ä.
1. One person.	ī'n-yu a-taú-zīk.	12. He divides into portions.	pa-tŭk-tu-á.
2. Two persons.	īn-yu mŭd-ro.	13. Are you making snow-shoes?	tŭg-ä-lu'-lī-bi?
3. Three persons.	pī'ñ-a-sun ī'n-nu-īn.		
4. Few men.	īn-yu-ki-tu-än.		
5. Many men.	īn-yu-gi-ŭ'k-tu-än.		
6. What a number of men!	īn-yu-kák-pa-sī'l-yä!	*Possession.*	
7. All the men.	mŭ'k-wä ī'n-nu-īt.		
8. Some men.	īn-yu-gi-ŭ'k-tu-än.	1. My hands.	wŭ'ñ-ä a-dī-gát-ka.
9. No man.	īn-yu-ait-yo.[14]	2. I have no tobacco.	ti-bax-ot-ait-yŭñ-ä.
10. Another man.	ī'n-yu ád-la.	3. You have no tobacco.	ti-bax-ot-ait-tu-tīn.
11. One woman.	añ-na a-taú-zīk.	4. He has no tobacco.	ti-bax-ot-ait-yo.
12. Two women.	añ-na-qī'ñ-na..	5. Ye have no tobacco.	ti-bax-ot-ait-yu-sĕ.
13. Three women.	añ-na-qaíñ-naíñ.		

[1] "Little labret."
[2] "Little sun."
[3] "Little kettle."
[4] "Little gun."
[5] "Onomatopœic."
[6] "15-er."
[7] Lit. "arrow."
[8] "paú-rä."
[9] "Little bullets."
[10] "big iglu."
[11] mī'ñ-un=black lead.
[12] ī'g-ní-a " fire."
[13] " big canoe."
[14] " There is nobody."
[15] Phoca fœtida.
[16] Where there are only two.
[17] Where there are more than two.

VOCABULARY COLLECTED AMONG THE ESKIMOS, &c.—Continued.

English.	Eskimo.	English.	Eskimo.

Possession—Continued.

6. They have no tobacco. — ti-bax-ot-ait-yu-än.
7. I have plenty of tobacco. — ti-bax u-tĭ-kă'k-tûñ-ä.
8. You have plenty of tobacco. — ti-bax-u-tĭ-kă'k-tu-tín.
9. Whose dog is this? — ki'ä-ó-kwa-kĭ'm-mea?
10. Whose party is this? — kĭt-kun tä'd-wä.
11. This is Angoru's party. — Añ-o-rút-kun tû'd-wä.
12. Hero is Ittû's dog. — Ĭ't-tûb kĭ'm-mea tû'd-wä.
13. Whose bow is this? — ki'ä ó-kwa pi-zŸk-aĭ?
14. Whose knife is this? — ki-ä ó-kwa sä-vĭk?
15. Whose are all these hands? — kit-kun mû'k-wä äd-rĭ-gai?
16. Nûgeru's (possessions). — Nûg ĕ-rút-kun.[1]
17. At Nûgeru's. — Nûg-ĕ-rút-kun-nĭ.
18. To Nûgeru's. — Nûg-ĕ-rút-kun-nun.
19. A tern's bill. — ut-yu-tá-kĭb si'-go.
20. A woman of soapstone. — tu-näk-tû'p-ku-nĭ-ä.[2]

Intransitive verbs, &c.

1. I am hungry. — kák-tûñ-ä.
2. I become hungry. — kák-sĭ-ruñ-ä.
3. I shall become hungry. — kák-sĭ-nĭ-ä'k-tûñ-ä.
4. You are hungry. — kák-tu-tín.
5. You become hungry. — kák-sĭ-ru-tĭn.
6. You will become hungry. — kak-sĭ-nĭ-ä'k-tu-tín.
7. Ye are hungry. — kák-tu-sĕ.
8. Ye become hungry. — kák-sĭ-ru-sĕ.
9. Ye will become hungry. — kak-sĭn-ĭ-ä'k-tu-sĕ.
10. He is hungry. — kák-to.
11. He becomes hungry. — kák-ĭ-ro.
12. He will become hungry. — kak-sĭn-ĭ-ä'k-to.
13. They are hungry. — kak-tu-än.
14. They become hungry. — kák-sĭ-ru-än.
15. They will become hungry. — kák-sĭ-nĭ-ä'k-tu-än.
16. I am making water (urinating). — ku-ĭ-jä'k-tûñ-ä.
17. I was making water. — ku-ĭ-jäk-tû'ñ-ĕ-rûñ-ä.
18. I am going to make water. — ku-ĭ-jäk-tu-nĭ-ä'k-tûñ-ä.
19. Ittû is making water. — ku-ĭ-jä'k-to.
20. I am talking. — ŏk-hä'k-tûñ.
21. I was talking. — ŏk-hä'k-tûñ-ĕr-ûñ-ä.
22. I will talk. — ŏk-hä'k-tu-nĭ-ä'k-tûñ-ä.
23. You were talking. — ŏk-häk-tûñ-ĕ-rú-tĭn.
24. He is talking. — ŏk-hä'k-to.
25. It-tû is talking. — Ĭ't-tu ŏk-hä'k-to.
26. I am singing. — a-tö'k-tûñ-ä.
27. I was singing. — a-tök-tûñ-e-rûñ-ä.
28. I will sing. — a-tök-tu-nĭ-ä'k-tûñ-ä.
29. You were singing. — a-tök-tûñ-e-rú-tĭn.
30. He is singing. — a-tö'k-to.
31. Ittû is singing. — a-tö'k to Ĭ't-tñ.
32. I am laughing. — Ĭg-lû'k-tûñ-ä.
33. He is laughing. — Ĭg-lû'k-to.
34. He is smiling. — ku-mu-yúk-tu-ä.
35. I am walking. — pi-so-ä'k-tûñ-ä.
36. He is walking. — pi-so-ä'k-to.
37. Ittû is running. — Ĭ't-tñ ak-paúk-tu-ä.
38. The bird is flying. — tĭ'ñ-mia ĭz-ĭ-kfu'l-yĕ-ru-ä.
39. Ittû's knife is bad. — Ĭ't-tûñ sä-vĭk a-sĭ-ru-ä.
40. I am cold. — a-la-pák-tûñ-ä, ki-yĭn-ä'k-tûñ-ä.
41. He will become cold. — a-la-pak-sĭ-nĭ-ä'k-to.
42. I am getting warm. — u-nä'k-sĭ-rûñ-ä.
43. He will become warm. — u-näk-sĭ-nĭ-ä'k-to.
44. It is cold. — ki-yĭn-äk-pa-sĭ'l-yä!
45. It is hot! — u-näk-pa-sĭ'l-yä!
46. It is dark! — ta-pa-sĭ'l-yä!
47. It will become cold to-morrow. — u-blá-xo al-a-pak-sĭn-ĭ-ä'k-to.
48. If it is cold to-morrow I shall not go. — u-blá-xo al-a-pak-pút, aud-lau-ĭ-ûñ-Ÿt-yûñ-ä.
49. A stone sinks in the water. — uj-ya-rûñ kĭ'm-mĕ-ro i-mû'-mi.
50. Who is that (man)? — kin-aú-na?[3]
51. Lie down (to a dog)! — a-ko-wĭ'd'-Ĭl.[4]
52. Lie low! pl. — a-wûñ-ä-rĭn (S.), a-wûñ-a-rĭ't-yĕ (P.).
53. Go away! — Ĭg-lú-mun-Ÿt-yĕ!
54. Go home! pl. — tu-pĕñ-mun-Ÿt-yĕ!
55. Go home! (to the tent). — kai(ny) (S.), kait-yĕ (P.).
56. Come! — kai-li.
57. Let him come! — ta'k-tu-tĭn.
58. You darken (the window). — Ĭs-Ÿñ-ĕ-ro.
59. He went in, entered. — Ĭs-Ÿñ-a-ba?
60. Did he enter? —

Intransitive verbs, &c.—Continued.

61. I did not enter. — Ĭs-Ÿû-ai't-yûñ-ä.
62. Shall I came in? — Ÿs-ûk-lûñ-ä?
63. Come in! — Ĭs-a-rÿn-(go)!
64. Shall I come? — kai'-lûñ-ä?
65. What shall I (do)? — cú-lûñ-ä!
66. What do you (want)? — cú-ru-tĭn?
67. Where are you going? — su-nlä'k-pĭn (S.), su-nĭ-ä'k-pĭ-sĕ (P.)?
68. I am not going (any) where. — su-nĭ-ûñ-Ÿt-yûñ-ä.
69. I am going home. — Ĭg-lu-mun-ai-nĭ-ä'k-tûñ-ä.
70. When will you go south? — kä-ko-go pauñ-a-nĭ-ä'k-pĭ?
71. To-morrow I will go east. — u-blä-xun-go ka-wûñ-a-nĭ-ä'k-tûñ-ä.
72. Whither will ye go? — cú-mun Ĭl-Ĭp-si al-ûk-ta-nĭ-ä'k-pĭ-sĭ?
73. When it becomes good or gets well. — na-kuo-sĭ'k-pút.
74. It will become good. — na-kuo-sĭn-Ĭ-ä'k-to.
75. —— will be plenty. — a-ma-dra-nĭ-ä'k-to.
76. If or when —— shall be plenty. — a-ma-drák-pút.
77. When —— was plenty. — a-ma-dräñ-mút.
78. I forget. — wû'ñ-ä pu-ĭ'-gu-a.
79. You forget. — Ÿl-u-ĭt pu-ĭ-gi.
80. I forgot completely. — pu-ĭ-gäk-sĭm-ĕr-û'ñ-ä.
81. They will come, be here. — pĭn-Ĭ-ä'k-tun.
82. They will not come. — pĭn-Ĭ-ûñ-Ÿt-tun.
83. I am going to stay. — a-kŭt-gĭn-Ĭ-ä'k-tûñ-ä.
84. It has gone out (pipe, &c.). — kam-Ĭv-wañ-nä.
85. They dive (ducks). — ä'g-lûk-tu-än.
86. They come up (ducks). — kû'k-Ĭ-myu-än.
87. There will be a dance. — u-a mĭ-nĭ-ä'k-to.
88. Dance! — n-ö'-nĭ-tĭn (S.), u-ö'-mĭt-yĕ (P.).
89. I am drunk. — tûñ-ä'k-tûñ-ä.
90. I cut. — wû'ñ-ä pĭ-lûk-ä.
91. I sew. — wû'ñ-ä ki-lĕ-ä.
92. I've hurt my shin. — kĭñ-a-drák-tuñ-ä.
93. I hit my nose, make it bleed. — pu-sĭ-käk-tuñ-ä.
94. I bump my head. — a-pŏk-tuñ-ä.
95. I bump my forehead. — ka-ti-tuñ-ä.
96. I hurt my knee. — sĭt-ko-äk-tuñ-ä.
97. I crack my crazy-bone. — Ĭt-kut-sĭ-äk-tuñ-ä.
98. My foot's asleep. — ka-kĭl-Ĭ-säk-si-ruñ-ä.[5]
99. He falls in the water. — nä-kok-to.
100. He falls backwards. — nĭ-wéak-to.
101. He falls sideways. — Ĭu-nä'k-to.
102. He falls forward. — pu-tu-kĬ't-to, pa-sák-to.
103. He falls into the water. — Ĭ-mák-to.
104. He falls by slipping on his heels. — ko-ai-ja-kĕ't-yu-ä.
105. He falls by slipping on his toes. — ko-ai-jañ-nä'k-tu-ä.
106. He almost falls by slipping on his heels. — ko-ai-ja-kĕt-kai-äk-to.
107. He shoots at a target. — nŏk-sa-rák-tu-ä.
108. He (the deer) has antlers. — nûg-ĕ-ru-Ÿt-yo.
109. What are you laughing at? — cú-bĭ Ĭg-lû'k-pĭ?
110. You strut with your elbows out. — añ-u-tau-kwák-tu-tĭn.[6]
111. It is bad. — pi-lû'k-tu-ä.
112. It is very bad. — pi-lu-pĭ'k-su-ä.
113. It is done with, over. — pi-yû'k-so. Interrog. pi-yû'k-pa?
114. I want. — wûñ-ä pi-sĭ-kĭ-ga.
115. I want my jacket. — a-tĭ'-gĭ-lûñ-ä.
116. I want some water. — i'-muk-lûñ-ä.
117. I want a chew (of tobacco). — wĭ'-läk-sĭm-uñ.
118. He puts on his boots. — kûm-nĭk-tä'k-to.
119. He puts on his boots. — a-tĭ-gĭ-ró.
120. He puts on his mittens. — aĭt-kät-Ĭ-ró.
121. He puts on his breeches. — kä'k-a-lĭk-sö.
122. Wake up! — ĭt-ûg-Ĭ-cá!
123. Give me a light! I want to smoke. — Ÿg-nŸñ-mĭñ! ku-kŏg-lûñ-ä.
124. Where have you been to? — cú-mun kĭd-lĬ-ĭñ-a-bwĭ?
125. How long will you be? (on a journey) — kap-si-nĭk-si-nĭk-tä-lu-tĭn?
126. Is it far? — u-ma-sĭ'k-pa?
127. Is it near? — kai-nĭ't-pa?
128. It has sunk, fallen under (water). — ka-tûk-sĭ-mĕ-ro tä-sû'm-mä.
129. Ho (the bird) has flown. — tĭñ-Ĭk-sĭ'm-ĕr-o.
130. Your shoe-string is broken. — sĭñ-yú'k-su-tĭn.

---

[1] Household, party, &c.
[2] "Ku-nĭ-ä," jargon for woman. Danish.
[3] = ki-na ú-na?
[4] Third person singular.
[5] "I become numb."
[6] Cf. añ-u-tá-ó, breast-fin.

VOCABULARY COLLECTED AMONG THE ESKIMOS, &c.—Continued.

Intransitive verbs, &c.—Continued.

English.	Eskimo.
131. Tie your shoe-strings!	sĭñ-yĕr-ĭ'n !
132. I have no shoe-strings.	sĭñ-jĭ'k-tŭñ-ä.
133. He weighs.	u-ko-mai-sĭ-lák-to.
134. Take one! (one of two).	ai-pa pĭ'k-sa-rĭñ !
135. Get out of the way!	ka-ki-ól-lĭ-ä'k-sl-ga!
136. He sits down.	et-tŭ-ä.
137. He is angry.	sa-perg-nä'k-to, sa-perg-sák-to.
138. He is raving.	u-mĭ-näk-to. Inter. u-mĭ-nä'k-pa.
139. They are copulating.	ku-yŭ'k-tu-än.
140. I come.	kai'-rŭñ-ä.
141. Thou comest.	kai-ru-tĭn.
142. He comes.	kai'-ro.
143. We come.	kai-ru-xun.
144. Ye come.	kai-ru-sĕ.
145. They come.	kai-ru-än.
146. I came.	kai-mĕ-rŭñ-ä.
147. Thou camest.	kai-mĕ-ru-tĭn.
148. He came.	kai-mĕ-ro.
149. We came.	kai'-mĕ-ru-xun.
150. Ye came.	kai-mĕ-ru-sĕ.
151. They came.	kai-mĕ-ru-än.
152. I shall come.	kai-nĭ-ä'k-tŭñ-ä.
153. Thou wilt come.	kai-nĭ-ä'k-tu-tĭn.
154. He will come.	kai-nĭ-ä'k-to.
155. We two will come.	kai-nĭ-ä'k-tu-xu.
156. You two will come.	kai-nĭ-ä'k-tu-xun.
157. They two will come.	kai-nĭ-ä'k-tu-xun.
158. We shall come.	kai-nĭ-ĭ'k-tu-xun.
159. Ye will come.	kai-nĭ-ä'k-tu-sĕ.
160. They will come.	kai-nĭ ä'k-tun.
161. If, when, &c., he shall come.	kai'-pŭt.¹
162. When or because he came.	kaiñ-mŭt.²
163. I came not.	kaiñ-ait-yŭñ-ä.
164. Thou camest not.	kaiñ-ait-tu-tĭn.
165. He came not.	kaiñ-ait-yo.
166. Ye came not.	kaiñ-ait-yu-sĕ.
167. I shall not come.	kai-nĭ-ŭñ-ĭ't-yŭñ-ä.
168. Wilt thou come?	kai-nĭ-ä'k-pi?
169. Will he come?	kai-nĭ-ä'k-pa?
170. Will ye come?	kai-nĭ-ä'k-pĭ-sĕ?
171. I eat.	nĕ'x-ĕ-rŭñ-ä.
172. Thou eatest.	nĕ'x-ĕ-ru-tĭn.
173. He eats.	nĕ'x-ĕ-rŭ-ä.
174. Ye eat.	nĕ'x-ĕ-ru-sĕ.
175. They eat.	nĕ'x-ĕ-ru-än.
176. I sleep.	si-nĭ'k-tŭñ-ä.
177. Thou sleepest.	si-nĭ'k-tu-tĭn.
178. He sleeps.	si-nĭ'k-tu-ä.
179. We two sleep.	si-nĭ'k-tu-ŭ'ñ-nĭ.
180. They two sleep.	si-nĭ'k-tu-ŭn.
181. We sleep.	si-nĭ'k-tu-ŭ'ñ-nĭ.
182. Ye sleep.	si-nĭ'k-tu-sĕ.
183. They sleep.	si-nĭ'k-tu-ŭn, si-nĭ'k-tun.
184. I shall sleep.	si-nĭñ-nĭ-ä'k-tŭñ-ä.
185. When, because, he slept.	si-nĭ'g-mŭt.¹
186. I do not sleep.	si-nĭñ-ĭ't-yŭñ-ä.
187. I shall not sleep.	si-nĭñ-nĭ-ñ-ĭ't-yŭñ-ä.
188. Are you asleep?	si-nĭ'k-pi?
189. Is he asleep?	si-nĭ'k-pa?
190. I am scared.	ku-ga-lŭk-tŭñ-ä.
191. Thou art scared.	ku-ga-lŭk-tu-tĭn.
192. He is scared.	ku-ga-lŭk-tu-ä.
193. Ye are scared.	ku-ga-lŭk-tu-sĕ.
194. I am not scared.	ku-ga-lŭñ-ait-yŭñ-ä.
195. Art thou scared?	ku-ga-lŭk-pi?
196. Is he scared?	ku-ga-lŭk-pa?
197. Are ye scared?	ku-ga-lŭk-pĭ-sĕ.
198. I lie (tell a —).	tcŭk-a-la-rŭ'ñ-ä.
199. Thou liest.	tcŭk-a-lä-ru-tĭn.
200. He lies.	tcŭk-a-lu-rŭ-ä.
201. Ye lie.	tcŭk-a-lru-sĕ.
202. They lie.	tcŭk-a-lŭ-tu-ru-ä.
203. When, because, he lied.	tcŭ'k-a-lo-mŭt.²
204. I do not lie.	tcŭk-a-lo-wĭ't-yŭñ-a.
205. I steal.	tig-a-lĭ'k-tŭñä.
206. Thou stealest.	tig-a-lĭ'k-tu-tĭn.
207. He steals.	tig-a-lĭ'k-tu-ä.
208. Ye steal.	tig-a-lĭ'k-tu-sĕ.
209. They steal.	tig-a-lĭ'k-tu-än.
210. I will not steal.	tig-a-lĭk-nĭ-ŭñ-ĭ'k-tŭñ-ä.
211. I go.	a-lŭk-tŭk-tŭ'ñ-ä.
212. He goes.	a-lŭk-täk-to.
213. I went.	a-lŭk-tä-mĕ-rŭñ-ä.

Intrasitive verbs, &c.—Continued.

English.	Eskimo.
214. I have gone.	a-lŭk-tŭk-sĭ'-mĕ-rŭñ-ä.
215. I shall go.	a-lŭk-ta-nĭ-ä'k-tŭñ-ä.
216. I did not go.	a-lŭk-tŭñ-ait-yŭñ-ä.
217. I do not know.	nĕl-u-rŭ'ñ-ä.
218. I do not know it.	wŭ'ñ-ä nĕl-u-ga-gä.
219. You did not know.	ĭ'l-uĭt nĕl-u-gĭ, nĕl-u-ĭ'.
220. I hear.	tu-sá-rŭñ-ä.
221. I heard.	wŭ'ñ-ä tu-sá-ga-ga.
222. You heard.	ĭ'l-u-ĭt tu-sá-gĭ.
223. I saw.	wŭ'n-ä tau-tŭ'k-ki-ga.
224. I do not see.	tau-tŭñ-ait-yŭñ-ä.
225. I did not see.	tau-tŭñ-aĭ't-kĭt-ka.
226. Did you see?	tau-tŭ'k-pi-u?
227. Did ye see?	tau-tŭ'k-pi-u-sĕ?
228. I killed.	wŭ'ñ-ä tu-kŭt-kĭ-ga.
229. Thou killedst.	ĭ'l-u-ĭt tu-kŭt-kĭ.
230. He killed.	tu-kŭt-ka.
231. I die, am dead.	tu-ku-rŭ'ñ-ä.
232. I am not dead.	tu-kuñ-ait-yŭñ-ä.
233. Kakaguna nearly died.	nu-na-mĭ-sĭ-nĭk-kai-äk-to Ka-ka-gú-nä.
234. It is spoiled.	pĭ-lŭk-sĭ'm-ĕ-ro.

Adjectives and participles.

English.	Eskimo.
1. Thick.	si-lĭ'k-tu-ä.
2. Thin, slender.	a-mĭ't-yu-ä.
3. Square.	ĭt-kañ-rä.
4. Round.	kai-ŭ'k-su-ä.
5. New, young.	nŭ-ta.
6. Old.	ú-tu-ka.
7. Near.	kai-nĭ't-yu-ä.
8. Far.	u-ma-zĭ'k-su.
9. Good.	nĭ-kŭ-rŭk.
10. Bad.	a-sĭ'-rŭk.
11. Heavy.	u-ko-mait-yu-ä.
12. Light.	a-kĕ't-yu-ä.
13. Clean.	ĭp-kĭ't-yä.
14. Strong.	sŭ'ñ-ĭ-ru-ä, cu-ä'ñ-ĭ-ru-ä.
15. Killed.	tu-kŭt'-kä.
16. Landed, on top.	ka-kĭ't-kä.
17. Frozen.	kĭ-kĭ't-kä.
18. Lost.	ta-mŭ'k-tä.
19. Big.	áñ-o-ru, -ä.
20. Little.	mĭ'k-ĭ-ru-ä.
21. Long.	tŭ'k-ĭ-ru-ä.
22. Short.	nait-yu-ä.
23. Elongated in shape, but short.	tŭk-ĭ-tĭ'g-ĭ-ru-ä.
24. Pretty long.	tŭk-ĭ-ṭál-o-ä'k-to.
25. Cold.	al-a-ná.
26. Hot.	u-nä'k-tu-ä.
27. Full.	sĭ-la-wĭ't-tu.
28. Broken.	na-wĭ't-kä.
29. Returned, brought back.	kai-lĭ-wĭñ-ĭ't-kä.
30. For sale.	a-kĭ-tcŭ(k), a-kĭ-tä.
31. Netted.	na-pĭ't-to.
32. Blown away.	tĭñ-ĭ't-kä.
33. Inside-out.	ud-lĭ-lú-go.
34. Fast.	cu-kaĭ-ro.
35. Hard.	aĭt-yu-ĭ't-yu-ä, sĭ's-ĭ-ru-ä.
36. Slow.	cu-kaĭt-to.
37. Soft.	a-kĭ't-yu-ä.

Adverbs.

English.	Eskimo.
1. Not.	pĭ'-djŭk, pĭ'-cäk, pĭ-tco, pĭd-la, pĭ'!a
2. Up.	pŭñ-mä.
3. Upwards.	pŭñ-mŭ'ñ-ä.
4. Down.	sŭ'm-mä.
5. Downwards.	sŭm-mŭ'ñ-ä.
6. Underneath.	tä-sŭ'm mä.
7. Yonder.	ṣtá-mä (in sight). ṭaĭ'ñ-ä (out of sight).
8. Indoors.	tät-ka-nä.
9. This way!	ta-mŭñ-a-lu.
10. Thus.	tai-mä-nä.
11. Here, in the house.	ta-má-nĭ ĭg-lú-mĭ.

¹ Future subjunctive.   ² Past subjunctive.

VOCABULARY COLLECTED FROM THE ESKIMOS, &c.—Continued.

English.	Eskimo.	English.	Eskimo.
Interjections.		*Conjunctions.*	
1. Yes, here, take it, come (to a dog).	añ!	1. And, also (enclitic).	—lu, —lu; —mī′g·lu, —mī′g·lu.
2. No.	ná-gä.	2. More, again (enclitic).	—su-lī.
3. Where's?	nau, nau —— -mī, nau —-. Ï′m-nä?	3. Thus, then, so.	á-sī.
4. Come on!	kĕ′-tai!¹	4. Only.	ḳī-sī′m-ī.
5. Get out! Go on!	a-tai! a-tai-já.		
6. Stop! Stay!	á-kûn! a-kû-já.	*Prepositions (enclitic.)*	
7. Hark!	á-tû.		
8. Get on!	kû! kû!²	1. In, on, with.	—mī, -nī.⁶
9. Come!	tû′l-lä!²	2. To, for (motion, purpose.)	—mun, nun.⁷
10. Encore!	ki, ki!		
11. Bless me! (surprise, &c.).	ä′k-qlá!	*Intensive, diminutive, &c., terminations.*	
12. Holloa!	kwau!		
13. What?	ca! cû-ä!	1. Big.	—pûk, —pûñ.⁸
14. Indeed, alas!	naû-mī.³	2. Very.	—pai-yá.⁹
15. Don't know!	aí-tou.⁴	3. Little.	—pa-lu, —ka-lu.¹⁰
16. Don't know, perhaps?	a-ki-ä! a-ka-nó.⁴	4. Bad.	—pī-lu.
17. Make haste!	kĕl-ï′m-ä!	5. Terminations of empha- { sis.	—go.¹¹
18. Oh!	a-na-ná.⁵		—a-mi.¹¹

¹ French, "allons."
² Driving and leading dogs.
³ With a negative idea frequently.
⁴ Exclamation of ignorance or possibility.
⁵ Cry of pain.
⁶ Example, sī-kó-mī, "on the ice."
⁷ Example, ïg-lú-mun, "to the house;" nä-nú-mun, "for bears."

⁸ Example, u-mī-äk-pûk, "ship." Ku-pûñ, "Great river."
⁹ Example, na-kur-pai-yá! "It is very good."
¹⁰ Caressing, example, "kï′m-mī-pa-lu!" "Dear little puppy!"
¹¹ One or both appended to a word for emphasis, "kapsingóami?" "How many, pray?" "Amadráktungo," "Very many, indeed."

ALPHABET.

a, as in *far, farther;* Gm. *haben;* Sp. *ramo.*
ă, nearly as in *what, not;* Gm. *man :* as *oi* in Fr. *toi.*
ä, as in *hat, man.*
â, as in *law, all, lord;* Fr. *or.*
ai, as in *aisle,* as *i* in *pine, find;* Gm. *Hain.*
âi, as *oi* in *boil, soil;* Sp. *eyendo, coyote.*
au, as *ou* in *out,* as *ow* in *how;* Gm. *Haus;* Sp. *auto.*
b, as in *blab;* Gm. *beben :* Fr. *belle;* Sp. *bajar.*
c, as *sh* in *shall;* Gm. *schellen;* Fr. *charmer.*
ç, as *th* in *thin, forth.*
¢, as *th* in *then, though.*
d, as in *dread;* Gm. *das;* Fr. *de;* Sp. *dedo.*
e, as in *they;* Gm. *Dehnung;* Fr. *dé;* Sp. *qué.*
ĕ, as in *then;* Gm. *denn;* Fr. *sienne;* Sp. *comen.*
'f, as in *fife;* Gm. *Feuer;* Fr. *feu;* Sp. *fumar.*
g, as in *gig;* Gm. *geben;* Fr. *goût;* Sp. *gozar.*
h, as in *ha, he;* Gm. *haben.*
i, as in *pique;* Gm. *ihn;* Fr. *île;* Sp. *hijo.*
ĭ, as in *pick;* Gm. *will.*
j, as *z* in *azure; j,* in Fr. *Jacques;* Portuguese *Joao.*
k, as in *kick;* Gm. *Kind;* Fr. *quart;* Sp. *querir.*
l, as in *lull;* Gm. *lallen;* Fr. *lourd;* Sp. *lento.*
m, as in *mum;* Gm. *Mutter;* Fr. *me;* Sp. *menos.*
n, as in *nun;* Gm. *Nonne;* Fr. *ne;* Sp. *nada.*
ñ, as *ng* in *sing, singer;* Sp. *luengo.*
o, as in *note;* Gm. *Bogen;* Fr. *nos.*
ŏ, nearly as in (N. E.) *home;* Gm. *soll;* Fr. *sotte;* It. *sotto,* Sp. *sol.*
p, as in *pipe;* Gm. *Puppe;* Fr. *poupe;* Sp. *popa.*
q, as *ch* in Gm. *ich,* or *ch* in *ach,* if the former is not found.
r, as in *roaring;* Gm. *rühren;* Fr. *rare;* Sp. *razgar.*
s, as in *sauce;* Gm. *Sack;* Fr. *sauce;* Sp. *sordo.*
t, as in *touch;* Gm. *Tag;* Fr. *tâter;* Sp. *tomar.*
u, as in *rule;* Gm. *du;* Fr. *doux;* Sp. *uno.*
ŭ, as in *pull, full;* Gm. *und.*
ü, as in Gm. *kühl;* Fr. *tu.*
û, as in *but;* Fr. *pleuvoir.*
v, as in *valve;* Fr. *veux;* Sp. *volver;* and as *w* in Gm. *wenn.*
w, as in *wish;* nearly as *ou* in Fr. *oui.*
x, nearly as the Arabic *ghain* (the sonant of *q*).
y, as in *you;* Sp. *ya;* as *j* in Gm. *ja.*
z, as *z* and *s* in *zones;* Gm. *Hase;* Fr. *zèle;* Sp. *roza.*
dj, as *j* in *judge.*
hw, as *wh* in *when;* Sp. *huerta.*
hy, as in *hue.*
ly, as *lli* in *million;* as *ll* in Fr. *brilliant;* Sp. *llano;* and as *gl* in It. *moglié.*
ñg, as in *finger, linger.*
ny, as *ni* in *onion;* as *ñ* in *cañon;* Fr. *agneau;* Sp. *maraña.*
tc, as *ch* in *church,* and *c* in It. *cielo;* Sp. *achaque.*

Excessive prolongation of a vowel should be marked thus: $a+$, $â+$, $ü+$.

Nasalized vowels should be written with a superior *n,* thus: e^n, $ŏ^n$, $ŭ^n$, a^n, ai^n.

An aspirated sound should be marked by an inverted comma, thus: $b^{'}$, $d^{'}$.

An exploded sound or hiatus should be marked by an apostrophe, thus: *b',* *d'.*

Synthetic sounds should be written with the letter which represents the sound which seems to be most commonly emitted.

Syllables should be separated by hyphens. In connected texts hyphens should be omitted.

The accented syllable of every word should be marked by an acute accent, thus: *tcu-ar'-u-ûm-pu-rún-kĕnt.*

From *Report of the International Polar Expedition to Point Barrow, Alaska* (1885)

APPENDIX 10

Artifact Plates Accompanying the 1885 Report

John Murdoch

From *Report of the International Polar Expedition to Point Barrow, Alaska* (1885)

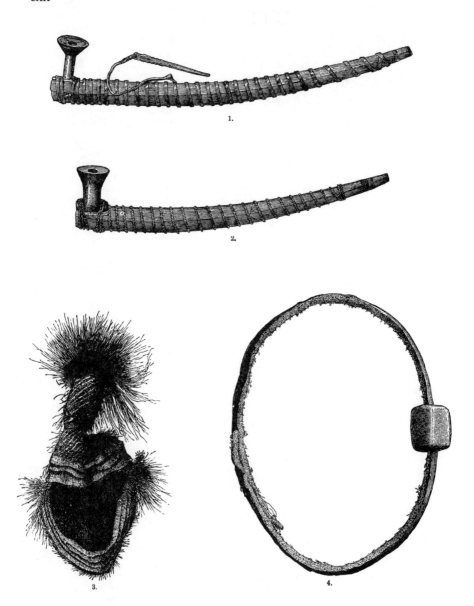

PLATE I.

PIPES, ETC. POINT BARROW ESKIMOS.

1. Tobacco-pipe with bowl of brass, inlaid with copper; stem of wood in two sections, held together by sealthong.
   Steel picker attached by a thong. ⅓. No. 89288.
2. Similar pipe with bowl of antler, wound with twine of braided sinew. ⅓. No. 89291.
3. Tobacco pouch of reindeer skin, trimmed with fur. ⅓. No. 89805.
4. Man's bracelet of walrus-hide, ornamented with a bead of soapstone. Natural size. No. 89388.

(Drawn by C. F. Trill.)

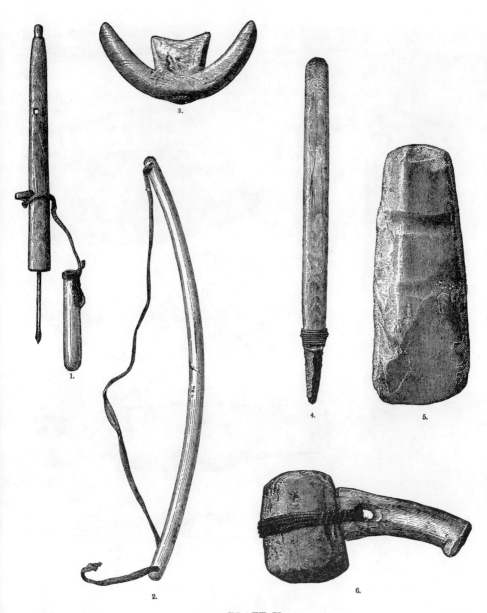

PLATE II.

TOOLS. POINT BARROW ESKIMOS.

1. Steel-pointed bow-drill, with ivory sheath. ½. Nos. 89502 and 89447.
2. Ivory drill-bow. ⅓. No. 89515.
3. Wooden mouth-piece, with stone socket for drill. ⅓. No. 89500.
4. Flint-pointed hand-drill. ⅓. No. 89626.
5. Ground adze-head of jade. ½. No. 56667.
6. Stone maul, with wooden haft. Head of light greenish, massive pectolite. ⅓. **No. 56635.**

(Drawn by C. F. Trill.)

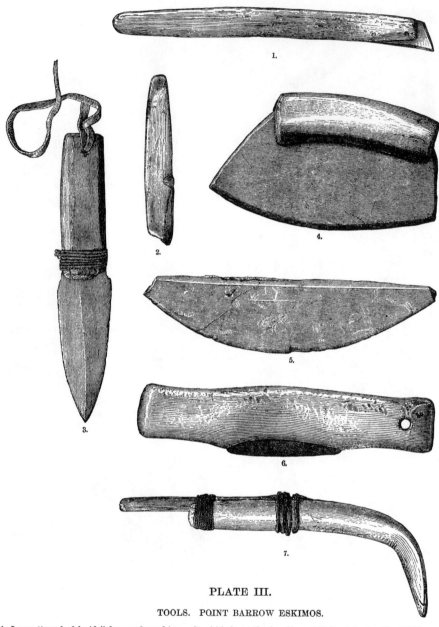

PLATE III.

TOOLS. POINT BARROW ESKIMOS.

1. Large "crooked knife" for wood-working. Steel blade, antler handle. *Left-handed.* ⅛. No. 89283.
2. Small "crooked knife" for cutting bone or ivory. ⅛. No. 89632.
3. Man's knife of slate, with wooden handle. Antique. ½. No. 89584.
4. Woman's knife of black slate, handle of antler. ½. No. 89682.
5. Blade of a similar knife of polished light green jade. ½. No. 56660.
6. "Shave" for scraping whalebone, with steel blade and ivory handle. Natural size. No. 89306.
7. Tool for flaking flints. A rod of hard bone, mounted in an ivory handle. ½. No. 89262.

(Drawn by C. F. Trill.)

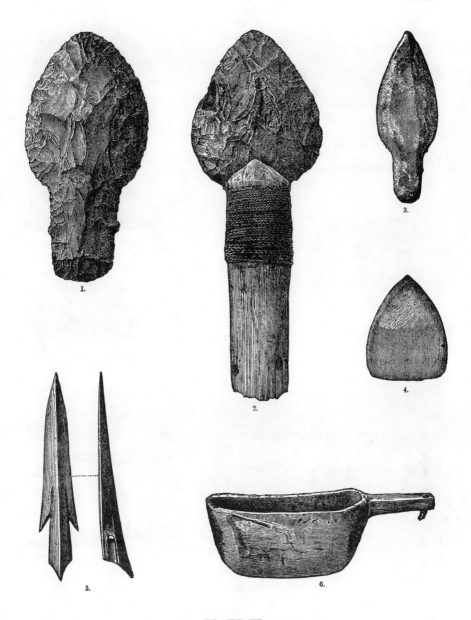

PLATE IV.

SPEAR-HEADS, ETC.   POINT BARROW ESKIMOS.

1. Black flint whale-lance head. ½.   No. 56679.
2. Similar head with part of shaft. ½.   No. 89596.
3. Head for deer-lance, of polished olive-green jade. ½.   No. 89610.
4. Ground slate blade for whaling harpoon. ½.   No. 89606.
5. Antique bone toggle-head for seal harpoon. Back and side view. ½. **No. 89378.**
6. Drinking-cup of fossil ivory. ⅛.   No. 89830.

(Drawn by C. F. Trill.)

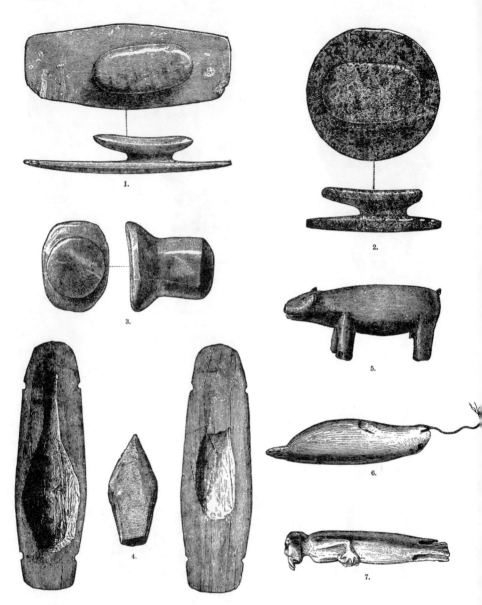

PLATE V.

LABRETS AND WORKS OF ART, POINT BARROW ESKIMOS.

1. Antique single labret of polished light green jade. Back and side view. Natural size. **No. 89705.**
2. Sienite labret, one of a pair. Back and side view. Natural size. No. 56716.
3. Plug labret of bright green stone (jade?). Front and side view. Natural size. **No. 89706.**
4. Slate lancet for cutting labret-holes, with wooden case. Natural size. No. 89721.
5. Polar bear carved in soapstone. ½. No. 89566.
6. Ivory carving, dead seal with drag-line. ½. No. 89330.
7. Ivory carving, grotesque figure, "walrus-man." ½. No. 89332.

(Drawn by C. F. Trill.)

ETHNOLOGICAL RESULTS

OF THE

POINT BARROW EXPEDITION.

BY

JOHN MURDOCH,

Naturalist and Observer, International Polar Expedition to
Point Barrow, Alaska, 1881–1883.

MAP
OF
NORTHWESTERN ALASKA
Showing the region known to the Point Barrow Eskimo
Based on the U.S. Coast & Geodetic Survey
map of Alaska. 1884, with additions from the U.S.C.&G.S.
"General Chart of Alaska" 1889, and from Eskimo account.
Eskimo names given in the form used at Point Barrow.
Names of "tribes" underlined thus Kuñmûdlûñ
Compiled by JOHN MURDOCH
1889

CONTENTS.

ILLUSTRATIONS.

9 ETH——2

THE HUNTING GROUNDS
OF THE
POINT BARROW ESKIMO.
Based on Lieut P.H.Ray's Map of
Explorations in Northwestern Alaska,
Signal Service, U.S.A. 1885
Compiled by
John Murdoch

ETHNOLOGICAL RESULTS OF THE POINT BARROW EXPEDITION.

By John Murdoch.

INTRODUCTION.

The International Polar Expedition to Point Barrow, Alaska, was organized in 1881 by the Chief Signal Officer of the Army, for the purpose of cooperating in the work of circumpolar observation proposed by the International Polar Conference. The expedition, which was commanded by Lieut. P. H. Ray, Eighth Infantry, U. S. Army, sailed from San Francisco July 18, 1881, and reached Cape Smyth, 11 miles southwest of Point Barrow, on September 8 of the same year. Here a permanent station was established, where the party remained until August 28, 1883, when the station was abandoned, and the party sailed for San Francisco, arriving there October 7.

Though the main object of the expedition was the prosecution of the observations in terrestrial magnetism and meteorology, it was possible to obtain a large collection of articles illustrating the arts and industries of the Eskimo of the region, with whom the most friendly relations were early established. Nearly all of the collection was made by barter, the natives bringing their weapons, clothing, and other objects to the station for sale. Full notes on the habits and customs of the Eskimo also were collected by the different members of the party, especially by the commanding officer; the interpreter, Capt. E. P. Herendeen; the surgeon, Dr. George Scott Oldmixon, and myself, who served as one of the naturalists and observers of the expedition. It fell to my share to take charge of and catalogue all the collections made by the expedition, and therefore I had especially favorable opportunities for becoming acquainted with the ethnography of the region. Consequently, upon the return of the expedition, when it was found that the ethnological observations would occupy too much space for publication in the official report,[1] all the collections and notes were intrusted to me for the purpose of preparing a special report. The Smithsonian Institution, through the kindness of the late Prof. Spencer F. Baird, then secretary, furnished

---

[1] Report of the International Polar Expedition to Point Barrow, Alaska, by Lieut. P. H. Ray, Washington, 1885.

a room where the work of studying the collection could be carried on, and allowed me access to its libraries and to the extensive collections of the National Museum for the purposes of comparison. The Director of the Bureau of Ethnology, Maj. J. W. Powell, kindly agreed to furnish the illustrations for the work and to publish it as part of his annual report, while the Chief Signal Officer, with the greatest consideration, permitted me to remain in the employ of his Bureau until the completion of the work.

Two years were spent in a detailed analytical study of the articles in the collection, until all the information that could be gathered from the objects themselves and from the notes of the collectors had been recorded. Careful comparisons were made with the arts and industries of the Eskimo race as illustrated by the collections in the National Museum and the writings of various explorers, and these frequently resulted in the elucidation of obscure points in the history of the Point Barrow Eskimo. In the form in which it is presented this work contains, it is believed, all that is known at the present day of the ethnography of this interesting people.

Much linguistic material was also collected, which I hope some time to be able to prepare for publication.

The observations are arranged according to the plan proposed by Prof. Otis T. Mason in his "Ethnological Directions, etc.," somewhat modified to suit the circumstances. In writing Eskimo words the alphabet given in Powell's "Introduction to the Study of Indian Languages" has been used, with the addition v for an obscure a (like the final a in *soda*), $ə$ for a similar obscure e, and $ö$ for the sound of the German $ö$ or French *eu*.

I desire to express my gratitude to the late Prof. Spencer F. Baird, Secretary of the Smithsonian Institution, to the late Gen. William B. Hazen, Chief Signal Officer of the Army, and to Maj. J. W. Powell, Director of the Bureau of Ethnology, for their kindness in enabling me to carry on these investigations. Grateful acknowledgment is due for valuable assistance to various members of the scientific staff of the National Museum, especially to the curator of ethnology, Prof. Otis T. Mason, and to Mr. William H. Dall. Valuable suggestions were received from Mr. Lucien M. Turner, Dr. Franz Boas, the late Dr. Emil Bessels, and Dr. H. Rink, of Christiania.

LIST OF WORKS CONSULTED.

The following list is not intended for a complete bibliography of what has been written on the ethnography of the Eskimo, but it is believed that it contains most of the important works by authors who have treated of these people from personal observation. Such of the less important works have been included as contain any references bearing upon the subject of the study.

As it has been my object to go, whenever possible, to the original sources of information, compilations, whether scientific or popular, have not been referred to or included in this list, which also contains only the editions referred to in the text.

ARMSTRONG, ALEXANDER. A personal narrative of the discovery of the Northwest Passage; with numerous incidents of travel and adventure during nearly five years' continuous service in the Arctic regions while in search of the expedition under Sir John Franklin. London, 1857.

BACK, GEORGE. Narrative of the Arctic land expedition to the mouth of the Great Fish River and along the shores of the Arctic Ocean, in the years 1833, 1834, and 1835. Philadelphia, 1836.

BEECHEY, FREDERICK WILLIAM. Narrative of a voyage to the Pacific and Beering's Strait to cooperate with the polar expeditions: performed in His Majesty's ship Blossom, under the command of Capt. F. W. Beechey, etc., etc., etc., in the years 1825, 1826, 1827, and 1828. London, 1831.

BESSELS, EMIL. Die amerikanische Nordpol-Expedition. Leipzig, 1878.

—— The northernmost inhabitants of the earth. An ethnographic sketch. <American Naturalist, vol. 18, pp. 861–882. 1884.

—— Einige Worte über die Inuit (Eskimo) des Smith-Sundes, nebst Bemerkungen über Inuit-Schädel. <Archiv für Anthropologie, vol. 8, pp. 107–122. Braunschweig, 1875.

BOAS, FRANZ. The Central Eskimo. In Sixth Annual Report of the Bureau of Ethnology, pp. 399-669. Washington, Government Printing Office, 1888.

BRODBECK, J. Nach Osten. Untersuchungsfahrt nach der Ostküste Grönlands, vom 2. bis 12. August 1881. Niesky, 1882.

CHAPPELL, E. (Lieut., R. N.). Narrative of a voyage to Hudson's Bay in His Majesty's ship Rosamond, containing some account of the northeastern coast of America, and of the tribes inhabiting that remote region. London, 1817.

CHORIS, L. Voyage Pittoresque autour du Monde, avec des portraits des sauvages d'Amérique, d'Asie, d'Afrique, et des iles du Grand Océan; des paysages, des vues maritimes, et plusieurs objets d'histoire naturelle; accompagné de descriptions par M. le Baron Cuvier, et M. A. de Chamisso, et d'observations sur les crânes humains par M. le Docteur Gall. Paris, 1822.

COOK, JAMES, and KING, JAMES. A voyage to the Pacific Ocean, undertaken by the command of His Majesty for making discoveries in the northern hemisphere, to determine the position and extent of the west side of North America; its distance from Asia; and the practicability of a northern passage to Europe, in the years 1776, 1777, 1778, 1779, and 1780. London, 1784. 3 vols. (Commonly called "Cook's Third Voyage.")

"CORWIN." Cruise of the revenue steamer Corwin in Alaska and the N. W. Arctic Ocean in 1881. Notes and memoranda. Medical and anthropological; botanical; ornithological. Washington, Government Printing Office, 1883.

CRANTZ, DAVID. The history of Greenland: containing a description of the country and its inhabitants; and particularly a relation of the mission carried on for above these thirty years by the Unitas Fratrum, at New Herrnhuth and Lichtenfels, in that country. 2 volumes. London, 1767.

DALL, WILLIAM HEALY. Alaska and its Resources. Boston, 1870.

—— On masks, labrets, and certain aboriginal customs, with an inquiry into the bearing of their geographical distribution. <Third Annual Report of the Bureau of Ethnology to the Secretary of the Smithsonian Institution. 1881. Washington, Government Printing Office, 1884.

—— Tribes of the extreme northwest. <Contributions to North American Ethnology, vol. 1. Washington, Government Printing Office, 1877.

[DAVIS, JOHN]. The first voyage of Master John Dauis, vndertaken in June 1585: for the discoverie of the Northwest Passage. Written by John Janes Marchant, Seruant to the worshipfull M. William Sanderson. <Hakluyt, "The principal navigations, voiages, etc.," pp. 776–780. London, 1589.

[DAVIS, JOHN]. The second voyage attempted by Master John Dauis with others
    for the discoverie of the Northwest passage, in Anno 1586. <Hakluyt,
    "The principal navigations, voiages, etc.," pp. 781–786. London, 1589.
——— The third ·voyage Northwestward, made by John Dauis, Gentleman, as chiefe
    Captaine and Pilot generall, for the discoverie of a passage to the Isles of the
    Molucca, or the coast of China, in the yeere 1587. Written by John Janes,
    Seruant to the aforesayd M. William Sanderson. <Hakluyt, "The princi-
    pal navigations, voiages, etc.," pp. 789–792. London, 1589.
DEASE, PETER W., and SIMPSON, THOMAS. An account of the recent arctic dis-
    coveries by Messrs. Dease and Simpson. <Journal of the Royal Geographi-
    cal Society of London, vol. 8, pp. 213-225. London, 1838.
EGEDE, HANS. A description of Greenland. Showing the natural history, situation,
    boundaries, and face of the country; the nature of the soil; the rise and prog-
    ress of the old *Norwegian* colonies; the ancient and modern inhabitants;
    their genius and way of life, and produce of the soil; their plants, beasts,
    fishes, etc. Translated from the Danish. London, 1745.
ELLIS, H. A voyage to Hudson's Bay, by the Dobbs Galley and California, in the
    years 1746 and 1747, for discovering a northwest passage. London, 1748.
FRANKLIN, SIR JOHN. Narrative of a journey to the shores of the Polar Sea in the
    years 1819–20–21–22. Third edition, 2 vols. London, 1824.
——— Narrative of a second expedition to the shores of the Polar Sea in the years 1825,
    1826, and 1827. Including an account of the progress of a detachment to the
    eastward, by John Richardson. London, 1828.
[FROBISHER, MARTIN]. The first voyage of M. Martine Frobisher to the Northwest for
    the search of the straight or passage to China, written by Christopher Hall,
    and made in the yeere of our Lord 1576. <Hakluyt, "The principal navi-
    gations, voiages, etc.," pp. 615–622. London, 1589.
——— The second voyage of Master Martin Frobisher, made to the West and Northwest
    Regions, in the yeere 1577. With a description of the Countrey and people.
    Written by Dionise Settle. <Hakluyt, "The principal navigations, voi-
    ages, etc.," pp. 622–630. London, 1589.
——— The third and last voyage into Meta Incognita, made by M. Martin Frobisher,
    in the year 1578. Written by Thomas Ellis. <Hakluyt, "The principal
    navigations, voiages, etc.," pp. 630–635. London, 1589.
GILDER, W. H. Schwatka's search. Sledging in the arctic in quest of the Franklin
    records. New York, 1881.
GRAAH, W. A. (Capt.). Narrative of an expedition to the east coast of Greenland,
    sent by order of the King of Denmark, in search of the lost colonies.
    Translated from the Danish. London, 1837.
HAKLUYT, RICHARD. The principall navigations, voiages and discoveries of the
    English nation, made by Sea or over Land, to the most remote and farthest
    distant Quarters of the earth at any time within the compasse of these 100
    yeeres. London, 1589.
HALL, CHARLES FRANCIS. Arctic researches and life among the Esquimaux: being
    the narrative of an expedition in search of Sir John Franklin, in the years
    1860, 1861, and 1862. New York, 1865.
——— Narrative of the second arctic expedition made by Charles F. Hall: his voyage
    to Repulse Bay, sledge journeys to the Straits of Fury and Hecla and to King
    William's Land, and residence among the Eskimos during the years 1864–'69.
    Washington, Government Printing Office, 1879.
HEALY, M. A. Report of the cruise of the revenue marine steamer Corwin in the
    Arctic Ocean in the year 1885. Washington, Government Printing Office,
    1887.
HOLM, G. Konebaads-Expeditionen til Grønlands Østkyst 1883–'85. <Geografisk
    Tidskrift, vol. 8, pp. 79–98. Copenhagen, 1886.

HOLM,G. and GARDE, V. Den danske Konebaads-Expeditionen til Grønlands Østkyst, populært beskreven. Copenhagen, 1887.

HOOPER, C. L. (Capt.). Report of the cruise of the U. S. revenue steamer Thomas Corwin, in the Arctic Ocean, 1881. Washington, Government Printing Office, 1884.

HOOPER, WILLIAM HULME (Lieut.). Ten months among the tents of the Tuski, with incidents of an arctic boat expedition in search of Sir John Franklin, as far as the Mackenzie River and Cape Bathurst. London, 1853.

KANE, ELISHA KENT (Dr.). Arctic explorations in the years 1853, '54, '55. Two vols. Philadelphia, 1856.

—— The U. S. Grinnell expedition in search of Sir John Franklin. A personal narrative. New York, 1853.

KIRKBY, W. W. (Archdeacon). A journey to the Youcan, Russian America. <An- nual Report of the Board of Regents of the Smithsonian Institution for the year 1864, pp. 416–420. Washington, 1865.

KLUTSCHAK, HEINRICH W. Als Eskimo unter den Eskimos. Eine Schilderung der Erlebnisse der Schwatka'schen Franklin-aufsuchungs-expedition in den Jahren 1878–'80. Wien, Pest, Leipzig, 1881.

KOTZEBUE, O. VON. A voyage of discovery into the South Sea and Beering's Straits, for the purpose of exploring a northeast passage, undertaken in the years 1815–1818. Three volumes. London, 1821.

KRAUSE, AUREL (Dr.). Die Bevolkerungsverhältnisse der Tschuktscher-Halbinsel. <Deutsche geographische Blätter, vol. 6, pp. 248–278. Bremen, 1883.

—— and ARTHUR. Die Expedition der Bremer geographischen Gesellschaft nach der Tschuktscher-Halbinsel. <Deutsche geographische Blätter, vol. 5, pp. 1–35, 111–133. Bremen, 1882.

—— Die wissenschaftliche Expedition der Bremer geographischen Gesellschaft nach dem Küstengebiete an der Beringsstrasse. <Deutsche geographische Blät- ter, vol. 4, pp. 245–281. Bremen, 1881.

KUMLIEN, LUDWIG. Contributions to the natural history of Arctic America, made in connection with the Howgate polar expedition, 1877–78. Bulletin of the U. S. National Museum, No. 15. Washington, Government Printing Office, 1879.

LISIANSKY, UREY. A voyage round the world, in the years 1803, '4, '5, and '6, per- formed by order of His Imperial Majesty Alexander the First, Emperor of Russia, in the ship Neva. London, 1814.

LYON, G. F. (Capt.). The private journal of Captain G. F. Lyon, of H. M. S. Hecla, during the recent voyage of discovery under Captain Parry. Boston, 1824.

M'CLURE, ROBERT LE MESURIER (Capt.). See Osborn, Sherard (editor).

MACKENZIE, ALEXANDER. Voyages from Montreal, on the river St. Lawrence, through the continent of North America, to the Frozen and Pacific Oceans, in the years 1789 and 1793. London, 1802.

MAGUIRE, ROCHFORT (Commander). Proceedings of Commander Maguire, H. M. dis- covery ship "Plover." < Parliamentary Reports, 1854, XLII, pp. 165–185. London, 1854.

—— Proceedings of Commander Maguire, Her Majesty's discovery ship "Plover." < Further papers relative to the recent arctic expedition in search of Sir John Franklin, etc., p. 905 (second year). Presented to both houses of Par- liament, January, 1855. London.

MORGAN, HENRY. The relation of the course which the Sunshine, a bark of fiftie tunnes, and the Northstarre, a small pinnesse, being two vessels of the fleet of M. John Dauis, held after he had sent them from him to discouer the pass- age between Groenland and Island. Written by Henry Morgan, seruant to M. William Sanderson, of London. <Hakluyt, "The principall navigations, voiages, etc.," pp. 787–9. London, 1589.

MURDOCH, JOHN. The retrieving harpoon; an undescribed type of Eskimo weapon < American Naturalist, vol. 19, 1885, pp. 423–425.

MURDOCH, JOHN. On the Siberian origin of some customs of the western Eskimos.
     < American Anthropologist, vol. 1, pp. 325-336. Washington, 1888.
—— A study of the Eskimo bows in the U. S. National Museum. < Smithsonian
     Report for 1884, pt. II, pp. 307-316. Washington, Government Printing
     Office, 1885.
NORDENSKIÖLD, ADOLF ERIC. The voyage of the Vega round Asia and Europe.
     Translated by Alexander Leslie. 2 vols. London, 1881.
OSBORN, SHERARD (editor). The discovery of the northwest passage by H. M. S. In-
     vestigator, Capt. R. M'Clure, 1850, 1851, 1852, 1853, 1854. Edited by Com-
     mander Sherard Osborn, from the logs and journals of Capt. Robert Le M.
     M'Clure. Appendix: Narrative of Commander Maguire, wintering at Point
     Barrow. London, 1856.
PARRY, WILLIAM EDWARD (Sir). Journal of a voyage for the discovery of a north-
     west passage from the Atlantic to the Pacific; performed in the years
     1819-'20, in His Majesty's ships Hecla and Griper. Second edition. London,
     1821.
—— Journal of a second voyage for the discovery of a northwest passage from the
     Atlantic to the Pacific; performed in the years 1821-'22-'23, in His Majesty's
     ships Fury and Hecla. London, 1824.
PETITOT, EMILE FORTUNÉ STANISLAS JOSEPH, (Rev.). Géographie de l'Athabascaw-
     Mackenzie. < Bulletin de la Société de Géographie, [6] vol. 10, pp. 5-12,
     126-183, 242-290. Paris, 1875.
—— Vocabulaire Français-Esquimaux, dialecte des Tchiglit des bouches du
     Mackenzie et de l'Anderson, précédé d'une monographie de cette tribu et de
     notes grammaticales. Vol. 3 of Pinart's "Bibliothèque de Linguistique et d'
     Ethnographie Américaines."
PETROFF, IVAN. Report on the population, industries, and resources of Alaska.
     < Tenth Census of the U. S. Washington, Government Printing Office,
     1884.
POWELL, JOSEPH S. (Lieut.). Report of Lieut. Joseph S. Powell: Relief expedition
     to Point Barrow, Alaska. < Signal Service Notes, No. V, pp. 13-23. Wash-
     ington, Office of the Chief Signal Officer, 1883.
RAE, JOHN (Dr.). Narrative of an expedition to the shores of the Arctic Sea in 1846
     and 1847. London, 1850.
RAY, PATRICK HENRY (Lieut.). Report of the International Polar Expedition to
     Point Barrow, Alaska. Washington, Government Printing Office, 1885.
—— Report of Lieut. P. Henry Ray: Work at Point Barrow, Alaska, from Septem-
     ber 16, 1881, to August 25, 1882. < Signal Service Notes, No. V, pp. 35-40.
     Washington, Office of the Chief Signal Officer, 1883.
RICHARDSON, JOHN (Sir.). Arctic searching expedition: A journal of a boat voyage
     through Rupert's Land and the Arctic Sea, in search of the discovery ships
     under command of Sir John Franklin. 2 volumes. London, 1851.
—— Eskimos, their geographical distribution. < Edinburgh New Philosophical
     Journal, vol. 52, pp. 322-323. Edinburgh, 1852.
—— The polar regions. Edinburgh, 1861.
RINK, HENRIK [Johan] (Dr.). Die dänische Expedition nach der Ostküste Grönlands,
     1883-1885. < Deutsche geographische Blätter, vol. 8, pp. 341-353. Bremen,
     1885.
—— Danish Greenland, its people and its products. London, 1877.
—— The Eskimo tribes. Their distribution and characteristics, especially in regard
     to language. Meddelelser om Grønland, vol. 11. Copenhagen, 1887.
—— Die Östgrönlander in ihrem Verhältnisse zu den ubrigen Eskimostämmen.
     < Deutsche geographische Blätter, vol. 9, pp. 228-239. Bremen, 1886.
—— Østgrønlænderne i deres Forhold til Vestgrønlænderne og de øvrige Eskimostam-
     mer. < Geografisk Tidskrift, vol. 8, pp. 139-145. Copenhagen, 1886. (Nearly
     the same as the above.)

RINK, HENRIK [Johan]. Tales and Traditions of the Eskimo, with a sketch of their habits, language, and other peculiarities. Translated from the Danish. Edinburgh, 1875.

ROSS, JOHN. Appendix to the narrative of a second voyage in search of a Northwest passage, and of a residence in the arctic regions during the years 1829, 1830, 1831, 1832, 1833. London, 1835.

—— Narrative of a second voyage in search of a northwest passage, and of a residence in the arctic regions during the years 1829, 1830, 1831, 1832, 1833. Philadelphia, 1835.

—— A voyage of discovery, made under the orders of the admiralty in His Majesty's ships Isabella and Alexander, for the purpose of exploring Baffin's Bay, and inquiring into the probability of a northwest passage. London, 1819.

SCHWATKA, FREDERICK. The Netschilluk Innuit. <Science, vol. 4, pp. 543–5. New York, 1884.

—— Nimrod in the North, or hunting and fishing adventures in the arctic regions. New York, 1885.

SCORESBY, WILLIAM, Jr. (Captain). Journal of a voyage to the northern whale-fishery; including researches and discoveries on the eastern coast of Greenland, made in the summer of 1822, in the ship Baffin, of Liverpool. Edinburgh, 1823.

SEEMANN, BERTHOLD. Narrative of the voyage of H. M. S. Herald, during the years 1845–'51, under the command of Captain Henry Kellett, R. N., C. B.; being a circumnavigation of the globe and three cruises to the arctic regions in search of Sir John Franklin. Two vols. London, 1853.

SIMPSON, JOHN (Dr.). Observations on the western Eskimo, and the country they inhabit; from notes taken during two years at Point Barrow. <A selection of papers on arctic geography and ethnology. Reprinted and presented to the arctic expedition of 1875 by the Royal Geographical Society ("Arctic Blue Book"), pp. 233–275. London, 1875. (Reprinted from "Further papers," etc., Parl. Rep., 1855.)

SIMPSON, THOMAS. Narrative of the discoveries on the north coast of America, effected by the officers of the Hudson's Bay Company during the years 1836–39. London, 1843.

SOLLAS, W. J. On some Eskimos' bone implements from the east coast of Greenland. <Journal of the Anthropological Institute of Great Britain and Ireland, vol. 9, pp. 329–336. London, 1880.

SUTHERLAND, P. C. (Dr.). On the Esquimaux. <Journal of the Ethnological Society of London, vol. 4, pp. 193–214. London, 1856.

WRANGELL, FERDINAND VON. Narrative of an expedition to the Polar Sea in the years 1820, 1821, 1822, and 1823. Edited by Maj. Edward Sabine. London, 1840.

The people whose arts and industries are represented by the collection to be described are the Eskimo of the northwestern extremity of the continent of North America, who make permanent homes at the two villages of Nuwŭk and Utkiavwĭñ. Small contributions to the collection were obtained from natives of Wainwright Inlet and from people of the Inland River (Nunatañmiun) who visited the northern villages.

Nuwŭk, "the Point," is situated on a slightly elevated knoll at the extremity of Point Barrow, in lat. 71° 23′ N., long. 156° 17′ W., and Utkiavwĭñ, "the Cliffs," at the beginning of the high land at Cape Smyth, 11 miles southwest from Nuwŭk. The name Utkiavwĭñ was explained as meaning "the high place, whence one can look out," and was said to be equivalent to ĭkpĭk, a cliff. This name appears on the various maps of this region under several corrupted forms, due to carelessness or inability to catch the finer distinctions of sound. It first appears on Capt. Maguire's map[1] as "Ot-ki-a-wing," a form of the word very near the Eskimo pronunciation. On Dr. Simpson's map[2] it is changed to "Ot-ke-a-vik," which on the admiralty chart is misprinted "Otkiovik." Petroff on his map[3] calls it "Ootiwakh," while he gives an imaginary village "Ootkaiowik, Arctic Ocean," of 55 inhabitants, in his census of the Arctic Division (op. cit., p. 4), which does not appear upon his map.

Our party, I regret to say, is responsible for the name "Ooglaamie" or "Uglaamie," which has appeared on many maps since our return. Strictly speaking this name should be used only as the official name of the United States signal station. It arose from a misunderstanding of the name as heard the day after we arrived, and was even adopted by the natives in talking with us. It was not until the second year that we learned the correct form of the word, which has been carefully verified.

The inhabitants of these two villages are so widely separated from their neighbors—the nearest permanent villages are at Point Belcher and Wainwright Inlet, 75 miles southwest, and Demarcation Point, 350 miles east[4]—and so closely connected with each other by intermarriage and common interests, that they may be considered as a single people. In their hunting and trading expeditions they habitually range from the neighborhood of Refuge Inlet along the coast to Barter Island, going inland to the upper waters of the large rivers which flow northward into the Arctic Ocean east of Point Barrow. Small parties occasionally travel as far as Wainwright Inlet and more rarely to Point Hope, and

---

[1] Parl. Reports, 1854, vol. 42, p. 186.

[2] Further Papers, &c., Parl. Rep. (1855).

[3] Report on the population, etc., of Alaska.

[4] Capt. E. E. Smith, who in command of a steam whaler penetrated as far east as Return Reef in the summer of 1885, says that the natives told him there was no permanent village west of Herschel Island.

some times as far as the Mackenzie River. The extent of their wanderings will be treated of more fully in connection with their relations to the other natives of the Northwest. They appear to be unacquainted with the interior except for about 100 miles south of Point Barrow.

The coast from Refuge Inlet runs nearly straight in a generally northeast direction to Point Barrow, and consists of steep banks of clay, gravel, and pebbles, in appearance closely resembling glacial drift, bordered by a narrow, steep beach of pebbles and gravel, and broken at intervals by steep gulleys which are the channels of temporary streams running only during the period of melting snow, and by long, narrow, and shallow lagoons, to whose edges the cliffs slope gradually down, sometimes ending in low, steep banks. The mouths of these lagoons are generally rather wide, and closed by a bar of gravel thrown up by the waves during the season of open water. In the spring, the snow and ice on the land melt months before the sea opens and flood the ice on the lagoons, which also melts gradually around the edges until there is a sufficient head of water in the lagoon to break through the bar at the lowest point. This stream soon cuts itself a channel, usually about 20 or 30 yards wide, through which the lagoon is rapidly drained, soon cutting out an open space of greater or less extent in the sea ice. Before the sea opens the lagoon is drained down to its level, and the tide ebbs and flows through the channel, which is usually from knee-deep to waist-deep, so that the lagoon becomes more or less brackish. When the sea gets sufficiently open for waves to break upon the beach, they in a short time bring in enough gravel to close the outlet. The cliffs gradually decrease in height till they reach Cape Smyth, where they are about 25 feet high, and terminate in low knolls sloping down to the banks of the broad lagoon Isûtkwɐ, which is made by the confluence of two narrow, sinuous gulleys, and is only 10 feet deep in the deepest part.

Rising from the beach beyond the mouth of this lagoon is a slight elevation, 12 feet above the sea level, which was anciently the site of a small village, called by the same name as the lagoon. On this elevation was situated the United States signal station of Ooglaamie. Beyond this the land is level with the top of the beach, which is broad and nearly flat, raised into a slight ridge on the outer edge. About half a mile from the station, just at the edge of the beach, is the small lagoon Imérnyɐ, about 200 yards in diameter, and nearly filled up with marsh. From this point the land slopes down to Elson Bay, a shallow body of water inclosed by the sandspit which forms Point Barrow. This is a continuation of the line of the beach, varying in breadth from 200 to 600 yards and running northeast for 5 miles, then turning sharply to the east-southeast and running out in a narrow gravel spit, 2 miles long, which is continued eastward by a chain of narrow, low, sandy islands, which extend as far as Point Tangent. At the angle of the point the land is slightly elevated into irregular turf-covered knolls, on which the

village of Nuwŭk is situated. At various points along the beach are
heaps of gravel, sometimes 5 or 6 feet in height, which are raised by the
ice. Masses of old ice, bearing large quantities of gravel, are pushed
up on the beach during severe storms and melt rapidly in the summer,
depositing their load of gravel and pebbles in a heap. These masses
are often pushed up out of reach of the waves, so that the heaps of
gravel are left thenceforth undisturbed.

Between Imernyɐ and Elson Bay (Tă'syûk) is a series of large shallow lagoons, nearly circular and close to the beach, which rises in a regular sea-wall. All have low steep banks on the land side, bordered with
a narrow beach. The first of these, I'kpĭlĭñ ("that which has high
banks"), breaks out in the spring through a narrow channel in the beach
in the manner already described, and is salt or brackish. The next is
fresh and connected with Ikpĭlĭñ by a small stream running along behind the beach. It is called Sĭ'n-nyû, and receives a rivulet from a
small fresh-water lake 3 or 4 miles inland. The third, Imê'kpûñ ("great
water"), is also fresh, and has neither tributary nor outlet. The fourth,
Imêkpû'niglu, is brackish, and empties into Elson Bay by a small stream.
Between this stream and the beach is a little fresh-water pond close to
the bend of Elson Bay, which is called Kĭkyûktă'ktoro, from one or two
little islands (kĭkyû'ktɐ) near one end of it.

Back from the shore the land is but slightly elevated, and is marshy
and interspersed with many small lakes and ponds, sometimes connected by inconsiderable streams. This marsh passes gradually into
a somewhat higher and drier rolling plain, stretching back inland from
the cliffs and growing gradually higher to the south. Dr. Simpson, on
the authority of the Point Barrow natives, describes the country as
" uniformly low, and full of small lakes or pools of fresh water to a distance of about 50 miles from the north shore, where the surface becomes
undulating and hilly, and, farther south, mountainous."[1] This description has been substantially verified by Lieut. Ray's explorations. South
of the usual deer-hunting ground of the natives he found the land decidedly broken and hilly, and rising gradually to a considerable range of
mountains, running approximately east and west, which could be seen
from the farthest point he reached.[2]

The natives also speak of high rocky land " a long way off to the
east," which some of them have visited for the purpose of hunting the
mountain sheep. The low rolling plain in the immediate vicinity of
Point Barrow, which is all of the country that could be visited by our
party when the land was clear of snow, presents the general appearance of a country overspread with glacial drift. The landscape is
strikingly like the rolling drift hills of Cape Cod, and this resemblance
is increased by the absence of trees and the occurrence of ponds in all
the depressions. There are no rocks in situ visible in this region, and

---

[1] Arctic papers, p. 233.
[2] Report U. S. International Polar Expedition to Point Barrow, p. 28.

large bowlders are absent, while pebbles larger than the fist are rare. The surface of the ground is covered with a thin soil, supporting a rather sparse vegetation of grass, flowering plants, creeping willows, and mosses, which is thicker on the higher hillsides and forms a layer of turf about a foot thick. Large tracts of comparatively level ground are almost bare of grass, and consist of irregular hummocks of black, muddy soil, scantily covered with light-colored lichens and full of small pools. The lowlands, especially those back of the beach lagoons, are marshes, thickly covered with grass and sphagnum. The whole surface of the land is exceedingly wet in summer, except the higher knolls and hillsides, and for about 100 yards back from the edge of the cliffs. The thawing, however, extends down only about a foot or eighteen inches. Beyond this depth the ground is perpetually frozen for an unknown distance. There are no streams of any importance in the immediate neighborhood of Point Barrow. On the other hand, three of the rivers emptying into the Arctic Ocean between Point Barrow and the Colville, which Dr. Simpson speaks of as "small and hardly known except to persons who have visited them,"[1] have been found to be considerable streams. Two of these were visited by Lieut. Ray in his exploring trips in 1882 and 1883. The first, Kua′ru, is reached after traveling about 50 miles from Point Barrow in a southerly direction. It has been traced only for a small part of its course, and there is reason to believe, from what the natives say, that it is a tributary of the second named river. Lieut. Ray visited the upper part of the second river, Kulugrua (named by him "Meade River"), in March, 1882, when he went out to join the native deer hunters encamped on its banks, just on the edge of the hilly country. On his return he visited what the natives assured him was the mouth of this river, and obtained observations for its geographical position. Early in April, 1883, he again visited the upper portion of the stream, and traced it back some distance into the hilly country. The intermediate portion has never been surveyed. At the time of each of his visits the river was, of course, frozen and the ground covered with snow, but he was able to see that the river was of considerable size, upwards of 200 yards wide where he first reached it, about 60 miles from its mouth, and showing evidences of a large volume of water in the spring. It receives several tributaries. (See maps, Pls. I and II.)

The third river is known only by hearsay from the natives. It is called Ĭ′kpĭkpûñ (Great Cliff), and is about 40 miles (estimated from day's journeys) east of Kulu′grua. It is described as being a larger and more rapid stream than the other two, and so deep that it does not freeze down to the bottom on the shallow bars, as they say Kulu′grua does. Not far from its mouth it is said to receive a tributary from the east flowing out of a great lake of fresh water, called Tă′syûkpûñ (Great Lake.) This lake is separated from the sea by a comparatively

---

[1] Op. cit., p. 235.

narrow strip of land, and is so large that a man standing on the northern shore can not see the "very high" land on the southern. It takes
an umiak a day to travel the length of the lake under sail with a fair
wind, and when the Nunatañmiun coming from the south first saw the
lake they said "Taxaio!" (the sea).

On Capt. Maguire's map[1] this lake is laid down by the name
"Taso'kpoh" "from native report." It is represented as lying between
Smith Bay and Harrison Bay, and connected with each by a stream.
Maguire seems to have heard nothing of Ikpikpûñ. This lake is not
mentioned in the body of the report. Dr. Simpson, however,[2] speaks of
it in the following words: "They [i. e., the trading parties when they
reach Smith Bay] enter a river which conducts them to a lake, or rather
series of lakes, and descend another stream which joins the sea in Harrison Bay." They are well acquainted with the Colville River, which in
their intercourse with us they usually called "the river at Nï'galĕk,"
Nï'galĕk being the well known name of the trading camp at the mouth.
It was also sometimes spoken of as the "river of the Nunatañmiun."
The Mackenzie River is known as "Kupûñ" (great river). We found
them also acquainted with the large unexplored river called "Kok" on
the maps, which flows into Wainwright Inlet. They called it "Ku" (the
river). The river "Cogrua," which is laid down on the charts as emptying into Peard Bay, was never mentioned by the Point Barrow natives,
but we were informed by Capt. Gifford, of the whaler *Daniel Webster*,
who traveled along the coast from Point Barrow to Cape Lisburne after
the loss of his vessel in 1881, that it is quite a considerable stream. He
had to ascend it for about a day's journey—20 miles, according to Capt.
Hooper[3]—before he found it shallow enough to ford.

CLIMATE.

The climate of this region is thoroughly arctic in character, the mean
annual temperature being 8° F., ranging from 65° to −52° F. Such
temperatures as the last mentioned are, however, rare, the ordinary
winter temperature being between −20° and −30° F., rarely rising
during December, January, February, and March as high as zero, and
still more rarely passing beyond it. The winter merges insensibly by
slow degrees into summer, with occasional "cold snaps," and frosty
nights begin again by the 1st of September.

The sun is entirely below the horizon at Point Barrow for 72 days in
the winter, beginning November 15, though visible by refraction a day
or two later at the beginning of this period and a day or two earlier at
the end. The midday darkness is never complete even at the winter
solstice, as the sun is such a short distance below the horizon, but the
time suitable for outdoor employments is limited to a short twilight
from 9 a. m. to 3 p. m. There is, of course, an equal time in the summer

---

[1] Parl. Rep., 1854, vol. 42, opp. p. 186.   [2] Op. cit., p. 265.   [3] Corwin Report, p. 72.

when the sun is continually above the horizon, and for about a month before and after this period the twilight is so bright all night that no stars are visible.

The snowfall during the winter is comparatively small. There is probably not more than a foot of snow on a level anywhere on the land, though it is extremely difficult to measure or estimate, as it is so fine and dry that it is easily moved by the wind and is constantly in motion, forming deep, heavy, hard drifts under all the banks, while many exposed places, especially the top of the sand beach, are swept entirely clean. The snow begins to soften and melt about the first week in April, but goes off very slowly, so that the ground is not wholly bare before the middle or end of June. The grass, however, begins to turn green early in June, and a few flowers are seen in blossom as early as June 7 or 8.

Rain begins to fall as early as April, but cold, snowy days are not uncommon later than that date. There is a good deal of clear, calm weather during the winter, and extremely low temperatures are seldom accompanied by high wind. Violent storms are not uncommon, however, especially in November, during the latter part of January, and in February. One gale from the south and southwest, which occurred January 22, 1882, reached a velocity of 100 miles an hour. The most agreeable season of the year is between the middle of May and the end of July, when the sea opens. After this there is much foggy and cloudy weather.

Fresh-water ponds begin to freeze about the last week in September, and by the first or second week in October everything is sufficiently frozen for the natives to travel with sledges to fish through the ice of the inland rivers. Melting begins with the thawing of the snow, but the larger ponds are not clear of ice till the middle or end of July. The sea in most seasons is permanently closed by freezing and the moving in of heavy ice fields from about the middle of October to the end of July. The heavy ice in ordinary seasons does not move very far from the shore, while the sea is more or less encumbered with floating masses all summer. These usually ground on a bar which runs from the Seahorse Islands along the shore parallel to it and about 1,000 yards distant, forming a "barrier" or "land-floe" of high, broken hummocks, inshore of which the sea freezes over smooth and undisturbed by the pressure of the outer pack.

Sometimes, however, the heavy pack, under the pressure of violent and long-continued westerly winds, pushes across the bar and is forced up on the beach. The ice sometimes comes in with great rapidity. The natives informed us that a year or two before the station was established the heavy ice came in against the village cliffs, tearing away part of the bank and destroying a house on the edge of the cliff so suddenly that one of the inmates, a large, stout man, was unable to escape through the trap-door and was crushed to death. Outside of the land-floe the ice is a broken pack, consisting of hummocks of fragmentary old and new ice, interspersed with comparatively level fields of the former. During the

early part of the winter this pack is most of the time in motion, sometimes moving northeastward with the prevailing current and grinding
along the edge of the barrier, sometimes moving off to sea before an off-
shore wind, leaving "leads" of open water, which in calm weather are
immediately covered with new ice (at the rate of 6 inches in 24 hours),
and again coming in with greater or less violence against the edges of
this new ice, crushing and crumpling it up against the barrier. Portions
of the land-floe even float off and move away with the pack at this season.

The westerly gales of the later winter, however, bring in great quantities of ice, which, pressing against the land-floe, are pushed up into
hummocks and ground firmly in deeper water, thus increasing the breadth
of the fixed land-floe until the line of separation between the land-floe
and the moving pack is 4 or 5 or sometimes even 8 miles from land. The
hummocks of the land-floe show a tendency to arrange themselves in
lines parallel to the shore, and if the pressure has not been too great
there are often fields of ice of the season not over 4 feet thick between
the ranges of hummocks, as was the case in the winter of 1881–'82. In
the following year, however, the pressure was so great that there were
no such fields, and even the level ice inside of the barrier was crushed
into hummocks in many places.

After the gales are over there is generally less motion in the pack,
until about the middle of April, when easterly winds usually cause
leads to open at the edge of the land-floe. These leads now continue to
open and shut, varying in size with the direction and force of the wind.
As the season advances, especially in July, the melting of the ice on
the surface loosens portions of the land-floe, which float off and join the
pack, bringing the leads nearer to the shore. In the meantime the level
shore ice has been cut away from the beach by the warm water running
down from the land and has grown "rotten" and full of holes from the
heat of the sun. By the time the outside ice has moved away so as to
leave only the floes grounded on the bar the inside ice breaks up into
loose masses, moving up and down with wind and current and ready
to move off through the first break in the barrier. Portions of the remaining barrier gradually break off and at last the whole finally floats
and moves out with the pack, sometimes, as in 1881—a very remarkable
season—moving out of sight from the land.

This final departure of the ice may take place at any time between
the middle of July and the middle of August. East of Point Barrow
we had opportunities only for hasty and superficial observations of the
state of the ice. The land floe appears to form some distance outside
of the sandy islands, and from the account of the natives there is much
open water along shore early in the season, caused by the breaking up
of the rivers. Dr. Simpson[1] learned from the natives that the trading
parties which left the Point about the 1st of July found open water at
Dease Inlet. This is more definite information than we were able to
obtain. We only learned that they counted on finding open water a
few days' journey east.

THE PEOPLE.

PHYSICAL CHARACTERISTICS.

In stature these people are of a medium height, robust and muscular, "inclining rather to spareness than corpulence,"[2] though the fullness of the face and the thick fur clothing often gives the impression of the latter. There is, however, considerable individual variation among them in this respect. The women are as a rule shorter than the men, occasionally almost dwarfish, though some women are taller than many of the men. The tallest man observed measured 5 feet 9½ inches, and the shortest 4 feet 11 inches. The tallest woman was 5 feet 3 inches in height, and the shortest 4 feet ½ inch. The heaviest man weighed 204 pounds and the lightest 126 pounds. One woman weighed 192 pounds and the shortest woman was also the lightest, weighing only 100 pounds.[3] The hands and feet are small and well shaped, though the former soon become distorted and roughened by work. We did not observe the peculiar breadth of hands noticed by Dr. Simpson, nor is the shortness of the thumb which he mentions sufficient to attract attention.[4] Their feet are so small that only one of our party, who is much below the ordinary size, was able to wear the boots made by the natives for themselves. Small and delicate hands and feet appear to be a universal characteristic of the Eskimo race and have been mentioned by most observers from Greenland to Alaska.[5]

The features of these people have been described by Dr. Simpson,[6] and are distinctively Eskimo in type, as will be seen by comparing the accompanying portraits (Figs. 1, 2, 3, and 4, from photographs by Lieut. Ray) with the many pictures brought from the eastern Arctic

---

[1] Op. cit., p. 264.

[2] Simpson, op. cit., p. 238.

[3] See Report of Point Barrow Expedition, p. 50, for a table of measurements of a number of individuals selected at random from the natives of both villages and their visitors.

[4] Op. cit., p. 238.

[5] Davis (1586) speaks of the "small, slender hands and feet" of the Greenlanders. Hakluyt's Voyages, etc. (1589), p. 782.

"Their hands and feet are little and soft." Crantz, vol. 1, p. 133 (Greenland).

Hands and feet "extremely diminutive," Parry 1st Voy., p. 282 (Baffin Land).

"Their hands and feet are small and well formed." Kumlien Contrib., p. 15 (Cumberland Gulf).

"Feet extraordinarily small." Ellis, Voyage, etc., p. 132 (Hudson Strait).

Franklin (1st Exp., vol. 2, p. 180) mentions the small hands and feet of the two old Eskimo that he met at the Bloody Fall of the Coppermine River.

" . . . boots purchased on the coast were seldom large enough for our people." Richardson Searching Exp., i, p. 344 (Cape Bathurst).

"Their hands and feet are small." Petroff, Report, etc., p. 134 (Kuskoquim River).

Chappell (Hudson Bay, pp. 59, 60) has a remarkable theory to account for the smallness of the extremities among the people of Hudson Strait. He believes that "the same intense cold which restricts vegetation to the form of creeping shrubs has also its effect upon the growth of mankind, preventing the extremities from attaining their due proportion"!

[6] Op. cit., p. 238.

9 ETH——3

FIG. 1.—Unalina, a man of Nuwŭk.

regions by various explorers, some of which might easily pass for portraits of persons of our acquaintance at Point Barrow.[1]

The face is broad, flat, and round, with high cheek bones and rather
low forehead, broad across the brow and narrowing above, while the
head is somewhat pointed toward the crown.   The peculiar shape of the

FIG. 2.—Mûmûñina, a woman of Nuwŭk.

head is somewhat masked by the way of wearing the hair, and is best
seen in the skull.   The nose is short, with little or no bridge (few Eskimo were able to wear our spring eye-glasses), and broad, especially
across the alæ nasæ, with a peculiar rounded, somewhat bulbous tip,

[1] One young man at Point Barrow looks remarkably like the well known "Eskimo Joe," as I remember him in Boston in the winter of 1862-'63.

and large nostrils.   The eyes are horizontal,[1] with rather full lids, and
are but slightly sunken below the level of the face.

The mouth is large and the lips full, especially the under one.   The
teeth are naturally large, and in youth are white and generally regular,
but by middle age they are generally worn down to flat-crowned stumps,
as is usual among the Eskimo.   The color of the skin is a light yellowish

FIG. 3.—Akabiana, a youth of Utkiavwiñ.

brown, with often considerable ruddy color on the cheeks and lips.
There appears to be much natural variation in the complexion, some
women being nearly as fair as Europeans, while other individuals seem
to have naturally a coppery color.[2]   In most cases the complexion appears darker than it really is from the effects of exposure to the weather.
All sunburn very easily, especially in the spring when there is a strong
reflection from the snow.

---

[1] The expression of obliquity in the eyes, mentioned by Dr. Simpson (op. cit., p. 239), seems to me to
have arisen from the shape of the cheek bones.   I may be mistaken, however, as no careful comparisons were made on the spot.

[2] Frobisher says of the people of Baffin Land: "Their colour is not much unlike the sunburnt countrie
man." Hakluyt's Voyages, etc. (1589), p. 627.

The old are much wrinkled, and they frequently suffer from watery eyes, with large sacks under them, which begin to form at a comparatively early age. There is considerable variation in features, as well as complexion, among them, even in cases where there seems to be no suspicion of mixed blood. There were several men among them with decided aquiline noses and something of a Hebrew cast of countenance.

FIG. 4.—Puka, a young man of Utkiavwiñ.

The eyes are of various shades of dark brown—two pairs of light hazel eyes were observed—and are often handsome. The hair is black, perfectly straight, and very thick. With the men it is generally coarser than with the women, who sometimes have very long and silky hair, though it generally does not reach much below the shoulders. The eyebrows are thin and the beard scanty, growing mostly upon the upper lip and chin, and seldom appearing under the age of 20. In this they resemble most Eskimo. Back,[1] however, speaks of the "luxuriant

---

[1] Journey, etc., p. 289.

beards and flowing mustaches" of the Eskimo of the Great Fish River. Some of the older men have rather heavy black mustaches, but there is much variation in this respect. The upper part of the body (as much is commonly exposed in the house) is remarkably free from hair. The general expression is good humored and attractive.

The males, even when very young, are remarkable for their graceful and dignified carriage. The body is held erect, with the shoulders square and chest well thrown out, the knees straight, and the feet firmly planted on the ground. In walking they move with long swinging elastic strides, the toes well turned out and the arms swinging.

I can not agree with Dr. Simpson that the turning out of the toes gives "a certain peculiarity to their gait difficult to describe."[1] I should say that they walked like well built athletic white men. The women, on the other hand, although possessing good physiques, are singularly ungraceful in their movements. They walk at a sort of shuffling half-trot, with the toes turned in, the body leaning forward, and the arms hanging awkwardly.[2]

A noticeable thing about the women is the remarkable flexibility of the body and limbs, and the great length of time they can stand in a stooping posture. (See Fig. 5 for a posture often assumed in working.)

FIG. 5.—Woman stretching skins.

Both men and women have a very fair share of muscular strength. Some of the women, especially, showed a power of carrying heavy loads superior to most white men. We were able to make no other comparisons of their strength with ours. Their power of endurance is very great, and both sexes are capable of making long distances on foot. Two men sometimes spend 24 hours tramping through the rough ice in search of seals, and we knew of instances where small parties made journeys of 50 or 75 miles on foot without stopping to sleep.

The women are not prolific. Although all the adults are or have been married, many of them are childless, and few have more than two children. One woman was known to have at least four, but investigations of this sort were rendered extremely difficult by the universal custom

---

[1] Op. cit., p. 238.   [2] Cf. Simpson, op. cit., p. 240.

of adoption. Dr. Simpson heard of a "rare case" where one woman had borne seven children.[1] We heard of no twins at either village, though we obtained the Eskimo word for twins. It was impossible to learn with certainty the age at which the women first bear children, from the impossibility of learning the age of any individuals in the absence of any fixed method of reckoning time. Dr. Simpson states that they do not commonly bear children before the age of 20,[2] and we certainly saw no mothers who appeared younger than this. We knew of but five cases of pregnancy in the two villages during the 2 years of our stay. Of these, one suffered miscarriage, and of the other four, only two of the infants lived more than a short time. It is exceedingly difficult, for the reasons stated above, to form any estimate of the age to which these people live, though it is natural to suppose that the arduous and often precarious existence which they lead must prevent any great longevity. Men and women who appeared to be 60 or over were rare. Yûksĭ'ña, the so-called "chief" of Nuwŭk, who was old enough to be a man of considerable influence at the time the *Plover* wintered at Point Barrow (1852–'54), was in 1881 a feeble, bowed, tottering old man, very deaf and almost blind, but with his mental faculties apparently unimpaired. Gray hair appears uncommon. Even the oldest are, as a rule, but slightly gray.

PATHOLOGY.

Diseases of the respiratory and digestive organs are the most frequent and serious ailments from which they suffer. The former are most prevalent toward the end of summer and early in winter, and are due to the natives sleeping on the damp ground and to their extreme carelessness in exposing themselves to drafts of wind when overheated. Nearly everyone suffers from coughs and colds in the latter part of August, and many deaths occur at this season and the beginning of winter from a disease which appears to be pneumonia. A few cases, one fatal, of hemorrhage of the lungs were observed, which were probably aggravated by the universal habit of inhaling tobacco smoke. The people suffer from diarrhea, indigestion, and especially from constipation.

Gonorrhea appears common in both sexes, but syphilis seems to be unknown in spite of the promiscuous intercourse of the women with the whalemen. One case of uterine hemorrhage was observed. Cutaneous diseases are rare. A severe ulcer on the leg, of long standing, was cured by our surgeon, to whose observations I am chiefly indebted for what I have to say about the diseases of these people; and one man had lost the cartilage of his nose and was marked all over the body with hideous scars from what appeared to be some form of scrofulous disease. A single case of tumor on the deltoid muscle was observed. Rheumatism is rather frequent. All are subject to snow blindness in the spring, and

---

[1] Op. cit., p. 254. [2] Op. cit. p. 254.

sores on the face from neglected frost bites are common. Many are blind in one eye from what appears to be cataract or leucoma, but only one case of complete blindness was noticed. Dr. Sutherland states that he does not recollect a single instance of total blindness among the Eskimo that he saw in Baffin Land, and expresses the opinion that "An individual in such a state would be quite unfit for the life of toil and hardship to which the hardy Esquimaux is exposed. The neglect consequent upon this helpless condition most probably cuts off its afflicted objects."[1]

This seems quite reasonable on a priori grounds, but nevertheless the blind man at Cape Smyth had lived to middle age in very comfortable circumstances, and though supported to a great extent by his relatives he was nevertheless able to do a certain share of work, and had the reputation of being a good paddler for a whaling umiak.

Injuries are rare. One man had lost both feet at the ankle and moved about with great ease and rapidity on his knees. All are subject to bleeding at the nose and usually plug the bleeding nostril with a bunch of deer hair.[2]

This habit, as it has been termed, of vicarious hemorrhage seems to be characteristic of the Eskimo race wherever they have been met with, and has been supposed to be a process of nature for relieving the fullness of the circulatory system caused by their exclusively animal diet.[3]

Natural deformities and abnormalities of structure are uncommon, except strabismus, which is common and often, at least, congenital. One boy in Utkiavwiñ had his forehead twisted to one side, probably from some accident or difficulty during delivery. His intelligence did not seem to be impaired. The people are, as a rule, right handed, but that left-handed persons occasionally occur is shown by their having a word for a left-handed man. We also collected a "crooked knife," fitted for use with the left hand.[4]

PSYCHICAL CHARACTERISTICS.

As a rule they are quick-witted and intelligent, and show a great capacity for appreciating and learning useful things, especially mechanical arts. In disposition they are light-hearted and cheerful, not easily cast down by sorrow or misfortune, and though sometimes quick-tempered, their anger seldom lasts long.[5] They have a very keen sense of humor, and are fond of practical jokes, which they take in good part,

---

[1] Journ. Ethnol. Soc., vol. 4, p. 206.

[2] Compare what Davis wrote in 1586 of the Greenlanders: "These people are much given to bleed, and, therefore, stoppe theyr noses with deere hayre or the hayre of an elan." Hakluyt, Voyages, etc., 1589, p. 782.

[3] Egede, Greenland, p. 120; Crantz, vol. 1, p. 234 (Greenland); Southerland, Journ. Ethnol. Soc., vol. IV, p. 207 (Baffin Land); Chappell, "Hudson Bay," p. 74 (North Shore of Hudson Strait); Lyon, Journal, p. 18 (Hudson Strait); Franklin, 1st Exp., I, p. 29 (Hudson Strait); Parry, 2d Voy., p. 544 (Igluilik); Hooper, Tents of the Tuski, p. 185 (Plover Bay, Siberia).

[4] I have an indistinct recollection of having once seen a left-handed person from Nuwŭk.

[5] Holm calls the East Greenlanders "et meget livligt Folkefærd" Geogr. Tidskrift, vol. 8, p. 96.

even when practiced on themselves.   They are generally peaceable. We did not witness a single quarrel among the men during the two years of our stay, though they told us stories of fatal quarrels in former years, in which firearms were used.   Liquor may have been the cause of these fights, as it is said to have been of the only suicide I ever heard of among them, which I am informed by Capt. E. E. Smith, the whaling master already referred to, occurred in 1885 at Nuwŭk.   Disagreements between man and wife, however, sometimes lead to blows, in which the man does not always get the best of it.

When the station was first established many of the natives began pilfering from our stores, but they soon learned that by so doing they cut themselves off from the privilege of visiting the station and enjoying the opportunity for trading which it afforded, and were glad to promise to refrain from the practice.   This promise was very well observed, though I think wholly from feelings of self-interest, as the thieves when detected seemed to have no feeling of shame.   Some, I believe, never yielded to the temptation.   There was seldom any difficulty in obtaining restitution of stolen articles, as the thief's comrades would not attempt to shield him, but often voluntarily betrayed him.   They acknowledged that there was considerable thieving on board of the ships, but the men of Utkiavwĭñ tried to lay the blame on the Nuwŭk people, and we may suppose that the charge was reciprocated, as was the case regarding the theft of the *Plover's* sails.[1]   We also heard of occasional thefts among themselves, especially of seals left on the ice or venison buried in the snow, but men who were said to be thieves did not appear to lose any social consideration.

Robbery with violence appears to be unknown.   We never saw or heard of the "burglar-alarm" described by Dr. Simpson,[2] which I am inclined to believe was really a "demon trap" like that described by Lieut. Ray (see below, under Religion).

They are in the main truthful, though a detected lie is hardly considered more than a good joke, and considerable trickery is practiced in trading.   For instance, soon after the station was established they brought over the carcass of a dog, with the skin, head, feet, and tail removed, and attempted to sell it for a young reindeer; and when we began to purchase seal-oil for the lamps one woman brought over a tin can nearly filled with ice, with merely a layer of oil on top.

Clothing and other articles made especially for sale to us were often very carelessly and hastily made, while their own things were always carefully finished.[3]

Their affection for each other, especially for their children, is strong,

---

[1] Simpson, op. cit., p. 248.

[2] Op. cit., p. 247.

[3] Compare Nordenskiöld's experience in Siberia.   The "Chukches" sold him skinned foxes with the head and feet cut off for hares, (Vega, vol. 1, p. 448), young ivory gulls for ptarmigan, and a dog's skull for a seal's (vol. 2, p. 137).   Besides, "While their own things were always made with the greatest care, all that they did especially for us was done with extreme carelessness" (ibid).   The Eskimos at Hotham Inlet also tried to sell Capt. Beechey fishskins sewed together to represent fish.   (Voyage, p. 285.)

though they make little show of grief for bereavement, and their minds are easily diverted by amusements.   I am inclined to believe, however, from some cases I have observed, that grief is deeper and more permanent than superficial appearances would indicate.

Their curiosity is unbounded, and they have no hesitation in gratifying it by unlimited questioning.   All who have read the accounts of the Eskimo character given by explorers in other parts of the Arctic regions will recognize this as a familiar trait.   We also found the habit of begging at first quite as offensive among some of these people as other travelers have found it, but as they grew better acquainted with us they ceased to beg except for trifling things, such as a chew of tobacco or a match.   Some of the better class never begged at all.   Some of them seemed to feel truly grateful for the benefits and gifts received, and endeavored by their general behavior, as well as in more substantial ways, to make some adequate return.   Others appeared to think only of what they might receive.

Hospitality is a universal virtue.   Many of them, from the beginning of our acquaintance with them, showed the greatest friendliness and willingness to assist us in every way, while others, especially if there were many of them together, were inclined to be insolent, and knives were occasionally drawn in sudden fits of passion.   These "roughs," however, soon learned that behavior of this sort was punished by prompt ostracism and threats of severer discipline, and before the first nine months were past we had established the most friendly relations with the whole village at Cape Smyth.   Some of those who were at first most insolent became afterwards our best friends.   Living as these people do at peace with their neighbors, they would not be expected to exhibit the fierce martial courage of many other savages, but bold whalemen and venturous ice-hunters can not be said to lack bravery.

In their dealings with white men the richer and more influential among them at least consider themselves their equals if not their superiors, and they do not appreciate the attitude of arrogant superiority adopted by many white men in their intercourse with so-called savages. Many of them show a grace of manner and a natural delicacy and politeness which is quite surprising.   I have known a young Eskimo so polite that in conversing with Lieut. Ray he would take pains to mispronounce his words in the same way as the latter did, so as not to hurt his feelings by correcting him bluntly.[1]

TRIBAL PHENOMENA.

We were unable to discover among these people the slightest trace of tribal organization or of division into gentes, and in this our observations agree with those of all who have studied the Eskimos elsewhere. They call themselves as a race "In'uĭn," a term corresponding to the

---

[1] Compare Vega, vol. 1, p. 489.   The Chukches were "so courteous as not to correct but to adopt the mistakes in the pronunciation or meaning of words that were made on the *Vega*."

"Inuit" of other dialects, and meaning "people," or "human beings." Under this name they include white men and Indians as well as Eskimo, as is the case in Greenland and the Mackenzie River district, and probably also everywhere else, though many writers have supposed it to be applied by them only to their own race.

They have however special names for the former two races. The people of any village are known as "the inhabitants of such and such a place;" for instance, Nuwŭ'ñmiun, "the inhabitants of the point;" Utkiavwĭñmiun, "the inhabitants of Utkiávwĭñ;" Kuñmiun (in Greenlandic "Kungmiut"), "the people who live on the river." The people about Norton Sound speak of the northern Eskimo, especially those of Point Barrow and Cape Smyth, as "Kûñmû'dlĭñ," which is not a name derived from a location, but a sort of nickname, the meaning of which was not ascertained. The Point Barrow natives do not call themselves by this name, but apply it to those people whose winter village is at Demarcation Point (or Herschel Island, see above, p. 26). This word appears in the corrupted form "Kokmullit," as the name of the village at Nuwŭk on Petroff's map. Petroff derived his information regarding the northern coast at second-hand from people who had obtained their knowledge of names, etc., from the natives of Norton Sound.

The people of the two villages under consideration frequently go backward and forward, sometimes removing permanently from one village to the other, while strangers from distant villages sometimes winter here, so that it was not until the end of the second year, when we were intimately acquainted with everybody at Utkiavwĭñ, that we could form anything like a correct estimate of the population of this village.[1] This we found to be about 140 souls. As well as we could judge, there were about 150 or 160 at Nuwŭk. These figures show a great decrease in numbers since the end of 1853, when Dr. Simpson[2] reckoned the population of Nuwŭk at 309. During the 2 years from September, 1881, to August, 1883, there were fifteen deaths that we heard of in the village of Utkiavwĭñ alone, and only two children born in that period survived. With this ratio between the number of births and deaths, even in a period of comparative plenty, it is difficult to see how the race can escape speedy extinction, unless by accessions from without, which in their isolated situation they are not likely to receive.[3]

SOCIAL SURROUNDINGS.

CONTACT WITH UNCIVILIZED PEOPLE.

Other Eskimo.—The nearest neighbors of these people, as has been stated above, are the Eskimo living at Demarcation Point (or Herschel

---

[1] See "Approximate Census, etc.," Report of Point Barrow Exp., p. 49.

[2] Op. cit., p. 237.

[3] Petroff's estimate (Report, etc., p. 4) of the number of natives on this part of the Arctic coast is much too large. He gives the population of "Ootiwakh" (Utkiavwĭñ) as 225. Refuge Inlet (where there is merely a summer camp of Utkiavwĭñmiun), 40, and "Kokmullit," 200. The supposed settlement of 50 inhabitants at the Colville River is also a mere summer camp, not existing in the winter.

Island), eastward, and those who inhabit the small villages between Point Belcher and Wainwright Inlet. These villages are three in number. The nearest to Point Belcher, Nuna'ria, is now deserted, and its inhabitants have established the new village of Sida'ru nearer the inlet. The third village consists of a few houses only, and is called A'tŭně. The people of these villages are so closely connected that they are sometimes spoken of collectively as Sida'ruñmiun. At a distance up the river, which flows into Wainwright Inlet, live the Ku'ñmiun, "the people who live on the river." These appear to be closely related to the people of the first village below Wainwright Inlet, which is named Kĭlauwitawĭñ. At any rate, a party of them who came to Cape Smyth in the spring of 1883 were spoken of indifferently as Kuñmiun or Kĭlauwitawĭ'ñmiun.

Small parties from all the villages occasionally visit Point Barrow during the winter for the purpose of trade and amusement, traveling with sledges along the land ice where it is smooth, otherwise along the edge of the cliffs; and similar parties from the two northern villages return these visits. No special article of trade appears to be sought at either village, though perhaps the southern villages have a greater supply of skins of the bearded seal, fit for making umiak covers, as I knew of a load of these brought up for sale, and in the spring of 1883 a party went down to the inlet in search of such skins. Single families and small parties like that from Kĭlauwitawĭñ, mentioned above, sometimes spend the whaling season at Point Barrow, joining some of the whaling crews at the northern villages. The people that we saw from these settlements were very like the northern Eskimos but many of them spoke a perceptibly harsher dialect, sounding the final consonants distinctly.

The people at Point Hope are known as Tĭkera'ñmiun "inhabitants of the forefinger (Point Hope)," and their settlement is occasionally visited by straggling parties. No natives from Point Hope came north during the 2 years of our stay, but a party of them visited the *Plover* in 1853.[1] We found some people acquainted by name with the Kuwû'ñmiun and Silawĭ'ñmiun of the Kuwûk (Kowak or "Putnam") and Silawik Rivers emptying into Hotham Inlet, and one man was familiar with the name of Sisualĭñ, the great trading camp at Kotzebue Sound. We were unable to find that they had any knowledge of Asia ("Kokhlitnuna,") or the Siberian Eskimo, but this was probably due to lack of properly directed inquiries, as they seem to have been well informed on the subject in the *Plover's* time.[2]

With the people of the Nu'natăk (Inland) River, the Nunatañmiun, they are well acquainted, as they meet them every summer for purposes of trading, and a family or two of Nunatañmiun sometimes spend the

---

[1] Maguire, NW. Passage, p. 384.

[2] It is to be regretted that the expedition was not supplied with a copy of Dr. Simpson's excellent paper, as much valuable information was missed for lack of suggestions as to the direction of inquiries.

winter at the northern villages. One family wintered at Nuwŭk in 1881–'82, and another at Utkiavwĭñ the following winter, while a widower of this "tribe" was also settled there for the same winter, having married a widow in the village. We obtained very little definite information about these people except that they came from the south and descended the Colville River. Our investigations were rendered difficult by the engrossing nature of the work of the station, and the trouble we experienced, at first, in learning enough of the language to make ourselves clearly understood. Dr. Simpson was able to learn definitely that the homes of these people are on the Nunatăk and that some of them visit Kotzebue Sound in the summer, while trading parties make a portage between the Nunatăk and Colville, descending the latter river to the Arctic Ocean.[1] I have been informed by the captain of one of the American whalers that he has, in different seasons, met the same people at Kotzebue Sound and the mouth of the Colville. We also received articles of Siberian tame reindeer skin from the east, which must have come across the country from Kotzebue Sound.

These people differ from the northern natives in some habits, which will be described later, and speak a harsher dialect. We were informed that in traveling east after passing the mouth of the Colville they came to the Kûñmû'dlĭñ ("Kangmali enyuin" of Dr. Simpson and other authors) and still further off "a great distance" to the Kupûñ or "Great River"—the Mackenzie—near the mouth of which is the village of the Kupûñmiun, whence it is but a short distance inland to the "great house" (iglu'kpûk) of the white men on the great river (probably Fort Macpherson). Beyond this we only heard confused stories of people without posteriors and of sledges that run by themselves without dogs to draw them. We heard nothing of the country of Kĭtiga'ru[2] or of the stone-lamp country mentioned by Dr. Simpson.[3] The Kûñmûdlĭñ are probably, as Dr. Simpson believes, the people whose winter houses were seen by Franklin at Demarcation Point,[4] near which, at Icy Reef, Hooper also saw a few houses.[5]

As already stated, Capt. E. E. Smith was informed by the natives that there is now no village farther west than Herschel Island, where there is one of considerable size. If he was correctly informed, this must be a new village, since the older explorers who passed along the coast found only a summer camp at this point. He also states that he found large numbers of ruined iglus on the outlying sandy islands along the coast, especially near Anxiety Point. We have scarcely any information about these people, as the only white men who have seen them had little intercourse with them in passing along the coast.[6] The

---

[1] Op. cit., pp. 234 and 236.

[2] This was the name of a girl at Nuwŭk.

[3] Op. cit., p. 269.

[4] Second Exp., p. 142.

[5] Tents of the Tuski, p. 255.

[6] All the published information there is about them from personal observation can be found in Franklin, Second Exp., p. 142; T. Simpson, Narrative, pp. 118–123; and Hooper, Tents, etc., pp. 255–257 and 260.

Point Barrow people have but slight acquaintance with them, as they see them only a short time each summer. Captain Smith, however, informs me that in the summer of 1885 one boat load of them came back with the Point Barrow traders to Point Barrow, where he saw them on board of his ship. There was a man at Utkiavwĭñ who was called " the Kûñmû′dlĭñ." He came there when a child, probably, by adoption, and was in no way distinguishable from the other people.

Father Petitot appears to include these people in the "Taρèoρmeut" division of his "Tchiglit" Eskimo, whom he loosely describes as inhabiting the coast from Herschel Island to Liverpool Bay, including the delta of the Mackenzie,[1] without locating their permanent villages. In another place, however, he excludes the "Taρèoρmeut" from the "Tchiglit," saying, "Dans l'ouest, les *Tchiglit* communiquaient avec leurs plus proches voisins les Taρèoρ-meut,"[2] while in a third place[3] he gives the country of the "Tchiglit" as extending from the Coppermine River to the Colville, and on his map in the same volume, the "Tareormeut" are laid down in the Mackenzie delta only. According to his own account, however, he had no personal knowledge of any Eskimo west of the Mackenzie delta. These people undoubtedly have a local name derived from that of their winter village, but it is yet to be learned.

It is possible that they do consider themselves the same people with the Eskimo of the Mackenzie delta, and call themselves by the general name of "Taρèoρmeut" (= Taxaiomiun in the Point Barrow dialect), "those who live by the sea." That they do not call themselves "Kûñmû′dlĭñ" or "Kanmali-enyuin" or "Kangmaligmeut" is to my mind quite certain. The word "Kûñmû′dlĭñ," as already stated, is used at Norton Sound to designate the people of Point Barrow (I was called a "Kûñmû′dlĭñ" by some Eskimo at St. Michaels because I spoke the Point Barrow dialect), who do not recognize the name as belonging to themselves, but have transferred it to the people under consideration. Now, "Kûñmû′dlĭñ" is a word formed after the analogy of many Eskimo words from a noun kûñmæ and the affix lĭñ or dlĭñ (in Greenlandic lik), "one who has a ——." The radical noun, the meaning of which I can not ascertain, would become in the Mackenzie dialect kρagmaρk (using Petitot's orthography), which with -lik in the plural would make kρagmalit. (According to Petitot's "Grammaire" the plural of -lik in the Mackenzie dialect is -lit, and not -gdlit, as in Greenlandic). This is the name given by Petitot on his map to the people of the Anderson River,[4] while he calls the Anderson River itself Kρagmalik.[5] The father, however, had but little personal knowledge of the natives of the Anderson, having made but two, apparently brief, visits to their village in 1865, when he first made the acquaintance of the Eskimo. He afterwards became fairly intimate with the Eskimo of the Mackenzie

[1] Monographie, p. xi.
[2] Ibid, p. xvi.
[3] Bull. de la Société de Géographie, 6e sér., vol. 10, p. 256.
[4] See also Monographie, etc., p. xi, where the name is spelled Kρamalit
[2] Vocabulaire, etc., p. 76.

delta, parties of whom spent the summers of 1869 and 1870 with him. From these parties he appears to have obtained the greater part of the information embodied in his Monographie and Vocabulaire, as he explicitly states that he brought the last party to Fort Good Hope "autant pour les instruire à loisir que pour apprendre d'eux leur idiome."[1] Nothing seems to me more probable than that he learned from these Mackenzie people the names of their neighbors of the Anderson, which he had failed to obtain in his flying visits 5 years before, and that it is the same name, " Kûñmû′dlïñ," which we have followed from Norton Sound and found always applied to the people just beyond us. Could we learn the meaning of this word the question might be settled, but the only possible derivation I can see for it is from the Greenlandic кarmaк, a wall, which throws no light upon the subject. Petitot calls the people of Cape Bathurst Kρagmaliveit, which appears to mean " the real Kûñmû′dlïñ " (" Kûñmû′dlïñ " and the affix -vik, " the real").

The Kupûñmiun appear to inhabit the permanent villages which have been seen near the western mouth of the Mackenzie, at Shingle Point[2] and Point Sabine,[3] with an outlying village, supposed to be deserted, at Point Kay.[4] They are the natives described by Petitot in his Monographie as the Taρèoρmeut division of the Tchiglit, to whom, from the reasons already stated, most of his account seems to apply. There appears to me no reasonable doubt, considering his opportunities for observing these people, that Taρèoρmeut, "those who dwell by the sea," is the name that they actually apply to themselves, and that Kupûñmiun, or Kopagmut, "those who live on the Great River," is a name bestowed upon them by their neighbors, perhaps their western neighbors alone, since all the references to this name seem to be traceable to the authority of Dr. Simpson. Should they apply to themselves a name of similar meaning, it would probably be of a different form, as, according to Petitot,[5] they call the Mackenzie Kuρvik, instead of Kupûk or Kupûñ.

These are the people who visit Fort Macpherson every spring and summer,[6] and are well known to the Hudson Bay traders as the Mackenzie River Eskimo. They are the Eskimo encountered between Herschel Island and the mouth of the Mackenzie by Franklin, by Dease and Simpson, and by Hooper and Pullen, all of whom have published brief notes concerning them.[7]

We are still somewhat at a loss for the proper local names of the last

---

[1] Bull. Soc. de Géog., 6ᵉ sér., vol. 10, p. 39.
[2] T. Simpson, Narrative, p. 112.
[3] Hooper, Tents, etc., p. 264.
[4] Ibid, p. 263.
[5] Bull. Soc. de Géog., 6 sér., vol. 10, p. 182.
[6] Petitot, Monographie, etc., pp. xvi and xx.
[7] Franklin, 2d Exp., pp. 99–101, 105–110, 114–119 and 128; T. Simpson, Narrative, pp. 104–112; Hooper, Tents, etc., pp. 263–264. There is also a brief note by the Rev. W. W. Kirkby, in a "Journey to the Youcan." Smithsonian Report for 1864. These, with Petitot's in many respects admirable Monographie, comprise all the information regarding these people from actual observation that has been published. Richardson has described them at second hand in his "Searching Expedition" and "Polar Regions." The "Kopagmute" of Petroff (Report, etc., p. 125) are a purely hypothetical people invented to fill the space between "the coast people in the north and the Athabascans in the south."

labret-wearing Eskimo, those, namely, of the Anderson River and Cape Bathurst. That they are not considered by the Taρèoρmeut as belonging to the same "tribe" with themselves is evident from the names Kρagmalit and Kρagmaliveit, applied to them by Petitot. Sir John Richardson, the first white man to encounter them (in 1826), says that they called themselves "Kitte-garrœ-oot,"[1] and the Point Barrow people told Dr. Simpson of country called "Kit-te-ga'-ru" beyond the Mackenzie.[2] These people, as well as the Taρèoρmeut, whom they closely resemble, are described in Petitot's Monographie, and brief notices of them are given by Sir John Richardson,[3] McClure,[4] Armstrong,[5] and Hooper.[6] The arts and industries of these people from the Mackenzie to the Anderson, especially the latter region, are well represented in the National Museum by the collections of Messrs. Kennicott, Ross, and MacFarlane. The Point Barrow people say that the Kupûñmiun are "bad;"[7] but notwithstanding this small parties from the two villages occasionally travel east to the Mackenzie, and spend the winter at the Kupûñmiun village, whence they visit the "great house," returning the following season. Such a party left Point Barrow June 15, 1882, declaring their intention of going all the way to the Mackenzie. They returned August 25 or 26, 1883, when we were in the midst of the confusion of closing the station, so that we learned no details of their journey. A letter with which they were intrusted to be forwarded to the United States through the Mackenzie River posts reached the Chief Signal Officer in the summer of 1883 by way of the Rampart House, on the Porcupine River, whence we received an answer by the bearer from the factor in charge. The Eskimo probably sent the letter to the Rampart House by the Indians who visit that post.

The intercourse between these people is purely commercial. Dr. Simpson, in the paper so often quoted, gives an excellent detailed description of the course of this trade, which agrees in the main with our observations, though we did not learn the particulars of time and distance as accurately as he did. There have been some important changes, however, since his time. A small party, perhaps five or six families, of "Nunatañmiun" now come every summer to Point Barrow about the end of July, or as soon as the shallow bays along shore are open. They establish themselves at the summer camping ground at Pérnyɐ, at the southwest corner of Elson Bay, and stay two or three weeks, trading with the natives and the ships, dancing, and shooting ducks. The eastward-bound parties seem to start a little earlier than formerly (July 7, 1853, July 3, 1854,[8] June 18, 1882, and June 29, 1883). From all accounts their rela-

---

[1] Franklin, 2d Exp., p. 203.
[2] Ibid., p. 269.
[3] Franklin, 2d Exp., pp. 193, 203 and 230; Searching Exp., and Polar Regions, p. 300.
[4] N. W. Passage, pp. 84–98.
[5] Personal Narrative, p. 176.
[6] Tents, etc., pp. 343–348.
[7] Compare what Petitot has to say—Monographie, etc., p. xiii and passim—about the turbulent and revengeful character of the "Tchiglit."
[8] Dr. Simpson, op. cit., p. 264.

tions with the eastern people are now perfectly friendly. We heard nothing of the precautionary measures described by Dr. Simpson,[1] and the women talked frequently of their trading with the Kûñmû′dlῐñ and even with the Kupûñmiun.[2] We did not learn definitely whether they met the latter at Barter Point or whether they went still farther east.

Some of the Point Barrow parties do not go east of the Colville. The articles of trade have changed somewhat in the last 30 years, from the fact that the western natives can now buy directly from the whalers iron articles, arms, and ammunition, beads, tobacco, etc. The Nunatañmiun now sell chiefly furs, deerskins, and clothing ready made from them, woodenware (buckets and tubs), willow poles for setting nets, and sometimes fossil ivory. The double-edged Siberian knives are no longer in the market and appear to be going out of fashion, though a few of them are still in use. Ready-made stone articles, like the whetstones mentioned by Dr. Simpson,[3] are rarely, if ever, in the market. We did not hear of the purchase of stone lamps from the eastern natives. This is probably due to a cessation of the demand for them at Point Barrow, owing to the falling off in the population.

The Kûñmû′dlῐñ no longer furnish guns and ammunition, as the western natives prefer the breech-loading arms they obtain from the whalers to the flintlock guns sold by the Hudson Bay Company. The trade with these people seems to be almost entirely for furs and skins, notably black and red fox skins and wolverine skins. Skins of the narwhal or beluga are no longer mentioned as important articles of trade.

In return for these things the western natives give sealskins, etc., especially oil, as formerly, though I believe that very little, if any, whalebone is now carried east, since the natives prefer to save it for trading with the ships in the hope of getting liquor, or arms and ammunition, and various articles of American manufacture, beads, kettles, etc. I was told by an intelligent native of Utkiavwῐñ that brass kettles were highly prized by the Kupûñmiun, and that a large one would bring three wolverine skins,[4] three black foxskins, or five red ones. One woman was anxious to get all the empty tin cans she could, saying that she could sell them to the Kûñmû′dlῐñ for a foxskin apiece. We were told that the eastern natives were glad to buy gun flints and bright-colored handkerchiefs, and that the Nunatañmiun wanted blankets and playing-cards.

Indians.—They informed us that east of the Colville they sometimes met "Itkû′dlῐñ," people with whom they could not converse, but who were friendly and traded with them, buying oil for fox skins. They were said to live back of the coast between the Colville and the Mackenzie, and were described as wearing no labrets, but rings in their ears and noses. They wear their hair long, do not tonsure the crown, and are dressed in jackets of skin with the hair removed, without hoods, and

---

[1] Op. cit., p. 265.

[2] In the Plover's time they were left a day's journey in the rear.

[3] Op. cit., p. 266.

[4] T. Simpson saw iron kettles at Camden Bay which had been purchased from the western natives at two wolverine skins apiece. Narrative, p. 171.

ornamented with beads and fringe. We saw one or two such jackets in Utkiavwĩñ apparently made of moose skin, and a few pouches of the same material, highly ornamented with beads. They have long flint-lock guns, white man's wooden pipes, which they value highly, and axes—not adzes—with which they "break many trees." We easily understood from this description that Indians were meant, and since our return I have been able to identify one or two of the tribes with tolerable certainty.

They seem better acquainted with these people than in Dr. Simpson's time, and know the word "kŭtchin," people, in which many of the tribal names end. We did not hear the names Ko'yukan or Itkalya'ruin which Dr. Simpson learned, apparently from the Nunatañmiun.[1] I heard one man speak of the Kŭtcha Kutchin, who inhabit the "Yukon from the Birch River to the Kotlo River on the east and the Porcupine River on the north, ascending the latter a short distance."[2]

One of the tribes with which they have dealings is the "Rat Indians" of the Hudson Bay men, probably the Vunta'-Kŭtchin,[3] from the fact that they visit Fort Yukon. These are the people whom Capt. Maguire met on his unsuccessful sledge journey to the eastward to communicate with Collinson. The Point Barrow people told us that "Magwa" went east to see "Colli'k-sina," but did not see him, only saw the Itkŭdlĩñ. Collinson,[4] speaking of Maguire's second winter at Point Barrow, says: "In attempting to prosecute the search easterly, an armed body of Indians of the Koyukun tribe were met with, and were so hostile that he was compelled to return." Maguire himself, in his official report,[5] speaks of meeting *four* Indians who had followed his party for several days. He says nothing of any hostile demonstration; in fact, says they showed signs of disappointment at his having nothing to trade with them, but his Eskimo, he says, called them Koyukun, which he knew was the tribe that had so barbarously murdered Lieut. Barnard at Nulato in 1851. Moreover, each Indian had a musket, and he had only two with a party of eight men, so he thought it safer to turn back. However, he seems to have distributed among them printed "informa-tion slips," which they immediately carried to Fort Yukon, and return-ing to the coast with a letter from the clerk in charge, delivered it to Capt. Collinson on board of the *Enterprise* at Barter Island, July 18, 1854. The letter is as follows:

FORT YOUCON, *June 27, 1854.*

The printed slips of paper delivered by the officers of H. M. S. *Plover* on the 25th of April, 1854, to the Rat Indians were received on the 27th of June, 1854, at the Hudson Bay Company's establishment, Fort Youcon. The Rat Indians are in the

---

[1] "The inland Eskimo also call them Ko'-yu-kan, and divide them into three sections or tribes. * * * One is called I't-ka-lyi [apparently the plural of Itkŭdlĩñ], * * * the second It-kal-ya'-ruin [differ-ent or other Itkŭdlĩñ]," op. cit., p. 269.

[2] Dall, Cont. to N. A. Ethn., vol. 1, p. 30, where they are identified with Itkalyaruin of Simpson.

[3] Ibid., p. 31.

[4] Arctic Papers, p. 119.

[5] Further papers, etc., pp. 905 et seq.

habit of making periodical trading excursions to the Esquimaux along the coast.
They are a harmless, inoffensive set of Indians, ever ready and willing to render
any assistance they can to the whites.

WM. LUCAS HARDISTY,

Clerk in charge.[1]

Capt. Collinson evidently never dreamed of identifying this "harmless, inoffensive set of Indians" with "an armed body of Indians of the
Koyukun tribe." It is important that his statement, quoted above,
should be corrected lest it serve as authority for extending the range of
the Koyukun Indians [2] to the Arctic Ocean. The Point Barrow people
also know the name of the U′na-kho-tānā,[3] or En′akotina, as they pronounce it. Their intercourse with all these Indians appears to be rather
slight and purely commercial. Friendly relations existed between the
Rat Indians and the "Eskimos who live somewhere near the Colville"
as early as 1849,[4] while it was still "war to the knife" between the Peel
River Indians and the Kupûñmiun.[5]

The name Itkû′dlĭñ, of which I′t-ka-lyi of Dr. Simpson appears to be
the plural, is a generic word for an Indian, and is undoubtedly the same
as the Greenland word erкilek—plural erкigdlit—which means a fabulous "inlander" with a face like a dog. "They are martial spirits and
inhuman foes to mankind; however, they only inhabit the east side of
the land."[6] Dr. Rink[7] has already pointed out that this name is in use
as far as the Mackenzie River—for instance, the Indians are called
"eert-kai-lee" (Parry), or "it-kagh-lie" (Lyon), at Fury and Hecla Strait;
ik-kil-lin (Gilder), at the west shore of Hudson Bay, and "itkρe′le′it"
(Petitot) at the Mackenzie. Petitot also gives this word as itkpe′lit in
his vocabulary (p. 42.) These words, including the term Ingalik, or
In-ka-lik, applied by the natives of Norton Sound to the Indians,[8] and
which Mr. Dall was informed meant "children of a louse's egg," all
appear to be compounds of the word erкeк, a louse egg, and the affix
lik. (I suspect erкilek, from the form of its plural, to be a corruption
of "erкiliк," since there is no recognized affix -leк in Greenlandic.)

Petitot[9] gives an interesting tradition in regard to the origin of this
name: "La tradition Innok dédaigne de parler ici des Peaux-Rouges.
L'áyant fait observer á mon narrateur A*ρviuna*: 'Oh!' me repondait-il,
'il ne vaut pas la peine d'en parler. Ils naquirent aussi dans l'ouest, sur
l'ile du Castor, des larves de nos poux. C'ést pourquoi nous les nom-
mons Itkρe′le′it."

CONTACT WITH CIVILIZED PEOPLE.

Until the visit of the *Blossom's* barge in 1826 these people had never
seen a white man, although they were already in possession of tobacco
and articles of Russian manufacture, such as copper kettles, which they

---

[1] Arctic Papers, p. 144.

[2] Koyû′-ku′kh-otā′nā, Dall, Cont. to N. A. Eth., p. 27.

[3] Ibid., p. 28.

[4] Hooper, Tents, etc., p. 276.

[5] Ibid., p. 273.

[6] Crantz, vol. 1, p. 208.

[7] Journ. Anthrop. Inst.. 1885, p. 244.

[8] Dall, Alaska, p. 28, and Contrib., vol. 1, p. 25.

[9] Monographie, p. xxiv.

had obtained from Siberia by way of the Diomedes. Mr. Elson's party landed only at Refuge Inlet, and had but little intercourse with the natives. His visit seemed to have been forgotten by the time of the *Plover's* stay at Point Barrow, though Dr. Simpson found people who recollected the visit of Thomas Simpson in 1837.[1] The latter, after he had left the boats and was proceeding on foot with his party, first met the Nuwŭñmiun at Point Tangent, where there was a small party encamped, from whom he purchased the umiak in which he went on to Point Barrow. He landed there early in the morning of August 4, and went down to the summer camp at Pernyɐ, where he stayed till 1 o'clock in the afternoon, trading with the natives and watching them dance. On his return to Point Tangent some of the natives accompanied him to Boat Extreme, where he parted from them August 6, so that his whole intercourse with them was confined to less than a week.[2]

The next white men who landed at Point Barrow were the party in the *Plover's* boats, under Lieuts. Pullen and Hooper, on their way to the Mackenzie, and the crew of Mr. Sheddon's yacht, the *Nancy Dawson*, in the summer of 1849. The boats were from July 29 to August 3 getting from Cape Smyth past Point Barrow, when the crews were ashore for a couple of days and did a little trading with the natives, whom they found very friendly. They afterwards had one or two skirmishes with evil-disposed parties of Nuwŭñmiun returning from the east in the neighborhood of Return Reef. The exploring ships *Enterprise* and *Investigator* also had casual meetings with the natives, who received tobacco, etc., from the ships.

The depot ship *Plover*, Commander Maguire, spent the winters of 1852–'53 and 1853–'54 at Point Barrow, and the officers and crew, after some misunderstandings and skirmishes, established very friendly and sociable relations with the natives. The only published accounts of the *Plover's* stay at Point Barrow are Commander Maguire's official reports, published in the Parliamentary Reports (Blue Books) for 1854, pp. 165–185, and 1855, pp. 905 et seq., and Dr. Simpson's paper, already mentioned. Maguire's report of the first winter's proceedings is also published as an appendix to Sherard Osborne's "Discovery of the Northwest Passage."

We found that the elder natives remembered Maguire, whom they called "Magwa," very well. They gave us the names of many of his people and a very correct account of the most important proceedings, though they did not make it clear that the death of the man mentioned in his report was accidental. They described "Magwa" as short and fat, with a very thick neck, and all seemed very much impressed with the height of his first lieutenant, "Epi'ana" (*Vernon*,) who had "lots of guns."

It was difficult to see that the *Plover's* visit had exerted any permanent influence on these people. In fact, Dr. Simpson's account of their habits and customs would serve very well for the present time, except

---

[1] Op. cit., p. 264.   [2] Narrative, pp. 146–168.

in regard to the use of firearms. They certainly remembered no English. Indeed, Dr. Simpson says[1] that they learned hardly any. The *Plover's* people probably found it very easy to do as we did and adopt a sort of jargon of Eskimo words and "pigeon English" grammar for general intercourse. Although, according to the account of the natives, there was considerable intercourse between the sailors and the Eskimo women, there are now no people living at either village who we could be sure were born from such intercourse, though one woman was suspected of being half English. She was remarkable only for her large build, and was not lighter than many pure-blooded women.

Since 1854, when the first whalers came as far north as the Point, there has hardly been a season in which ships have not visited this region, and for a couple of months every year the natives have had considerable intercourse with the whites, going off to the ships to trade, while the sailors come ashore occasionally. We found that they usually spoke of white men as "kablu'na;" but they informed us that they had another word, "tû'n-nyĭn," which they used to employ among themselves when they saw a ship. Dr. Simpson[2] says that they learned the word "kabluna" from the eastern natives, but that the latter (he gives it Tan'-ning or Tan'-gin) came from the Nunata'ñmiun. He supposes it to apply to the Russians, who had regular bath days at their posts, and says it is derived from tan-nikh-lu-go, to wash or cleanse the person.

The chief change resulting from their intercourse with the whites has been the introduction of firearms. Nearly all the natives are now provided with guns, some of them of the best modern patterns of breechloaders, and they usually succeed in procuring a supply of ammunition. This is in some respects a disadvantage, as the reindeer have become so wild that the natives would no longer be able to procure a sufficient number of them for food and clothing with their former appliances, and they are thus rendered dependent on the ships. On the other hand, with a plentiful supply of ammunition it is easier for them to procure abundance of food, both deer and seals, and they are less liable to famine than in former times.

There is no reason to fear, as has been suggested, that they will lose the art of making any of their own weapons except in the case of the bow. With firearms alone they would be unable to obtain any seals, a much more important source of food than the reindeer, and their own appliances for sealing are much better than any civilized contrivances. Although they have plenty of the most improved modern whaling gear, they are not likely to forget the manufacture of their own implements for this purpose, as this important fishery is ruled by tradition and superstition, which insists that at least one harpoon of the ancient pattern must be used in taking every whale. All are now rich in iron, civilized tools, canvas and wreck wood, and in this respect their condition is improved.

---

[1] Op. cit., p. 251.   [2] Op. cit., p. 271.

They have, however, adopted very few civilized habits. They have contracted a taste for civilized food, especially hard bread and flour, but this they are unable to obtain for 10 months of the year, and they are thus obliged to adhere to their former habits. In fact, except in regard to the use of firearms and mechanics' tools, they struck me as essentially a conservative people.

Petroff[1] makes the assertion that in late years their movements have been guided chiefly by those of the whalers. As far as we could observe they have not changed the course or time of their journeys since Dr. Simpson's time, except that they have given up the autumn whaling, possibly on account of the presence of the ships at that season. Of course, men who are rich in whalebone now stay to trade with the ships, while those who have plenty of oil go east. They are not absolutely dependent on the ships for anything except ammunition, and even during the short time the ships are with them they hardly neglect their own pursuits.

The one unmitigated evil of their intercourse with the whites has been the introduction of spirits. Apart from the direct injury which liquor does to their health, their passionate fondness for it leads them to barter away valuable articles which should have served to procure ammunition or other things of permanent use. It is to be hoped, however, that the liquor traffic is decreasing. The vigilance of the revenue cutter prevents regular whisky traders from reaching the Arctic Ocean, and public opinion among the whaling captains seems to be growing in the right direction.

Another serious evil, which it would be almost impossible to check, is the unlimited intercourse of the sailors with the Eskimo women. The whites can hardly be said to have introduced laxity of sexual morals, but they have encouraged a natural savage tendency, and have taught them prostitution for gain, which has brought about great excesses, fortunately confined to a short season. This may have something to do with the want of fertility among the women.

Our two years of friendly relations with these people were greatly to their advantage. Not only were our house and our doings a constant source of amusement to them, but they learned to respect and trust the whites. Without becoming dependent on us or receiving any favors without some adequate return either in work or goods, they were able to obtain tobacco, hard bread, and many other things of use to them, all through the year. Our presence prevented their procuring more than trifling quantities of spirits, and though the supply of breech-loading ammunition was pretty well cut off, they could get plenty of powder and shot for their muzzle loaders. The abundance of civilized food was undoubtedly good for them, and our surgeon was able to give them a great deal of help in sickness.

In all their intercourse with the whites they have learned very little

---

[1] Report, etc., p. 125.

English, chiefly a few oaths and exclamations like "Get out of here," and the words of such songs as "Little Brown Jug" and "Shoo Fly," curiously distorted. They have as a rule invented genuine Eskimo words for civilized articles which are new to them.[1] Even in their intimate relations with us they learned but few more phrases and in most cases without a knowledge of their meaning.

There are a few Hawaiian words introduced by the Kanaka sailors on the whaleships, which are universally employed between whites and Eskimo along the whole of the Arctic coast, and occasionally at least among the Eskimo themselves. These are *kau-kau*,[2] food, or to eat; *hana-hana*, work; *pŭnĭ-pŭnĭ*, *coitus*, and *pau*, not. *Wahíne*, woman, is also used, but is less common. Another foreign word now universally employed among them in their intercourse with the whites, and even, I believe, among themselves, is "kuníɐ" for woman or wife. They themselves told us that it was not an Eskimo word—"When there were no white men, there was no *kuniɐ*"—and some of the whalemen who had been at Hudson Bay said it was the "Greenland" word for woman. It was not until our return to this country that we discovered it to be the Danish word *kone*, woman, which in the corrupted form "coony" is in common use among the eastern Eskimo generally in the jargon they employ in dealing with the whites. *Kuniɐ* is "coony" with the suffix of the third person, and therefore means "his wife." It is sometimes used at Point Barrow for either of a married couple in the sense of our word "spouse."

NATURAL RESOURCES.

ANIMALS.

These people are acquainted with the following animals, all of which are more or less hunted, and serve some useful purpose.

Mammals.—The wolf, amáxo (Canis lupus griseo-albus), is not uncommon in the interior, but rarely if ever reaches the coast. Red and black foxes, kaiă'ktûk (Vulpes fulvus fulvus and argentatus), are chiefly known from their skins, which are common articles in the trade with the eastern natives, and the same is true of the wolverine, ka'vwĭñ (Gulo luscus), and the marten, kabweatyía (Mustela americana). The arctic fox, tĕrĭgûniɐ (Vulpes lagopus), is very abundant along the coast, while the ermine (Putorius erminea) and Parry's spermophile (Spermophilus empetra empetra) are not rare. The last is called sĭksĭñ. Lemmings, a'vwĭñɐ, of two species (Cuniculus torquatus and Myodes obensis) are

---

[1] See list of "New Words," Rep. Point Barrow Exp., p. 57.

[2] The history of this word, which also appears as a Chuckch word in some of the vocabularies collected by Nordenskiöld's expedition, is rather curious. Chamisso (Kotzebue's Voyage, vol. 2, p. 392, foot-note) says that this is a Hawaiian corruption of the well-known "Pigeon-English" (he calls it Chinese) word "chow-chow" recently (in 1816–'17) adopted by the Sandwich Islanders from the people with whom they trade. I am informed that the word is not of Chinese origin, but probably came from India, like many other words in "Pigeon-English." Chamisso also calls *pŭnĭ-pŭnĭ* a Chinese word, but I have been able to learn nothing of its origin.

very abundant some years, and they recognize a tiny shrewmouse (Sorex forsteri). This little animal is called ugrúnɐ, a word corresponding to the name ugssungnaʞ given to the same animal in Labrador, which, according to Kleinschmidt,[1] is an ironical application of the name of the largest seal, ugssuk (ugru at Point Barrow), to the smallest mammal known to the Eskimo. The same name is also applied at Point Barrow to the fossil ox, whose bones are sometimes found. The most abundant land animal, however, is the reindeer, tŭ′ktu (Rangifer tarandus grœnlandicus), which is found in winter in great herds along the upper waters of the rivers, occasionally coming down to the coast, and affords a very important supply of food.

The moose, tŭ′ktuwŭñ, or "big reindeer" (Alce machlis), is well known from the accounts of the Nunatañmiun, who bring moose skins to trade. Some of the natives have been east to hunt the mountain sheep, i′mnêɐ (Ovis canadensis dalli), and all are familiar with its skin, horns, and teeth, which they buy of the eastern natives. The musk ox, umíñmau (Ovibos moschatus), is known only from its bones, which are sometimes found on the tundra. Inland, near the rivers, they also find a large brown bear, ă′kqlak, which is probably the barren ground bear, while on the ice-pack, the polar bear, nä′nu (Thalassarctos maritimus), is not uncommon, sometimes making raids on the provision storehouses in the villages.

The most important sea animal is the little rough seal, nĕtyĭʞ (Phoca fœtida), which is very abundant at all seasons. Its flesh is the great staple of food, while its blubber supplies the Eskimo lamps, and its skin serves countless useful purposes. The great bearded seal, úgru (Erignathus barbatus), is less common. It is especially valued for its hide, which serves for covering the large boats and making stout harpoon lines. Two other species of seal, the harbor seal, kasigía (Phoca vitulina), and the beautiful ribbon seal, kaixólĭñ (Phoca fasciata), are known, but both are uncommon, the latter very rare.

Herds of walrus, ai′bwêk (Odobænus obesus), pass along the coast in the open season, generally resting on cakes of floating ice, and are pursued for their hides and ivory as well as their flesh and blubber. Whales, akbwêk, of the species Balæna mysticetus, most pursued for its oil and whalebone, travel along the coast in the leads of open water above described from the middle of April to the latter part of June in large numbers, and return in the autumn, appearing about the end of August. White whales, kĭlĕlua (Delphinapterus sp.), are not uncommon in the summer, and they say the narwhal, tugálĭñ (Monodon monoceros), is occasionally seen. They are also acquainted with another cetacean, which they call áxlo, and which appears from their description to be a species of Orca.

Birds.—In the spring, that is during May and the early part of June, vast flocks of migrating ducks pass to the northeast, close to the shore,

---

[1] Grønlandsk Ordbog, p. 386.

a few only remaining to breed, and return at the end of the summer
from the latter part of July to the end of September. Nearly all the
returning birds cross the isthmus of Point Barrow at Pernyɐ where the
natives assemble in large numbers for the purpose of taking them.
These migrating birds are mostly king ducks, kĭñalĭñ (Somateria spectabilis), Pacific eiders, amau′lĭñ (S. v-nigra), and long-tailed ducks,
a′dyigi′a, a′hadlĭñ (Clangula hyemalis), with smaller numbers of the
spectacled eider, ka′waso (Arctonetta fischeri), and Steller's ducks, ĭgni-
kau′kto (Eniconetta stelleri). At the rivers they also find numbers of
pintails, i′vwûgɐ (Dafila acuta), which visit the coast in small numbers
during the migrations. Geese of three species, the American white-
fronted goose, nû′glûgruɐ (Anser albifrons gambeli), the lesser snow-
goose, kû′ño (Chen hyperborea), and the black brant, nûglû′gnɐ (Branta
nigricans), are not uncommon on the coast both during the migrations
and the breeding season, but the natives find them in much greater
abundance at the rivers, where they also find a species of swan, ku′gru,
probably Olor columbianus, which rarely visits the coast.

Next in importance to the natives are the gulls, of which the Point
Barrow gull, nau′yɐ (Larus barrovianus), is the most abundant all through
the season, though the rare rosy gull, kă′ñmaxlu (Rhodostethes rosea),
appears in multitudes late in the autumn. The ivory gull (Gavia alba),
nariyalbwûñ, and Sabine's gull, yûkû′drĭgûgi′ɐ (Xema Sabinii), are uncommon, while the Arctic tern, utyuta′kĭn (Sterna paradisea), is rather
abundant, especially about the sandspits of Nuwŭk. All these species,
particularly the larger ones, are taken for food.

Three species of loons are common: the great white-billed loon, tu′dlĭñ
(Urinator adamsi), and the Pacific and red-throated divers (U. pacificus
and lumme), which are not distinguished from each other but are both
called kă′ksau. They also occasionally see the thick-billed guillemot
a′kpa (Uria lomvia arra), and more often the sea-pigeon, sêkbwɐk (Ce-
phus mandtii). The three species of jaegers (Stercorarius pomarinus,
parasiticus, and longicaudus) are not distinguished from one another
but are all called isuñɐ. They pay but little attention to the numerous
species of wading birds which appear in considerable abundance in the
migrations and breeding season, but they recognize among them the
turnstone, tûlĭ′gwa (Arenaria interpres), the gray plover, ki′raio′n (Charadrius squatarola), the American golden plover, tu′dlĭñ (C. dominicus),
the knot, tu′awi′a (Tringa canutus), the pectoral and Baird's sandpipers,
(T. maculata and bairdii), both called ai′bwûkiɐ, the red-backed sandpiper, mêkapĭñ (T. alpina pacifica), the semipalmated sandpiper, nĭwĭl-
ĭwĭ′lûk (Ereunetes pusillus), the buff-breasted sandpiper, nu′dluayu
(Tryngites subruficollis), the red phalarope, sabrañ (Chrymophilus fuli-
carius), and the northern phalarope, sabrañɐ (Phalaropus lobatus).
The last is rare at Point Barrow, but they see many of them near the
Colville. The little brown crane, tutĭ′drĭgɐ (Grus canadensis), is also
rare at the Point, but they say they find many of them at the mouth of
Kulu′grua.

Of land birds, the most familiar are the little snow bunting, amaulig̈e (Plectrophenax nivalis), the first bird to arrive in the spring, the Lapland longspur, nĕssau'dlig̈e (Calcarius lapponicus), and two species of grouse, the willow grouse (Lagopus lagopus) and the rock ptarmigan (L. rupestris), which are both called akû'dĭgĭn. These two birds do not migrate, but are to be seen all winter, as is also the well known snowy owl,u'kpĭk (Nyctea nyctea). A gerfalcon,kĭ'drĭgûmĭñ (Falco rusticolus), is also sometimes seen, and skins and feathers of the golden eagle, tĭ'ñ-mieͅkpûk, "the great bird" (Aquila chrysætos), are brought from the east for charms and ornaments. The raven, tulúeͅ (Corvus corax sinuatus), was not seen at Point Barrow, but the natives are familiar with it and have many of its skins for amulets. Several species of small land birds also occur in small numbers, but the natives are not familiar with them and call them all "sû'ksaxíeͅ." This name appears to mean "wanderer" or "flutterer," and probably belongs, I believe, to the different species of redpolls (Aegiothus).

Fishes.—A few species only of fish are found in the salt water. Of these the most abundant are the little polar cod (Boreogadus saida), which is plentiful through the greater part of the year, and is often an important source of food, and the capelin, añmû'grûñ (Mallotus villosus), which is found in large schools close to the beach in the middle of summer. There are also caught sometimes two species of sculpins, kû'naio (Cottus quadricornis and decastrensis), and two species of Lycodes, kú-graun (L. turnerii and coccineus). In the gill nets at Elson Bay they also catch two species of salmon (Onchorhynchus gorbuscha and nerka) and a whitefish (Coregonus laurettæ) in small numbers, and occasionally a large trout (Salvelinus malma). The last-named fish they find sometimes in great numbers, near the mouth of the Colville.

The greatest quantities of fish are taken in the rivers, especially Kuaru and Kulugrua, by fishing through the ice in the winter. They say there are no fish taken in Ikpikpûñ, and account for this by explaining that the former two rivers freeze down to the bottom on the shallow bars inclosing deep pools in which the fish are held, while in the latter the ice never touches the bottom, so that the fish are free to run down to the sea. The species caught are the small Coregonus laurettæ, two large whitefish (C. kennicottii and nelsoni), and the burbot, tita'liñ (Lota maculosa). They speak of a fish, sulukpau'ga (which appears to mean "wing-fin" and is applied in Greenland to a species of Sebastes), that is caught with the hook in Kulugrua apparently only in summer, and seems from the description to be Back's grayling (Thymallus signifer). In the river Ku is caught a smelt, ĭthoa'nĭñ (Osmerus dentex). In the great lake, Tă'syûkpûñ (see above, p. 29), they tell of an enormous fish "as big as a kaiak." They gave it no name, but describe it as having a red belly and white flesh. One man said he had seen one 18 feet long, but another was more moderate, giving about 3 feet as the length of the longest he had seen.

Insects and other invertebrates.—Of insects, they recognize the trouble-some mosquito, kiktoriɐ (Culex spp.), flies, humblebees, and gadflies (Œestrus tarandi), both of which they seem much afraid of, and call i′gu-tyai, and the universal louse, ku′mɐk. All the large winged insects, including the rare butterflies and moths and crane flies, are called tû-kĭlû′kica, or tûkilûkĭdja′ksûn, which is also the name of the yellow poppy (Papaver nudicaule). We were told that "by and by" the poppies would turn into "little birds" and fly away, which led us to suppose that there was some yellow butterfly which we should find abundant in the later summer, but we saw none either season. A small spider is sometimes found in the Eskimo houses, and is called pidrairu′rɐ, "the little braider." They pay but little attention to other invertebrates, but are familiar with worms, kupidro, a species of crab, kinau′rɐ, (Hyas latifrons), and the little branchipus, iritu′ña (Greenlandic issitôrak, "the little one with big eyes"), of the fresh water-pools. Cockles (Buc-cinum, etc.) are called siu′tigo (Gr. sinterok, from siut, ear), and clams have a name which we failed to obtain. Jellyfish are called ipiaru′rɐ, "like bags." They say the "Kûñmudlĭñ" eat them!

PLANTS.

Few plants that are of any service to man grow in this region. The willows, ŭ′kpĭk, of various species, which near the coast are nothing but creeping vines, are sometimes used as fuel, especially along the rivers, where they grow into shrubs 5 or 6 feet high. Their catkins are used for tinder and the moss, mû′nĭk, furnishes wicks for the lamps. We could find no fruit that could be eaten. A cranberry (Vaccinium vitis-idæa) occurs, but produced no fruit either season. No use is made of the different species of grass, which are especially luxuriant around the houses at Utkiavwĭñ, where the ground is richly manured with various sorts of refuse,[1] though the species of mosses and lichens furnish the rein-deer with food easily reached in the winter through the light covering of snow. Little attention is paid to the numerous, and sometimes showy, flowering plants. We learned but two names of flowers, the one mentioned above, tûkĭlû′kica, tûkĭlûkĭdja′ksûn, which seemed to be applied to all striking yellow or white flowers, such as Papaver, Ranun-culus, and Draba, and mai′sun, the bright pink Pedicularis. All the wood used in this region, except the ready-made woodenware and the willow poles obtained from the Nunatañmiun, comes from the drift on the beach. Most of this on the beach west of Point Barrow appears to come from the southwest, as the prevailing current along this shore is to the northeast, and may be derived from the large rivers flowing into Kotzebue Sound, since it shows signs of having been long in the water. The driftwood, which is reported to be abundant east of Point Barrow, probably comes from the great rivers emptying into the Arctic

---

[1] "The oil had acted as a manure on the soil, and produced a luxuriant crop of grass from 1 to 2 feet high" (village at Point Atkinson, east of the Mackenzie). Richardson Searching Exp., vol. 1, p. 254.

Ocean. This wood is sufficiently abundant to furnish the natives with all they need for fuel and other purposes, and consists chiefly of pine, spruce, and cottonwood, mostly in the form of water-worn logs, often of large size. Of late years, also, much wood of the different kinds used in shipbuilding has drifted ashore from wrecks.

MINERALS.

The people of this region are acquainted with few mineral substances, excluding the metals which they obtain from the whites. The most important are flint, slate, soapstone, jade, and a peculiar form of massive pectolite, first described by Prof. F. W. Clarke [1] from specimens brought home by our party. Flint, ánma, was formerly in great demand for arrow and spear heads and other implements, and according to Dr. Simpson [2] was obtained from the Nunatañmiun. It is generally black or a slightly translucent gray, but we collected a number of arrowheads, etc., made of jasper, red or variegated. A few crystals of transparent quartz, sometimes smoky, were also seen, and appeared to be used as amulets. Slate, ulu′ksɐ, "material for a round knife," was used, as its name imports, for making the woman's round knife, and for harpoon blades, etc. It is a smooth clay slate, varying in hardness, and light green, red, purple, dark gray, or black in color. All the pieces of soft gray soapstone, tună′ktɐ, which are so common at both villages, are probably fragments of the lamps and kettles obtained in former years from the eastern natives. The jade is often very beautiful, varying from a pale or bright translucent green to a dark olive, almost black, and was formerly used for making adzes, whetstones, and occasionally other implements. The pectolite, generally of a pale greenish or bluish color, was only found in the form of oblong, more or less cylindrical masses, used as hammerheads. Both of these minerals were called kau′dlo, and were said to come "from the east, a long way off," from high rocky ground, but all that we could learn was very indefinite. Dr. Simpson was informed [3] that the stones for making whetstones were brought from the Kuwûk River, so that this jade is probably the same as that which is said to form Jade Mountain, in that region.

Bits of porphyry, syenite, and similar rocks are used for making labrets, and large pebbles are used as hammers and net sinkers. They have also a little iron pyrites, both massive and in the form of spherical concretions. The latter were said to come from the mouth of the Colville, and are believed by the natives to have fallen from the sky. Two other kinds of stone are brought from the neighborhood of Nu′ɐsŭknan, partly, it appears, as curiosities, and partly with some ill defined mystical notions. The first are botryoidal masses of brown limonite, resembling bog iron ore, and the other sort curious concretions, looking like the familiar "clay stones," but very heavy, and apparently containing a

---

[1] U. S. Geol. Surv., Bull. 9, p. 9, 1884.   [2] Op. cit., p. 266.   [3] Op. cit., p. 266.

great deal of iron pyrites. White gypsum, used for rubbing the flesh side of deerskins, is obtained on the seashore at a place called Tû′tyĕ, "one sleep" east from Point Barrow.

Bituminous coal, alu′a, is well known, though not used for fuel. Many small fragments, which come perhaps from the vein at Cape Beaufort,[1] are picked up on the beach. Shaly, very bituminous coal, broken into small square fragments, is rather abundant on the bars of Kulugrua, whence specimens were brought by Capt. Herendeen. A native of Wainwright Inlet gave us to understand that coal existed in a regular vein near that place, and told a story of a burning hill in that region. This may be a coal bed on fire, or possibly "smoking cliffs," like those seen by the *Investigator* in Franklin Bay.[2] We also heard a story of a lake of tar or bitumen, ádngun, said to be situated on an island a day's sail east of the point. Blacklead, mĭ′ñun, and red ocher are abundant and used as pigments, but we did not learn where they were obtained. Pieces of amber are sometimes found on the beach and are carried as amulets or (rarely) made into beads. Amber is called aúmɐ, a word that in other Eskimo dialects, and probably in this also, means "a live coal." Its application to a lump of amber is quite a striking figure of speech.

CULTURE.

MEANS OF SUBSISTENCE.

FOOD.

Substances used for food.—The food of these people consists almost entirely of animal substances. The staple article of food is the flesh of the rough seal, of which they obtain more than of any other meat. Next in importance is the venison of the reindeer, though this is looked upon as a kind of dainty.[3] Many well developed fœtal reindeer are brought home from the spring deer hunt and are said to be excellent eating, though we never saw them eaten. They also eat the flesh of the other three species of seal, the walrus, the polar bear, the "bowhead" whale, the white whale, and all the larger kinds of birds, geese, ducks, gulls, and grouse. All the different kinds of fish appear to be eaten, with the possible exception of the two species of Lycodes (only a few of these were caught, and all were purchased for our collection) and very little of a fish is wasted except the hardest parts. Walrus hide is sometimes cooked and eaten in times of scarcity. Mollusks of any kind are rarely eaten, as it is difficult to procure them. After a heavy gale in the autumn of 1881, when the beach was covered with marine animals, mostly lamellibranch mollusks with their shells and softer parts broken off by

---

[1] Hooper found coal on the beach at Nuwŭk in 1849, showing that this coal has not necessarily been thrown over from ships. Tents of the Tuski, p. 221.

[2] Discovery of the Northwest Passage, p. 100.

[3] The Eskimo of Iglulik "prefer venison to any kind of meat." Parry, 2d Voyage, p. 510.

the violence of the surf, we saw one woman collect a lapful of these "clam-heads," which she said she was going to eat. The "blackskin" (epidermis) of the whale is considered a great delicacy by them, as by all the other Eskimo who are able to procure it, and they are also very fond of the tough white skin or gum round the roots of the whalebone.[1]

We saw and heard nothing of the habit so generally noticed among other Eskimo and in Siberia of eating the half-digested contents of the stomach of the reindeer, but we found that they were fond of the fæces taken from the rectum of the deer. I find that this curious habit has been noticed among Eskimo only in two other places—Greenland in former times and Boothia Felix. The Greenlanders ate "the Dung of the Rein-deer, taken out of the Guts when they clean them; the Entrails of Partridges and the like Out-cast, pass for Dainties with them."[2] The dung of the musk ox and reindeer when fresh were considered a delicacy by the Boothians, according to J. C. Ross.[3] The entrails of fowls are also considered a great delicacy and are carefully cooked as a separate dish.[4]

As far as our observations go these people eat little, if any, more fat than civilized man, and, as a rule, not by itself. Fat may occasionally be eaten (they are fond of the fat on the inside of duck skins), but they do not habitually eat the great quantities of blubber spoken of in some other places[5] or drink oil, as the Hudson Bay Eskimo are said to do by Hall, or use it as a sauce for dry food, like the natives of Norton Sound. It is usually supposed and generally stated in the popular accounts of the Eskimo that it is a physiological necessity for them to eat enormous quantities of blubber in order to obtain a sufficient amount of carbon to enable them to maintain their animal heat in the cold climate which they inhabit. A careful comparison, however, of the reports of actual observers[6] shows that an excessive eating of fat is not the rule, and is perhaps confined to the territory near Boothia Felix.

Eggs of all kinds, except, of course, the smallest, are eagerly sought for, but the smaller birds are seldom eaten, as it is a waste of time and ammunition to pursue them. We saw this people eat no vegetable substances, though they informed us that the buds of the willow were sometimes eaten. Of late years they have acquired a fondness for many kinds of civilized food, especially bread of any kind, flour, sugar, and molasses, and some of them are learning to like salt. They were very

---

[1] Compare Hooper, Tents, etc. "This, which the Tuski call their sugar," p. 174; and Hall, Arctic Researches, p. 132 (Baffin Land).

[2] Egede, Greenland, p. 136.

[3] Appendix to Ross's 2d Voyage, p. xix.

[4] Compare the passage from Egede, just quoted, and also Kumlien, Contributions, etc., p. 20, at Cumberland Gulf.

[5] For instance, Schwatka says that the Nĕtcĭllĭk of King William Land devour enormous quantities of seal blubber, "noticeably more in summer than the other tribes," viz, those of the western shores of Hudson's Bay (Science, vol. 4, p. 544). Parry speaks of the natives of the Savage Islands, Hudson's Strait, eating raw blubber and sucking the oil remaining on the skins they had emptied (2d Voyage, p. 14).

[6] See for example Egede's Greenland, p. 134; Crantz, History of Greenland, vol. 1, p. 144; Dall, Alaska, passim; Hooper Tents of the Tuski, p. 170; Nordenskiöld, Vega, p. 110.

glad to purchase from us corn-meal "mush" and the broken victuals from the table. These were, however, considered as special dainties and eaten as luncheons or as a dessert after the regular meal. The children and even some of the women were always on the watch for the cook's slop bucket to be brought out, and vied with the ubiquitous dogs in searching for scraps of food. Meat which epicures would call rather "high" is eaten with relish, but they seem to prefer fresh meat when they can get it.

Means of preparing food.—Food is generally cooked, except, perhaps, whale-skin and whale-gum, which usually seem to be eaten as soon as obtained, without waiting for a fire. Meat of all kinds is generally boiled in abundance of water over a fire of driftwood, and the broth thus made is drunk hot before eating the meat. Fowls are prepared for boiling by skinning them. Fish are also boiled, but are often eaten raw, especially in winter at the deer-hunting camps, when they are frozen hard. Meat is sometimes eaten raw or frozen. Lieut. Ray found one family in camp on Kulugrua who had no fire of any kind, and were eating everything raw. They had run out of oil some time before and did not like to spend time in going to the coast for more while deer were plentiful.

When traveling in winter, according to Lieut. Ray, they prefer frozen fish or a sort of pemmican made as follows: The marrow is extracted from reindeer bones by boiling, and to a quantity of this is added 2 or 3 pounds of crushed seal or whale blubber, and the whole beaten up with the hands in a large wooden bowl to the consistency of frozen cream. Into this they stir bits of boiled venison, generally the poorer portions of the meat scraped off the bone, and chewed up small by all the women and children of the family, "each using some cabalistic word as they cast in their mouthful."[1] The mass is made up into 2-pound balls and carried in little sealskin bags. Flour, when obtained, is made into a sort of porridge, of which they are very fond. Cooking is mostly done outside of the dwelling, in the open air in summer, or in kitchens opening out of the passageway in winter. Little messes only, like an occasional dish of soup or porridge, are cooked over the lamps in the house. This habit, of course, comes from the abundant supply of firewood, while the Eskimo most frequently described live in a country where wood is very scarce, and are obliged to depend on oil for fuel.

Time and frequency of eating.—When these people are living in the winter houses they do not, as far as we could learn, have any regular time for meals, but eat whenever they are hungry and have leisure. The women seem to keep a supply of cooked food on hand ready for any one to eat. When the men are working in the kû′dyĭgi, or " club house," or when a number of them are encamped together in tents, as at the whaling camp in 1883, or the regular summer camp at Pe′rnyû, the women at intervals through the day prepare dishes of meat, which the

_____

[1] Lieut. Ray's MS. notes.

men eat by themselves.   When in the deer-hunting camps, according
to Lieut. Ray, they eat but little in the morning, and can really be said
to take no more than one full meal a day, which is eaten at night when
the day's work is done.[1]   When on the march they usually take a few
mouthfuls of the pemmican above described before they start out in
the morning, and rarely touch food again till they go into camp at
night.

When a family returns from the spring deer hunt with plenty of venison they usually keep open house for a day or two.   The women of the
household, with sometimes the assistance of a neighbor or two, keep
the pot continually boiling, sending in dishes of meat at intervals,
while the house is full of guests who stay for a short time, eating,
smoking, and chatting, and then retire to make room for others.   Messes
are sometimes sent out to invalids who can not come to the feast.   One
household in the spring of 1883 consumed in this way two whole reindeer in 24 hours.   They use only their hands and a knife in eating meat,
usually filling the mouth and cutting or biting off the mouthful.   They
are large eaters, some of them, especially the women, eating all the time
when they have plenty, but we never saw them gorge themselves in the
manner described by Dr. Kane (2d Grinnell Exp., passim) and other
writers.

Their habits of hospitality prevent their laying up any large supply
of meat, though blubber is carefully saved for commercial use, and they
depend for subsistence, almost from day to day, on their success in
hunting.   When encamped, however, in small parties in the summer they
often take more seals than they can consume.   The carcasses of these,
stripped of their skins and blubber, are buried in the gravel close to the
camp, and dug up and brought home when meat becomes scarce in the
winter.

DRINKS.

The habitual drink is water, which these people consume in great
quantities when they can obtain it, and like to have very cold.   In the
winter there is always a lump of clean snow on a rack close to the lamp,
with a tub under it to catch the water that drips from it.   This is replaced in the summer by a bucket of fresh water from some pond or
lake.   When the men are sitting in their open air clubs at the summer
camps there is always a bucket of fresh water in the middle of the circle, with a dipper to drink from.   Hardly a native ever passed the station without stopping for a drink of water, often drinking a quart of
cold water at a time.   When tramping about in the winter they eat
large quantities of ice and snow, and on the march the women carry
small canteens of sealskin, which they fill with snow and carry inside
of their jackets, where the heat of the body melts the snow and keeps

---

[1] "They have no set Time for Meals, but every one eats when he is hungry, except when they go to
sea, and then their chief Repast is a supper after they are come home in the Evening." (Egede, Greenland, p. 135. Compare also, Crantz, vol. 1, p. 145.)

it liquid. This great fondness for plenty of cold water has been often noticed among the Eskimo elsewhere, and appears to be quite characteristic of the race.[1] They have acquired a taste for liquor, and like to get enough to produce intoxication. As well as we could judge, they are easily affected by alcohol. Some of them during our stay learned to be very fond of coffee, "ka'fe," but tea they are hardly acquainted with, though they will drink it. I have noticed that they sometimes drank the water produced by the melting of the sea ice along the beach, and pronounced it excellent when it was so brackish that I found it quite undrinkable.

NARCOTICS.

The only narcotic in use among these people is tobacco, which they obtain directly or indirectly from the whites, and which has been in use among them from the earliest time when we have any knowledge of them. When Mr. Elson, in the *Blossom's* barge, visited Point Barrow, in 1826, he found tobacco in general use and the most marketable article.[2] This undoubtedly came from the Russians by way of Siberia and Bering Strait, as Kotzebue found the natives of the sound which bears his name, who were in communication with the Asiatic coast by way of the Diomedes, already addicted to the use of tobacco in 1816. It is not probable that tobacco was introduced on the Arctic coast by way of the Russian settlements in Alaska. There were no Russian posts north of Bristol Bay until 1833, when St. Michael's Redoubt was built. When Capt. Cook visited Bristol Bay, in 1778, he found that tobacco was not used there,[3] while in Norton Sound, the same year, the natives "had no dislike to tobacco."[4] Neither was it introduced from the English posts in the east, as Franklin found the "Kûñmû'dlĭû" not in the habit of using it—"The western Esquimaux use tobacco, and some of our visitors had smoked it, but thought the flavor very disagreeable,"[5]—nor had they adopted the habit in 1837.[6]

When the *Plover* wintered at Point Barrow, according to Dr. Simpson's account,[7] all the tobacco, except a little obtained from the English discovery ships, came from Asia and was brought by the Nunatañmiun. At present the latter bring very little if any tobacco, and the supply is obtained directly from the ships, though a little occasionally finds its way up the coast from the southwest.

---

[1] See, for instance, Egede: "Their Drink is nothing but Water" (Greenland, p. 134), and, "Furthermore, they put great Lumps of Ice and Snow into the Water they drink, to make it cooler for to quench their Thirst" (p. 135). "Their drink is clear water, which stands in the house in a great copper vessel, or in a wooden tub. * * * They bring in a supply of fresh water every day * * * and that their water may be cool they choose to lay a piece of ice or a little snow in it" * * * (Crantz, vol. 1, p. 144). Compare, also, Parry, 2d voy., p. 506, where the natives of Iglulik are said to drink a great deal of water, which they get by melting snow, and like very cold. The same fondness for water was observed by Nordenskiöld in Siberia (Vega, vol. 2, p. 114)

[2] Beechey, Voyage, p. 308.

[3] Third Voyage, vol. 2, p. 437.

[4] Ibid, 2, p. 479.

[5] Second Exp., p. 130.

[6] See T. Simpson, Narrative, p. 156.

[7] Op. cit., pp., 235, 236, 266.

They use all kinds of tobacco, but readily distinguish and desire the sorts considered better by the whites. For instance, they were eager to get the excellent quality of "Navy" tobacco furnished by the Commissary Department, while one of our party who had a large quantity of exceedingly bad fine-cut tobacco could hardly give it away. A little of the strong yellow "Circassian" tobacco used by the Russians for trading is occasionally brought up from the southwest, and perhaps also by the Nunatañmiun, and is very highly prized, probably because it was in this form that they first saw tobacco. Snuff seems to be unknown; tobacco is used only for chewing and smoking. The habit of chewing tobacco is almost universal. Men, women, and even children, though the latter be but 2 or 3 years old and unweaned,[1] when tobacco is to be obtained, keep a "chew," often of enormous size, constantly in the mouth. The juice is not spit out, but swallowed with the saliva, without producing any signs of nausea. The tobacco is chewed by itself and not sweetened with sugar, as was observed by Hooper and Nordenskiöld among the "Chukches."[2] I knew but two adult Eskimo in Utkiavwĭñ who did not chew tobacco, and one of these adopted the habit to a certain extent while we were there.

Tobacco is smoked in pipes of a peculiar pattern called kui'nyʉ, of which the collection contains a series of ten specimens.

Of these, No. 89288 [705],[3] figured in Ray's Point Barrow Report, Ethnology, Pl. I, Fig. 1, will serve as a type. The bowl is of brass, neatly inlaid on the upper surface with a narrow ring of copper close to the edge, from which run four converging lines, 90° apart, nearly to the center. Round the under surface are also three concentric rings of copper. The wooden stem appears to be willow or birch, and is in two longitudinal sections, held together by the lashing of sealskin thong which serves to attach the bowl to the stem. This lashing was evidently put on wet and allowed to shrink on, and the ends are secured by tucking under the turns. The whipping at the mouthpiece is of fine sinew thread. A picker of steel for cleaning out the bowl is attached to the stem by a piece of seal thong, the end of which is wedged under the turns of the lashing. The remaining pipes are all of the same general pattern, but vary in the material of the bowl and in details of execution. The stems are always of the same material and put together in the same way, but are sometimes lozenge-shaped instead of elliptical in section. The lashing is sometimes of three-ply sinew braid. The bowl shows the greatest variation, both in form and material.

Fig. 6a (No. 56737 [10], from Utkiavwĭñ) has an iron bowl, noticeable for the ornamentation of the shank. The metal work has all been done with the file except the fitting of the saucer to the shank. This has evidently been heated and shrunk on. Three pipes have bowls of

---

[1] Compare J. Simpson, op. cit., p. 250, and Nordenskiöld, Vega, vol. 2, p. 116.

[2] Tents, etc., p. 83; Vega, vol. 2, p. 116.

[3] The numbers first given are those of the National Museum; the numbers in brackets are those of the collector.

smoothly ground stone. No. 89289 [1582] (Fig. 6b from Utkiavwĭñ) is of rather soft greenish gray slate. No. 89290 [864] is of the same shape, but of hard greenish stone, while the third stone pipe (No. 89291 [834], from Utkiavwĭñ), of gray slate, is of quite a different pattern. Three of the series have bowls of reindeer antler, lined with thin sheet brass, and one a bowl of walrus ivory, lined with thin copper. (See Fig. 6c, Nos. 89285 [954], 89286 [915], and 89287 [1129].)

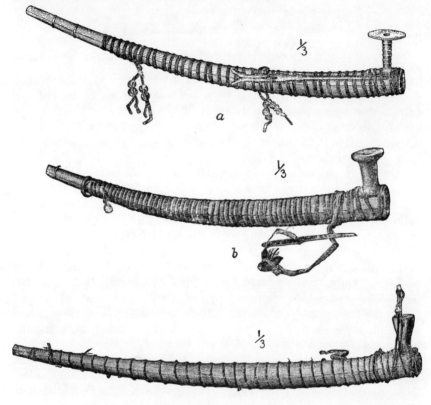

FIG. 6.—Pipes: a, pipe with metal bowl; b, pipe with stone bowl; c, pipe bowl of antler or ivory.

Antler and stone pipes of this pattern and rather small are usually carried by the men out of doors, while the more elaborate metal pipes, which are often very large and handsome (I have seen some with a saucer at least 3 inches in diameter) are more frequently used in the house and by the women. The stem is usually 1 foot or 13 inches long, though pipes at least 18 inches long were seen.

To most pipes are attached pickers, as in the type specimen. The picker is in all cases of metal, usually iron or steel, but sometimes of copper (see the pickers attached to pipes above). When not in use the point is tucked under the lashing on the stem. The pipes are readily taken apart for cleaning.

No. 89292 [1752] (Fig. 7) is an extemporized pipe made in a hurry by a man who wished to smoke, but had no pipe.

It is simply a rough willow stick, slightly whittled into shape, split and hollowed out like a pipestem. It is held together by a whipping of sinew thread and a lashing of deerskin thong, fastened by a slip-

FIG. 7.—Pipe made of willow stick.

knot at one end, the other being tucked in as usual. A small funnel-shaped hole at one end serves for a bowl, and shows by its charred surface that it has been actually used. This pipe was bought from one of the "Nunatañmiun," who were in camp at Pernyû in 1883, and shows its inland origin in the use of the deerskin thong. A coast native would have used seal thong.

The pipe is carried at the girdle, either with the stem thrust inside the breeches or in a bag attached to the belt. No. 56744 [55] (Utkiavwĭñ) is the only specimen of pipe bag in the collection. It is a long, narrow, cylindric bag, made of four white ermine skins, with two hind legs and two tails forming a fringe round the bottom, which is of dressed deerskin, in one piece, flesh side out. The band round the mouth is of gray deerskin, running only two-thirds of the way round. The piece which fills the remaining third runs out into the strap for fastening the bag to the belt. The ornamental strips on two of the longitudinal seams and round the bottom are of deerskin. The seams are all sewed "over and over" on the "wrong" side with sinew thread. This is an unusually handsome bag.

Tobacco is carried in a small pouch of fur attached to the girdle, and tucked inside of the breeches, or sometimes worn under the jacket, slung round the neck by a string or the necklace. The collection contains three of these, of which No. 89803 [889] (Fig. 8a) will serve as a typical specimen.

It is made by sewing together two pieces of wolverine fur, hair out, of the same shape and size, and round the mouth of this a band of short-haired light-colored deerskin, also hair out, with the ends meeting at one side in a seam corresponding to one of the seams of the wolverine fur. The mouth is ornamented with a narrow band of wolverine fur, the flesh side, which is colored red, turned out. It is closed by a piece of seal thong about 5 inches long, one end of which is sewed to the middle of the seam in the deerskin band and the other passed through a large blue glass bead and knotted. This string is wound two or three times round the neck of the bag, and the bight of it tucked under the turns. The seams are all sewed "over and over" on the "wrong" side with sinew thread.

These tobacco pouches are usually of a similar pattern, often slightly narrowed at the neck, and generally fringed round the mouth with a narrow strip of wolverine fur as above. They are often ornamented with tags of wolverine fur on the seams (as in No. 89804 [1341, Fig. 8*b*]), and borders of different colored skin. No. 89805 [1350] is very elaborately ornamented. It is made of brown deerskin, trimmed with white deerskin clipped close and bordered with narrow braids of blue and red worsted, and little tags of the latter. According to Dr. Simpson,[1] these bags are called "del-la-mai'-yu." We neglected to obtain the proper names for them, as we always made use of the lingua franca "tiba' púksak," bag for tiba' (tobacco). No. 89903 [889] contains a specimen of tobacco as prepared for smoking by the Eskimo. This consists

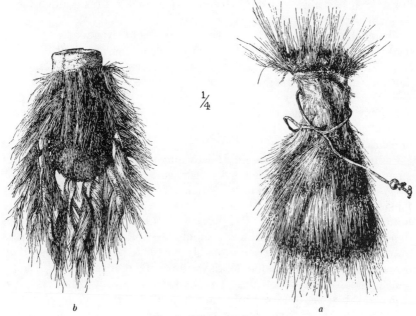

$\frac{1}{4}$

b   *a*

FIG. 8.—Tobacco pouches.

of common black Cavendish or "Navy" tobacco, cut up very fine, and mixed with finely chopped wood in the proportion of about two parts of tobacco to one of wood. We were informed that willow twigs were used for this purpose. Perhaps this may have some slight aromatic flavor, as well as serving to make the tobacco go further, though I did not recognize any such flavor in some tobacco from an Eskimo's pouch that I once smoked and found exceedingly bad. The smell of an Eskimo's

---

[1] Op. cit., p. 243.

pipe is different from any other tobacco smoke and is very disagreeable. It has some resemblance to the smell of some of the cheaper brands of North Carolina tobacco which are known to be adulterated with other vegetable substances. The method of smoking is as follows: After clearing out the bowl with the picker, a little wad of deer hair, plucked from the clothes in some inconspicuous place, generally the front skirt of the inner jacket, is rammed down to the bottom of the bowl. This is to prevent the fine tobacco from getting into the stem and clogging it up. The bowl is then filled with tobacco, of which it only holds a very small quantity. The mouthpiece is placed between the lips, the tobacco ignited, and all smoked out in two or three strong inhalations. The smoke is very deeply inhaled and allowed to pass out slowly from the mouth and nostrils, bringing tears to the eyes, often producing giddiness, and almost always a violent fit of coughing. I have seen a man almost prostrated from the effects of a single pipeful. This method of smoking has been in vogue since the time of our first acquaintance with these people.[1]

Though they smoke little at a time, they smoke frequently when tobacco is plentiful. Of late years, since tobacco has become plentiful, some have adopted white men's pipes, which they smoke without inhaling, and they are glad to get cigars, and, since our visit, cigarettes. In conversation with us they usually called all means for smoking "pai'pa," the children sometimes specifying "pai'pa-sigya'" (cigar) or "mûkpara-pai'pa," paper-pipe (cigarette). The use of the kui'nyɐ, which name appears to be applied only to the native pipes, seems to be confined to the adults. We knew of no children owning them, though their parents made no objection to their chewing tobacco or owning or using clay or wooden pipes which they obtained from us. They carry their fondness for tobacco so far that they will even eat the foul oily refuse from the bottom of the bowl, the smallest portion of which would produce nausea in a white man. This habit has been observed at Plover Bay, Siberia.[2] Tobacco ashes are also eaten, probably for the sake of the potash they contain, as one of the men at Utkiavwĩñ was fond of carbonate of soda, which he told the doctor was just like what he got from his pipe. Pipes of this type, differing in details, but all agreeing in having very small bowls, frequently of metal, and some contrivance for opening the stem, are used by the Eskimo from at least as far south as the Yukon delta (as shown by the collections in the National Museum) to the An-

---

[1] See T. Simpson: "Not content with chewing and smoking it, they swallowed the fumes till they became sick, and seemed to revel in a momentary intoxication." Point Barrow (1837), Narrative, p. 156. Also Kotzebue: "They chew, snuff, smoke, and even swallow the smoke." Kotzebue Sound (1816) Voyage, vol. 1, p. 237. Beechey also describes the people of Hotham Inlet in 1826 as smoking in the manner above described, obtaining the hair from a strip of dogskin tied to the pipe. Their tobacco was mixed with wood. Voyage, p. 300. Petitot (Monographie, etc., p. xxix) describes a precisely similar method of smoking among the Mackenzie Eskimos. Their tobacco was "melangé à de la ráclure de saule" and the pipe was called "kwiñeρk," (Vocabulaire, p. 54).

[2] See Hooper, Tents, etc., p. 177, and Dall, Alaska. p. 81.

derson River and Cape Bathurst,[1] and have even been adopted by the
Indians of the Yukon, who learned the use of tobacco from the Eskimo.
They are undoubtedly of Siberian origin, as will be seen by comparing
the figure of a "Chukch" pipe in Nordenskiöld's Vega, vol. 2, p. 117,
Fig. 7, and the figure of a Tunguse pipe in Seebohm's "Siberia in Asia"
(p. 149), with the pipes figured from our collection. Moreover, the
method of smoking is precisely that practiced in Siberia, even to the
proportion of wood mixed with the tobacco.[2]

The consideration of the question whence the Siberians acquired this
peculiar method of smoking would lead me beyond the bounds of the
present work, but I can not leave the subject of pipes without calling
attention to the fact that Nordenskiöld[3] has alluded to the resemblance
of these to the Japanese pipes. A gentleman who has spent many
years in China also informs me that the Chinese pipes are of a very
similar type and smoked in much the same way.[4] The Greenlanders
and eastern Eskimo generally, who have learned the use of tobacco
directly from the Europeans, use large-bowled pipes, which they smoke
in the ordinary manner. In talking with us the people of Point Barrow
call tobacco " tiba' " or " tibakï," but among themselves it is still known
as ta'wak, which is the word found in use among them by the earliest
explorers.[5] "Tiba" was evidently learned from the American whalers,
as it was not in use in Dr. Simpson's time. It is merely an attempt to
pronounce the word tobacco, but has been adopted into the Eskimo

---

[1] This is an interesting fact, as it shows that the Eskimo from Demarcation Point east learned to
smoke from the people of Point Barrow, and not from the English or the northern Indians, who use
pipes "modeled after the clay pipes of the Hudson Bay Company." (Dall, Alaska, p. 81, Fig. A.)
They acquired the habit some time between 1837, when T. Simpson found them ignorant of the use of
tobacco (see reference above, p. 65), and 1849, when they were glad to receive it from Pullen and Hooper.
(Tents, etc., p. 258.) Petitot (Monographie, etc., p. xxvi) states that the Eskimo of the Mackenzie
informed him that the use of tobacco and the form of the pipe, with blue beads, labrets, and other things,
came through the neighbors from a distant land called "Nate'ρovik," which he supposes to mean St.
Michaels, but which, from the evidence of other travelers, is much more likely to mean Siberia.

The Eskimo geography, on which Fr. Petitot relies so strongly, is extremely vague west of Barter
Island, and savors of the fabulous almost as much as the Point Barrow stories about the eastern natives.
The evidence which leads Fr. Petitot to believe "Nate'ρovik" to be St. Michaels is rather peculiar.
The Mackenzie natives call the people who are nearest to Nate'ρovik on the north "the Sedentary."
Now, the people who live nearest to St. Michaels on the north are the "Sedentary American Tchu-
katchis "(!); therefore Nate'ρovik is probably St. Michaels. (" Le nom *Natépovik* semble convenir à
l'ancien fort russe Michaëlowski, en ce que la tribu innok la plus voisine de ce poste, vers le nord, est
désignée par nos Tchiglit sous le nom d' *Apkwam-méut* ou de Sédentaires; or telle est la position
géographique qui convient aux sédentaires Tchukatches américains, dont la limite la plus septen-
trionale, selon le capitaine Beechey, est la pointe Barrow.") A slight acquaintance with the work of
of Dall and other modern explorers in this region would have saved Fr. Petitot from this and some
other errors.

[2] See Wrangell, Narrative of an Expedition, etc., p. 58. "The Russians here [at Kolymsk, 1820]
smoke in the manner common to all the people of northern Asia; they draw in the tobacco smoke,
swallow it, and allow it to escape again by the nose and ears (!)." The tobacco is said to be mixed
with "finely powdered larch wood, to make it go further" (ibid.). See also Hooper, Tents, etc.: "Generally, I believe, about one-third part of wood is used" (pp. 176 and 177; and Nordenskiöld, Vega, vol.
2, p. 116.)

[3] See also Petitot, Monographie, etc., p. xxix.

[4] See Beechey, Voyage, p. 323; T. Simpson, Narrative, p. 156—"tobacco, which * * * they call
tawāc, or tawākh, a name acquired of course from Russian traders;" Hooper, Tents, etc., p. 239; also
Maguire and J. Simpson, loc. cit. passim. Petitot calls ta'wak "mot français corrompu "!

language sufficiently to be used as the radical in compound words such as "tiba'xutikă'ktûñɐ," "I have a supply of tobacco." There is no evidence that anything else was smoked before the introduction of tobacco, and no pipes seen or collected appear older than the time when we know them to have had tobacco.[1]

HABITATIONS.

The winter house (*ĭ'glu*).—The permanent winter houses are built of wood[2] and thickly covered with clods of earth. Each house consists of a single room, nearly square, entered by an underground passage about 25 feet long and 4 to 4½ feet high. The sloping mound of earth which

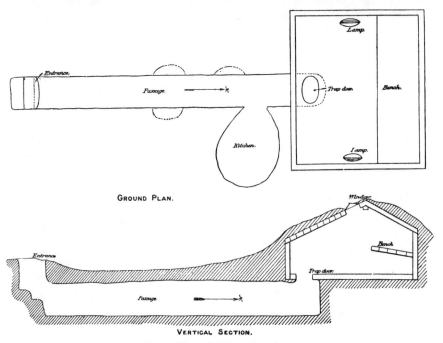

GROUND PLAN.

VERTICAL SECTION.

FIG. 9.—Plans of Eskimo winter house.

covers the house, grading off insensibly to the level of the ground, gives the houses the appearance of being underground, especially as the land on which they stand is irregular and hilly. Without very careful measurements, which we were unable to make, it is impossible to tell whether the floor is above or below the surface of the ground. It is certainly not very far either way. I am inclined to think that a space

---

[1] Since the above was written, the word for pipe, "kuinyɐ," has been found to be of Siberian origin. See the writer's article "On the Siberian origin of some customs of the Western Eskimos" (American Anthropologist, vol. 1, pp. 325–336).

[2] In some of the older houses, the ruins of which are still to be seen at the southwest end of the village of Utkiavwĭñ, whales' bones were used for timbers. Compare Lyon Journal, p. 171, where the winter huts at Iglulik are described as "entirely constructed of the bones of whales, unicorns, walruses, and smaller animals," with the interstices filled with earth and moss.

at or near the top of a hillock is simply leveled to receive the floor. In this case the back of the house on a hill side, like some in Utkiavwĭñ, would be underground.

The passage is entered at the farther end by a vertical shaft about 6 feet deep in the center of a steep mound of earth. Round the mouth is a square frame or combing of wood, and blocks of wood are placed in the shaft to serve as steps. One or two houses in Utkiavwĭñ had ship's companion ladders in the shaft. This entrance can be closed with a piece of walrus hide or a wooden cover in severe weather or when the family is away. The passage is about 4 feet wide and the sides and

Fig. 10.—Interior of iglu, looking toward door.

roof are supported by timbers of whalebone. On the right hand near the inner end is a good-sized room opening from the passage, which has a wooden roof covered with earth, forming a second small mound close to the house, with a smoke hole in the middle, and serves as a kitchen, while various dark and irregular recesses on the other side serve as storerooms. The passage is always icy and dark.

At the inner end of the passage a circular trapdoor in the floor opens into the main room of the house, close to the wall at the middle of one end. The floor is at such a height from the bottom of the tunnel that a man standing erect in the tunnel has his head and shoulders in the room. These rooms vary somewhat in dimensions, but are generally about 12 or 14 feet long and 8 or 10 feet wide. The floor, walls, and roof are made of thick planks of driftwood, dressed smooth and neatly fitted together, edge to edge. The ridgepole runs across the house and the roof slopes toward each end. The two slopes are unequal, the front, or that towards the entrance, being considerably the longer. The walls are vertical, those at the ends being between 3 and 4 feet high, while the sides run up to 6 or 7 feet at the ridgepole. The wall planks run up and down, and those of the roof from the ridge to the ends of the house, where there is a stout horizontal timber. In some houses the walls are made of paneled bulkheads from some wrecked whaler.

In the front of the house over the trapdoor there are no planks for a space of about 2 feet. The lower part of this space is filled in with short transverse beams, so as to leave a square hole close to the ridge. This hole has a stout transverse beam at the top and bottom and serves as a window. When the house is occupied it is covered by a translucent membrane made of strips of seal entrail sewed together and stretched

Fig. 11.—Interior of iglu, looking toward bench.

over two arched sticks of light wood—whalebone was used in Dr. Simpson's time[1]—running diagonally across from corner to corner. The window is closed with a wooden shutter when the house is shut up in winter, but both apertures are left open in summer. Just above the window, close to the ridgepole, is a little aperture for ventilation. Across the back of the room runs a platform or banquette, about 30 inches high in front and sloping back a little, which serves as a sleeping and lounging place. It is about 5 feet wide, and the front edge comes nearly under the ridgepole. It is made of thick planks running across the house, and supported at each end by a horizontal beam, the end of which projects somewhat beyond the bench and is supported by a round post. At each side of the house stands a lamp, and over these are suspended racks in the shape of small ladders for drying clothing,[2] etc. Deerskin blankets

---

[1] Op. cit., p. 256.
[2] Compare Hooper, Tents, etc., p. 46: "Small lattice shelves * * * on which moccasins * * * are put to dry." Plover Bay. See also plate to face p. 160 Parry's Second Voyage.

for the bed, which are rolled up and put under the bench when not in use, and a number of wooden tubs of various sizes—I counted nine tubs and buckets in one house in Utkiavwiñ—complete the furniture.

Two families usually occupy such a house, in which case each wife has her own end of the room and her own lamp, near which on the floor she usually sits to work. Some houses contain but one family and others more. I knew one house in Utkiavwiñ whose regular occupants were thirteen in number, namely, a father with his wife and adopted daughter, two married sons each with a wife and child, his widowed sister with her son and his wife, and one little girl. This house was also the favorite stopping-place for people who came down from Nuwŭk to spend the night. The furniture is always arranged in the same way. There is only one rack on the right side of the house and two on the left. Of these the farther from the lamp is the place for the lump of snow. In this same corner are kept the tubs, and the large general chamber pot and the small male urinal are near the trap door. Dishes of cooked meat are also kept in this corner. This leaves the other corner of the house vacant for women visitors, who sit there and sew. Male visitors, as well as the men of the house when they have nothing to do, usually sit on the edge of the banquette.

In sleeping they usually lie across the banquette with their feet to the wall, but sometimes, when there are few people in the house, lie lengthwise, and occasionally sleep on the floor under the banquette. Petitot says that in the Mackenzie region only married people sleep with their heads toward the edge of the banquette. Children and visitors lie with their heads the other way.[1] (See Fig. 9, ground plan and section of house, and Figs. 10 and 11, interior, from sketches by the writer. For outside see Fig. 12, from a photograph by Lieut. Ray).

At the back of the house is a high oblong scaffolding, made by setting up tall poles of driftwood, four, six, or eight in number, and fastening on cross pieces about 8 or 10 feet from the ground, usually in two tiers, of which the lower supports the frames of the kaiaks and the upper spears and other bulky property. Nothing except very heavy articles, such as sledges, boxes, and barrels, is ever left on the ground. A man can easily reach this scaffold from the top of the house, but it is high enough to be out of reach of the dogs. The cross pieces are usually supported on crotches made by lashing the lower jaw of a walrus to the pole, so that one ramus lies along the latter. Scaffolds of this sort, usually spoken of as "caches" or "cache frames," are of necessity used among the Eskimos generally, as it is the only way in which they can protect their bulky property.[2]

---

[1] Monographie, etc., p. xxiii.

[2] See for instance, Crantz, History of Greenland, vol. 1, p. 141; Franklin, 1st Exped., vol. 2, p. 194 (Coppermine River); 2d Exped., p. 121 (Mouth of the Mackenzie, where they are made of drift logs stuck up so that the roots serve as crotches to hold the cross pieces); Hooper, Tents, etc., pp. 48, 228, and 343 (Plover Bay, Point Barrow, and Toker Point); J. Simpson, op. cit., p. 256 (Point Barrow); Nordenskiöld, Vega, vol. 2, p. 92 (Pitlekaj).

Around Norton Sound, however, they use a more elaborate structure, consisting of a regular little house 6 feet square, raised 6 to 10 feet from the ground on four posts.[1]

Belonging to each household, and usually near the house, are low scaffolds for the large boats, rows of posts for stretching lines of thong, and one or more small cellars or underground rooms framed with whales' bones, the skull being frequently used for a roof, which serve as store-houses for blubber. These may be called "blubber rooms."

These winter houses can only be occupied when the weather is cold enough to keep the ground hard frozen. During the summer the passageways are full of water, which freezes at the beginning of winter

Fig. 12.—House in Utkiavwiñ.

and is dug out with a pickax. The people of Utkiavwiñ began to come to us to borrow our pickax to clean out their iglus about September 24, 1882, and all the houses were vacated before July 1, both seasons.

This particular form of winter house, though in general like those built by other Eskimo, nevertheless differs in many respects from any described elsewhere. For instance, the Greenland house was an oblong flat-roofed building of turf and stones, with the passageway in the middle of one side instead of one end, and not underground. Still, the door and windows were all on one side, and the banquette or "brix" only on the side opposite the entrance. The windows were formerly made of seal entrails, and the passage, though not underground, was still lower than the floor of the house, so that it was necessary to step up at each end.[2]

A detailed description of the peculiar communal house of the East

[1] Dall, Alaska, p. 13.

[2] Egede, Greenland, p. 114; Crantz, History of Greenland, vol. 1, p. 139; Rink, Tales and Traditions, p. 7.

Greenlanders, of which there is only one at each village, will be found in Capt. Holm's paper in the Geografisk Tidskrift, vol. 8, pp. 87–89. This is the long house of West Greenland, still further elongated till it will accommodate "half a score of families, that is to say, 30 to 50 people." John Davis (1586) describes the houses of the Greenlanders "neere the Sea side," which were made with pieces of wood on both sides, and crossed over with poles and then covered over with earth.[1]

At Iglulik the permanent houses were dome shaped, built of bones, with the interstices filled with turf, and had a short, low passage.[2] No other descriptions of permanent houses are to be found until we reach the

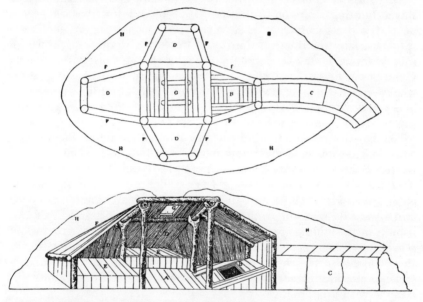

FIG. 13.—Ground plan and section of winter house in Mackenzie region.

people of the Mackenzie region, who build houses of timbers, of rather a peculiar pattern, covered with turf, made in the form of a cross, of which three or all four of the arms are the sleeping rooms, the floor being raised into a low banquette.[3] (See Fig. 13.) Petitot[4] gives a very excellent detailed description of the houses of the Anderson River people. According to his account the passageway is built up of blocks of ice. He mentions one house with a single alcove like those at Point Barrow.[5]

We have no description of the houses at the villages between Point Barrow and Kotzebue Sound, but at the latter place was found the

---

[1] Hakluyt, Voyages, etc. (1589), p. 788.

[2] Lyon, Journal, p. 171.

[3] See Fig. 13, ground plan and section, copied from Petitot, Monographie, etc., p. XXIII.

[4] Monographie, etc., p. XXI.

[5] See also Franklin, 2d Exped., p. 121 (Mouth of the Mackenzie), and pp. 215 and 216 (Atkinson Island, Richardson. A ground plan and section closely resembling Petitot's are given here); and Hooper, Tents, etc., p. 243 (Toker Point).

large triple house described by Dr. Simpson, and compared by him
with that described by Richardson, though in some respects it more
closely resembles those seen by Hooper.[1] This house really has a fire-
place in the middle, and in this approaches the houses of the southern
Eskimo of Alaska. According to Dr. Simpson,[2] "a modification of the
last form, built of undressed timber, and sometimes of very small dimensions, with two recesses opposite each other, and raised a foot above the
middle space, is very common on the shores of Kotzebue Sound," but he
does not make it plain whether houses like those used at Point Barrow
are not used there also.

This form of house is very like the large snow houses seen by Lieut.
Ray at hunting camps on Kulugrua. Dr. Simpson describes less permanent structures which are used on the rivers, consisting of small trees
split and laid "inclining inward in a pyramidal form towards a rude
square frame in the center, supported by two or more upright posts.
Upon these the smaller branches of the felled trees are placed, and the
whole, except the aperture at the top and a small opening on one side,
is covered with earth or only snow."[2] These buildings, and especially
the temporary ones described by Dr. Simpson, used on the Nunatak,
probably gave rise to the statement we heard at Point Barrow that
"the people south had no iglus and lived only in tents." The houses at
Norton Sound are quite different from the Point Barrow form. The
floor, which is not planked, is 3 or 4 feet under ground, and the passage
enters one side of the house, instead of coming up through the floor,
and a small shed is built over the outer entrance to the passage. The fire
is built in the middle of the house, under the aperture in the roof which
serves for chimney and window, and there is seldom any banquette, but
the two ends of the room are fenced off by logs laid on the ground, to
serve as sleeping places, straw and spruce boughs being laid down and
covered with grass mats.[3]

The houses in the Kuskokwim region are quite similar to those just
described, but are said to be built above ground in the interior, though
they are still covered with sods.[4] There are no published accounts of the
houses of the St. Lawrence islanders, but they are known to inhabit subterranean or partly underground earth-covered houses, built of wood,
while the Asiatic Eskimo have abandonded the old underground houses,
which were still in use at the end of the last century, and have adopted
the double-skin tent of the Chukches.[5] In addition to the cases quoted by
Dall, Capt. Cook speaks of finding the natives of St. Lawrence Bay in
1778 living in partly underground earth-covered houses.[6]

---

[1] See ante.
[2] Op. cit., p. 258.
[3] Dall, Alaska, pp. 13 and 14, diagram on p. 13.
[4] Petroff, Report, etc., p.15.
[5] See Dall, Cont. to N. A. Ethn., vol. 1, p. 105. Mr. E. W. Nelson tells me, however, that the village
at East Cape, Siberia, is composed of real iglus.
[6] Third Voyage, vol. 2, p. 450.

Arrangement in villages.—The village of Utkiavwĭñ occupies a narrow strip of ground along the edge of the cliffs of Cape Smyth, about 1,000 yards long, and extending some 150 yards inland. The houses are scattered among the hillocks without any attempt at regularity and at different distances from each other, sometimes alone, and sometimes in groups of two contiguous houses, which often have a common cache frame. Nuwŭk, from Dr. Simpson's account[1] and what we saw in our hurried visits, is scattered in the same way over the knolls of Point Barrow, but has its greatest extension in an east and west direction. From Simpson's account (ibid.) double houses appear more common at Nuwŭk than at Utkiavwĭñ, and he even speaks of a few threefold ones. All the houses agree in facing south. This is undoubtedly to admit the greatest amount of light in winter, and seems to be a tolerably general custom, at least among the northern Eskimo.[2]

The custom of having the dwelling face south appears to be a deeply rooted one, as even the tents in summer all face the same way.[3]

The tents on the sandspit at Plover Bay all face west. The same was observed by the Krause brothers at East Cape.[4] At Utkiavwĭñ there are twenty-six or twenty-seven inhabited houses. The uninhabited are mostly ruins and are chiefly at the southwest end of the village, though the breaking away of the cliffs at the other end has exposed the ruins of a few other old houses. Near these are also the ruins of the buildings destroyed by the ice catastrophe described above (p. 31). The mounds at the site of the United States signal station are also the ruins of old iglus. We were told that "long ago," before they had any iron, five families who "talked like dogs" inhabited this village. They were called Isû′tkwamiun. Similar mounds are to be seen at Pernyû, near the present summer camp. About these we only learned that people lived there "long ago." We also heard of ruined houses on the banks of Kulugrua.

Besides the dwellings there are in Utkiavwĭñ three and in Nuwŭk two of the larger buildings used for dancing, and as workrooms for the men, so often spoken of among other Eskimo.

Dr. Simpson states[5] that they are nominally the property of some of the more wealthy men. We did not hear of this, nor did we ever hear the different buildings distinguished as "So-and-so's," as I am inclined to think would have been the case had the custom still prevailed. They are called kû′dyĭgi or kû′drĭgi (karrigi of Simpson), a word which corresponds, mutatis mutandis, with the Greenlandic kagsse, which means, first, a circle of hills round a small deep valley, and then a circle of

[1] Op. cit., p. 256.
[2] For example, I find it mentioned in Greenland by Kane, 1st Grinnell Exp., p. 40; at Iglulik by Parry, 2d Voy., p. 499; and at the mouth of the Mackenzie by Franklin, 2d Exp., p. 121, as well as by Dr. Simpson at Nuwŭk, op. cit., p. 256.
[3] Frobisher says the tents in Meta Incognita (in 1577) were "so pitched up, that the entrance into them, is alwaies South, or against the Sunne." Hakluyt's Voyages, etc., (1589) p. 628.
[4] Geographische Blätter, vol. 5, p. 27.
[5] Op. cit., p. 259.

people who sit close together (and then, curiously enough, a brothel). At Utkiavwïñ they are situated about the middle of the village, one close to the bank and the others at the other edge of the village. They are built like the other houses, but are broader than long, with the ridgepole in the middle, so that the two slopes of the roof are equal, and are not covered with turf, like the dwellings, being only partially banked up with earth.

The one visited by Lieut. Ray on the occasion of the "tree dance" was 16 by 20 feet and 7 feet high under the ridge, and held sixty people. In the fall and spring, when it is warm enough to sit in the kû′dyïgi without fire and with the window open, it is used as a general lounging place or club room by the men. Those who have carpentering and similar work to do bring it there and others come simply to lounge and gossip and hear the latest news, as the hunters when they come in generally repair to the kû′dyïgi as soon as they have put away their equipments.

They are so fond of this general resort that when nearly the whole village was encamped at Imêkpûñ in the spring of 1883, to be near the whaling ground, they extemporized a club house by arranging four timbers large enough for seats in a hollow square near the middle of the camp. The men take turns in catering for the club, each man's wife furnishing and cooking the food for the assembled party when her husband's turn comes. The club house, however, is not used as a sleeping place for the men of the village, as it is said to be in the territory south of Bering Strait,[1] nor as a hotel for visitors, as in the Norton Sound region.[2] Visitors are either entertained in some dwelling or build temporary snow huts for themselves.

The kû′dyïgi is not used in the winter, probably on account of the difficulty of warming it, except on the occasions of the dances, festivals, or conjuring ceremonies. Crevices in the walls are then covered with blocks of snow, a slab of transparent ice is fitted into the window, and the house is lighted and heated with lamps. Buildings of this sort and used for essentially the same purposes have been observed among nearly all known Eskimo, except the Greenlanders, who, however, still retain the tradition of such structures.[3] Even the Siberian Eskimo, who have abandoned the iglu, still retained the kû′dyïgi until a recent date at least, as Hooper saw at Oong-wy-sac a performance in a "large tent, apparently erected for and devoted to public purposes (possibly as a council room as well as a theater, for in place of the

---

[1] Petroff, Report, etc., p. 128.

[2] Dall, Alaska, p. 16.

[3] See Rink, Tales and Traditions, p. 8; also Geografisk Tidskrift, vol. 8, p. 141. Speaking of buildings of this sort, Dr. Rink says: "Men i Grønland kjendes de vel kun af Sagnet. Paa Øer Disko vil man have paavist Ruinen af en saadan Bygning, som besynderlig nok særlig sagdes at have været benyttet til Festligheder af erotisk Natur." Boas, "The Central Eskimo," passim; Lyon, Journal, p. 325 (Iglulik); Richardson, in Franklin's 2d Exp., pp. 215–216 (Atkinson Island); Petitot, Monographie, etc., xxx; "Kéchim, ou maison des assemblées;" Beechey, Voyage, p, 268 (Point Hope); Dall, Alaska, p. 16 and elsewhere; Petroff, Rep. p. 128 and elsewhere.

usual inner apartments only a species of bench of raised earth ran round it)."[1] These buildings are numerous and particularly large and much used south of Bering Strait, where they are also used as steam bath houses.[2]

Snow houses (*apúya*).—Houses of snow are used only temporarily, as for instance at the hunting grounds on the rivers, and occasionally by visitors at the village who prefer having their own quarters. For example, a man and his wife who had been living at Nuwŭk decided in the winter of 1882–'83 to come down and settle at Utkiavwĭñ, where the woman's parents lived. Instead of going to one of the houses in the village, they built themselves a snow house in which they spent the winter. The man said he intended to built a wooden house the next season. These houses are not built on the dome or beehive shape so often described among the Eskimo of the middle region of Dr. Rink.[3]

The idea naturally suggests itself that this form of building is really a snow *tupek* or tent, while the form used at Point Barrow is simply the iglu built of snow instead of wood. When built on level ground, as in the village, the snow house consists of an oblong room about 6 feet by 12, with walls made of blocks of snow, and high enough for a person to stand up inside. Beams or poles are laid across the top, and over these is stretched a roof of canvas. At the south end is a low narrow covered passage of snow about 10 feet long leading to a low door not over 2½ feet high, above which is the window, made, as before described, of seal entrail. The opening at the outer end of the passage is at the top, so that one climbs over a low wall of snow to enter the house.

At the right side of the passage, close to the house, is a small fire-place about 2½ feet square and built of slabs of snow, with a smoke hole in the top and a stick stuck across at the proper height to hang a pot on. When the first fire is built in such a fireplace there is considerable melting of the surface of the snow, but as soon as the fire is allowed to go out this freezes to a hard glaze of ice, which afterwards melts only to a trifling extent. Opposite to the door of the house, which is protected by a curtain of canvas, corresponding to the Greenlandic ubkuaᴋ, "a skin which is hung up before the entrance of the house,"[4] the floor is raised into a banquette about 18 inches high, on which are laid boards and skins. Cupboards are excavated under the banquette, or in the walls, and pegs are driven into the walls to hang things on.

---

[1] Tents, etc., p. 136.

[2] See references to Dall and Petroff, above.

[3] Parry, 2nd Voy., p. 160 and plate opposite; Franklin, 1st Exped. vol. 2, pp. 43–47, ground plan, p. 46; Boas, "Central Eskimo," pp. 539–553; Kumlien, Contributions, etc., p. 31; Petitot, Monographie, etc., p. xvii (a full description with a ground plan and section on p. xix), and all the popular accounts of the Eskimo.

[4] Grønlandsk Ordbog, p. 404; Kane's 1st Grinnell Exp., p. 40, calls it a "skin-covered door." Compare, also, the skin or matting hung over the entrance of the houses at Norton Sound, Dall, Alaska, p. 13, and the bear-skin doors of the Nunatañmiun and other Kotzebue Sound natives, mentioned by Dr. Simpson, op. cit., p. 259.

As such a house is only large enough for one family, there is only one lamp, which stands at the right-hand side of the house[1].

At the hunting grounds, or on the road thither in the winter, a place is selected for the house where the snow is deeply drifted under the edge of some bank, so that most of the house can be made by excavation. When necessary, the walls are built up and roofed over with slabs of snow. Such a house is very speedily built. The first party that goes over the road to the hunting ground usually builds houses at the end of each day's march, and these serve for the parties coming later, who have simply to clear out the drifted snow or perhaps make some slight repairs. On arriving at the hunting ground they establish themselves in larger and more comfortable houses of the same sort; generally for two families. Lieut. Ray, who visited these camps, has drawn the plan represented in Fig. 14. There is a banquette, *a*, at each end of the room,

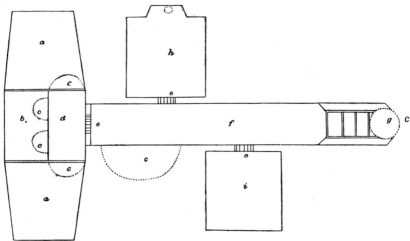

FIG. 14.—Ground plan of large snow house.

which is much broader than long (compare the form of house common at Kotzebue Sound, mentioned above, p. 78), but only one lamp, on a low shelf of snow, *b*, running across the back of the room and excavated below into a sort of cupboard. There are also similar cupboards, *c*, at different places in the walls, and a long tunnel, *f*, with the usual storerooms, *i*, and kitchen, *h*, from which a branch tunnel often leads to an adjoining house. The floor is marked *d*, the entrance to the tunnel *g*, and the door *e*. The house is lighted by the seal-gut windows of the iglu brought from the village.

On going into camp the railed sled is stuck points down into the snow and net-poles, or ice-picks, thrust through the rails, making a temporary cache frame,[2] on which are hung bulky articles—snowshoes and

[1] Compare Dr. Simpson's description, op. cit., p. 259.
[2] Compare the woodcut on p. 406, vol. 1, of Kane's 2d Exp., where two sleds are represented as stuck up on end with their "upstanders" meeting to form a platform—Smith Sound.

guns.[1] Small storehouses of snow or ice are built to contain provisions. In the autumn many such houses are built in the village, of slabs of clear fresh-water ice about 4 inches thick cemented together by freezing. These resemble the buildings of fresh-water ice at Iglulik, described by Capt. Lyon.[2]

Other temporary structures of snow, sometimes erected in the village, serve as workshops. One of these, which was built at the edge of the village in April, 1883, was an oblong building long enough to hold an umiak, giving sufficient room to get around it and work, and between 6 and 7 feet high. The walls were of blocks of snow and the roof of canvas stretched over poles. One end was left open, but covered by a canvas curtain, and a banquette of snow ran along each side. It was lighted by oblong slabs of clear ice set into the walls, and warmed by several lamps. Several men in succession used this house for repairing and rigging up their umiaks, and others who had whittling to do brought their work to the same place.

Such boat shops are sometimes built by digging a broad trench in a snowbank and roofing it with canvas. Women dig small holes in the snow, which they roof over with canvas and use for work-rooms in which to dress seal skins. In such cases there is probably some superstitious reason, which we failed to learn, for not doing the work in the iglu. The tools used in building the snow houses are the universal wooden snow-shovel and the ivory snow-knife, for cutting and trimming the blocks. At the present day saws are very much used for cutting the blocks, and also large iron knives (whalemen's "boarding knives," etc.) obtained from the ships.

Tents (*tupĕk*).—During the summer all the natives live in tents, which are pitched on dry places upon the top of the cliffs or upon the gravel beach, usually in small camps of four or five tents each. A few families go no farther than the dry banks just southwest of the village, while the rest of the inhabitants who have not gone eastward trading or to the rivers hunting reindeer are strung along the coast. The first camp below Utkiavwĭñ is just beyond the double lagoon of Nunava, about 4 miles away, and the rest at intervals of 2 or 3 miles, usually at some little inlet or stream at places called Sê'kqluka, Nakĕ'drixo, Kuosu'gru, Nună'ktuau, Ĭpersua, Wă'lăkpa (Refuge Inlet, according to Capt. Maguire's map, Parl. Rep. for 1854, opp. p. 186), Er'nĭvwĭñ, Sĭ'ñaru, and Sa'kămna. It is these summer camps seen from passing ships which have given rise to the accounts of numerous villages along this coast. There is usually a small camp on the beach at Sĭ'nnyû and one at Imê'kpûñ, while a few go to Pernyû even early in the season.

As the sea opens the people from the lower camps travel up the coast and concentrate at Pernyû, where they meet the Nuwuñmiun, the Nuna-

---

[1] Firearms can not be carried into a warm room in cold weather, as the moisture in the air immediately condenses on the cold surface of the metal.

[2] Journal, p. 204; see also the plate opposite p. 358 of Parry's 2d Voyage.

tañmiun traders, and the whalemen, and are joined later in the season by the trading parties returning from the east, all of whom stop for a few days at Pernyû. On returning to the village also, in September, the tents are pitched in dry places among the houses and occupied till the latter are dry enough to live in. Tents are used in the autumnal deer hunts, before snow enough falls to build snow houses. In the spring of 1883, when the land floe was very heavy and rough off Utkiavwĭñ, all who were going whaling in the Utkiavwĭñ boats went into camp with their families in tents pitched on the crown of the beach at Imêk pûñ, whence a path led off to the open water.

The tents are nowadays always made of cloth, either sailcloth obtained from wrecks or drilling, which is purchased from the ships. The latter is preferred as it makes a lighter tent and both dark blue and white are used. Reindeer or seal skins were used for tents as lately as 1854. Elson saw tents of sealskin lined with reindeer skin at Refuge Inlet,[1] and Hooper mentions sealskin tents at Cape Smyth and Point Barrow.[2] Dr. Simpson gives a description of the skin tents at Point Barrow.[3] Indeed, it is probable that canvas tents were not common until after the great "wreck seasons" of 1871 and 1876, when so many whaleships were lost. The Nunatañmiun at Pernyû had tents of deerskin, and I remember also seeing one sealskin tent at the same place, which, it is my impression, belonged to a man from Utkiavwĭñ. Deerskin tents are used by the Anderson River natives,[4] while sealskins are still in use in Greenland and the east generally.[5] The natives south of Kotzebue Sound do not use tents, but have summer houses erected above ground and described as "generally log structures roofed with skins and open in front."[6] That they have not always been ignorant of tents is shown by the use of the word "topek" for a dwelling at Norton Sound.[7]

The tents at Point Barrow are still constructed in a manner very similar to that described by Dr. Simpson (see reference above). Four or five poles about 12 feet long are fastened together at the top and spread out so as to form a cone, with a base about 12 feet in diameter. Inside of these about 6 feet from the ground is lashed a large hoop, upon which are laid shorter poles (sometimes spears, umiak oars, etc.). The canvas cover, which is now made in one piece, is wrapped spirally round this

---

[1] Beechey's Voyage, p. 315.

[2] Tents, etc., pp. 216, 225.

[3] Op. cit., p. 260.

[4] MacFarlane MSS. and Petitot, Monographie, etc., p. xx, "des tentes coniques (*tuppepk*) en peaux de renne."

[5] See Rink, Tales, etc., p. 7 ("skins" in this passage undoubtedly means sealskins, as they are more plentiful than deerskins among the Greenlanders, and were used for this purpose in Egede's time—Green, land, p. 117; and Kumlien, op. cit., p. 33.). In east Greenland, according to Holm, "Om Sommeren bo Angsmagsalikerne i Telte, der ere betrukne med dobbelte Skind og have Tarmskinds Forhæng." Geogr. Tids., vol. 8, p. 89. In Frobisher's description of Meta Incognita (in 1577), he says: "Their houses are tents made of seale skins, pitched up with 4 Firre quarters, foure square, meeting at the toppe, and the skinnes sewed together with sinewes, and layd thereupon." Hakluyt's Voyages, etc. (1589), p. 628. See also Boas, "Central Eskimo."

[6] Petroff, op. cit., p. 128.

[7] Dall, Alaska, p. 13.

frame, so that the edges do not meet in front except at the top, leaving a triangular space or doorway, filled in with a curtain of which part is a translucent membrane, which can be covered at night with a piece of cloth.   A string runs from-the upper corner of the cloth round the apex of the tent and comes obliquely down the front to about the middle of the edge of the other end of the cloth.   The two edges are also held together by a string across the entrance.   Heavy articles, stones, gravel, etc., are laid on the flap of the tent to keep it down, and spears, paddles, etc., are laid up against the outside.   (See Fig. 15, from a photograph by Lieut. Ray.)

Inside of the tent there is much less furniture than in the iglu, as the lamp is not needed for heating and lighting, and the cooking is done outdoors on tripods erected over fires.   The sleeping place is at the

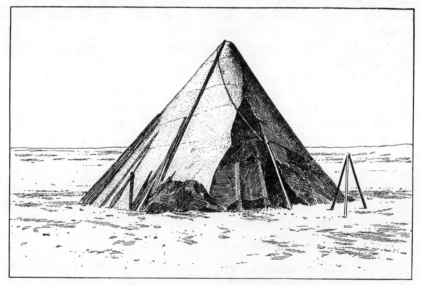

FIG. 15.—Tent on the beach at Utkiavwiñ.

back of the tent, and is usually marked off by laying a log across the floor, and spreading boards on the ground.   Not more than one family usually occupy a tent.   The tents at the whaling camp mentioned above were, at first, fitted out with snow passages and fireplaces like a snow hut, and many had a low wall of snow around them, but these had all melted before the camp was abandoned.

These tents differ considerably in model from those in use in the east, though all are made by stretching a cover over radiating poles.   For example, the tents in Greenland have the front nearly vertical,[1] while at Cumberland Gulf two sets of poles connected by a ridgepole are used, those for the front being the shorter.[2]   The fashion at Iglulik is some-

---

[1] Egede, Greenland, p. 117; Crantz, vol. 1, p. 141; Rink, Tales, etc., p. 7.
[2] Kumlien, op. cit., p. 33.

what similar.[1] Small rude tents only large enough to hold one or two, people are used as habitations for women during confinement, and for sewing rooms when they are working on deerskins in the autumn. Tents for the latter purpose are called "su'dliwĭñ," the place for working.

HOUSEHOLD UTENSILS.

FOR HOLDING AND CARRYING FOOD, WATER, ETC.

Canteens (i'mutĭn).—None of the canteens, the use of which has been described above (under "Drinks"), were obtained for the collection. They were seen only by Lieut. Ray and Capt. Herendeen, who made winter journeys with the natives. They describe them as made of seal-skins and of small size. I find no published mention of the use of such canteens among the Eskimo elsewhere, except in Baffin Land.[2]

Wallets, etc.—Food and such things are carried in roughly made bags of skin or cloth, or sometimes merely wrapped up in a piece of skin or entrail, or whatever is convenient. Special bags, however, are used for bringing in the small fish which are caught through the ice. These are flat, about 18 inches or 2 feet square, and made of an oblong piece of sealskin, part of an old kaiak cover, doubled at the bottom and sewed up each side, with a thong to sling it over the shoulders.

Buckets and tubs.—Buckets and tubs of various sizes are used for holding water and other fluids, blubber, flesh, entrails, etc., in the house,

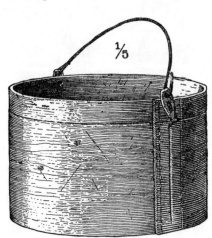

and are made by bending a thin plank of wood (spruce or fir) round a nearly circular bottom and sewing the ends together. These are probably all obtained from the Nunatañmiun, as it would be almost impossible to procure suitable wood at Point Barrow. The collection contains four specimens—two tubs and two buckets.

No. 56764 [370] (Fig. 16) will serve as a type of the water bucket (kûtau'ʁ). A thin strip of spruce 8 inches wide is bent round a circular bottom of the same wood 10¼ inches in diameter. The edge of the latter is slightly rounded and

FIG. 16.—Wooden bucket.

fits into a shallow croze one-fourth inch from the lower edge of the strip. The ends of the strip overlap 3½ inches and are sewed together with narrow strips of whalebone in two vertical seams of short stitches, one

---

[1] See Parry's 2nd Voyage, p. 271 and plate opposite. Compare also Chappell, "Hudson Bay," pp. 75–77, figure on p. 75.

[2] "When out traveling, they mostly carry their water supply in a seal's stomach, prepared for the purpose." Kumlien, op. cit., p. 41. Compare also Hall, Arctic Researches, p. 584.

seam close to the outer end, which is steeply chamfered off and painted red, and the other 1·6 inches from this. Both seams are countersunk in shallow grooves on the outer part. The bucket is ornamented with a shallow groove running round the top, and a vertical groove between the seams. These grooves and the seam grooves are painted red. The bail is of stout iron wire fastened on by two ears of white walrus ivory cut into a rude outline of a whale, and secured by neat lashings of whalebone passing through corresponding holes in the ear and the bucket. The bucket has been some time in use.

No. 56763 [369] is a bucket with a bail, and very nearly of the same shape and dimensions. It has, however, a bail made of rope yarns braided together, and the ears are plain flat pieces of ivory. Buckets of this size, with bails, are especially used for water, particularly for bringing it from the ponds and streams. The name "kûtaue" corresponds to the Greenlandic kátauaκ, "a water-pail with which water is brought to the house."[1]

No. 89891 [1735] (Fig. 17), which is nearly new, is a very large tub (ilulĭ'kpûñ, which appears to mean "a capacious thing") without a bail, and is 11 inches high and 20 in diameter.

FIG. 17.—Large tub.

The sides are made of two pieces of plank of equal length, whose ends overlap alternately and are sewed together as before. The bottom is in two pieces, one large and one small, neatly fastened together with two dowels, and is not only held in by having its edge chamfered to fit the croze, but is pegged in with fourteen small treenails. The seams, edges, and two ornamental grooves around the top are painted red as before.

No. 89890 [1753] is smaller, 9·7 inches high and 14·5 in diameter. It has no bail, and is ornamented with two grooves, of which the lower is painted with black lead. The bottom is in two equal pieces, fastened together with three dowels. This is a new tub and has the knotholes neatly plugged with wood. There are a number of these tubs in every house. They are known by the generic name of imusiáru (which is applied also to a barrel, and which means literally "an unusual cup or dipper," small cups of the same shape being called i'musyû), but have special names signifying their use. For instance, the little tub about 6 inches in diameter, used by the males as a urinal, is called kúvwĭñ ("the place for urine.") One of these large tubs always stands to catch the drip from the lump of snow in the house, and those of the largest size, like No. 89891 [1735], are the kind used as chamber pots.

Vessels of this sort are in use throughout Alaska, and have been observed among the eastern Eskimo where they have wood enough to

---

[1] Grønl. Ordbog., p. 135.

make them. For instance, the Eskimo of the Coppermine River "form very neat dishes of fir, the sides being made of thin deal, bent into an oval form, secured at the ends by sewing, and fitted so nicely to the bottom as to be perfectly water-tight."[1] There are specimens in the Museum from the Mackenzie and Anderson Rivers, described in the MacFarlane MS. as "pots for drinking with, pails for carrying and keeping water, and also as chamber pots. Oil is also sometimes carried in them in winter."

In some places where wood is scarce vessels of a similar pattern are made of whalebone. Vessels "made of whalebone, in a circular form, one piece being bent into the proper shape for the sides," are mentioned by Capt. Parry on the west shore of Baffins Bay,[2] and "circular and oval vessels of whalebone" were in use at Iglulik.[3] This is the same as the Greenlandic vessel called pertaᴋ (a name which appears to have been transferred in the form pĭ'túño to the wooden meat bowl at Point Barrow), "a dish made of a piece of whalebone bent into a hoop, which makes the sides, with a wooden bottom inserted."[4] Nordenskiöld speaks of vessels of whalebone at Pitlekaj, but does not specify the pattern.[5] Whalebone dishes were used at Point Barrow, but at the present day only small ones for drinking-cups are in general service. One large dish was collected. (Fig. 18. No. 89850 [1199]).

A strip of whalebone 4¼ inches wide is bent round a nearly circular bottom of cottonwood so as to form a small tub. The edges of the bot-

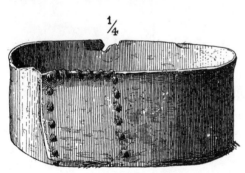

¼

FIG. 18.—Whalebone dish.

tom are chamfered to fit a shallow croze in the whalebone. The overlapping ends of the whalebone are sewed together with a strip of whalebone in long stitches. This dish is quite old and impregnated with grease. Vessels of this kind are uncommon, and it is probable that none have been made since whalebone acquired its present commercial value.

They were very likely in much more general use formerly, as when there was no such market for whalebone as at present it would be cheaper to make tubs of this material than to buy wooden ones. In corroboration of this view it may be noted that Dr. Simpson does not mention woodenware among the articles brought for sale by the Nunatañmiun.[6] The small whalebone vessels will be described under drinking cups, which see.

[1] Franklin, 1st Exp., vol. 2, p. 181.
[2] First Voy., p. 286.
[3] Second Voy., p. 503.

[4] Grønl. Ordbog., p. 293.
[5] Vega, vol. 2, p. 124.
[6] Op. cit., p. 266.

Meat bowls.—(Pĭ'tûño, see remarks on p. 88.) Large wooden bowls are used to hold meat, fat, etc., both raw and cooked, which are generally served on trays. These are of local manufacture and carved from blocks of soft driftwood. The four specimens collected are all made of cottonwood, and, excepting No. 73570 [408], have been long in use and are thoroughly impregnated with grease and blood.

No. 89864 [1322] (Fig. 19) will serve as the type. This is deep and nearly circular, with flat bottom and rounded sides. The brim is ornamented with seven large sky-blue glass beads imbedded in it at equal intervals, except on one side, where there is a broken notch in the place of a bead.

Another, No. 89863 [1320], is larger and not flattened on the bottom, and the brim is thinner. It is also provided with a bail of seal thong, very neatly made, as follows: One end of the thong is knotted with a single knot into one of the holes so as to leave one long part and one short part (about 3 inches). The long part is then carried across and through the

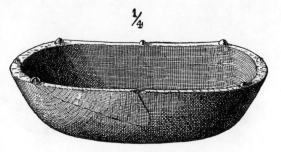

FIG. 19.—Meat bowl.

other hole from the outside, back again through the first hole and again across, so that there are three parts of thong stretched across the bowl. The end is then tightly wrapped in a close spiral round all the other parts, including the short end, and the wrapping is finished off by tucking the end under the last turn. The specimen shows the method of mending wooden dishes, boxes, etc., which have split. A hole is bored on each side of the crack, and through the two is worked a neat lashing of narrow strips of whalebone, which draws the parts together.

In No. 89865 [1321], which has been split wholly across, there are six such stitches, nearly equidistant, holding the two parts together. This bowl is strengthened by neatly riveting a thin flat "strap" of walrus ivory along the edge across the end of the crack. These three bowls are of nearly the same shape, which is the common one. The new bowl (No. 73570 [408]) is of a less common shape, being not so nearly hemispherical as the others, but shaped more like a common milk pan. It is ornamented with straight lines drawn in black lead, dividing the surface into quadrants. These were probably put on to catch the white man's eye, as the bowl was made for the market. Dishes of this description are common throughout Alaska (see the National Museum collections) and have been noted at Plover Bay.[1]

---

[1] Hooper, Tents, etc., p.147.

Pots of stone and other materials (*u'tkuziñ*).—In former times, pots of soapstone resembling those employed by the eastern Eskimo, and probably obtained from the same region as the lamps, were used for cooking food at Point Barrow, but the natives have so long been able to procure metal kettles directly or indirectly from the whites (Elson found copper kettles at Point Barrow in 1826)[1] that the former have gone wholly out of use, and at the present day fragments only are to be found. There are four such fragments in the collection, of which three are of the same model and one quite different.

No. 89885–6 [1559] (Fig. 20) is sufficiently whole to show the pattern of the first type. It is of soft gray soapstone. A large angular gap is broken from the middle of one side, taking out about half of this side,

¼

Fig. 20.—Stone pot

and a small angular piece from the bottom. From the corner of this gap the pot has been broken obliquely across the bottom, and mended in three places with stitches of whalebone made as described under No. 89865 [1321]. One end is cut down for about half its height, and the edge carried round in a straight line till it meets the gap in the broken side. This end appears to have been pieced with a fresh piece of stone, as there are holes for stitches in the edge of the whole side and in the upper edge of the broken side. There are also two "stitch holes" at the other side of the gap, showing how it was originally mended. A low transverse ridge across the middle of the whole end was probably an ornament. Holes for strings by which the pot was hung up are bored one-fourth to one-half inch from the brim. Two of these are bored obliquely through the corners, which are now broken off. The holes in the sides close to the corners were probably made to take the place of these. The pot is neatly and smoothly made, and the brim is slightly rounded. It shows signs of great age, and is blackened with soot and crusted with oil and dirt.[2]

Nos. 89886 [680] and 89868 [1096] are much less complete. They are the broken ends of pots slightly smaller than the above, but of precisely the same pattern, even to the ornamental transverse ridge across the end.[3] The string holes are bored through the corners as before, and

---

[1] Beechey's Voyage, p. 572.

[2] This specimen was broken in transportation, and the pieces received different Museum numbers. It is now mended with glue.

[3] Compare these pots with the two figured in Parry's 2d Voyage (plate opposite p. 160). The smaller of these has a ridge only on the end, but on the larger the ridge runs all the way round. The plate also shows how the pots were hung up. See also Fig. 1, plate opposite p. 548.

in both pots are holes showing where they have been mended by whalebone stitches, fragments of which are still sticking in one pot. This
method of mending soapstone vessels by sewing is mentioned by Capt.
Parry as practiced at Iglulik.[1]

No. 89883 [1097] (Fig. 21) is a small pot of a quite different shape,
best understood from the figure. Round the edge are eight holes for
strings nearly equidistant. The outside is rough, especially on the
bottom. One of the sides is much gapped, and the acute tip has been
broken off obliquely and mended with a stitch of whalebone. The care
used in mending these vessels shows that they were valuable and not
easily replaced. I can
find no previous mention
of the use of stone ves-
sels for cooking on the
western coast, and there
are no specimens in the
National Museum collec-
tions. The only Eskimo
stone vessels are a couple
of small stone bowls from
Bristol Bay. These are
very much the shape of

¼

FIG. 21.—Small stone pot.

the wooden bowls above described, and appear to have been used as oil
dishes and not for cooking, as the inside is crusted with grease, while the
outside is not blackened. On the other hand, stone cooking pots are
very generally employed even now by the eastern Eskimos, and have
been frequently described.[2] The close resemblance of the pots from
Point Barrow to those described by Capt. Parry, taken in connection
with Dr. Simpson's statement[3] that the stone lamps were brought from
the east, renders it very probable that the kettles were obtained in the
same way. The absence of this utensil among the southern Eskimo of
Alaska is probably due to the fact that being inhabitants of a well
wooded district they would have no need of contrivances for cooking
over a lamp.

I obtained three fragments of pottery, which had every appearance
of great age and were said to be pieces of a kind of cooking-pot which
they used to make "long ago, when there were no iron kettles." The
material was said to be earth (nu'na), bear's blood, and feathers,[4]
and appears to have been baked. They are irregular fragments (No.

[1] 2d Voyage, p. 502.

[2] I need only refer to Crantz, who describes the "bastard-marble kettle," hanging "by four strings
fastened to the roof, which kettle is a foot long and half a foot broad, and shaped like a longish box"
(vol. 1, p. 140); the passage from Parry's 2d Voyage, referred to above; Kumlien, op. cit., p. 20 (Cumberland Gulf); Boas, "Central Eskimo," p. 545; and Gilder, Schwatka's Search, p. 260 (West Shore
of Hudson Bay).

[3] Op. cit., pp. 267–269.

[4] Compare the cement for joining pieces of soapstone vessels mentioned by Boas ("Central Eskimo,"
p. 526) consisting of "seal's blood, a kind of clay, and dog's hair."

89697 [1589], Fig. 22) of perhaps more than one vessel, which appears to have been tall and cylindrical, perhaps shaped like a bean-pot, pretty smooth inside, and coated with dried oil or blood, black from age. The outside is rather rough, and marked with faint rounded transverse ridges, as if a large cord had been wound round the vessel while still soft. The largest shard has been broken obliquely across and mended with two stitches of sinew, and all are very old and black.

Beechey (Voyage, p. 295) speaks of "earthen jars for cooking" at Hotham Inlet in 1826 and 1827, and Mr. E. W. Nelson has collected a

FIG. 22.—Fragments of pottery.

few jars from the Norton Sound region, very like what those used at Point Barrow must have been. Choris figures a similar vessel in his Voyage Pittoresque, Pl. III (2d), Fig. 2, from Kotzebue Sound. Metal kettles of various sorts are now exclusively used for cooking, and are called by the same name as the old soapstone vessels, which it will be observed corresponds to the name used by the eastern Eskimo. Light sheet-iron camp-kettles are eagerly purchased and they are very glad to get any kind of small tin cans, such as preserved meat tins, which they use for holding water, etc., and sometimes fit with bails of string or wire, so as to use them for cooking porridge, etc., over the lamp. They had learned the value of these as early as Maguire's time,[1] as had the people of Plover Bay in 1849.[2]

Bone crushers.—In preparing food it is often desirable to break the large bones of the meat, both to obtain the marrow and to facilitate the trying out of the fat for making the pemmican already described. Deer bones are crushed into a sort of coarse bone-meal for feeding the dogs when traveling. For this purpose heavy short-handled stone mauls are used. These tools may have been formerly serviceable as hammers for driving treenails, etc., as the first specimen obtained was described as "savik-pidjûk-nunamisinĭ′ktuᴇ-kau′tᴇ" (literally "iron-not-dead-hammer"), or the hammer used by those now dead, who had no iron. For this purpose, however, they are wholly superseded by iron hammers, and are now only used for bone crushers. The collection contains a large series of these implements, namely, 13 complete mauls and 13 unhafted heads. All are constructed on the same general plan, consisting of an oblong roughly cylindrical mass of stone, with flat ends, mounted on the expanded end of a short haft, which is applied to the middle of one side of the cylinder and is slightly curved, like the handle of an adz. Such a haft is frequently made of the "branch" of a reindeer antler, and the expanded end is made by cutting off a portion of the "beam" where the branch joins it. A haft so made is naturally elliptical and slightly curved at right angles to the longer diameter of the ellipse, and is applied to the head so that the greatest thickness and therefore the greatest strength comes in the line of the blow, as in a civilized ax or hammer. The head and haft are held together by a lashing of thong or three-ply braid of sinew, passing through a large hole in the large end of the haft and round the head. This lashing is put on wet and dries hard and tight.[3] It follows the same general plan in all the specimens, though no two are exactly alike. The material of the heads, with three exceptions (No. 56631 [222], gray porphyry; No. 89654 [906], black quartzite, and No. 89655 [1241], coarse-grained gray syenite), is massive pectolite (see above, p. 60), generally of a pale greenish or bluish gray color and slightly translucent, sometimes dark and opaque. No. 56635 [243] will serve as the type of these implements.[4]

The head is of light bluish gray pectolite, and is lashed with a three-ply braid of reindeer sinew to a haft of some soft coniferous wood, probably spruce, rather smoothly whittled out and soiled by handling. The transverse ridge on the under side of the butt is to keep the hand from slipping off the grip. The whole is dirty and shows signs of considerable age.

---

[1] See Further Papers, etc., p. 909.

[2] Hooper, Tents, etc., p. 57.

[3] We saw this done on No. 56634 [83], the head and haft of which were brought in separate and put together by an Eskimo at the station.

[4] Figured in Ray's Point Barrow Report, Ethnology, Pl. II, Fig. 6.

These mauls vary considerable in size. The largest is 7·1 inches long and 2·5 in diameter, and the smallest 2·1 inches long by 2·4. This is a very small hammer, No. 56634 [83] having a haft only 4·7 inches long. The haft is usually about 5 inches long. The longest (belonging to one of the smaller heads, 4 inches by 2) is 7·2 inches long, and the shortest (belonging to a slightly larger head, 4·7 by 3·1 inches) is 4·5 inches. The largest two heads, each 7·1 by 2·5 inches, have hafts 5 inches long.

The lashing of all is put on in the same general way, namely, by securing one end round the head and through the eye, then taking a varia-

FIG. 23.—Stone maul.

ble number of turns round the head and through the hole, and tightening these up by wrapping the end spirally round all the parts, where they stretch from head to haft on each side. Seal thong, narrow or broad, is more generally used than sinew braid (only three specimens out of the thirteen have lashings of sinew). When broad thong is used the loop is made by splicing, as follows: A slit is cut about 1½ inches from the end of the thong, and the end is doubled in a bight and passed through this slit. The end is then slit and the other end of the thong passed through it and drawn taut, making a splice which holds all the tighter for drawing on it. A simple loop is tied in sinew braid.

The following figures will illustrate the most important variations in the form of this implement. Fig. 23, No. 56634 [83] from Utkiavwĭñ, has a head of light gray pectolite, slightly translucent, and evidently ground flat on the faces,

FIG. 24.—Stone maul.

and the haft is of reindeer antler, with a slight knob at the butt. A square piece of buckskin is doubled and inserted between the head and haft. The lashing is of fine sealskin twine, and the spiral wrapping is carried wholly round the head. This was the first stone maul collected, and was put together at the station, as mentioned above. It is rather smaller than usual. Fig. 24, No. 56637 [196], from Utkiavwĭñ, has the head of grayish pectolite, rough and unusually large. The haft is of some soft coniferous wood soaked with grease. It is nearly round, instead of elliptical, with an irregular knob at the butt, and not curved, but fastened obliquely to the head. The loop of double thong attached to the haft is probably to go round the wrist.

Fig. 25, No. 56639 [161], from Utkiavwĭñ, is of pectolite, the upper and lower faces almost black and the sides light gray. The haft is of

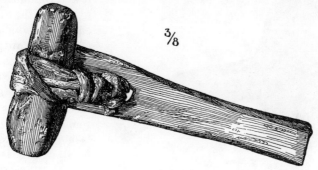

$\frac{3}{8}$

FIG. 25.—Stone maul.

hard wood and unusually long (7·2 inches). It is noticeable for being at-tached at right angles to the head, by a very stout lashing of thong of the usual kind, and further tightened by a short flat stick wedged in below the head on one side. There appears to have been a similar "key" on the other side. This is an unusual form.

Fig. 26, No. 89654 [906], is from Nuwŭk. The head is an oblong, nearly cylindrical, water-worn pebble of black quartzite, 7·1 inches long; the haft is of reindeer ant-ler, and the lashing of seal thong.

Fig. 27, No. 89655 [1241], from Utkiavwĭñ. The head of this maul is a long pebble of rather coarse-grained gray sy-enite, and is peculiar in having a shallow groove roughly worked out round the middle to keep the lashing from slip-ping. It is 4·7 inches long and 3·1 in diameter.

$\frac{3}{8}$

FIG. 26.—Stone maul.

The haft is of reindeer antler 4·5 inches long, and the lashing of seal thong peculiar only in the large number of turns in the spiral wrappings.

Fig. 28, No. 89657 [877], from Nuwŭk. This is peculiar in having the haft fitted into a deep angular groove on one side of the head, which is of pectolite and otherwise of the common pattern. The haft of reindeer antler and the lashing of broad thong are evidently newer than the head and are clumsily made and put on, the latter making several turns about one side of the haft as well as through it and round the head.

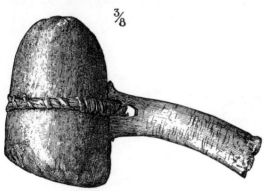

³⁄₈

None of the unmounted heads, which are all of pectolite, are grooved in this way to receive the haft, but No. 56658 [205] has two shallow, incomplete grooves round the middle for lashings, and No. 56655 [218], which is nearly square in section, has shallow notches on the edges for the same purpose. One specimen of the series comes from Sidaru, but differs in no way from specimens from the northern villages.

FIG. 27.—Stone maul.

Stone mauls of this type have previously been seldom found among the American Eskimo. The only specimens in the Museum from America are two small unhafted maul heads of pectolite, one from Hotham Inlet and the other from Cape Nome, and a roughly made maul from Norton Sound, all collected by Mr. Nelson. The last is an oblong piece of dark-colored jade rudely lashed to the end of a short thick stick, which has a lateral projection round which the lashing passes instead of through a

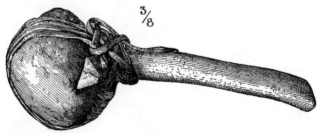

³⁄₈

FIG. 28.—Stone maul.

hole in the haft. Among the "Chukches" at Pithkaj, however, Nordenskiöld found stone mauls of precisely the same model as ours and also used as bone crushers. He observed that the natives themselves ate the crushed bone after boiling it with blood and water.[1] Lieut. Ray saw only dogs fed with it in the interior. Nordenskiöld does not men-

---

[1] Vega, vol. 2, p. 113; figures on p. 112.

tion the kind of stone used for these tools, but the two in the National
Museum, collected by Mr. Nelson at Cape Wankarem, are both of
granite or syenite and have a groove for the lashing. (Compare No.
89655 [1241], fig. 27.)

In addition to the above-described stone mauls, there are in the collection five nearly similar mauls of heavy bone, which have evidently

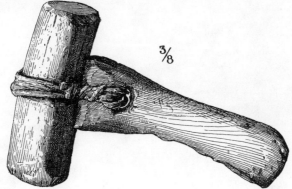

FIG. 29.—Bone maul.

served the same purpose. They were all brought over for sale from
Utkiavwiñ at about the same time, and from their exceedingly oily condition were evidently brought to light in rummaging round in the old
"blubber-rooms," where they have long lain forgotten. Four of these
differ in no respect from the stone mauls except in having the heads
made of whale's rib; the fifth is all in one piece.

The following figures will illustrate the general form of these imple-

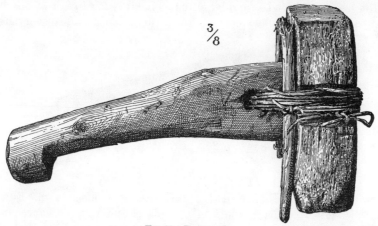

FIG. 30.—Bone maul.

ments: Fig. 29, No. 89847 [1046]: The head is a section of a small rib,
4·8 inches long, and has a deep notch on each side to receive the lashing.
The haft is probably of spruce (it is so impregnated with grease that it

is impossible to be sure about it), and is rough and somewhat knobby, with a rounded knob on the butt and two shallow finger notches on the under side of the grip. It is attached by a lashing of stout thong of the ordinary pattern. Fig. 30, No. 89849 [1047]: The head is a straight four-sided block of whale's rib, 6 inches long. The deep notches for the lashing, one on each side, are 1 inch behind the middle. The haft is a

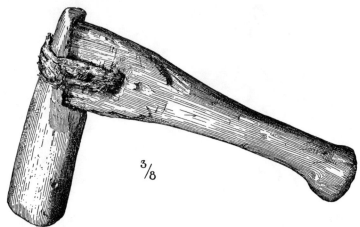

Fig. 31.—Bone maul.

roughly whittled knotty piece of spruce, and instead of a knob has a thick flange on the lower side of the butt. The lashing is of fourteen or fifteen turns of seal twine, and keyed upon each side by a roughly split stick thrust in under the head. Fig. 31, No. 89846 [1048]: This is peculiar in having the haft not attached at or near the middle of the head, but at one end, which is shouldered to receive it. The haft is of the common pattern and attached as usual, the lashing being made of very stout

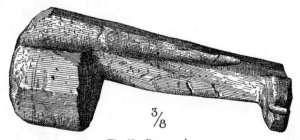

Fig. 32.—Bone maul.

sinew braid. The head is a section of a small rib 6 inches long. Fig. 32, No. 89845 [1049]: This is made in one piece, and roughly carved with broad cuts from a piece of whale's jaw. The grooves and holes in the bone are the natural canals of blood vessels. All these mauls are battered on the striking face, showing that they have been used.

At the first glance it seems as if we had here a series illustrating the development of the stone hammer. Fig. 32 would be the first form, while the next step would be to increase the weight of the head by lashing a large piece of bone to the end of the haft, instead of carving the whole laboriously out of a larger piece of bone. The substitution of the still heavier stone for the bone would obviously suggest itself next. The weak point in this argument, however, is that the advantage of the transition from the first to the next form is not sufficiently obvious. It seems to me more natural to suppose that the hafted stone hammer has been developed here, as is believed to have been the case elsewhere, by simply adding a handle to the pebble which had already been used as a hammer without one. These bone implements are then to be considered as makeshifts or substitutes for the stone hammer, when stones suitable for making the latter could not be procured. Now, such stones are rare at Point Barrow, and must be brought from a distance or purchased from other natives; hence the occasional use of such makeshifts as these. This view will account for the rarity of these bone hammers, as well as the rudeness of their construction. No. 89845 [1049] would thus be merely the result of individual fancy and not a link in the chain of development.

FOR SERVING AND EATING FOOD.

TRAYS.

Cooked food is generally served in large shallow trays more or less neatly carved from driftwood and nearly circular or oblong in shape.

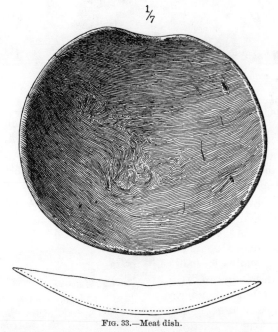

$\frac{1}{7}$

FIG. 33.—Meat dish.

The collection contains two specimens of the circular form and three oblong ones. All but one of these have been long in use and are very greasy. No. 73576 [392] (Fig. 33) has been selected as the type of the circular dishes (i'libiɐ). This is very smoothly carved from a single piece of pine wood. The brim is rounded, with a large rounded gap in one side, where a piece has probably been broken out. The brim is slightly cracked and chipped. The vessel is very greasy and shows marks inside where meat has been cut up in it. No. 89867 [1323] is a very similar dish, and made of the same material, but elliptical instead of circular, and larger, being 22·5 inches long, 15·5

⅛

FIG. 34.—Oblong meat dish.

broad, and 2·1 deep. It has been split in two, and mended with whalebone stitches in the manner previously described.

No. 73575 [223] (Fig. 34) is a typical oblong dish. It is neatly hollowed out, having a broad margin painted with red ocher. It measures 24 inches in length, is made of pine, rather roughly carved on the outside, and is new and clean. This is a common form of dish. Fig. 35, No.

⅛

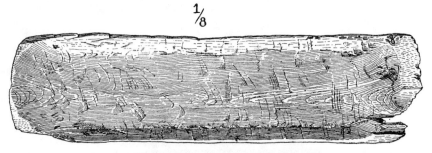

FIG. 35.—Oblong meat dish; very old.

89868 [1377], is an old tray of an unusual form. It is rudely hewn out of a straight piece of plank, 34·8 inches long, showing inside and out the marks of a dull adz, called by the seller "kau'dlo tu'mai," "the footprints of the stone (scil. adz)." The excavation is shallow and leaves a margin of 2 inches at one end, and the outside is roughly beveled off at the sides and ends. The holes near the ends were evidently for handles of thong. The material is spruce, discolored and somewhat greasy. Fig. 36, No. 89866 [1376], was said by the native who brought it over for sale to be especially intended for fish. It is much the shape of No. 73575 [223], but broader, slightly deeper, and more

⅒

FIG. 36.—Fish dish.

curved. The brim is narrow and rounded and the bottom smoothly rounded off. It measures 23·3 inches in length, and is made of pine. It has been deeply split in two places and stitched together with whalebone in the usual way. Trays and dishes of this sort are in general use among all Eskimo,[1] and are sometimes made of tanned sealskins.[2]

DRINKING VESSELS.

Whalebone Cup (*I'musyû*).—One of the commonest forms of drinking vessels is a little tub of whalebone of precisely the same shape as the large whalebone dish described above (p. 88). Of these there are five specimens in the collection, all from Utkiavwĭñ. No. 89853 [1302] (Fig. 37) will serve as the type. It is 4·6 inches long and made by binding a strip of black whalebone round a spruce bottom, and sewing together the ends, which over-lap each other about 1½ inches, with coarse strips of whalebone.

FIG. 37.—Whalebone cup.

There are two vertical seams three-fourths inch apart. The bottom is held in by fitting its slightly chamfered edge into a shallow croze cut in the whalebone. All these cups are made almost exactly alike, and nearly of the same size, varying only a fraction of an inch in height, and from 4·2 to 5·5 inches in length. The only variation is in the distance the ends overlap and the number of stitches in the seams. Such cups are to be found in nearly every house, and one is generally kept conveniently near the water bucket. Though the pattern is an ancient one, they are still manufactured. No. 56560 [654] was found among the débris of one of the ruined houses at Utkiavwĭñ, and differs from the modern cups only in having the ends sewed together with one seam instead of two, while No. 89851 [1300], though it has been in actual use, was made after our arrival, as the bottom is made of a piece of one of our cigar boxes.

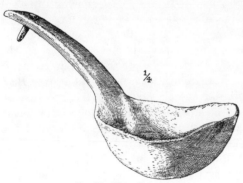

FIG. 38.—Horn dipper.

Dippers of horn are in very general use for drinking water. These are all of essentially the same shape, and are made of the light yellow translucent horn of the mountain sheep. There are three specimens in our collection, of which No. 56534 [28] (Fig. 38) has been selected as the type. This is made of a single piece of pale yellow translucent horn,

---

[1] See for example, Crantz, vol. 1, p. 144, Greenland; Parry, 2d. Voy., p. 503, Iglulik; and Hooper, Tents, etc., p. 170, Plover Bay.

[2] Bessels, Naturalist, Sept. 1884, p. 867.

apparently softened and molded into shape, cut only on the edges and the handle.   A stout peg of antler is driven through the handle, 1 inch from the tip, and projects behind, serving as a hook by which to hang the dipper on the edge of a bucket.   The other two are similar in shape and size, but No. 89831 [1293] has no peg, and has one side of the handle cut into a series of slight notches to keep the hand from slipping, while No. 89832 [1577] is rather straighter and has a smaller, shallower bowl, and the grip of the handle roughened with transverse grooves.   Fig. 39, No. 89739 [774], is a horn dipper, but one that is very old and of a

FIG. 39.—Horn dipper.

pattern no longer in use.   The bowl, which is much broken and gapped, is oval and deep, with a thick handle at one end, running out in the line of the axis of the bowl.   This handle, which is the thick part of the horn, near the tip, is flat above, rounded below, and has its tip slightly rounded, apparently by a stone tool. Just where the bowl and handle meet there is a deep transverse saw-cut, made to facilitate bending the handle into its place.   The material is horn, apparently of the mountain sheep, turned brown by age and exposure.   The specimen had been long lying neglected round the vil-lage of Utkiavwĭñ.

Horn dippers of the same general pattern as these are common throughout Alaska.   The Museum collection contains a large series of such utensils, collected by Mr. Nelson and others.   The cups and dip-pers of musk-ox horn found by Parry at Iglulik are somewhat different in shape.[1]   Those made of the enlarged base of horn[2] have a short handle and a nearly square bowl, while the hollow top of the horn is used for a cup without alteration beyond sometimes bending up the end, which serves as a handle.[3]   Curiously enough, cups of this last pattern appear not to be found anywhere else except at Plover Bay, eastern Siberia, where very similar vessels (as shown by the Museum collections) are made from the horn of the Siberian mountain sheep. An unusual form of dipper is beautifully made of fossil ivory.   Such cups are rare and highly prized.   We saw only three, one from each village, Nuwŭk, Utkiavwĭñ, and Sidaru, and all were obtained for the collection.   They show signs of age and long use.   They differ some-what in shape and size, but each is carved from a single piece of ivory and has a large bowl and a straight handle.   No. 56535 [371] (Fig. 40), which will serve as the type of the ivory dipper (i'musyû, kĭlĭgwû'garo), is neatly carved from a single piece of fine-grained fossil ivory, yel-lowed by age.   The handle, polished by long use, terminates in a blunt, recurved, tapering hook, which serves the purpose of the peg in the

[1] Second Voyage, p. 503.
[2] See Fig. 26, plate opposite p. 550.
[3] See Figs. 8 and 9, opposite p. 548.

horn dipper. The rounded gap in the brim opposite the handle is an accidental break. Another, No. 89830 [1259], from Sidaru, is a long trough-like cup, with rounded ends and a short flat handle at one end, made of a short transverse section of a rather small tusk, keeping the natural roundness of the tusk, but cut off flat on top and excavated. A wooden peg, like those in the horn dippers, is inserted in the end of the handle. This cup is especially interesting from its resemblance to the one obtained by Beechey (Voyage, Pl. I, Fig. 4) at Eschscholtz

FIG. 40.—Dipper of fossil ivory.

Bay, from which it differs only in being about 2 inches shorter and deeper in proportion. Thomas Simpson speaks of obtaining an ivory cup from some Point Barrow natives at Dease Inlet exactly like the one figured by Beechey, but with the handle broken off.[1] Fig. 41, No. 89833 [933], from Nuwŭk, has a large bowl, nearly circular, with a broad, straight handle and a broad hook. The part of the bowl to which the handle is attached, a semicircular piece 3 inches long and $1\frac{3}{4}$ wide, has been split out with the grain of the tusk, and mended with three stitches, in this case of sinew, in the usual manner. There was an old gap in the brim opposite to the handle, and the edges of it have been

FIG. 41.—Dipper of fossil ivory.

freshly and roughly whittled down. The ornamentation of the outside and handle, consisting of narrow incised lines and small circles, each with a dot in the center, is well shown in the figure. These engravings were originally colored with red ocher, but are now filled with dirt and are nearly effaced by wear on the handle. This dipper is not of such fine quality of ivory as the other two. It is not unlikely that all these vessels were made by the natives around Kotzebue Sound, where ivory is plenty, and where Beechey, as quoted above, found one so like one of ours. We were informed by the owner that No. 56535 [371] was obtained from the Nunatañmiun.

---

[1] Narrative, p. 148.

Spoons and ladles.—Each family has several spoons of various sizes, and narrow shallow ladles of horn, bone, etc. The large spoon is for stirring and ladling soup, etc. There is only one specimen in the collection, No. 89739 [1352] (Fig. 42). This is a new one, made by a native of Utkiavwĭñ, whom I asked to make himself a new spoon and bring

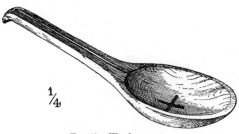

FIG 42.—Wooden spoon.

me his old one. He, however, misunderstood me and brought over the new one, which Lieut. Ray purchased, not knowing that I had especially asked for the old one. These spoons seem to be in such constant use that the natives did not offer them for sale. This specimen is smoothly carved from a single piece of pine, and painted all over, except the inside of the bowl, with red ocher. A cross of red ocher is marked in the middle of the bowl, and there is a shallow groove, colored with blacklead, along the middle of the handle on top. The length is 13·2 inches. A small spoon of light-colored horn, No. 89416 [1379], has a bowl of the common spoon shape with a short, flat handle. Spoons of this sort were not seen in use, and as this is new and evidently made for sale it

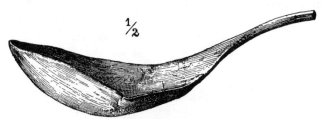

FIG. 43.—Horn ladle.

may be meant for a copy of one of our spoons. The narrow ladles of horn or bone may formerly have been used for eating before it was so easy to get tin pots, but at present are chiefly used for dipping oil, especially for filling the lamp. The collection contains one of horn and four of bone.

No. 89415 [1070], Fig. 43, is made of a single piece of mountain-sheep horn, dark brown from age and use, softened and molded into shape.

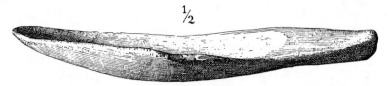

FIG. 44.—Bone ladle.

It is impregnated with oil, showing that it has been long in use. This utensil closely resembles a great number of specimens in the Museum from the more southern parts of Alaska. No. 89411 [1294] (Fig. 44) is a typical bone ladle. The material is rather coarse-grained, compact bone from a whale's rib or jawbone. No. 89414 [1013] closely resembles this but is a trifle larger. The other two specimens are interesting as showing an attempt at ornamentation. No. 89412 [1102] (Fig. 45, from Nuwŭk) is carved smoothly into a rude, flattened figure of a whale (Balaena mysticetus). The flukes form the handle and the belly is hollowed out into the bowl of the ladle. No. 89413 [934] (Fig. 46, from Utkiavwĭñ) has the handle carved into a rude bear's head, which has the eyes, nostrils, and outline of the mouth incised and filled in with

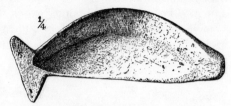

FIG. 45.—Bone ladle in the form of a whale.

dark oil dregs. All these ladles have the curved side of the bowl on the left, showing that they were meant to be used with the right hand. The name, kĭliu′tᴇ, obtained for these ladles is given in the vocabulary collected by Dr. Oldmixon as "scraper," which seems to be the etymological meaning of the word. These implements may be used for scraping blubber from skins, or the name may correspond in meaning to the

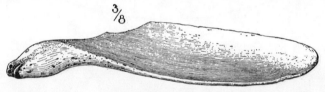

FIG. 46.—Bone ladle.

cognate Greenlandic kiliortût, "a scraper; especially a mussel shell (a natural scraper)." The resemblance of these ladles to a mussel shell is sufficiently apparent for the name to be applied to them. Indeed, they may have been made in imitation of mussel shells, which the Eskimo, in all probability, like so many other savages, used for ladles as well as scrapers.

MISCELLANEOUS HOUSEHOLD UTENSILS.

Lamps (*kódlö*).—Mention has already been made of the stone lamps or oil-burners used for lighting and warming the houses, which, in Dr. Simpson's time, were obtained by trading from the "Kûñmû′dlĭñ," who in turn procured them from other Eskimo far to the east. These are flat, shallow dishes, usually like a gibbous moon in outline, and are of two sizes: the larger house lamp, 18 inches to 3 feet in length, and the small traveling lamp, 6 or 8 inches long. The latter is used in the temporary snow huts when a halt is made at night. In each house are usually two lamps, one standing at each side, with the curved side against the wall, and raised by blocks a few inches from the floor. In one large house, that of old Yûksĭ′ña, the so-called "chief," at Nuwŭk, there were three lamps, the third standing in the right-hand front corner of the house. The dish is filled with oil, which is burned by means of a wick of moss fibers arranged along the outer edge. Large lamps are usually divided into three compartments, of which the middle is the largest, by wooden partitions called sä'potĭn (corresponding to the Greenlandic saputit, "(1) a dam across a stream for catching fish, (2) a dam or dike in general"), along which wicks can also be arranged. The women tend the lamps with great care, trimming and arranging the wick with little sticks. The lamp burns with scarcely any smoke and a

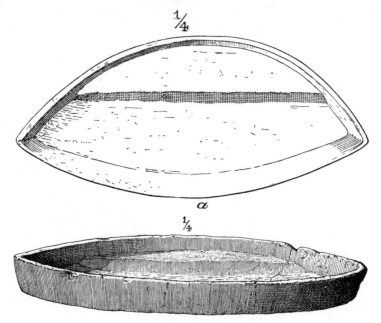

Fig. 47.—Stone house lamp.

bright flame, the size of which is regulated by kindling more or less of the wick, and is usually kept filled by the drip from a lump of blubber stuck on a sharp stick (ajû'ksûxbwĭñ) projecting from the wall about a foot above the middle of the lamp.[1]

In most houses there is a long slender stick (kukun, "a lighter"), which the man of the house uses to light his pipe with when sitting on the banquette, without the trouble of getting down, by dipping the end in the oil of the lamp and lighting this at the flame. The sticks used for trimming the wick also serve as pipe-lighters and for carrying fire across the room in the same way.[2] No food, except an occasional

[1] Compare the custom noticed by Parry, at Iglulik, of hanging a long thin strip of blubber near the flame of the lamp to feed it (2d Voyage, p. 502). According to Petitot (Monographie, etc., p. xviii), the lamps in the Mackenzie district are fed by a lump of blubber stuck on a stick, as at Point Barrow.

[2] Compare Nordenskiöld, Vega, vol. 2, p. 119: "The wooden pins she uses to trim the wick . . . are used when required as a light or torch . . . to light pipes, etc. In the same way other pins dipped in train-oil are used" (Pitlekaj), and foot-note on same page: "I have seen such pins, also oblong stones, sooty at one end, which, after having been dipped in train-oil, have been used as torches. . . . in old Eskimo graves in northwestern Greenland."

luncheon of porridge or something of the sort, is now cooked over these lamps. Two such lamps burning at the ordinary rate give light enough to enable one to read and write with ease when sitting on the banquette, and easily keep the temperature between 50° and 60° F. in the coldest weather. In the collection are three house lamps, two complete and one merely a fragment, and three traveling lamps.

Fig. 47 (No. 89879) [872] is a typical house lamp, though rather a small specimen. It is carved out of soft gray soapstone and is 17 inches long. The back is nearly vertical, while the front flares strongly outward. The back wall is cut down vertically inside with a narrow rounded brim and the front curves gradually in from the very edge to the bottom of the cavity, which is 1½ inches deep in the middle. The posterior third of the cavity is occupied by a flat, straight shelf with a sloping edge about 0·7 inch high. About a third of one end of the lamp

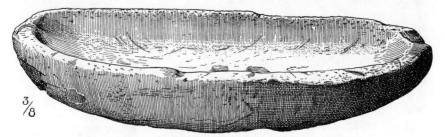

FIG. 48.—Sandstone lamp.

has been broken off obliquely and mended, as usual, with stitches. There are two of these neatly countersunk in channels. The specimen has been long in use and is thoroughly incrusted with oil and soot. No. 89880 [1731] (Fig. 48) is peculiar, from the material of which it is made. This is a coarse, gritty stone, rather soft, but much more difficult to work than the soapstone. It is rudely worked into something the same shape as the type, but has the cavity but slightly hollowed out, without a shelf, and only a little steeper behind than in front. The idea at once suggests itself that this lamp, which is very old and sooty, was made at Point Barrow and was an attempt to imitate the imported lamps with stone obtained from the beds reported by Lieut. Ray in Kulugrua. There is, of course, no means of proving this supposition. There is no mention of any material except soapstone being made into lamps by the Greenlanders or other eastern Eskimo, but the lamps from Kadiak and Bristol Bay in the National Museum are made of some hard gray stone.

Fig. 49, No. 56673 [133], is a traveling lamp, and is a miniature of the large lamp, No. 89879 [872], 8·7 inches long, 4·2 wide, and 1 inch high, also of soapstone and without a shelf. The front also is straighter, and the whole more roughly made. No. 89882 [1298] is another traveling lamp, also of soapstone, and made of about half of a large lamp. It has been used little if at all since it was made over, as the inside is almost new while the outside is coated with soot and grease. It is 6·3 inches long·

No. 89881 [1209] is a miniature of No. 89880, 8·1 inches long, and is made of the same gritty stone.

Suitable material is not at hand for the proper comparison of the lamps

FIG. 49.—Traveling lamp.

used by the different branches of the Eskimo race. All travelers who have written about the Eskimo speak of the use of such lamps, which agree in being shallow, oblong dishes of stone. Dr. Bessels[1] figures a lamp of soapstone from Ita, Smith Sound, closely resembling No. 89880, and a little lamp in the Museum from Greenland is of essentially the same shape, but deeper. The same form appears at Hudson Strait in the lamps collected by Mr. L. M. Turner, while those used at Iglulik are nearly semicircular.[2] South of Kotzebue Sound lamps of the shape so common in the east are used, but these, Mr. Turner informs me, are never made of soapstone, but always of sandstone, shale, etc. The people of Kadiak and the Aleuts anciently used lamps of hard stone, generally oval in shape, and sometimes made by slightly hollowing out one side of a large round pebble.[3] Such a rough lamp was brought by Lieut. Stoney, U. S. Navy, from Kotzebue Sound. No such highly finished and elaborate lamps as the large house lamps at Point Barrow are mentioned except by Nordenskiöld, who figures one from Siberia.[4] This lamp is interesting as the only one described with a ledge comparable to the shelf of No. 89879. Lamps from the region between

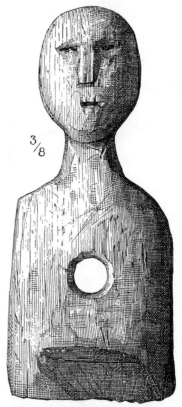

FIG. 50.—Socket for blubber holder.

Point Barrow and Boothia Felix are especially needed to elucidate the distribution and development of this utensil. The rudely hollowed peb-

[1] Naturalist, September, 1884, p. 867, Fig. 2.

[2] Parry, Second Voyage, Pl. opposite p. 548, Fig. 2.

[3] See Dall, Alaska, p. 387; and Petroff, Report, etc., p. 141. See also the collections of Turner and Fischer from Attu and Kadiak.

[4] Vega, vol. 2, p. 23, Fig. b on p. 22, and diagrams, p. 23.

ble of the ancient Aleut and the elaborate lamp of the Point Barrow Eskimo are evidently the two extremes of the series of forms, but the intermediate patterns are still to be described.

Fig. 50, No. 56492 [108], is a peculiar article of which only one specimen was collected. We were given to understand at the time of purchasing it that it was a sort of socket or escutcheon to be fastened to the wall above a lamp to hold the blubber stick described above. No such escutcheons, however, were seen in use in the houses visited. The article is evidently old. It is a flat piece of thick plank of some soft wood, 11·4 inches long, 4·2 broad, and about $1\frac{1}{2}$ thick, very rudely carved into a human head and body without arms, with a large round hole about $1\frac{1}{4}$ inches in diameter through the middle of the breast. The eyes and mouth are incised, and the nose was in relief, but was long ago split off. There is a deep furrow all around the head, perhaps for fastening on a hood.

CLOTHING.

MATERIAL.

The clothing of these people is as a rule made entirely of skins, though of late years drilling and calico are used for some parts of the dress which will be afterwards described. Petroff[1] makes the rather surprising statement that " a large amount of ready-made clothing finds its way into the hands of these people, who wear it in summer, but the excessive cold of winter compels them to resume the fur garments formerly in general use among them." Fur garments are in as general use at Point Barrow as they ever were, and the cast-off clothing obtained from the ships is mostly packed away in some corner of the iglu. We landed at Cape Smyth not long after the wreck of the *Daniel Webster*, whose crew had abandoned and given away a great deal of their clothing. During that autumn a good many men and boys wore white men's coats or shirts in place of the outer frock, especially when working or lounging about the station, but by the next spring these were all packed away and were not resumed again except in rare instances in the summer.

The chief material is the skin of the reindeer, which is used in various stages of pelage. Fine, short-haired summer skins, especially those of does and fawns, are used for making dress garments and underclothes. The heavier skins are used for everyday working clothes, while the heaviest winter skins furnish extra warm jackets for cold weather, warm winter stockings and mittens. The white or spotted skins of the tame Siberian reindeer, obtained from the "Nunatañmiun," are especially valued for full-dress jackets. We heard no mention of the use of the skin of the unborn reindeer fawn, but there is a kind of dark deerskin used only for edgings, which appears to be that of an exceedingly young deer. This skin is extremely thin, and the hair so short that it is almost invisible. Siberian deerskins can always be recognized by

---

[1] Report, etc., p. 125.

having the flesh side colored red,[1] while American-dressed skins are worked soft and rubbed with chalk or gypsum, giving a beautiful white surface like pipe-clayed leather.

The skins of the white mountain sheep, white and blue fox, wolf, dog, ermine, and lynx are sometimes used for clothing, and under jackets made of eider duck skins are rarely used. Sealskin dressed with the hair on is used only for breeches and boots, and for those rarely. Black dressed sealskin—that is, with the epidermis left on and the hair shaved off—is used for waterproof boots, while the white sealskin, tanned in urine, with the epidermis removed, is used for the soles of winter boots. Waterproof boot soles are made of oil-dressed skins of the white whale, bearded seal, walrus, or polar bear. The last material is not usually mentioned as serving for sole leather among the Eskimo. Nordenskiöld,[2] however, found it in use among the Chukches for this purpose. It is considered an excellent material for soles at Point Barrow, and is sometimes used to make boat covers, which are beautifully white. Heavy mittens for the winter are made of the fur of the polar bear or of dogskin. Waterproof outer frocks are of seal entrails, split and dried and sewed together. For trimmings are used deerskin of different colors, mountain-sheep skin, and black and white sealskin, wolf, wolverine, and marten fur, and whole ermine skins, as well as red worsted, and occasionally beads.

FIG. 51.—Man in ordinary deer-skin clothes.

STYLE OF DRESS.

Dr. Simpson[3] gave an excellent general description of the dress of these people, which is the same at the present day. While the same in general pattern as that worn by all other Eskimo, it differs in many details from that worn by the eastern Eskimo,[4] and most closely resembles the style in vogue at and near Norton Sound.[5] The man's dress (Fig. 51, from a photograph of Apaidyao) consists of the usual loose hooded frock, without opening except at the neck and wrists. This reaches just over the hips, rarely about to mid-thigh, where it is cut

---

[1] Compare Nordenskiöld, Vega, vol 2. p. 213.

[2] Vega, vol. 2, p. 98.

[3] Op. cit., pp. 241–245.

[4] See for example, Egede, p. 219; Crantz, vol. 1, p. 136; Bessels, Op. cit., pp. 805 and 868 (Smith Sound); Kane, 1st Grinnell Exp., pp. 45 (Greenland) and 132 (Cape York); Brodbeck, "Nach Osten," pp. 23, 24, and Holm, Geografisk Tidskrift, vol. 8, p. 90 (East Greenland); Parry, 2d Voy., pp. 494–6 (Iglulik); Boas, "Central Eskimo," pp. 554–6; Kumlien, loc. cit., pp. 22–25 (Cumberland Gulf); also, Frobisher, in Hakluyt's Voyages, 1589, etc., p. 628.

[5] Dall, Alaska, pp. 21 and 141.

off square, and is usually confined by a girdle at the waist. Under this garment is worn a similar one, usually of lighter skin and sometimes without a hood. The thighs are clad in one or two pairs of tight-fitting knee breeches, confined round the hips by a girdle and usually secured by a drawstring below the knee which ties over the tops of the boots. On the legs and feet are worn, first, a pair of long, deerskin stockings with the hair inside; then slippers of tanned sealskin, in the bottom of which is spread a layer of whalebone shavings, and outside a pair of close-fitting boots, held in place by a string round the ankle, usually reaching above the knee and ending with a rough edge, which is covered by the breeches. Dress boots often end with an ornamental border and a drawstring just below the knee. The boots are of reindeer skin, with white sealskin soles for winter and dry weather, but in summer waterproof boots of black sealskin with soles of white whale skin, etc., are worn. Overshoes of the same material, reaching just above the ankles, with a drawstring at the top and ankle strings, are sometimes worn over the winter boots. When traveling on snowshoes or in soft dry snow the boots are replaced by stockings of the same shape as the under ones, but made of very thick winter deerskins with the flesh side out.

Instead of breeches and boots a man occasionally wears a pair of pantaloons or tight-fitting trousers terminating in shoes such as are worn by the women. Over the usual dress is worn in very cold weather a circular mantle of deerskin, fastened by a thong at the neck—such mantles are nowadays occasionally made of blankets—and in rainy weather both sexes wear the hooded rain frock of seal gut. Of late years both sexes have adopted the habit of wearing over their clothes a loose hoodless frock of cotton cloth, usually bright-colored calico, especially in blustering weather, when it is useful in keeping the drifting snow out of their furs.

Both men and women wear gloves or mittens. These are of deerskin for ordinary use, but in extreme weather mittens of polar bear skin are worn. When hunting in winter it is the custom to wear gloves of thin deerskin under the bearskin mitten, so that the rifle can be handled without touching the bare hand to the cold iron. The women have a common trick of wearing only one mitten, but keeping the other arm withdrawn from the sleeve and inside of the jacket.

FIG. 52.—Womans' hood.

The dress of the women consists of two frocks, which differ from those of the men in being continued from the waist in two rather full rounded skirts at the front and back, reaching to or below the knee. A woman's frock is always distinguished by a sort of rounded bulge or pocket at the nape of the neck (see Fig. 52, from a sketch by the writer), which is intended to receive the head of the infant when carried in the jacket. The little peak at the top of the hood is also characteristic of the woman's frock. On her legs a woman wears a pair of tight-fitting deerskin pantaloons with the hair next the skin, and outside of these a similar pair made of the skins of deer legs, with the hair out, and having soles of sealskin, but no anklestrings. The outer pantaloons are usually laid aside in spring, and waterproof boots like the men's, but fastened below the knee with drawstrings, are worn over the under pantaloons. In the summer pantaloons wholly of waterproof sealskin are often put on. The women's pantaloons, like the men's breeches, are fastened with a girdle just above the hips. It appears that they do not stay up very well, as the women are continually " hitching" them up and tightening their girdles.

Until they reach manhood the boys wear pantaloons like the women, but their jackets are cut just like those of the men. The dress of the girls is a complete miniature of that of the women, even to the pocket for the child's head. Those who are well-to-do generally own several complete suits of clothes, and present a neat appearance when not engaged in dirty work. The poorer ones wear one suit on all occasions till it becomes shabby. New clothes are seldom put on till winter.

The outer frock is not often worn in the iglu, being usually taken off before entering the room, and the under one is generally dispensed with. Men habitually leave off their boots in the house, and rarely their stockings and breeches, retaining only a pair of thin deerskin drawers. This custom of stripping in the house has been noticed among all Eskimos whose habits have been described, from Greenland to Siberia. The natives are slow to adopt any modifications in the style of dress, the excellence and convenience of which has been so frequently commented upon that it is unnecessary to refer to it. One or two youths learned from association with us the convenience of pockets, and accordingly had " patch pockets" of cloth sewed on the outside of the skirt of the inner frock, and one young man in 1883 wore a pair of sealskin hip boots, evidently copies from our india-rubber wading boots. I now proceed to the description of the clothing in detail.

Head clothing.—The only head covering usually worn is the hood of the frock, which reaches to about the middle of the head, the front being covered by the hair. Women who are carrying children in the jacket sometimes wrap the head in a cloth. (I have an indistinct recollection of once seeing a woman with a deerskin hood, but was too busy at the time to make a note or sketch of it.) One man at Utkiavwïñ (Nägawau'ra, now deceased), who was quite bald on the forehead, used to protect the front of his head with a sort of false front of deerskin, tied round like a fillet. No specimens of any of these articles were obtained. Fancy conical caps are worn in the dances and theatrical performances, but these belong more properly under the head of Games and Pastimes (where they will be described) than under that of Clothing.

Frocks (atigĕ).—Two frocks are always worn by both sexes except in the house, or in warm weather, the inner (ílupa) with the hair next the skin, and the outer (kalûru′rɐ) with the hair out. The outer frock is also sometimes worn with the hair in, especially when it is new and the flesh side clean and white. This side is often ornamented with little tufts of marten fur and stripes of red ocher. The difference in shape between the frocks of the two sexes has been already mentioned. The man's frock is a loose shirt, not fitted to the body, widening at the bottom, and reaching, when unbelted, just below the hips. The skirts are cut off square or slightly rounded, and are a little longer behind than in front. The hood is rounded, loose around the neck, and fitted in more on the sides than on the nape. The front edge

FIG. 53.—Man's frock.

of the hood, when drawn up, comes a little forward of the top of the head and runs round under the chin, covering the ears.

There are in the collection three specimens, all rather elaborate dress frocks, to be worn outside. All have been worn. No. 56751 [184] (Fig. 53), brown deerskin, will serve as the type. The pattern can best

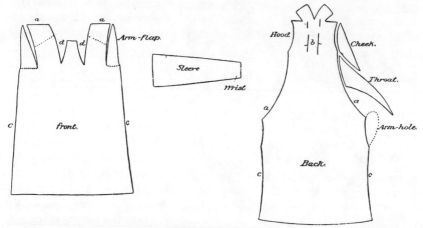

FIG. 54.—Pattern of man's deerskin frock.

be explained by reference to the accompanying diagrams (Fig. 54). The body consists of two pieces, front and back, each made of the

9 ETH——8

greater part of the skin of a reindeer fawn, with the back in the middle and the sides and belly coming at the edges. The head of the

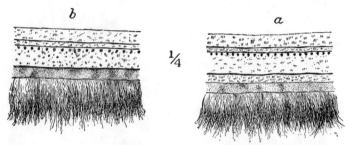

FIG. 55.—Detail of trimming, skirt and shoulder of man's frock.

animal is made into the hood, which is continuous with the back. Each sleeve is in two pieces, front and back, of the same shape, which are sewed together along the upper edge, but separated below by the

FIG. 56.—Man wearing plain, heavy frock.

arm flap of the front, which is bent down and inserted like a gusset from the arm-pit nearly to the wrist. A band of deerskin an inch broad is sewed round the edge of the hood, flesh side out. The trimming consists, first, of a narrow strip of long-haired wolfskin (taken from the middle of the back) sewed to the outer side of the binding of the hood, its ends separated by the chin piece, so that the long hairs form a fringe around the face. Similar strips are sewed round each wrist with the fur inward. The binding round the skirt (Fig. 55a) is $2\frac{1}{4}$ inches broad. The light-colored strips are clipped mountain sheep skin, the narrow pipings are of the dark brown skin of a very young fawn, the little tags on the second strip are of red worsted and the fringe is of wolverine fur, sewed on with the flesh side, which is colored red, probably with ocher, outward. A band of similar materials, arranged a little differently (Fig. 55b) and 1¼ inches broad, is inserted into the body at each shoulder seam, so that the fringe makes a sort of epaulet. This jacket is 24·5 inches long from the chin to the bottom of the skirt, 21 inches wide across the shoulders, and 24·5 inches wide at the bottom.

Apart from the trimming this is a very simple pattern. There are no seams except those absolutely necessary for producing the shape, and the best part of each skin is brought where it will show most, while the poorer portions are out of sight under the arms.

The chief variation in deerskin frocks is in the trimming. All have the hood fitted to the head and throat, with cheek and throat pieces, and these are invariably white or light colored, even when the frock is made of white Siberian deer skin. When possible the head of the deer

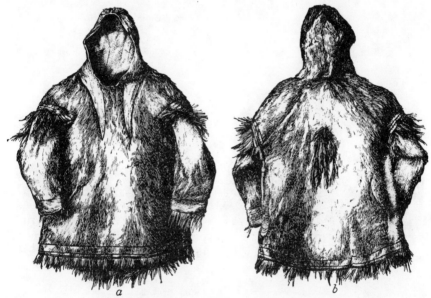

FIG. 57.—Man's frock of mountain sheepskin, front and back.

is always used for the back of the hood, as Capt. Parry observed to be the custom at Iglulik.[1] A plain frock is sometimes used for rough work, hunting, etc. This has no fringe or trimming round the hood, skirt, or wrists, the first being smoothly hemmed or bound with deer-skin and the last two left raw-edged. Fig. 56 shows such a jacket, which is often made of very heavy winter deerskin. Most frocks, how-ever, have the border to the hood either of wolf or wolverine skin, in the latter case especially having the end of the strips hanging down like tassels under the chin. The long hairs give a certain amount of protection to the face when walking in the wind.[2] Instead of a fringe the hood sometimes has three tufts of fur, one on each side and one above.

---

[1] Second Voy., p. 537.　　　[2] Compare Dall, Alaska, p. 22.

Trimmings of edging like that above described, or of plain wolverine fur round the skirts and wrists, are common, and the shoulder straps rather less so.   Frocks are sometimes also fringed on the skirts and seams with little strips of deerskin, after what the Point Barrow people called the "Kûñmûdlĭñ" fashion.[1]   Nearly all the natives wear outer frocks of deerskin, but on great occasions elaborately made garments of other materials are sometimes seen.   Nos. 56758 [87] (Fig. 57, a and b) and 56757 [11] (Fig. 58, a and b) are two such frocks.   No. 56758 [87] is of mountain sheep skin, nearly white.   As shown in the diagrams (Fig. 59, a, b, c,) the general pattern is not unlike the type described, but there are more pieces in the hood and several small gussets are inserted to improve the set of the garment.   The trimmings are shoulder

a   b

FIG. 58.—Man's frock of ermine skins, front and back.

straps, and a border round the skirt of edging like that described above, and the seams of the throat pieces are piped with the dark almost hairless deerskin, which sets them off from the rest of the coat.   The wrists have narrow borders of wolf fur, and there was a wolfskin fringe to the hood, which was removed before the garment was offered for sale.

No. 56757 [11] is a very handsome garment (Fig. 58).   The body and sleeves are of white and brown (winter and summer) ermine skins arranged in an elegant pattern, and the hood of reindeer and mountain sheep skin.   This is the only frock seen in which the hood is not fitted to the sides of the throat by curved and pointed throat pieces, after the fashion universal among the western Eskimo, from Cape Bathurst at least to Norton Sound.   The pattern of the hood is shown by the dia-

---

[1] There are several frocks so trimmed in the National Museum, from the Mackenzie and Anderson region,

gram (Fig. 60 a). The middle piece is the skin of a reindeer head, the two cheek pieces and median chin piece of mountain sheep skin. When the hood is put together the lower edge of it is sewed to the neck of the body, which has the back and front of nearly the same size and shape (diagram, Fig. 60 b), though the back is a little longer in the

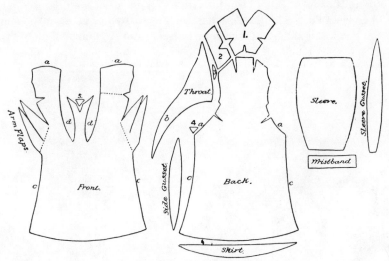

FIG. 59.—Pattern of sheepskin frock.

skirt. There is no regular seam on the shoulders, where irregular bits of white ermine skin are pieced together so as to fit. From the armpit on each side runs a narrow strip of sheepskin between back and front. The sleeve is a long piece made of three white ermine skins put together lengthwise, doubled above, with a straight strip of sheepskin let in below, and enlarged near the body by two triangular gussets (front and back) let in between the ermine and sheepskin. The wristbands are broad pieces of sheepskin. The skirts are of white ermine skins pieced together irregularly, but the skins composing the front, back, and sleeves are split down the back of the animal and neatly cut into long rectangular pieces, with the feet and tails still attached. They are arranged in a pattern of vertical stripes, two skins fastened together end to end making a stripe, which is the same on the front and the back. There

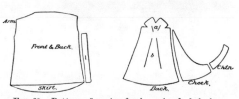

FIG. 60.—Pattern of ermine frock. a, hood; b, body.

is a brown stripe down the middle, then two white stripes on each side, and a brown stripe on each edge. The hood is bound round the edge with white sheepskin and bordered with wolfskin. There are shoulder straps and a border round the skirt of edging of the usual materials, but slightly different arrangement, and tagged with small red glass beads.

The former owner of this beautiful frock (since dead) was always very elegantly dressed. His deerskin clothes were always much trimmed, and he owned an elegant frock of foxskins, alternately blue and white, with a hood of deerskin, which we did not succeed in obtaining for the collection. (The "jumper of mixed white and blue fox pelts," seen by Dr. Kane at Ita,[1] must have been like this.)

The woman's frock differs from that worn by the men, in the shape of the hood and skirts, as mentioned above, and it is also slightly fitted

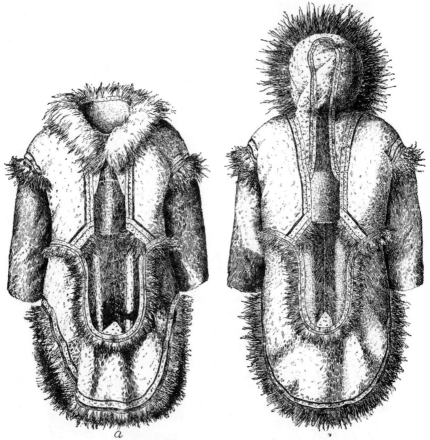

FIG. 61.—Woman's frock, front and back.

in to the waist and made to "bag" somewhat in the back, in order to give room for carrying the child. The pattern is considerably different from that of the man's frock, as will be seen from the description of the type specimen (the only one in the collection), No. 74041 [1791] (Fig. 61, a and b), which is of deerskin. The hood is raised into a little point on top and bulges out into a sort of rounded pocket at the nape. This is a holiday garment, made of strips of skin from the shanks and belly of the reindeer, pieced together so as to make a pattern of alternating

---

[1] Second Grinnell Exp., vol. 1, p. 203.

light and dark stripes. The pattern is shown in the diagram, Fig. 62. The sleeves are of the same pattern as those of No. 56751 [184]. The edge of the hood is bound with deerskin, hair outwards. Trimming: a strip of edging (Fig. 63) in which the light stripes are clipped white mountain sheepskin, the dark pipings brown, almost hairless, fawnskin, and the tags red worsted, is inserted in the seam between 7 on each side and 6 and 2, and a similar strip between the inner edge of 3, 2, 7, 9, and 1. A broader strip of similar insertion, fringed below with marten fur, with the flesh side out

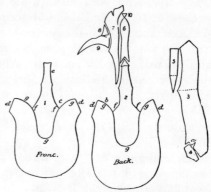

FIG. 62.—Pattern of woman's frock.

and colored red, runs along the short seam *ffff*. The seam between 9 and 7 has a narrow piping of thin brown deerskin, tagged with red worsted. A strip of edging, without tags and fringed with marten fur (Fig. 64), is inserted in the seam *gggg*. The border of the skirt is 1 inch wide (Fig. 64). The dark stripe is brown deerskin, the white, mountain sheep, and the fur, marten, with the red flesh side out. The fringes are double strips of white deerskin sewed to the inside of the last seam, about 3 inches apart. The shoulder straps are of edging like that at *g*, but have the fur sewed on so as to show the red flesh side. The hood has a fringe of wolfskin sewed to the outside of the binding. This frock measures 45 inches in the back, 32 in the front, 19 across the shoulders, and 17 at the waist. The skirts are 21 inches wide, the front 18, and the back 20 inches long. The pieces 7, 8, and 9 of the hood are white. This is an unusually handsome garment.

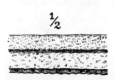

FIG. 63.—Detail of edging, woman's frock.

FIG. 64.—Details of trimming, woman's frock.

Deerskin garments rarely have the ornamental piecing seen in this frock. Each one of the numbered parts of the pattern is generally in one piece. The pieces 8 and 9 are almost universally white, and 7 is often so. About the same variety in material and trimming is to be found as in the men's frocks, though deer and mountain sheep skins were the only materials seen used, and the women's frocks are less often seen without the fringe round the hood. Plain deerskin frocks are often bordered round the skirts with a fringe cut from deerskin. The women nowadays often line the outer frock with drilling, bright calico, or even bedticking, and then wear it with this side out.

The frocks for both sexes, while made on the same general pattern as those of the other Eskimo, differ in many details from those of eastern America. For instance, the hood is not fitted in round the throat with the pointed throat pieces or fringed with wolf or wolverine skin until we reach the Eskimo of the Anderson River. Here, as shown by the specimens in the National Museum, the throat pieces are small and wide apart, and the men's hoods only are fringed with wolverine skin. The women's hoods are very large everywhere in the east for the better accommodation of the child, which is sometimes carried wholly in the hood.[1]

The hind flap of the skirt of the woman's frock, except in Greenland, has developed into a long narrow train reaching the ground, while the front flap is very much decreased in size (see references just quoted). The modern frock in Greenland is very short and has very small flaps (see illustrations in Rink's Tales, etc., pp. 8 and 9), but the ancient fashion, judging from the plate in Crantz's History of Greenland, referred to above, was much more like that worn by the western Eskimo. In the Anderson and Mackenzie regions the flaps are short and rounded and the front flap considerably the smaller. There is less difference in the general shape of the men's frocks. The hood is generally rounded and close fitting, except in Labrador and Baffin Land, where it is pointed on the crown. The skirt is sometimes prolonged into rounded flaps and a short scallop in front, as at Iglulik and some parts of Baffin Land.[2] Petitot[3] gives a full description of the dress of a "chief" from the Anderson River. He calls the frock a "blouse échancrée par côté et terminée en queues arrondies par devant et par derrière." The style of frock worn at Point Barrow is the prevalent one along the western coast of America nearly to the Kuskokwim. On this river long hoodless frocks reaching nearly or quite to the ground are worn.[4] The frock worn in Kadiak was hoodless and long, with short sleeves and large armholes beneath these.[5]

The men of the Siberian Eskimo and sedentary Chukches, as at Plover Bay, wear in summer a loose straight-bottomed frock without a hood, but with a frill of long fur round the neck. The winter frock is described as having "a square hood without trimmings, but capable of being drawn, like the mouth of a bag, around the face by a string in-

---

[1] Egede, p. 131; Crantz, i, p. 137 and Pl. III. (Greenland); Bessels, op. cit., p. 865 (Smith Sound—married women only); Parry, 2nd Voy., p. 494, and numerous illustrations, passim (Iglulik); Packard, Naturalist Vol. 19, p. 6, Pl. XXIII (Labrador), and Kumlien, l. c., p. 33 (Cumberland Gulf). See also several specimens in the National Museum from Ungava (collected by L. M. Turner) and the Mackenzie and Anderson rivers (collected by MacFarlane). The hoods from the last region, while still much larger and wider than those in fashion at Point Barrow, are not so enormous as the more eastern ones. The little peak on the top of the woman's hood at Point Barrow may be a reminiscence of the pointed hood worn by the women mentioned by Bessels, op. cit.

[2] Parry, 2d Voy., p. 494, and 1st Voy., p. 283.

[3] Monographie, etc., p. xiv.

[4] Petroff, op. cit., p. 134, Pls. 4 and 5. See also specimens in the National Museum.

[5] Petroff, op. cit., p. 139, and Liscansky, Voy., etc., p. 194.

serted in the edge."[1]   According to Nordenskiöld,[2] the men at Pitlekaj
wear the hoodless frock summer and winter, putting on one or two separate hoods in winter.   The under hood appears to be like one or two
which I saw worn at Plover Bay, namely, a close-fitting nightcap of
thin reindeer skin tied under the chin.   The
dress of the Siberian women consists of frock
and baggy kneebreeches in one piece, sewed
to tightfitting boots reaching to the knees.[3]

Mantles.—"Circular" mantles of deerskin,
fastened at the neck by a thong, and put on
over the head like a poncho, are worn by the
men in very cold weather over their other
clothes when lounging in the open air about
the village or watching at a seal hole or tend-
ing the seal nets at night.   The cloaks are
especially affected by the older men, who,
having grown-up sons or sons-in-law, do not
have to go sealing in winter, and spend a
great deal of their time in bright weather
chatting together out of doors.   There is

FIG. 65.—Man's cloak of deerskin.

one specimen in the collection, No. 56760 [94] (Fig. 65).   It is made of
fine summer doe-reindeer skin, in three pieces, back and two sides of
dark skin, sewed to a collar of white skin from the belly of the animal.

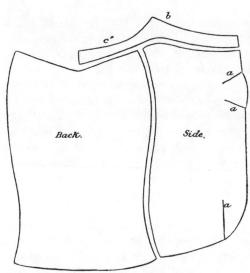

FIG. 66.—Pattern of man's cloak.

For pattern see diagram
(Fig. 66).   The seams at *a*
are gored to make the cloak
hang properly from the
shoulder.   The collar is in
two pieces, joined in the
middle, and the edge *c* is
turned over toward the hair
side and "run" down in a
narrow hem.   The points *b*
of the collar are brought
together in the middle and
joined by a little strap of
deerskin about an inch
long, so that the edge *c*
makes a round hole for the
neck.   The width of the
mantle is 60 inches and its
depth 39.   It is worn with

the white flesh side out, as is indicated by the seams being sewed "over

[1] Dall, Alaska, p. 379.

[2] Vega, vol. 2, p. 98.

[3] Nordenskiöld, Vega, vol. 2, p. 100 and Fig. on p. 57; Dall, Alaska, p. 379 and plate opposite.   I also noticed this dress at Plover Bay in 1881.   Compare also Krause Brothers, Geogr. Blätter, vol. 5, No. 1, p. 5,
where the dress along the coast from East Cape to Plover Bay is described as we saw it at Plover Bay.

and over" on the hair side. All the mantles seen were essentially of the same pattern. The edge is sometimes cut into an ornamental fringe, and the flesh side marked with a few narrow stripes of red ocher. This garment appears to be peculiar to northwestern America. No mention is to be found of any such a thing except in Mr. MacFarlane's MS. notes, where he speaks of a deerskin blanket "attached with a line across the shoulders in cold weather," among the Anderson River Eskimo. We have no means at present of knowing whether such cloaks are worn by the coast natives between Point Barrow and Kotzebue Sound, but one was worn by one of the Nunata'ñmiun who were at Nuwŭk in the autumn of 1881.

Rain-frocks.—The rain-frock (silû'ña) is made of strips of seal or walrus intestines about 3 inches broad, sewed together edge to edge. This material is light yellowish brown, translucent, very light, and quite waterproof. In shape the frock resembles a man's frock, but the hood comes well forward and fits closely round the face. It is generally plain, but the seams are nowadays sewed with black or colored cotton for ornament. The garment is of the same shape for both sexes, but the women frequently cover the flesh side of a deerskin frock with strips of entrail sewed together vertically, thus making a garment at once waterproof and warm, which is worn alone in summer with the hair side in. These gut shirts are worn over the clothes in summer when it rains or when the wearer is working in the boats. There are no specimens in the collection.

The kaiak jacket of black sealskin, so universal in Greenland, is unknown at Point Barrow. The waterproof gut frocks are peculiar to the western Eskimo, though shirts of seal gut, worn between the inner and outer frock, are mentioned by Egede (p. 130) and Crantz[1] as used in Greenland in their time. Ellis also[2] says: "Some few of them [i. e., the Eskimo of Hudsons Strait] wear shifts of seals' bladders, sewed together in pretty near the same form with those in Europe." They have been described generally under the name *kamleïka* (said to be a Siberian word) by all the authors who have treated of the natives of this region, Eskimo, Siberians, or Aleuts. We saw them worn by nearly all the natives at Plover Bay. One handsome one was observed trimmed on the seams with rows of little red nodules (pieces of the beak of one of the puffins) and tiny tufts of black feathers.

The cotton frock, already alluded to as worn to keep the driving snow out of the furs, is a long, loose shirt reaching to about midleg, with a round hole at the neck large enough to admit the head. This is generally of bright-colored calico, but shirts of white cotton are sometimes worn when hunting on the ice or snow. Similar frocks are worn by the natives at Pitlekaj.[3]

---

[1] Vol. 1, p. 137.

[2] Voyage to Hudsons Bay, p. 136.

[3] Nordenskiöld, Vega, vol. 2, p. 98.

ARM CLOTHING.

Mittens.—The hands are usually protected by mittens (aitkă′ti) of different kinds of fur. The commonest kind are of deerskin, worn with the flesh side out. Of these the collection contains one pair, No. 89828 [973] (Fig. 67). They are made of thick winter reindeer skin, with the white flesh side outward, in the shape of ordinary mittens but short and not narrowed at the wrists, with the thumb short and clumsy. The seams are all sewed "over and over" on the hair side. These mittens are about 7½ inches long and 4½ broad. The free part of the thumb is only 2¼ inches long on the outer side. Such mittens are the ordinary hand covering of men, women, and children. In extreme cold weather or during winter hunting, very heavy mittens of the same shape, but gathered to a wristband, are worn. These are made of white bearskin for men and women, for children of dog-skin, with the hair out. When the hand covered with such a mitten is held upon the windward side of the face in walking, the long hair affords a very efficient protection against the wind. The long stiff hair of the bear-skin also makes the mitten a very convenient brush for re-

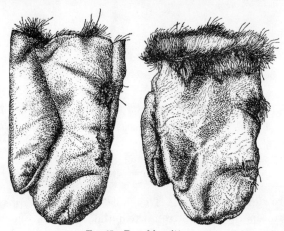

FIG. 67.—Deerskin mittens.

moving snow and hoar frost from the clothes. It is even sometimes used for brushing up the floor.

In the MacFarlane collection are similar mittens from the Mackenzie region. Petitot[1] says the Anderson River "chief" wore pualuk "mitaines en peau de morse, aussi blanches et aussi soyeuses que de belle laine." These were probably of bearskin, as a mitten of walrus skin is not likely to be "blanche" or "soyeuse." Gloves are worn under these as at Point Barrow. All these mittens are short in the wrist, barely meeting the frock sleeve, and leaving a crack for the cold to get in, which is partially covered by the usual wolf or wolverine skin fringe of the sleeve. I have already mentioned the common habit among the women of carrying only one mitten and drawing one arm inside of the frock.[2] The men, except when hunting, frequently wear only one of these heavy mittens, which are called pu′alu. Waterproof mittens of black sealskin, coming well up over the forearm, were also observed, but not obtained. I do not remember ever seeing them in use.

---

[1] Monographie, etc., p. xv.
[2] Compare Parry, 2d Voy., p. 494, where a similar habit is mentioned at Iglulik.

Gloves.—Gloves of thin deerskin, worn with the hair in, and often elegantly ornamented, are used with full dress, especially at the dances. As already stated, the men wear such gloves under the pualu when shooting in the winter. When ready to shoot, the hunter slips off the mitten and holds it between his legs, while the glove enables him to cock the rifle and draw the trigger without touching the cold metal with his bare hands. There are two pairs of gloves in the collection. No. 89829 [974] (Fig. 68) illustrates a very common style called a′drigûdrĭn. They are made of thin reindeer skin, with the white flesh side out, and

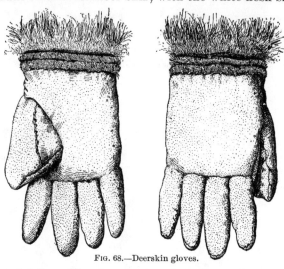

FIG. 68.—Deerskin gloves.

are rights and lefts. The short and rather clumsy fingers and thumbs are separate pieces from the palm, which is one straight, broad piece, doubled so as to bring the seam on the same side as the thumb. The thumbs are not alike on both hands. The outside piece of the thumb runs down to the wrist on the left glove, but is shorter on the right, the lower 2 inches of the edge seam being between the edges of the palm piece. Each finger is a single piece doubled lengthwise and sewed over the tip and down one side. The wrists are ornamented with an edging of two narrow strips of clipped mountain sheep skin, bordered with a narrow strip of wolverine fur with the reddened flesh side out. These gloves were made for sale and are not well mated, one being 8½ inches, with fingers (all of the same length) 4½ inches long, while the other is 8 inches long with fingers of 3½ inches. No. 56747 [128] is a pair of gloves made in the same way but more elaborately ornamented. There is a band of deerskin but no fringe round the wrist. The back of the hand is covered with brown deerskin, hair out, into which is inserted the square ornamental pattern in which the light stripes are white deerskin and the dark pipings the usual almost hairless fawn-skin. Gloves like this type are the most common and almost universally have a fringe round the wrist. They are also usually a little longer-wristed than the mittens.

Mittens are universally employed among the Eskimo, but gloves with fingers, which, as is well known, are a much less warm covering for the hand than mittens, are very rare. They are in use at Norton Sound [1] and in the Mackenzie district,[2] and have even been observed among the Arctic Highlanders of Smith Sound, who, however, generally wear mittens.[3] Dr. Simpson [4] mentions both deerskin and bearskin mittens as used at Point Barrow, but makes no reference to gloves. The natural inference from this is that the fashion of wearing gloves has been introduced since his time. It is quite probable that the introduction of firearms has favored the general adoption of gloves. The following hypothesis may be suggested as to the way the fashion reached Point Barrow: We may suppose that the Malimiut of Norton Sound got the idea directly from the Russians. They would carry the fashion to the Nunatañmiun at Kotzebue Sound, who in their turn would teach it to the Point Barrow traders at the Colville, and these would carry it on to the eastern natives.

LEG AND FOOT CLOTHING.

Breeches (*kǎ'kli*).—The usual leg-covering of the men is one or two pairs of knee breeches, rather loose, but fitted to the shape of the leg. They are very low in front, barely covering the pubes, but run up much higher behind, sometimes as high as the small of the back. They are held in place by a girdle of thong round the waist, and are usually fastened below the knee, over the boots, by a drawstring. There is one pair in the collection, No. 56759 [91], Fig. 69. They are of short-haired brown reindeer skin, from the body of the animal, worn with the hair out. The waist is higher behind than in front, and each leg is slightly gathered to a band just below the knee. Pattern (see diagram, Fig. 70): There are two pieces in each leg, the inside and the outside. The

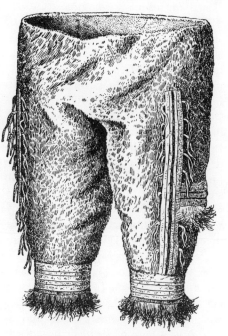

FIG. 69.—Man's breeches of deerskin.

spaces between the edges *e* of the two legs is filled by the gusset,

---

[1] Dall, Alaska, pp. 23, 152, and 153. He speaks of the thumb (p. 23) as "a triangular, shapeless protuberance"; a description which applies well to those in our collection.

[2] MacFarlane MS., and Petitot, Monographie, etc., p. xv.

[3] Bessels, Naturalist, vol. 18, p. 865.

[4] Op. cit., p. 242.

made of five pieces, which covers the pubes. The crotch is reinforced by a square patch of white deerskin sewed on the inside. The trimming consists of strips of edging. The first strip (Fig. 71) is 1½ inches wide, and runs along the front seam, inserted in the outside piece, to the knee-band, beginning 5 inches from the waist. The light strips

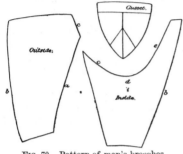

FIG. 70.—Pattern of man's breeches.

are of clipped mountain sheepskin; the dark one of dark brown deerskin; the pipings of the thin fawn skin, and the tags of red worsted. The edges of the strip are fringed with narrow double strips of mountain sheepskin 2 inches long, put on about 1½ inches apart. A straight strip, 2 inches wide, is inserted obliquely across the outside piece from seam to seam. It is of the same materials, but differs slightly in pattern. The knee-band is of the same materials and 2½ inches deep. The length from waist to knee is 24 inches behind, 23 in front; the girth of the leg 24 inches round the thigh and 14 round the knee. These represent a common style of full-dress breeches, and are worn with a pair of trimmed boots held up by drawstrings They are always worn with the hair out and usually over a pair of deerskin drawers. The ordinary breeches are of heavier deerskin, made perfectly plain, being usually worn alone, with the hair turned in. When a pair of under breeches is worn, however, the hair of the outer ones is turned out. Trimmed breeches are less common than trimmed frocks, as the plain breeches when new are often worn for full dress. The clean, white flesh side presents a very neat appearance. The skin of the rough seal is sometimes, but rarely, used for summer breeches,

³⁄₈

FIG. 71.—Trimming of man's breeches.

which are worn with the hair out. With this exception, breeches seem to be invariably made of deerskin. This garment is practically universal among the Eskimo and varies very little in pattern.

Pantaloons (*kûmûñ*).—The women and children, and occasionally the men, wear pantaloons (stricly speaking), i. e., tight-fitting trousers continuous with the foot covering. Of the two pairs of pantaloons in the collection, No. 74042 [1792] (Fig. 72) will serve as the type. The shoes with sealskin moccasin soles and deerskin uppers are sewed at the ankles to a pair of tight-fitting deerskin trousers, reaching above the hips and higher behind than in front. Pattern (diagram, Fig. 73a): Each leg is composed of four long pieces (front 1, outside 2, back 3, and inside 4), five gussets (one on the thigh 5, and four on the calf, 6, 6, 6, 6), which enlarges the garment to fit the swell of the calf and thigh and the half-waistband (7). The two legs are put together by joining the edges *d d d* of the opposite legs and sewing the gusset (8) into the space in front with its base joined to the edges *e e* of the two legs. The sole of each shoe is a single piece of white tanned sealskin with the grain side out, bent up about 1¼ inches all round the foot, rounded at the toe and heel and broadest across the ball of the foot. The toe and heel are "gathered" into shape by crimping the edge vertically. A space of about 3½ inches is left uncrimped on each side of the foot. (The process of crimping these soles will be described under the head of boots and shoes, where it properly belongs). Around the top of this sole is sewed a narrow band of white sealskin, sewed "over and over" on the edge of the uncrimped space, but "run" through the gathers at the ends, so as to draw them up. The upper is in two pieces (heel, 9, and toe, 10). The heel piece is folded round the heel, and the toe piece doubled along the line *f*, and the curved edges *g g* joined to the straight edges *h h*, which makes the folded edge *f*, fit the outline of the instep. The bottom is then cut off accurately to fit the sole and sewed to the edge of the band. The trousers and shoes are sewed together at the ankles. The whole is made of the short-haired skin from the deer's legs.

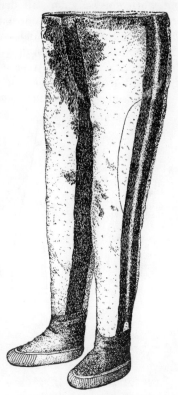

FIG. 72.—Woman's pantaloons.

Pieces 2, 4, 7, 8, 9, and 10 are of dark brown skin (10 put on so that the tuft of coarse hair on the deer's ankle comes on the outside of the wearer's ankle), while the remaining pieces are white, making a pleasing pattern of broad stripes. The inner edge of 5 is piped with dark brown fawnskin, and a round piece of white skin is inserted at the bottom of 2. No. 56748 [136] is a pair of pantaloons of nearly the same pattern (see diagram, Fig. 73*b*) and put together in a similar way. These pantaloons have soles of sealskin with the hair left on and worn inside, and are made of deer leg-skin, wholly dark brown, except the gussets on the calf, which are white. There is a piece of white skin let out, 2, as before, and the ankle tuft is in the same position.

From the general fit of these garments they appear to be all made on essentially the same pattern, probably without greater variations than those already described. When worn by the women the material is usually, if not always, the skin of reindeer legs, and most commonly of the pattern of No. 56748 [136], namely, brown, with white leg gussets. Pantaloons wholly of brown skin are quite common, especially for everyday wear, while striped ones, like No. 74042 [1792], are much less usual and worn specially for full dress. Children's pantaloons are always brown, and I have seen one pair, worn by a young lad, of lynx skin. The two or three pairs which we saw worn by men were wholly brown. These pantaloons of leg skin with sealskin soles are always worn with the hair out and usually over a pair of under pantaloons of the same shape, but made of softer skins with longer hair, which is worn next the skin, and with stocking feet. The outer pantaloons are discarded

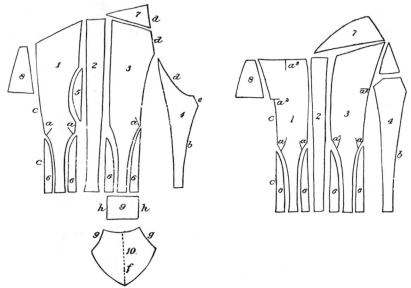

Fig. 73.—Patterns of woman's pantaloons.

in summer and the inner ones only worn, the feet being protected by sealskin waterproof boots, as already stated. The waterproof sealskin pantaloons mentioned in the same connection do not fit so neatly, as they are made with as few seams as possible (usually only one, up the leg) to avoid leakage. They are sewed with the waterproof seam, and held up round the ankle by strings, like the waterproof boots to be described further on. This last-mentioned garment seems to be peculiar to the Point Barrow region (including probably Wainwright Inlet and perhaps the rest of the coast down to Kotzebue Sound). No mention of such a complete protection against wet is to be found in any of the published accounts of the Eskimo elsewhere, nor are there any specimens in the Museum.[1]

---

[1] Dr. Simpson's language (op. cit., p. 243) is a little indefinite ("The feet and legs are incased in water-tight sealskin boots"), but probably refers to these as well as to the knee boots. The "outside coat of the same material," and the boots and outside coat "made all in one, with a drawing string round the face," mentioned in the same place, appears to have gone wholly out of fashion since his time. At all events, we saw neither, though we continually saw the natives when working in the boats, and these garments, especially the latter, could hardly have failed to attract our attention.

Boots and breeches united in this way so as to form pantaloons are peculiar to the west of America, where they are universally worn from the Mackenzie district westward and southward. We have no specimens of women's leg coverings from the Mackenzie district, but Petitot[1] describes them thus: "Le pantalon * * * fait corps avec la chaussure." In the east the women always wear breeches separate from the boots, which usually differ from those of the men in their size and length, often reaching to the hips.[2]

Stockings.—Next to the skin on the feet and legs the men wear stockings of deerskin, usually of soft, rather long-haired skin, with the hair in. These are usually in three pieces, the leg, 1, toe piece, 2, and sole, 3 (see diagram, Fig. 74). A straight strip about 1 inch wide often runs round the foot between the sole and the other pieces. Stockings of this pattern, but made of very thick winter deerskin, are substituted for the outer boots when deer-hunting in winter in the dry snow, especially when snowshoes are used. They are warm; the flesh side sheds the snow well and the thick hair acts as a sort of wadding which keeps the feet from being galled by the bars and strings of the snowshoes. Many of the deer-hunters in 1883 made rough buskins of this pattern out of the skins of freshly killed deer simply dried, without further preparation.

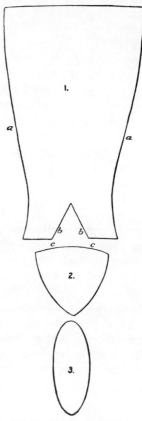

FIG. 74.—Pattern of stocking.

Boots and shoes.—Over the stockings are worn boots or shoes with uppers of various kinds of skin, with the hair on, or black tanned sealskin, always fitted to heelless crimped moccasin soles of some different leather, of the pattern which, with some slight modifications of form, is universal among the Eskimo. These soles are made as follows: A "blank" for the sole is cut out, of the shape of the foot, but a couple of inches larger all round. Then, beginning at one side of the ball of the foot, the toe part is doubled over toward the inside of the sole, so that the edges just match. The two parts are then pinched together with

---

[1] Monographie, etc., p. xv.

[2] Bessels, Naturalist, vol. 18, p. 865, Smith Sound; Egede, p. 131, and Crantz, vol. 1, p. 138, Greenland; Parry, 2d Voy., p. 495 and 496, Iglulik, and Kumlien, op. cit., p. 23, Cumberland Gulf. Also in Labrador, see Pl. XVII, Naturalist, vol. 19, No. 6. The old couple whom Franklin met at the Bloody Fall of the Coppermine appear to have worn pantaloons, for he speaks of their "tight leggings sewed to shoes" (1st Exp., vol. 2, p. 180).

the teeth along a line parallel to the folded edge and at a distance
from it equal to the depth of the intended fold.   This bitten line runs
from the edge of the leather as far as it is intended to turn up the side
of the sole.   A series of similar folds is carried round the toe to a point
on the other side of the sole opposite the starting point.   In the same
way a series of crimps is carried round the heel, leaving an uncrimped
space of 2 or 3 inches on each side of the foot.   The sole is then sewed
to a band or to the edge of the upper, with the thread run through each
fold of the crimps.   This gathers the sole in at the heel and toe and
brings the uncrimped part straight up on each side of the shank.   When
the folds are all of the same length and but slightly gathered the sole is
turned up nearly straight, as at the heel usually, and at the toe also of
waterproof boots.   When the folds are long and much gathered the sole
slopes well in over the foot.   Some boots, especially those intended for full
dress, have the sole deeper on the sides than at the toe, so that the top of
the sole comes to a point at the toe.   The ordinary pattern is about the
same height all round and follows the shape of the foot, being rather more
gathered in over the toe than at the heel.   The "blank" for the sole is cut
out by measuring the size of the foot on the leather and allowing by eye
the margin which is to be turned up.   The crimping is also done by
eye.   Any irregularity in the length of the crimps can be remedied by
pressing out the crease.   I have never seen at Point Barrow the ivory
knives, such as are used at Norton Sound for arranging the crimps.

Different kinds of leather are used for the soles, and each kind is
supposed to be best suited for a particular purpose.   The beautiful
white urine-tanned sealskin is used for winter wear when the snow is
dry, but is not suited for standing the roughness and dampness of the
salt-water ice.   For this purpose sealskin dressed with the hair on and
worn flesh side out is said to be the very best, preferable even to the
various waterproof skins used for summer boot soles.   For waterproof
soles are used oil-dressed skins[1] of the walrus, bearded seal, polar bear,
or, best of all, the white whale.   This last makes a beautiful light yellow
translucent leather about 0·1 inch thick, which is quite durable and
keeps out water for a long time.   It is highly prized and quite an article
of trade among the natives, a pair of soles usually commanding a good
price.   These Eskimo appear to be the only ones who have discovered
the excellence of this material for waterproof soles, as there is no mention to be found of its use elsewhere.   The "narwhal skin" spoken of
by Dr. Simpson[2] is probably this material, as he calls it "Kel-lel'-lu-a,"
which is the ordinary word for white whale at Point Barrow.   The narwhal is very rare in these waters, while the white whale is comparatively
abundant.   Dr. Simpson appears not to have seen the animal from which
the skin was obtained.   It is, however, by no means impossible that *some*
skins of the narwhal, which when dressed would be indistinguishable

[1] Probably prepared like the boat covers described by Crantz, vol. 1, p. 167, by drying them without
removing all of their own blubber.

[2] Op. cit., pp. 242–266.

from the white whale skins, are obtained from the eastern natives or elsewhere. Such crimped soles are in use among the Eskimo everywhere, varying but little in general pattern. The Greenland boots are specially noticeable for the neatness of the crimping, while specimens in the Museum from the central region are decidedly slovenly in their workmanship. The boots worn by the natives of Plover Bay have the sole narrowed at the shank and hardly coming over the foot except at the toe and heel, where they are crimped, but less deeply than usual. This style of sole very much resembles those of a pair of Kamchatdale boots in the National Museum, which, however, are turned up without crimping, as is the case with the boots used by the Aleuts on the Commander Islands, of which Dr. L. Stejneger has kindly shown me a specimen. There is a folded "welt" of sealskin in the seam between the upper and sole of the Plover Bay boots. I am informed by Capt. Herendeen that the natives have been taught to put this in by the whalemen who every year purchase large numbers of boots on

FIG. 75.—Man's boot of deerskin.

the Siberian coast, for use in the Arctic. Similar welts, which are very unusual on Eskimo boots, are to be seen on some brought by Mr. Nelson from Kings Island and Norton Sound. The winter boots usually have uppers of deerskin, generally the short-haired skin from the legs. Mountain-sheep skin is sometimes used for full-dress boots, and sealskin with the hair out for working boots. The latter is not a good material, as the snow sticks to it badly. There are four pairs of men's winter boots in the collection, from which No. 56750 [111] (Fig. 75) has been selected as the type of the everyday pattern. They are made of deer-leg skin with white sealskin soles. Leg and upper are in four pieces,[1] back 1, two sides 2 2, and front 3; 1 and 3 are gored at *a a a* to fit the swell

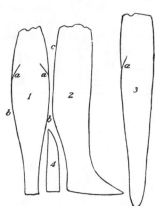

FIG. 76.—Pattern of deerskin boot.

of the calf; 1 and 3 are of dark skin, and 2 2 lighter colored, especially along the middle. The bottom is cut off accurately to fit the sole but the top is left irregular, as this is concealed by the breeches. The boots are

[1] See diagram, Fig. 76.

held up round the ankles by two tie-strings of sealthong, sewed in between the sole and the band, one on each side just under the middle of the ankle.   They are long enough to cross above the heel, pass once or

twice round the ankle, which fits more loosely than the rest of the boot, and tie in front.   On each heel is a large round patch of sealskin with the hair on and pointing toward the toe (to prevent slipping).   These patches are carefully "blind-stitched" on so that the stitches do not show on the outside.

Boots of this style are the common everyday wear of the men, sometimes made wholly of dark deerskin and sometimes variegated. They are often made of a pattern like that of the lower part of the women's pantaloons; that is, with the uppers separate from the leg pieces, which are brown, with four white gussets on the calf.   Fig. 77, No. 56759 [91], is one of a pair of full-dress boots of a slightly different pattern.   The leg pieces are the same in number as in No. 56750, and put together in the same way, but 2 and 3 are of a different shape.[1]   They are made of deerleg skins, each piece with a lighter streak down the middle.   The soles are of white sealskin, finely crimped, with the edge coming

FIG. 77.—Man's dress boot of deer-skin.

to a point at the toe, and the five ornamental bands are of sealskin, alternately black and white.   A strip of edging three-fourths of an inch wide is inserted in the seam between 2 and 3 on each side.   The light stripes are mountain-sheep skin and the dark ones the usual young fawnskin, tagged with red worsted.   The leg reaches to just below the knee, and is hemmed over on the inside, to hold the drawstring, which comes out behind.   There are strings at the ankles as before.

Fig. 79, No. 89834 [770], is one of a pair of almost precisely the same pattern as the last, but made of mountain-sheep skin.   The soles are more deeply turned up all round and have three ornamental bands of sealskin around the edge, black, white, and black.   Edging is inserted into both the seams on each side.   It is of strips of moun-

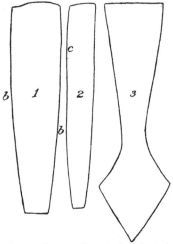

FIG. 78.—Pattern of man's dress boot of deerskin.

---

[1] See diagram, Fig. 78.

tain-sheep skin and a dark brown deerskin, tagged with red worsted, with the edge which laps over the side piece cut into oblique tags. There are no tiestrings, as the soles are turned up high enough to stay in place without them. These boots were brought from the east by one of the Nuwŭk trading parties in 1882. Fig. 80, No. 56749 [110], is also a full-dress boot, with soles like the last and no tiestrings. The leg is of two pieces of dark brown deerskin with the hair clipped short. These pieces are shaped like 2 in No. 56750, and the inner is larger, so that it laps round the leg, bringing the seam on the outside. The leg is enlarged to fit the swell of the calf by a large triangular gusset from the knee to the midleg, meeting the inside piece in an oblique seam across the calf. Instead of a hem, the top of the leg has a half-inch band sewed round it and a binding for the drawstring above this. Edging is inserted in the front seam, and obliquely across the outside of the leg. That in the front seam is three narrow strips of deerskin, dark in the middle and light on each side. The other is of mountain-sheep skin in three strips, piped with fawnskin and tagged with worsted.

FIG. 79.—Man's dress boot of skin of mountain sheep.

The boots belong with the breeches, No. 56759. They fairly represent the style of full-dress boots worn with the loose-bottomed breeches. They all have drawstrings just below the knee, and often have no tie-strings at the ankles. The eastern Eskimo are everywhere described as wearing the boots tied at the top with a drawstring and the bottoms of the breeches usually loose and hanging down on them. Tying down the breeches over the tops of the boots, as is done at Point Barrow, is an improvement on the eastern fashion, as it closes the garments at the knee so as to prevent the entrance of cold air. The same result is obtained in an exactly opposite way by the people of Smith Sound, who, according to Bessels (Naturalist, vol. 18, p. 865), tie the boots over the breeches.

All fur garments, including boots, are sewed in the same way, usually with reindeer sinew, by fitting the edges together and sewing them "over and over" on the "wrong" side. The waterproof boots of black sealskin, however, are sewed with an elaborate double seam, which is quite waterproof, and is made as follows: The two pieces are put together, flesh side to flesh side, so that the edge of one projects beyond the other, which is then "blind-stitched" down by sewing it "over and over" on the edge, taking pains to run the stitches only part way through the other piece. The seam is then turned and the edge of

the outer piece is turned in and "run" down to the grain side of the under with fine stitches which do not run through to the flesh side of it. Thus in neither seam are there holes through both pieces at once. The sewing is done with fine sinew thread and very fine round needles (the women used to ask for "little needles, like a hair"), and the edge of the leather is softened by wetting it in the mouth. A similar waterproof seam is used in sewing together boat covers.

There is one pair of waterproof boots in the collection (No. 76182 [1794] Fig. 81). The tops are of black dressed sealskin, reaching to the knee and

FIG. 80.—Pair of man's dress boots of deerskin.   especially full on the instep and

ankle, which results from their being made with the least possible number of seams, to reduce the chance of leaking. The soles are of white whale skin, turned up about 1½ inches all around. The leg and upper are made all in one piece so that the double water-tight seam runs down the front of the leg to the instep, and then diagonally across the foot to the quarter on one side. The bottom is cut off accurately to fit the top of the sole. The edges of the upper and the sole are put together so that the inside of the former comes against the inside of the latter, and the two are "run" together with fine stitches, with a stout double under-thread running through them along the surface of the upper. The ornamental band at the top is of white sealskin "run" on with strong dark thread, and the checkered pattern is made by drawing a strip of black skin through slits in the white. Round the top of the band is sewed a binding of black sealskin, which holds a drawstring of sinew braid. The sole is kept up in shape and the boot made to fit round the ankle by a string of sealskin twine passed through four loops, one on each side just back of the ball of the foot, and one on each quarter. These loops are made of little strips of white whale skin, doubled over and sewed to the edge of the sole on the outside. The ends of the string are passed through the front loop so that the bight comes across the ball of the foot, then through the hinder loops, and are crossed above the heel, carried once or twice around the ankle, and tied in front.

Such boots are universally worn in summer. The men's boots are usually left with an irregular edge at the top, and are held up by the breeches, while the women's usually have white bands around the tops with drawstrings. Half-boots of the same material, reaching to mid-leg, without drawstrings, or shoes reaching just above the ankle with a string round the top are sometimes worn over the deerskin boots. Similar shoes of deerskin are sometimes worn in place of boots.

Waterproof boots of black seal-skin are universally employed by Eskimo and by the Aleuts. These boots stand water for a long time without getting wet through, but when they become wet they must be turned inside out and dried very slowly to prevent them from shrinking, and worked soft with a stone

FIG. 81.—Woman's waterproof sealskin boot.

skin-dressing tool or the teeth. The natives prefer to dry them in the sun. When the black epidermis wears off this leather is no longer waterproof, so that the women are always on the watch for white spots, which are mended with water-tight patches as soon as possible.

In the early spring, before it thaws enough to render waterproof boots

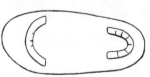

FIG. 82.—Sketch of "ice-creepers" on boot sole.

necessary, the surface of the snow becomes very smooth and slippery. To enable themselves to walk on this surface without falling, the natives make a kind of "creeper" out of strips of sealskin. These are doubled lengthwise, and generally bent into a half-moon or horseshoe shape, with the folded edges on the outside of the curve, sewed on the toe and heel of the sealskin sole, as represented in Fig. 82.

PARTS OF DRESS.

Belts (*tapsĭ*).—The belt which is used to hold up the pantaloons or breeches is simply a stout strip of skin tied round the waist. The girdle, which is always worn outside of the frock, except when the weather is warm or the wearer heated by exercise, is very often a similar strap of deerskin, or perhaps wolfskin. Often, however, and especially for full dress, the men wear a handsome belt woven from feathers, and the women one made of wolverines' toes. There are in the collection two of the former and one of the latter.

No. 89544 [1419] (Fig. 83*a*) has been chosen as the type of a man's belt. It is 35 inches long and 1 inch broad, and made of the shafts of feathers woven into an elegant pattern, bordered on the edges with deerskin, and terminating in a leather loop at one end and a braided string at the other. The loop is a flat piece of skin of the bearded seal, in which is cut a large oblong eye. The weaving begins at the square end of the loop. The warp consists of nine long strands sewed through the inner face of the leather so as to come out on the hinder edge. The middle strand is of stout sinew braid, ending in a knot on the

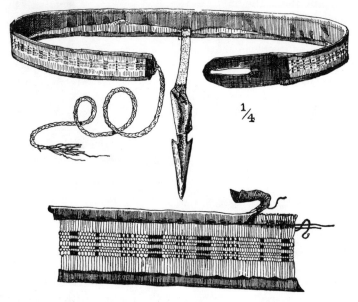

Fig. 83.—Man's belt woven of feathers. The lower cut shows detail of pattern.

inner side of the leather. The four on each side are of fine cotton twine or stout thread, each two being one continuous thread passing through the leather and out again. The woof is the shafts of small feathers regularly woven, the first strand woven over and under, ending over the warp, the next under and over, ending under the warp, and so on alternately, each strand extending about one-fourth inch beyond the outer warp-strand on each side. This makes the pattern shown in Fig. 83*b*, a long stitch on each side, three very short ones on each side of the middle, and a slightly longer one in the middle. The strips of feathers forming the woof are not joined together, but one strip is woven in as far as it will go, ending always on the inner side of the belt, a new strip beginning where the other ends. The shafts of black feathers, with a few of the barbs attached, are woven into the woof at tolerably regular intervals. Each black strand starts under the first strand of the warp, making the outer and inner of the three short stitches on each side black. This produces a checkered pattern along the middle of the belt (see enlarged section, Fig. 83b). The woof strands are driven home tightly and their ends are secured on each side by a double thread of cotton sewed into the corner of the leather loop. One thread runs along the outside of the belt and the other along the inside, passing between the ends of the feathers about every ten feathers and making a turn round the outer thread, as in Fig. 84. The edges of the belt are trimmed off even and bound with

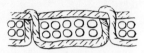

FIG. 84. — Diagram showing method of fastening the ends of feathers in belt.

a narrow strip of deerskin with the flesh side out and painted red. The binding of the upper edge makes an irregular loose lining on the inside of the belt. Across the end of the belt is sewed on each side a narrow strip of sealskin, and the ends of the warp are gathered into a three-ply braid 16 inches long, which is used to fasten the belt by drawing it through the loop and knotting it. An ancient bone spearhead is attached to the belt as an amulet by a stout strap.

No. 89543 [1420] is a similar belt worn in precisely the same way, but with the black feathers introduced in a different pattern. The weaving is done by hand with the help of some little tools, to be described under implements for making and working fiber. Belts of

3/8

FIG. 85.—Woman's belt of wolverine toes.

this style appear to be peculiar to the Point Barrow region. Indeed, girdles of any kind are seldom worn over the jacket by the men in the eastern regions.

The women never wear anything except a simple strip of skin or the wolvervine belt mentioned above. No. 89542 [1421], Fig. 85, is one of these. It is made of nine strips of dark brown skin from round the foot of the wolverine, sewed together end to end. Each strip, except the one at the end, has a claw at the lower corner (on some of the strips the bit of skin bearing the claws is pieced in) so that there are

eight nearly equidistant claws making a fringe round the lower edge
of the belt. There is a hole at each end into which is half-hitched the
end of a narrow strip of deerskin about 8 inches long. These strings
serve to tie the girdle. This belt is 33 inches long and 1½ inches wide,
and has been worn so long that the inside is very dirty. Such belts
are very valuable and highly prized, and are worn exclusively by the
women.

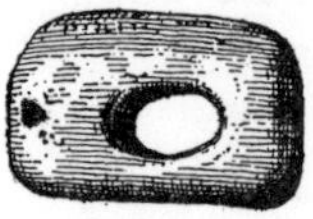

Fig. 86, No. 89718 [1055], is an object which is quite uncommon and
seldom if ever now seen in use. It is of walrus ivory,
very old and yellow. It served as a belt-fastener (táp-
sĭgʋ). I have seen a brass clock wheel used on a girl's
belt for the same purpose. This specimen is very old,
neatly made, and polished smooth, probably from long
use.

FIG. 86.—Belt-fast-
ener.

Ornaments.—In addition to the trimmings above described there are
certain ornamental appendages which belong to the dress, but can not
be considered as essential parts of any garments, like the trimmings.
For instance, nearly every male in the two villages wears dangling from
his back between the shoulders an ermine skin either brown or white,
or an eagle's feather, which is transferred to the new garment when the old
one is worn out. This is perhaps an amulet as well as an ornament, as Dr.
Simpson states.[1] An eagle's feather is often worn on the outside of the
hood, pendant from the crown of the head. Attached to the belt are various amulets (to be described under the head of "Religion") and at the
back always the tail of an animal, usually a wolverine's. Very seldom
a wolf's tail is worn, but nearly all, even the boys, have wolverine
tails, which are always saved for this purpose and used for no other.
This habit among the Eskimo of western America of wearing a tail at
the girdle has been noticed by many travelers, and prevails at least as
far as the Anderson River, since Petitot,[2] in describing the dress of the
Anderson River "chief," says: "par derrière il portait aux reins une
queue épaisse et ondoyante de renard noir." According to him[3] it is
the *women* of that region, who wear, "à titre de talismans, des defroques
empaillées de corbeau, de faucon, ou d'hermine." The custom of wearing an ermine skin on the jacket was observed by Dr. Armstrong of the
Investigator at Cape Bathurst.[4]

PERSONAL ADORNMENT.

SKIN ORNAMENTATION.

Tattooing.—The custom of tattooing is almost universal among the
women, but the marks are confined almost exclusively to the chin and
form a very simple pattern. This consists of one, three, five, or perhaps as

---

[1] Op. cit., p. 243.   [3] Ibid.
[2] Monographie, etc., p. xiv.   [4] Personal Narrative, p. 176.

many as seven vertical lines from the under lip to the tip of the chin, slightly radiating when there are more than one. When there is a single line, which is rather rare, it is generally broad, and the middle line is sometimes broader than the others. The women as a rule are not tattooed until they reach a marriageable age, though there were a few little girls in the two villages who had a single line on the chin. I remember seeing but one married woman in either village who was not tattooed, and she had come from a distant settlement, from Point Hope, as well as we could understand.

Tattooing on a man is a mark of distinction. Those men who are, or have been, captains of whaling umiaks that have taken whales have marks to indicate this tattooed somewhere on their persons, sometimes forming a definite tally. For instance, Añoru had a broad band across each cheek from the corners of the mouth (Fig. 87, from a sketch by the writer), made up of many indistinct lines, which was said to indicate "many whales." Amaiyuna had the "flukes" of seven whales in a line across his chest, and Mû´ñialu had a couple of small marks on one forearm. Niăksára, the wife of Añoru, also had a little mark tattooed in each corner of her mouth, which she said were "whale marks," indicating that she was the wife of a successful whaleman. Such marks, according to Petitot (Monographie, etc., p. xv) are a part of the usual pattern in the Mackenzie district— "deux traits aux commissures de la bouche." One or two men at Nuwŭk had each a narrow line across the face, over the bridge of the nose, which

FIG. 87.—Man with tattooed cheeks.

were probably also "whale marks," though we never could get a definite answer concerning them.[1]

The tattooing is done with a needle and thread, smeared with soot or gunpowder, giving a peculiar pitted appearance to the lines. It is rather a painful operation, producing considerable inflammation and swelling, which lasts several days. The practice of tattooing the women is almost universal among the Eskimo, from Greenland to Kadiak, including the Eskimo of Siberia, the only exception being the

---

[1] Compare the custom observed by H. M. S. *Investigator*, at Cape Bathurst, where, according to McClure (Discovery of the Northwest Passage, p. 93), a successful harpooner has a blue line drawn across his face over the bridge of the nose; or, according to Armstrong (Personal Narrative, p. 176), he has a line tattooed from the inner angle of the eye across the cheek, a new one being added for every whale he strikes. Petitot, however (Monographie, etc., p. xxv), says that in this region whales are "scored" by tattooing crosses on the shoulder, and that a murderer is marked across the nose with a couple of horizontal lines. It is interesting to note in this connection that one of the "striped" men at Nuwŭk told us that he had killed a man. According to Holm, at Angmagsalik (east Greenland), "Mændene ere kun undtagelsvis tatoverede og da kun med enkelte mindre Streger paa Arme og Haandled, for at kunne harpunere godt" (Geogr. Tids., vol. 8, p. 88). Compare also Hooper, Tents, etc., p. 37, "Men only make a permanent mark on the face for an act of prowess, such as killing a bear, capturing a whale, etc.;" and Parry, 2d Voyage, p. 449, where some of the men at Iglulik are said to be tattooed on the back of the hand, as a souvenir of some distant or deceased person.

natives of Smith Sound, though the custom is falling into disuse among the Eskimo who have much intercourse with the whites.[1]

The simple pattern of straight, slightly diverging lines on the chin seems to prevail from the Mackenzie district to Kadiak, and similar

FIG. 88.—Woman with ordinary tattooing.

chin lines appear always to form part of the more elaborate patterns, sometimes extending to the arms and other parts of the body, in fashion among the eastern Eskimo[2] and those of Siberia, St. Lawrence Island, and the Diomedes.

Fig. 88, from a sketch made on the spot by the writer, shows the Point Barrow pattern.

Painting.—On great occasions, such as dances, etc., or when going whaling, the face is marked with a broad streak of black lead, put on with the finger, and usually running obliquely across the nose or one cheek.[3] Children, when dressed up in new clothes, are also frequently marked in this way. This may be compared with the ancient custom among the people of Kadiak of painting their faces "before festivities or games and before any important undertaking, such as the crossing of a wide strait or arm of the sea, the sea-otter chase, etc."[4]

HEAD ORNAMENTS.

Method of wearing the hair.—The men and boys wear their hair combed down straight over the forehead and cut off square across in front, but hanging in rather long locks on the sides, so as to cover the ears. There is always a small circular tonsure on the crown of the head, and a strip is generally clipped down to the nape of the neck. (See Fig. 89, from a sketch from life by the writer.) The natives believe that this clipping of the back of the head prevents snow blindness in the spring. The people of the Mackenzie district have a different theory. "La large

---

[1] Bessels, Naturalist, vol. 18, p. 875 (Smith Sound); Egede, p. 132, and Crantz, vol. 1, p. 138, already given up by the Christian Greenlanders (Greenland); Holm, Geogr. Tids., vol. 8, p. 88, still practiced regularly in east Greenland; Parry, 1st Voyage, p. 282 (Baffin Land); 2d Voyage, p. 498 (Iglulik); Kumlien, Contrib., p. 26 (Cumberland Gulf, aged women chiefly); Boas, "Central Eskimo," p. 561; Chappell, "Hudson Bay," p. 60 (Hudson Strait); Back, Journey, etc., p. 289 (Great Fish River); Franklin, 1st Exped., vol. 2, p. 183 (Coppermine River); 2d Exped., p. 126 (Point Sabine); Petitot, Monographie, etc., p. xv (Mackenzie district); Dall, "Alaska," pp. 140, 381 (Norton Sound, Diomede Islands, and Plover Bay); Petroff, Report, etc., p. 139 (Kadiak); Lisiansky, Voyage, p. 195 (Kadiak in 1805, "the fair sex were also fond of tattooing the chin, breasts, and back, but this again is much out of fashion"); Nordenskiöld, Vega, vol. 2, pp. 99, 100, 251, and 252, with figures (Siberia and St. Lawrence Island); Krause brothers, Geographische Blätter, vol. 5, pp. 4, 5 (East Cape to Plover Bay); Hooper, Tents, etc., p. 37, "Women were tattooed on the chin in diverging lines" (Plover Bay); Rosse, Cruise of the *Corwin*, p. 35, fig. on p. 36 (St. Lawrence Island).

Frobisher's account, being the earliest on record, is worth quoting: " * * * The women are marked on the face with blewe streekes downe the cheekes and round about the eies" (p. 621). * * * "Also, some of their women race their faces proportionally, as chinne, cheekes, and forehead, and the wristes of their hands, whereupon they lay a colour, which continueth dark azurine" (p. 627). Hakluyt's Voyages, etc., 1589.

[2] Holm (East Greenland) says: "et Paar korte Streger paa Hagen" (Geogr. Tids. vol. 8, p. 88).

[3] Compare Kotzebue's Voy., vol. 3, p. 296, where Chamisso describes the natives of St. Lawrence Bay, Siberia, as having large quantities of fine graphite, with which they painted their faces.

[4] Petroff Report, etc., p. 139.

tonsure que portent nos Tchiglit a pour but, m'ont-ils dit, de permettre au soleil de rechauffer leur cerveau et de transmettre par ce moyen sa bienfaisante chaleur à leur cœur pour les faire vivre."[1] Some of the Nunatañmiun and one man from Kilauwïtaiwïñ that we saw wore their front hair long, parted in the middle, and confined by a narrow fillet of leather round the brow. The hair on the tonsure is not always kept clipped very close, but sometimes allowed to grow as much as an inch long, which probably led Hooper to believe that the tonsure was not common at Point Barrow.[2] It is universal at the present day, as it was in Dr. Simpson's time.[3] The western Eskimo generally crop or shave the crown of the head, while those of the east allow their hair to grow pretty long, sometimes clipping it on the forehead. The practice of clipping the crown appears to be general in the Mackenzie district,[4] and was occasionally observed at Iglulik by Capt. Parry (2d Voy., p. 493). The natives of St. Lawrence Island and the Siberian coast carry this custom to an extreme, clipping the whole crown, so as to leave only a fringe round the head.[5] The women dress their

hair in the fashion common to all the Eskimo except the Greenlanders and the people about the Mackenzie and Anderson Rivers, where the women bring the hair up from behind into a sort of high top-knot, with the addition in the latter district of large bows or pigtails on the sides.[6] The hair is parted in the middle from the forehead to the nape of the neck, and gathered into a club on each side behind the ear. The club is either simply braided

FIG. 89.—Man's method of wearing the hair.

or without further dressing twisted and lengthened out with strips of leather, and wound spirally for its whole length with a long string of small beads of various colors, a large flat brass button being stuck into the hair above each club. The wife of the captain of a whaling umiak wears a strip of wolfskin in place of the string of beads when the boat is "in commission" (as Capt. Herendeen observed).

Some of the little girls wear their hair cut short behind. The hair is not arranged every day. Both sexes are rather tidy about arranging their hair, but there is much difference in this between individuals. The marrow of the reindeer is sometimes used for pomatum. Baldness

---

[1] Petitot, Monographie, etc., p. xxxi.

[2] Tents, etc., p. 225.

[3] Op. cit., p. 238.

[4] Petitot, Monographie, etc., p. xxxi. See also Franklin, 2d·Exp., p. 118.

[5] See also Nordenskiöld, Vega, vol. 2, pp. 9 and 252, and figures passim, especially pp. 84 and 85; Hooper, Tents, etc., p. 27; and Dall, Alaska, p. 381.

[6] See Kane, 2d Grinnell Exp. Many illustrations, passim, Smith Sound; Egede, p. 132, and Crantz, vol. 1, p. 128, Greenland; Brodbeck, "Nach Osten," p. 23, and Holm, Geogr. Tids., vol. 8, p. 90, East Greenland; Frobisher, in Hakluyt, Voyages, etc. (1589), p. 627, Baffin Land; Parry, 2d Voy., p. 494, and Lyon, Journal, p. 230, Iglulik; Petitot, Monographie, etc., p. xxix, Mackenzie district; Hooper, Tents, etc., pp. 257, Icy Reef, and 347, Maitland Id.; Franklin, 2d Exp., p. 119, Point Sabine; Dall, Alaska, pp. 140 and 381, Norton Sound and Plover Bay. See also references to Nordenskiöld, given above, and Krause Bros., Geographische Blätter, vol. 5, pt. 1, p. 5.

in either sex is rare. I do not remember ever seeing a bald woman, and there were only two bald men at the two villages. Neither of these men was very old.

Head-bands.—Some of the men and boys wear across the forehead a string of large blue glass beads, sometimes sewed on a strip of deer-skin. Occasionally, also a fillet is worn made of the skin of the head of a fox or a dog, with the nose coming in the middle of the forehead. Such head-dresses are by no means common and seem to be highly prized, as they were never offered for sale. MacFarlane (MS.) speaks of a similar head-dress worn at the Anderson River, "generally made of the skin of the fore part of the head skins of wolves, wolverines, and marmots. Very often, however, a string of beads is made use of instead." Another style of head-dress is the badge of a whaleman, and is worn only when whaling (and, I believe, at the ceremonies in the spring preparatory to the whaling). This seems to be very highly prized, and is, perhaps, "looked upon with superstitious regard."[1] None were ever offered for sale and we had only two or three opportunities of seeing it. It consists of a broad fillet of mountain-sheep skin, with pendants of flint, jasper, or crystal, rudely flaked into the shape of a whale (see under "Amulets," where specimens are described and figured), one in the middle of the brow and one over each ear. Some of them are also fringed with the incisor teeth of the mountain sheep attached by means of a small hole drilled through the end of the root, as on the dancing cap (see under "Games and Pastimes"). The captain and harpooner of a whaling crew which I saw starting out in the spring of 1882 each wore one of these fillets. The harpooner's had only the whale pendants, but the captain's was also fringed with teeth. This ornament closely resembles the fillet fringed with deer's teeth, observed by Capt. Parry at Iglulik,[2] which "was understood to be worn on the head by men, though we did not learn on what occasions."

Earrings (*nógolu*).—Nearly all the women and girls perforate the lobes of the ears and wear earrings. The commonest pattern is a little hook of ivory to which are attached pendants, short strings of beads, etc. Large, oblong, dark-blue beads and bugles are specially desired for this purpose. Cheap brass or "brummagem" earrings are sometimes worn nowadays. The fashion in earrings seems to have changed somewhat since Dr. Simpson's time, as I do not remember ever having seen the long strings of beads hanging across the breast or looped up behind as he describes them.[3] At present, one earring is much more frequently worn than a pair. There are in the collection two pairs of the ivory hooks for earrings, which, though made for sale, are of the ordinary pattern. Of these No. 89387 [1340] (Fig. 90) will serve as the type. They are of coarse, white walrus ivory.

---

[1] See Dr. Simpson, op. cit., p. 243. Compare also Brodbeck, "Nach Osten" (p. 23). Speaking of "ein Kopf- oder Stirnband," he says: "Vielleicht gilt es ihnen als eine Art von Zauberschützmittel, denn es ist um kein Geld zu haben. Drängt man sie, so sagen sie wohl, es sei nicht ihr eigen."

[2] Second Voy., p. 498 and Fig. 7, pl. opposite p. 548.

[3] Op. cit., p. 241.

No. 89386 [1340] is a similar pair of earrings, in which the hook projects at right angles and terminates in a flat, round button. Both of the specimens are of the usual pattern, but very roughly made. The custom of wearing earrings is very general among the Eskimo. I need only refer to the descriptions of dress and ornaments already quoted.

Labrets.—As has been stated by all travelers who have visited Point Barrow since the time of Elson, all the adult males wear the labrets or stud-shaped lip ornaments. The discussion of the origin and extent of this habit, or even a comparison of the forms of labrets in use among the Eskimo, would lead me far beyond the scope of the present work.[1] They are or have been worn by all the Eskimo of western America, including St. Lawrence Island and the Diomedes, from the most southern point of their range to the Mackenzie and Anderson district, and were also worn by Aleuts in ancient times.[2] East of the Mackenzie district no traces of the habit are to be observed. Petitot[3] says that Cape Bathurst is the most eastern point at which labrets are worn. The custom of wearing them at this place is perhaps recent, as Dr. Armstrong, of the *Investigator*, expressly states that he saw none there in 1850. At Plover Bay, eastern Siberia, however, I noticed one or two men with a little cross or circle tattooed under each corner of the mouth, just in the position of the labret. This may be a reminiscence of an ancient habit of wearing labrets, or may have been done in imitation of the people of the Diomedes and the American coast.

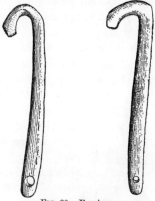

FIG. 90.—Earrings.

At Point Barrow at the present day the lip is always pierced for two labrets, one at each corner of the mouth, though one or both of them are frequently left out. They told us, however, that in ancient times a single labret only was worn, for which the lip was pierced directly in the middle. Certain old and large-sized labrets in the collection are said to have been thus worn. The incisions for the labrets appear to be made about the age of puberty, though I knew one young man who had been married for some months before he had the operation performed. From the young man's character, I fancy shyness or timidity, as suggested by Dr. Simpson,[4] had something to do with the delay. Contrary to Dr. Simpson's experience, I did not see a single man above the age of 18 or 19 who did not wear the labrets. It seems hardly probable that ability

---

[1] This subject has been thoroughly treated by Mr. W. H. Dall in his admirable paper in the Report of the Bureau of Ethnology, No. 3 for 1881–'82, pp. 67–203.

[2] See Dall, Contrib., etc., vol. 1, p. 87, and the paper just referred to.

[3] Monographie, etc., p. xxvi.

[4] Op. cit., p., 241.

to take a seal entitles a boy to wear labrets, as he suggests. We knew a number of boys who were excellent seal hunters and even able to manage a kaiak, but none had their lips pierced under the age of 14 or 15, when they may be supposed to have reached manhood. The incisions are at first only large enough to admit a flat-headed pin of walrus ivory, about the diameter of a crow quill, worn with the head resting against the gum. These are soon replaced by a slightly stouter pair, and these again by stouter ones, until the holes are stretched to a diameter of about one-half inch, when they are ready for the labrets.

We heard of no special ceremonies or festivals connected with the making of these incisions, such as Dall observed at Norton Sound,[1] but in the one case where the operation was performed at the village of Utkiavwĭñ during our stay, we learned that it was done by a man outside of the family of the youth operated upon. We were also informed that the incisions must be made with a little lancet of slate. The employment of an implement of ancient form and obsolete material for this purpose indicates, as Dall says in the passage referred to above, "some greater significance than mere ornamentation."

The collection contains two specimens of such lancets. No. 89721 [1153] (figured in Rept. Point Barrow Expedition, Ethnology, Pl. v, Fig. 4) is the type. A little blade of soft gray slate is carefully inclosed in a neat case of cottonwood. The blade is lanceolate, 1·3 inches long, 0·6 broad, and 0·1 thick, with a short, broad tang. The faces are somewhat rough, and ground with a broad bevel to very sharp cutting edges. The case is made of two similar pieces of wood, flat on one side and rounded on the other, so that when put together they make a rounded body 3 inches long, slightly flattened, and tapering toward the rounded ends, of which

FIG. 91.—Plug for enlarging labret hole.

one is somewhat larger than the other. Round each end is a narrow, deep, transverse groove for a string to hold the two parts together. A shallow median groove connects these cross grooves on one piece, which is hollowed out on the flat face into a rough cavity of a shape and size suitable to receive the blade, which is produced into a narrow, deep groove at the point, probably to keep the point of the blade from being dulled by touching the wood. The other piece, which serves as a cover, has merely a rough, shallow, oval depression near the middle. The whole is evidently very old, and the case is browned with age and dirt.

No. 89579 [1200] is a similar blade of reddish purple slate, mounted in a rough haft of bone. Fig. 91, No. 89715 [1211], is one of a pair of bone models, made for sale, of the ivory plugs used for enlarging the holes for the labrets, corresponding in size to about the second pair used. It is roughly whittled out of a coarse-grained compact bone, and closely

[1] Alaska, p. 141.

resembles the plugs figured by Dall from Norton Sound,[1] but lacks the hole in the tip for the transverse wooden peg, which is not used at Point Barrow. One youth was wearing the final size of plugs when we landed at the station. These were brought to a point like the tip of a walrus tusk, and had exactly the appearance of the tusks of a young walrus when they first protrude beyond the lip. The labrets worn at Point Barrow at the present day are usually of two patterns. One is a large, flat, circular disk about 1½ inches in diameter, with a flat stud on the back something like that of a sleevebutton, and the other a thick cylindrical plug about 1 inch long, and one-half inch in diameter, with the protruded end rounded and the other expanded into an oblong flange, presenting a slightly curved surface to the gum. These plug labrets are the common fashion for everyday wear, and at the present day, as in Dr. Simpson's time, are almost without exception made of stone. Granite or syenite, porphyry, white marble, and sometimes coal (rarely jade) are used for this purpose.

One of the Nunatañmiun wore a glass cruet-stopper for a labret, and many natives of Utkiavwĭñ took the glass stopples of Worcestershire sauce bottles, which were thrown away at the station, and inserted them in the labret holes for everyday wear, sometimes grinding the round top into an oblong stud. There is one specimen of the plug labret in the collection. Labrets of all kinds are very highly prized, and it was almost impossible to obtain them.[2] Though we repeatedly asked for them and promised to pay a good price, genuine labrets that had been worn or that were intended for actual use were very rarely offered for sale, though at one time a large number of roughly made models or imitations were brought in. The single specimen of the plug labret (tu′tɐ) is No. 89700 [1163] (figured in Point Barrow Report, Ethnology, Pl. v, Fig. 3). It is a cylindrical plug of hard, bright green stone (jade or hypochlorite), 1·1 inches long and 0·6 in diameter at the outer end, which is rounded off, tapering slightly inward and expanded at the base into an elliptical disk 1·2 inches long and 0·9 broad, slightly concave on the surface which rests against the teeth and gum. The specimen is old and of a material very unusual at Point Barrow. Fig. 92, No. 89719 [1166], from Nu-wŭk, may also be called a plug labret, but is of a very unusual pattern, and said to be very old. It has an oblong stud of walrus ivory surmounted by a large, transparent, slightly greenish glass bead, on top of which is a small, translucent, sky-blue bead. The beads are held on by a short wooden peg, running through the perforations of the beads and a hole drilled through the ivory. There is a somewhat similar labret in the Museum collection (No. 48202)

Fig. 92.—Labret of beads and ivory.

---

[1] Alaska, p. 140.

[2] The men whom Thomas Simpson met at or near Barter Island sold their labrets, but demanded a hatchet or a dagger for a pair of them (Narrative, p. 119).

from Cape Prince of Wales, also very old. It is surmounted by a single oblong blue bead.

I saw but one other labret made of whole beads, and this had three good sized oval blue beads, in a cluster, projecting from the hole. It was worn by a man from Nuwŭk. This may be compared with a specimen from the Mackenzie district, No. 7714, to which two similar beads are attached in the same way. The disk labret is the pattern worn on full-dress occasions, seldom when working or hunting. One disk and one plug labret are frequently worn. Disk labrets are made of stone, sometimes of syenite or porphyry, but the most fashionable kind is made of white marble, and has half of a large, blue glass bead cemented on the center of the disk. These are as highly prized as they were in Dr. Simpson's time, and we consequently did not succeed in procuring a specimen.

I obtained one pair of syenite disk labrets, No. 56716 [197] (figured in Point Barrow Rept., Ethnology, Pl. v, Fig. 2). Each is a flat circular disk (1·7 and 1·6 inches in diameter, respectively) of rather coarse-grained black and white syenite, ground very smooth, but not polished. On the back of each is an elliptical stud, like that of a sleeve-button, 1·2 and 1·1 inches long and 0·8 and 0·6 broad, respectively.

Fig. 93, No. 2083, is one of the blue and white disks said to come from the Anderson River. This is introduced to represent those worn at Point Barrow, which are of precisely the same pattern. The disk is of white marble, 1½ inches in diameter, and in the center of it is cemented,

apparently with oil dregs, half of a transparent blue glass bead, three-quarters of an inch in diameter, around the middle of which is cut a shallow groove. Similar marble disks without the bead are sometimes worn. These

FIG. 93.—Blue and white labret from Anderson River.

blue and white labrets appear to be worn from Cape Bathurst to the Kaniag peninsula, including the Diomede Islands (see figure on p. 140 of Dall's Alaska). There are specimens in the Museum from the Anderson River and from the north shore of Norton Sound and we saw them worn by the Nunatañmiun, as well as the natives of Point Barrow and Wainwright Inlet. The beads, which are larger than those sold by the American traders, were undoubtedly obtained from Siberia, as Kotzebue, in 1816, found the people of the sound which bears his name wearing labrets "ornamented with blue glass beads."[1] The high value set on these blue-bead labrets has been mentioned by Franklin[2] and T. Simpson,[3] as well as by Dr. Simpson.[4] The last named seems to be the

[1] Voyage, vol. 1, p. 210. Labrets of precisely the same pattern as the one described are figured in the frontispiece of this volume. (See also Choris, Voyage Pittoresque).
[2] 2d Exp., p. 118.
[3] Narrative, p. 119.
[4] Op. cit., p. 239.

first to recognize that the disks were made of marble. All previous writers speak of them as made of walrus ivory.

There are still at Point Barrow a few labrets of a very ancient pattern, such as are said to have been worn in the middle of the lip. These are very rarely put on, but are often carried by the owners on the belt as amulets. All that we saw were of light green translucent jade, highly polished. I obtained one specimen, No. 89705 [866] (figured in Point Barrow Rept., Ethnology, Pl. v, Fig. 1), a thin oblong disk of light green, translucent, polished jade, 2·6 inches long, 1·1 wide in the middle, and 0·8 wide at the ends, with the outer face slightly convex. On the back is an oblong stud with rounded ends, slightly curved to fit the gums.

Labrets of this material and pattern do not seem to be common anywhere. Beechey saw one in Kotzebue Sound 3 inches long and 1½ wide,[1] and there is a large and handsome one in the Museum brought by Mr. Nelson from the lower Yukon. A similar one has recently been received from Kotzebue Sound.

Fig. 94, No. 89712 [1169], from Sidaru is a labret of similar shape, 3 inches long and 1½ broad, but made of compact bone, rather neatly carved and ground smooth. It shows some signs of having been worn. There are marks on the stud where it appears to have been rubbed

FIG. 94—Oblong labret of bone.

against the teeth, and it is probably genuine. The purchase of this specimen apparently started the manufacture of bone labrets at Utkiavwĩn, where no bone labrets, old or new, had previously been seen. For several days after we bought the specimen from Sidaru the natives continued to bring over bone labrets, but all so newly and clumsily made

FIG. 95.—Oblong labret of soapstone.

that we declined to purchase any more than four specimens. About the same time they began to make oblong labrets out of soapstone (a material which we never saw used for genuine labrets), like Fig. 95, No. 89707 [1215]. The purchase of three specimens of these started a wholesale manufacture of them, and we stopped purchasing.

The oblong labret appears to have been still in fashion as late as 1826, for Elson saw many of the men at Point Barrow wearing oblong labrets of bone (*cf.* No. 89712 [1169] and stone, 3 inches long and 1 broad.[2] Unfortunately, he does not specify whether they were worn in pairs or

---

[1] Voyage, p. 249.   [2] Beechey's Voy.. p. 308.

singly, and if singly, as would be natural from their size and shape, whether in the middle of the lip or at one side.

Nos. 89304 [1713], 89716 [1042], and 89717 [1031] (Fig. 96) are very old labrets, which are interesting from their resemblance to the ancient Aleutian single labrets found by Dall in the cave on Amaknak Island.[1] No. 89304 [1713] is an elliptical plug of bituminous coal, with a projecting flange round the base, which is slightly concave to fit the curve of the jaw. This labret is very old and was said to have been found in one of the ruined houses in Utkiavwīñ. The other two labrets are of walrus ivory and of similar shape, but have the flange only at the ends of the base. All of these three are large, the largest being 2·2 inches wide and

FIG. 96.—Ancient labrets.

0·7 thick, and the smallest 1·3 by 0·5, so that they required a much larger incision in the lip than is at present made. In connection with what has been said of the ancient habit of wearing labrets in the middle of the lip, it is interesting to note that Nordenskiöld saw men at Port Clarence who had, besides the ordinary labret holes, "a similar hole forward in the lip."[2] The various portraits of natives previously inserted show the present manner of wearing the labrets at Point Barrow.

NECK ORNAMENTS.

Most of the women and girls wear necklaces made of strings of beads, large or small, frequently strung together with much taste. The tobacco pouch is often attached to this necklace.

ORNAMENTS OF THE LIMBS.

Bracelets.—The women all wear bracelets, which are sometimes strings of beads, but more commonly circles of iron, brass, or copper wire, of which several are often worn on the same wrist, after the fashion of bangles. The men also sometimes wear bracelets. These consist of cir-

---

[1] See Contrib., etc., vol. 1, p. 89, and the two upper figures on the plate opposite.
[2] Vega, vol. 2, p. 233.

cles of narrow thong, upon which are strung one or two large beads or a couple of Dentalium shells (pû'tû).[1]

We brought home one pair of men's bracelets (newly made), one of which (89388 [1355]) is figured in Point Barrow Rept. Ethnology, Pl. I, Fig. 4. They are made of strips of seal thong 0·2 inch broad, bent into rings (9·4 and 8·6 inches in circumference, respectively), with the ends slightly overlapping and sewed together. On each is strung a cylindrical bead of soapstone about one-half inch long and of the same diameter. A single bracelet is generally worn.

Finger-rings.—Both sexes now frequently wear brass finger-rings, called katû'kqlĕrûñ, from katû'kqlûñ, the middle finger, upon which the ring is always worn.

MISCELLANEOUS ORNAMENTS.

Beads.—In addition to the ornaments already described, the women use short strings of beads, buttons, etc., to ornament various parts of the dress, especially the outer side of the inner frock (i'lupa), and strings of beads are often attached to various objects, such as pipes, tobacco pouches, etc. One or two women were also observed to wear large bunches of beads and buttons attached to the inner girdle in front so as to hang down between the legs inside of the pantaloons. A similar strange custom was observed by Beechey at Hotham Inlet, where a young woman wore a good-sized metal bell in the same uncomfortable manner.[2] These people appear to have attempted the manufacture of beads in former times, when they were not so easily obtained as at present. There is in the collection a

FIG. 97.—Beads of amber.

string of four small beads made from amber picked up on the beach (Fig. 97, No. 89700 [1716]). They are of dark honey-colored transparent amber, about one-third inch long and one-half inch diameter at the base. Such beads are very rare at the present day. The above specimens were the only ones seen.

TOILET ARTICLES.

The only object in use among these people that can be considered a toilet article is the small hair comb (i^dlai'utĭn), usually made of walrus ivory.

The collection contains ten specimens, from which No. 56566*b* [182] (Fig. 98*a*) has been selected as the type. It is made of walrus ivory (from near the root of the tusk). When in use, it is held with the tip of the forefinger in the ring, the thumb and middle finger resting on each

---

[1] There is in the collection a bunch of five of these shells (No. 89530 [1357], which are scarce and highly valued as ornaments. Mr. R. E. C. Stearns, of the U. S. National Museum, has identified the species as Dentalium Indianorum Cpr. (probably = *D. pretiosum*, Sby.), called "alĭkotci'k" by the Indians of northwest California, and "hiqua" (J. K. Lord) or "hya-qua" (F. Whymper) by the Indians round Queen Charlotte Sound.

[2] Voyage, p. 295.

side of the neck. This is perhaps the commonest form of the comb, though it is often made with two curved arms at the top instead of a ring, as in Fig. 98*b*, No. 56569 [194], or sometimes with a plain top, like No. 56572 [210] (Fig. 98*c*). Nine of the ten combs, all from Utkiavwĭñ, are of walrus ivory, but No. 89785 [1006], which was the property of Ilû'bwga, the Nunatañmiun, who spent the winter of 1882–'83 at Utki-

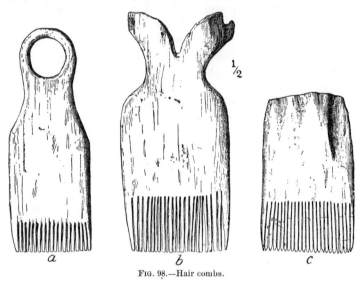

FIG. 98.—Hair combs.

avwĭñ, is made of reindeer antler. This was probably made in the interior, where antler is more plentiful than ivory. All these combs are made with great care and patience. The teeth are usually cut with a saw, but on one specimen the maker used the sharp edge of a piece of tin, as we had refused to loan him a fine saw. This kind of comb is very like that described by Parry from Iglulik.[1]

IMPLEMENTS FOR GENERAL USE.

TOOLS.

Knives.—All the men are now supplied with excellent knives of civilized manufacture, mostly butcher knives or sheath knives of various patterns, which they employ for numerous purposes, such as skinning and butchering game, cutting up food, and rough whittling. Fine whittling and carving is usually done with the "crooked knife," to be described further on. In whittling the knife is grasped so that the blade projects on the ulnar side of the hand and is drawn toward the workman. A pocketknife, of which they have many of various patterns, is used in the same way. I observed that the Asiatic Eskimo at Plover Bay held the knife in the same manner. Capt. Lyon, in describing a man whit-

---

[1] 2nd Voyage, p. 194, Fig. 12, Pl. opp. p. 548.

tling at Winter Island, says: "As is customary with negroes, he cut toward the left hand and never used the thumb of the right, as we do, for a check to the knife."[1] This apparently refers to a similar manner of holding the knife. Before the introduction of iron, knives appear to have been always made of slate, worked by grinding. We obtained twenty-six more or less complete knives, most of which are genuine old implements, which have been preserved as heirlooms or amulets. These knives are either single or double edged, and the double-edged knives may be divided into four classes, according to their shape. The first class consists of rather small knives with the edges straight or only slightly curved, tapering to a sharp or truncated point, with the butt terminating in a short broad tang slightly narrower than the blade, which is inserted in the end of a straight wooden haft, at least as long as the blade. The commonest material is a hard, dark purple slate, though some are of black or dark gray slate. Of this class we have three complete knives and five blades without the haft.

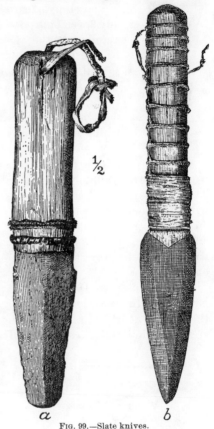

FIG. 99.—Slate knives.

No. 89584 [1107] (figured in Point Barrow Rept., Ethnology, Pl. III, Fig. 3), will represent this class. It is a blade of dark purple slate, ground smooth, 3·5 inches long, tapering from a width of 1·3 inches at the butt, with curved edges to a sharp point, and beveled on both faces from the middle line to the edges, and the flat tang is inserted into a cleft in the end of a straight haft of spruce. The blade is secured by a whipping of about fifteen turns of sinew braid lodged in a broad shallow groove round the end of the haft. In a hole in the other end of the haft is looped a short lanyard of seal thong. Fig. 99a, No. 89581 [1011], is a knife of the same class and about the same size, having a haft 4 inches and a blade 3 inches long. The blade is secured by two lashings, of which the first is a narrow strip of whalebone, and the other of sinew braid. The materials of blade and haft are the same as before. No. 89585 [1710] (Fig. 99b), has a blade of dark gray slate, and the haft, which appears to be of cottonwood, is in two longitudinal sections. The

---

[1] Journal, p. 92.

lashing which holds these two sections together is of braided sinew. Of the blades, the only sharp-pointed one, No. 56684 [228] (Fig. 100), is like the blade of 89584 [1107], but rather larger. The others all have rounded or truncated points and are not over 3½ inches long, including the tang, but otherwise closely resemble the blades already described. They all show signs of considerable age and several of them are nicked and gapped on the edge from use. Knives of this class are not like any in use at the present day, and it was not possible to learn definitely whether this shape served any special purpose. We were, however, given to understand that the sharp-pointed ones were sometimes, at least, used for stabbing. Perhaps they were used specially for cutting up the smaller animals.

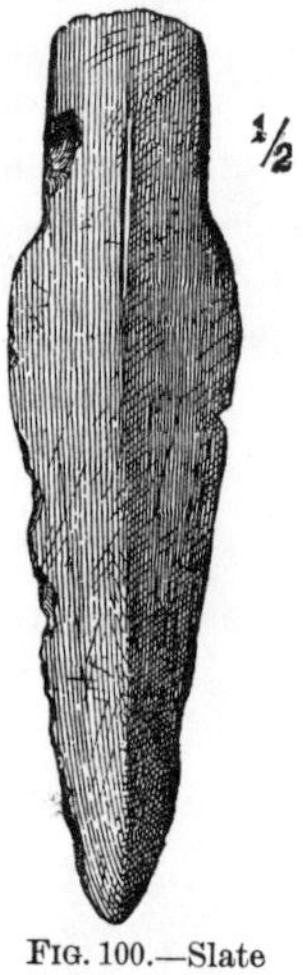

The second class, of which there are four specimens, is not unlike the first, but the blade is short and broad, with strongly curved edges, and always sharp pointed, while the haft is always much longer than the blade. Instead of being evenly beveled off on both faces from the middle line to the edges, they are either slightly convex, worked down gradually to the edge, or flat with narrowly beveled edges. They are all small knives, the longest being 8·3 inches long, with the blade projecting 3·1 inches from the haft, and the shortest 4·9 inches, with the blade projecting only 1·4 inches.

FIG. 100.—Slate knife-blade.

Fig. 101, No. 89583 [1305], is a knife of this class, with the blade a nearly equilateral triangle (1·4 inches long and

FIG. 101.—Slate knife.

1·3 inches wide at the base), with a flat wooden haft as wide as the blade and 3½ inches long, cleft at the tip and lashed with thirteen or fourteen turns of sinew braid. The holes near the butt of the haft were probably to receive a lanyard. Fig. 102, No. 89591 [1016], is another form of the same class. The blade is secured by a single rivet of wood.

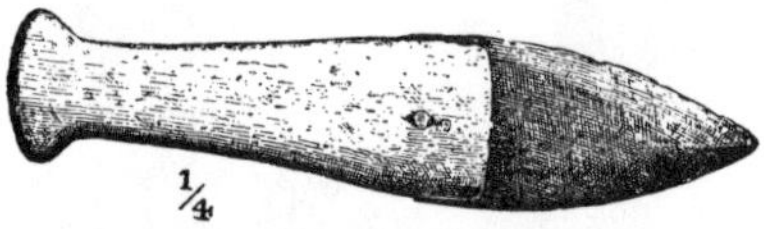

FIG. 102.—Slate knife.

The third class consists of large knives, with long, broad, lanceolate blades, and short straight hafts. There is only one complete specimen, No. 89592 [1002], Fig. 103.

FIG. 103.—Slate hunting-knife.

This has a blade of soft, light greenish slate, 6 inches long and 2·6 inches broad, with the edges broadly beveled on both faces. The haft of spruce is in two longitudinal sections, put together so as to inclose the short tang of the blade, and is secured by a tight whipping of eighteen turns of fine seal twine, and painted with red ocher. This knife is new and was made for sale, but is undoubtedly a correct model of an ancient pattern, as No. 56676 [204] (Fig. 104), which is certainly ancient, appears to be the blade of just

FIG. 104.—Blade of slate hunting-knife.

such a knife. We were told that the latter was intended for cutting blubber. This perhaps means that it was a whaling knife. Mr. Nelson brought home a magnificent knife of precisely the same pattern, made of light green jade.

The two knives, representing the fourth class, are both new and made for sale, having blades of soft slate. As we obtained no genuine knives of this pattern, it is possible that they are merely commercial fabrications. The two knives are very nearly alike, but the larger, No.

FIG. 105.—Large slate knife.

89590 [984] (Fig. 105), is the more carefully made. The blade is of light greenish gray slate, 6·2 inches long and 2 inches broad, and is straight nearly to the tip, where it curves to a sharp point, making a blade like that of the Roman gladius. The haft is a piece sawed out of the beam of an antler, and has a cleft sawed in one end to receive the short broad tang of the blade. The whipping is of sinew braid.

The single-edged knives were probably all meant specially for cutting food, and are all of the same general pattern, varying in size from a blade only 2½ inches long to one of 7 inches. The blade is generally more strongly curved along the edge than on the back and is usually sharp-pointed. It is fitted with a broad tang to a straight haft, usually shorter than the blade. There are in the collection four complete knives and five unhafted blades. No. 89597 [1052] (Fig. 106) is a typical knife of this kind. The blade is of black slate, rather rough, and

FIG. 106.—Large single-edged slate knife.

is 5·6 inches long (including the tang). The tang, which is about one-half inch long and the same breadth, is lashed *against* one end of the flat haft of bone which is cut away to receive it, with five turns of stout seal thong. No. 89594 [1053] differs from the preceding only in having the tang inserted in a cleft in the end of the haft, and No. 89589*a*

[1054] has the back more curved than the edge, the haft of antler and
the lashing of whalebone. All three are of very rude workmanship.
No. 89587 [1587] is a small knife with a truncated point and the tang
imbedded without lashing in the end of a roughly made haft of bone.

Most of the blades are those of knives similar to the type, more
smoothly finished, but No. 56712 [226] (Fig. 107a) is noticeable for the

extreme "belly" of the edge and the
smoothness with which the faces are
beveled from back to edge. Such
knives approach the woman's round
knife (ulu, ulu′ra). No. 89601 [776]
(Fig. 107b) is almost double-edged,
the back being rounded off. Fig.
108, No. 89631 [1081], is a very remarkable form of slate knife, of
which this was the only specimen
seen. In shape it somewhat resem.
bles a hatchet, having a broad tri-

FIG. 107.—Blades of knives.

angular blade with a strongly curved cutting edge, along the back of which
is fitted a stout haft of bone 12½ inches long. The blade is of soft, dark
purple slate, ground smooth, and resembles the modern knives in having
the sharp cutting edge beveled almost wholly on one face. The haft is
the foreshaft of an old whale harpoon, and is made of whale's bone.
The back of the blade is fitted into a deep narrow saw cut, and held on
by three very neat lashings of narrow strips of whalebone, each of which
passes through a hole drilled through the blade close to the haft and
through a pair of vertical holes in the haft on each side of the blade.
These holes converge towards the back of the haft and are joined by
a deep channel, so that the lashing is countersunk below the surface of

FIG. 108.—Peculiar slate knife.

the haft. This implement was brought down from Nuwŭk and offered
for sale as a knife anciently used for cutting off the blubber of a whale.
The purchaser got the impression that it was formerly attached to a
long pole and used like a whale spade. On more careful examination
after our return it was discovered that the haft was really part of an old
harpoon and that the lashings and holes to receive them were evidently
newer than the haft.

It is possible that the blade may have been long ago fitted to the haft and that the tool may have been used as described. That knives of this sort were occasionally used by the Eskimo is shown by a specimen in the Museum from Norton Sound. This is smaller than the one described but has a slate blade of nearly the same shape and has a haft, for hand use only, put on in the same way.

With such knives as these the cut is made by *drawing* the knife toward the user instead of pushing it away, as in using the round knife. We found no evidence that these Eskimo ever used knives of ivory (except for cutting snow) or ivory knives with bits of iron inlaid in the edge, such as have been observed among those of the East.

Fig. 109, No. 89477 [1422], is a very extraordinary implement, which was brought down from Point Barrow and which has evidently been exposed alongside of some corpse at the cemetery. The blade is a long, flat, thin piece of whale-bone wedged between the two parts of the haft, which has been sawed lengthwise for $6\frac{1}{2}$ inches to receive it.

¼

FIG. 109—Knife with whalebone blade.

The haft is a slender piece of antler. No other specimens of the kind were seen, nor have similar implements, to my knowledge, been observed elsewhere. The natives insisted that it was genuine, and was formerly used for cutting blubber.

I have introduced four figures of old iron or steel knives, of which we have six specimens, in order to show the way in which the natives in early days, when iron was scarce, utilized old case-knives and bits of tools, fitting them with hafts of their own make. All agree in having the edge beveled on the upper face only. All the knives which they obtain from the whites at the present day are worked over with a file so as to bring the bevel on one face only. Fig. 110, No. 89296 [970], from Nuwŭk, has a blade of iron, and the flat haft is made of two longitudinal sections of reindeer antler, held together

½

FIG. 110—Small iron knife.

with four large rivets nearly equidistant. The two which pass through the tang are of brass and the other two of iron. The blade is 3·6 inches long, the haft 4·1 long and 0·9 broad. Fig. 110, No. 89294 [901], from Utkiavwĭñ, has a short, thick, and sharp-pointed blade, and is hafted in the same way with antler, one section of the haft being cut out to receive the short, thick tang. The first two rivets are of iron, the other three of brass and not quite long enough to go wholly through the haft. The blade is barely 2 inches long. Fig. 111*a*, No. 89297 [1125], from Nuwŭk, has a short blade, $2\frac{1}{4}$ inches long, and the two sections of the

haft are held together, not by rivets, but by a close spiral lashing of
stout seal thong extending the whole length of the haft. No. 89293
[1330], Fig. 111*b*, from Utkiavwĭñ, has a peculiarly shaped blade, which
is a bit of some steel tool imbedded in the end of a straight bit of
antler 4 inches long. One of these knives, not figured, is evidently
part of the blade of an old-fashioned curved case knife. It is stamped

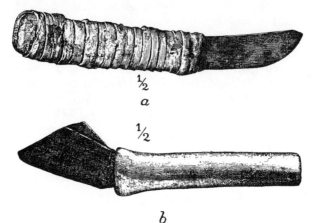

FIG. 111.—Small iron knives.

with the name "Wilson," and underneath this are three figures, of
which only ◇ can be made out. This may be a table knife bought or
stolen from the *Plover* in 1852–'54.

There is in the collection one large double-edged knife (Fig. 112, No.
89298 [1162]) of precisely the same form as the slate hunting knife (Fig.
103) and Mr. Nelson's jade knife previously mentioned. The blade is of
thick sheet iron, which has in it a couple of rivet holes, and the haft
of reindeer antler in two sections, held together by a large copper rivet

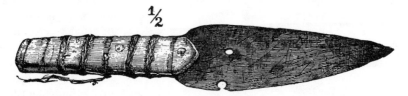

FIG. 112.—Iron hunting knife.

at each end and a marline of sinew braid. Each edge has a narrow
bevel on one face only, the two edges being beveled on opposite faces.
There are a small number of such knives still in use, especially as hunting
knives (for cutting up walrus, one man said). They are considered to
be better than modern knives for keeping off evil spirits at night. As
is not unusual, the antiquity of the object has probably invested it with
a certain amount of superstitious regard. These knives are undoubtedly
the same as the "double-edged knives (pan'-na)" mentioned by Dr.

Simpson (op. cit., p. 266) as brought for sale by the Nunatañmiun, who obtained them from the Siberian natives, and which he believes to be carried as far as the strait of Fury and Hecla. It would be interesting to decide whether the stone hunting knives were an original idea of the Eskimo, or whether they were copies, in stone, of the first few iron knives obtained from Siberia; but more material is needed before the matter can be cleared up.

The natives of Point Barrow, in ordinary conversation, call all knives savĭk, which also means *iron*, and is identically the same as the word used in Greenland for the same objects. If, then, there was a time, as these people say, when their ancestors were totally ignorant of the use of iron—and the large number of stone implements still found among them is strongly corroborative of this—the use of this name indicates that the first iron was obtained from the east, along with the soapstone lamps, instead of from Siberia. Had it first come from Siberia, as tobacco did, we should expect to find it, like the latter, called by a Russian or Siberian name.

Like all the Eskimo of North America from Cape Bathurst westward, the natives of Point Barrow use for fine whittling and carving on wood, ivory, bone, etc., "crooked knives," consisting of a small blade, set on the under side of the end of a long curved haft, so that the edge, which is beveled only on the upper face, projects about as much as that of a spokeshave. The curve of blade and haft is such that when the under surface of the blade rests against the surface to be cut the end of the haft points up at an angle of about 45°. This knife differs essentially from the crooked carving knife so generally used by the Indians of North America. As a rule the latter has only the blade (which is often double edged) curved and stuck into the end of a straight haft. These knives are at the present time made of iron or steel and are of two two sizes, a large knife, mĭ'dlĭñ, with a haft 10 to 20 inches long, intended for working on wood, and a small one, savigro'n (lit. "an instrument for shaving"), with a haft 6 or 7 inches long and intended specially for cutting bone and ivory. Both sizes are handled in the same way. The knife is held close to the blade between the index and second fingers of the right hand with the thumb over the edge, which is toward the workman. The workman draws the knife toward him, using his thumb as a check to gauge the depth of the cut. The natives use these knives with very great skill, taking off long and very even shavings and producing very neat workmanship.[1]

There are in the collection four large knives and thirteen small ones. No. 89278 [787] (Fig. 113) will serve as the type of the large knives. The haft is a piece of reindeer antler, flat on one face and rounded on the other, and the curve is toward the rounded face. The flat face is hollowed out by cutting away the cancellated tissue from the bend to

---

[1] Compare this with what Capt. Parry says of the workmanship of the people of Iglulik (2d Voy.,p. 336). The almost exclusive use of the double-edged pan'na is the reason their work is so "remarkably coarse and clumsy."

the tip, and the lower edge is sloped off so that the end of the haft is flat and narrow, with a slight twist. The blade is riveted to the flat face of the haft with three iron rivets, and is a piece of a saw counter-sunk flush with the surface of the haft, so that it follows its curvature. The cutting edge is beveled only on the upper face. The lower edge of the haft, from the blade to the place where it begins to narrow, is pierced with eleven equidistant holes, through which is laced a piece of seal-skin thong, the two parts crossing like a shoe-lacing, to prevent the

½

FIG. 113.—Large crooked knife.

hand from slipping. The ornamental pattern on the upper face of the haft is incised and was originally colored with red ocher, but is now filled with dirt.

Fig. 114, No. 89780 [1004*d*], is a very long hafted knife (the haft is 12·3 inches long), but otherwise resembles the type, though not so elaborately ornamented. The blade is also a bit of a saw. It is pro-vided with a sheath 3¼ inches long, made of black sealskin with the black side out, doubled over at one side, and sewed "over and over" down the other side and round one end. To the open end is sewed a bit of thong with a slit in the end of it into which one end of a lanyard of seal twine 15 inches long is fastened with a becket-hitch. When the

⅓

FIG. 114.—Large crooked knife, with sheath.

sheath is fitted over the blade the lanyard is passed through a hole in the haft and made fast by two or three turns around it. Such sheaths are often used by careful workmen. This particular knife was the property of the "inlander" Ilû'bwgᴇ, previously mentioned. No. 89283 [967], from Nuwŭk, is interesting as being the only left-handed tool we obtained. The fourth knife has a blade with a cutting edge of 3½ inches, while that of each of the others is 3 inches.

The small knife differs little from the mĭ'dlĭñ except in having the haft very much shorter and not tapered off at the tip. Fig. 115*a*, No. 56552 [145], from Utkiavwĭñ, shows a common form of this kind of knife, though the blade usually has a sharp point like those of the large knives, projecting beyond the end of the haft. This knife has a blade of iron riveted on with two iron rivets to a haft of reindeer antler. The edges of the haft close to the blade are roughened with crosscuts to prevent slipping.

The blades of the small knives are frequently inserted into a cleft in the edge of the haft, as in Fig. 115*b*, 89632 [827], and 89277 [1172]. The blade, in such cases, is secured by wedging it tightly, with sometimes the addition of a lashing of thong through a hole in the haft and round the heel of the blade. The blade is usually of steel, in most cases a bit of

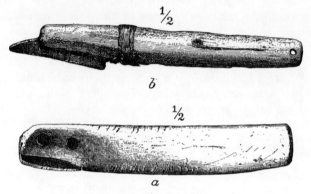

FIG. 115.—Small crooked knives.

a saw and the haft of reindeer antler, generally plain, unless the circular hollows, such as are to be seen on No. 89277 [1172], which are very common, are intended for ornament. Fig. 116, No. 89275 [1183], from Ut-kiavwiñ, is a rather peculiar knife. The haft, which is the only one seen of walrus ivory, is nearly straight, and the unusually long point of the blade is strongly bent up. The rivets are of copper. This knife, the history of which we did not obtain, was very likely meant both for wood and ivory. It is old and rusty and has been long in use.

FIG. 116.—Crooked knife.

All of the crooked knives in the collection are genuine implements which have been actually in use, and do not differ in type from the crooked knives in the Museum from the Mackenzie district, Kotzebue Sound, and other parts of Alaska. Similar knives appear to be used among the Siberian Eskimo and the Chukches, who have adopted their habits. Hooper (Tents, etc., p. 175), mentions "a small knife with a bent blade and a handle, generally made of the tip of a deer's horn," as one in general use at Plover Bay, and handled in the same skillful way as at Point Barrow.[1]   Among the Eskimo of the central region they are almost entirely unknown.   The only mention I have seen of such tools is in Parry's Second Voyage (p. 504), where he speaks of seeing at Iglulik "several open knives with crooked wooden handles," which he thinks "must have been obtained by communication alongshore with Hudson Bay."   I can find no specimen, figure, or description of the sa'nat ("tool"), *the* tool par excellence of the Greenlanders, except the following definition in Kleinschmidt's "Grønlandsk Ordbog": "2. Specially a narrow, long-hafted knife, which is sharpened on one side and slightly curved at the tip (and which is a Greenlander's chief tool)."   This seems to indicate that this knife, so common in the West, is equally common in Greenland.[2]

Whether these people used crooked knives before the introduction of iron is by no means certain, though not improbable.   Fig. 117*a*, No. 89633 [1196], from Utkiavwïñ, is a knife made by imbedding a flake of gray flint in the lower edge of a haft of reindeer antler, of the proper shape and curvature for a mïdlïñ handle.   The haft is soiled and

a

b

FIG. 117.—Crooked knives, flint bladed.

undoubtedly old, while the flaked surfaces of the flint do not seem fresh, and the edge shows slight nicks, as if it had been used.   Had this knife been followed by others equally genuine looking, I should have no hesitation in pronouncing it a prehistoric knife, and the ancestor of the present steel one.   The fact, however, that its purchase gave rise to the manufacture of a host of flint knives all obviously new and more and more clumsily made, until we refused to buy any more, leads me to suspect that it was fabricated with very great care from old material, and skillfully soiled by the maker.

Ten of these knives of flint were purchased within a fortnight before we detected the deceit.   Fig. 117*b*, No. 89636 [1212] is one of the best of these counterfeits, made by wedging a freshly flaked flint blade into the haft of an old savigrón, which has been somewhat trimmed to receive the blade and soiled and charred to make it look old.   Other more carelessly made ones had clumsily carved handles of whale's bone, with roughly flaked flints stuck into them and glued in with oil dregs. All of these came from Utkiavwïñ.   Another suspicious circumstance is that a few days previously two slate-bladed crooked knives had been brought down from Nuwŭk and accepted without question as ancient. On examining the specimens since our return, I find that while the hafts are certainly old, the blades, which are of soft slate easily worked,

---

[1] Lisiansky also mentions "a small crooked knife" (Voyage, p. 181), as one of the tools used in Kadiak in 1805.

[2] A specimen has lately been received at the National Museum.   It is remarkably like the Indian knife in pattern.

are as certainly new.   Fig. 118a, 118b, represent these two knives
(89580 [1062], 89586 [1061]), which have the blades lashed on with deer
sinew.   It is worthy of note in this connection that there are no stone
knives of this pattern in the museum from any other locality.

The women employ for all purposes for which a knife or scissors could
be used a semicircular knife of the same general type as those described
by every writer from the days of Egede, who has had to deal with the

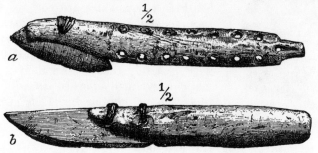

FIG. 118.—Slate-bladed crooked knives.

Eskimo.   The knives at the present day are made of steel, usually, and
perhaps always, of a piece of a saw blade, which gives a sheet of steel of
the proper breadth and thickness, and are manufactured by the natives
themselves.   Dr. Simpson says[1] that in his time they were brought
from Kotzebue Sound by the Nunatañmiun, who obtained them from the
Siberian Eskimo.   There are in the collection three of these steel knives,
all of the small size generally called ulúre ("little úlu").   No. 56546 [14]
has been picked out for description (Fig. 119).

FIG. 119—Woman's knife, steel blade.

The blade is wedged into a handle of walrus
ivory.   The ornamentation on the handle is
of incised lines and dots blackened.   The cutting edge of the blade is beveled on one face
only.   This knife represents the general
shape of knives of this sort, but is rather
smaller than most of them.   I have seen some knives with blades fully
5 or 6 inches long and deep in proportion.   The handle is almost always
of walrus ivory and of the shape figured.   I do not remember ever
seeing an úlu blade secured otherwise than by fitting it tightly into a
narrow slit in the handle, except in one case, when the handle was part
of the original handle of the saw of which the knife was made, left
still riveted on.

It is not necessary to specify the various purposes for which these
knives are used.   Whenever a woman wishes to cut anything, from her
food to a thread in her sewing, she uses an úlu in preference to anything
else.   The knife is handled precisely as described among the eastern
Eskimo, making the cut by pushing instead of drawing,[2] thus differing
from the long-handled round knife mentioned above.   Knives of this

---

[1] Op. cit., p. 266.   [2] See for example, Kumlien, op. cit., p. 26,

pattern are very generally used among the western Eskimo, but in the east the blade is always separated from the handle by a short shank, as in our mincing knives.

The natives of Point Barrow used round knives long before the introduction of iron. There are in the collection twenty-three more or less

FIG. 120.—Woman's knife, slate blade.

complete round knives of stone, most of which are genuine implements that have been used. Of these a few, which are perhaps the more recent ones, have blades not unlike the modern steel knife. For instance, No. 89680 [1106] Fig. 120, has a blade of hard gray mica slate of almost precisely the modern shape, but both faces are gradually worked down to the cutting edge without a bevel on either. The handle is very large and stout and made of coarse whale's bone. This knife was said to have come from the ruined village at Pernyᴇ. Fig. 121, No. 89679 [971], from Nuwŭk, was made for sale, but is perhaps a model of a form sometimes used. The shape of the blade is quite different from those now in use, in having the cutting edge turned so strongly to the front. The handle is of oak and the blade of rather hard, dark purple slate. Fig. 122, 89689 [985], also from Nuwŭk, and made for the market, is introduced to show a method of hafting which may have been formerly employed. The haft is of reindeer

FIG. 121. — Woman's knife, slate blade.

antler in two longitudinal sections, between which the blade is wedged. These two sections are held together by lashings of sinew at each end, passing through holes in each piece and round the

FIG. 122.—Woman's knife, slate blade.

ends. These lashings being put on wet, have shrunk so that the blade is very tightly clasped between the two parts of the handle. The commoner form of these stone knives, however, has the back of the blade much longer, so that the sides are straight instead of oblique and usually round off gradually at the ends of the cutting edge without being produced into a point at either end. No. 89682 [958] is a form intermediate between this and the modern shape, having a blade with a long back, but produced into a sharp point at one end. The handle is of reindeer antler and the blade rather soft black slate. This specimen is a very cleverly counterfeited antique.

No. 89636 [1122], Fig. 123, approaches yet nearer the ancient shape, but still has one end slightly produced. The handle is also of reindeer

FIG. 123. — Woman's knife, slate blade.

antler, which seems to have been very commonly used with the slate blades. The lashing round the blade close to the handle is of seal thong, with the end wound spirally round all the parts on both sides and neatly tucked in. It seems to serve no purpose beyond enlarging the handle so as to make it fit the hand better. One beautiful blade of light olive green, clouded jade, No. 89675 [1170], belonged to a knife of this pattern. The older pattern is represented by No. 89676 [1586], a small knife blade from Ukiavwĭñ, which has been kept as an amulet. No. 56660 [129], is a blade of the same type, but elongated, being 7½ inches long and 2 broad.

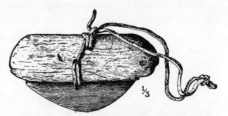

FIG. 124.—Woman's ancient slate-bladed knife.

This is a very beautiful implement of pale olive jade, ground smooth. The bevel along the back of each of these blades indicates that they were to be fitted into a narrow slit in a long haft, like that of No. 89684 [886], Fig. 124, from Nuwŭk. Though both blade and handle of this specimen are very old, and have been put together in their present shape for a long time, the handle, which is of whale's bone, evidently belonged to a longer blade, which fitted in the cleft without the need of any lashing. Fig. 125, No. 89693 [874], shows a form of handle evidently of very great antiquity,

FIG. 125.—Ancient bone handle for woman's knife.

as the specimen shows signs of great age. It was purchased from a native of Utkiavwĭñ. It is made of a single piece of coarse whale's bone. It was intended for a blade at least 7 inches long.

Fig. 126, No. 56672 [191], from Utkiavwĭñ, is a very crude, large knife, intended for use without a handle. It is of rough, hard, dark purplish

FIG. 126.—Large knife of slate.

slate. The upper three-quarters of both faces are almost untouched cleavage surfaces, but the lower quarter is pretty smoothly ground down to a semicircular cutting edge, which is somewhat nicked from use.

The angular grooves on the two faces were evidently begun with the intention of cutting the knife in two. We were told that this large knife was specially for cutting blubber. It is a genuine antique.

While ground slate is a quite common material for round knives, flint appears to have been rarely used. We obtained only three of this material. No. 89690 [1311] is a flint knife hafted with a rough, irregular lump of coarse whale's bone. The blade is a rather thin " spall " of light gray flint, flaked round the edges into the shape of a modern ulúr̦ɐ blade, with a very strongly curved cutting edge. Though the handle is new, the flaking of the blade does not seem fresh, so that it is possibly a genuine old blade fitted with a new haft for the market. A similar flint blade, more neatly flaked, was brought from Kotzebue Sound by Lieut. Stoney, U. S. Navy, in 1884. The other two flint knives are interesting from being made for use without handles.

No. 89691 [1360], Fig. 127, from Sidaɐu, is an oblong, wedge-shaped spall of gray flint, of which the back still preserves the natural surface of the pebble. It is slightly shaped by coarse flaking along the back and one end, and the edge is finely flaked into a curved outline rounding up at the ends. The specimen is old and dirty, and was probably preserved as a sort of heirloom or amulet. No. 89692 [1178] is a similar

⅓

FIG. 127.—Woman's knife of flaked flint.

spall from a round pebble. Such knives as these are evidently the first steps in the development of the round knife. The shape of the spalls, produced by breaking a round or oval pebble of flint, would naturally suggest using them as knives, and the next step would be to improve the edge by flaking. The greater adaptability of slate, from its softness and easy cleavage, for making such knives would soon be recognized, and we should expect to find, as we do, knives like No. 56672 [191]. The next step would naturally be to provide such a knife with a haft at the point where the stone was grasped by the hand, while reducing this haft so as to leave only just enough for the grasp and cutting away the superfluous corners of the blade would give us the modern form of the blade. Round knives of slate are not peculiar to Point Barrow, but have been collected in many other places in northwestern America.[1]

The relationship between these knives and the semilunar slate blades found in the North Atlantic States has already been ably discussed by Dr. Charles Rau.[2] It must, however, be borne in mind that while these are sufficiently " fish-cutters " to warrant their admission into a book on fishing, the cutting of fish is but a small part of the work they do. The name " fish-cutter," as applied to these knives, would be no more

---

[1] See, especially, Dall, Contrib., vol. 1, pp. 59 and 79, for figures of such knives from the caves of Unalashka.

[2] Prehistoric Fishing, pp. 183–188.

distinctive than the name "tobacco-cutter" for a Yankee's jack-knife.[1]

Adzes (udlimau).—Even at the present day the Eskimo of Point Barrow use no tool for shaping large pieces of woodwork, except a short-handled adz, hafted in the same manner as the old stone tools which were employed before the introduction of iron. Though axes and hatchets are frequently obtained by trading, they are never used as such, but the head is removed and rehafted so as to make an adz of it. This habit is not peculiar to the people of Point Barrow. There is a hatchet head, mounted in the same way, from the Anderson River, in the Museum collection, and the same thing was noted in Hudson's Strait by Capt. Lyon[2] and at Iglulik by Capt. Parry.[3] Mr. L. M. Turner informs me that the Eskimo of Ungava, on the south side of Hudson's Strait, who have been long in contact with the whites, have learned to use axes. The collection contains two such adzes made from small hatchets. No. 89873 [972], Fig. 128, is the more typical of the two. The blade is the head of a small hatchet or tomahawk lashed to the haft of oak with a stout thong of seal hide. The lashing is one piece, and

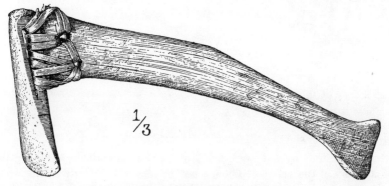

FIG. 128.—Hatchet hafted as an adz.

is put on wet and shrunk tightly on. This tool is a little longer in the haft than those commonly used, and the shape and material of the haft is a little unusual, it being generally elliptical in section and made of soft wood.

Fig. 129, No. 56638 [309], from Utkiavwĭñ, is a similar adz, but the head has been narrowed by cutting off pieces from the sides (done by filing part way through and breaking the piece off), and a deep transverse groove has been cut on the front face near the butt. Part of the lashing is held in this groove as well as by the eye, the lower half of which is filled up with a wooden plug. The haft is peculiar in being a

---

[1] It is but just to Dr. Rau to say that he recognized the fact that these implements are not exclusively fish-cutters, and applies this name only to indicate that he has treated of them simply in reference to their use as such. The idea, however, that these, being slightly different in shape from the Greenland *olu* or ulu, are merely fish knives, has gained a certain currency among anthropologists which it is desirable to counteract.

[2] Journal, p. 28.

[3] 2d Voyage, p. 536, and pl. opp. p. 548, fig. 3.

piece of reindeer antler which has been reduced in thickness by sawing
out a slice for 8 inches from the butt and bringing the two parts together
with four stout wooden treenails about 1½ inches apart. This is preferable to trimming it down to a proper thickness from the surface, as
the latter process would remove the compact tissue of the outside and
expose the soft inside tissue. The whipping of seal thong just above
the flange of the butt helps to give a better grip and, at the same time,
to hold the parts together. As before, there are two large holes for
the lashing. Adzes of this sort are used for all large pieces of wood
work, such as timbers for boats, planks, and beams for houses, etc.
After roughly dressing these out with the adz they are neatly smoothed
off with the crooked knife, or sometimes, of late years, with the plane.
The work of "getting out" the large pieces of wood is almost always
done where the drift log lies on the beach. When a man wants a new
stem or sternpost for his umiak, or a plank to repair his house, he
searches along the beach until he finds a suitable piece of driftwood,

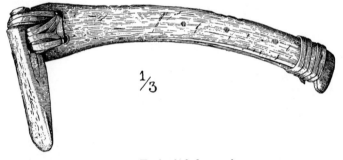

FIG. 129.—Hatchet hafted as an adz.

which he claims by putting a mark on it, and sometimes hauls up out
of the way of the waves. Then, when he has leisure to go at the work,
he goes out with his adz and spends the day getting it into shape and
reducing it to a convenient size to carry home, either slung on his back
or, if too large, on a dog-sled. A man seldom takes the trouble to carry
home more of a piece of timber than he actually needs for the purpose
in hand.

The adz was in general use long before the introduction of iron.
There is in the collection a very interesting series of ancient tools,
showing the gradual development of the implement from a rude oblong
block of stone worked down to a cutting edge on one end, to the
steel adzes of the present day. They have, however, not even yet
learned to make an eye in the head of the tool in which to insert the
haft, but all tools of this class—adzes, hammers, picks, and mattocks—
are lashed, with one face resting against the expanded end of the haft.
Firmness is obtained by putting the lashing on wet and allowing it to
shrink tight. Nearly all these ancient adzes are of jade, a material
well adapted for the purpose by its hardness, which, however, renders

it difficult to work. Probably the oldest of these adzes is No. 56675 [69], Fig. 130, which has been selected as the type of the earliest form we have represented in the collection. This is of dark olive green, almost black, jade, 7·2 inches long, 2·8 wide, and 1·3 thick, and smoothly ground on the broader faces. The cutting edge is much broken from long use. One broad face is pretty smoothly ground, but left rough at the butt end. The other is rather flatter, but more than half of it is irregularly concave, the natural inequalities being hardly touched by grinding. Like the other dark-colored jade tools, this specimen is very much lighter on a freshly fractured surface. The dark color is believed to be due to long contact with greasy substances.

FIG. 130.—Adz-head of jade.

FIG. 131.—Adz-head of jade.

No. 89662 [900], from Nuwŭk, is an exceedingly rough adz of similar shape, but so slightly ground that it is probably one that was laid aside unfinished. From the battered appearace of the ends it seems to have been used for a hammer. It is of the same dark jade as the preceding. No. 89689 [792], from Utkiavwīñ, is of rather light olive, opaque jade and a trifle better finished than the type, while No. 89661 [1155], Fig. 131, also from Utkiavwīñ, is a still better piece of workmanship, the curve of the faces to the cutting edge being very graceful. The interesting point about this specimen is that a straight piece has been cut off from one side by sawing down smoothly from each face almost to the middle and breaking the piece off. We were informed that this was done to procure rods of jade for making knife sharpeners. We were informed that these stones were cut in the same way as marble and freestone are cut with us, namely, by sawing with a flat blade of iron and sand and water. A thin lamina of hard bone was probably used before the introduction of iron. Possibly a reindeer scapula, cut like the one made into a saw (No. 89476 [1206], Fig. 147), but without teeth, was used for this purpose.

That such stone blades were used with a haft is shown by the only hafted specimen, No. 56628 [214], Fig. 132, from Nuwŭk. This is a rather small adz. The head of dark green jade differs from those already de-

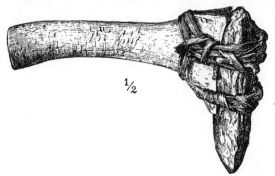

FIG. 132.—Hafted jade adz.

scribed only in dimensions, being 4 inches long, 2·1 wide, and 1·7 thick. The haft is of reindeer antler and in shape much like that of No. 56638 [309], but has only one hole for the lashing. The lashing is of the usual stout seal thong and put on in the usual fashion. No. 89673 [1423] is an old black adz from Sidaru of the same pattern as those described, but very smoothly and neatly made. About one-half of this specimen has been cut off for whetstones, etc.

The next step is to make the lashing more secure by cutting transverse grooves on the upper face of the head to hold the thong in place. This has been done on No. 56667 [215], figured in Point Barrow Rept., Ethnology, Pl. II, Fig. 5, an adz of dark olive green jade, from Utkiavwiñ, which shows two such grooves, broad and shallow, running across the upper face. Of these two classes the collection contains thirteen unhafted specimens and one hafted specimen,

FIG. 133.—Adz-head of jade and bone.

FIG. 134.—Adz-head of bone and iron, without eyes.

all of jade. As cutting these grooves in the stone is a laborious process, the device of substituting some more easily worked substance for the back part of the head would naturally suggest itself.

Fig. 133, No. 89658 [1072], from Utkiavwiñ, has a long blade of black stone with the butt slightly tapered off and imbedded in a body of whale's bone, which has a channel 1 inch wide, for the lashing, cut round

it and a shallow socket on the face to receive the end of the haft.   Adz
heads of this same type continued in use till after the introduction of
iron, which was at first utilized by inserting a flat blade of iron into
just such a body, as is shown in Fig. 134 (No. 89877 [752], from the cemetery at Utkiavwĭñ).

From this type to that shown in Fig. 135 (No. 89876 [696] brought
by the natives from the ruins on the Kulugrụa) the transition is easy.
Suppose, for the greater protection of the lashings, we *inclose* the chan-

nels on the sides of the head — in
other words, bore holes instead of cutting grooves—we have exactly this
pattern, namely, vertical eyes on each
side of the head joined by transverse
channels on the upper face.   The
specimen figured has on each side two
oblong slots with a round eye between them.   The blade is of iron,
Fig. 136, No. 56640 [260] has two eyes
on each side, and shows a different
method of attaching the blade, which
is countersunk flush with the upper
surface of the body and secured with
three stout iron rivets.   The next step
is to substitute horizontal eyes for the
vertical ones, so as to have only one

FIG. 135.—Adz-head of
bone and and iron,
with vertical eyes.

FIG. 136.—Adz-head of
bone and iron, with
vertical eyes.

set of holes to thread the lashings through.   This is seen in No. 89869
[878], Fig. 137, from Nuwŭk, which in general pattern closely resembles
No. 89876 [696], but has three large horizontal eyes instead of the vertical ones.   The blade is of iron and the haft of whale's bone.   The
lashing is essentially the same as that of the modern adz, No. 56638
[309].

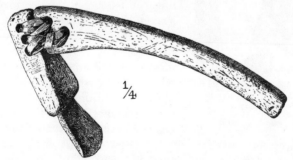

FIG. 137.—Hafted bone and iron adz.

That this final type of hafting was reached before stone had gone
out of use for such implements is shown by Fig. 138, No. 89839 [769],
from Utkiavwĭñ, which, while very like the last in shape, has a blade

of hard, dark purple slate. The haft is of reindeer antler. The lashing has the short end *knotted* to the long part after making the first
round, instead of being slit to receive the latter. Otherwise it is of
the usual pattern. These composite adzes of bone and stone or iron
seemed to have been common at the end of the period when stone was
exclusively used and when iron first came into use in small quantities,
and a good many have been preserved until the present day. We
obtained four hafted and six unhafted specimens, besides seven jade
blades for such composite adzes, which are easily recognizable by

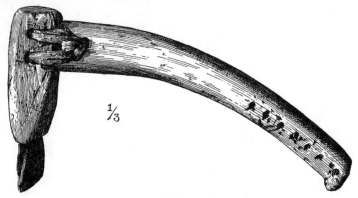

FIG. 138.—Hafted bone and stone adz.

their small size and their shape. They are usually broad and rather
thin, and narrowed to the butt, as is seen in Fig. 139, No. 56685 [71], a
beautiful little adz of bright green jade 2·8 inches long and 2·3 wide,
from Utkiavwiñ. No. 56670 [246] also from Utkiavwiñ, is a similar
blade of greenish jade slightly larger,
being 3·4 inches long and 2 inches wide.
No. 89670 [1092] is a tiny blade of hard,
fine-grained black stone, probably oil-
soaked jade, only 1·7 inches long and 1·5
wide. It is very smoothly ground. Such
little adzes, we were told, were especially
used for cutting bone. The implement,[1]
which Nordenskjöld calls a "stone
chisel," found in the ruins of an old Eskimo house at Cape North, is evidently the
head of one of these little bone adzes, as is

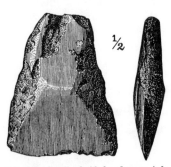

FIG. 139.—Small adz-blade of green jade.

plainly seen on comparing this figure with the larger adzes figured above.

I have figured two more composite adzes, which are quite different
from the rest. No. 89838 [1109], Fig. 140, has a blade of neatly flaked
gray flint, but this as well as the unusually straight haft is newly

---

[1] Figured in the Voyage of the *Vega*, vol. 1, p. 444, Fig. 1.

made. These are fitted to a very old bone body, which when whole was not over 3 inches long, and was probably part of a little bone adz. There is no evidence that these people ever used flint adzes. Fig. 141, No. 89872 [785], is introduced to show how the native has utilized an old cooper's adz, of which the eye was probably broken, by fitting it with a bone body.

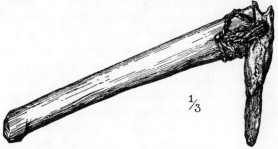

FIG. 140.—Hafted adz of bone and flint.

While the adzes already described appear to have been the predominating types, another form was sometimes used. Fig. 142, No. 89874 [964], from Nuwŭk, represents this form. The haft is of whale's rib, 1 foot long, and the head of *bone*, apparently whale's scapula, 5·6 inches long and 2·8 inches wide on the edge. There is an adze in the Museum from the Mackenzie River region with a *steel* blade of precisely the same pattern. That adzes of this pattern sometimes had stone blades is

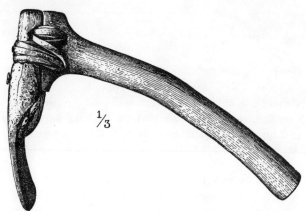

FIG. 141.—Old cooper's adz, rehafted.

probable. No. 89840 [1317], is a clumsily made *commercial* tool of this type, with a small head of greenish slate. It has an unusually straight haft, which is disproportionately long and thick.

All these adzes, ancient and modern, are hafted upon essentially the same pattern. The short curved haft, the shape of which is sufficiently well indicated by the figures, seems to have been generally made of whale's rib or reindeer antler, both of which have a natural curve suited to the shape of the haft. A "branch" of a reindeer's antler is particularly well suited for the haft of a small adze. Not only does it have naturally the proper dimensions and a suitable curve, but it is very easy, by cutting out a small segment of the "beam" where the "branch" starts from it, to make a flange of a convenient shape for fitting to the head. Antler is besides easily obtained, not only when the deer is killed for food, but by picking up shed antlers on the tundra, and is consequently employed for many purposes. The haft usually has a knob at the tip to keep the hand from slipping, and the grip is sometimes roughened with cross cuts or wound with thong. There are usually as many holes for the lashing as there are eyes in the head, though there are two holes when the head has only one large eye. On the bone heads, the surfaces to which the haft is applied and the channels for the lashings are roughened with cross cuts to prevent slipping. The lashing always follows the same general plan, though no two adzes are lashed exactly alike. The plan may be summarized as follows: One end of the

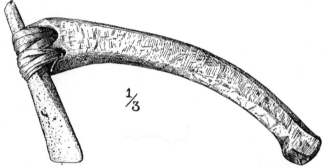

FIG. 142.—Adz with bone blade.

thong makes a turn through one of the holes in the haft, and around or through the head. This turn is then secured, usually by passing the long end through a slit in the short end and hauling this loop taut, sometimes by knotting the short end to the long part, or by catching the short end down under the next turn. The long part then makes several turns round or through the head and through the haft, sometimes also crossing around the latter, and the whole is then finished off by wrapping the end two or three times around the turns on one side and tucking it neatly underneath. This is very like the method of lashing on the heads of the mauls already described, but the mauls have only one hole in the haft, and there are rarely any turns around the latter.

Jade adz blades, like those already described, have been brought by Mr. Nelson from Kotzebue Sound, the Diomedes, St. Michaels, etc., and one came from as far south as the Kuskoquim River.

Chisels.—We collected a number of small short handled chisels, resembling the implements called "trinket makers," of which there are so many in the National Museum. We never happened to see them in actual use, but were informed that they were especially designed for working on reindeer antler. Of the eight specimens collected No. 89302 [884], Fig. 143, has been selected as a type of the antler chisel (kī′ñnusa). The blade is of steel, and the haft is of reindeer antler, in two longitudinal sections, put together at right angles to the plane of the blade, held

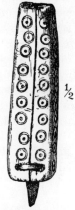

together by a stout round bone treenail 2½ inches from the butt. The square tip of the blade is beveled on both faces to a rough cutting edge. Fig. 144 (No. 89301) [1000] has a small blade with an oblique tip *not* beveled to an edge, and a haft of walrus ivory yellowed from age, and ornamented with rows of rings, each with a dot in the center, all incised and colored with red ocher. The two parts of the haft are fastened together by a stout wooden treenail and a *stitch* of whalebone.

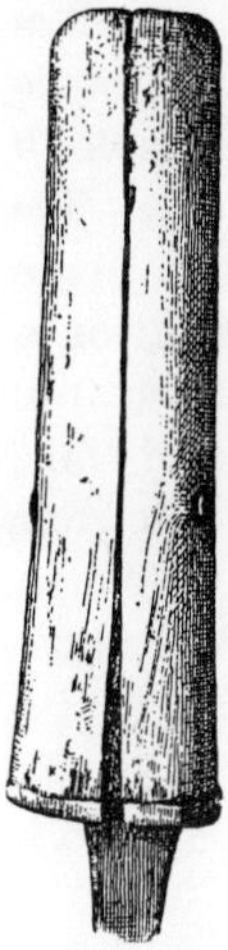

The rest of the steel-bladed chisels, four in number, are all of about the same size and hafted with antler. The blades are somewhat irregular in shape, but all have square or oblique tips and no sharp edge. Three of them have

FIG. 143.—Antler chisel.

FIG. 144.—Antler chisel.

the sections of the haft put together as described, and fastened by a treenail and a whipping of seal twine or sinew braid at the tip. One has the two sections put together in the plane of the blade and fastened with a large copper rivet, which also passes through the butt of the blade, and three stout iron ones. The hafts of all these tools show signs of much handling. The remaining two specimens have blades of black flint. No. 89637 [1207], has a haft of walrus ivory, of the usual pattern, fastened together by a bone treenail and two stitches, one of sinew braid and one of seal thong. The lashing of seal twine near the tip serves to mend a crack. The haft is old and rusty about the slot into which the blade is fitted, showing that it originally had an iron blade. The flint blade was probably put in to make it seem ancient, as there was a special demand for prehistoric articles. No. 89653 [1290], Fig. 145, is nothing

FIG. 145.—Spurious tool, flint blade.

but a fanciful tool made to meet this demand. The haft is of light-brown mountain sheep horn, and the blade of black flint. Such flint-bladed tools may have been used formerly, but there is no proof that they were.

Whalebone shaves.—There is in use at Point Barrow, and apparently not elsewhere among the Eskimo, a special tool for shaving whalebone, a substance which is very much used in the form of long, thin strips for fastening together boat timbers, whipping spear shafts, etc. The thin, long shavings which curl up like "curled hair," are carefully saved and used for the padding between stocking and boot. Whalebone is also sometimes shaved for this special purpose. The tool is essentially a little spokeshave about 4 inches long, which is held by the index and second finger of the right hand, one on each handle, with the thumb pressed against one end, and is drawn toward the workman. The collection contains three specimens of the ordinary form (sávige), represented by No. 89306 [885] (figured in Point Barrow Report, Ethnology, Pl. III, Fig. 6). This has a steel blade and a haft of walrus ivory. The upper face of the haft is convex and the under flat, and the blade, which is beveled only on the upper face, is set at a slight inclination to the flat face of the haft. The edge of the blade projects 0·2 inch from the haft above and 0·3 below. The hole at one end of the haft is for a lanyard to hang it up by. The other two are of essentially the same pattern, but have hafts of reindeer antler.

The collection also contains six tools of this description, with stone blades, but they are all new and very carelessly made, with hafts of coarse-grained bone. The shape of the tools is shown in Fig. 146, No. 89649 [1213], from Utkiavwĭñ, which has a rough blade of soft, light

FIG. 146.—Whalebone shave, slate blade.

greenish slate. The other five have blades of black or gray flint, roughly flaked. All these blades are glued in with oil dregs. No. 89652 [1225] is like the others in shape, but more neatly made, and is peculiar in having a blade of hard, compact bone. This is inserted by sawing a deep, narrow slit along one side of the haft from end to end. The blade is wedged into the middle of the slit, the ends of which are neatly filled in with slips of the same material as the haft. This was the only tool of the kind seen. It is very probable that shaves of stone were formerly used, though we obtained no genuine specimens. The use of oblong chips of flint for this purpose would naturally suggest itself to a savage, and the convenience of fitting these flakes into a little haft would soon occur to him. No. 89616 [1176] is such an oblong flint, flaked to an edge on one face, which is evidently old, and which was said to have been used for shaving whalebone. The material is black flint. Whalebone is often shaved nowadays with a common knife. The slab of bone is laid upon the thigh and the edge of the knife pressed firmly against it, with the blade perpendicular to the surface of the slab, which is drawn rapidly under it.

Saws.—If the Eskimo had not already invented the saw before they became acquainted with the whites they readily adopted the tool even when they had scanty materials for making it. Crantz[1] speaks of "a little lock saw" as one of a Greenlander's regular tools in his time, and Egede[2] mentions handsaws as a regular article of trade. Capt. Parry[3]

---

¹ History of Greenland, vol. 1, p. 149.   ² Greenland, p. 175.   ³ 2d Voyage, p. 536.

found the natives of Iglulik, in 1821–1823, using a saw made of a notched piece of iron. On our asking Nĭkawa'alu, one day, what they had for tools before they got iron he said that they had drills made of seal bones and saws made of the shoulder blade of the reindeer. Some time afterwards he brought over a model of such a saw, which he said was exactly like those formerly used. Fig. 147, No. 89476 [1206], represents this specimen. It

FIG. 147.—Saw made of deer's scapula.

is made by cutting off the anterior edge of a reindeer's scapula in a straight line parallel to the posterior edge and cutting fine saw teeth on this thin edge. The spine is also cut off nearly flat. This makes a tool very much like a carpenter's backsaw, the narrow part of the scapula forming a convenient handle.

Fig. 148, No. 56559 [15], shows how other implements were utilized before it was easy to obtain saws in plenty. It is a common case knife stamped on the blade, "Wilson, Hawksworth, ———n & Co., Sheffield," which perhaps came from the *Plover*, with saw teeth cut on the edge. It was picked up at the Utkiavwĭñ cemetery, where it

FIG. 148.—Saw made of a case-knife.

had been exposed with a corpse. Saws are now a regular article of trade, and most of the natives are provided with them of various styles and makes. The name for saw is uluă'ktun.

Drills and borers.—The use of the bow drill appears to be universal among the Eskimo. Those at present employed at Point Barrow do not differ from the large series collected at the Mackenzie and Anderson rivers by MacFarlane. The drill is a slender rod of steel worked to a drill point and imbedded in a stout wooden shaft, which is tapered to a rounded tip. This fits into a stone socket imbedded in a wooden block, which is held between the teeth, so that the point of the drill can be pressed down against the object to be drilled by the head, leaving both hands free to work the short bow, which has a loose string of thong long enough to make one turn round the shaft. The collection contains ten of these modern steel or iron drills, fifteen bows, and seven mouthpieces. No. 89502 [853], figured in Point Barrow Rept., Ethnology, Pl. II, Fig. 1, has been selected as a typical drill (niă'ktun). The drill is a cylindrical rod of steel beaten out into a small lanceolate point, which is filed sharp on the edges. The shaft is made of hard wood. The remaining drills are of essentially the same pattern, varying in total length from about 11 inches to 16½.

Fig. 149, No. 89499 [968] shows a somewhat unusual shape of shaft. The lashings round the large end are to keep it from splitting any more than it has done already. The drill is of iron and the shaft of spruce, which was once painted with red ocher.

No. 89497 [819] (Fig. 150) has a ferrule of coarse-grained bone neatly pegged on with two small pegs of the same material. This is unusual

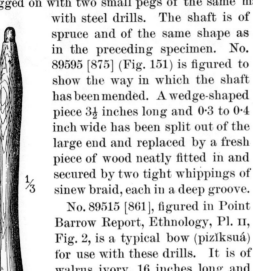

with steel drills. The shaft is of spruce and of the same shape as in the preceding specimen. No. 89595 [875] (Fig. 151) is figured to show the way in which the shaft has been mended. A wedge-shaped piece 3½ inches long and 0·3 to 0·4 inch wide has been split out of the large end and replaced by a fresh piece of wood neatly fitted in and secured by two tight whippings of sinew braid, each in a deep groove.

No. 89515 [861], figured in Point Barrow Report, Ethnology, Pl. II, Fig. 2, is a typical bow (pizĭksuá) for use with these drills. It is of walrus ivory, 16 inches long and oval in section. Through each end is drilled a transverse hole. A string of seal thong 21 inches long is looped into one of these holes by passing one end of the thong through the hole, cutting a slit in it, and passing the other end through this. The other end is passed through the other hole and knotted at the tip.

FIG. 149.—Bow drill.

These bows vary slightly in dimensions, but are not less than a foot or more than 16 inches long, and are almost always of walrus ivory. No. 89508 [956] (Fig. 152), is an old and rudely made bow of whalebone, which is more strongly arched than usual, and has the string attached to notches at the ends instead of into holes. This was said to belong with an old bone drill, No. 89498 [956]. Both came from Nuwŭk. These bows are often highly ornamented both by carving and with incised patterns colored with red ocher or soot. The following figures are introduced to show some of the different styles of ornamentation.

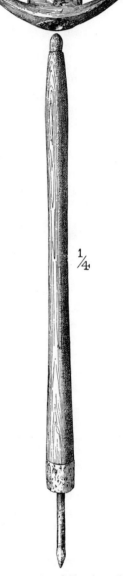

FIG. 150.—Bow drill and mouthpiece.

Fig. 153a, No. 56506 [298] is unusually broad and flat and was probably made for a handle to a tool bag. Such handles, however, appear to be also used for drill bows. The tips of this bow represent seals heads, and have good sized sky-blue glass beads inserted for eyes. The rest of the ornamentation is incised and blackened. Fig. 153*b*, No. 89421 [1260], from Utkiavwĭñ, is a similar bow, which has incised on the back figures of men and animals, which, perhaps, tell of some real event. Mr. L. M. Turner informs me that the natives of Norton Sound keep a regular record of hunting and other events engraved in this way upon their drill bows, and that no one ever ventures to falsify these records. We did not learn definitely that such was the rule at Point Barrow, but we have one bag-handle marked with whales, which we were told indicated the number killed by the owner. Fig. 153*c*, No. 89425 [1732], from Utkiavwĭñ, is a similar bow, ornamented on the back with simply an incised border colored red. On the other side are the figures of ten bearded seals, cross-hatched and blackened. These are perhaps a "score." Fig. 153*d*, No. 89509 [914], from Nuwŭk, is a bow of the common pattern, but ornamented by carving the back into a toothed keel.

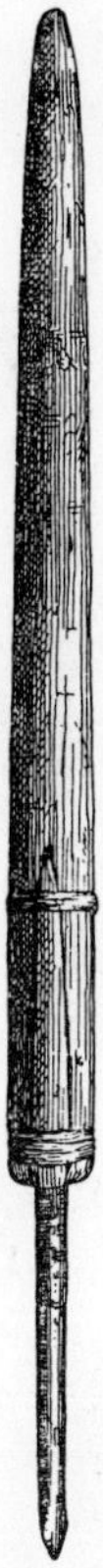

¼

Fig. 153*e*, No. 89510 [961], from Utkiavwĭñ, is ornamented on one side only with an incised pattern, which is blackened. Fig. 153*f*, No. 89511 [961], also from Utkiavwĭñ, has, in addition to the incised and blackened pattern, a small transparent sky-blue glass bead inlaid in the middle of the back. Fig. 153*g*, No. 89512 [836], from the same place, is a flat bow with the edges carved into scallops. The incised line along the middle of the back is colored with red ocher. The string is made of sinew braid.

Fig. 154, No. 89777 [1004*b*], which belongs in the "kit" of Ilû'bw'ga, the Nunatañmiun, previously mentioned, is interesting from having been lengthened 3¼ inches by riveting on a piece of reindeer antler at one end. The two pieces are neatly joined in a "lap splice" about 2 inches long and fastened with three iron rivets. The owner appears to have concluded that his drill bow was too short when

FIG. 151.—
Bow drill.

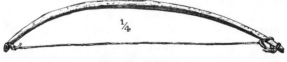

FIG. 152.—Drill bow.

he was at home, in the interior, where he could obtain no walrus ivory. The incised pattern on the back is colored with red ocher.

The mouthpiece (kĭ'ñmia) consists of a block of hard stone (rarely iron), in which is hollowed out a round cup-like socket, large enough to receive the tip of the drill shaft, imbedded in a block of wood of a suitable size to hold between the teeth. This block often has curved flanges

9 ETH——12

on each side, which rest against the cheeks. Such mouthpieces are
common all along the coast from the Anderson River to Norton Sound,
as is shown by the Museum collection. No. 89500 [800], figured in Point
Barrow Report, Ethnology, Pl. II, Fig. 3, is a type of the flanged mouthpiece. The block is of pine, carved into a thick, broad arch, with a
large block on the inside. Into the top of the arch is inlaid a piece of gray

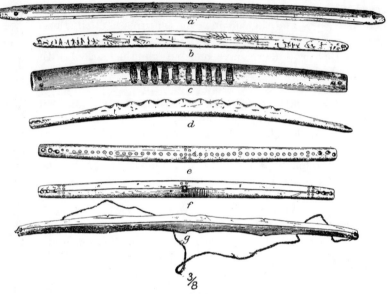

FIG. 153.—Drill bows.

porphyry with black spots, which is slightly convex on the surface, so as
to project a little above the surface of the wood. In the middle of the
stone is a cup-shaped cavity one-half inch in diameter and of nearly the
same depth. This is a rather large mouthpiece, being 6 inches across
from one end of the arch to the other.

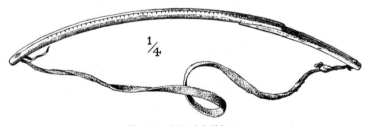

FIG. 154.—Spliced drill bow.

There are two other specimens of the same pattern, both rather smaller.
No. 89503 [891], Fig. 150, from Nuwŭk, has the stone of black and white
syenite. This specimen is very old and dirty, and worn through to the
stone on one side, where the teeth have come against it. No. 89787
[1004c], Fig. 155, is almost exactly the same shape as the type, but has

for a socket a piece of iron 1·1 inches square, hollowed out as usual.
The outside of the wood has been painted with red ocher, but this is
mostly worn off.   This mouthpiece belonged to Ilû'bw'ga.

Fig. 156, No. 89505 [892], from
Utkiavwĭñ, represents the pattern which is perhaps rather
commoner than the preceding.
The wood, which holds the
socket of black and white syenite, is simply an elliptical
block of spruce.   The remain-

FIG. 155.—Drill mouthpiece, with iron socket.

ing three specimens are of the same pattern and of the same material as
the last, except No. 89507 [908], from Nuwŭk, in which the wood is oak.
As it appears very old, this wood may have come from the *Plover*.

When not in use, the point of the drill is sometimes protected with a
sheath.   One such sheath was obtained, No. 89447 [1112], figured in Point Barrow Report, Ethnology, Pl. II, Fig. 1.   It is
of walrus ivory, 3·6 inches long.   The end of a piece of thong
is passed through the eye and the other part fastened round
the open end with a marline-hitch, catching down the end.
This leaves a lanyard 9¼ inches long, which is hitched or
knotted round the shaft of the drill when the sheath is fitted
over the point.

The drills above described are used for perforating all sorts
of material, wood, bone, ivory, metal, etc., and are almost the
only boring implements used, even
awls being unusual.   Before the introduction of iron, the point was made
of one of the small bones from a seal's
leg.   We obtained four specimens of
these bone drills, of which two, at
least, appear to be genuine.   No.
89498 [956], Fig. 157, is one of these,
from Nuwŭk.   The shaft is of the

FIG. 156.—Drill mouthpiece without wings.

ordinary pattern and made of some hard wood, but the point
is a roughly cylindrical rod of bone, expanding at the point,
where it is convex on one face and concave on the other and
beveled on both faces into two cutting edges, which meet in
an acute angle.   The larger end of the shaft has been split
and mended by whipping it for about three-quarters of an
inch with sinew braid.   No. 89518 [1174], is apparently also
genuine, and is like the preceding, but beveled only on the
concave face of the point, which is rather obtuse.   No. 89519
[1258] was made for the market.   It has a rude shaft of whale's
bone, but a carefully made bone point of precisely the pattern
of the modern iron ones.   No. 89520 [1182] has no shaft, and appears to
be an old unfinished drill fitted into a carelessly made bone ferrule.

FIG. 157—
Bone-pointed
drill.

The drill at the present day is always worked with a bow, which allows one hand to be used for steadying the piece of work. We were informed, however, that formerly a cord was sometimes used without the bow, but furnished with a transverse handle at each end.

We collected six little handles of ivory, carved into some ornamental shape, each with an eye in the middle to which a thong could be attached. All were old, and we never saw them in use. The first two were collected at an early period of our acquaintance with these people, and from our imperfect knowledge of the language we got the impression that they were handles to be attached to a harpoon line.

We were not long, however in finding out that the harpoon has no such appendage, and when the other four came in a year later, at a time

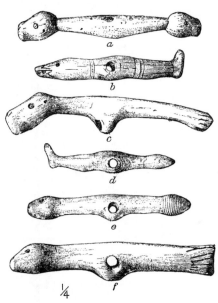

¼

FIG. 158.—Handles for drill cords.

when the press of other work prevented careful inquiry into their use, we supposed that they were meant for handles to the lines used for dragging dead seals, as they somewhat resemble such an implement. On our return home, when I had opportunities for making a careful study of the collection, I found that none of the drag lines, either in our own collection or in those of the Museum, had handles of this description. On the other hand, I found many similar implements in Mr. Nelson's collection labeled "drill-cord handles," and finally one pair (No. 36319, from Kashunuk, near Cape Romanzoff), still attached to the drill cord. These handles are almost identical in shape with No. 89458 [835], from Utkiavwĭñ. This leaves no doubt in my mind that the so-called "drag-line handles" in our collection are nothing more than handles for drill cords, now wholly obsolete and supplanted by the bows already described. I have figured all six of these handles to show the different patterns of ornamentation. They are all made of walrus ivory, and are all "odd" handles, no two being mates. Fig. 158a (No. 56526) [86], is 5·2 inches long, and light blue beads are inserted for eyes in the seal's heads. The eye for the drill cord is made by boring two median holes at the middle of one side so that they meet under the surface and make a longitudinal channel.

Fig. 158b (No. 56527 [23] from Utkiavwĭñ), is 4·3 inches long, and is very accurately carved into the image of a man's right leg and foot, dressed in a striped deerskin boot. The end opposite to the foot is the head of some animal, perhaps a wolf, with bits of dark wood inlaid for eyes. The eye is a simple large transverse hole through the thigh.

Fig. 158c (No. 89455 [929] from Nuwŭk), is 5·9 inches long. The eye is drilled lengthwise through a large lump projecting from the middle of one side. Small blue beads are inlaid for the eyes, and one to indicate the male genital opening.

Fig. 158d (No. 89456 [930] from Nuwŭk) is like No. 56527 [23], but represents the left foot and is not so artistically carved. It is 3·7 inches long.

Fig. 158e (No. 89457 [925] from Nuwŭk) is 4·7 inches long, and resembles No. 89455 [929], but has instead of the seal's tail and flippers a large ovoid knob ornamented with incised and blackened rings. The "eye" is bored transversely.

Fig. 158f (No. 89458 [835] from Utkiavwĭñ) differs from No. 89455 [925] in having a transverse eye, and being less artistically carved. Bits of lead are inlaid for the eyes. It is 4·4 inches long. The name of this implement is kû'ñ-i.

We obtained six specimens of an old flint tool, consisting of a rather long thick blade mounted in a straight haft about 10 inches long, of which we had some difficulty in ascertaining the use. We were at last able to be quite sure that they were intended for drilling, or rather reaming out, the large cavity in the base of the ivory head of a whale harpoon, which fits upon the conical tip of the fore-shaft. The shape of the blade is well fitted for this purpose. It is not unlikely that such tools, worked as these are, by hand, preceded the bone drills for boring all sorts of objects, and that the habit of using them for making the whale harpoon was kept up from the same conservatism founded on superstition which surrounds the whole whale fishery. (See under "Whale fishing," where the subject will be more fully discussed.) No. 89626 [870], figured in Point Barrow Report, Ethnology, Pl. II, Fig. 4, is a typical implement of this class (itaun, i'tûgetsau'). The blade is of black flint, flaked, 2 inches long, imbedded in the end of a haft of spruce, 10·5 inches long. The blade is held in place by whipping the cleft end of the haft with sinew braid.

Two of the other specimens, No. 89627 [937] and No. 89628 [912], are of essentially the same pattern and material, but have rounded hafts. No. 89629 [960] and No. 89630 [1068], Figs. 159a, 159b, have blades of the same pattern, but have hafts fitted for use with the mouthpiece and bow, showing that sometimes, at least in later times, these tools were so used. No. 89625 [1217] (Fig. 160) has no haft, but the blade, which is rather narrow in proportion to its length (2·3 inches by 0·5), is fitted into a short ferrule of antler, with a little dovetail on the edge for attaching it to the haft.

Of awls we saw only one specimen, which, perhaps, ought rather to be considered a little hand drill. This is No. 89308 [1292], Fig. 161, from Utkiavwĭñ. The point is the tip of a common three-cornered file, sharpened down. It is imbedded in a handle of fossil ivory which has turned a light yellowish brown from age. Its total length is 2·8 inches.

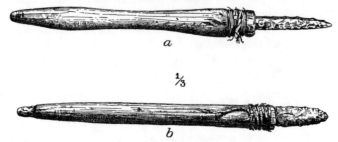

$\frac{1}{3}$

FIG. 159.—Flint-bladed reamers.

Hammers.—At the present day nearly every man has been able to procure an iron hammer of some kind, which he uses with great handiness. Before the introduction of iron, in addition to the bone and stone mauls above described as bone crushers, unhafted pebbles of convenient shape were also employed. No. 56661 [274] is such a stone. It is an ovoid water-worn pebble of greenish gray quartzite, $3\frac{1}{2}$ inches long. The ends are battered, showing how it had been used. It was brought from one of the rivers in the interior by one of the natives of Utkiavwĭñ.

Files.—Files of all kinds are eagerly sought after by the natives, who use them with very great skill and patience, doing nearly all their metal work with these tools. For instance, one particularly ingenious native converted his Winchester rifle from a rim fire to a central fire with nothing but a file. To do this he had to make a new firing pin, as the firing pin of the rim-fire gun is too short to reach the head of the cartridge. He accomplished this by accurately cutting off, to the proper length, an old worn-out three-cornered file. He then filed off enough of each edge so that the rod fitted evenly in the cylindrical hole where the firing pin works. The work was done so carefully that the new firing pin worked perfectly, and he had only to complete the job by cutting off his central fire cartridge shells to a proper length to fit the chamber of the gun.

$\frac{3}{4}$

FIG. 160.—Flint-bladed reamer.

$\frac{3}{4}$

FIG. 161.—Awl.

They have almost no knowledge of working metal with the aid of heat, as is natural from the scarcity of fuel. I have, however, seen them roughly temper small articles, such as fire steels, etc., by heating them in the fire and quenching them in cold water. One native very neatly mended a musket barrel which had been cracked by firing too heavy a charge. He cut a section from another old barrel of somewhat larger caliber, which he heated until it had expanded enough to slip down over the crack, and then allowed it to shrink on.

Whetstones (ipiksaun).—Knives are generally sharpened with a file, cutting a bevel, as before mentioned, on one face of the blade only. To "set" or "turn" the edge they use pieces of steel of various shapes, generally with a hole drilled in them so that they can be hung to the breeches belt by a lanyard. One man, for instance, used about half of

FIG. 162.—Jade whetstones.

a razor blade for this purpose, and another a small horseshoe magnet. In former times they employed a very elegant implement, consisting of a slender rod of jade from 3 to 7 inches long, with a lanyard attached to an eye in the larger end. These were sometimes made by cutting a piece from one of the old jade adzes in the manner already described. There are a few of these whetstones still in use at the present day, and they are very highly prized. We succeeded in obtaining nine specimens, of which No. 89618 [801], Fig. 162a, has been selected as the type. It is of hard black stone, probably jade, 6·3 inches long. Through the wider end is drilled a large eye, into which is neatly spliced one end of a stout flat braid of sinew 4¾ inches long.

The remaining whetstones are of very much the same pattern. I have figured five of them, to show the slight variations. Fig. 162*b* (No. 56662 [393], from Utkiavwĭñ) is of light grayish green jade, smoothly polished and 4·1 inches long. It is chamfered only on the small end at right angles to the breadth, and has the eye prolonged into ornamental grooves on the two opposite faces. The long lanyard is of common sinew braid. No. 56663 [229] (from the same village) is of olive green, slightly translucent jade, 6·8 inches long, and elliptical in section, also chamfered only at the small end. The lanyard, which is a strip of seal thong 9 inches long, is secured in the eye, as described before, with two slits, one in the standing part through which the end is passed and the other in the end with the standing part passed through it. No. 89617 [1262] (from Sidaru) is of olive green, translucent jade, 6·1

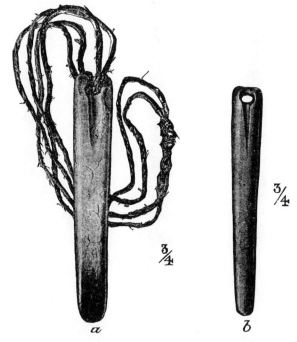

Fig. 163.—Jade whetstones.

inches long, and shaped like the type, but chamfered only at the small end. The lanyard of seal thong is secured in the eye by a large round knot in one end. No. 89619 [837] (from Utkiavwĭñ) is of bright green, translucent jade, 5·1 inches long, and unusually thick, its greatest diameter being 0·6 inch. The tip is gradually worked off to an oblique edge, and it has ornamental grooves running through the eye like No. 56662 [393].

No. 89620 [865] (from Nuwŭk) is shaped very much like the type, but has the tip tapered off almost to a point. It is of olive green, slightly translucent jade and is 7 inches long. The lanyard is a piece of sinew braid with the ends knotted together and the bight looped into the eye. A large sky-blue glass bead is slipped on over both parts of the lanyard and pushed up close to the loop. Fig. 163a (No. 89621 [757], from Utkiavwïñ) is very short and broad (3·6 inches by 0·6), is chamfered at both ends, and has the ornamental grooves at the eye. The material is a hard, opaque, bluish gray stone, veined with black.

A whetstone of similar material was brought by Lieut. Stoney from Kotzebue Sound. The long lanyard is of sinew braid. Fig. 163b (No. 89622 [951], also from Utkiavwïñ) is a very small, slender whetstone, 3·3 inches long, of dark olive green semitranslucent jade, polished. The tip is not chamfered, but tapers to a blunt point. It has the ornamental grooves at the eye. These are undoubtedly the "stones for making . . . whetstones, or these ready-made" referred to by Dr. Simpson (Op. cit., p. 266) as brought by the Nunatañmiun from the people of

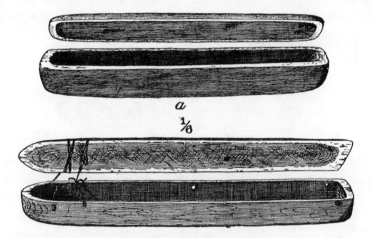

FIG. 164.—Wooden tool boxes.

the "Ko-wak River." A few such whetstones have been collected on other parts of the northwest coast as far south as the northern shore of Norton Sound. The broken whetstone mentioned above is of a beautiful bluish green translucent jade. Bits of stone are also used for whetstones, such as No. 89786 [1004f], which belong in Ilû′bw'ga's tool bag. They are two rough, oblong bits of hard dark gray slate, apparently split off a flat, weathered surface.

Tool boxes and bags.—We collected six specimens of a peculiarly shaped long, narrow box, carved from a single block of wood, which we were informed were formerly used for holding tools. They have gone out of fashion at the present day, and there are but few of them left. No. 89860 [1152], Fig. 164a, represents the typical shape of this box. It is carved from a single block of pine. The cover is slightly hollowed on the under side and is held on by two double rings of twine (one of seal twine and the other of sinew braid), large enough to slip over the end. Each ring is made by doubling a long piece of twine so that the two parts are equal, passing one end through the bight and knotting it to the other. The box and cover seem to have been painted inside and out with red ocher. On the outside this is mostly faded and worn off and covered with dirt, but inside it has turned a dark brown. Fig. 164*b* (No. 89858 [1319], from Utkiavwïñ,) is a similar box, 21·1 inches long. The cover is held on by a string passing over little hooked ivory studs close to the edge of the box. There were originally five of these studs, two at each end and one in the middle of one side. The string started from one of these studs at the pointed end. This stud is broken and the string fastened into a hole close to it. To fasten on the cover the string was carried over and hooked under the opposite stud, then crossed over the cover to the middle stud, then across to the end stud on the other side, and the loop on the end hooked onto the last stud.

No. 89859 [1318] is a smaller box (19 inches long) of the same pattern, with only four studs. The cover has three large blue glass beads,

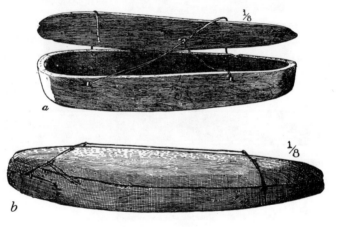

FIG. 165.—Large wooden tool boxes.

like those used for labrets, inlaid in a line along the middle. No. 89858 [1144], from Utkiavwïñ, is the shape of the type, but has a thicker cover and six stud holes in the margin. No. 89861 [1151], Fig. 165*a*, from the same place, is shaped something like a violin case, 22·2 inches long. The cover has been split and "stitched" together with whalebone, and a crack in the broader end of the box has been neatly mended by pegging on, with nine little wooden treenails, a strap of reindeer antler of the same width as the edge and following the curve of its outline. There are four studs, two at each end. The string is made fast to one at the smaller end, carried over to the opposite one, then crossed to the opposite stud at the other end and back under the last one, a bight of the end being tucked under the string between the two last-mentioned studs. The string is made of sinew braid, rope-yarns, and a long piece of seal thong. It was probably at first all of sinew braid, and, gradually growing too short by being broken and knotted together again, was lengthened out with whatever came to hand.

No. 89862 [1593], Fig. 165b, is a large box, of a very peculiar shape, best understood from the figure. The outside is much weathered, but appears to have been roughly carved, and the excavation of the box and cover is very rudely done, perhaps with a stone tool. A hole in the larger end is mended by a patch of wood chamfered off to fit the hole and sewed on round the edges with "over-and-over" stitches of whalebone. The string is arranged in permanent loops, under which the cover can be slipped off and on.

The arrangement, which is rather complicated, is as follows: On one side of the box, one-half inch from the edge and about 7 inches from each end, are two pairs of holes, one-half inch apart. Into each pair is fastened, by means of knots on the inside, a loop of very stout sinew braid, 3 inches long, and similar loops of seal thong, 5 inches long, are

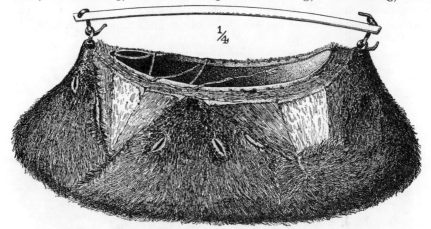

FIG. 166.—Tool bag of wolverine skin.

fastened into corresponding pairs of holes on the other side. A piece of seal thong is fastened with a becket-hitch into the loop of seal thong at the small end of the box, passes through both braid loops on the other side, and is carried over through the loop of seal thong at the large end. The end of the thong is knotted into one of the pairs of holes left by the breaking away of a stitch at the edge of the wooden patch above mentioned.

All these boxes are very old and were painted inside with red ocher, which has turned dark brown from age. Tools are nowadays kept in a large oblong, flat satchel, ĭkqûxbwĭñ, which has an arched handle of ivory or bone stretched lengthwise across the open mouth. These bags are always made of skin with the hair out, and the skins of wolverines' heads are the most desired for this purpose. The collection contains four such bags. No. 89794 [1018], Fig. 166, is the type of these bags. The bottom of the bag is a piece of short-haired brown deerskin, with the hair out, pieced across the middle.   The sides and ends are made of the skins of four wolverine heads, without the lower jaw, cut off at the nape and spread out and sewed together side by side with the hair outward and noses up.   One head comes on each end of the bag and one on each side, and the spaces between the noses are filled out with gussets of deerskin and wolverine skin.   A narrow strip of the latter is sewed round the mouth of the bag.   The handle is of walrus ivory, 14½ inches long and about one-half inch square.   There is a vertical hole through it one-half inch from each end, and at one end also a transverse hole between this and the tip.   One end of the thong which fastens the handle to the bag is drawn through this hole and cut off close to the surface.   The other end is brought over the handle and down through the vertical hole and made fast with two half-hitches into a hole through the septum of the nose of the head at one end of the bag. The other end of the handle is fastened to the opposite nose in the same way, but the thong is secured in the hole by a simple knot in the end above.   On one side of the handle is an unfinished incised pattern.

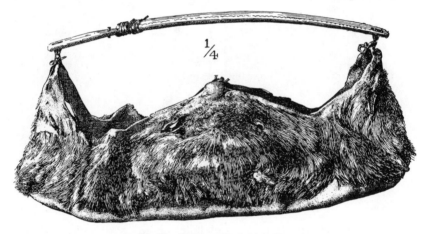

FIG. 167.—Tool bag of wolverine skin.

Fig. 167, No. 89776 [1004], is a similar bag, made of four wolverine heads with the lower jaws attached.   The bottom is of stout leather without hair.   The mouth is tied up by a bit of thong passed through the nostrils of the two side heads so that it can spread open only about 1¾ inches.   The handle is broad and flat, made of walrus ivory, and ornamented with an incised border on top.   One end is broken and pieced out with reindeer antler secured by a clumsy "fishing" of seal twine, which is passed through holes in the two parts.   The pieces seem to have been riveted together as in the drill bow, No. 89777 [1004b] (Fig. 154), which belongs to this bag.   There is a rivet still sticking in the antler.   It is possible that the ivory may have broken in the process of riveting the two together.   The handle has two vertical holes at each end for the thong, by which it is fastened to the end noses, both in the median line and joined by a short channel on top of the handle. This bag was the property of the Nunatañmiun Ilûbw'ga, so frequently mentioned, and was purchased with all its contents.

These are two bow drills, one large and one small (Figs. 168a and 168b, Nos. 89778 and 89779 [1004a]); a drill bow (Fig. 154, No. 89777 [1004b]); a mouthpiece (Fig. 155, No. 89787 [1004c]); a large crooked knife with a sheath (Fig. 114, No. 89780 [1004d]); a flint flaker (No. 89752 [1004e]); a comb for deerskins (Fig. 169, No. 89781 [1005]); a haircomb made of antler (No. 89785 [1006]); a fishhook (No. 89783 [1007]); and a small seal harpoon head (No. 89784 [1008]).

$\frac{1}{3}$

a   b

FIG. 168.—Drills belong-
ing to the tool bag.

No. 89796 [1118], from Nuwŭk, is of rather unusual materials. The bottom is of brown reindeer skin and the sides and ends are the heads of two wolves and a red fox. The wolf heads meet on one side, and the fox head is put in between them on the other. The fox head has no lower jaw, and one wolf head has only the left half of the lower jaw. The vacant spaces around the mouth are filled by triangular gussets of wolf and reindeer skin. The eyeholes are patched on the inside with deerskin. It has no handle. No. 89795 [1309], the remaining bag, is of the usual pattern, but carelessly made of small pieces of deerskin, with a handle of coarse-grained whale's bone. It was probably made for sale.

$\frac{1}{2}$

FIG. 169.—Comb for deerskins in the tool bag.

I have figured four handles of such bags to show the style of ornamentation. Fig. 170a (No. 89420 [1111], from Nuwŭk) has incised figures of men and reindeer on the back, once colored with ocher, of which traces can still be seen. This is perhaps a hunting score. (See remarks on this subject under "Bow drills.") Fig. 170b (No. 89423 [996], from Utkiavwĭñ) is a very elaborate handle, with scalloped edges and fluted back, which is also ornamented with an incised pattern colored with red ocher. The other side is covered with series of the incised circles, each with a dot in the center, so frequently mentioned. Fig. 170c (No. 89424 [890], from Nuwŭk) has on the under side two rows of figures representing the flukes and "smalls" of whales. This is the specimen already mentioned, which the natives called an actual score. The series of twenty-six tails were said to be the record of old Yûksĭ'ña ("Erksinra" of Dr. Simpson), the so-called "chief" at Nuwŭk. All the above handles are of walrus ivory, and have been in actual use. Fig. 170c (No. 56513

[43], from Utkiavwĭñ) is a handle of different material (reindeer antler) and of somewhat different pattern. One end is neatly carved into an exceedingly accurate image of the head of a reindeer which has shed

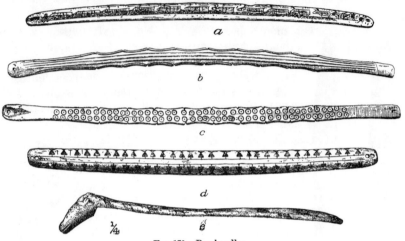

FIG. 170.—Bag handles.

its antlers, with small blue beads inlaid for the eyes. The back of the handle is ornamented with an incised pattern colored with red ocher. We were told that such handles were sometimes fitted to the wooden buckets, but I never saw one so used.

No. 89798 [1075], Fig. 171, is a bag of rather unusual pattern, the only one of the kind we saw. The bottom is a single round piece, 9

FIG. 171—Bag of leather.

inches in diameter, of what seems to be split skin of the bearded seal, flesh side out, and the rest of the bag is of white-tanned seal leather. The sides are of five broad pieces (6, 4½, 4, 5½, and 5 inches broad at the bottom, respectively, narrowing to 2½, 1½, 1¼, 2, and 2½, respectively, at the top), alternating with five straight strips, respectively 1½, 1, 1⅓, 1¼, and 1½ inches broad. The edges of these strips overlap the edges of the broad pieces, and are neatly stitched with two threads, as on the soles of the waterproof boots. The outer thread, which is caught in the loop of each stitch of the other, is a slender filament of black whale-bone. This produces a sort of embroidery. The neck is stitched to the bag with the same seam, but the hem at the mouth is merely "run" round with sinew. This bag was probably for holding small tools and similar articles.

WEAPONS.

As would naturally be expected from what has been said of the peaceful character of these people, offensive weapons, specially intended for use against men, are exceedingly rare. In case of quarrels between individuals or parties the bows, spears, and knives intended for hunting or general use would be turned against their enemies. Even their rifles, nowadays, are kept much more for hunting than as weapons of offense, and the revolvers of various patterns which many of them have obtained from the ships are chiefly carried when traveling back and forth between the two villages as a protection against a possible bear. We, however, obtained a few weapons which were especially designed for taking human life. One of these was a little club (tĭ′glun) (No. 89492 [1310], Fig. 172, from Utkiavwĭñ) made of the butt end of an old pickax head of whale's bone, with the point cut down to a blunt end. It is 6·4 inches long and meant to be clenched in the hand like a dagger, and used for striking blows, probably at the temple. The transverse grooves for hafting give a good hold for the fingers. This was the only weapon of the kind seen.

½

FIG. 172.—Little hand-club.

We collected a single specimen of a kind of slung shot, No. 89472 [905] (Fig. 173), made of a roughly ovoid lump of heavy bone, the symphysis of the lower jaw of a walrus, 3⅛ inches long. At the smaller end two large holes are bored in obliquely so as to meet under the surface and form a channel through which is passed a slip of white seal skin about 15 inches long, the ends of which fasten together with two slits, so as to make a loop. This may be compared with the stone balls used by the ancient Aleuts for striking a man on the temple.

The commonest weapon of offense was a broad dagger made of a bone of the polar bear. This was said to be especially meant for killing a "bad man," possibly for certain specified offenses or perhaps in cases of insanity. Insane persons were sometimes killed in Greenland, and the act was considered "neither decidedly admissi-

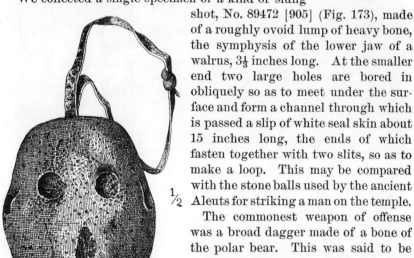

½

FIG. 173.—Slungshot made of walrus jaw.

ble nor altogether unlawful."[1] The use of bears' bones for these weapons points to some superstitious idea, perhaps having reference to the ferocity of the animal. We collected five specimens of these daggers, of which No. 89484 [767], Fig. 174, has been selected as the type. It is the distal end of the ulna of a polar bear, with the neck and condyles forming the hilt, and the shaft split so as to expose the medullary cavity and cut into a pointed blade. It is very old, blackened, and crumbling on the surface, and is a foot long.

Fig. 175a, No. 89475 [988], from Nuwŭk, is made of a straight splinter from the shaft of one of the long bones, 9¾ inches long. No. 89480 [1141], from Utkiavwĭñ, has a roughly whittled hilt and a somewhat twisted blade, rather narrow, but widened to a sharp lanceolate point. It is 12 inches long. No. 89481 [1175], from the same place,

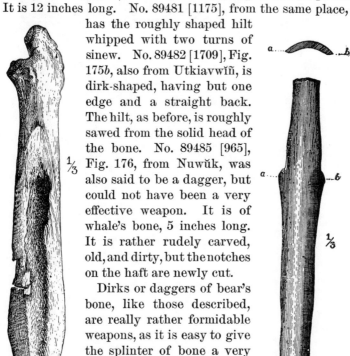

has the roughly shaped hilt whipped with two turns of sinew. No. 89482 [1709], Fig. 175b, also from Utkiavwĭñ, is dirk-shaped, having but one edge and a straight back. The hilt, as before, is roughly sawed from the solid head of the bone. No. 89485 [965], Fig. 176, from Nuwŭk, was also said to be a dagger, but could not have been a very effective weapon. It is of whale's bone, 5 inches long. It is rather rudely carved, old, and dirty, but the notches on the haft are newly cut.

Dirks or daggers of bear's bone, like those described, are really rather formidable weapons, as it is easy to give the splinter of bone a very keen point. The Museum contains a bone dagger curiously like these Eskimo weapons, but made of the bone of the

FIG. 174.—Dagger of grizzly bear, and used by bear's bone. the Indians of the McCloud

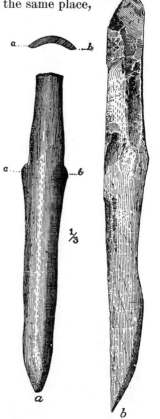

FIG. 175.—Bone daggers.

River, northern California. They believe that the peculiar shape of the point, having a hollow (the medullary cavity) on one face, like the Eskimo daggers, causes the wound to bleed internally.

---

[1] Rink, Tales and Traditions, p. 35.

PROJECTILE WEAPONS.

Firearms.—When Dease and Simpson first met these people, in 1837, they had no firearms, but the next party of whites who came in contact with them (Pullen and Hooper, in 1849) found the "chief" in possession of an old shaky musket of English make, with the name "Barnett" on the lock.[1] Hooper believed this to be the gun lost by Sir John Franklin's party in 1826.[2] This gun was, however, often seen by the people of the *Plover* (in fact, Capt. Maguire kept it on board of the *Plover* for some time[3]), and was found to have on the lock, besides the name "Barnett," also the date, "1843," so that of course it was not lost in 1826. Armstrong[4] also mentions seeing this gun, which, the natives told him, they had procured "from the other tribes to the south ward." In the summer of 1853 they began to purchase guns and ammunition from the eastern natives. Yûksĭña and two other men each bought a gun this year.[5]

As the whalers began to go to Point Barrow in 1854, the opportunity for obtaining firearms has been afforded the natives every year since then, so that they are now well supplied with guns, chiefly of American manufacture. That all their firearms have not been obtained from this source is probable from the fact they have still in their possession a number of smoothbore percussion guns, double and single barreled, of Russian manufacture. They are all stamped in Russian with the name of Tula, a town on the Oopa, 105 miles south of Moscow, which has received the name of the "Sheffield and Birmingham of Russia," from its vast manufactory of arms, established by Peter the Great. These guns must have come from the "Nunatañmiun," who obtained them either from

½

FIG. 176.—So-called dagger of bone.

the Siberian traders or from the Russians at Norton Sound through the Malemiut. Both smoothbore and rifled guns are in general use. The smoothbores are of all sorts and descriptions, from an old flintlock musket to more or less valuable single and double percussion fowling-pieces. Three of the natives now (1883) have cheap double breechloaders and one a single breechloader (made by John P. Lovell, of Boston). Guns in general are called "cupûñ," an onomatopœic word in general use in western America, but many of the different kinds have special names. For instance, a double gun is called madro'lĭñ (from *madro, two*). The rifles are also of many different patterns. The kind preferred by the natives is the ordinary Winchester brass-mounted 15-shot repeater, which the whalers and traders purchase cheaply at wholesale. This is

---

[1] Hooper, Tents, etc., p. 239.
[2] Franklin, 2d Exp., p. 148. In the hurry of leaving Barter Island "one of the crew of the *Reliance* left his gun and ammunition."
[3] See McClure's N. W. Passage, p. 390.
[4] Narrative, p. 109.
[5] Maguire, Further Papers, p. 907.

called akĭmiɐlĭñ ("that which has fifteen," sc., shots). The whalers are also in the habit of buying up all sorts of cheap or second-hand guns for the Arctic trade, so that many other kinds of guns are also common. Of breechloaders, we saw the Sharpe's rifle, savĭgro′lĭñ (from a fancied resemblance between the crooked lever of this gun and the crooked knife, savigro′n); other patterns of Winchester; the Spencer repeater, kai′psualĭñ (from kaipsĭ, cartridge); the peculiar Sharps-Hankins, once used in the U. S. Navy, and which was the favorite weapon of the rebel Boers in South Africa; the Peabody-Martini, made in America for the Turkish Government, marked on the rear sight with Turkish figures, and, exposed with a corpse at the cemetery, one English Snider. The regulation Springfield rifles belonging to the post, which were often loaned to the natives for the purpose of hunting, were called mûkpara′lĭñ (from *mûkpara′*, book, referring to the breech action, which opens like a book).

They formerly had very few muzzle-loading rifles, but of late years, since the law against trading arms to the natives has been construed to refer solely to breech-loading rifles, the whalers have sold them yäger rifles, of the old U. S. Army pattern, Enfield rifles, ship's muskets with the Tower mark on them, and a sort of bogus rifle made especially for trade, in imitation of the old-fashioned Kentucky rifle, but with grooves extending only a short distance from the muzzle. They of course depend on the ships for their supplies of ammunition, though the Nunatañmiun sometimes bring a few cartridges smuggled across from Siberia. They naturally are most desirous to procure cartridges for the rim-fire Winchester guns, as these are not intended to be used more than once. They have, however, invented a method of priming these rim-fire shells so that they can be reloaded. A common "G. D." percussion cap is neatly fitted into the rim of the shell by cutting the sides into strips which are folded into slits in the shell, a little hole being drilled under the center of the cap to allow the flash to reach the powder. This is a very laborious process, but enables the natives to use a rifle which would otherwise be useless. Such cartridges reloaded with powder and home-made bullets—they have many bullet molds and know how to use them—are tolerably effective. Great care must be taken to insert the cartridge right side up, so that the cap shall be struck by the firing pin, which interferes with using the gun as a repeater.

They are very careless with their rifles, allowing them to get rusty, and otherwise misusing them, especially by firing small shot from them in the duck-shooting season. As a rule they are very fair shots with the rifle, but extremely lavish of ammunition when they have a supply. The only economy is shown in reloading cartridges and in loading their shotguns, into which they seldom put a sufficient charge. In spite of this some of them shoot very well with the shotgun, though many of them show great stupidity in judging distance, firing light charges of shot at short rifle range (100 to 200 yards). Though they mold their own bullets, I have never known any of them to attempt making shot or slugs. This, which they call kăkrúra (little bullets, from kă'kru, originally meaning *arrow* and now used for *bullet* as well) is always obtained from the whites. The gun is habitually carried in a case or holster long enough to cover the whole gun, made of sealskin, either black-tanned or with the hair on the outside. This, like the bow case, from which it is evidently copied, is slung across the back by a thong passing round the shoulders and across the chest. This is the method universally practiced for carrying burdens of all sorts. The butt of the gun is on the right side, so that it can be easily slipped out of the holster under the right arm without unslinging it. Revolvers are also carried slung in holsters on the back in the same way. Ammunition is carried in a pouch slung over the shoulder. They are careless in handling firearms and ammunition. We knew two men who shot off the tip of the forefinger while filing cartridges which had failed to explode in the gun.

Whaling guns.—In addition to the kinds of firearms for land hunting above described a number of the natives have procured from the whalemen, either by purchase or from wrecks, whaling guns, such as are used by the American whalers, in place of the steel lance for dispatching the whale after it is harpooned. These are of various patterns, both muzzle and breech loading, and they are able to procure nearly every year a small supply of the explosive lances to be shot from them. They use them as the white men do for killing harpooned whales, and also, when the leads of open water are narrow, for shooting them as they pass close to the edge of the ice.

Bows (pízĭ'ksĕ).—In former times the bow was the only projectile weapon which these people possessed that could be used at a longer range than the "dart" of a harpoon. It was accordingly used for hunting the bear, the wolf, and the reindeer, for shooting birds, and in case of necessity, for warfare. It is worthy of note, in this connection, as showing that the use of the bow for fighting was only a secondary consideration, that none of their arrows are regular "war arrows" like those made by the Sioux or other Indians; that is, arrows to be shot with the breadth of the head horizontal, so as to pass between the horizontal ribs of a man. Firearms have now almost completely superseded the bow for actual work, though a few men, too poor to obtain guns, still use them.

Every boy has a bow for a plaything, with which he shoots small birds and practices at marks. Very few boys, however, show any great skill with it. We never had an opportunity of seeing an adult shoot with the bow and arrow; but they have not yet lost the art of bowmaking. The newest boys' bows are as skillfully and ingeniously constructed as the old bows, but are of course smaller and weaker. The bow in use among these people was the universal sinew-backed bow of

the Eskimo carried to its highest degree of efficiency.[1] It was of what
I have called the "Arctic type," namely, a rather short bow of spruce,
from 43 to 52 inches in length, nearly elliptical in section, but flatter on
the back than on the belly, and slightly narrowed and thickened at the
handle. The greatest breadth was usually about 1¼ inches and the
thickness at the handle about three-fourths of an inch. The ends were
often bent up as in the Tatar bow, and were sometimes separate pieces
mortised on. Strength and elasticity was given to the brittle spruce
by applying a number of strands of sinew to the back of the bow in
such a way that drawing the bowstring stretched all these elastic cords,
thus adding their elasticity to that of the wood. This backing was
always a continuous piece of a three-ply braid of sinew, about the size
of stout pack thread, and on a large bow often 40 or 50 yards long. It
began, as on all Eskimo bows which I have been able to examine (ex-

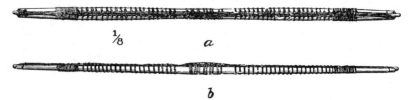

FIG. 177.—Boy's bow from Utkiavwïñ.

cept those from St. Lawrence Island and the mainland of Siberia—
my "western type"), with an eye at one end of the cord looped over
one nock of the bow, usually the upper. The cord was then laid on the
back of the bow in long strands running up and down and round the
nocks, as usual on the other types of bow, but after putting on a number of these, began running backward and forward between the bends
(if the bow was of the Tatar shape), or between corresponding points
on a straight bow, where they were fastened with complicated hitches
around the bow in such a way that the shortest strands came to the
top of the backing, which was thus made to grow thicker gradually
toward the middle of the bow, where the greatest strength and elasticity were needed. When enough strands had been laid on they
were divided into two equal parcels and twisted from the middle into
two tight cables, thus greatly increasing the tension to be overcome in
drawing the bow. These cables being secured to the handle of the
bow, the end of the cord was used to seize the whole securely to the
bow.

This seizing and the hitches already mentioned served to incorporate
the backing very thoroughly with the bow, thus equalizing the strain
and preventing the bow from cracking. This made a very stiff and
powerful bow, capable of sending an arrow with great force. We were
told by a reliable native that a stone-headed arrow was often driven by

[1] See the writer's paper on the subject of Eskimo bows in the Smithsonian Report for 1884, Part II,
pp. 307–316.

one of these bows wholly through a polar bear, "if there was no bone."
Three bows only were obtained: One from Nuwŭk, one from Utkiavwĭñ (a lad's bow), and one from Sidaru.

The bow from Utkiavwĭñ, No. 89904 [786] (Fig. 177), though small,
is in some respects nearer the type than the other
two, and has been selected for description. The body
of the bow is a single piece of the heart of a log of
spruce driftwood 36¼ inches long, elliptical in section,
flattened more on the back than on the belly. It is
tapered to the nocks, which are small club-shaped
knobs, and narrowed and thickened at the handle.
The backing is of round three-ply braid of sinew in
one continuous piece. The string is a round four-ply
braid with a loop at each end, made by tying a single
knot in the standing part, passing the end through
this and taking a half hitch with it round the standing
part (Fig. 178). The upper loop is a little the larger.

No. 89245 [25] (Fig. 179), from Nuwŭk, is a full-
sized man's bow, which is old and
has been long in use. It is of the
same material, and is 47·3 inches
long. Its greatest breadth is 1⅓
inches, and it is 0·8 inch thick at
the handle. It is slightly narrowed
and thinned off from the broadest part to about 6
inches from each tip, and is then gradually thickened
to the nocks and bent up so that the ends make an
angle of about 45° with the bow when unstrung. The
ends are separate pieces fitted on at the bends. The
ends of the body are chamfered off laterally to a wedge
which fits into a corresponding notch in the end piece,
making a scarf 3¼ inches long, which is strengthened
by a curved strap of antler, convex above and thickest in the middle, fitting into the bend on the back.
The joint is held together wholly by the backing.

We never saw bows of this pattern made and consequently did not learn how the bending was accomplished. The method is probably the same as that
seen by Capt. Beechey in 1826, at Kotzebue Sound
(Voyage, p. 575). The bow was wrapped in wet
shavings and held over the fire, and then pegged
down on the ground (probably on one side), into shape. A strip of rawhide (the split skin of the bearded seal, with the grain side out), 1 inch
wide, runs along the back from bend to bend under the backing. The
chief peculiarity of this bow is the third cable, above the other two, and
the great and apparently unnecessary complication of the hitches.

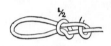

FIG. 178.—Loop at end of bowstring.

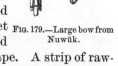

FIG. 179.—Large bow from Nuwŭk.

No. 72771 [234], from Sidaru (Fig. 180*a* and *b*), is a bow with bent ends like the last, but all in one piece and smaller. Its length is 43½ inches and its greatest breadth 1⅛. The backing has only two cables, and its chief peculiarity is in having the loose end of the last strand twisted into one of the cables, while the seizing, of the same pattern as in the last bow, is made of a separate piece. The workmanship of this

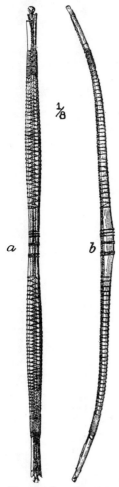

FIG. 180.—Large bow from Sidaru.

bow is particularly neat, and it is further strengthened with strips of rawhide (the skin of the bearded seal, split), under the backing. The method of making the string is very ingenious. It appears to have been made on the bow, as follows: Having the bow sprung back one end of a long piece of sinew twine was made fast temporarily to the upper nock, leaving an end long enough to finish off the bowstring. The other end was carried round the lower nock and the returning strand half-hitched round the first snugly up to the nock, and then carried round the upper nock and back again. This was repeated, each strand being half-hitched round all the preceding at the lower nock until there were eight parallel strands, and an eye fitted snugly to the lower nock. The bight was then slipped off the upper nock, the end untied and the whole twisted tight. This twisted string is now about 2 inches too long, so the upper eye is made by doubling over 2 inches of the end and stopping it down with the free end mentioned above, thus making a long eye of seven strands. With the end, six similar strands are added to the eye, each being stopped to the twist with a half hitch. The end is neatly tucked in and the strands of the eye twisted tightly together.

In my paper on Eskimo bows, already mentioned, I came to the conclusion that the bows formerly used by the Eskimo of western North America and the opposite coast of Asia were constructed upon three well defined types of definite geographical distribution, and each easily recognized as a development of a simple original type still to be found in Baffin Land in a slightly modified form. These three types are:

I. The Southern type, which was the only form used from the island of Kadiak to Cape Romanzoff, and continued in frequent use as far as Norton Sound, though separated by no hard and fast line from

II. The Arctic type, to which the bows just described belong, in use from the Kaviak peninsula to the Mackenzie and Anderson rivers; and

III. The Western type, confined to St. Lawrence Island and the mainland of Siberia.

I have shown how these three types differ from each other and from the original type, and have expressed the opinion that these differences result from the different resources at the command of the people of different regions. I have also endeavored to account for the fact that we find sporadic examples of the Arctic type, for instance as far south as the Yukon, by the well known habits of the Eskimo in regard to trading expeditions.

Outside of the region treated in my paper above referred to, there is very little material for a comparative study of Eskimo bows, either in the Museum or in the writings of travelers. Most writers have contented themselves with a casual reference to some of the more salient peculiarities of the weapon without giving any detailed information. Beginning at the extreme north of Greenland, we find that the so-called "Arctic Highlanders" have hardly any knowledge of the bow. Dr. Kane saw none during his intercourse with them, but Dr. Bessels[1] mentions seeing one bow, made of pieces of antler spliced together, in the possession of a man at Ita. In Danish Greenland, the use of the bow has been abandoned for many years. When Crantz[2] wrote it had already gone out of use, though in Egede's[3] time it was still employed. It appears to have been longer than the other Eskimo bows. Nordenskiöld[4] reproduces a picture of a group of Greenlanders from an old painting of the date of 1654 in the Ethnographical Museum of Copenhagen. The man holds in his left hand a straight bow, which appears to have the backing reaching only part way to the ends like a western bow without the end cables, and yet twisted into two cables. If this representation be a correct one, this arrangement of the backing, taken in connection with what Crantz and Egede say of the great length of the bow, would be an argument in favor of my theory that the St. Lawrence Island bow was developed from the primitive form by lengthening the ends of the bow without lengthening the backing. The addition of the end cables would then be an after invention, peculiar to the western bow. In Baffin Land the bow is very rudely made, and approaches very closely to my supposed primitive form. Owing to the scarcity of wood in this region the bow was frequently made of reindeer antler, a substance still more unsuitable for the purpose than the soft coniferous woods used elsewhere. There are in the Museum three specimens of such antler bows, brought from Cumberland Gulf by Mr. Kumlien.

---

[1] Naturalist, vol 8, No. 9, p. 869.

[2] "In former times they made use of bows for land game; they were made of soft fir, a fathom in length, and to make it the stiffer it was bound round with whalebone or sinews." History of Greenland, vol. 1, p. 146.

[3] "Their Bow is of an ordinary Make, commonly made of Fir Tree, . . . and on the Back strengthened with Strings made of Sinews of Animals, twisted like Thread." "The Bow is a good fathom long." Greenland, p. 101.

[4] Voyage of the Vega, vol. 1, p. 41.

The first mention of the Eskimo bow with sinew backing will be found in Frobisher's account of his visit to Meta Incognita in 1577:[1] "Their bowes are of wood of a yard long, sinewed on the back with strong sinewes, not glued too, but fast girded and tyed on. Their bowe strings are likewise sinewes."

Of the bow used at the straits of Fury and Hecla we have a most excellent figure in Parry's Second Voyage (Pl. opposite p. 550, Fig. 22), and the most accurate description to be found in any author. It is, in fact, as exact a description as could be made from an external examination of the bow. From the figure the bow appears to have been almost of the arctic type, having an unusual number of strands (sometimes sixty, p. 511) which are not, however, twisted, but secured with a spiral wrapping, as on southern bows. The backing is stopped to the handle, but not otherwise seized. It appears to have been rather a large bow, as Parry gives the length of one of their best bows, made of a single piece of fir, as "4 feet 8 inches" (p. 510). "A bow of one piece is, however, very rare; they generally consist of from two to five pieces of bone of unequal lengths, fastened together by rivets and treenails" (p. 511). Parry also speaks of the use of wedges for tightening the backing. Schwatka[2] speaks of the Netyĭlĭk of King Williams Land as using bows of spliced pieces of musk-ox horn or driftwood, but gives no further description of them. Ellis[3] describes the bow in use at Hudson's Strait in 1746 as follows:

Their greatest Ingenuity is shown in the Structure of their Bows, made commonly of three Pieces of Wood, each making a part of the same Arch, very nicely and exactly joined together. They are commonly of Fir or Larch, which the English there call Juniper, and as this wants Strength and Elasticity, they supply both by bracing the Back of the Bow with a kind of Thread or Line made of the Sinew of their Deer, and the Bowstring of the same material. To make them draw more stiffly, they dip them into Water, which causes both the Back of the Bow and the String to contract, and consequently gives it the greater force.[4]

Ellis's figure (plate opposite p. 132) shows a bow of the Tatar shape, but gives no details of the backing, except that the latter appears to be twisted.

We have no published descriptions of the bows used in other regions.

As far as I have been able to ascertain, the practice of backing the bow with cords of sinew is peculiar to the Eskimo, though some American Indians stiffen the bow by gluing flat pieces of sinew upon the back.

One tribe of Indians, the "Loucheux" of the Mackenzie district, however, used bows like those of the Eskimos, but Sir Alexander Mackenzie[5] expressly states that these were obtained from the Eskimo.

[1] Hakluyt's Voyages, 1589, p. 628.
[2] Science, vol. 4 , 98, p. 543.
[3] Voyage to Hudson's Bay, p. 138.
[4] Compare what I have already said about the backing being put on wet.
[5] Voyages from Montreal . . . to the Frozen and Pacific Oceans, p. 48.

Arrows.—With these bows were used arrows of various patterns adapted for different kinds of game. There are in the collection fifty-one arrows, which are all about the same length, 25 to 30 inches. In describing these arrows I shall employ the terms used in modern archery [1] for the parts of the arrow. The greatest variation is in the shape and size of the pile. The stele is almost always a straight cylindrical rod, almost invariably 0·4 inch in diameter, and ranging in length from 20 to 28 inches. Twenty-five inches is the commonest length, and the short steles, when not intended for a boy's bow, are generally fitted with an unusually long pile. From the beginning of the feathering the stele is gradually flattened above and below to the nock, which is a simple notch almost always 0·2 inch wide and of the same depth. The stele is sometimes slightly widened just in front of the nock to give a better hold for the fingers. The feathering is 6 or 7 inches long, consisting of two, or less often, three feathers. (The set of sixteen arrows from Sidaru, two from Nuwŭk, and one from Utkiavwĭñ, have three feathers. The rest of the fifty-one have two.) The shaft of the feather is split and the web is cut narrow, and tapered off to a point at each end (Fig. 181). The ends of the feathers are fastened to the stele with whippings of fine

FIG. 181.—Feathering of the Eskimo arrow.

sinew, the small end of the feather which, of course, comes at the nock, being often wedged into a slit in the wood (with a special tool to be described below), or else doubled back over a few turns of the whipping and lashed down with the rest. The small end of the feather is almost always twisted about one turn, evidently to make the arrow revolve in flight, like a rifle ball. Generally, if not universally, the feathering was made of the feathers of some bird of prey, falcon, eagle, or raven, probably with some notion of giving to the arrow the death-dealing quality of the bird. Out of the fifty-one arrows in the collection, only nine are feathered with gull's feathers, and of these all but two are new, or newly feathered for sale to us.[2] Dr. Simpson[3] says that in his time "feathers for arrows and head-dresses," probably the eagles' feathers previously mentioned, were obtained in trade from the "Nunatañmiun."

Four kinds of arrows were used: the bear arrow, of which there were three varieties, the deer arrow, the arrow for geese, gulls, and other large fowl, and the blunt headed arrow for killing small birds without mangling them.

---

[1] Encyclopedia Britannica, 9th edition, article Archery.

[2] On this subject of using the feathers of birds of prey for arrows, compare Crantz, History of Greenland, i, p. 146, "the arrow . . . winged behind with a couple of raven's feathers." Bessels, Naturalist, vol. 18, pt. 9, p. 869 (the three arrows at Ita had raven's feathers). Parry, 2d Voyage, p. 511, "Toward the opposite end of the arrow are two feathers, generally of the spotted owl, not very neatly lashed on;" and Kumlien, Contributions, p. 37, "The feather-vanes were nearly always made from the primaries of *Strix scandiaca* or *Graculus carbo*." The last is the only mention I find of using any feathers except those of birds of prey.

[3] Op. cit., p. 266.

Bear arrows.—These are of three kinds, all having a broad, sharp pile, often barbed. The first kind has a pile of flaked flint, called kŭki ("claw" or "nail"), and was known as kŭkĭ′ksadlĭñ ("provided or fitted with claw material"). Of this kind we have eight complete arrows and one shaft.

No. 89240 [25], Fig. 182, will serve as the type. The pile is of black flint, double edged and sharp pointed, 2 inches long, with a short tang inserted into a cleft in the end of the stele, and secured by a whipping of about fifteen turns of fine sinew. The stele is of spruce, 25½ inches

⅛

FIG. 182.—Flint-headed arrow (kukĭksadlĭñ).

long and four-tenths inch in diameter, and painted with red ocher from the feathering to 5 inches from the pile. The three feathers, apparently those of the gyrfalcon, have their ends simply whipped to the stele. They are 6 inches long. This is one of the two arrows from Nuwŭk with three feathers.

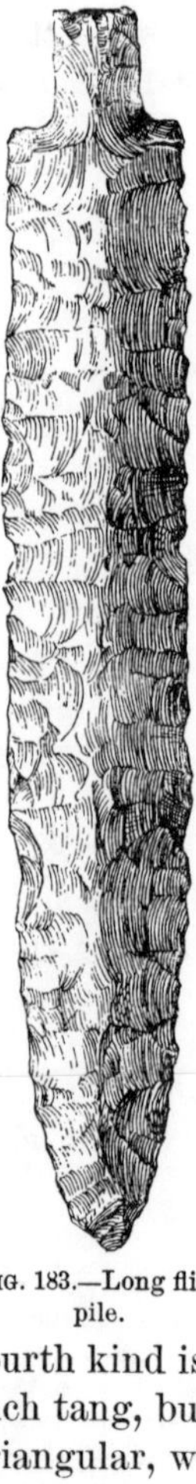

No. 72780 [234 *a*], from Sidaru, is feathered with three raven feathers, of which the small ends are wedged into slits in the wood. The pile is of brown jasper, long and lancet-tipped, expanding into rounded wings at each side of the base. The stele is peculiar only in being slightly widened in front of the nock. It is of pine, 26·8 inches long, and painted with two rings, one red and one green, at the middle of the feathering.

The only variations of importance in these arrows are in the shape of the pile, which is made of black or gray flint, or less often of jasper, mostly variegated, brown and gray. There are four patterns to be found in the series of eight arrows and twenty-two stone piles. The first is long and narrow, like No. 56704 [232], Fig. 183, from Utkiavwĭñ, which is of gray flint. The next is similar in shape, but shorter, as shown in Fig. 182 (No. 89240 [25], from Nuwŭk), which is only 2 inches long, exclusive of the tang. The third pattern, which is less common than the others, is about the size of the last, but rhomboidal in shape (Fig. 184, No. 56691*c* [64*c*], from Utkiavwĭñ, of dark grayish brown flint, rather coarsely flaked). The fourth kind is very short, being not over 1½ inches, including the half-inch tang, but is 1 inch broad, thick and convex on both faces. It is triangular, with a square base and curved edges (Fig. 185, No. 56702*b* [113*b*], from Utkiavwĭñ, newly made for sale).

FIG. 184.—Short flint pile.

FIG. 183.—Long flint pile.

No stone arrow or dart heads made by these people have anything like barbs except the square shoulders at the base. They seem never to have attained to the skill in flint-working which enabled many other savages to make the beautiful barbed heads so often seen. To keep the flint-headed arrow from dropping out of the wound they hit upon the contrivance of mounting it not directly in the stele but in a piece of bone upon which barbs could be cut, or, as is not unlikely, having already the deer arrow with the barbed head of antler, they added the flint head to this, thus combining the penetration of the flint arrow with the holding power of the other. I was at first inclined to think that this piece of bone bore the same relation to the rest of the arrow as the fore shaft of many Indian arrows, and was to be considered as part of the stele. Considering, however, that its sole function is to furnish the pile with barbs, it evidently must be considered as part of the latter. I shall designate it as "after-pile." Arrows with this barbed "after-pile" form

FIG. 185.—Heart-shaped flint pile.

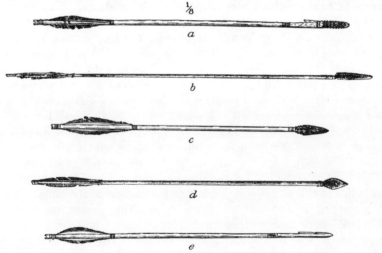

⅛

a

b

c

d

e

FIG. 186.—Arrows: (*a*) Arrow with "after-pile" (ipudlĭgadlĭñ); (*b*) arrow with iron pile (savidlĭñ; (*c*) arrow with iron pile (savidlĭñ); (*d*) arrow with copper pile (savidlĭñ); (*e*) deer-arrow (nûtkodlĭñ).

the second kind of bear arrows, which are called ipudlĭ′gadlĭñ ("having the ipu′dlĭgʉ" [Gr. ipuligak, the similar bone head of a seal lance with iron tip]). After the introduction of iron, metal piles sometimes replaced the flint in arrows of this kind. We collected eight with flint and two with metal piles. No. 72787 [234*a*], Fig. 186*a*, has been selected to illustrate this form of arrow. This pile is of gray flint with the tang wedged by a slip of sealskin into the tip of the after-pile, which is cleft to receive it and kept from splitting by a whipping of sinew. The after-pile is fitted into the tip of the stele with a rounded sharp-pointed tang, slightly enlarged just above the tip. It is of reindeer antler. The rest of the arrow does not differ from those previously described. The stele is of pine and is feathered with three gyrfalcon feathers.

Two others from Sidaru have only a single barb on the after-pile, but the other four have two, one behind the other on the same side. No. 89237 [164], from Utkiavwĭñ, differs in no respect from the single-barbed flint arrows from Sidaru, but No. 72763 [164], from the same village, has four small barbs on the after-pile, which is unusually (nearly 7 inches) long, and a pile of sheet brass. This has the basal angles on each side cut into three small, sharp, backward-pointing teeth. The total length of this arrow is 28 inches.

The after-piles of all arrows except one were of reindeer antler, which is another reason for supposing that this form of arrow is a modification of the deer arrow. After the introduction of iron, this metal or copper was substituted for the flint pile of the kukĭ′ksadlĭñ, making the third and last form of bear arrow, the sa′vĭdlĭñ ("fitted with iron"). This arrow differs from the others only in the form of the pile, which is generally broad and flat, and either rhomboidal, with the base cut into numerous small teeth, or else triangular, with a shank. The barbs are usually bilateral.

No. 72758 [25], from Nuwŭk, represents the first form. The pile is of iron, rough and flat, 2½ inches long. No. 72770 [241b], from Utkiavwĭñ, is of the same form. No. 72760 [165], Fig. 186c, from Utkiavwĭñ, has a similar pile 3·3 inches long, but has each of the under edges cut into four sharp, backward-pointing teeth. No. 72778 [234b], Fig. 186d, has a pile of sheet copper 2·3 inches long, of the same shape, but with six teeth. This arrow came from Sidaru. No. 72765 [25], from Nuwŭk, is a long, narrow iron pile with three bilateral barbs, all simple.

Nos. 72755 [25], from Nuwŭk, 72759 [25], also from Nuwŭk, and 72764 [165], from Utkiavwĭñ, show the shanked form. The first is triangular, with a flat shank and a simple barb at each angle of the base. It is of steel (piece of a saw) and 2·8 inches long. The second resembles No. 72760 [165], with more teeth, mounted on a slender cylindrical shank 1½ inches long. It is of iron and 3·9 inches long. The third is a long pile with a sinuate outline and one pair of simple bilateral barbs, and a flat shank one-half inch long. Nos. 72757 [25] (Fig. 186b) and 72762 [25], both from Nuwŭk, are peculiar in being the only iron-pointed arrows with unilateral barbs. The piles are made of the two blades of a pair of large scissors, cut off at the point, with enough of the handle left to make a tang. The unilateral barb is filed out on the back of the blade, which has been beveled down on both faces to a sharp edge. All of these broadheaded arrows have the breadth of the pile at right angles to the plane of the nock, showing that they are not meant to fly like the Sioux war arrows. Although iron makes a better material for arrow piles and is more easily worked than flint, the quivers which some men still carry at Point Barrow contain flint as well as iron headed arrows. They are probably

kept in use from the superstitious conservatism already mentioned.   It
is certain that the man who raised a couple of wolf cubs for the sake of
their fur was obliged by tradition to have a flint-headed arrow to kill
them with.   These arrows, we were informed, were especially designed
for hunting " nä′nu," the polar bear, but of course they also served for
use against other dangerous game, like the wolf and brown bear, and

FIG. 187.—Pile of deer arrow (nûtkǎñ).

there is no reason to believe that they were not also shot at reindeer,
though the hunter would naturally use his deer arrows first.

Deer arrows have a long trihedral pile of antler from 4 to 8 inches
long, with a sharp thin-edged point slightly concaved on the faces like
the point of a bayonet.   Two of the edges are rounded, but the third is
sharp and cut into one or more simple barbs.   Behind the barb
the pile takes the form of a rounded shank, ending in a shoulder
and a sharp rounded tang a little enlarged above the point.

No. 72768 [162], Fig. 186e from Utkiavwïñ, has a pile 3½ inches
long with two barbs.   The pile of No. 89238 [162] from the same
village is 3½ inches long and has but one barb, while that of
No. 89241a [162] is 7·8 inches long and has three barbs.   The
rudely incised figure on the shank of No. 89238 [162] represents
a wolf, probably a talisman to make the arrow as fatal to the
deer as the wolf is.   No. 56588 [13], Fig. 187, is a pile for one of
these arrows slightly peculiar in shape, being elliptical in section, with one edge sharp and two-barbed and a four-sided point.
The figure shows well the shape of the tang.   The peculiarity
of these arrows is that the pile is not fastened to the shaft, but
can easily be detached.[1]   When such an arrow was shot into a
deer the shaft would easily be shaken out, leaving the sharp
barbed pile in the wound.

The Eskimo told us that a deer wounded in this way would
"sleep once and die," meaning, apparently, that death would
ensue in about twenty-four hours, probably from peritonitis.
The bone pile is called nû′tkǎñ, whence comes the name of the
arrow, nû′tko′dlïñ.   We collected ten arrows and three piles of
this pattern.   No. 89460 [1263], Fig. 188, is a peculiar bone arrow
pile, perhaps intended for a deer arrow.   It is 7 inches long and
made of one of the long bones of some large bird, split lengthwise so that it is rounded on one side and deeply concave on
the other, with two thin rounded edges tapered to a sharp point.   Each

½

FIG. 188.—
"Kûñmû-
dlïñ " ar-
row pile.

---

[1]Compare the passage in Frobisher's Second Voyage (Hakluyt, 1589, p. 628).   After describing the
different forms of arrowheads used by the Eskimo of "Meta Incognita" (Baffin Land) in 1577 he
says: "They are not made very fast, but lightly tyed to, or else set in a nocke, that upon small occasion the arrowe leaveth these heads behind them."

edge has three little barbs about the middle of the pile. This was the only arrowhead of the kind seen at Point Barrow, and the native who sold it said it was a "Kûñmûd′liñ" arrow. I was pleased to find the truth of this corroborated by the Museum collection. There are two arrows from the Mackenzie region (Nos. 1106 and 1906) with bone piles of almost the same form.

For shooting gulls, geese, and other large fowl they used an arrow with a straight polygonal pile of walrus ivory, 5 or 6 inches long and about one-half inch in diameter, terminating in a somewhat obtuse polygonal point, and having one or more unilateral barbs. These piles are generally five-sided, though sometimes trihedral, and have a long, rounded tang inserted into the end of the shaft. Fig. 189a (No. 89349 [119] from Utkiavwĭñ), represents one of these arrows with a five-sided pile 5·5 inches long, with four simple barbs. The rest of the arrow does not differ from the others described. No. 89238 [25], from Nuwŭk, has a trihedral pile 6·6 inches long, with a single barb. Another from Nuwŭk (No. 89241 [25]) has a trihedral pile 5·3 inches long, with two barbs, and one from Utkiavwĭñ (No. 89241 [119]) has a five-sided pile with three barbs. The remaining three, from Sidaru, all have five-sided piles with one barb.

Arrows of this pattern are called tuga′liñ (from tu′ga, walrus ivory). There are also in the collection two small arrows of this pattern suited for a boy's bow. They are only 25 inches long, and have roughly trihedral sharp-pointed ivory piles about 4 inches long, without barbs. (No. 89904a [786] from Utkiavwĭñ). These arrows are new and rather carelessly made, and were intended for the lad's bow (No. 89904 [786]) already described. The three kinds of arrows which have been described all have the pile secured to the stele by a tang fitting into a cleft or hole in the end of the latter, which is kept from splitting by whipping it with sinew for about one-half inch.

The fourth kind, the blunt bird arrow (kĭ′xodwain), on the other hand, has the pile cleft to receive the wedge-shaped tip of the stele and secured by a whipping of sinew.

⅛

a   b

FIG. 189.—Arrows: (a) fowl arrow (tugaliñ); (b) bird arrow (kixodwain).

The four arrows of this kind in the collection are almost exactly alike, except that three of them, belonging to the set from Sidaru, have three feathers. Fig. 189b, No. 72773 [234c] from Sidaru represents the form of arrow. The pile is of hard bone 2·3 inches long. A little rim at each side of the butt keeps the whipping of sinew from slipping off. The rest of the arrow differs from the others described only in having the end of the stele chamfered down to a wedge-shaped point to fit into the pile.

This is the kind of arrow mostly used by the boys, whose game is almost exclusively small birds or lemmings. Nowadays the bone pile is often replaced by an empty cartridge shell, which makes a very good head. I have seen a phalarope transfixed at short range by one of these cartridge-headed arrows. An assortment of the different kind of arrows is usually carried in the quiver. The lot numbered 25, from Nuwŭk, which I believe to be a fairly average set, contains two flint-headed bear arrows, one barbed bear arrow with a steel pile, six bear arrows with iron piles, one deer arrow, two fowl arrows, and one bird arrow.

As I have already said, all these arrows are flattened above and below at the nocks. This indicates that they were intended to be held to the string and let go after the manner of what is called the "Saxon release," namely, by hooking the ends of the index and second fingers round the string and holding the arrow between them, the string being released by straightening the fingers. This is the "release" which we actually saw employed both by the boys and one or two men who showed us how to draw the bow. This method of release has been observed at Cumberland Gulf[1] and at East Cape, Siberia, and is probably universal among the Eskimo, as all the Eskimo arrows in the National Museum are fitted for this release. There is ample material in the Museum collections for a comparative study of Eskimo arrows, which I hope some day to be able to undertake, when the material is in a more available condition. One or two references to other regions will not, however, be out of place. The arrow with a barbed bone after-pile seems a very general form, being represented in the Museum from most of the Alaskan regions, as well as from the Mackenzie. Scoresby mentions finding the head of one of these at the ancient settlements in east Greenland.[2] The arrow, however, described by Capt. Parry[3] has a real foreshaft of bone, not a barbed after pile. One of these arrows from the Mackenzie has the after pile barbed on both sides, the only instance, I believe, in the Museum of a bilaterally-barbed Eskimo arrow where the pile is not wholly of metal.

Bow cases and quivers.—The bow and arrows were carried in a bow case and quiver of black sealskin, tied together side by side and slung across the back in the same manner as the gun holster already described. We obtained one case and quiver which belong with the bow and arrows (No. 25, from Nuwŭk) and a single quiver with the bow and arrows (No. 234, from Sidaru.) The case, No. 89245 [25], Fig. 190a (pizĭ′ksĭzax), is of such a shape that the bow can be carried in it strung and ready for use. It is made by folding lengthwise a piece of black sealskin with the flesh side in and sewing up one side "over and over" from the outside. The bag is wide enough—6 inches at the widest part—to allow the bow to slip in easily when strung, and the small end

---

[1] "In shooting this weapon the string is placed on the first joint of the first and second fingers of the right hand." (Kumlien, Contributions, p. 37.)

"Beim Spannen wird der Pfeil nicht zwischen Daumen und Zeigefinger, sondern zwischen Zeige- und Mittelfinger gehalten," Krause Brothers, Geographische Blätter, vol. 5, p. 33.

[2] Voyage to the Northern Whale Fishery, p. 187.

[3] 2d Voyage, p. 511, and figured with the bow (22) on Pl. opposite p. 550.

is bent up into the shape of the end of the bow. Along the folded edge are three round holes about 10 inches apart, through which a round stick was formerly thrust, coming out from the inside through the first hole, in through the second and out through the third again. This served to hold the case in shape when the bow was withdrawn, and to its ends were fastened the thong for slinging it across the shoulders. It was gone from the specimen before we obtained it.

The quiver (No. 89240–1 [25], Fig. 190*b*) is a long, straight bag of the same material, open at one end, with a seam down one side, and the

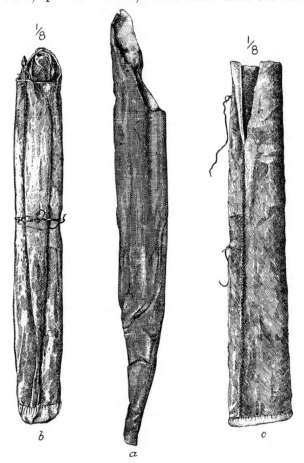

FIG. 190.—Bow case and quivers.

edge of the mouth opposite to the seam forming a rounded flap 2 inches long. The other end is closed by an elliptical cap of white tanned seal skin, turned up about 2 inches all round, and crimped round the ends like a boot sole. Its extreme length is 30 inches, and its circumference 1 foot. Inside along the seam is a roughly rounded rod of wood about ½ inch in diameter, with one end, which is pointed, projecting about 1½ inches through a hole in the bottom, and the other projecting about 1 inch beyond the mouth, where it is secured by a bit of thong knotted through a couple of small holes in the bag close to the edge and passing round a notch on the stick. The stick serves to stiffen the quiver when there are no arrows in it. A bit of thong is knotted round the middle, one end being hitched into a loop on the other, for tightening up the quiver and confining the arrows.

The quiver from Sidaru (No. 72788 [234] Fig. 190*c*) is like the preceding, but larger at the bottom than at the mouth. The latter is 8½ inches in circumference and the former 12¾, and the seam is left open for about 7½ inches from the mouth to facilitate getting at the arrows. The stiffening rod is made of pine, and does not project through the bottom or reach the edge of the mouth. It is held in by two pieces of thong about 10 inches long, which also serve to fasten it to the bow case. This quiver is nearly new.

It is probable that the form of the bow case and quiver varied but little, among the American Eskimo at least. Those figured by Capt. Lyon[1] are almost exactly like the ones we collected at Point Barrow, even to the crimped cap on the bottom of the quiver. A similar set belong with a lad's bow in the Museum

FIG. 192.—Cap for quiver rod.

from Point Hope (No. 63611). Nordenskiöld, however, figures a very elaborate flat quiver,[2] in use at Pitlekaj, which is evidently of genuine Asiatic origin.

Some pains seem to have been bestowed on ornamenting the quiver in former times, when the bow was in more general use. Fig. 191, No. 56505 [231], from Nuwŭk, represents what we understood had been a stiffening rod for a quiver or bow case. It is of reindeer antler, 17 inches long, and one end is very neatly carved into the head and shoulders of a reindeer, with small, blue glass beads inserted for the eyes. The lanceolate point at the tip was probably made with an idea of improving it for sale. The hole at the back of the neck is for a thong to fasten it on with. A similar reindeer head of antler, Fig. 192, No. 89449 [1066], also from Nuwŭk, seems to have been a cap for a quiver stick. The back of the neck makes a half-ferrule, in which are three holes for rivets or treenails.

Bracers.—In shooting the bow, the wrist of the bow hand was pro-

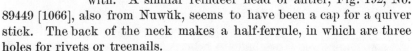

FIG. 191.—Quiver rod.

⅓

---

[1] Parry's 2d Voyage, Pl. opposite p. 550, Fig. 24.
[2] Vega, vol. 2, p. 106.

tected from being chafed by the bowstring by a small shield or "bracer" of bone or horn, strapped on with a thong: We never saw these in use,

as the bow is so seldom employed except by the children. Two of these, newly made, were offered for sale. I will describe one of these, No. 89410*b* [1233], Fig. 193.

It is of pale yellow mountain sheep horn, convex on the outer face and concave on the inner and considerably arched lengthwise. In the middle are two straight longitudinal narrow slots, which serve no apparent pur-

FIG. 193.—Bracer.

pose except ornament. The short slot near the edge at the middle of each side, however, is for the thongs which strap the bracer to the wrist. One of these is short and made into a becket by fastening the ends together with double slits. One end of the other is passed through the slot, slit, and the other end passed through this and drawn taut. A knot is tied on the free end. This thong is just long enough to fasten on the bracer by passing round the wrist and catching the knot in the loop opposite. The other, No. 89410*a* [1233], is like this, but 1 inch shorter and nearly flat. The arch of the specimen figured is probably unintentional and due to the natural shape of the material, as it does not fit well to the wrist. It is probable that these people used a flat bracer, as Fig. 194, No. 89350 [1382], from Utkiavwĭñ, is apparently such an implement. It is a thin elliptical plate of hard bone, 2½ inches long and 1½ wide, with two rows of holes crossing at right angles in the middle. The holes at the side were probably for the thong and the others for ornament, as some of them go only part way through. Four small pebbles are lodged in the four holes around the center in the form of a cross.

Mr. Nelson collected several specimens of bracers from Kotzebue Sound and St. Lawrence Island. These are all slightly larger than our specimens, and bent round to fit the wrist. They are of bone or copper. When Beechey visited Kotzebue Sound, in 1826, he found the bracer in general use.[1] I find

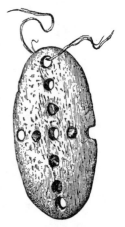

FIG. 194.—Bracer of bone.

no other mention of this implement in the writers who have described the Eskimo.

Bird darts.—For capturing large birds like ducks or geese, sitting on the water, especially when they have molted their wing feathers so as to be unable to escape by flight, they use the universal Eskimo weapon, found from Greenland to Siberia, namely, a dart with one or more points at the tip, but carrying a second set of three ivory prongs

---

[1] "They buckle on a piece of ivory, called *mun-era,* about 3 or 4 inches long, hollowed out to the wrist, or a guard made of several pieces of ivory or wood fastened together like an iron-holder." Voyage, p. 575.

in a circle round the middle of the shaft. The object of these prongs is
to increase the chance of hitting the bird if he is missed
by the head of the dart. They always curve forward,
so that the points stand out a few inches from the
shaft, and are barbed on the inner edge in such a way
that, though the neck of a fowl will easily pass in between the prong and the shaft, it is impossible to draw
it back again. The weapon is in very general use at
Point Barrow, and is always thrown from the boat with
a handboard (to be described below). It can be darted
with considerable accuracy 20 or 30 yards. We seldom
saw this spear used, as it is chiefly employed in catching molting fowl, in the summer season, away from the
immediate neighborhood of the station. It is called
nuiă′kpai, which is a plural referring to the number
of points, one of which is called nuiă′kpûk ("the great
nuiăk").[1]

No. 89244 [1325], Fig. 195, from Utkiavwĭñ, has been
selected as the type of this weapon. The shaft is of
spruce, 61⅛ inches long and 0·7 inch in diameter at the
head. The end of the butt is hollowed out to fit the
catch of the throwing board. The head, of white walrus ivory, is fitted into the cleft end of the shaft with
a wedge-shaped tang as broad as the shaft. The head
and shaft are held together by a spaced lashing of
braided sinew. To the enlargement of the shaft, 22
inches from the butt, are fastened three curved prongs
of walrus ivory at equal distances from each other
round the shaft. The inner side of each prong is cut
away obliquely for about 2 inches, so that when this
edge is applied to the shaft, with the point of the prong
forward, the latter is about 1 inch from the shaft. Each
prong has two little ridges on the outside, one at the
lower end and the other about 1 inch above this. They
are secured to the shaft by three separate lashings of
sinew braid, two narrow ones above the ridges just
mentioned and one broad one just below the barb. In
making this the line is knotted round one prong, then
carried one-third of the distance round the shaft to the
prong; half hitched round this, and carried round next
the next prong; half hitched round this, and carried
round to the starting point, and half hitched round

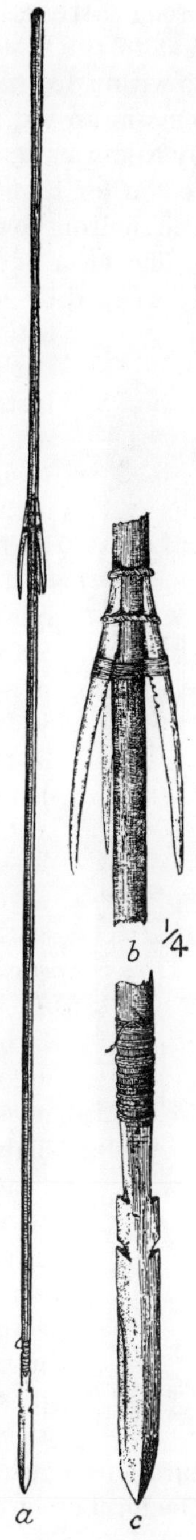

_b_   ¼

---

[1] This word appears to be a diminutive of the Greenlandic nuek—nuik, now
used only in the plural, nugfit, for the spear. These changes of name may represent corresponding changes in the weapon in former times, since, unless we
may suppose that the bird dart was made small and called the "little nuik,"
and enlarged again after the meaning of the name was forgotten, it is hard to see any sense in the
present name, "big little nuik."

_a_   _c_

FIG. 195.—Bird dart.

this. It goes around in this way seven times, and then is carried one prong farther, half hitched again, and the end taken down and made fast to the first narrow lashing. The shaft is painted with red ocher to within 13½ inches (the length of the throwing board) from the butt. This is an old shaft and head fitted with new prongs, and was made by Nĭkawa′alu, who was anxious to borrow it again when getting ready to start on his summer trip to the east, where he would find young ducks and molting fowl.

The form of head seen in this dart appears to be the commonest. It is called by the same name, nû′tkăñ, as the bone head of the deer arrow. There is considerable variation in the number of barbs, which are always bilateral, except in one instance, No. 56590 [122], Fig. 196, from Utkiavwĭñ, which has four barbs on one side only. It is 7¼ inches long exclusive of the tang. Out of eight specimens of such heads one has one pair of barbs, one two pairs, two three pairs, one four unilateral barbs, one five pairs, one six pairs, and one seven pairs. The total length of these heads is from 9 inches to 1 foot, of which the tang makes about 2 inches, and they are generally made of walrus ivory, wherein they differ from the nugfit of the Greenlanders, which, since Crantz's time[1] has always had a head of iron. Iron is also used at Cumberland Gulf, as shown by the specimens in the National Musuem. Fig. 197 represents a very ancient spearhead from Utkiavwĭñ, No. 89372 [760]. It is of compact whale's bone, darkened with age and impregnated with oil. It is 8·7 inches long and the other end is beveled off into a wedge-shaped tang roughened with crosscuts on both faces, with a small hole for the end of a lashing as on the head of No. 89244 [1325]. This was called by the native who sold it the head of a seal spear, ă′kqlĭgûk, and it does bear some slight resemblance to the head of weapon used in Greenland and called by a similar name[2] (agdligak). The roughened tang, however, indicates that it was intended to be fixed permanently in the shaft, and this, taken in connection with its strong resemblance to the one-barbed head of the Greenland nugfit[3] as well as to the head of the Siberian bird dart figured by Nordenskiöld[4], makes it probable that it is really the form of bird dart head anciently used at Point Barrow. It is pos-

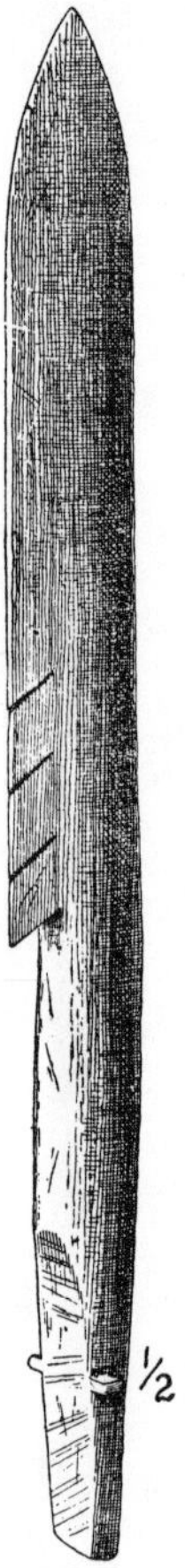

FIG. 196.—Point for bird dart.

FIG. 197.—Ancient point for bird dart.

---

[1] History of Greenland, vol. 1, p. 148.
[2] Crantz, vol. 1, p. 147, and Figs. 6 and 7, Pl. v.
[3] Ibid., Fig. 8.
[4] Vega, vol. 2, p. 105, Fig. 5.

sible that this pattern has been so long out of use that the natives have forgotten what this old point was made for and supposed it to belong to a seal spear.

One of the eight heads of the ordinary pattern in the collection, No. 56592 [284], a genuine one, old and dirty, is made of coarse-grained whale's bone, an unusual material. No. 89373 [948], from Utkiavwĭñ, an ivory head of a good typical shape, has been figured (Fig. 198) to show a common style of orna- menting these heads. A narrow incised line, colored with red ocher, runs along the base of the barbs on each side for about three-fourths the length of the blade. These heads are sometimes secured by treenails as well as by a simple lashing, as is shown by the holes through the tang of this specimen.

An improvement on this style of dart, which appears to be less common, has two prongs at the tip instead of a sharp head, so that the bird may be caught if struck on the neck with the point of the spear. No. 89905 [1326], Fig. 199, from Utkiavwĭñ, is one of this pattern. The two prongs are fastened on with a lashing of fine sinew braid. The rest of the dart does not differ from the one described except in the method of attaching the three prongs at the middle (Fig. 199b). These are fitted into slight grooves in the wood and secured by two neat lashings of narrow strips of whalebone, one just above a little ridge at the lower end of each prong and one through little holes in each prong at the top of the oblique edge. Each lashing consists of several turns with the end closely wrapped around them. There is one specimen, No. 89242 [526], in the collection which not only has not the prongs at the middle, but lacks the enlargement of the shaft to receive them. The head is undoubtedly old and gen- uine, but the shaft and fittings, though dirty, look suspiciously fresh. I am inclined to believe that this head was mounted for sale by a man who had no prongs ready made, and was in too much of a hurry to get his price to stop to make them. Imperfect or unfinished objects were frequently offered for sale.

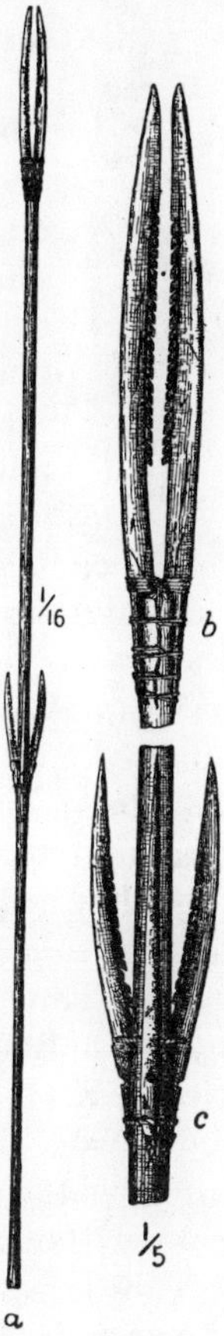

FIG. 198.— Point for bird dart.

FIG. 199.—Bird dart with double point.

The bird darts used at Point Barrow, and by the western Eskimo generally, are lighter and better finished than those used in the east. The latter have a heavy shaft, which is four-sided in Baffin Land, and the prongs are crooked and clumsy.[1]

---

[1] See Crantz's figure referred to above; also one in Parry's second voyage, Pl. opposite p. 550, Fig. 19, and Rink, Tales., etc., Pl. opposite p. 12.

Fig. 200, No. 89380 [793], is a fragment of a very ancient narwhal ivory spearhead, dark brown from age and shiny from much handling, which appears to have been worn as an amulet. It was said to have come

from the east and to belong to a bird dart, though it does not resemble any in use at the present day in this region. It is a slender four-sided rod, having on one side three short oblique equidistant simple barbs. The resemblance of this specimen to the bone dart heads from Scania figured by Dr. Rau[1] is very striking.

Seal darts.—The Eskimo of nearly all localities use a dart or small harpoon to capture the smaller marine animals, with a loose, barbed head of bone fitted into a socket in the end of the shaft, to which it is attached by a line of greater or less length. It is always contrived so that when the head is struck into the quarry, the shaft is detached from the head and acts as a drag upon the animal. This is effected by

FIG. 200.—Ancient ivory dart head.

attaching an inflated bladder to the shaft, or else by attaching the line with a martingale so that the shaft is dragged sideways through the water. Nearly all Eskimo except those of Point Barrow, as shown in the National Museum collections and the figures in Crantz[2] and Rink[3], use weapons of this kind of considerable size, adapted not only to the capture of the small seals (*Phoca vitulina* and *P. fœtida*), but also to the pursuit of the larger seals, the narwhal and beluga. At Point Barrow, however, at the present day, they employ only a small form of this dart, not over 5 feet long, with a little head, adapted only for holding the smallest seals. That they formerly used the larger weapon is shown by our finding a single specimen of the head of such a spear, No. 89374 [1281] Fig. 201. It is of hard, compact bone, impregnated with oil, 8·1 inches long. The flat shank is evidently intended to fit into a socket. The two holes through the widest part of the shank are for attaching the line.

This is very like the head of the weapon called *agligak* (modern Greenlandic agdligak̲), figured by Crantz, and referred to above, except that the barbs are opposite each other. Mr. Lucien M. Turner tells me that it is precisely like the head of the dart used at Norton Sound for capturing the beluga. The native who sold this specimen called it "nuiă′kpai nû′tkoa," "the point of a bird dart," to which it does bear some resemblance, though the shape of the butt and the line holes indicate plainly that it was a *detachable* dart head. Probably, as in the case of the ancient bird dart point, No. 89372 [760], referred to above, this weapon has been so long disused that the natives have forgotten what it was. The name ă′kqlĭgûk, evidently the same as the

FIG. 201.— Bone dart head.

[1] Prehistoric fishing, Figs. 94 and 95, p. 73.
[2] History of Greenland, vol. 1, p. 147, Pl. v, Figs. 6 and 7.
[3] Tales, etc., Pl. opposite p. 12 ("bladder arrow").

Greenlandic *agdligak*, is still in use, but was always applied to the old bone harpoon heads, which are, however, of the toggle-head pattern (described below). It seems as if the Point Barrow natives had for-

gotten all about the ă′kqlĭgûk except that it was a harpoon with a bone head for taking seals. At the present time the small bladder float, permanently attached to the shaft of the harpoon, is never used at Point Barrow. That it was used in ancient times is shown by our finding in one of the ruined houses

FIG. 202.—Nozzle for bladder float.

in Utkiavwĭñ a very old broken nozzle for inflating one of these floats. Fig. 202, No. 89720 [756], is this specimen, which was picked up by Capt. Herendeen. This is a rounded tube of fossil ivory, 1·3 inches long and about one-half inch in diameter, slightly contract-ed toward one end and then expanded into a stout collar. At the other is a stout longi-tudinal flange, three-fourths inch long, perforated with an oblong slot. Between the flange and the collar the sur-face is roughened with cross-cuts, and the other end is still choked with the remains of a wooden plug. This nozzle was inserted into a hole in the blad-der as far as the flange and secured by tying the bladder above the collar. The whole was then secured to the shaft by a lashing through the slot, and could be inflated at pleas-ure and corked up with the wooden plug.

As I have already said, the only harpoon of this kind now used at Point Barrow is a small one intended only for the capture of small seals. It has no bladder, but the rather long line is attached to the shaft by a martingale which makes the shaft drag sideways

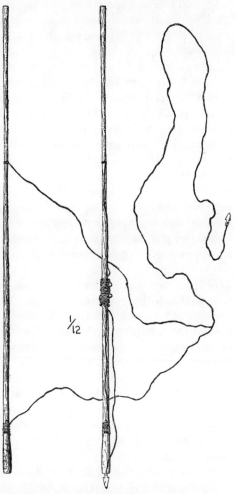

¹⁄₁₂

FIG. 203.—Seal dart.

through the water. Three of these little darts, which are thrown with a handboard like the bird dart, make a set. The resistance of the shafts

of these three spears darted into the seal in succession is said to be sufficient to fatigue the seal so that he can be easily approached and dispatched. We never saw these weapons used, though they are very common, as they are intended only for use from the kaiak, which these people
seldom use in the neighborhood of the villages. When in the *umiak*,
shooting with the rifle is a more expeditious means of taking seals. We
collected three sets of these darts (kúkigû).

No. 89249*b* [523], Fig. 203, has been selected for description. The shaft
is of spruce, 54½ inches long, and 0·8 inch in diameter at the tip, tapering
slightly almost to the butt, which is hollowed on the end to fit the catch
of the throwing board. The foreshaft is of white walrus ivory 5 inches
long, and is fitted into the tip of the shaft with a wedge-shaped tang.
This foreshaft, which has a deep oblong slot to receive the head in the
middle of its flat tip, serves the double purpose of making a strong
solid socket for the head and giving sufficient weight to the end of the
dart to make it fly straight. The head is a simple flat barbed arrow-head
of hard bone 2·3 inches long and one-half inch broad across the barbs,
with a flat tang, broadest in the middle, where there is a hole for attaching the line. This head simply serves to attach the drag of the shaft
to the seal as it is too small to inflict a serious wound. It is fastened to
the shaft by a martingale made as follows: One end of a stout line of
sinew braid 5½ feet long is passed through the hole in the head and secured by tying a knot in the end. The other end of this line divides
into two parts not quite so stout, one 3 feet long, the other 2 feet 8
inches. The latter is fastened to the shaft 18½ inches from the butt by
a single marling hitch with the end wedged into a slit in the wood and
seized down with fine sinew. The longer part serves to fasten the foreshaft to the shaft, and was probably put on separately and worked into
the braiding of the rest of the line at the junction. The foreshaft is
kept from slipping out by a little transverse ridge on each side of the
tang. When the weapon is mounted for use the two parts of the bridle
are brought together at the middle of the shaft and wrapped spirally
around it till only enough line is left to permit the head to be inserted
in the socket, and the bight of the line is secured by tucking it under
the last turn. When a seal is struck with this dart his sudden plunge
to escape unships the head. The catch of the martingale immediately
slips; the latter unrolls and drags the shaft through the water at right
angles to the line. The shaft, besides acting as a drag on the seal's
motions, also serves as a float to indicate his position to the hunter, as
its buoyancy brings it to the surface before the seal when the latter
rises for air.

The shaft is usually painted red except so much of the end as lies in
the groove of the throwing-board, in the act of darting. These darts
vary but little in size and material, and are all of essentially the same
pattern. They are always about 5 feet in length when mounted for
use. (The longest is 64⅛ inches, and the shortest 57.) The head, as

well as the foreshaft, is sometimes made of walrus ivory, and the latter sometimes of whale's bone. The chief variation is in the length of the martingale, and the details of the method of attaching it. No two are precisely alike. The foreshaft is generally plain, but is occasionally highly ornamented, as is shown in Fig. 204, No. 56516 [105]. The figures are all incised and colored, some with ocher and some with soot.

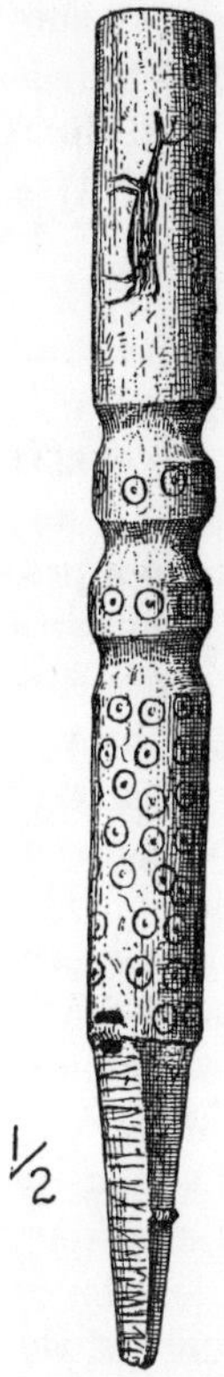

Both of the kinds of darts above described are thrown by means of a hand board or throwing-board. This is a flat, narrow board, from 15 to 18 inches long, with a handle at one end and a groove along the upper surface in which the spear lies with the butt resting against a catch at the other end. The dart is propelled by a quick motion of the wrist, as in casting with a fly-rod, which swings up the tip of the board and launches the dart forward. This contrivance, which practically makes of the hand a lever 18 inches long, enables the thrower by a slight motion of the wrist to impart great velocity to the dart. The use of this implement is universal among the Eskimo, though not peculiar to them. The Green-

½

FIG. 204.—Fore-
shaft of seal dart.

landers, however, not only use it for the two kinds of darts already mentioned, but have adapted it to the large harpoon.[1] This is undoubtedly to adapt the large harpoon for use from the kaiak, which the Greenlanders use more habitually than most other Eskimo. On the other hand, the people of Baffin Land and the adjoining regions, as well as the inhabitants of northeastern Siberia, use it only with the bird dart.[2] Throughout western North America the throwing-board is used essentially as at Point Barrow. Prof. O. T. Mason has given[3] an interesting ac-

¼

¼

a　　　*b*

FIG. 205.—Throwing board for darts.

count of the different forms of throwing-board used by the Eskimo and Aleuts of North America.

---

[1] Crantz, vol. 1, p. 146, Pl. v, Figs. 1 and 2, and Rink as quoted above, also Kane, First Exp., p. 478.
[2] Parry, Second Voyage, p. 508 (Iglulik); and Nordenskiöld, Vega, vol. 2, p. 105, Fig. 5.
[3] Smithsonian Report for 1884, part II, pp. 279–289.

We obtained five specimens of the form used at Point Barrow. No. 89233 [523], Fig. 205a, belonging to the set of seal darts bearing the same collector's number, has been selected as the type. This is made of spruce, and the hole is for the forefinger. A little peg of walrus ivory, shaped like a flat-headed nail, is driven through the middle of the tip so that the edge of the head just projects into the groove. This fits into the hollow in the butt of the dart and serves to steady it. It is painted red on the back and sides. Fig. 205b, No. 89235 [60], differs from this in having a double curve instead of being flat. A slight advantage is gained by this as in a crooked lever. The catch is a small iron nail. The others are essentially the same as the type. No. 89234 [528], has a small brass screw for the catch, and No. 89902 [1326], has an ivory peg of a slightly different shape, the head having only a projecting point on one side. They are generally painted with red ocher except on the inside of the groove. There appears to be no difference between throwing-boards meant for seal darts and those used with the bird dart.

Unfortunately I had no opportunity of observing accurately how the handle was grasped, but it is probably held as seen by Beechey at Eschscholtz Bay,[1] namely, with the forefinger in the hole, the thumb and middle finger clasped round the spear, and the third and little fingers clasping the handle under the spear. This seems a very natural way of holding it. Of course, the fingers release the spear at the moment of casting. All the throwing-boards from Point Barrow are right-handed.

Harpoons.—All kinds of marine animals, including the smaller seals, which are also captured with the darts just described and with nets, are pursued with harpoons of the same general type, but of different patterns for the different animals. They may be divided into two classes—those intended for throwing, which come under the head of projectile weapons, and those which do not leave the hand, but are thrust into the animal. These fall properly under the head of thrusting weapons. Both classes agree in having the head only attached permanently to the line, fitted loosely to the end of the shaft, and arranged so that when struck into the animal it is detached from the shaft, and turns under the skin at right angles to the line, like a toggle, so that it is almost impossible for it to draw out.

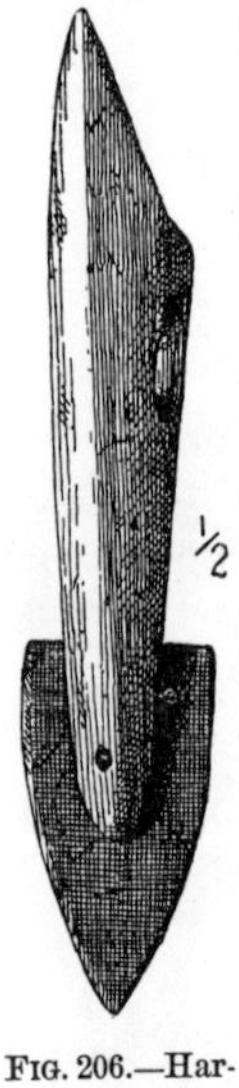

No. 89793 [873], Fig. 206, is a typical toggle head of this kind, intended for a walrus harpoon (túkᵄ), and will be described in full, as the names of the different parts will apply to all heads of this class. The *body* is a conoidal piece, 4½ inches in length, and flattened laterally so that at the widest part it is 1 inch wide and 0·7 thick. On one side, which may be called the *lower*, it is cut off straight for about half the

FIG. 206.—Harpoon head.

½

longer diameter, while the upper side is produced into a long, four-sided spur, the *barb*. The *line hole* is a round hole about one-fourth inch in diameter, a little back of the middle of the body, at right angles to its longer diameter. From this, on each side, run shallow *line grooves* to the base of the body, gradually deepening as they run into the line hole. In the middle of the base of the body is the deep, cup-shaped *shaft-socket*, which fits the conical tip of the shaft or fore shaft. In the tip of the body is cut, at right angles to the longer diameter of the body, and therefore at right angles to the plane of the barb, the narrow *blade slit*, 1·1 inches deep, into which fits, secured by a single median rivet of whalebone, the flat, thin *blade* of metal (brass in this case). This is triangular, with curved edges, narrowly beveled on both faces, and is 1·9 inches long and 1 broad.

The body is sometimes cut into faces so as to be hexagonal instead of elliptical in section as in Fig. 207 (No. 89791 [873]), ⅓ and intermediate forms are common. When such a head is mounted for use a bight of the line or *leader*, a short line for connecting the head with the main line, runs through the line hole so that the head is slung in a loop in the end of the line. The tip of the shaft is then fitted into the shaft socket and the line brought down the shaft with the parts of the loop on each side resting in the line grooves and is made fast, usually so that a slight pull will detach it from the shaft. When the animal is struck the blade cuts a wound large enough to allow the head to pass in beyond the barb. The struggles of the animal make the head slip off the tip of the shaft and the strain on the line immediately toggles it across the wound. The toggle head of the whale harpoon is called kia¢ron, of the walrus harpoon, tukɐ, and of the seal harpoon, naulɐ. They are all of essentially the same pattern, differing chiefly in size.

FIG. 207.—Harpoon head.

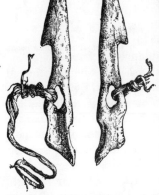

FIG. 208.—Ancient bone harpoon head.

There is in the collection an interesting series of old harpoon heads, showing a number of steps in the development of the modern pattern of harpoon head from an ancient form. These heads seem to have been preserved as amulets; in fact one of them is still attached to a belt. They are not all of the same kind, but since the different kinds as mentioned above practically differ only in size, their development was probably the same. The earliest form in the collection is No. 89382 [1383], Fig. 208, from Nuwŭk, which is evidently very old, as it is much worn and weathered. It is a single flat piece of fine-grained bone 3 inches long, pointed at the end and provided with a single unilateral barb. Behind this it is narrowed and then widened into a broad flat base produced on one side into a sharp barb, in the same plane as the other barb,

which represents the blade, but on the opposite side. The line hole is large and irregularly triangular, and there are no line grooves. Instead of a shaft socket bored in the solid body, one side of the body is excavated into a deep longitudinal groove, which was evidently converted into a socket by a transverse band, probably of sealskin, running round the body, and kept in place by a shallow transverse groove on the convex side of it. A harpoon head with the socket made by inclosing a groove with thongs was seen by Dr. Kane at Smith Sound.[1]

The next form, No. 89331 [932], Fig. 209a, has two bilateral barbs to the blade part, thus increasing its holding power. Instead of an open transverse groove to hold the thong, it has two slots parallel to the socket groove running obliquely to the other side, where they open into a shallow depression.

FIG. 209.—Harpoon heads: (a) ancient bone harpoon head; (b) variant of the type.

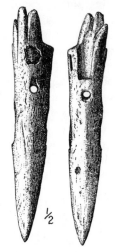

FIG. 210.—Bone harpoon head.

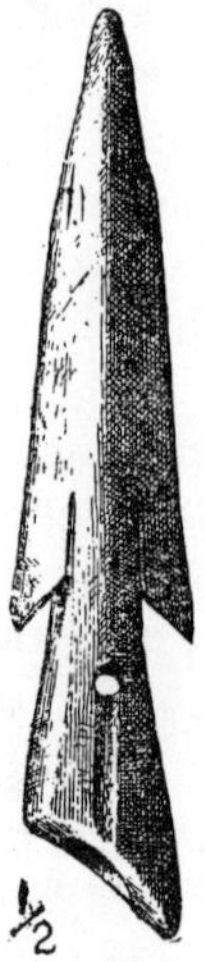

Figs. 209b and 210, Nos. 89544 [1419] and 89377 [766], are variants of this form, probably intended for the larger seal, as the blade part is very long in proportion. No. 89544 [1419] is interesting from its close resemblance to the spear head figured by Nordenskiöld[2] from the ancient "Onkilon" house at North Cape. No. 89377 [766] is a peculiar form, which was perhaps not general, as it has left no descendants among the modern harpoon. Instead of the bilateral blade barbs it has an irregular slot on each side, which evidently served to hold a blade of stone, and the single barb of the body is replaced by a cluster of four, which are neither in the plane of the blade nor at right angles to it, but between the two. No modern harpoon heads from Point Barrow have more than two barbs on the body. The next improvement was to bore the shaft socket instead of making it by inclosing a groove with thongs. This is shown in Fig. 211 (No. 89379 [795], from Utkiavwiñ), which is just like No. 89544 [1419] except in this respect. The line grooves first appear at this stage of the development.

FIG. 211.—Bone harpoon head.

---

[1] Second Grinnell Exp., vol. 1, Figs. on pp. 412 and 413.   [2] Vega, vol. 1, p. 444, Fig. 5.

The next step was to obtain greater penetration by substituting a triangular blade of stone for the barbed bone point, with its breadth still in the plane of the body barb. This blade was either of slate (No. 89744 [969] from Nuwŭk) or of flint, as in Fig. 212 (No. 89748 [928], also from Nuwŭk). Both of these are whale harpoons, such as are sometimes used even at the present day.

Before the introduction of iron it was discovered that if the blade were inserted at right angles to the plane of the body barb the harpoon would have a surer hold, since the strain on the line would always draw it at right angles to the length of the wound cut by the blade. This is shown in Fig. 213 (No. 56620 [199], a walrus harpoon head from Utkiavwĭñ), which has the slate blade inserted in this position. Substituting a metal blade for the stone one gives us the modern toggle head, as already described. That the insertion of the stone blade preceded the rotation of the plane of the latter is, I think, conclusively shown by the whale harpoons[1] already mentioned, in spite of the fact that

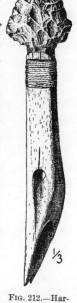

we have a bone harpoon head in the collection, No. 89378 [1261], figured in Point Barrow report, which is exactly like No. 89379 [795], except that it has the

FIG. 212.—Harpoon head, bone and stone.

blade *at right angles* to the plane of the body barb. This is, however, a newly made model in reindeer antler of the ancient harpoon, and was evidently made by a man so used to the modern pattern that he forgot this important distinction. The development of this spear head has been carried no further at Point Barrow. At one or two places, however, namely, at Cumberland Gulf in the east[2] and at Sledge Island in the west (as shown in Mr. Nelson's collec-

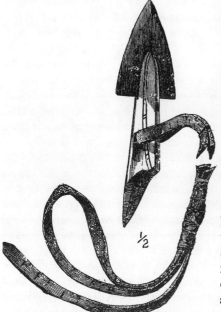

FIG. 213.—Harpoon head, bone and stone.

tion), they go a step further in making the head of the seal harpoon, body and blade, of one piece of iron. The shape, however, is the same as those with the ivory or bone body.

---

[1] Compare, also, the walrus harpoon figured by Capt. Lyon, Parry's Second Voyage, Pl. opposite p. 550, Fig. 13.

[2] See Kumlien, Contributions, p. 35, and Boas, "Central Eskimo," p. 473, Fig. 393.

All of the Eskimo race, as far as I have any definite information, use toggle harpoon-heads. There are specimens in the National Museum from Greenland, Cumberland Gulf, the Anderson and Mackenzie region, and from the Alaskan coast from Point Barrow to Kadiak, as well as from St. Lawrence Island, which are all of essentially the same type, but slightly modified in different localities. The harpoon head in use at Smith Sound is of the same form as the walrus harpoon heads used at Point Barrow, but appears always to have the shaft socket made by a groove closed with thongs.[1]   In Danish Greenland, however, the body has an extra pair of bilateral barbs below the blade. The Greenlanders have, as it were, substituted a metal blade for the point only of the barbed blade portion of such a bone head as No. 89379 [795].[2]

Curiously enough, this form of the toggle head appears again in the Mackenzie and Anderson region, as shown by the extensive collections of Ross, MacFarlane, and others. In this region the metal blade itself is often cut into one or more pairs of bilateral barbs. At the Straits of Fury and Hecla, Parry found the harpoon head, with a body like the walrus harpoon heads at Point Barrow,[3] but with the blade *in the plane* of the body barb. Most of the pictures scattered through the work represent the blade in this position, but Fig. 19 on the same plate has the blade at right angles to the barb, so that the older form may not be universal. At Cumberland Gulf the form of the body is considerably modified, though the blade is of the usual shape and in the ordinary position. The body is flattened at right angles to the usual direction, so that the thickness is much greater than the width. It always has two body barbs. On the western coast the harpoon heads are much less modified, though there is a tendency to increase the number of body barbs, at the same time ornamenting the body more elaborately as we go south from Bering Strait. Walrus harpoon heads with a single barb, hardly distinguishable from those used at Point Barrow, are in the collection from the Diomedes and all along the northern shore of Norton Sound, and one also from the mouth of the Kuskoquim. They are probably also used from Point Barrow to Kotzebue Sound. At St. Lawrence Island and on the Asiatic shore they are the common if not the universal form.[4] The seal harpoon head (naulᴇ) at Point Barrow appears always to have the body barb split at the tip into two, and this is the case rarely with the tu'kᴇ. This form, which appears occasionally north of Norton Sound (Port Clarence, Cape Nome), appears to be more common south of this locality, where, however, a pattern with the barb divided into three points seems to be the prevailing form. I will now proceed to the description of the different forms of harpoon with which these toggle heads are used.

---

[1] Kane, 2d Grinnell Exp., vol. 1, pp. 412 and 413 (Fig. 1), and Bessells, Naturalist, vol. 18, pt. 9, p. 869, Figs. 6–12.

[2] Crantz, vol. 1, p. 146, and Pl. v, Figs. 1 and 2, and Rink Tales, etc., Pl. opposite p. 10.

[3] 2d Voyage, Pl. opposite p. 550, Fig. 13.

[4] Museum collections and Nordenskiöld, Vega, vol. 2, p. 105, Fig. 1. This figure shows the blade *in he plane* of the barb, but none of the specimens from Plover Bay are of this form.

Throwing-harpoons are always thrown from the hand without a throwing-board or other assistance, and are of two sizes, one for the walrus and bearded seal, and one for the small seals. Both have a long shaft of wood to the tip of which is attached a heavy bone or ivory foreshaft, usually of greater diameter than the shaft and somewhat club-shaped. This serves the special purpose of giving weight to the head of the harpoon, so it can be darted with a sure aim. The native name of this part of the spear, ukumailuta (Greenlandic, okimailutaκ, *weight*), indicates its design. This contrivance of weighting the head of the harpoon with a heavy foreshaft is peculiar to the western Eskimo. On all the eastern harpoons (see figures referred to above and the Museum collections) the foreshaft is a simple cap of bone no larger than the shaft the tip of which it protects. Between the foreshaft and the toggle-head is interposed the *loose shaft* (i'gimû), a slender rod of bone whose tip fits into the shaft socket of the head, while its butt fits loosely in a socket in the tip of the foreshaft. It is secured to the shaft by a thong just long enough to allow it to be unshipped from the foreshaft. This not only prevents the loose shaft from breaking under a lateral strain, but by its play facilitates unshipping the head. On these harpoons intended for throwing, this loose shaft is always short. This brings the weight of the foreshaft close to the head, while it leaves space enough for the head to penetrate beyond the barb.

The walrus harpoon varies in size, being adapted to the strength and stature of the owner. Of the six in our collection, the longest, when mounted for use, is 9 feet 6 inches long, and the shortest 5 feet 8 inches. The ordinary length appears to be about 7 feet. It has a long, heavy shaft (ipua) of wood, usually between 5 and 6 feet long and tapering from a diameter of 1½ inches at the head to about 1 inch at the butt. The head is not usually fastened directly to the line, but has a leader of double thong 1 to 2 feet long, with a becket at the end into which the main line is looped or hitched. At the other end of the line, which is about 30 feet long, is another becket to which is fastened a float consisting of a whole sealskin inflated. When the head is fitted on the tip of the loose shaft the line is brought down to the middle of the shaft and hooked by means of a little becket to an ivory peg (ki'lerb-wĩñ) projecting from the side of the shaft. The eastern Eskimo have, in place of the simple becket, a neat little contrivance consisting of a plate of ivory lashed to the line with a large slot in it which hooks over the catch, but nothing of the sort was observed at Point Barrow.

The harpoon thus mounted is poised in the right hand with the fore-finger resting against a curved ivory projection (ti'ka) and darted like a white man's harpoon, the float and line being thrown overboard at the same time. When a walrus is struck the head slips off and toggles as already described; the line detaches itself from the catch, leaving the shaft free to float and be picked up. The float is now fastened to the walrus, and, like the shaft of the seal dart, both shows his whereabouts and acts as a drag on his movements until he is "played" enough for the hunters to come up and dispatch him. This weapon is called u′nakpûk, "the great u′na or spear." U′na (unâk, u′nañ) appears to be a generic term in Eskimo for harpoon, but at Point Barrow is now restricted to the harpoon used for stabbing seals as they come up to their breathing holes.

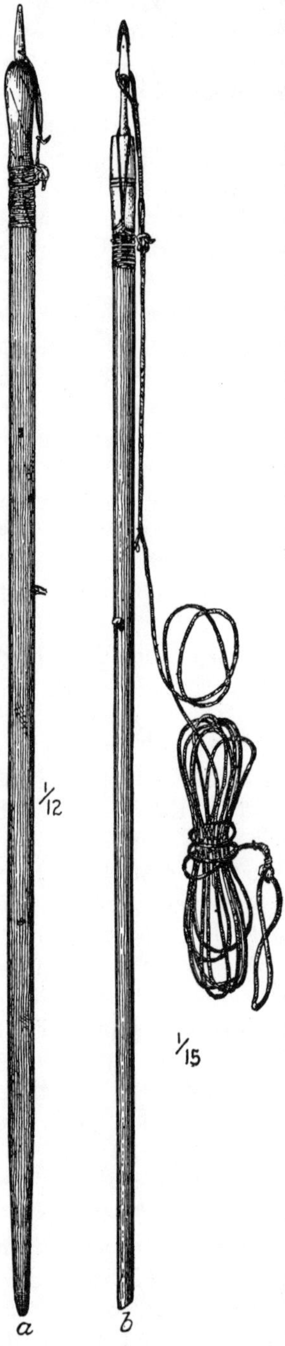

We collected six of these walrus harpoons complete and forty-two separate heads. Of these, No. 56770 [534], Fig. 214a, has the most typical shaft and loose shaft. The shaft is of spruce 71 inches long, roughly rounded, and tapering from a diameter of 1½ inches at the tip to 0·8 at the butt. The foreshaft is of white walrus ivory, 6·7 inches long, exclusive of the wedge-shaped tang which fits into a cleft in the tip of the shaft. It is somewhat club-shaped, being 1·6 inches in diameter at the tip and tapering to 1·3 just above the butt, which expands to the diameter of the shaft, and is separated from the tang by a square transverse shoulder. The shaft and foreshaft are fastened together by a whipping of broad seal thong, put on wet, one end passing through a hole in the foreshaft one-quarter inch from the shaft, and kept from slipping by a low transverse ridge on each side of the tang. In the tip of the foreshaft is a deep, round socket to receive the loose shaft, which is a tapering rod of walrus ivory 4·4 inches long, shouldered off at the butt, which is 0·7 inch in diameter, to a blunt, rounded tang 0·9 inch long. It fits loosely into the foreshaft up to the shoulder, and is secured by a piece of narrow seal thong which passes through a transverse hole one-half inch above the shoulder. The end is spliced to the standing part with double slits about 6 inches from the loose shaft, and the other end makes a couple of turns outside of the lashing on the shaft mentioned above and is secured with two half-hitches.

The line catch (ki′lerbwĭñ) is a little, blunt, backward-pointing hook of ivory inserted in the shaft 17 inches from the tip and projecting about one-third inch. Ten and one-fourth inches farther back and 90

FIG. 214.—Walrus harpoons.

¹⁄₁₂

¹⁄₁₅

a   b

degrees round the shaft from the line catch is the finger rest—a conical recurved piece of ivory 1 inch high, with a flat base, resting against the shaft and secured by a lashing of whalebone, which passes through two corresponding holes, one in the rest and one in the shaft. The head and line belonging to this harpoon are intended for hunting the bearded seal, and will be described below. No. 56772 [536], Fig. 214b, from Utkiavwĩñ, is fitted with fairly typical walrus gear. 'The head is of the typical form, 6 inches long, with a conoidal body of walrus ivory, ornamented with incised lines colored with red ocher, and a blade of steel secured by a whalebone rivet. The "leader," which is about 15 inches long, is made by passing one end of a piece of stout walrus-hide thong about one-quarter inch wide through the line hole and doubling it with the head in the bight, so that one part is about 6 inches the longer. The two parts are stopped together about 2 inches from the head with a bit of sinew braid. The ends are joined and made into a becket, as follows: The longer end is doubled back for 7 inches and a slit cut through both parts about 2 inches from the end. The shorter end is passed through this slit, and a slit is cut 5 inches from the end of this, through which the loop of the other end is passed and all drawn taut. The whole joint is then tightly seized with sinew braid so as to leave a becket 3 inches and a free end 4 inches long. This becket is looped into an eye 1½ inches long at the end of the main line, made by doubling over 5 inches of the end and stopping the two parts firmly together with sinew braid. The line is of the hide of the bearded seal, about the same diameter as the leader, and 27 feet long. It is in two nearly equal parts, spliced together with double slits, firmly seized with sinew braid. There is a becket about 8 inches long at the other end of the line for attaching the float, made by doubling over the end and tying a carrick bend, the end of which is stopped back to the standing part with sinew braid. The becket to hook upon the line catch is a bit of sinew braid, fastened to the line 2½ feet from the head, as follows: One end being laid against the line it is doubled in a bight and the end is whipped down to the line by the other end, which makes five turns round them.

I will now consider the variations of the different parts of these harpoons in detail, beginning with the head. Our series is so large, containing in all forty-eight heads, besides some spare blades, that it probably gives a fair representation of the common variations. The longest of this series is 6 inches long and the shortest 3½, but by far the greater number are from 4½ to 5 inches long. Their proportions are usually about as in the types figured, but the long head just figured (No. 56772 [534]) is also unusually slender. Sheet brass is the commonest material for the blade (thirty blades are of this material), though iron or steel is sometimes used, and rarely, at present, slate. There is one slate-bladed head in the series (No. 56620 [199]) figured above, and four blades for such heads. The blade is commonly of the shape of the type figured, triangular with curved edges, varying from a rather long

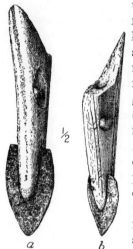

triangle like the slate blade just mentioned to a rather short one with very strongly curved edges like Fig. 215a (No. 89750 [1038]), which is peculiar as the only walrus harpoon head with a body of reindeer antler. It also has an iron blade and a rivet of iron, not seldom with rounded basal angles so as to be almost heart-shaped, like Fig. 215b (No. 56621 [283]). A less common shape of blade is lanceolate, with the base cut off square as in Fig. 216a (No. 89764 [940]). Only eight blades out of the series are of this shape. A still more peculiar shape of blade, of which we saw only one specimen, is shown in Fig. 216b (No. 89790 [943]). This is made of brass. It was perhaps meant for an imitation of the barbed blades used at the Mackenzie, of which I have already spoken.

FIG. 215.—Typical walrus-harpoon heads.

The blade, when of metal, is generally fastened in with a single rivet. One only out of the whole number has two rivets, and three are simply wedged into the blade slit. The slate blades appear never to have been riveted; Nordenskiöld, however, figures a walrus harpoon from Port Clarence[1] with a jade blade riveted in. The rivet is generally made of whalebone, but other materials are sometimes used. For instance, in the series collected two have rivets of iron, two of wood, and five of rawhide. The body is generally made of white walrus ivory, (five of those collected are of hard bone, and one already mentioned and figured, No. 89750 [1038], Fig. 215a, is of reindeer antler), and the hexagonal shape, often with rounded edges, and the line grooves continued to the tip, as in Fig. 217a, No. 89757 [947], appears to be the commonest. Three out of the forty-eight have four-sided bodies. It is

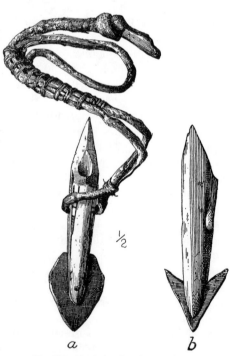

FIG. 216.—Typical walrus-harpoon heads.

unusual for the body barb to be bifurcated, as is common farther south.

[1] Vega, vol. 2, p. 229, Fig. 3.

Only three out of the forty-eight show this peculiarity, of which No. 56613 [53], Fig. 217*b*, is an example.

The specimens figured show the different styles of ornamentation, which always consist of incised patterns colored with red ocher or rarely with soot. These never represent natural objects, but are always conventional pat-
terns, generally a single or double border on two or more faces with short oblique cross-lines and branch-
es. Harpoon heads at Point Barrow are probably never ornamented with the "circles and dots," so common on other implements and on the harpoons of the southern Eskimo.

Twenty-eight of the heads still have the leaders attached to them. The object of this short line is to enable the hunter to readily de-
tach a broken head and put on a fresh one without going to the trouble of undoing a splice, which must be made strong to keep the head from

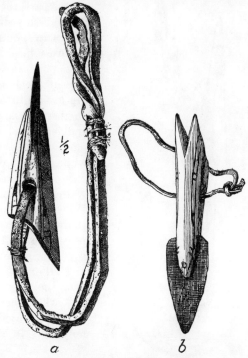

FIG. 217.—Typical walrus-harpoon heads.

separating from the line. It is made of a stout piece of rawhide thong, the skin of the walrus or bearded seal, about one-third inch in diameter,

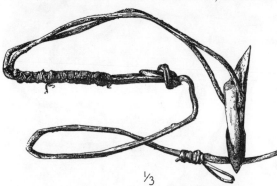

FIG. 218.—Walrus-harpoon head, with leader.

and usually from 2 to 3 feet long. It is al-
ways passed through the line hole, as in the specimen described, and the ends are made into a becket for attaching the line, with an end left to serve as a handle for pulling the two beck-
ets apart when the main line ends in a becket. Occasionally (two are made this way) the longer end is simply doubled in a bight, and the three parts are then seized together with sinew braid, but it is generally made with a splice, the details of which differ slightly on the different leaders.

The commonest method is that already described. When the longer end is doubled over, a slit is cut through both parts close to the end of this through which the shorter end is passed. A slit is then cut a few inches from the tip of this part, the bight of the becket passed through this slit and all drawn taut. This makes a very strong splice. Fourteen beckets are spliced in this way. A variation of this splice has a slit only through the end part of the longer end, the shorter end being passed through and slit as before. In one becket the standing part of the longer end is passed through the slit of the end part before going through the line hole, while the rest of the becket is made as before. A reversed splice is found on three of the leaders, which is made as follows: When the long end is doubled over, the short end is slit as usual and the longer end passed through this and slit close to the tip. Through this slit is passed the head and all drawn taut. The splice is always firmly seized with sinew braid. The main line, which serves to attach the head to the float, is always made of stout thong, preferably the skin of the bearded seal (very fine

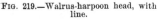

FIG. 219.—Walrus-harpoon head, with line.

lines are sometimes made of beluga skin), about one-third inch square, and, when properly made, trimmed off on the edges so as to be almost round. It is about 10 yards long It is fastened into the becket of the leader with a becket hitch tied

FIG. 220.—Walrus-harpoon head, with line.

upside down (No. 56771 [535], Fig. 218), or by means of a small becket, made either as on the specimen described (No. 56770 [536], Fig. 219), or spliced with double slits. The long becket at the other end for attaching the float is made either by tying a carrick bend with the end stopped back to the standing part (Fig. 220, No. 56767 [531]), or by splicing (Fig. 221, No. 56769).

The loose shaft varies very little in shape, though it is sometimes rounded off at the butt without a shoulder, but the line which secures this to the foreshaft is put on differently on each of the six spears. Five of them have the end simply passed through the hole in the loose shaft and spliced to the standing part, but two (the type figured and No. 56768 [532]) have the other end carried down and hitched round the tip of the shaft; another has it passed through a hole in the foreshaft, taken $1\frac{1}{2}$ turns round this and knotted (No. 56771 [535]); another has a loop as long as the foreshaft with the short end passed under the first turn of the shaft lashing before it is spliced, and the long end secured as on the first mentioned; and the fifth has the end passed through a hole in the foreshaft and carried down and wrapped round the shaft lashing. The sixth has one end passed through a hole in the smallest part of the foreshaft and knotted at the end, the other end carried up through the hole in the loose shaft and down to a second hole in the foreshaft close to the first, then up through the loose shaft, and down through the first hole, and tucked under the two parts on the other side.

The foreshaft is made of walrus ivory or the hard bone of the walrus jaw and varies little in form and dimensions. It is sometimes ornamented by carving, as in No. 56772 [536], or by incised patterns, as in Fig. 222, No. 56538 [98], and generally has one or two deep longitudinal notches in the thickest part, in which the lines can be drawn snugly down. It usually is joined to the shaft by a stout, wedge-shaped tang, which fits into a corresponding cleft in the shaft, and is secured by wooden treenails and a wrapping of seal thong or sinew braid, sometimes made more secure by passing

Fig. 221.—Walrus-harpoon head, with line.

one end through holes in the foreshaft. No. 56768 [532] is peculiar in having the tang on the shaft and the corresponding cleft in the foreshaft. The shaft itself varies little in shape and proportions, and at

the present day is sometimes made of ash or other hard wood obtained from the ships. The line catch is generally a little hook of ivory or hard bone like the one described, but two specimens have small screws fastened into the shaft to serve this purpose. The finger rest is ordinarily of the same shape as on the type and fastened on in the same way, but No. 56771 [535] has this made of a knob of ivory elaborately carved into a seal's head. The eyes are represented by round bits of ivory with pupils drilled in them inlaid in the head. This is evidently the knob of a seal drag (see below) as the longitudinal perforation from chin to nape now serves no purpose. It is fastened on by a lashing of whalebone, which runs round the shaft and through a transverse hole in the knob.

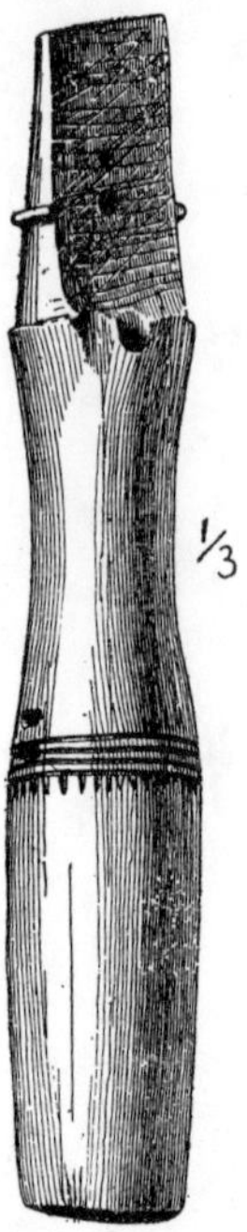

Harpoons closely resembling these in type are used by the Eskimo of western North America wherever they habitually hunt the walrus. At many places this heavy spear is armed at the butt with a long sharp pick of ivory like the smaller seal spear. Two of these large harpoons appear to be rigged especially for the pursuit of the bearded seal, as they have heads which are of precisely the same shape and material as the small seal harpoons in the collection. Both these heads have lanceolate iron blades, conoidal antler bodies with double barbs, and are more slender than the walrus harpoon heads. No. 56770 [534], Fig. 219, has a head 4 inches long and 0·7 broad at the widest part, and fastened to a very long line (12 fathoms long) without a leader, the end being simply passed through the line hole and seized down to the standing part with sinew braid. This is the method of attaching the head of the small seal harpoons. This line is so long that it may have been held in the boat and not attached to a float. No. 56768 [532], however, has a leader with a becket of the ordinary style. Fig. 223, No. 56611 [89], is a head similar to those just described, and probably, from its size, intended for large seals. It is highly ornamented with the usual reddened incised pattern.

FIG. 222.—Foreshaft of walrus harpoon.

The throwing harpoon for small seals is an exact copy in miniature of the walrus harpoon, with the addition of a long bayonet-shaped pick of ivory at the butt. The line, however, is upwards of 30 yards long, and the end never leaves the hand. The line is hitched round the shaft back of the line catch, which now only serves to keep the line from slipping forward, as the shaft is never detached from the line. This harpoon is used exclu-

FIG. 223.—Harpoon head for large seals.

sively for retrieving seals that have been shot in open
holes or leads of water within darting distance from the
edge of the solid ice, and is thrown precisely as the
walrus harpoon is, except that the end of the line is
held in the left hand. In traveling over the ice the
line with the head attached is folded in long hanks
and slung on the gun case at the back. The rest of
the weapon is carried in the hand and serves as a staff
in walking and climbing among the ice, where the
sharp pick is useful to prevent slipping and to try
doubtful ice, and also enables the hunter to break
away thin ice at the edge of the hole, so as to draw
his game up to the solid floe. It can also serve as a
bayonet in case of necessity. This peculiar form of
harpoon is confined to the coast from Point Barrow to
Bering Strait, the only region where the seal is hunted
with the rifle in the small open holes of water.[1]

Since my note in the Naturalist was written, I have
learned from Mr. Henry Balfour, of the museum at Ox-
ford, that their collection contains two or three specimens of this very pattern of harpoon, undoubtedly collected by some of the officers of the *Blossom*. Consequently, my theory that the retrieving harpoon was a
modern invention, due to the introduction of firearms,
becomes untenable, as the *Blossom* visited this region
before firearms were known to the Eskimo. It was
probably originally intended for the capture of seals
"hauled out" on the ice in the early summer. There is
no doubt, however, that it is at the present day used
for nothing but retrieving.

Though this weapon was universally used at Point
Barrow, we happened to obtain only two specimens,
possibly because the natives thought them too necessary an implement to part with lightly. No. 89907
[1695], Figs. 224, 225, has a new shaft, etc., but was
used several times by the maker before it was offered
for sale. Such a retrieving harpoon is called naúlĭg̑e.
The shaft (ipúa) is of ash, 4 feet 5 inches long and 1
inch in diameter, tapering very slightly to each end.
The ice pick (túu) of walrus ivory, 14 inches long and
1 inch wide, has a round tang fitting into a hole in the
butt of the shaft. Close to the shaft a small hole is
drilled in one edge of the pick, and through this is
passed a bit of seal thong, the ends of which are laid
along the shaft and neatly whipped down with sinew
braid, with the end wedged into a slit in the wood.

$\frac{1}{10}$

FIG. 224.—Retrieving
seal harpoon.

[1] See the writer's note on this weapon, American Naturalist, vol. 19, p. 423.

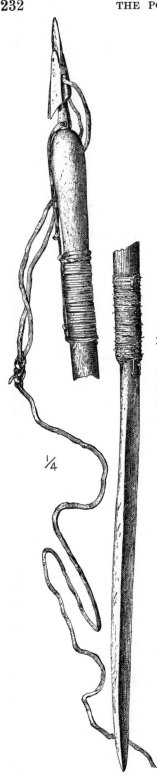

FIG. 225.—Details of retrieving seal harpoon.

¼

The foreshaft (ukumailuta) is of walrus ivory, 4½ inches long and 1½ inches in diameter at the thickest part, and secured to the shaft by a whipping (nĭ'mxa) of seal thong. The loose shaft (ígimû) is also of ivory and 2 inches long and secured by a thong (ĭpíuta) spliced into a loop through the hole at the butt, as previously described. The end is hitched round the tip of the shaft with a marling hitch, followed by a clove hitch below the whipping. The ivory finger rest (ti'ka) is fastened on with a lashing of whip cord (white man's) passing round the shaft. The line catch (ki'lerbwĭñ), which was of ivory and shaped like those on the walrus harpoons, has been lost in transportation. The head differs only in size from those just described as intended for the bearded seal, except in having a hexagonal body. It is 3·3 inches long and has a blade of iron fastened into a body of walrus ivory with a single wooden rivet. While there is no detachable leader, the head is attached by a separate piece of the same material to the line (tûkăksia), which is 86 feet 10 inches long and made of a single piece of fine seal thong about one-eighth inch thick. This shorter piece is about 27 inches long and is passed through the line hole and doubled so that one part is a little the longer. It is fastened strongly to the end of the line by a complicated splice made as follows: A slit is cut in the end of the main line through which are passed both ends of the short line. The longer part is then slit about 2 inches from the end and the shorter part passed through the slit, and a slit cut close to the end of it, through which the longer end is passed. The whole is then drawn taut and the longer end clove hitched round the main line.

No. 89908 [1058] is one of these spears rigged ready for darting. The line is secured at about the middle of the shaft with a couple of marling hitches. This specimen, except the head, is new and was rather carelessly made for the market. It has neither line catch nor finger rest. The foreshaft and ice pick are lashed in with sinew braid, which is first knotted round the tip of the shaft and then hitched round with a series of left-handed soldier's hitches. The end of the thong which holds the loose shaft is passed through the hole in it and knotted and the other end hitched into the pulley at the smallest part of the foreshaft. The head is like that of the preceding, but has a conoidal body of reindeer antler, a common material for seal-harpoon heads, and the line, which is of stout sinew braid

43 feet long, is attached to it simply by passing the end through the line hole and tying it with a clove hitch to the standing part 9½ inches from the head. This spear is about the same size as the preceding. These weapons are all of the same general pattern, but vary in length according to the height of the owner. The heads for these harpoons, as well as for the other form of seal harpoon, are usually about 3 inches long, and, as a rule, have lanceolate blades. The body is generally conoidal, often made of reindeer antler, and always, apparently, with a double barb. It is generally plain, but sometimes orna-

FIG. 226.—Jade blade for seal harpoon.

mented like the walrus-harpoon heads. No. 89784 [1008] was made by Ilû′bw'ga, the Nunatañmeun, when thinking of coming to winter at Utkiavwĭñ. He had had no experience in sealing, having apparently spent all his winters on the rivers inland, and this harpoon head seems to have been condemned as unsatisfactory by his new friends at Utkiavwĭñ. It looks like a very tolerable naula, but is unusually small, being only 2½ inches long.

We saw only one stone blade for a seal harpoon, No. 89623 [1418], Fig. 226. This is of light olive green jade, and triangular, with peculiarly dull edges and point. Each face is concaved, and there is a hole for a rivet. (Compare the jade-bladed harpoon figured by Nordenskiöld and referred to above.) It is 2 inches long and 0·7 inch wide at the base. It appears to have been kept as an amulet. The other form of seal harpoon comes properly under the next head.

THRUSTING WEAPONS.

Harpoons.—For the capture of seals as they come up for air to their breathing holes or cracks in the ice a harpoon is used which has a short wooden shaft, armed, as before, with an ice pick and a long, slender, loose shaft suited for thrusting down through

FIG. 227.—Seal harpoon for thrusting.

the small breathing hole.   It carries a núalᴇ like the other harpoon, but has only a short line, the end of which is made fast permanently to the shaft.   Such harpoons are used by all Eskimo wherever they are in the habit of watching for seals at their breathing holes.   The slender part of the shaft, however, is not always loose.[1]   The foreshaft is simply a stout ferrule for the end of the shaft.   These weapons are in general use at Point Barrow and are very neatly made.

We obtained two specimens, of which No. 89910 [1694], Fig. 227, will serve as the type.   The total length of this spear when rigged for use is 5 feet 3 inches.   The shaft is of spruce, 20½ inches long and 1·1 inches in the middle, tapering to 0·9 at the ends.   At the butt is inserted, as before, an ivory ice pick (túu) of the form already described, 13¾ inches long and lashed in with sinew braid.   The foreshaft (kátû) is of walrus ivory, nearly cylindrical, 5¾ inches long and 0·9 inch in diameter, shouldered at the butt and fitted into the tip of the shaft with a round tang.   The latter is very neatly whipped with a narrow strip of white whalebone, which makes eleven turns and has the end of the last turn forced into a slit in the wood and wedged with a round wooden peg.   Under this whipping is the bill of a tern as a charm for good luck.   (As the boy who pointed this out to me said, "Lots of seals.")

The loose shaft (ígimû) is of bone, whale's rib or jaw, and has two transverse holes above the shoulder to receive the end of the assembling

line (sábromia), which not only holds the loose shaft in place, but also connects the other parts of the shaft so that in case the wood breaks the pieces will not be dropped.   It is a long piece of seal thong, of which one end makes a turn round the loose shaft between the holes; the other end is passed through the lower hole,

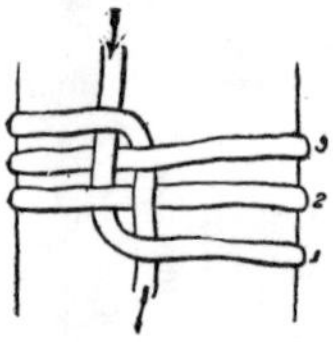

FIG. 228.—Diagram of lashing on shaft.

then through the upper and carried down to the tip of the shaft, where it is hitched just below the whalebone whipping, as follows: three turns are made round the shaft, the first over the standing part, the second under, and the third over it; the end then is passed under 3, over 2, and under 1 (Fig. 228), and all drawn taut; it then runs down the shaft almost to the butt-lashing and is secured with the same hitch, and the end is whipped around the butt of the ice pick with five turns.   The head (naúlᴇ) is of the ordinary pattern, 2·8 inches long, with a copper blade and antler body.   The line (túkăktĭn) is a single piece of seal thong 9 feet long, and is fastened to the head without a leader, by simply passing the end through the line-hole, doubling it over and stopping it to the standing part so as to make a becket 21 inches long.   The other end is made fast round the shaft and assembling line just back of the middle, as follows: An eye is made at the end of the line, by cutting a slit close to the tip and pushing a bight of the line through this.   The end then makes a turn round the shaft, and the other end, with the head, is passed through this eye and drawn taut.   When mounted for use, the head is fitted on the tip of the loose shaft as usual

---

[1] Parry, Second Voyage, p. 507, Iglulik.

and the line brought down to the tip of the shaft and made fast by two or three round turns with a bight tucked under, so that it can be easily slipped. It is also confined to the loose shaft by the end of the assembling line, which makes one or two loose turns round it. The slack of the line is doubled into "fakes" and tucked between the shaft and assembling line.

The other specimen is of the same pattern, but slightly different proportions, having a shaft 18½ inches long and a pick 19 inches long. The loose shaft is of ivory, and there are lashings of white whalebone at each end of the shaft. The assembling line is hitched round the foreshaft as well as round the two ends of the shaft, and simply knotted round the pick. The line is of very stout sinew braid, and has an eye neatly spliced in the end for looping it round the shaft. Fig. 229, No. 89551 [1082], is a model of one of these harpoons, made for sale. It is 16¼ inches long, and correct in all its parts, except that the whole head is of ivory, even to having the ends of the shaft whipped with light-colored whalebone. The shaft is of pine and the rest of walrus ivory, with lines of sinew braid. We also collected four loose shafts for such harpoons. One of these, No. 89489 [802], is of whale's bone and unusually short, only 14 inches long. It perhaps belonged to a lad's spear. The other three are long, 20 to 25 inches, and are made of narwhal ivory, as is shown by the spiral twist in the grain.

The harpoon used for the whale fishery is a heavy, bulky weapon, which is never thrown, but thrust with both hands as the whale rises under the bows of the umiak. When not in use it rests in a large ivory crotch, shaped like a rowlock, in the bow. The shaft is of wood and 8 or 9 feet long, and there is no loose shaft, the bone or ivory foreshaft being tapered off to a slender point of such a shape that the head easily unships. This foreshaft is not weighted, as in the walrus harpoon, since this is not necessary in a weapon which does not leave the hand. The harpoon line is fitted with two inflated sealskin floats.

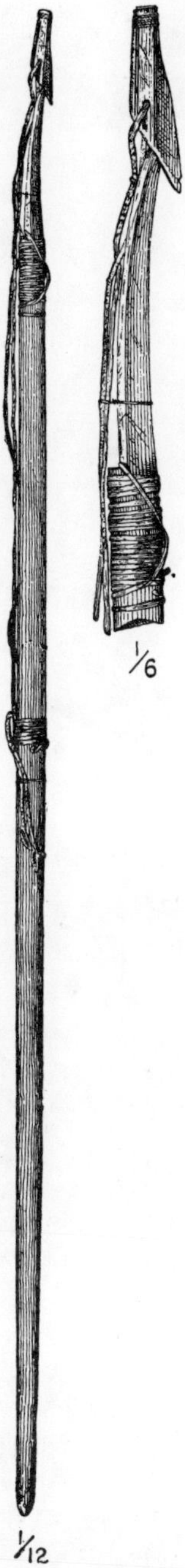

No complete, genuine whaling harpoons were ever offered for sale, but a man at Nuwûk made a very excellent reduced model about two-thirds the usual size (No. 89909 [1023], Fig. 230), which will serve as the type of this weapon

FIG. 229.— Model of a seal harpoon.

⅓

⅙

1/12

FIG. 230.— Large model of a whale harpoon.

(a′jyûñ). This is 6 feet 11 inches in length when rigged for use. The

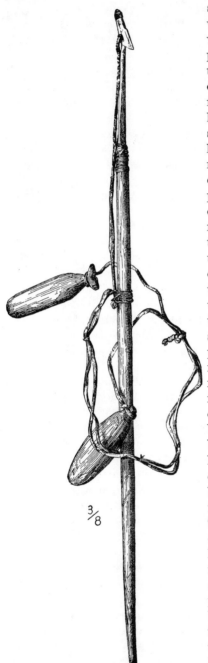

shaft is of pine, 5 feet 8½ inches long, with its greatest diameter (1½ inches) well forward of the middle and tapered more toward the butt than toward˙ the tip, which is chamfered off on one side to fit the butt of the foreshaft (igimû), and shouldered to keep the lashing in place. The foreshaft is of whale's bone, 11½ inches long, three-sided with one edge rounded off, and tapers from a diameter of 1 inch to a tapering rounded point 1½ inches long, and slightly curved away from the flat face of the foreshaft. It will easily be seen that the shape of this tip facilitates the unshipping of the head. The butt is chamfered off on the flat face to fit the chamfer of the shaft, and the whole foreshaft is slightly curved in the same direction as the tip. It is secured to the shaft by a stout whipping of seal thong. The head is 7 inches long, and has a body of walrus ivory, which is ornamented with incised patterns colored red with ocher, and a blade of dark reddish brown jasper, neatly flaked. This blade is not unlike a large arrow head, being triangular, with curved edges, and a short, broad tang imbedded in the tip of the body, which is seized round with sinew braid. The body is unusually long and slender and is four sided, with a single long, sharp barb, keeled on the outer face. The line hole and line grooves are in the usual position, but the peculiarity of the head is that the blade is inserted with its breadth in the plane of the body barb. In other words, this head has not reached the last stage in the development of the

3/8

FIG. 231.—Model of whale harpoon with floats.   toggle-head. The line is of stout thong (the skin of the bearded seal) and about 8½ feet long. It is passed through the line hole, doubled in the middle, the two parts are firmly stopped together with sinew in four places, and in the ends are cut long slits for looping on the floats. When the head is fitted on the foreshaft the line is secured to the flat face of the foreshaft by a little stop made of a single strand of sinew, easily broken. About 28 inches from the tip of the shaft the line is doubled forward and the bight stopped to the shaft with six turns of seal thong, so that the line is held in place and yet can be easily de-tached by a straight pull. The ends are then doubled back over the lashing and stopped to the shaft with a single thread of sinew.

Fig. 231 is a toy model of the whale harpoon, No. 56562 [233], 18½ inches long, made of pine and ivory, and shows the manner of attaching the floats, which are little blocks of spruce roughly whittled into the shape of inflated seal-skins. A piece of seal thong 13½ inches long has its ends looped round the neck of the floats and the harpoon-line is looped into a slit in the middle of this line.

Fig. 232.—Flint blade for whale harpoon.

We collected thirteen heads for such harpoons, which have been in actual use, of which two have flint blades like the one described, two have brass blades, and the rest either blades of slate or else no blades. The flint blades are either triangular like the one described or lanceolate and are about 3 inches long exclusive of the tang. The three separate flint blades which we obtained (Fig. 232, No. 56708 [114], from Utkiavwïñ, is one of these, made of black flint) are about 1 inch shorter and were perhaps intended for walrus har-poons, though we saw none of these with flint blades. They are all newly made for the market.

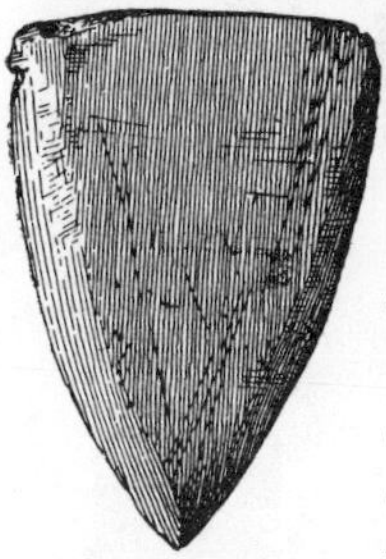

The slate blades of which we collected eleven, some old and some new, besides those in the heads, are all triangular, with curved edges, as in Fig. 233 (No. 56709 [139] from Utkiavwïñ, made of soft purple slate), except one new one, No. 56697a [188a], which has the corners cut off so as to give it a rhomboidal shape. The cor-ners are sometimes rounded off so that they are nearly heart-shaped. These blades are usually about 2¾ inches long and 2 broad; two unusually large ones are 3 inches long and nearly 2¼ broad, and one small one 2·1 by 1·6 inches, and are simply wedged into the blade slit without a rivet. The brass blades are of the same shape.

FIG. 233.—Slate blade for whale harpoon.

The common material for the body seems to have been rather coarse whale's bone, from the rib or jaw. Only two out of the thirteen have ivory bodies, and these are both of the newer brass-bladed pattern. The body is very long and slender, being usually about 8 or 8½ inches long (one is 9¼ inches long) and not over 1½ inches broad at the widest part.

It is always cut off very obliquely at the base, and the part in front of the line hole is contracted to a sort of shank, as in Fig. 234 (No.

89747 [1044]), a head with slate blade (broken) and bone body. This represents a very common form in which the shank is four-sided, while back of the middle the outer face of the barb rises into a ridge, making this part of the body five-sided. The edges of the shank are sometimes rounded off so as to make this part elliptical in section, and all the edges of the body except the keel, on the outer face of the barb, are frequently rounded off as in Fig. 235*a*, No. 89745 [1044], which has a slate blade wedged into the bone body with a bit of old cloth and a wooden wedge. Fig. 235*b*, No. 56602 [157], from Utkiavwĭñ, is a head of the same shape, but has a brass blade and a body of ivory. This blade is wedged in with deer hair, but the other brass-bladed harpoon, No. 56601 [137], has a single rivet of whalebone.

FIG. 234.—Body of whale harpoon head.

The blade slit, and consequently the blade, is always in the plane of the barb, which position, as I have said before, corresponds to the last step but one in the develop-

ment of the harpoon-head. When the blade is of flint and inserted with a tang, the tip of the body is always whipped with sinew braid, as in Fig. 212, No. 89748 [928], from Nuwŭk. This specimen is remarkable as being the only one in the series with a double point to the barb. These bodies are sometimes ornamented with incised lines, in conventional patterns, as shown in the different figures. A short incised mark somewhat resembling an arrow (see above, Fig. 234, No. 89747 [1044]) may have some significance as it is repeated on several of the heads. Harpoon-heads of this peculiar pattern are to be found in the Museum collection from other localities. As we should naturally expect, they have been found at the Diomede Islands, St. Lawrence Island, and Plover Bay. It is very interesting, however, to find a specimen of precisely the same type from Greenland, where the modern harpoons are so different from those used in the west.

FIG. 235.—Whale harpoon heads.

That the line connecting the head with the float line is not always so

long in proportion as represented on the two models is shown by Fig.
236, No. 89744 [969], the only specimen obtained with any part of the
line attached. A piece of stout wal-
rus-hide thong 2 feet long is passed
through the line-hole and doubled
in two equal parts, which are firmly
stopped together with sinew about
2 inches from the head. Another
piece of similar thong 4 feet 2 inches
long is also doubled into two equal
parts and the ends firmly spliced to
those of the short piece thus: The
two ends of the long piece are slit
and one end of the short piece passed
through each slit. One of these ends
is then slit and through it are passed
the other end of the short piece and
the bight of the
long piece, and all
is drawn taut and
securely seized
with sinew. The
becket thus

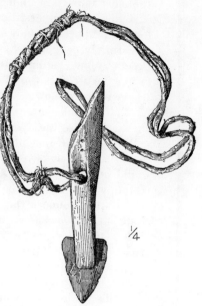

FIG. 236.—Whale harpoon head with "leader."

formed was probably looped directly into the bight of
the float line.

The foreshaft is much larger than that of the model,
though of the same shape. No. 56537 [97], Fig. 237,
from Utkiavwĭñ, is of walrus-ivory and 15.8 inches
long with a diameter of 1½ inches at the butt. The
oblong slot at the beginning of the chamfer is to
receive the end of the lashing which secured this to
the shaft. This form of foreshaft is very well adapted
to insure the unshipping of the toggle-head, but lacks
the special advantage of the loose-shaft, namely, that
under a violent lateral strain it unships without breaking. The question at once suggests itself, why was
not the improvement that is used on all the other
harpoons applied to this one? In my opinion, the
reason for this is the same as for retaining the form
of toggle-head, which, as I have shown, is of an ancient pattern.

That is to say, the modern whale harpoon is the
same pattern that was once used for all harpoons,
preserved for superstitious reasons. It is a well
known fact, that among many peoples implements,
ideas, and language have been preserved in connection with religious

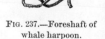

FIG. 237.—Foreshaft of
whale harpoon.

ceremonies long after they have gone out of use in every-day life. Now, the whale fishing at Port Barrow, in many respects the most important undertaking in the life of the natives, is so surrounded by superstitious observances, ceremonies to be performed, and other things of the same nature as really to assume a distinctly religious character. Hence, we should naturally expect to find the implements used in it more or less archaic in form. That this is the case in regard to the toggle-head I think I have already shown. It seems to me equally evident that this foreshaft, which contains the loose shaft and foreshaft, undifferentiated, is also the older form.

Why the development of the harpoon was arrested at this particular stage is not so easily determined. A natural supposition would be that this was the form of harpoon used by their ancestors when they first began to be successful whalemen.

That they connect the idea of good luck with these ancient stone harpoons is shown by what occurred at Point Barrow in 1883. Of late years they have obtained from the ships many ordinary "whale-irons," and some people at least had got into the habit of using them.

Now, the bad luck of the season of 1882, when the boats of both villages together caught only one small whale, was attributed to the use of these "irons," and it was decided by the elders that the *first* harpoon struck into the whale must be a stone-bladed one such as their forefathers used when they killed many whales.

In this connection, it is interesting to note a parallel custom observed at Point Hope. Hooper[1] says that at this place the beluga must always be struck with a *flint* spear, even if it has been killed by a rifle shot.

Lances.—As I have said on a preceding page, some of the natives now use bomb-guns for dispatching the harpooned whale, and all the whaleboats are provided with steel whale lances obtained from the ships. In former times they used a large and powerful lance with a broad flint head. They seem to have continued the use of this weapon, probably for the same reasons that led them to retain the ancient harpoon for whaling until they obtained their present supply of steel lances, as we found no signs of iron whale lances of native manufacture, such as are found in Greenland and elsewhere. We obtained nine heads for stone lances (kaluwiɐ) and one complete lance, a very fine specimen (No. 56765 [537], Fig. 238), which was brought down as a present from Nuwŭk. The broad, sharp head is of light gray flint, mounted on a shaft of spruce 12 feet 6 inches long. It has a broad, stout tang inserted in the cleft end of the

FIG. 238.—Whale lan

---

[1] Corwin Report, p. 41.

shaft. The shaft is rhomboidal in section with rounded edges, and tapers from a breadth of 2 inches and a thickness of 1 at the tip to a butt of 0·7 inch broad and 1 thick. The tip of the shaft has a whipping of sinew-braid 1¾ inches deep, "kackled" down on both edges, one end of the twine on each edge, so that the hitch made by one end crosses the round turn of the other, making in all twenty-six turns. The shaft has been painted red for 1½ inches below the whipping.

No. 89596 [1032] is the head and 5 inches of the shaft of a similar lance. The head is of black flint, and the sinew-braid forms a simple whipping. The remaining heads are all unmounted. I have figured several of them to show the variations of this now obsolete weapon. Fig. 239, No. 56677 [49], from Utkiavwĭñ, is of gray flint chipped in large flakes. The total length is 6·9 inches. The small lugs on the edges of the tang are to keep it from slipping out of the whipping. No. 56679 [239], also from Utkiavwĭñ, is of black flint and broader than the preceding. Its length is 6·3 inches. No. 56680 [394], from the same village, is of light bluish gray flint and very broad. It

½

FIG. 239.—Flint head of whale lance.

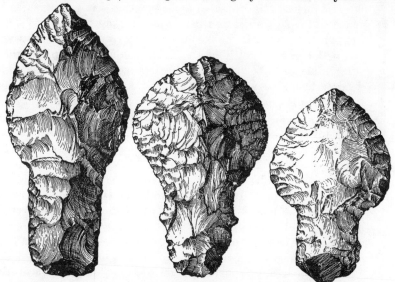

FIG. 240.—Flint heads for whale lances.

is 5·4 inches long. No. 56681 [5], from Utkiavwĭñ, is another broad

9 ETH——16

head of black flint, 6 inches long. Fig. 240a, No. 89597 [1034], from
Nuwŭk, is of black flint, and unusually long in proportion, running into
the tang with less shoulder than usual. Much of the original
surface is left untouched on one face. This is probably very old.
No. 89598 [1361] is a head of similar shape of dark gray flint from
Sidaru. It is 6 inches long. Fig. 240b, No. 89599 [1373], from
the same place and of similar material, is shaped very like the
head of a steel lance. It is 5 inches long. Fig. 240c, No. 89600
[1069], from Utkiavwĭñ, is still broader in proportion and almost
heart-shaped. It is of bluish gray flint and 4·8 inches long.
These heads probably represent most of the different forms in
use. Only two types are to be recognized among them, the long-
pointed oval with a short tang, and the broad leaf-shaped head
with a rather long tang, which appears to be the commoner form.

We obtained one newly made lance of a pattern similar to the
above, but smaller, which was said to be a model
of the weapon used in attacking the polar bear
before the introduction of firearms. The name,
pû′nnû, is curiously like the name panna given
by Dr. Simpson and Capt. Parry to the large
double-edged knife. The specimen, No. 89895
[1230], Fig. 241, came from Utkiavwĭñ. It has a
head of gray flint 3½ inches long, exclusive of the
tang, roughly convex on one face, but flat and
merely beveled at the edges on the other. The
edges are finely serrate. The shaft is of spruce,
6 feet 8 inches long, rounded and somewhat flattened at the tip, which is 1 inch wide and tapering to a diameter of 0·7 at the butt, and is painted
red with ocher. The tip has a slight shoulder to keep the whipping in place. The tang is wedged in with bits of leather and
secured by a close whipping of sinew braid 1¼ inches deep. Fig.
242, No. 89611 [1034], from Nuwŭk, was probably the head of such
a lance, although it is somewhat narrower and slightly shorter.
Its total length is 3·4 inches. The other two large lance-heads,
No. 56708a [114a] and No. 56708b [114b], are both new, but were
probably meant for the bear lance. They are of gray flint, 3½
inches long, and have the edges regularly serrate.

One form of lance is still in general use. It has a sharp metal
head, and a light wooden shaft about 6 feet long. It is used in
the kaiak for stabbing deer swimming in the water, after the
manner frequently noticed among other Eskimo.[1] A pair of
these spears is carried in beckets on the forward deck of the
kaiak. On approaching a deer one of them is slipped out of the
becket and laid on the deck, with the butt resting on the combing of

FIG. 242.—Flint
head for bear lance.

½

FIG. 241.—
Bear
lance.

½/12

---

[1] Parry, 2d Voy., p. 512 (Iglulik); Kumlien, Contributions, p. 54 (Cumberland Gulf); Schwatka,
Science, vol. 4, No. 98, p. 544 (King Williams Land).

the cockpit. The hunter then paddles rapidly up alongside of the deer, grasps the lance near the butt, as he would a dagger, and stabs the animal with a quick downward thrust. This spear is called kă′pun, which in the Point Barrow dialect exactly corresponds to the Greenlandic word kapût, which is applied to the long-bladed spear or long knife used for dispatching a harpooned seal.[1] The word kă′pun means simply "an instrument for stabbing."

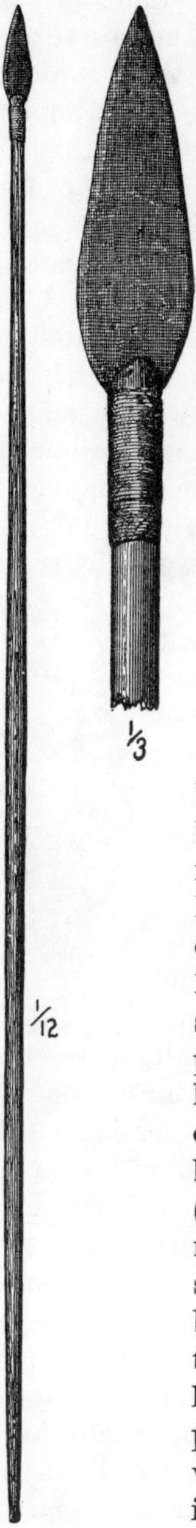

No. 73183 [524], Figs. 243a, 243b (head enlarged), will serve as a type of this weapon, of which we have two specimens. All that we saw were essentially like this. The head is iron, 4¾ inches long exclusive of the tang, and 1½ inches broad. The edges are narrowly beveled on both faces. The shaft is 6 feet 2 inches long, and tapers from a diameter of 0·8 inch about the middle to about one-half inch at each end. The tip is cleft to receive the tang of the head, and shouldered to keep the whipping from slipping off. The latter was of sinew braid and 2 inches deep. The shaft is painted with red ocher.

The other has a shaft 6 feet 4 inches long, but otherwise resembles the preceding. The heads for these lances are not always made of iron. Copper, brass, etc., are sometimes used. No. 56699 [166] is one of a pair of neatly made copper lance heads. It is 5·9 inches long and 1½ wide, and ground down on each face to a sharp edge without a bevel, except just at the point. Before the introduction of iron these lances had stone heads, but were otherwise of the same shape. Fig. 244 represents the head and 6 inches of the shaft of one of these (No. 89900 [1157] from Nuwŭk). The shaft is new and rather carelessly made of a rough, knotty piece of spruce, and is 5 feet 5¾ inches long. The head is of black flint and 2 inches long, exclusive of the tang, and the tip of the shaft is whipped with a narrow strip of light-colored whalebone, the end of which is secured by passing it through a slit in the side of the shaft and wedging it into a crack on the opposite side. This is an old head newly mounted for the market, and the head is wedged in with a bit of blue flannel.

⅓

1/12

FIG. 243.—Deer lance.

FIG. 244.—Part of deer lance, with flint head.

½

No. 89897 [1324], Fig. 245, from Utkiavwĭñ, on the other hand, is an old shaft 5 feet 7½ inches long, fitted with a new head, which is very broad, and shaped like the head of a bear lance. It is of variegated

---

[1] Crantz, vol. 1, p. 147, Pl. v, Fig. 5; and Kane, 1st Grinnell Exp., p. 479 (fig. at bottom).

jasper, brown and gray, and has a piece of white sealskin lapped over the cleft of the shaft at each side of the tang so that the edges of the two pieces almost meet in the middle. They are secured by a spaced whipping of sinew braid. This shaft, which is painted red, evidently had a broad head formerly, as it is expanded at the tip. No. 89896 [1324] is the mate to this, evidently made to match it. We also obtained one other flint-headed lance. The mate to No. 89900 [1157], No. 89898 [1157], has a head of dark gray slate 2·3 inches long. This spear appears to be wholly old, except the whipping of sinew braid. The shaft is of spruce, 5 feet 4¾ inches long, and painted red with ocher. We also collected three stone heads for such lances. Fig. 246, No. 38711 [148], from Utkiavwiñ, shows the shape of the tang. It is of gray flint, and 3·7 inches long. No. 89610 [1154] is a beautiful lance head of polished olive green jade, 4·3 inches long. The hole in the tang is probably not intended for a rivet, as none of the lance heads which we saw were fastened in this way. It is more likely that it was perforated for attaching it to the belt as an amulet. We were told that this lance head was brought from the west. A large slate lance head found by Nordenskiöld[1] in the old "Onkilon" house at North Cape is of precisely the same shape as these deer-lance heads, but from its size was probably intended for a whale lance.

THROWING WEAPONS.

The only throwing weapon which these people use is a small bolas, designed for catching birds on the wing. This consists of six or seven small ivory balls, each attached to a string about 30 inches long, the ends of which are fastened together to a tuft of feathers, which serves as a handle and perhaps directs the flight of the missile. When not in use the strings are shortened up, as in Fig. 247, No. 75969 [1793], for convenience in carrying and to keep them from tangling, by tying them into slip knots, as follows: All the strings being straightened out and laid parallel to each other, they are doubled in a bight, with the end under the standing part, the bight of the end passed through the preceding bight, which is drawn up close, and so on, usually five or six times, till the strings are sufficiently shortened. A pull on the two ends slips all these knots and the strings come out straight and untangled.

The bolas is carried knotted up in a pouch slung round the neck, a native frequently carrying several sets. When a flock of ducks is seen approaching, the handle is grasped in the right

FIG. 245.—Deer lance, flint head.

FIG. 246.—Flint head for deer lance.

½

1/12

[1] Vega, vol. 1, p. 444, Fig. 7.

hand, the balls in the left, and the strings are straightened out with a quick pull.   Letting go with the left hand the balls are whirled round the head and let fly at the passing flock.   The balls spread apart in flying through the air, so as to cover considerable space, like a charge of shot, and if they are stopped by striking a duck, the strings immediately wrap around him and hamper his flight so that he comes to the ground.   The natives said that the balls flew with sufficient force to stun a duck or break his wing, but we never happened to see any taken except in the way just described.   A duck is occasionally left with sufficient freedom of motion to escape with the bolas hanging to him.   The weapon is effective up to 30 or 40 yards, but the natives often throw it to a longer distance, frequently missing their aim.   It is universally employed, especially by those who have no guns, and a good many ducks are captured with it.   In the spring, when the

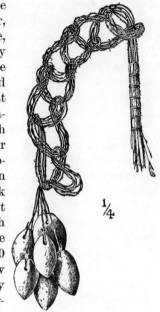

FIG. 247.—Bird bolas, looped up for carrying.

ducks are flying, the women and children hardly ever stir out of the house without one or more of these.

We brought home one specimen of this implement (kelaui̯-tau′ti̯n), No. 75969 [1793], Fig. 248, which is new and has the balls rather carelessly made.   The balls, which are six in number, are of walrus ivory, 1·6 to 1·8 inches long and 1 inch in diameter (except one which is flattened, 2 inches long and 1·3 wide; they are usually all of the same shape).   Through the larger end is drilled a small hole, the ends of which are joined by a shallow groove running over the end, into which the ends of the strings are fastened by three half-hitches each.   There is one string of sinew braid to each set of two balls, doubled in the middle so that all six parts are equal and about 28 inches long.   They are fastened to the feather handle as follows: Nine wing feathers of the eider duck are laid side by side, butt to point, and doubled in the middle so that the quills and vanes stand up on all sides.   The middle of each string is laid across the bight of the feathers, so that the six parts come out on all sides between the feathers.   The latter are then lashed tightly together with a bit of sinew braid, by passing the end over the bend of the feathers and tying with the rest of the string round the feathers.

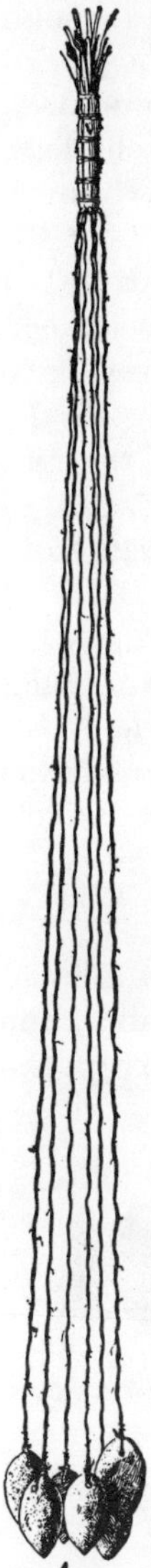

FIG. 248.—Bird bolas, ready for use.

These weapons are generally very much like the specimen described, but vary somewhat in the shape and material of the balls, which are sometimes simply ovoid or spherical, and often made of single teeth of the walrus, instead of tusk ivory. Bone is also sometimes used. In former times, the astragalus bones of the reindeer, perforated through the ridge on one end were used for balls. No. 89490 [1342], is a pair of such bones tied together with a bit of thong, which appear to have been actually used. No. 89537 [1251] from Utkiavwĭñ is a very old ball, which is small (1·1 inches long) and unusually flat. It appears to have been kept as a relic.

There is very little information to be found concerning the extent of the region in which this implement is used, either in the Museum col lections or in the writings of authors. A few points, however, have been made out with certainty. The bolas are unknown among all the Eskimo east of the Anderson River, and the only evidence that we have of their use at this point is an entry in the Museum catalogue, to which I have been unable to find a corresponding specimen. Dease and Simpson, in 1837, did not observe them till they reached Point Barrow.[1] They were first noticed by Beechey at Kotzebue Sound in 1826.[2] Mr. Nelson's collections show that they are used from Point Barrow along the Alaskan coast, at least as far south as the Yukon delta, and on St. Lawrence Island, while for their use on the coast of Siberia as far as Cape North, we have the authority of Nordenskiöld,[3] and the Krause Brothers.[4]

HUNTING IMPLEMENTS OTHER THAN WEAPONS.

Floats.—I have already spoken of the floats (apotû′kpûñ) of inflated sealskin used in capturing the whale and walrus. We obtained one specimen, No. 73578 [538] Fig. 249. This is the whole skin, except the

¹⁄₁₂

FIG. 249.—Seal skin float.

head, of a male rough seal (Phoca fœtida), with the hair out. The car cass was carefully removed without making any incision except round the neck and a few inches down the throat, and skinned to the very

---

¹ T. Simpson's Narrative, p. 156.

² Voyage, p. 574.

³ Vega, vol. 2, p. 109, and Fig. 3, p. 105.

⁴ Geographische Blätter, vol. 5, pt. 1, p. 32. See also Rosse, Arctic Cruise of the Corwin, p. 34.

toes, leaving the claws on. All natural or accidental apertures are care
fully sewed up, except the genital opening, into which is inserted a ring
of ivory, which serves as a mouthpiece for inflating the skin and is
corked with a plug of wood. The cut in the throat is carefully sewed
up, and the neck puckered together, and wrapped with seal thong into
a slender shank about 1 inch long, leaving a flap of skin which is wrapped
round a rod of bone 4 inches long and 1 in diameter, set across the
shank, and wound with thong. This makes a handle for looping on the
harpoon line.

All the floats used at Point Barrow are of the same general pattern
as this, and are generally made of the skin of the rough seal,
though skins of the harbor seal (P. vitulina) are sometimes used.
One of these floats is attached to the walrus harpoon, but two are used
in whaling.[1] Five or six floats are carried in each boat, and are inflated
before starting out. I have seen them used for seats during a halt on
the ice, when the boat was being taken out to the "lead." The use of
these large floats is not peculiar to Point Barrow. They are employed
by all Eskimo who pursue the larger marine mammals.

Flipper toggles.—We collected two pairs of peculiar implements, in
the shape of ivory whales about 5 inches long, with a perforation in the
belly through which a large thong could be attached. We understood
that they were to be fastened to the ends of a stout thong and used
when a whale was killed to toggle his flippers together so as to keep
them in place while towing him to the ice, by cutting holes in the flippers and passing the ivory through. We unfortunately never had an
opportunity of verifying this story. Neither pair is new. Fig. 250a
represents a pair of these implements (kǎ′gotĭñ) (No. 56580 [227]).
They are of white walrus ivory. In the middle of each belly is excavated a deep, oblong cavity about three-fourths of an inch long and one-
half wide, across the middle of which is a stout transverse bar for the
attachment of the line. One is a "bow-head" whale (Balæna mysticetus), 4½ inches long, and the other evidently intended for a "California gray" (Rhachinectes glaucus). It has light blue glass beads
inserted for eyes and is the same length as the other.

Fig. 250 (No. 56598 [407]) is a similar pair, which are both "bowheads"
nearly 5 inches long. Both have cylindrical plugs of ivory inserted for
eyes, and are made of a piece of ivory so old that the surface is a light
chocolate color. The name, kǎgotĭñ, means literally "a pair of toggles."

Harpoon boxes (u′dlun or u′blun, literally "a nest.")—The slate harpoon
blades already described were very apt to be lost or broken, so they
always carried in the boat a supply of spare blades. These were kept
in a small box carved out of a block of soft wood, in the shape of the
animal to be pursued.

---

[1] I learn from our old interpreter, Capt. E. P. Herendeen, who has spent three years in whaling at
Point Barrow since the return of the expedition, that a third float is also used. It is attached by a
longer line than the others, and serves as a sort of "telltale," coming to the surface some time ahead
of the whale.

Fig. 251a represents one of these boxes (No. 56505 [138]) intended for spare blades for the whale harpoon. This is rather neatly carved from a single block of soft wood, apparently spruce, though it is very old and much weathered, in the shape of a "bowhead" whale, 9½ inches long. The ends of the flukes are broken short off, and show traces of having been mended with wooden pegs or dowels. The right eye is indicated by a simple incision, but a tiny bit of crystal is inlaid for the left. Two little bits of crystal are also inlaid in the middle of the back. The belly is flat and excavated into a deep triangular cavity, with its base just forward of the angle of the mouth and the apex at the

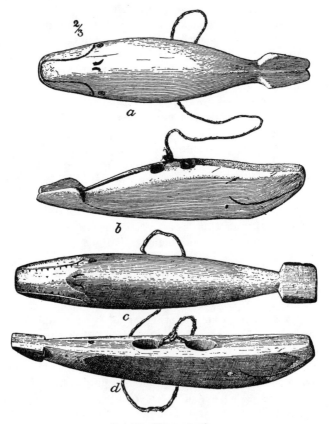

FIG. 250.—Flipper toggles.

"small." It is beveled round the edge, with a shoulder at the base and apex, and is covered with a flat triangular piece of wood beveled on the under face to fit the edge of the cavity. About half of one side of the cover has been split off and mended on with two "stitches" of whalebone fiber. The cover is held on by three strings of seal thong passing through holes in each corner of the cover and secured by a knot in the end of each string. They then pass through three corresponding holes in the bottom of the cavity, leaving outside of the back two ends 7 inches and one 15 long, which are tied together. The cover can be lifted wholly off and then drawn back into its place by pulling the string.

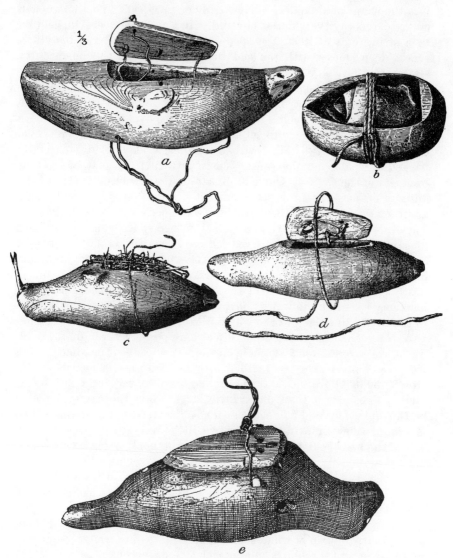

FIG. 251.—Boxes for harpoon heads.

We collected seven such whale-harpoon boxes, usually about 9 to $9\frac{3}{4}$ inches long. Nearly all have bits of crystal, amber, or pyrite, inlaid for the eyes and in the middle of the back, and the cover is generally rigged in the way described. No. 56502 [198], from Utkiavwïñ, is a large whale, a foot long, and has the tail bent up, while the animal is usually represented as if lying still. It has good-sized sky-blue beads inlaid for the eyes.

Fig. 251b (No. 89733 [1161], from Nuwŭk) represents a small box 4⅓ inches long, probably older than the others, and the only one not carved into the shape of a whale. It is roughly egg-shaped and has no wooden cover to the cavity, which is covered with a piece of deerskin, held on by a string of seal thong wrapped three times around the body in a rough, deep groove, with the end tucked under. In this box are five slate blades for the whale harpoon.

We also collected two boxes for walrus harpoons made in the shape of the walrus, with ivory or bone tusks. No. 89732 [860], Fig. 251c, from Nuwŭk, is old, and 7 inches long, and has two oval bits of ivory, with holes bored to represent the pupils, inlaid for the eyes. There is no cover, but the cavity is filled with a number of slate blades, carefully packed in whalebone shavings. There is a little eyebolt of ivory at each end of the cavity. One end of a bit of sinew braid is tied to the anterior of these, and the other carried down through the hinder one, and then brought up and fastened round the body with a marling hitch. The other (No. 56489 [127], is new and rather roughly made, 5 inches long and painted all over with red ocher. It has a cover, but no strings.

No. 56501 [142], Fig. 251d, from Utkiavwĭñ, is for carrying harpoon blades for the chase of the bearded seal (Erignathus barbatus), and is neatly carved into the shape of that animal. It is 7·4 inches long and has ivory eyes like the walrus box, No. 89732 [860]. The cover is fitted to the cavity like those of the whale boxes, but is held on by one string only, a piece of seal thong about 3 feet long passing through the middle of the cover and out at a hole on the left side, about one-fourth inch from the cavity. The box is filled with raveled rope-yarns. Fig. 251e (No. 89730 [981], from Utkiavwĭñ) is like this, but very large, 9·3 inches long. The cover is thick and a little larger than the cavity, beveled on the upper face and notched on each side to receive the string, which is a bit of sinew braid fastened to two little ivory hooks, one on each side of the body. It is fastened to the right hook, carried across and hooked around the left-hand one, then carried over and hooked round the other, and secured by tucking a bight of the end under the last part. The box contains several slate blades. We also collected one other large seal box (No. 89731 [859], from Nuwŭk), very roughly carved, and 9·8 inches long. The cover is fitted into the cavity and held on by a narrow strip of whalebone running across in a transverse groove in the cover and through a hole in each side of the box.

Nets (*ku'bra*).—The smaller seals are captured in large-meshed nets of rawhide. We brought home one of these, No. 56756 [109], Figs 252a–252b (detail of mesh). This is a rectangular net, eighteen meshes long and twelve deep, netted of fine seal thong with the ordinary netting knot. The length of the mesh is 14 inches.

Such nets are set under the ice in winter, or in shoal water along the shore by means of stakes in summer. In the ordinary method of setting the net under the ice two small holes are cut through the ice the length of the net apart, and between them in the same straight line is cut a third

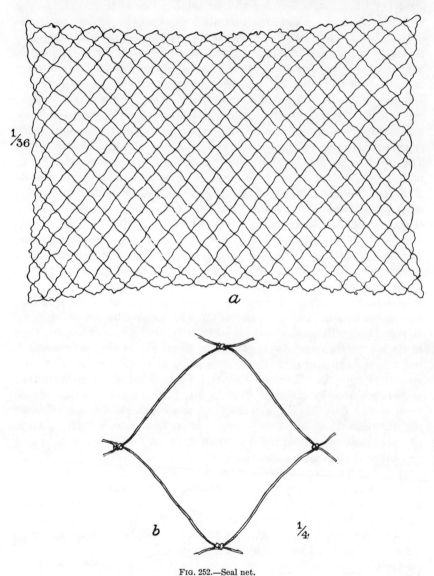

FIG. 252.—Seal net.

large enough to permit a seal to be drawn up through it. A line with a plummet on the end is let down through one of the small holes, and is hooked through the middle hole, with a long slender pole of willow, often made of several pieces spliced together, with a small wooden hook on the end. The line is then detached from the plummet and fastened to one upper corner of the net, and a second line is let down through the other small hole and made fast in the same way to the other upper corner. By pulling on these lines the net is drawn down through the middle and stretched like a curtain under the ice, while a line at the middle serves to haul it up again. The end lines are but loosely made fast to lumps of ice, so that when a seal strikes the net nothing hinders his wrapping it completely around him in his struggles to escape. When the hunter, who is usually watching his net, thinks the seal is sufficiently entangled he hauls him up through the large hole and sets the net again.

I had no opportunity of observing whether any weights or plummets were used to keep down the lower edge of the net. These nets are now universally employed, but one native spoke of a time "long ago" when there were no nets and they captured seals with the spear (u'nɐ) alone. The net was used in seal catching in Dr. Simpson's time, though he makes but a casual reference to it,[1] and Beechey found seal nets at Kotzebue Sound in 1826.[2] The net is very generally used for sealing among the Eskimo of western America and in Siberia. We observed seal nets set with stakes along the shore of the sandspit at Plover Bay, and Nordenskiöld speaks of seal nets " set in summer among the ground ices along the shore,"[3] and at open leads in the winter, but gives no description of the method of setting these nets beyond mentioning the "long pole which was used in setting the net,"[4] as none of his party ever witnessed the seal fishery.[5] I am informed by Mr. W. H. Dall that the winter nets in Norton Sound are not set under the ice as at Point Barrow, but with stakes in shoal water wherever there are open holes in the ice. "Ice nets" are spoken of as in use for sealing in Greenland, but I have been able to find no description of them. As they are not spoken of by either Egede or Crantz I am inclined to believe that they were introduced by the Europeans.[6] Mr. L. M. Turner informs me that such is the case at Ungava Bay on the southern shore of Hudson Strait, where they use a very long net set under the ice very much as at Point Barrow. I can find no mention of the use of seal nets among any other of the eastern Eskimo.

It is well known that seals have a great deal of curiosity, and are easily attracted by any unusual sounds, especially if they are gentle and long-continued. It is therefore easy to entice them into the nets by making such noises, for instance, gentle whistling, rattling on the ice with the pick, and so forth. Two special implements are also used for this purpose. The first kind I have called:

---

[1] Op. cit., p. 262.

[2] Voyage, pp. 295, 574.

[3] Vega, vol. 2, p. 108.

[4] Ibid., p. 98.

[5] See also the reference to Hooper's Corwin Report, quoted below under Hunting.

[6] See, however, the writer's paper in the American Anthropologist, vol. 1, p. 333.

Seal calls (adrigautĭn).—This implement consists of three or four claws mounted on the end of a short wooden handle, and is used to make a gentle noise by scratching on the ice. It is a common implement, though I never happened to see it in use. We obtained six specimens, of which No. 56555 [90] Fig. 253*a*, is the type. It is 11½ inches long. The round handle is of ash, the claws are those of the bearded seal, secured by a lashing of sinew braid, with the end brought down on the under side to a little blunt, backward-pointing hook of ivory, set into the wood about 1 inch from the base of the arms.

Fig. 253*b* (No. 56557 [93] from Utkiavwĭñ) is 9½ inches long and has four prongs. The haft is of spruce, and instead of an ivory hook there is a round-headed stud of the same material, which is driven wholly through the wood, having the point cut off flush with the upper sur-

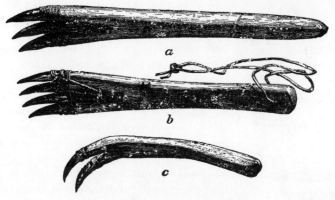

FIG. 253.—Scratchers for decoying seals.

face. It has a lanyard of seal twine knotted into the hole in the haft. The other two specimens of this pattern, Nos. 56556 [100] and 56558 [51] have each three claws, and hafts of soft wood, painted with red ocher, with lanyards, and are respectively 10·4 and 10·7 inches long. One has an ivory hook, but the other in place of this has a small iron nail, and is ornamented with a medium-sized sky-blue glass bead inlaid in the back. The other two are both new and small, being respectively 7·5 and 7·6 inches long. The hafts are made of reindeer antler and have only two prongs. No. 89467 [1312] from Utkiavwĭñ, has the haft notched on each side, and has an irregular stud of bone for securing the lashing.

No. 89468 [1354], Fig. 253*c*, from Utkiavwĭñ, has no stud and the claws are simply held on by a slight lashing of twisted sinew. Both of these were made for the market, but may be models of a form once used. There are two old seal calls in the Museum from near St. Michaels, made of a piece of reindeer antler, apparently the spreading brow antler, in which the sharp points of the antler take the place of claws.

The use of this implement, as shown by Mr. Nelson's collection, extends or extended from Point Barrow to Norton Sound. He collected specimens from St. Lawrence Island and Cape Wankarem in Siberia. Nordenskiöld speaks of the use of this implement at Pitlekaj and figures a specimen.[1] The other instrument appears to be less common. I have called it a seal rattle.

Seal rattle.—We obtained only two specimens, No. 56533 [409], which seem to be a pair. Fig. 254 is one of these. It is of cottonwood and 4 inches long, roughly carved into the shape of a seal's head and painted red, with two small transparent blue glass beads inlaid for the eyes. The neat becket of seal thong consists of three or four turns with the end wrapped spirally around them. The staple on which the ivory

FIG. 254.—Seal rattle.

pendants hang is of iron. This is believed to be a rattle to be shaken on the ice by a string tied to the becket for the purpose of attracting seals to the ice net. It was brought in for sale at a time during our first year when we were very busy with zoological work, and as something was said about "nĕtyĭ" and "kubra" ("seal" and "net") the collector concluded that they must be floats for seal nets, and they were accordingly catalogued as such and laid away. We never happened to see another specimen, and as these were sent home in 1882 we learned no more of their history. The late Dr. Emil Bessels, however, on my return called my attention to the fact that in the museum at Copenhagen there is a single specimen very similar to these, which was said to have been used in the manner described above. It came from somewhere in eastern America. There is one, he told me, in the British Museum from Bering Strait. The National Museum contains several specimens collected by Mr. Nelson at Point Hope. It is very probable that this is the correct explanation of the use of these objects, as it assigns a function to the ivory pendants which would otherwise be useless. They have been called "dog bells," but the Eskimo, at Point Barrow, at least, are not in the habit of marking their dogs in any way.

Seal indicators.—When watching for a seal at his breathing hole a native inserts in the hole a slender rod of ivory, which is held loosely in place by a cross piece or a bunch of feathers on the end. When the seal rises he pushes up this rod, which is so light that he does not notice it, and thus warns the hunter when to shoot or strike with his spear. Most of the seal hunting was done at such a distance from the station that I remember only one occasion when this implement was

---

[1] Vega, vol. 2, p, 117, Fig. 3.

seen in use. We collected two specimens, of which No. 56507 [104], Fig. 255*a*, will serve as the type. It is of walrus ivory, 14½ inches long and 0·3 in diameter, with a small lanyard of sinew. The curved cross piece of ivory, 1⅓ inches long, is inserted into a slot one-fourth of an inch from the end and secured by a little treenail of wood.

Fig. 255*b* (No. 89454 [1114], from Nuwŭk) is a similar indicator, 13½ inches long and flat (0·3 inch wide and 0·1 thick). The upper end is carved into scallops for ornament and has a small eye into which

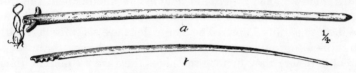

FIG. 255.—Seal indicators.

was knotted a bit of whalebone fiber. The tip is beveled off with a concave bevel on both faces to a sharp edge, so that it can be used for a "feather setter" (ĭgugwau) in feathering arrows. Such implements are mentioned in most popular accounts of the Eskimo of the east, and Capt. Parry describes it from personal observation at Iglulik.[1] I have been unable to find any mention of its use in western America, and have seen no specimens in the National Museum.

Sealing stools.—When a native is watching a seal-hole he frequently has to stand for hours mo-
tionless on the ice. His feet would become exceedingly cold, in spite of the excellence of his foot covering, were it not for a little three-legged stool about 10 inches high upon which he stands. This stool is made of wood, with a triangular top just large enough to accommodate a man's feet, with the heels together over one leg of the stool, and the other two legs supporting the toes of each foot, respectively.

FIG. 256.—Sealing stool.

The stool is neatly made, and is as light as is consistent with strength. It is universally employed and carried by the hunter, slung on the gun cover with the legs projecting behind.

When the hunter has a long time to wait he generally squats down so as almost to sit on his heels, holding his gun and spear in readiness, and wholly covered with one of the deerskin cloaks already described. They sometimes use this stool to sit on when waiting for ducks to fly over the ice in the spring.

---

[1] Second Voyage, p. 510; also pl. opposite p. 550, Fig. 17.

We brought home two specimens of this common object (nĭgawaú-otĭn). No. 89887 [1411], Fig. 250, will serve as the type. The top is of spruce, 8¾ inches long and 10¾ wide. The upper surface is flat and smooth, the lower broadly beveled off on the edges and deeply excavated in the middle, so that there are three straight ridges joining the three legs, each of which stands in the middle of a slight prominence. The object of cutting away the wood in this way is to make the stool lighter, leaving it thick only at the points where the pressure comes. The large round hole in the middle, near the front, is for convenience in picking it up and hanging it on the cache frâme, where it is generally kept. The three legs are set into holes at each corner, spreading out so as to stand on a base larger than the top of the stool. Where they fit into the holes they are 0·7 inch in diameter, tapered slightly to fit the hole, and then tapering down to a diameter of one-third inch at the tip. On the under side of the top they are braced with a lashing of stout seal thong. A split on the right-hand edge of the top has been mended, as usual, with a stitch of whalebone. This stool is quite old and has been actually used.

No. 89888 [1412], from the same village, is new and a little larger, but differs from the type only in having a triangular instead of a round hole in the top and no lashing. Those of our party who landed at Sidaru September 7, 1881, saw one of these stools hanging up in the then vacant village, and there is a precisely similar stool in the Museum from the Anderson region.

MacFarlane, in his manuscript notes, describes the use of these stools as follows: "Both tribes kill seals under ice; that is, they watch for them at their holes (breathing) or wherever open water appears. At the former they generally build a small snow house somewhat like a sentinel's box, on the bottom of which they fix a portable three-cornered stool, made of wood. They stand on this and thereby escape getting cold feet, as would be the case were they to remain for any time on ice or snow in the same immovable position." Beyond this I find no mention of the use of any such a utensil, east or west, except in Greenland, where, however, they used a sort of one-legged chair to sit on, as well as a footstool, which Egede pictures (Pl. 9) as oval, with very short legs.[1]

Seal drags (*uksiu′tiñ.*)—Every seal hunter carries with him a line for dragging home his game, consisting of a stout thong doubled in a bight about 18 inches long, with an ivory handle or knob at the other end. The bight is looped into an incision in the seal's lower jaw, while the knob serves for attaching a longer line or the end of a dog's harness. The seal is dragged on his back and runs as smoothly as a sled. We

---

[1] "They first look out for Holes, which the Seals themselves make with their Claws about the Bigness of a Halfpenny; after they have found any Hole, they seat themselves near it upon a Chair, made for the Purpose; and as soon as they perceive the Seal coming up to the Hole and put his snout into it for some Air, they immediately strike him with a small Harpoon." Egede, Greenland, p. 104.

"The seals themselves make sometimes holes in the Ice, where they come and draw breath; near such a hole a Greenlander seats himself on a stool, putting his feet on a lower one to keep them from the cold. Now when the seal comes and puts its nose to the hole, he pierces it instantly with his harpoon." Crantz, History of Greenland, vol. 1, p. 156.

collected eight of these drag lines, from which I have selected No. 56624 [44], Fig. 257a, as the type.

This consists of a stout thong of rawhide (the skin of the bearded

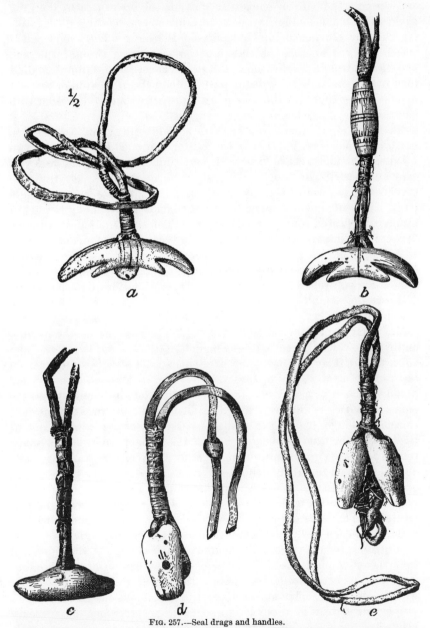

FIG. 257.—Seal drags and handles.

seal) 0·3 inch wide and 37 inches long, and doubled in a bight so that one end is about 2½ inches the longer. These ends are fastened into a handle of walrus ivory, consisting of three pieces, namely: a pair of

9 ETH——17

neatly carved mittens, respectively 1·9 and 1·8 inches long, put together
wrist to wrist with the palms up; and lying across the joint above, a
little seal 1¼ inches long, belly down. A hole runs through each wrist
and through the belly of the seal. The mittens are ornamented on the
back with a blackened incised pattern, and the seal has blue glass beads
for eyes and blackened incised spots on the back. The longer end of
the thong runs up through the right mitten, across through the seal,
and down through the left mitten. It is then passed through a slit 1
inch from the end of the shorter part and slit itself. Through this slit
is passed the bight of the thong, all drawn up taut and seized with
sinew braid.

No. 89467 [755], from Utkiavwĭñ, is a similar drag, put together in
much the same way, but it has the mittens doweled together with two
wooden pins, and a seal's head with round bits of wood inlaid for eyes,
ears, and nostrils, in place of the seal. The longitudinal perforation in
this head shows that it was originally strung lengthwise on one of these
lines. The "double slit splice" of the two ends of the thong is worked
into a complicated round knot, between which and the handle the two
parts of the line are confined by a tube of ivory 1 inch long, ornamented
with deeply incised patterns. Fig. 257b is the upper part of a line (No.
56622 [36], from Utkiavwĭñ), with a similar tube 1¾ inches long, and a
handle carved from a single piece into a pair of mittens like the others.

No. 56625 [81], also from Utkiavwĭñ, is almost exactly similar to the
one first described, but has the seal belly up. Fig. 257c (No. 89470
[1337], from the same village) has a seal 2·3 inches long for the handle,
and No. 56626 [212], from Utkiavwĭñ, is like it. No. 89469a [755a] Fig.
257d, from Utkiavwĭñ, has for a handle the head of a bearded seal 1·6
inches long, neatly carved from walrus ivory, with round bits of wood
inlaid for the eyes and ears. It is perforated longitudinally from the
chin to the back of the head, and a large hole at the throat opens into
this. The longer end of the thong is passed in at the chin and out at
the back of the head; the shorter, in at the back of the head and out at
the throat; the two ends brought together between the standing parts
and all stopped together with sinew braid.

No. 56627 [45], Fig. 257e, has a handle made of two ivory bears' heads,
very neatly carved, with circular bits of wood inlaid for eyes, and perforated like the seal's head just described. The thong is doubled in the
middle and each end passed through one of the heads lengthwise, so as
to protrude about 7 inches. About 4 inches of end is then doubled
over, thrust through the throat hole of the opposite head, and brought
down along the standing parts. All the parts are stopped together
with sinew braid. This makes a small becket above the handle.

We collected seven knobs for these drag lines, of which six are seals'
heads and one a bear's. They are all made of walrus ivory, apparently
each a single tooth, and not a piece of tusk, and are about 1½ inches to
2 inches long. They are generally carved with considerable skill, and

often have the ears, roots of the whiskers, nostrils, and outline of the mouth incised and blackened, while small blue beads, bits of ivory, or wood are inlaid for the eyes. Implements of this sort are in common use among Eskimo generally wherever they are so situated as to be able to engage in seal-hunting. Mr. Nelson's collection contains specimens from as far south as Cape Darby.

Whalebone wolf-killers (ĭsĭbru).—Before the introduction of the steel traps, which they now obtain by trade, these people used a peculiar contrivance for catching the wolf. This consists of a stout rod of whalebone about 1 foot long and one-half inch broad, with a sharp point at each end. One of these was folded lengthwise in the form of a Z,[1] wrapped in blubber (whale's blubber was used, according to our informant, Nĭkawáalu), and frozen solid. It was then thrown out on the snow where the wolf could find and swallow it. The heat of the animal's body would thaw out the blubber, releasing the whalebone, which would straighten out and pierce the walls of the stomach, thus causing the

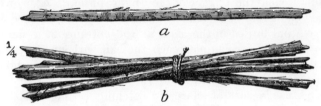

FIG. 258.—Whalebone wolf-killers.

animal's death. Nikawáalu says that a wolf would not go far after swallowing one of these blubber balls.

We collected four sets of these contrivances, one set containing seven rods and the others four each. Fig. 258*a* gives a good idea of the shape of one of these. It belongs to a set of seven, No. 89538 [1229], Fig. 258*b*, from Utkiavwĭñ, which are old and show the marks of having been doubled up. It is 12½ inches long, 0.4 broad, and 0.2 thick. The little notches on the opposite edges of each end were probably to hold a lashing of sinew which kept the folded rod in shape while the blubber was freezing, being cut by thrusting a knife through the partially frozen blubber, as is stated by Schwatka.[2] Two of the sets are new, but made like the others.

This contrivance is also used by the Eskimo of Hudson Bay[3] and at Norton Sound, where, according to Petroff,[4] the rods are 2 feet long and wrapped in seal blubber. The name ĭsĭ'bru appears to be the same as the Greenlandic (isavssok), found only in the diminutive isavssoraĸ, a provincial name for the somewhat similar sharp-pointed stick baited with blubber and used for catching gulls. The diminutive form of this

---

[1] It is twisted into "a compact helical mass like a watch-spring" in the Hudson Bay region. Schwatka, "Nimrod in the North," p. 133. See also Klutschak, "Als Eskimo," pp. 194, 195.

[2] "Nimrod in the North," p. 133.

[3] See Gilder, Schwatka's Search, p. 225; see also, Klutschak, "Als Eskimo," etc., pp. 194–5, where the whalebones are said to have little knives on the ends.

[4] Report, etc., p. 127.

word in Greenlandic may indicate that their ancestors once used the large wolf-killer, when they lived where wolves were found. The definition of uju'kuaĸ, the ordinary word for the gull-catcher (see below)—in the Grønlandske Ordbog—is the only evidence we have of the use of this contrivance in Greenland. This is one of the several cases in which we only learn of the occurrence of customs, etc., noted at Point Barrow, in Greenland, by finding the name of the thing in question defined in the dictionary.

Traps.—Foxes are caught in the winter by deadfalls or steel traps (nänori'a), set generally along the beach, where the foxes are wandering about in search of carrion thrown up by the sea. In setting the deadfalls a little house about 2 feet high is built, in which is placed the bait of meat or blubber. A heavy log of driftwood is placed across the entrance, with one end raised high enough to allow a fox to pass under it, and supported by a regular "figure of four" of sticks. The fox can not get at the bait without passing under the log, and in doing so he must touch the trigger of the "figure of four" (4), which brings down the log across his back. When a steel trap is used it is not baited itself, but buried in the snow at the entrance of a similar little house, so that the fox can not reach the bait without stepping on the plate of the trap and thus springing it. Many foxes are taken with such traps in the course of the winter.

The boys use a sort of snare for catching setting birds. This is simply a strip of whalebone made into a slip-noose, which is set over the eggs, with the end fastened to the ground, so that the bird is caught by the leg. Once or twice, when there was a light snow on the beach, we saw a native catching the large gulls as follows: He had a stick of hard wood, pointed at each end, to the middle of which was fastened one end of a stout string about 6 feet long. The other end was secured to a stake driven into the frozen gravel, and the stick wrapped with blubber and laid on the beach, with the string carefully hidden in the snow. The gull came along, swallowed the lump of blubber, and as soon as he tried to fly away the string made the sharp stick turn like a toggle across his gullet, the points forcing their way through, so that he was held fast. A similar contrivance, but somewhat smaller and made of bone, is used at Norton Sound for catching gulls and murres, a number of them being attached to a trawl line and baited with fish. Mr. Nelson collected a large number of these.[1] In regard to the use of this contrivance in Greenland, see above under "wolf-killers."

Snow-goggles.—The wooden goggles worn to protect the eyes from snow-blindness may be considered as accessories to hunting, as they are worn chiefly by those engaged in hunting or fishing, especially when deer-hunting in the spring on the snow-covered tundra or when in the whaleboats among the ice. They are simply a wooden cover for the

---

[1] See Dr. Rau's Prehistoric Fishing, p. 12. Fig. 2, p. 13, represents one of these from Norton Sound, and Figs. 3–8, a series of similar implements from the bone caves of France.

eyes, admitting the light by a narrow horizontal slit, which allows. only a small amount of light to reach the eye and at the same time gives sufficient range of vision. Such goggles are universally employed by the Eskimos everywhere [1] except in Siberia, where they use a simple shade for the eyes.[2]

We brought home four pairs of these goggles (í'dyĭgûñ), of which No 89894 [1708], Fig. 259, represents the common form. These are of pine wood, 5·8 inches long and 1·1 inches broad, and deeply excavated on the inside, with a narrow horizontal slit with thin edges on each side of the middle. In the middle are two notches to fit the nose, the one in the lower edge deep and rounded, the upper very shallow. The two holes in each end are for strings of sinew braid to pass round the head. They are neatly made and the outside is scraped smooth and shows traces of a coat of red ocher.

The history of this particular pair of goggles is peculiarly interesting. Though differing in no important respect from those used at the present day, they were found on the site of the ancient village of Isû'tkwa, where our station stood, buried at a depth of 27 feet in undisturbed frozen ground, and were uncovered in digging the shaft sunk by Lieut. Ray for obtaining earth temperatures.[3] The layer in which they were found was evidently an old sea beach, consisting of sand and gravel mixed

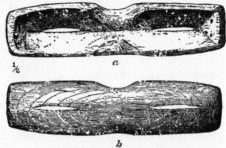

FIG. 259.—Wooden snow goggles.

with broken shells, among which Mya truncata was recognized. The amount of the superincumbent gravel and similar material above this object does not necessarily indicate any very great length of time since they were first buried, as will be readily understood from what I have said above (p. 28) about the rapidity with which high hummocks of gravel are pushed up by the ice. The unbroken layer of turf, however, nearly a foot thick, with which the ground was covered at this point, shows that a considerable period must have elapsed since the gravel had reached nearly to its present level.

The pattern of these goggles is to my mind a very decided proof that at that early date this region was inhabited by Eskimo not essentially different from its present inhabitants. Goggles worn at the present day are almost always of the shape of these, though I remember seeing one pair made in two pieces joined by short strings of beads across the nose. They are, I think, universally painted with red ocher on the outside and

[1] See Parry, 2d Voyage, p. 547, Iglulik and Hudson Strait, pl. opposite p. 548, Fig. 4, and pl. opposite p. 14; Crantz, History of Greenland, vol. 1, p. 234; Dall, Alaska, p. 195, figure (Norton Sound); also MacFarlane, MS., No. 2929 (Anderson River).

[2] Nordenskiöld, Vega, vol. 2, p. 99.

[3] Report U. S. International Polar Expedition to Point Barrow, p. 37.

blackened inside.   They were not always made of wood, as there are two specimens in the collection made of a piece of antler, following the natural curve of the beam, divided longitudinally, with the softer inside tissue hollowed out.

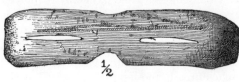

FIG. 260.—Bone snow goggles.

Fig. 260 (No. 89701 [763], from Utkiavwĭñ) represents one of these specimens.   I do not recollect ever seeing goggles of this material in actual use.   No. 89703 [754], Fig. 261, is an unusual pattern, having along the top a horizontal brim about one-half inch high, which serves for an additional shade to the eyes.   Above this are two oblique holes opening into the cavity inside, which are probably for the purpose of ventilation, to prevent the moisture from the skin from being deposited as frost on the inside of the goggles or on the eyelashes.   I do not remember having seen such goggles worn.   Dall figures

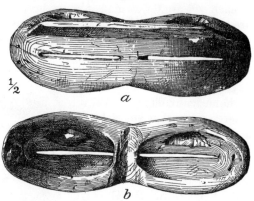

FIG. 261.—Wooden snow goggles, unusual form.

a similar pair from Norton Sound, and those brought by Mr. Turner from Ungava have a similar brim and ventilating holes.   The snow goggles mentioned in Parry's Second Voyage (p. 547) as occasionally seen at Iglulik, but more common in Hudson's Strait, appear to have resembled these, but had a brim 3 or 4 inches deep.

Meat - cache markers.—We purchased a couple of little ivory rods, each with a little bunch of feathers tied to one end, which we were told were used by the deer hunters to mark the place where they had buried the flesh of a deer in the snow.   This implement is called tû′kusia.

FIG. 262.—Marker for meat cache.

Fig. 262, represents one of these (No. 89531 [978] from Nuwŭk).   It is a flat, slender rod of white walrus ivory, 11½ inches long, and evidently broken off at the tip.   The other end is cut into ornamental notches, and ornamented with an incised pattern colored with red ocher, consisting of conventional lines and the figure of a reindeer on each face, a buck on one face and a doe on the other. Tied by a bit of sinew to the uppermost notch are four legs and three wing tips (three or four primaries, with the skin at the base) of the buff-breasted sandpiper (Tryngites subruficollis). This was evidently

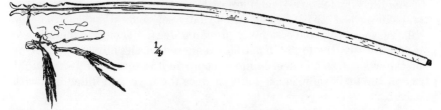

FIG. 263.—Marker for meat cache.

longer when new and perhaps was originally used for a seal indicator (which see above). Fig. 263 (No. 89453 [1581] from Utkiavwïñ) is a similar rod, the tip of which has been brought to an edge so that it can be used as a "feather-setter" in feathering arrows. The remains of two wing tips of some small bird are tied to one of the notches at the upper end.

METHODS OF HUNTING.

Having now described in detail all the weapons and other implements used in hunting, I am prepared to give an account of the time and methods of pursuing the different kinds of game.

The polar bear.—Bears are occasionally met with in the winter by the seal hunters, roaming about the ice fields at some distance from the shore. They usually run from a man and often do not make a stand even when wounded. Occasionally, however, a bear rendered bold by hunger comes in from the sea and makes an attack on some native's storehouse of seal meat even in the midst of the village. Of course, in such a case he has very little chance of escape, as the natives all turn out with their rifles and cut off his retreat. Two bears were killed in this way at Utkiavwïñ in the winter of 1882–'83. The bear is always attacked with the rifle, often with the help of dogs to bring him to bay. The umiaks when walrus hunting sometimes meet with bears among the loose ice. If the bear is caught in the water, there is very little difficulty in paddling up close enough to him to shoot him.

The wolf.—The wolf can hardly be considered a regular object of pursuit. Wolves are often seen and occasionally shot by deer hunters in the winter, and one family in the summer of 1883 managed to catch a couple of young wolf cubs alive, somewhere between Point Barrow and the Colville. These they brought home with them and kept them picketed on the tundra just outside of the village, with a little kennel of snow to shelter them, carefully feeding them till winter, when their fur had grown long enough for use in trimming hoods. They were then killed with a stone-headed arrow, which we were told was necessary for the purpose, and their skins dressed and cut into strips which were sold around the village. Superstition required that the man who killed these wolves should sleep outside of the house in a tent or snow hut for "one moon" after killing them. We did not learn the reason for this practice beyond that it would be "bad" to do otherwise.

The fox.—Foxes are sometimes shot, but are generally taken in the traps described above, which are usually set some distance from the village so as to avoid catching prowling dogs. Though generally exceedingly shy, the fox is sometimes rendered careless by hunger. One of the women at the deer-hunters' camp in the spring of 1882 caught one in the little snow house built to store the meat and killed him with a stick.

The reindeer.—Reindeer are comparatively scarce within the radius of a day's march from Point Barrow, though solitary animals and small parties are to be seen almost any day in the winter a few miles inland from the seacoast. In the autumn, which is the rutting season, they occasionally wander down to the lagoons back of the beach. Nearly every day in the autumn and winter, when the weather is not stormy, one or more natives are out looking for reindeer, usually traveling on snowshoes and carrying their rifles slung on their backs. The deer are generally very wild and often perceive a man and begin to run at a distance of a mile or two, though a rutting buck will sometimes fancy that a skin-clad Eskimo is a rival buck, and come toward him, especially if the hunter crouches down and keeps perfectly still.

The usual method of hunting is to walk off inland until a deer is sighted, when the hunter moves directly toward him at a rapid pace, without regard to the wind or attempting to conceal himself, which would be almost hopeless in such open country. As soon as the deer starts to run, the hunter quickens his pace—to a run, if he has "wind" enough—and follows the game as long as he can keep it in sight, trusting that the well known curiosity of the deer will induce it to "circle" round, in order to see what it is that is following him with such pertinacity. Should the deer turn, as often happens, especially if there is more than one of them, the hunter alters his course so as to head him off, and as soon as he gets within long rifle range opens fire, and keeps it up till the animal is hit or escapes out of range. Strange as it may seem, a number of deer are killed every winter in this way.

If a deer be killed, the hunter usually "butchers" him on the spot, and brings in as much of the meat as he can carry on his back, leaving the rest, carefully covered with slabs of snow to protect it from the foxes, to be brought in as soon as convenient by a dog sled, which follows the hunter's tracks to the place.

During the spring the deer retire some distance from the Point, and the does then drop their fawns. At this season nearly all the natives are busily engaged in the whale fishery, and pay little attention to the reindeer, so that we did not learn where they went to. When the fawns are perhaps a month old a small party, say a young man and his wife, sometimes makes a short journey to the eastward to procure fawn skins for clothing. They say that the fawns at this age can be caught by running them down. During the summer again the deer come down to the coast in small numbers, taking to the water in the lagoons, or even in the sea, when the flies become troublesome.

Sometimes in warm, calm weather the flies are so numerous that the deer is driven perfectly frantic, and runs along without looking where he is going, so that, as the natives say, a hunter who places himself in the deer's path has no difficulty in shooting him. Flies were unusually scarce both summers that we were at the station, so that we never had an opportunity of seeing this done. When a deer is seen swimming he is pursued with the kaiak and lanced in the manner already described. In July, 1883, one man from Utkiavwïñ made a short journey inland, "carrying" his kaiak from lake to lake, and killed two deer in this way without firing a shot. I believe this method of hunting is frequently practiced by the parties who go east for trading in the summer, and those who visit the rivers for the purpose of hunting.

The natives seemed to expect deer in summer at the lagoons, as along the isthmus between Imê'kpûñ and Imêkpûnïglu they had set up a range of stakes, evidently intended to turn the deer up the beach where he would be seen from the camp at Pernijû. Only one deer, however, came down either summer, and he escaped without being seen. This contrivance of setting up stakes to guide the deer in a certain direction is very commonly used by the Eskimo. Egede gives a curious description of the practice in Greenland in his day: They "chase them [i. e., the reindeer] by Clap-hunting, setting upon them on all sides and surrounding them with all their Women and Children to force them into Defiles and Narrow Passages, where the Men armed lay in wait for them and kill them. And when they have not People enough to surround them, then they put up white Poles (to make up the Number that is wanted) with Pieces of Turf to head them, which frightens the Deer and hinders it from escaping."[1] Pl. 4, of the same work, is a very curious illustration of this style of hunting.

A similar method is practiced at the Coppermine River, where the deer are led by ranges of turf toward the spot where the archer is hidden.[2] Franklin also noticed between the Mackenzie and the Colville similar ranges of driftwood stumps leading across the plain to two cairns on a hill,[3] and Thomas Simpson mentions a similar range near Herschel Island,[4] and double rows of turf to represent men leading down to a small lake near Point Pitt, for the purpose of driving the deer into the water where they could be speared.[5] This is

[1] Greenland, p. 62.
[2] Franklin, 1st Exped., vol. 2, p. 181.
[3] 2d Exped., p. 137.
[4] Narrative, p. 114.
[5] Ibid., p. 138.

similar to the practice described by Schwatka[1] among the "Netschilluk" of King William's Land, where a line of cairns as high as a man and 50 to 100 yards apart is built along a ridge running obliquely to the water. When deer are seen feeding near the water the men form a skirmish line from the last cairn to the water and advance slowly. The deer mistake the cairns for men and take to the water, where they are easily speared.

The most important deer hunt takes place in the late fall and early spring, when the natives go inland 50 or 75 miles to the upper waters of Kuaru and Kulugrua, where the deer are exceedingly plentiful at this season. Capt. Herendeen, who went inland with the deer hunters in the autumn of 1882, reports that the bottom lands of Kulugrua "looked like a cattle yard," from the tracks of the reindeer. They start as soon as it is possible to travel across the country with sledges, usually about the first of October, taking guns, ammunition, fishing tackle, and the necessary household utensils for themselves and their families, and stay till the daylight gets too short for hunting. In 1882, many parties got home about October 27 or 28. At this season there is seldom snow enough to build snow huts, so they generally live in tents, always close to the rivers from which they procure water for household use. The men spend their time hunting the deer, while the women bring in the game, attend to drying the skins and the household work, and catch whitefish and burbot through the ice of the rivers, which are now frozen hard enough for this purpose. Some of the old men and those who have not a supply of ammunition engage in the same pursuit.

A comparatively small number of the people go out to this fall deer hunt, which appears to be a new custom, adopted since Dr. Simpson's time. It was probably not worth while to go out after deer at seasons when there was not enough snow for digging pitfalls, since they depended chiefly on these for the capture of the reindeer before the introduction of firearms. Fully half of each village go out on the spring deer hunt, as they did in Maguire's time, the first parties starting out with the return of the sun, about January 23, and the others following in the course of two or three weeks, and remain out till about the middle of April, when it is time to come back for the whale fishery. The people of Utkiavwiñ always travel to the hunting grounds by a regular road, which is the same as that followed by Lieut. Ray in his exploring trips. They travel along the coast on the ice wherever it is smooth enough till they reach Sĭ'ñaru, and then strike across country, crossing Kuaru and reaching Kulugrua near the hill Nuasu'knan. (See map, Pl. II.)

The people from Nuwŭk travel straight across Elson Bay to the south till they reach nearly the same region. Some parties from Nuwŭk also hunt in the rough country between Kulugrua and Ikpĭkpûñ. As the sledges are heavily laden with camp equipage, provisions and oil for the lamps, they travel slowly, taking four or five days for the journey,

---

[1] Science, vol. 4, 9, pp. 543-544.

stopping for the night with tolerable regularity at certain stations where the first party that travels over the trail build snow huts, which are used by those who follow them. At the rivers they are scattered in small camps of four or five families, about a day's journey apart. As well as we could learn these camps are in regularly established places, where the same people return every year, if they hunt at all. It even seemed as if these localities were considered the property of certain influential families, who could allow any others they pleased to join their parties.[1] It is certain, at all events, that the people of Utkiavwĭñ did not hunt on the Ikpĭkpûñ with the men of Nuwŭk. At this season they live entirely in snow huts, often excavated in the deep drifts under the river bluffs, and the men hunt deer while the women, as before, catch fish in Kuaru and Kulugrua. None are taken in Ikpĭkpûñ. (See above, p. 58.)

Deer are generally very plentiful at this season, though sometimes, as happened in February, 1883, there comes a warm southerly wind which makes them all retreat farther inland for a few days. They are generally hunted by chasing them on snowshoes, in the manner already described, but with much better chances of success, since when a number of hunters are out in the same region the deer are kept moving, so that a herd started by one hunter is very apt to run within gunshot of another. The natives have generally very good success in this spring hunt. Two men who were hunting on shares for the station killed upward of ninety reindeer in the season of 1883. A great deal of the meat is, of course, consumed on the spot, but a good many deer are brought home frozen. They are skinned and brought home whole, only the heads and legs being cut off. The latter are disjointed at the knee and elbow. These frozen carcasses are usually cut up with a saw for cooking. At this season the does are pregnant, and many good-sized fetuses are brought home frozen. We were told that these were excellent food, though we never saw them eaten. For the first two or three days after the return of the deer hunters to the village all the little boys are playing with these fetuses, which they set up as targets for their blunt arrows.

Before starting for the deer hunt the hunters generally take the movable property which they do not mean to carry with them out of the house and bury it in the snow for safe keeping, apparently thinking that while a dishonest person might help himself to small articles left around the house, he could hardly go to work and dig up a cache without attracting the attention of the neighbors. If both families from a house go deer hunting, they either close it up entirely or else get some family who have no house of their own to take care of it during their absence. During the season, small parties, traveling light, with very little baggage, make flying trips to the village, usually to get a fresh supply of

---

[1] Dr. Richardson believes that the hunting grounds of families are kept sacred among the Eskimo. Searching Expedition, vol. 1, pp. 244, 351. See, also, the same author's paper, New Philosophical Journal, vol. 52, p. 323.

ammunition or oil, and at the end of the season a lucky hunter almost always sends in to borrow extra dogs and hire women and children to help bring in his game. The skins, which at this season are very thick and heavy, suitable only for blankets, heavy stockings, etc., are simply rough dried in the open air, and brought in stacked up on a flat sled. Lieut. Ray met a Nuwŭk party returning in 1882 with a pile of these skins that looked like a load of hay. With such heavy loads they, of course, travel very slowly. A few natives, especially when short of ammunition, still use at this season the snow pitfalls mentioned by Capt. Maguire.[1]

The following is the description of those seen by Lieut. Ray in 1883: A round hole is dug in the drifted snow, along the bank of a stream or lake. This is about 5 feet in diameter and 5 or 6 feet deep, and is brought up to within 2 or 3 inches of the surface, where there is only a small hole, through which the snow was removed. This is carefully closed with a thin slab of snow and baited by strewing reindeer moss and bunches of grass over the thin surface, through which the deer breaks as soon as he steps on it. The natives say that they sometimes get two deer at once.

This method of hunting the reindeer appears uncommon among the Eskimo. I find no mention of it except at Repulse Bay.[2] and among the Netsillingmiut, where dogs' urine is said to be sprinkled on the snow as a bait to attract the deer by its "Salzgehalt."[3] Lieut. Ray was informed by the natives that the "Nunatañmiun" also captured deer by means of a rawhide noose set across a regular deer path, when they discovered such. The noose is held up and spread by a couple of sticks, and the end staked to the ground with a piece of antler. A similar method was practiced by the natives of Norton Sound.[4] A few parties visit the rivers in summer for the purpose of hunting reindeer, but most of the natives are either off on the trading expeditions previously mentioned or else settled in the small camps along the coast, 3 or 4 miles apart, whence they occasionally go a short distance inland in search of reindeer.

The seal.—The flesh of the smaller seals forms such a staple of food, and their blubber and skin serve so many important purposes, that their capture is one of the most necessary pursuits at Point Barrow, and is carried on at all seasons of the year and in many different methods. During the season of open water many seals are shot from the umiaks engaged in whaling and walrus hunting or caught in nets set along the shore at Elson Bay. This is also the only season when seals can be captured with the small kaiak darts.

The principal seal fishery, however, begins with the closing of the sea, usually about the middle of October. When the pack ice comes in there are usually many small open pools, to which the seals resort for air. Most of the able-bodied men in the village are out every day armed

[1] Northwest Passage, Appendix, p. 387.

[2] Rae, Narratives, etc., p. 135.

[3] Klutschak, "Als Eskimo," etc., p. 131.

[4] Dall, Alaska, p. 147.

with the rifle and retrieving harpoon, traveling many miles among the ice hummocks in search of such holes. When a seal shows his head he is shot at with the rifle, and the hunter, if successful, secures his game with the harpoon. This method of hunting is practiced throughout the winter wherever open holes form in the ice. A native going to visit his nets or to examine the condition of the ice always carries his rifle and retrieving harpoon, in case he should come across an open hole where seals might be found. The hunt at this season is accompanied with considerable danger, as the ice pack is not yet firmly consolidated and portions of it frequently move offshore with a shift of the wind, so that the hunter runs the risk of being carried out to sea. The natives exercise considerable care, and generally avoid crossing a crack if the wind, however light, is blowing offshore; but in spite of their precautions men are every now and then carried off to sea and never return.

The hunters meet with many exciting adventures. On the morning of November 24, 1882, all the heavy ice outside of the bar broke away from the shore, leaving a wide lead, and began to move rapidly to the northeast, carrying with it three seal hunters. They were fortunately near enough to the village to be seen by the loungers on the village hill, who gave the alarm. An umiak was immediately mounted on a flat sled and carried out over the shore ice with great rapidity, so that the men were easily rescued. The promptness and energy with which the people at the village acted showed how well the danger was appreciated.

At this season of the year a single calm night is sufficient to cover all the holes and leads with young ice strong enough to support a man, and occasionally before the pack comes in the open sea freezes over. In this young ice the seals make their breathing holes (adlu), "about the Bigness of a Halfpenny," as Egede says, and the natives employ the stabbing harpoon for their capture. At the present day this is seldom used alone, but the seal is shot through the head as he comes to the surface, and the spear only used to secure him. Seals which have been shot in this way are sometimes carried off by the current before they can be harpooned. As far as I can learn, this practice of shooting seals at the adlu is peculiar to Point Barrow (including probably the rest of the Arctic coast as far as Kotzebue Sound), though the use of the *una*, as already stated, is very general.

This method of hunting can generally be prosecuted only a few days at a time, as the movements of the pack soon break up the fields of young ice, though new fields frequently form in the course of the season. After the January gales the pack is so firmly consolidated that there are no longer any open holes or leads, and when the spring leads open young ice seldom forms, so that this method of hunting is as a rule confined to the period between the middle of October and the early part of January.

With the departure of the sun, about the middle of November, begins the netting, which is the most important fishery of the year, but which can be prosecuted with success only in the darkest nights. The natives say that even a bright aurora interferes with the netting. At this season narrow leads of open water are often formed parallel to the shore, and frequently remain open for several days. The natives are constantly reconnoitering the ice in search of such leads, and when one is found nearly all the men in the village go out to it with their nets. A place is sought where the ice is tolerably level and not too thick for about a hundred yards back from the lead, at which distance the nets are set, often a number of them close together, in the manner already described, so that they hang like curtains under the ice, parallel to the edge of the open water. When darkness comes on the hunters begin to rattle on the ice with their ice picks, scratch with the seal call, or make some other gentle and continuous noise, which soon excites the curiosity of the seals that are swimming about in the open lead. One at length dives under the ice and swims in the direction of the sound, which of course leads him directly into the net, where he is entangled.

On favorable nights a great many seals are captured in this way. For instance, on the night of December 2, 1882, the netters from Utkiavwiñ alone took at least one hundred seals. Such lucky hauls are not common, however. As the weather at this season is often excessively cold, the seals freeze stiff soon after they are taken from the net, and if sufficient snow has fallen they are stacked up by sticking their hind flippers in the snow. This keeps them from being covered up and lost if the snow begins to drift. I have counted thirty seals, the property of one native, piled up in this way into a single stack. The women and children go out at their convenience with dog sleds and bring in the seals. A woman, however, who is at work on deerskin clothing must not touch a hand to the seals or the sled on which they are loaded, but may lend a hand at hauling on the drag line. When the seals are brought to the edge of the beach they must not be taken on land till each has been given a mouthful of fresh water. We did not learn the object of this practice, but Nordenskiöld, who observed a similar custom at Pitlekaj, was informed that it was to keep the leads from closing.[1]

When the lead keeps open for several days, or there is a prospect of its opening again, the hunter leaves his gear out on the ice, sometimes bringing his ice pick, scoop, and setting pole part way home and sticking them up in the snow alongside of the path. In 1884 a lead remained open for several days about 3 or 4 miles from the village, and the natives made a regular beaten trail out to it. When we visited the netting ground the lead had closed, but nearly all the men had left their gear sticking up near it, with the nets tied up and hung upon the ice picks. They had built little walls of snow slabs as a protection against the wind. The season for this netting ends with the January gales, which close the leads permanently.

---

[1] Vega, vol. 2, p. 130. Compare the custom observed in Baffin Land, of sprinkling a few drops of water on the head of the seal before it is cut up, mentioned by Hall, Arctic Researches, p. 573.

Later in the winter the seals resort to very inconsiderable cracks among the hummocks for air, and nets are set hanging around these cracks, so that a seal can not approach the crack without being caught. There was such a crack just in the edge of the rough land floe, not half a mile from Utkiavwiñ, in February, 1883, from which two men took several seals, visiting the nets every day or two. Those men who do not go off on the deer hunt keep one or more seal nets set all winter, either in this way or in the third method, which can be practiced only after the daylight has come back, when the ice is thick. At this season there are frequently to be found among the hummocks what the natives call i'glus, dome-shaped snow houses about 6 feet in diameter and 2 or 3 feet high, with a smooth round hole in the top, and communicating with the water. These are undoubtedly the same as the snow burrows described by Kumlien,[1] which the female seal builds to bring forth her young in.[2] They are curious constructions, looking astonishingly like a man's work. The natives told me that nets set at these places were for the capture of young seals (nĕtyiáru). It appears that these houses are the property of a single female only until her young one is able to take to the water, as a net is kept set at one of these holes, as well as I could understand, sometimes capturing several seals. The net is set flat under the hole, the corners being drawn out by cords let down through small holes in a circle round the main opening, through which the net is drawn. A seal rising to the surface runs his head through the meshes of the net. The small holes and sometimes the middle one are carefully covered with slabs of snow.

The officers of the revenue steamer *Corwin*, who made the sledge journey along the northeast coast of Siberia in the early summer of 1881, saw seal nets set in this way, flat, under air holes in the ice, with a hole for each corner of the net. When a seal was caught the net was drawn up through the middle hole with a hooked pole.[3] In 1883 they began setting these nets at Point Barrow about March 4, and probably about the same date the year before, though we did not happen to observe this method of netting until considerably later.

In June and July, when the ice becomes rotten and worn into holes, the seals "haul out" to bask in the sun, and are then stalked and shot. They are exceedingly wary at this season. The seal usually taken in the methods above described is the rough or ringed seal (Phoca fœtida), but in 1881 a single male ribbon seal (Histriophoca fasciata) was netted, and in 1882 a native shot one at the breathing hole, but it was carried away by the current before he could secure it. The natives said that they sometimes caught the harbor seal (P. vitulina) in the shore nets in Elson Bay. The bearded seal (Erignathus barbatus), whose skin is especially prized for making harpoon lines, boot soles, umiak covers,

---

[1] Contributions, p. 57.
[2] Hall, Arctic Researches, pp. 507 and 578, with diagrams.
[3] Hooper, Corwin Report, p. 25.

etc., is never very abundant, and occurs chiefly in the season of open water, when it is captured from the umiak with harpoon and rifle, but they are sometimes found in the winter, as two were killed at breathing holes in the rough ice January 8, 1883.

The walrus.—The walrus occurs only during the season of open water, and is almost always captured from the umiak with the large harpoon and rifle. The whaling boats usually find a few, especially late in the season, and after the trading parties have gone in the summer the natives who remain are generally out in the boats a good deal of the time looking for walrus and seals. As a general thing walrus are especially plenty in September, when much loose ice is moving backwards and forwards with the current, frequently sleeping in large herds upon cakes of ice. The boats, which are out nearly every day at this season with volunteer crews, not regularly organized as for whaling, paddle as near as they can to these sleeping herds and try to shoot them in the head, aiming also to "fasten" to as many as they can with the harpoon and float as they hurry into the water. A harpooned walrus is followed up with the boat and shot with the rifle when a chance is offered. Swimming walruses are chased with the boat and "fastened to" by darting the harpoon. When a walrus is killed it is towed up to the nearest cake of ice and cut up on the spot. We never knew of the kaiak being used in walrus-hunting, as is the custom among the eastern Eskimo.

The whale.—The pursuit of the "bowhead" whale (Balæna mysticetus), so valuable not only for the food furnished by its flesh and "blackskin" and the oil from its blubber, but for the whalebone, which serves so many useful purposes in the arts of the Eskimo and is besides the chief article of trade with the ships, is carried on with great regularity and formality. In the first place all the umialĭks (boat-owners) or those who are to be the captains of whaling umiaks, before the deer hunters start out in January, bring all the gear to be used in the whale fishery to the kŭ'dyĭgĭ, where it is consecrated by a ceremony consisting of drumming and singing, perhaps partaking of the nature of an incantation.

Capt. Herendeen was the only one of our party who witnessed this ceremony, which took place at Utkiavwĭñ on January 9, 1883, and he did not bring back a detailed account of the proceedings. During part of the ceremony all the umialĭks were seated in a row upon the floor, and a woman passed down the line marking each across the face with an oblique streak of blacklead. As soon as the deer hunters return in the spring they begin getting ready for the whales, covering the boats, fitting lines to harpoons, and putting gear of all sorts in perfect order. Every article to be used in whaling—harpoons, lances, paddles, and even the timbers of the boats—must be scraped perfectly clean.[1] This work is generally done by the umialĭk himself and his

---

[1] Compare Egede, Greenland, p. 102. The whale "can't bear sloven and dirty habits."

family, as the crews do not enter on their duties till the whaling actually commences. The crews are regularly organized for the season, and are made up during the winter and early spring. They consist of eight or ten persons to each boat, including the captain, who is always the owner of the boat, and sits in the stern and steers, using a larger paddle than the rest, and the harpooner, who occupies the bow. When a bombgun is carried it is intrusted to a third man, who sits in the waist of the boat, and whose duty it is to shoot the whale whenever he sees a favorable opportunity, whether it has been harpooned or not. The rest are simply paddlers.

When used for whaling, the umiak is propelled by paddles alone, sails and oars never being even taken on board. Men are preferred for the whaling crews when enough can be secured, otherwise the vacancies are filled by women, who make efficient paddlers. Some umialiks hire their crews, paying them a stipulated price in tobacco and other articles, and providing them with food during the season. Others ship men on shares. We did not learn the exact proportions of these shares in any case. They appear to concern the whalebone alone, as all seem to be entitled to as much of the flesh and blubber as they can cut off in the general scramble. At this season exploring parties are out every day examining the state of the ice to ascertain when the pack is likely to break away from the landfloe, and also to find the best path for the umiaks through the hummocks.

In 1882 the condition of the ice was such that the boats could be taken out directly from Utkiavwĭñ, by a somewhat winding path, to the edge of the land floe about five or six miles from the shore. This path was marked out by the seal-hunters during the winter, and some of the natives spent their leisure time widening and improving it, knocking off projecting points of ice with picks and whale spades, and filling up the worst of the inequalities. Much of the path, however, was exceedingly rough and difficult when it was considered finished. In 1883 the land floe was so rough and wide abreast of the village that no practicable path could be made, so all the whalemen with their families moved up to Imê′kpûñ and encamped in tents as already described (see p. 84) for the season. From this point a tolerably straight and easy path was made out to the edge of the land floe. The natives informed me as early as April 1 that it would be necessary for them to move up to Imê′kpûñ, adding that the ice abreast of the village was very heavy and would move only when warm weather came. This prediction was correct, as the season of 1883 was so late that no ships reached the station until August 1.

About the middle of April the natives begin anxiously to expect an east or southeast wind (nígyə) to drive off the pack and open the leads, and should it not speedily blow from that quarter recourse is had to supernatural means to bring it. A party of men go out and sit in a semicircle facing the sea on the village cliff, while one man in the middle beats a drum and sings a monotonous chant, interrupted by curious vibrating cries, accompanied with a violent shaking of the head from side to side. This ceremony is conducted with great solemnity, and the natives seemed disinclined to have us witness it, so that we learned very little about it. They, however, told us that the chant was addressed to a tuaña or spirit, requesting him to make the desired wind blow.[1] It does not appear to be necessary that the man who delivers the invocation should be a regular magician or " doctor." A succession of unsuccessful attempts were made in 1882, some of them by men who never to our knowledge practiced incantations on other occasions. During this period, and while the whaling is going on, no pounding must be done in the village, and it is not allowable even to rap with the knuckles on wood for fear of frightening away the whales.[2] It is interesting to find that at Norton Sound, where the whale is not pursued, this superstition has been transferred to the salmon fishery, one of the most important industries of the year. Mr. Dall[3] says: " While the fishery lasts no wood must be cut with an axe, or the salmon will disappear."

As soon as the lead opens, and sometimes before when the prospect looks promising, the boats are taken out to the edge of the land floe and kept out there during the season, which lasts till about the last week in June, when they are brought in and got ready for the summer expeditions. When the lead closes, as often happens, the boats are hauled up on the ice and many or all of the crews come home until there are prospects of open water. When there is open water, the boats are always on the lookout for whales, either cruising about in the lead or lying up at the edge of the floe, the crews eating and sleeping when they can get a chance and shooting seals and ducks when there are no whales in sight. The women and children travel back and forth between the village and the boats, carrying supplies of food for the whalemen.

In 1883, there was a regular beaten trail along the smooth shore ice between Imê'kpûñ and Utkiavwĭñ, where people were constantly traveling back and forth. When the boats are out no woman is allowed to sew, as was noticed by Dr. Simpson.[4] To carry the umiak out over the ice it is lashed on a flat sled and drawn by dogs and men. A description of one of these boats which I accompanied for part of its journey out to the open water, will show how a whaleboat is fitted out. The rifles, harpoons, lances, and other gear of the party were sent on ahead on a sled drawn by half a dozen dogs, with a woman to lead them. After these had made a short stage, they were unfastened from this

---

[1] Hall speaks of seeing the angeko " very busy ankooting on the hills "—" To try and get the pack ice out of the bay."—Arctic Res., p. 573.

[2] Compare Rink, Tales, etc., p. 55: " To the customs just enumerated may be added various regulations regarding the chase, especially that of the whale, this animal being easily scared away by various kinds of impurity or disorder."

[3] Alaska, p. 147.

[4] Loc. cit., p. 261.

sled and brought back and harnessed to the flat sled on which the umiak was lashed. The party, which consisted of five men and two women, one of whom remained with the sled load of gear, then started ahead, the women running in front of the dogs and the men pushing at the sides of the boat. The boat travels very easily and rapidly on smooth ice, but among the hummocks the men have hard work pushing and scrambling, and occasional stops have to be made to widen narrow places in the path and to chisel off projecting points of ice which might pierce the skin cover of the boat. When they came up to the first sled the women were again sent on with this while the men rested. The inflated sealskin floats, five or six in number, the whale harpoon, and whale spades, and ice picks were carried in the boats.

A whaling umiak always carries a number of amulets to insure success. These consisted in this case of two wolf skulls, a dried raven, the axis vertebra of a seal, and numerous feathers. The skin of a golden eagle is considered an excellent charm for whaling, and Nĭka-waalu was particularly desirous to secure the tip of a red fox's tail, which he said was a powerful amulet. The captain and harpooner wore fillets of mountain sheepskin, with a little crystal or stone image of a whale dangling at each side of the face, and the captain's fillet was also fringed with the incisor teeth of the mountain sheep. Both wore little stone whales attached to the breast of the jacket, and one woman and one or two of the men had streaks of black lead on their faces.[1]

When they are on the watch for whales the great harpoon is kept always rigged and resting in a crotch of ivory in the bow of the boat. When a whale is sighted they paddle up as close as possible and the harpooner thrusts the harpoon into him. The whale dives, with the floats attached to him, and the shaft, which is retained, is rigged for striking him when he rises again. The other boats, if any are near, join in the chase until the whale is so wearied that he can be lanced or a favorable opportunity occurs for shooting him. All boats in sight at the time the whale is struck, as I understood, are entitled to an equal share of the whalebone.

As soon as the whale is killed he is towed up to the edge of the land floe and everybody standing on the edge of the ice and in the boats begins hacking away, at random, at the flesh and blubber, some of them going to work more carefully to cut out the whalebone. The "cutting in" is managed without order or control, everybody who can be on the spot being apparently entitled to all the meat, blubber, and blackskin he or she can cut off. The same custom was practiced in Greenland, and is to this day in eastern Siberia.

[1] Compare Egede, Greenland, p. 102. "When they go a Whale-catching they put on their best Gear or Apparel, as if they were going to a Wedding Feast, fancying that if they did not come cleanly and neatly dressed the Whale, who can't bear sloven and dirty Habits, would shun them and fly from them."

See also Crantz, History of Greenland, Vol. I, p. 121. "They dress themselves in the best manner for it, because, according to the portentous sayings of their sorcerers, if any one was to wear dirty cloaths, especially such in which he had touched a dead corpse, the whale would escape, or, even if it was already dead, would at least sink."

While they are very particular in all superstitious observances regarding the whales, they are less careful about certain things, such as loud talking and firing guns at seals and fowl when they are waiting for whales, which really hurt their chances with the timid animals. They are less energetic than one would suppose in pursuit of the whale, according to Capt. Herendeen, who spent several days each season with the whaleboats. Instead of cruising about the lead in search of whales they are rather inclined to lie in wait for them at the edge of the floe, so that when the open water is wide many whales escape.

When the leads are very narrow the whales are sometimes shot with the bombgun from the edge of the ice. Success in this appears to be variable. In 1882 only one small whale was secured, and in 1883 one full-grown one, though several were struck and lost each season. The veteran whaling-master, Capt. L. C. Owen, informs me that one season the boats of these two villages captured ten. The season of 1885 was very successful. The natives of the two villages are reported to have taken twenty-eight whales. Capt. E. E. Smith, however, informs me that only seven of these were full-grown.

When actually engaged in whaling the umialik exercises a very fair degree of discipline, but at other times he seems hardly able to keep his men from straggling off to go home or to visit their seal nets, etc., so that he sometimes has to chase a whale "short-handed."

Nowhere else among the Eskimo does the whale fishery appear to be conducted in such regular manner with formally organized crews as upon this northwest coast. From all accounts the animal is only casually pursued elsewhere with fleets of kaiaks or umiaks manned by volunteer crews.[1]

The beluga or white whale is only casually pursued, and as far as I could learn is always shot with the rifle. It is not abundant.

Fowl.—During the winter months a few ptarmigan are occasionally shot, but the natives pay no special attention to birds until the spring migrations. The first ducks appear a little later than the whales, about the end of April or the first week of May, and from that time till the middle of June scarcely a day passes when they are not more or less plenty. The king ducks (Somateria spectabilis) are the first to appear, while the Pacific eiders (S. v-nigra) arrive somewhat later, and are more abundant towards the end of the migrations. At this season all women and children, and many men, go armed with the bolas, and everybody is always on the lookout for flocks of ducks. On four or five favorable days each season, at intervals of a week or ten days, there are great flights of eiders coming up in huge flocks of two or three hundred, stretched out in long diagonal lines. These flocks follow one another in rapid succession and keep the line of the coast, apparently striking straight across Peard Bay from the Seahorse Islands to a point

---

[1]See Egede, Greenland, p. 102; Crantz, History of Greenland, Vol. I, p. 121; Parry, 2d. Voy., p. 509 (Iglulik); McClure, Northwest Passage, p. 92 (Cape Bathurst).

four or five miles below Utkiavwĭñ, and most of them fly up along the smooth shore-ice to Pernyû or Point Barrow. Some flocks always fly up among the hummocks of the land floe, and a few others turn eastward below the village and continue their course to the northeast across the land.

On the days between the great flights there are always a few flocks passing, and some days when there is no flight along shore they are very abundant out at the open water, where the whalemen shoot them in the intervals of whaling. When a great flight begins the people at the village hasten out and form a sort of skirmish line across the shore ice from the shore to the hummocks, a few sometimes stationing themselves among the latter. They take but little pains to conceal themselves, frequently sitting out on the open ice-field on sealing stools or squares of bearskins. The ducks generally keep on their course without paying much attention to the men, and in fact one may often get a shot by running so as to head off an approaching flock. Firing, however, frightens them and makes them rise to a considerable height, often out of gunshot. Many ducks are taken with guns and bolas in these flights.

Rather late in the season the old squaws (Clangula hyemalis) pass to the northeast in large flocks, but usually go so high than none are taken. A good many of these, however, with a few eiders, geese, brant, and loons, remain and breed on the tundra, and are occasionally shot by the natives, though most of them are too busy with whaling and seal and walrus hunting to pay much attention to birds. Small parties of two or three lads or young men, sometimes with their wives, make short excursions inland to the small streams and sand islands east of Point Barrow, after birds and eggs, and the boys from the small camps along the coast towards Woody Inlet are always on the lookout for eggs and small birds, such as they can kill with their bows and arrows or catch in snares. They say that the parties which go east, and those which visit the rivers in summer, get many eggs and find plenty of ducks, geese, and swans, which have molted their flight feathers so that they are unable fly.

About the end of July the return migration of the ducks begins. At this season the flocks, which are generally smaller and more compact than in the spring, come from the east along the northern shore, and cross out to sea at the isthmus of Pernyû, where the natives assemble in large numbers to shoot them as well as to meet with the Nunatañmiun. All the people who have been scattered along the coast in small camps gradually collect at this season at Pernyû, and the returning eastern parties generally stop there two or three days; while, after they have brought their families back to the village, the men frequently walk up to Pernyû for a day or two of duck shooting. The tents are pitched just in the bend of Elson Bay, and north of them is a narrow place in the sandspit over which the ducks often pass. Here the natives dig shallow pits in the gravel, in which they post themselves with guns and bolas. A line of posts is set up along the bend of the beach from the tents almost to the outlet of Imêkpûniglu.

When a light breeze is blowing from the northeast the ducks, no matter how far off shore they are when first seen, always head for the point of land on the other side of this outlet, probably with the intention of following the line of lagoons and going out to sea farther down the coast, as they sometimes do. When, however, they reach this critical point they catch sight of the posts, and the natives who are watching them sharply set up a shrill yell. Frightened by this and by the line of posts, nine times out of ten, if the cry is given at the right moment, the ducks will falter, become confused, and, finally, collecting into a compact body will whirl along the line of posts, past the tents, flying close to the water, and turn out to sea at the first open space, which is just where the gunners are posted. This habit of yelling to frighten the ducks and bring them within gunshot has been observed on the Siberian cost in places where the ducks are in the habit of flying in and out from lagoons over low bars.[1] Should the wind blow hard from the east, however, or blow from any other quarter, the ducks do not fly in such abundance, nor do they pay much attention to the posts or the yelling, but often keep on their course down the lagoons, or head straight for the beach and cross wherever they strike it. The latter is generally the habit with the old squaws, who come rather late in the migrations, while the black brant (Branta nigricans) are more apt to go down the lagoons. A few pintail ducks (Dafila acuta), are occasionally shot at this season, and are sometimes found in the two little village ponds (Tûseraru). The shooting at Pernyû usually lasts till the middle or end of September, during which month the natives also shoot a good many gulls (Larus barrovianus and Rhodostethia rosea) as they fly along the shore.

IMPLEMENTS FOR FISHING.

Hooks and lines.—The streams and lakes in the immediate neighborhood of Point Barrow contain no fish, and there is comparatively little fishing in the sea. When the water first closes in the autumn narrow tide cracks often form at the very edge of the beach. At these cracks the natives frequently catch considerable numbers of Polar cod (Boreogadus saida) and small sculpins (Cottus quadricornis and C. decastrensis), with the hook and line. The tackle for this fishing consists of

---

[1] Von der Lagune aus pflegten jeden Morgen und Abend grosse Entenschaaren über den Ort hinweg nach dem Meere zu fliegen. Dann wurden durch Pfeifen und Schreien die Thiere so geängstigt, dass sie ihren Flug abwärts richteten und nun durch die mit grosser Sicherheit geworfene Schleuder oder durch Flintenschüsse erreicht werden konnten. (East Cape), Krause Brothers, Geographische Blätter, Vol. 5, pt. 1, p. 32.

"The birds were easily called from their course of flight, as we repeatedly observed. If a flock should be passing a hundred yards or more to one side, the natives would utter a long, peculiar cry, and the flock would turn instantly to one side and sweep by in a circuit, thus affording the coveted opportunity for bringing down some of their number." (Cape Wankarem), Nelson, Cruise of the Corwin, p. 100.

a short line of whalebone, provided with a little "squid" or artificial bait of ivory, and fastened to a wooden rod about 18 inches or 2 feet long. The lure, which is apparently meant to represent a small shrimp, is kept moving, and the fish bite at it. We brought home two complete sets of tackle for this kind of fishing, two lines without rods and twelve lures or hooks. No. 89548 [1733] Fig. 264, has been selected for description.

The line is 40 inches long and made of four strips of whalebone 0·1 inch wide, fastened together with what appear to be "waterknots." Two of these strips are of black whalebone, respectively 4½ and 9 inches long; the other two are of light colored whalebone and 15½ and 11 inches long. The light colored end is made fast to the eye in the small end of the hook as follows: The end is passed through the eye, doubled back

³⁄₄

FIG. 264.—Tackle for shore fishing.

and passed through a single knot in the standing part, and knotted round the latter with a similar knot (Fig. 265). This knot is the one generally used in fastening a fishing line to the hook. The other end is doubled in a short bight into which is becket-hitched one end of a bit of sinew thread about 3 inches long, and the other end is knotted into a notch at one end of the rod, as the whalebone would be too stiff to tie securely to the stick. The rod is a roughly whittled splinter of California redwood, 14½ inches long. The body of the lure is a piece of walrus ivory 1½ inches long. Through a hole in the large end of this is driven the barbless brass hook, with a broad thin plate at one end bent up, flush with the convex side. When not in use the line is reeled lengthwise on the rod, secured by a notch at each end of the latter, and the hook stuck into the wood on one side of the rod. The hook is wedged into the body of the lure with a bit of whalebone. The other specimen, No. 89547, [1733] from the same village, is almost exactly like this, but

FIG. 265.—Knot of line into hook.

has a slightly shorter line, made of three strips of bone, of which the lower two, as before, are of light colored whalebone. The object of using this material is probably to render the part of the line which is under water less conspicuous, as we use leaders and casting lines of transparent silkworm gut. The body of the lure is made of old brown walrus ivory. These lures are 1 inch to 1½ inches long, and vary little in the shape of the body which is usually made of walrus ivory, in most cases darkened on the surface by age or charring, so that when carved into shape it is parti-colored, black and white. The body is often ornamented with small colored beads inlaid for eyes and along the back (Fig. 266a, No. 56609 [153], from Utkiavwiñ).

The hook is usually of the shape described but is sometimes simply a slightly recurved spur about ½-inch long as in Fig. 266b (No. 56610 [160], also from Utkiavwĭñ). It is usually of brass or copper, rarely of iron. Two peculiar lures from Utkiavwĭñ, are No. 56705 [150a and 150b].

The first, a, has a body of brass of the usual shape, and a copper hook, and the other, b, has the body made of a strip of thin brass to the back of which is fastened a lump of lead or pewter. The hook appears to be made of a common copper tack. We were informed that these lures were also used for catching small fish, trout, smelts, and perhaps grayling in the rivers in summer. No. 89554 [950], Fig. 267a, from Utkiavwĭñ, is per-

FIG. 266.—Small fishhooks.

haps intended exclusively for this purpose, as it is larger than the others, (1.9 inch long) and highly ornamented with beads. Fig. 267b, No. 89783 [1007], is one of these beaded lures (2½ inches long), with an iron hook, undoubtedly for river fishing, as it belonged to the "inland" native, Ilû′bw′ga. It differs slightly in shape from the others, having two eyes at the small end into which is fastened a leader of sinew braid 3 inches long. On this are strung four blue glass beads and one red one.

No. ——[1] [151] Fig. 268, from Utkiavwĭñ, is a rod rigged for fishing in the rivers. The rod is a roughly whittled stick of spruce or pine, 27 inches long. One line is 43 and the other 36 inches long and each is made of two strips of whalebone of which the lower is light colored as usual. The shorter line carries a small plain ivory lure of the common pattern, and the longer one a little flat barbless hook of copper with a broad flat shank. This was probably scraped bright and used without bait. The lines are

FIG. 267.—Hooks for river fishing.

FIG. 268.—Tackle for river fishing.

reeled in the usual manner on the rod, and the hooks caught into notches on the sides of it. The small lures are called nĭ′ksĭñ.

---

[1] Museum number effaced.

When at the rivers in the autumn and early spring, they fish for burbot with a line carrying a peculiar large hook called iᵦkqlûñ, which is baited with a piece of whitefish. There are two forms of this hook, which is from 3 to 5¼ inches long. One form differs in size only from the small nĭ′ksĭn, but is always of white ivory and not beaded (Fig. 269, No. 89550 [780] from Utkiavwĭñ, which is 4½ inches long and has a copper hook). The hook is of copper, brass or iron. The other form, which is perhaps the commoner, has a narrow flat body, slightly bent, and serrated on the edges to give a firm attachment to the bait. This body is usually of antler, and has a copper or iron hook either spur-shaped or of the common form as in Fig. 270, No. 89553 [764] from Utkiavwĭñ, which has a body of walrus ivory 4 inches long and a copper hook. Of late years, small cod hooks obtained from the ships have been adapted to these bodies, as is seen in Fig. 271, No. 89552 [841] from Utkiavwĭñ. The shank of the hook has been half imbedded in a longitudinal groove on the flatter side of the body, with the bend of the hook projecting about ¼ inch beyond the tip of the latter. The ring of the hook has been bent open and the end sunk into the body. The hook is held on by two lashings of sinew, one at each end of the shank.

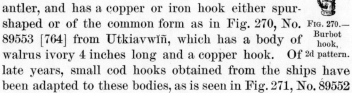

FIG. 270.—Burbot hook, 2d pattern.

⅓

FIG. 269.—Burbot hook, 1st pattern.

½

No. 56594 [32] from Utkiavwĭñ is like the preceding, but has a larger hook, which from the bend to the point is wrapped in a piece of deer skin with the flesh side out, and wound with sinew having a tuft of hair at the point of the hook. This is probably to hide the point when the hook is baited. No. 56594 [167] from Utkiavwĭñ, has the hook fastened to the back of the body instead of the flat side. The manner in which these hooks are baited is shown in Fig. 272, which represents a complete set of burbot tackle (No. 89546 [946]) brought in and sold by some Utkiavwĭñ natives, just as they had been using it in the autumn of 1882 at Kuaru or Kulugrua. A piece of whitefish, flesh and skin,

FIG. 271.—Burbot hook, made of cod hook.

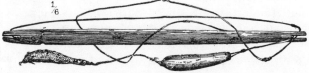

1/6

FIG. 272.--Burbot tackle, baited.

with the scales removed is wrapped round the hook so as to make a club-shaped body 4½ inches long and is sewed up along one side with cotton twine. The copper spur projects through the skin on the other side.

This hook would not hold the fish unless it were "gorged," but the voracious burbot always swallows its prey. In dressing these fish for the table, whitefish of considerable size were frequently found in them. The line is of whalebone like those already described but a little stouter, 78 inches long, and made of seven pieces, all black. The end of the line is fastened into an eye in the small end of a rough club-shaped sinker of walrus ivory, 4¾ inches long. There is another eye at the large end of the sinker, for the attachment of a leader of double sinew braid 5½ inches long connecting the hook with the sinker.

The reel, which serves also as a short rod, is of yellow pine 19½ inches long. When the line is reeled up, the hook is caught into the wood on one side of the reel. No. 89545 [946] is a similar set of baited tackle, bought from the same natives, differing from the preceding only in proportions, having a longer line—9 feet and 6 inches—and a somewhat larger bait. We also procured two sets of burbot tackle unbaited.

½

One of these (No. 56543 [33] from Utkiavwĭñ) has a whalebone line 14 feet long, and a roughly octahedral sinker of walrus ivory 3 inches long and 1½ in diameter. The hook, which is joined to the sinker as before by a leader of stout sinew braid, is of the second pattern, with serrated edges, and a copper hook. The leader is neatly spliced into this. The other, No. 56544 [187], also from Utkiavwĭñ, has no sinker and a hook with a club-shaped body and iron spur. It was probably put together for sale, as it is new. The sinkers, of which we collected five, besides those already mentioned, are always about the same weight and either club-shaped or roughly octahedral. They are always of walrus ivory and usually carelessly made. Fig. 273 (No. 56577 [260]) represents one of these sinkers (kíbica), on which there is some attempt at ornamentation. On the larger are two eyes and the outline of a mouth like a shark's, incised and filled in with black refuse oil.

FIG. 273.—
Ivory sinker.

A similar line and reel are used for catching polar cod in the spring and late winter through the ice at some distance from the shore. These lines are 10 or 15 fathoms long, and provided with a heavy sinker of ivory, copper, or rarely lead, to which are attached by whalebone leaders of unequal length, two little jiggers like Fig. 274 (the property of the writer, from Utkiavwĭñ). This is of white walrus ivory, 2⅛ inches long and ¾ in diameter at the largest part. The two slender hooks are of copper and are secured by wedges of whalebone. This makes a contrivance resembling the squid jigs used by our fishermen. These jiggers are sometimes made wholly of copper, which is scraped bright.

This fishery begins with the return of the sun, about the

¾

FIG. 274.—
Ivory jigger for
polar cod.

1st of February, and continues when the ice is favorable until the season is so far advanced that the ice has begun to melt and become rotten. The fish are especially to be found in places where there is a good-sized field of the season's ice, 3 or 4 feet thick, inclosed by hummocks, and they sometimes occur in very great numbers. In 1882 there was a large field of this kind about 2 miles from the village and the fishing was carried on with great success, but in 1883 the ice was so much broken that the fish were very scarce. Some lads caught a few early in the season, but the fishery was soon abandoned.

A hole about a foot in diameter is made through the ice with an ice pick, and the fragments dipped out either with the long-handled whale-bone scoop, or the little dipper made of two pieces of antler mounted on a handle about 2 feet long, which everybody carries in the winter. The line is unreeled and let down through the hole till the jigs hang about a foot from the bottom. The fisherman holds in his left hand the dipper above mentioned, with which he keeps the hole clear of the ice crystals, which form very quickly, and in his right the reel which he jerks continually up and down. The fish, attracted by the white "jiggers," begin nosing around them, when the upward jerk of the line hooks one of them in the under jaw or the belly. As soon as the fisherman feels the fish, he catches a bight of the line with the scoop in his left hand and draws it over to the left; then catches the line below this with the reel and draws it over to the right, and so on, thus reeling the line up in long hanks on these two sticks, without touching the wet line with his fingers.

When the fish is brought to the surface of the ice, he is detached from the barbless hook with a dextrous jerk, and almost instantly freezes solid. The elastic whalebone line is thrown off the stick without kinking and let down again through the hole. When fish are plentiful, they are caught as fast as they can be hauled up, sometimes one on each "jigger." If the fisherman finds no fish at the first hole he moves to another part of the field and tries again until he succeeds in "striking a school." The fish vary in abundance on different days, being sometimes so plentiful that I have known two or three children to catch a bushel in a few hours, while some days very few are to be taken. In addition to the polar cod, a few sculpins are also caught, and occasionally the two species of Lycodes (L. turnerii and coccineus) which voracious fish sometimes seize the little polar cod struggling on the "jigger" and are thus caught themselves. This fishery is chiefly carried on by the women, children, and old men, who go out in parties of five or six, though the hunters sometimes go fishing when they have nothing else to do. There were generally thirty or forty people out at the fishing-ground every day in 1882.

Jiggers of this pattern appear to be used at Pitlekaj, from Nordends-kiöld's description,[1] but I have seen no account either there or elsewhere

---

[1] Vega, vol. 2, p. 110.

of the peculiar method of reeling up the line such as we saw at Point Barrow. Lines of whalebone are very common among the Eskimo generally,[1] and perhaps this material is preferable to any other for fishing in this cold region, for not only does the elastic whalebone prevent kinking, but the ice which forms instantly on the wet line in winter does not adhere to it, but can easily be shaken off. No. 56545 [410] is a line 51 feet and 10 inches long and 0·05 inch in diameter, made of human hair, neatly braided in a round braid with four strands. This was called a fishing line, but was the only one of the kind seen. Fishhooks of the kind described, with a body of bone or ivory, which serves for a lure, armed with a spur or bent hook of metal, without a barb, seem to be the prevailing type amongst the Eskimo. In the region about Norton Sound (as shown by the extensive collections of Mr. Nelson and others) this is often converted into an elaborate lure by attaching pendants of beads, bits of the red beak of the puffin, etc. Crantz mentions a similar custom in Greenland of baiting a hook with beads.[2]

Nets (Kubra).—The most important fishery at the rivers is carried on by means of gill-nets, set under the ice, and visited every few days. In these are taken large numbers of all three species of whitefish (Coregonus kenicotti, C. nelsoni, and C. laurettæ.) The collection contains three specimens of these nets, two of whalebone and one of sinew. No. 56754 [147], Fig. 275, is a typical whalebone net. It is long and shallow, 79 meshes long and 21 deep, made of fine strips of whalebone fastened together as in the whalebone fishing lines. Most of the whalebone is black, but a few light colored strips are intermixed at random. The length of the mesh is $3\frac{1}{4}$ inches, and the knot used in making them is the ordinary netting-knot. When not

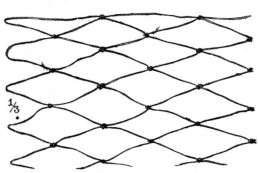

FIG. 275.—Section of whalebone net.

in use the net is rolled up into a compact ball and tied up with a bit of string. When set, this net is 21 feet 7 inches long and 3 feet 4 inches deep. The other whalebone net (No. 56753 [172], also from Utkiavwiñ), is similar to this, but slightly larger, being 87 meshes (25 feet) long and 22 (3 feet 9 inches) deep. The length of mesh is $3\frac{1}{2}$ inches.

---

[1] "Their Lines are made of Whalebones, cut very small and thin, and at the End tacked together." Egede, Greenland, p. 107. See also, Crantz, vol. 1, p. 95; Dall, Alaska, p. 148; and the Museum Collections which contain many whalebone lines from the Mackenzie and Anderson rivers, collected by MacFarlane, and from the whole western region, collected by Nelson.

[2] "Instead of a bait, they put on the hook a white bone, a glass bead, or a bit of red cloth" (when fishing for sculpins). History of Greenland, vol. 1, p. 95.

Fig. 276 (unit of web) is a net (No. 56752 [171] from the same village)
of the same mesh and depth, but 284 meshes
(60 feet) long and made of twisted sinew
twine.

FIG. 276.—Mesh of sinew net.

I had no opportunity of seeing the method of
setting these nets under the ice, but it is probably the same as that used in setting the seal nets.
When in camp at Pernyû in the summer, the
natives set these nets in the shoal water of Elson Bay, at right angles
to the beach, with a stake at each end of the net. They are set by a
man in a kayak, and in them are gilled considerable numbers of whitefish, two species of salmon (Oncorhynchus gorbuscha and O. nerka)
and an occasional trout (Salvelinus malma). They take these nets east
with them on their summer expeditions, but we did not learn the method
of using them at this season. Perhaps they are sometimes used for
seining on the beach, as Thomas Simpson says that the Eskimo at
Herschel Island (probably Kûñmûd′lïñ) sold his party "some fine salmon trout, taken in a seine of whalebone, which they dragged ashore
by means of several slender poles spliced together to a great length."[1]

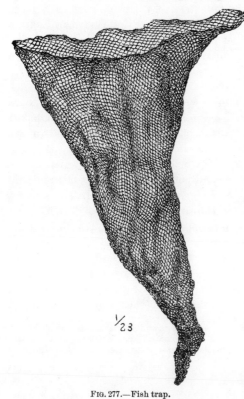

FIG. 277.—Fish trap.

An Utkiavwïñ native told
us that he found trout (Salvelinus malma) so plentiful
at or near the mouth of the
Colville, in 1882, that he fed
his dogs with them.

Fig. 277 is a peculiar net
or fish-trap (No. 56755 [190])
from Utkiavwïñ, the only
specimen of the kind seen.
It is a conical, wide-mouthed
bag, 8 feet 4 inches long and
$5\frac{1}{2}$ feet wide at the mouth,
netted all in one piece of
twisted sinew, with a $2\frac{1}{4}$-inch
mesh. This was brought
over for sale at an early date,
before we were well ac-
quainted with the natives,
and we only learned that it
was set permanently for
catching fish. Unfortunately, we never saw another
specimen, and through the
press of other duties never
happened to make further

---

[1] Narrative, p. 115.

inquiries about it. From its shape it would appear as if it were meant to be set in a stream with the mouth towards the current. This contrivance is called sápotĭn, which corresponds to the Greenlandic saputit, a dam for catching fish.

From all accounts, the natives east of the Anderson River region were ignorant of the use of the net before they made the acquaintance of the whites,[1] though they now use it in several places, as in Greenland and Labrador. The earliest explorers on the northwest coast, however, found both fish and seal nets in use, though, as I have already mentioned, the seal net was spoken of at Point Barrow as a comparatively recent invention. At the present day, nets are used all along the coast from the Mackenzie and Anderson rivers (see MacFarlane's Collection) as far south at least as the Yukon delta.[2] I have not been able to learn whether gill nets are used in the delta of the Kuskoquim. Petroff[3] mentions fish traps and dip nets merely. That the natives of Kadiak formerly had no nets I infer from Petroff's statement[4] that " of late they have begun to use seines of whale sinew." Nets are generally used on the Siberian coast. We observed them ourselves at Plover Bay, and Nordenskiöld[5] describes the nets used at Pitlekaj, which are made of sinew thread. It is almost certain that the American Eskimo learned the use of the net from the Siberians, as they did the habit of smoking, since the use of the gill net appears to have been limited to precisely the same region as the Siberian form of tobacco pipe.[6]

Spears.—The only evidence which we have of the use of spears for catching fish in this region is a single specimen, No. 89901 [1227], Fig. 278, from Utkiavwĭñ, which was newly and rather carelessly made for sale, but intended, as we were told, for spearing fish. This has a roughly whittled shaft, of spruce, 21½ inches long, armed at one end with three prongs. The middle prong is of whalebone, 4⅓ inches long, inserted into the tip of the shaft, which is cut into a short neck and whipped with sinew. The side prongs are also of bone, 9 inches long. Through the tip of each is driven a sharp, slender slightly recurved spur of bone, about 1½ inches long. Each prong is fastened to the shaft with two small wooden treenails, and they are braced with a figure-of-eight lashing of sinew through holes in the side prongs and around the middle one. The side prongs are somewhat elastic, so that when the spear is struck down

⅛

Fig. 278.—
Fish spear.

---

[1] The Greenlanders used a sort of sieve or scoop net, not seen at Point Barrow, for catching caplin (Mallotus villosus). Egede, Greenland, p. 108; and Crantz, vol. 1, p. 95. John Davis, however, says of the Greenlanders in 1586, "They make nets to take their fish of the finne of a whale." Hakluyt's Voyages, etc. (1589), p. 782.

[2] Dall, Alaska, p. 147; and Petroff, Report, etc., p. 127.

[3] Op cit., p. 73.

[4] Op cit., p. 142.

[5] Vega, vol. 2, p. 109.

[6] See the writer's paper in the American Anthropologist, vol. 1, pp. 325-336.

on the back of a fish they spring apart and allow the middle prong to
pierce him, and then spring back so that the spurs either catch in his
sides or meet below his belly, precisely on the principle of the "patent
eel spear." This implement is almost identical with one in the National
Museum from Hudson Bay, which appears to be in general use among
the eastern Eskimo.[1] The name, kăki′bua, is very nearly the same as
that used by the eastern natives (kākkĭe-wĕi, Parry, and kakívak,
Kumlien). This spear is admirably adapted for catching large fish in
shallow rocky streams where a net can not be used, or where they are
caught by dams in tidal streams in the manner described by Egede and
Crantz. There is so little tide, however, on the northwest coast, that
this method of fishing can not be practiced, and, as far as I know, there
is no locality in the range of the Point Barrow natives, a region of open
shoal beaches, and rivers free of rocks, where this spear could be used
in which a net would not serve the purpose much better. Taking into
consideration the scarcity of these spears and the general use of nets, I
am inclined to believe that this spear is an ancient weapon, formerly in
general use, but driven out of fashion by the introduction of nets.

FLINT WORKING.

These people still retain the art of making flint arrow and spear-
heads, and other implements such as the blades for the skin scrapers to be
hereafter described. Many of the flint arrowheads and spear points already described were made at Nuwŭk or Utkiavwĭñ especially for sale
to us and are as finely formed and neatly finished as any of the ancient
ones. The flints, in many cases water-worn pebbles, appear to have
been splintered by percussion into fragments of suitable sizes, and these
sharp-edged spalls are flaked into shape by means of a little instrument consisting of a short, straight rod of some hard material mounted
in a short curved haft. We collected nine of these tools (kĭ′gli) of
which two have no blades. No. 89262 [1223] figured in Point Barrow
Report, Ethnology, Pl. III, Fig. 7, has been selected as the type. The
handle is of walrus ivory, 7·8 inches long, straight and nearly cylindrical for about 4½ inches, then bending down like a saw handle and
spread out into a spatulate butt. Fitted into a deep groove on the top
of the handle so that its tip projects 1·8 inches beyond the tip of the
latter is a slender four-sided rod of whale's bone, 4·7 inches long. This
is held in place by two simple lashings, one of cotton twine and the
other of seal thong. The flint to be flaked is held in the left hand and

---

[1] Kumlien's description (Contributions, p. 37, Cumberland Gulf) would apply almost word for word
to this spear, and Captain Parry, (Second Voyage, p. 509) describes a very similar one in use at Iglulik.
The "Perch, headed with two sharp-hooked Bones," for spearing salmon—called in the Grønlandsk
Ordbog, kakiak, "en Lyster (med to eller tre Pigge")—mentioned by Egede (Greenland, p. 108) is probably the same thing, and a similar spear is spoken of by Rae (Narrative, p. 172) as in use at Repulse
Bay. A similar weapon, described by Dr. Rink as "Mit einem in brittischen Columbien vorkommenden
identisch," was found in east Greenland (Deutsche Geographische Blätter, vol. 9, p. 234). See the
description of the spear found by Schwatka at Back's Great Fish River (Nimrod in the North, p. 139),
also described by Klutschak (Als Eskimo, etc., p. 120).

pressed against the fleshy part of the palm which serves as a cushion and is protected by wearing a thick deer-skin mitten. The tool is firmly grasped well forward in the right hand with the thumb on top of the blade and by pressing the point steadily on the edge of the flint, flakes of the desired size are made to fly off from the under surface.

These tools vary little in pattern, but are made of different materials.

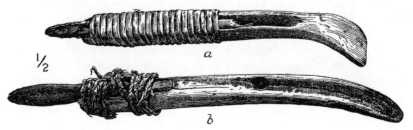

FIG. 279.—Flint flakers.

Hard bone appears to have been the commonest material for the blade, as three out of the seven blades are of this substance. One specimen (No. 89263 [796] from Utkiavwĭñ) has a blade of iron of the same shape but only 2 inches long. No. 89264 [1001] also from Utkiavwĭñ, Fig. 279a, has a short blade of black flint flaked into a four-sided rod 1½ inches long. This is held in place by a whipping of stout seal thong tightened by thrusting a splinter of wood in at the back of the groove.

Two specimens (Nos. 89260 [794] Fig. 279b and 89261 [1216] both from Utkiavwĭñ) have blades of the peculiar Nuᴇsuknan concretions previously described. Each is an oblong pebble wedged into the groove and secured by a lashing as usual. No. 89260 [794] has a haft of antler. This is rather the commonest material for the haft. Two specimens have hafts of walrus ivory and three of fossil ivory. The length of the haft is from 6 to 8 inches, of the blade 1·5 to 4·7 inches. Fig. 280 (No. 89265 [979] from Nuwŭk) is the haft of one of these tools, made of fossil ivory, yellow from age and stained brown in blotches, which shows the way in which the groove for the blade was excavated, namely, by boring a series of large round holes and cutting away the material between them. The remains of the holes are still to be seen in the bottom of the groove. The tip of this haft has been roughly carved into a bear's head with the eyes and nostrils incised and filled with

FIG. 280.—Haft of flint flaker. black dirt, and the eyes, nostrils, and mouth of a human face have been rudely incised on the under side of the butt and also blackened. All this carving is new and was done with the view of increasing the market value of the object. The original ornamentation consists of an incised pattern on the upper surface of the butt, colored with red ocher which has turned black from age and dirt.

Fig. 281 (No. 89782 [1004e]) is one of these tools, very neatly made, with a haft of reindeer antler and a bone blade, secured by a whipping of seal thong which belongs with the "kit" of tools owned by the "inland" native, Ilû'bw'ga. Mr. Nelson collected a number of specimens of this tool at various points on the northwest coast from Point Hope as far south as Norton Bay, but I can find no evidence of its use elsewhere.

⅓

FIRE MAKING.

Drills.—In former times fire was obtained in the method common to so many savages, from the heat developed by the friction of the end of a stick worked like a drill against a piece of soft wood. This instrument was still in use at least as late as 1837,[1] but appears to have been wholly abandoned at Point Barrow at the time of the *Plover's* visit, though still in use at Kotzebue Sound.[2]

FIG. 281.—Flint flaker with bone blade.

A native of Nuwŭk one day brought down for sale what he said was an exact model of the ancient fire drill, níootĭñ. This is No. 89822 [1080], Fig. 282. The drill is a stick of pine 12 inches long, shaped like the shaft of a common perforating drill, brought to a blunt but rounded

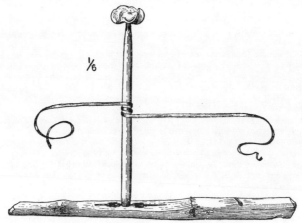

⅙

FIG. 282.—Fire drill with mouthpiece and stock.

point. This is worked by a string, without bow or handles, consisting of a strip of the skin of the bearded seal, 40 inches long, and has for a mouthpiece the astragalus bone of a reindeer, the natural hollow on one side serving as a socket for the butt of the drill.[3] The point of the drill

---

[1] "Their own clumsy method of producing fire is by friction with two pieces of dry wood in the manner of a drill."—(T. Simpson, Narrative, p. 162.)

[2] Dr. Simpson, op. cit., p. 242.

[3] Compare Nordenskiöld's figure of the fire drill in use at Pitlekaj (Vega, vol. 2, p. 121), which has a similar bone for a socket, held not in the mouth but in the left hand.

is made to work against the split surface of a stick of spruce 18 inches long, along the middle of which is cut a gash, to give the drill a start. Three equidistant circular pits, charred and blackened, were bored out by the tip of the drill, which developed heat enough to set fire to the sawdust produced. Tinder was probably used to catch and hold the fire.

Most authors who have treated of the Eskimo have described an instrument of this sort in use either in former times or at the present day.[1]

Among most Eskimo, however, a bow is used to work the drill. The only exceptions to this rule appears to have been the ancient Greenlanders and the people of Hudson Bay (see the passages from Hakluyt, Crantz, and Ellis, just quoted.) Chamisso, however,[2] speaks of seeing the Aleutians at Unalaska produce fire by means of a stick worked by a string making two turns about the stick and held and drawn with both hands, with the upper end of the stick turning in a piece of wood held in the mouth. When a piece of fir was turned against another piece of the same wood fire was often produced in a few seconds. This passage appears to have escaped the usually keen observation of Mr. W. H. Dall, who, speaking of the ancient Aleutians, says: " The 'fiddle-bow drill' was an instrument largely used in their carving and working bone and ivory; but for obtaining fire but two pieces of quarz were struck together," etc.[3]

---

[1] Bessels, Naturalist, vol. 18, pt. 9, p. 867, speaks of a fire drill used at Smith Sound with a bow and a mouthpiece of ivory.

A Greenlander; seen by John Davis, in 1586, " beganne to kindle a fire, in his manner: he took a piece of a boord, wherein was a hole halfe thorow: into that he puts the end of a roūd sticke like unto a bedstaffe, wetting the end thereof in traine, and in fashion of a turner, with a piece of lether, by his violent motion doth very speedily produce fire."—Hakluyt's Voyages, etc. (1589), p. 782.

"They take a short Block of dry Fir Tree, upon which they rub another Piece of hard Wood, till by the continued Motion the Fir catches Fire."—Egede, Greenland, p. 137.

"If their fire goes out, they can kindle it again by turning round a stick very quick with a string through a hole in a piece of wood."—Crantz, History of Greenland, vol. 1, p. 145.

Lyon (Journal, p. 210) says that at Iglulik they were able to procure "fire by the friction of a pin of wood in the hole of another piece and pressed down like a drill from above." This was worked with a bow and willow catkins were used for tinder. A man informed them that "he had learned it from his father rather for amusement than for utility; the two lumps of iron pyrites certainly answering the purpose a great deal better."

"They have a very dextrous Method of kindling Fire; in order to which, they prepare two small Pieces of dry Wood, which having made flat, they next make a small Hole in each, and having fitted into these Holes a little cylindrical Piece of Wood, to which a Thong is fastened, they whirl it about thereby with such a Velocity, that by rubbing the Pieces of Wood one against the other, this Motion soon sets them on fire."—Ellis, Voyage to Hudsons Bay, p. 234.

A picture of the process is given opposite page 132, in which a man holds the socket, while a woman works the thong (western shore of Hudson Bay, near Chesterfield Inlet).

Rae also mentions a similar drill used in the same region in 1847 (Narrative, p. 187); and there is a specimen in the National Museum, collected by MacFarlane, and said to be the kind "in use until lately" in the Mackenzie and Anderson region.

Dall figures a fire drill with bow and mouthpiece formerly in use at Norton Sound (Alaska, p. 142); and Hooper (Tents, etc., p. 187) describes a similar drill at Plover Bay.

From Nordenskiöld's account (Vega, vol. 2, p. 121) the fire drill seems to be still generally used by the natives at the Vega's winter quarters. He says that the women appeared more accustomed to the use of the drill than the men, and that a little oil was put on the end of the drill.

[2] Kotzebue's Voyage, vol. 3, p. 260.

[3] Contribution to N. A. Ethnology, vol. 1, p. 82.

I had no opportunity of seeing this drill manipulated, but I have convinced myself by experiment that the stick or "light-stock," to use Nordenskiöld's expression, must be held down by one foot, the workman kneeling on the other knee.

Flint and steel.—Fire is usually obtained nowadays by striking a spark in the ordinary method from a bit of flint with a steel, usually a bit of some white man's tool. Both are carried, as in Dr. Simpson's time, in a little bag slung around the neck, along with some tinder made of the down of willow catkins mixed with charcoal or perhaps gunpowder. The flints usually carried for lighting the pipe, the only ones I have seen, are very small, and only a tiny fragment of tinder is lighted which is placed on the tobacco. Lucifer matches (kĭlĭăksagau) were eagerly begged, but they did not appear to care enough for them to purchase them. Our friend Nĭkawáalu, from whom we obtained much information about the ancient customs of these people, told us that long ago, "when there was no iron and no flint"—"savik pĭñmût, ánma pĭñmût"[1]—they used to get "great fire" by striking together two pieces of iron pyrites. Dr. Simpson speaks[2] of two lumps of iron pyrites being used for striking fire, but he does not make it clear whether he saw this at Point Barrow or only at Kotzebue Sound. Iron pyrites appears to have been used quite generally among the Eskimo. Bessels saw it used with quartz at Smith Sound, with willow catkins for tinder[3] and Lyon mentions the use of two pieces of the same material, with the same kind of tinder, at Iglulik.[4] Willow catkins are also used for tinder at the Coppermine River.[5]

No. 89825 [1133 and 1722] are some of the catkins used for making the tinder, which were gathered in considerable quantities at the rivers. They are called kĭmmiuru, which perhaps means "little dogs," as we say "catkins" or "pussy willows."

Kindlings.—From the same place they also brought home willow twigs, 9 inches long, and tied with sinews into bunches or fagots of about a dozen or a dozen and a half each, which they said were used for kindling fires. (No. 89824 [1725].)

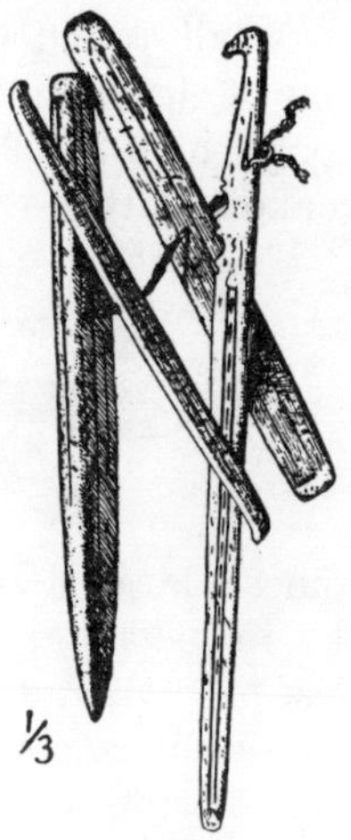

Bow-and-arrow making.—A complete set of bow-and-arrow tools consists of 4 pieces, viz: a marline spike, two twisters, and a feather setter, as shown in Fig. 283, No. 89465 [962], from Utkiavwĭñ. The pieces of this set are perforated and strung on a piece of sinew braid, 4 inches long, with a knot at each end.

⅓

FIG. 283.—Set of bow-and-arrow tools.

The Marline spike.—This is a flat, four-sided rod of walrus ivory, 5·6

---

[1] Compare this with Dr. Simpson's statement, quoted above, that stones for arrowheads were brought by the Nunatañmiun from the Ku'wûk River.
[2] Op. cit., p. 243.
[3] Naturalist, vol. 18, pt. 9, p. 867.
[4] Journal, pp. 210 and 231.
[5] Franklin, First Exped., vol. 2, p. 188.

inches long, tapering to a sharp rounded point at one end, and tapered slightly to the other, which terminates in a small rounded knob. It is very neatly made from, rather old yellow ivory, and ornamented on all four faces with conventional incised patterns colored with red ochre.

This implement is used in putting on the backing of a bow to raise parts of the cord when an end is to be passed under and in tucking in the ends in finishing off a whipping. It was probably also used in putting whippings or seizings on any other implements. We collected 10 of these tools, all quite similar, and made of walrus ivory, yellow from age and handling. They vary in length from 4½ to 6 inches, and are always contracted at the upper end into a sort of neck or handle, surmounted by a knob or crossbar. No. 89463 [836] Fig. 284, from Utkiavwĭñ has

FIG. 284.—Marline spike.

the crossbar carved very neatly into the figure of an Amphipod crustacean without the legs. The eyes, mouth, and vent are indicated by small round holes filled with some black substance, and there is a row of eight similar holes down the middle of the back. The tip of this tool, which is 5·9 inches long, has been concaved to an edge so as to make a feather-setter of it. Through the knob at the butt there is some-

FIG. 285.—Marline spike.

times a large round eye, as in Fig. 285 (No. 89464 [842] from Utkiavwĭñ, 4·7 inches long). These tools are sometimes plain, like the specimens last figured, and sometimes ornamented with conventional patterns of incised lines, colored with red ocher, like the others.

The twisters (No. 89465 [962]) are flat four-sided rods of walrus ivory, respectively 4·4 and 4·7 inches long. At each end one broad face is raised into a low transverse ridge about 0·1 inch high and the other rounded off, with the ridge on opposite faces at the two ends. They are ornamented on all four faces with longitudinal incised lines, colored with red ocher.

The use of these tools, which was discovered by actual experiment after our return to this country[1] is for twisting the strands of the sinew backing after it has been put on the bow into the cables already de-

[1] See the writer's paper on Eskimo bows, Smithsonian Report for 1884, pt. 2, p. 315.

scribed. The manner in which this tool is used is as follows: The end is inserted between the strands at the middle of the bow, so that the ridge or hook catches the lower strands, and the end is carried over through an arc of 180°, which gives the cable a half turn of twist. This brings the twister against the bow, so that the twisting can be carried no further in this direction, and if the tool were to be removed for a fresh start the strands would have to be held or fastened in some way, making the process a slow one. Instead, the tool is slid back between the strands till the other end comes where the first was, so that the hook. at this end catches the strand, and the workman can give to the cable another half turn of twist. This is continued until the cable is sufficiently twisted, the tool sliding back and forth like the handle of a vise. The tools are used in pairs, one being inserted in each cable and manipulated with each hand, so as to give the same amount of twist to each cable. At the present day, these tools are seldom used for bow making, since the sinew-backed bow is so nearly obsolete, but are employed in playing a game of the nature of pitch-penny. (See below, under games and pastimes.)

These tools, of which we collected twenty-six specimens, are all of walrus ivory, and of almost exactly the same shape, varying a little in size and ornamentation. They vary in length from 3 to 5·7 inches, but are usually about 4½ inches long. The commonest width is 0·4 inches, the narrowest being 0·3 and the width 0·7 broad, while the thickness is almost always 0·3, varying hardly 0·1 inch. Most of them are plain, but a few are ornamented with incised lines, and two are marked with "circles and dots" as in Fig. 286, one of a rather large pair (No. 56521

FIG. 286.—Twister for working sinew backing of bow.

[249] from Utkiavwĭñ). These are 5·4 inches long, neatly made and quite clean. All the others show signs of age and use.

There are large numbers of these tools in the National Museum from various points in the region where bows of the Arctic type are used, namely, from the Anderson River to Norton.Sound, and one from St. Lawrence Island, whence we have received no twisted bows. Their use was, however, not definitely understood, as they are described simply as "bow tools," "bow string twisters" or even "arrow polishers." Mr. Nelson informs me that the tool is now not used in Norton Sound, except for playing a game, as at Point Barrow, but that the natives told him that they were formerly used for tightening the backing on a bow and also for twisting the hard-laid sinew cord, which is quite as much, if not more, used at Norton Sound as the braid so common at Point Barrow. I find no mention of the use of this tool in any of the authors who have treated of the Eskimo, except the following in Capt. Beechey's vocabulary, collected at Kotzebue Sound: "Marline spike, small of ivory, for lacing bows—ke-poot-tak." The specimens from the Mackenzie and Anderson rivers are almost without exception made of hard bone, while walrus ivory is the common material elsewhere. The name (kapute) means simply a "twister."

The feather-setter (ĭ′gugwau) (No. 89465 [962]) is a flat, slender, rounded rod of walrus ivory, 7 inches long, with the tip abruptly concaved to a thin rounded edge. The faces are ornamented with a pattern of straight incised lines, colored with red ocher. This tool is used for squeezing the small ends of the feathering into the wood of the arrow shaft close

FIG. 287.—"Feather-setter."

to the nock. Fig. 287 is a similar tool (No. 89486 [1285] from Utkiavwĭñ) also of walrus ivory, 6 inches long, with the upper end roughly whittled to a sharp point. It is probably made of a broken seal indicátor or meat-cache marker. Several other ivory tools previously mentioned have been concaved to an edge at the tip so that they can be used as feather-setters. I do not find this tool mentioned by previous observers, nor have I seen any specimens in the National Museum.

Fig. 288 (No. 89459 [1282] from Utkiavwĭñ) represents an unusual

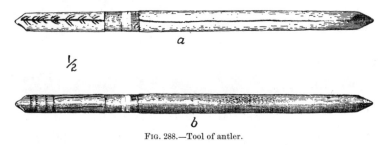

FIG. 288.—Tool of antler.

tool, the use of which was not ascertained in the hurry of trade. It has a point like that of a graver, and is made of reindeer antler, ornamented with a pattern of incised lines and bands, colored with red ocher, and was perhaps a marline spike for working with sinew cord.

SKIN-WORKING.

Scrapers (ikun).—For removing bits of flesh, fat, etc., from a "green" skin, and for "breaking the grain" and removing the subcutaneous tissue from a dried skin, the women, who appear to do most if not all of this work, use a tool consisting of a blunt stone blade, mounted in a short, thick haft of wood or ivory, fitting exactly to the inside of the hand and having holes or hollows to receive the tips of the fingers and thumb. The skin is laid upon the thigh and thoroughly scraped with this tool, which is grasped firmly in the right hand and pushed from the worker. This tool is also used for softening up skins which have become stiffened from being wet and then dried. The teeth appear to be less often used for such purposes than among the eastern Eskimo.

We obtained eighteen such scrapers, some without blades, and two unmounted blades. Every woman owns one of these tools. While they are all of the same general model, they vary a good deal in details. Four different forms or subtypes have been recognized in the series collected, all modifications of the form seen in Fig. 289, No. 89313 [955], which may be called the type. The blade is of brown jasper, rather coarsely flaked, 1·1 inches long. It is wedged with pieces of skin, into a deep slot in the tip of the handle, which is of fossil ivory, slightly yellowed from handling. The left side against

FIG. 289.—Skin scraper.

which the thumb rests is slightly flattened, and the right slightly excavated to receive the third and fourth fingers, which are bent round under the lobe, their tips pressing against the concave under surface of the latter. The fore and middle fingers rest upon the upper surface.

No. 89320 [1171] from Utkiavwiñ, without a blade, is of the same general pattern, but is slightly excavated on the left as well as the right side so as to make a sort of shank. It is of fossil ivory, stained a dingy orange from age and grease. The two incised circles and dots on the upper surface close to the slot make the end of the handle look like the head of a Lophius, which it is perhaps meant to represent. No. 89321 (858), an old fossil ivory handle, has the left side slightly hollowed to receive the tip of the thumb, and a median keel on the upper surface with a barely perceptible hollow on each side of it for the tips of the fingers. This is a step toward the second subtype as shown in Fig. 290 (No. 89317 [748] from Utkiavwiñ, which has no blade). This

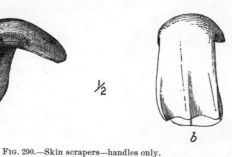

FIG. 290.—Skin scrapers—handles only.

is of fossil ivory, thicker and more strongly arched than the type described, deeply excavated below so as to form a broad lobe at the butt, with the upper surface deeply grooved to receive the tips of the fore and middle fingers, and a slight hollow on the left side for the thumb. This specimen is very neatly made and polished, and all the edges are rounded off. One-half of the handle (lengthwise) and the outer quarter of the other half are stained with age and grease a beautiful amber brown. This specimen was said to be as old as the time when men wore but one labret.

The only essential difference between this subtype and the preced-

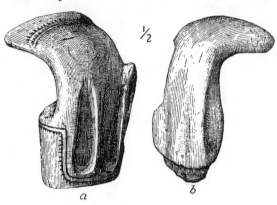

½

a

b

FIG. 291.—Skin scrapers.

ing is that the former has deep grooves or hollows for the thumb and two fingers. We collected five specimens of this pattern, all but one with handles of fossil ivory. The single exception, which came from Sidaru, has a handle of walrus ivory, yellowed with age and grease. This specimen (Fig. 291a, No. 89322 [1426]) has an unusually short blade (only 0·4 inch long), and is much cut out on the right side so as to make a sort of nick. Fig. 291b (No. 89314 [1780]) is a nearly new handle of this pattern, which was bought of the "Nunatañmiun," who came to Pernyû in 1883. It is very highly ornamented, both with incised patterns, colored black, and by carving the space between the unusually deep thumb hollow and those for the fingers into what seems to be meant for an ear, in high relief, colored red inside.

½

FIG. 292.—Skin scraper.

The third subtype has the lobe separated from the body on the right side only, leaving the left side unexcavated, except by the thumb-hollow, as is shown in Fig. 292 (No. 89316 [1177] from Utkiavwĭñ) which has a handle of yellowed fossil ivory and a black flint blade. No. 89310 [1071]

½

FIG. 293.—Peculiar modification of scraper.

Fig. 293, from Utkiavwĭñ, is a rather unusual modification of this pattern, with a wooden handle, in which the bottom is not cut out. The thumb groove is deepened into a large hole which opens into the excavation on the right side, while a large oblong slot on top, opening into these cavities, takes the place of the two finger hollows. The blade was of gray flint and rather longer than usual.

The last subtype which, according to my recollection, is the one most frequently seen in use at the present day, has the butt produced horizontally into a broad, flat lobe. The excavation of the right side may be continued through to the left in the form of a notch, as shown in Fig. 294 (No. 89315 [1365] from Sidaru) which has a blade of black flint and a handle of fossil ivory, with hollows for the thumb and fingers; or the left side may be unexcavated except for the thumb groove as in Fig. 295 (No. 89309 [1135] from Utkiavwĭñ). This specimen has a rather large wooden

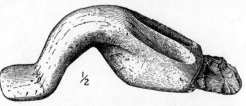

FIG. 294.—Skin scraper.

handle, with the grooves as before. It appears, however, to have been remodeled to fit a smaller hand than that of the original owner, as the thumb groove has been deepened for about two-thirds of its original length, and there is a deep, round hole in the middle of the groove for

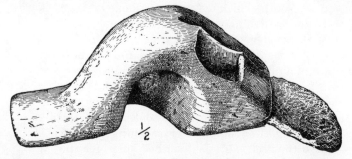

FIG. 295.—Skin scraper.

the second finger. The peculiarity of this specimen, however, is that it has a blade of sandstone, flat and rather thin, with a smooth, rounded edge. The natives told us that scraper blades of sandstone were the prevailing form in old times.

Fig. 296 (No. 89312 [1336] from Utkiavwĭñ) is another wooden handle,

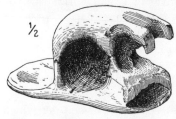

FIG. 296.—Skin scraper.

in which the excavation for the third and fourth fingers is merely a large round hole on the right side, while in front the handle is cut into two short lobes, between which in a deep groove the forefinger fits. There is a hollow for the thumb under the left lobe and one on the right for the middle finger. No. 89311 [1079] from the same village is almost exactly similar. These are the only two specimens of the kind which I recollect seeing. A rather large flint-bladed scraper with a wooden handle very much the shape of that of No. 89309 [1135] is the tool most generally used at the present day. The blades are all of the same general shape and vary in size from the little one above mentioned (No. 89322

[1426], Fig. 291*a*), only 0·4 inch long, to blades like No. 89612 [820], Fig. 297, from Utkiavwĭñ. This is newly made from light gray translucent flint and is 5 inches long. The name kibûgû, applied to this specimen by the native from whom it was purchased, appears to refer either to the material or the unusual size. The blade is ordinarily called kuki, "a claw." With the ivory handles a blade about 1 or 1½ inches is commonly used and with the wooden ones a considerably larger one, 2 to 3 inches in length. The handles vary in size to fit the hands of the owners, but are all too small for an average white man's hand. All that we collected are for the right hand.

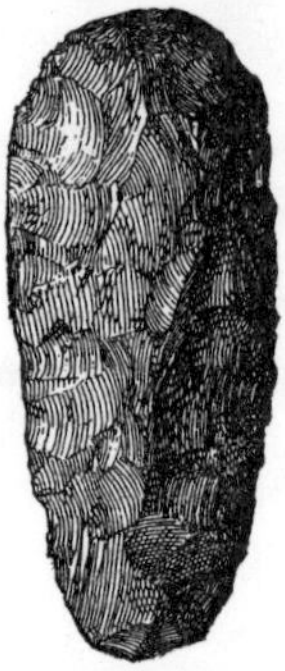

This pattern of skin scraper which appears from the Museum collections to be the prevailing one from Point Barrow to Norton Sound, is evidently the direct descendant of the form used still farther south, which consists of a stone or bone blade of the same shape, mounted on a wooden handle often a foot or 18 inches long, which has the other end bent down into a handle like the butt of a pistol. Shortening this handle (a process shown by specimens in the Museum) would bring the worker's hand nearer to the blade, thus enabling him to guide it better. Let this process be continued till the whole handle is short enough to be grasped in the hand and we have the first subtype described, of which the others are clearly improvements.

FIG. 297.—Flint blade for skin scraper.

A still more primitive type of scraper is shown by Fig. 298, No. 89651 [1295] from Utkiavwĭñ, the only specimen of the kind seen. This has a flint blade, like those of the modern scrapers, inserted in the larger end of a straight haft of reindeer antler, 5½ inches long. We did not learn the history of this tool in the hurry of trade, but from the shape of the blade it is evidently a scraper. Its use as a skin scraper is rendered still more probable by the fact that the scrapers used by some of the eastern Eskimo (there are specimens in the Museum from Cumberland Gulf and Pelly Bay) have straight handles, though shorter than this.

FIG. 298.—Straight-hafter scraper.

The Siberian natives use an entirely different form of scraper which has a long handle like that of a spoke-shave with a small blade of stone or iron in the middle and is worked with both hands.[1] Fig. 299 (No. 89488 [1578] from Utkiavwĭñ) is a tool which we never saw in use but which we were told was intended for scraping skins. It is probably an obsolete tool, as a knife would better serve the purpose of re-

---

[1] Nordenskiöld, Vega, vol. 2, pp. 122, and Fig. 1, p. 117.

moving the subcutaneous tissue, etc., while the stone scrapers just described are better for softening the skin.

It is the distal end of the "cannon" bone or metacarpal, of a reindeer,
6·2 inches long, with the two condyles forming the handle. At the other
end the posterior face of the shaft is chamfered off so as to expose the
medullary cavity for about 2½ inches, leaving a sharp edge on each
side. The tip is roughly broken off. The tool appears
to be old but the two condyles have been recently carved
rudely into two human faces, one male (with marks for
labrets) and the other female. There is a somewhat
similar tool in the Museum brought by Mr. Nelson from
Norton Sound.

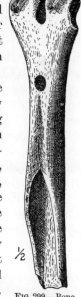

Scraper cups (óhovwĭñ).—In removing the last of the
blubber from the skins of seals or walruses when they
wish to save the oil, they scrape it off with a little oblong
cup of walrus ivory with a sharp edge at one or both
ends. The cup, of course, catches the oil which is transferred to a dish. These cups are sometimes, I believe,
also used for dipping oil. We collected ten of these cups,
of which No. 89251 [1287], Fig. 300a, will serve as the
type. This is 3·7 inches long, carved out of a single
piece of walrus ivory, and worked down from the inside
to a sharp edge on each end. The carving is smoothly
done on the outside, but more roughly within, where it
is somewhat hacked. It is stained a dark yellow with oil
and polished on the outside, probably by much handling.

½

FIG. 299.—Bone
scraper.

Fig. 300b (No. 89258 [1090] also from Utkiavwĭñ) is a similar cup, but has a sharp edge only at one end which is cut out in a
concave curve.

The ten cups in the collection are all about the same shape and size
and all of walrus ivory, stained yellow with oil. The largest is 4 inches
long and 2¾ wide, and the smallest, 3 by 2·1 inches. The majority are

½

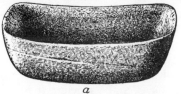

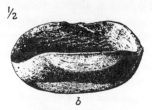

a

b

FIG. 300.—Scraper cups.

about 3½ by 2½ inches. Five of the ten have sharp edges at both ends,
the rest at one only. Mr. Nelson brought home specimens of this implement from Point Hope and St. Lawrence Island, but I do not find
it mentioned elsewhere.

With these tools and their knives, they do all the work of preparing
skins for clothing, boat covers, etc. I had no opportunity of seeing the

process in all its stages, and can therefore give only a general account of it. Deerskins are always dressed as furs, with the hair on. The skin is rough-dried in the open air, with considerable subcutaneous tissue adhering to it, and laid aside until needed. When wanted for use, a woman takes the skin and works it over carefully with a stone scraper on the flesh side, removing every scrap of subcutaneous tissue and "breaking the grain" of the skin, which leaves a surface resembling white chamois leather and very soft. This is then rubbed down with a flat piece of sandstone or gypsum, and finally with chalk, so that when finished it seems like pipeclayed leather. All furs are prepared in the same way. Small seal skins to be worn with the hair on are scraped very clean and, I think, soaked in urine, before they are spread out to dry. The black waterproof seal skin has the hair shaved off close to the skin, great care being taken to leave the epidermis intact, and also has a certain amount of tanning in urine. It is probable that a little of the blubber is left on these skins, to make them oily and waterproof.

When, however they wish to prepare the white-tanned seal skin, the skins are brought into the warm house, thawed out or dampened and then rolled up and allowed to ferment for several days, so that when they are unrolled hair and epidermis are easily scraped off together. The skin is then soaked in urine, stretched on a large hoop, and put out to dry in the sun and air. Many of these skins are prepared during the first sunny weather in the early spring. The skins of the large seal, walrus or bear when used for boat-covers or boot soles appear to be sweated in the same way, as the epidermis is always removed. We did not learn whether urine was employed on these skins, but I think from their ordinary appearance that they are simply stretched and dried in their own fat, as appears to be the case with the skin of the beluga, from which the epidermis is easily scraped without sweating.[1]

Combs for deerskins.—The loosened hairs on a deerskin garment are removed by means of a comb made of a section of the beam of an antler, hollowed out and cut into teeth on the end. This instrument probably serves also to remove vermin, as its name "kúmotĭn" looks very much as if derived from kúmŭk, louse. I must say, however, that the natives whom I asked if kúmotĭn had anything to do with kúmŭk said it had not. When vermin get troublesome in a garment, it is taken out on the tundra, away from the houses, and beaten with rods like a carpet. Very old garments when much infested with lice are taken out back of the village, cut into small pieces, and burned. It is no uncommon sight in the spring to see an old woman sitting out on the tundra, busy with her knife cutting up old clothes.

We brought home nine of these combs, of which No. 89354 [1879], Fig. 301a, has been selected as the type. It is 4¼ inches long and has

---

[1] Crantz describes the process of preparing boat covers as follows: "The boat skins are selected out of the stoutest seals' hides, from which the fat is not quite taken off; they roll them up, and sit on them, or let them lie in the sun covered with grass several weeks, 'till the hair will come off." History of Greenland, vol. 1, p. 167.

sixteen teeth about 1 inch long. The small holes near the other end are for a lanyard to hang it up by.

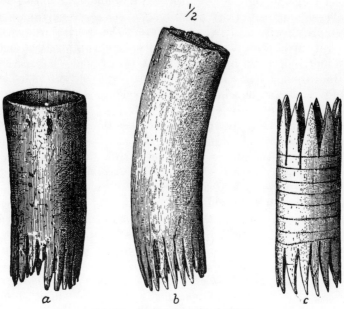

FIG. 301.—Combs for cleaning deerskins.

Six of these combs have teeth at one end only, the other three at both ends. These teeth are generally about fifteen in number, and 1 inch or a little over long. No. 89781 [1005], a very small comb only 2·9 inches long, which belonged to the "inland" native Ilûbw'ga, has twenty teeth 0·6 inch long. These combs are usually about 4 or 4½ inches long. No. 89556 [1017], Fig. 301b, from Utkiavwïñ is an unusually long comb, 5·3 inches long, which is peculiar in being solid except at the end which is cut into teeth.

Fig. 301c (No. 89359 [993]), from Utkiavwïñ is a double-ended comb, having ten teeth on one end and thirteen on the other. It is 4·1 inches long and made with considerable care, being ornamented with incised rings colored with red ocher. This is a common implement at Point Barrow, but seems unusual elsewhere. There is a single specimen from the Diomedes in Mr. Nelson's collection.

MANUFACTURE OF LINES OF THONG.

No tools are used for this purpose except a knife. I have seen a small jackknife used for cutting the fine seal skin lines. The workman takes a wet skin from which the hair and epidermis have been removed and sits down cross-legged on the ground with somebody else to hold the skin stretched for him. Then holding the knife vertically up with the edge away from him, he starts at one corner of the skin and cuts a narrow strip in one continuous piece, going round and round the skin, gathering and stretching the strip with the left hand. They do this work quite rapidly and with great skill, cutting single lines upward of 90 feet long and only one-eighth inch in diameter, almost perfectly even. These fine lines of seal-skin thong, which serve a great variety of purposes, are usually made when they are in the summer camps, before the breaking up of the ice. They are dried by stretching them between stakes 6 inches or a foot high, driven into the ground.

The stout thongs of the hide of the bearded seal, walrus, or beluga are usually made in the winter and stretched to dry between posts of whales' bones set up in the village, about breast high. While they are drying, the maker carefully trims and scrapes the edges with his knife, so as to make an almost round line.[1] The usual diameter is about 0·3 inch. These lines are not always made with such care, being often merely flat thongs. Fine deer-skin twine, or "babiche," as it is called by the voyageurs, for making the nettings of snow shoes, is made in the same way. A deer skin is dampened, rolled up, and put up over the lamp for a day or two to remove the hair by sweating, and then cut into a single long piece of fine thong.

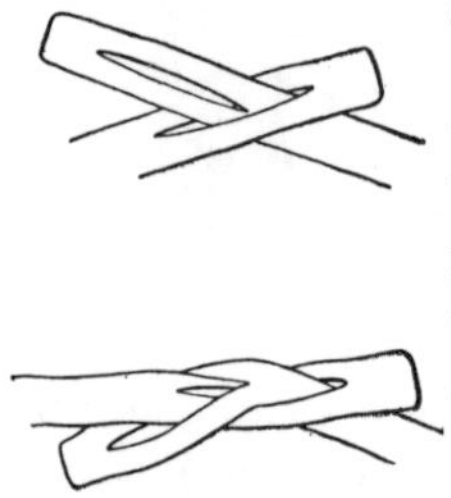

All the men do not appear able to do this fine work. For instance, our friend Mû'ñialu had the babiche for his new snowshoes made by his house-mate, the younger Tuñazu. When it is desired to fasten together two pieces of the stouter kinds of thong, what I have so often referred to as the "double-slit splice" is generally employed. This

FIG. 302.—Double-slit splice for rawhide lines.

is made as follows: The two ends to be joined together are each slit lengthwise, and one is passed through the slit in the other. The other end of this piece is then passed through the slit in the first piece, and drawn through so that the sides of each slit interlace like the loops of a square knot (see diagrams, Fig. 302). The splice is often further secured by a seizing of sinew braid. Most writers on the Eskimo have not gone sufficiently into the details of their arts to describe their methods of splicing. One writer,[2] however, in describing some Eskimo implements from East Greenland, describes and figures several splices somewhat of this nature, and one in particular especially complicated by crossing the sides of the slits and passing the end through several times. This method of uniting thongs is probably very general among the Eskimo and is also common enough among civilized people.

BUILDERS' TOOLS.

For excavating.—At the present day they are very glad to use white men's picks and shovels when they want to dig in the gravel or clean out the ice from their houses. They, however, have mattocks and pick

---

[1] Gilder describes a similar process of manufacturing these lines at Hudson's Bay. (Schwatka's Search, p. 176.)

[2] W. J. Sollas, in Jour. Anthrop. Inst. of Great Britain and Ireland, vol. 9, pp. 329-336.

axes (síkla) of their own manufacture, which are still in use. These are
always single-pointed and have a bone or ivory head, mounted like an
adz head on a rather short haft. The haft, like those of the mauls and
adzes already described, is never fitted into the head, but always applied
to the under surface of the latter and held on by a lashing of thong.

The only complete
implement of the
kind which we ob-
tained is No. 73574
[297], Fig. 303. The
head is of whale's
rib, 17¾ inches long.
The butt is shoul-
dered on the under
surface to receive
the haft and rough-
ened with crosscuts
to prevent slipping,
with two shallow

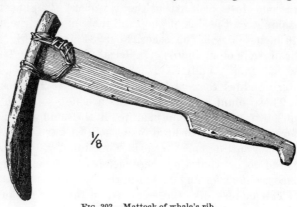

FIG. 303.—Mattock of whale's rib.

rough transverse notches on the upper surface for the lashings. The
haft is of pine, 24½ inches long. The lashing is of stout thong of bearded
seal hide, in two pieces, one of four turns passing through the hole, round
the front edge of the haft, over the lower notch in the head, and back
across the haft to the hole again. The ends are knotted together on top

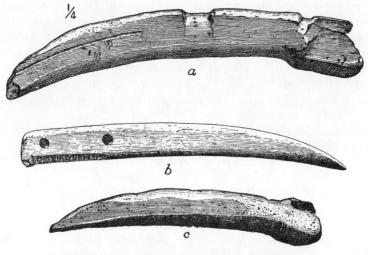

FIG. 304.—Pickax heads of bone, ivory, and whale's ribs.

of the head by becket-hitching one end into an eye in the other, made by
slitting it close to the tip and passing a bight of the standing part through
this slit. The other part is of seven turns, put on in the same way, but
crossing back of the haft, and started by looping one end round the
head and through the eye by means of an eye at the end made as before.

It is finished off by winding the end three or four times round these turns, so as to tighten them up, and hitching it round two of them on one side. This method of hafting differs in no essential respect from that used on the mauls and adzes above described.

We have also two heads for such mattocks, which hardly differ from the one described, except the No. 56494 [285] has the notches for the lashings on the side of the head instead of on the upper surface. It is 16 inches long. The other, No. 89843 [1043], Fig. 304a, is a very rude head made of an almost cylindrical piece of rib. This is a very old tool, which from its oily condition has evidently been long laid away in some blubber room at Utkiavwĭñ. It is 15·2 inches long.

These blunt-pointed mattocks are not so much used at present as picks with a sharp point mounted in the same way, and specially adapted for working in ice or hard frozen soil. I have, however, never seen them used for cutting holes in the ice for fishing, which some authors have supposed to be what they were meant for. Their shape makes them very inconvenient for any such a purpose, except when the ice is very thin.

The ice pick, like those carried on the butt of the spear, is under any circumstances a more serviceable tool. These sharp pickax heads are generally made of a walrus tusk, the natural shape of which requires very little alteration to fit it for the purpose. We collected three of these ivory heads, all very nearly alike, of which No. 56539b [96], Fig. 304b, will serve as the type. This is the tip of a good-sized walrus tusk, 14·2 inches long, preserving very nearly the natural outline of the tusk except at the point, where it is rounded off rather more abruptly above. It is keeled along the upper edge and on the lower edge at the point, so that the latter is four-sided, and the sides of the butt are flattened. On the under side the butt is cut off flat for about 3½ inches, leaving a low flange or ridge, and roughened with crosscuts to fit the end of the haft, and the butt is perforated with two large tranverse eyes for the lashing. The other two heads are almost exactly like this and very nearly the same size.

Sharp-pointed pick heads of whale's bone appear also to have been used, probably at an earlier date than the neatly finished ivory ones, as we collected three such heads, all very old and roughly made, and having notches or grooves for the lashings instead of eyes. Fig. 304c is one of these, No. 89844 [1315], from Utkiavwĭñ, very rudely cut from a piece of whale's rib, 12 inches long.

I do not recollect seeing any of these bone-headed picks in use, while the ivory-headed one was one of the commonest tools. This Eskimo tool is in use at Pitlekaj, a village supposed to be wholly inhabited by sedentary Chukches.[1]

TOOLS FOR SNOW AND ICE WORKING.

Snow knives.—For cutting the blocks of snow used in building the

---

[1] Nordenskiöld's figures, Vega, vol. 2, p. 123.

apu'ya, or snow hut, they at the present day prefer a saw or a large steel knife (for instance, a whaleman's boarding knife), if they can procure it, but they still have many of the large saber-shaped ivory knives so commonly used by the Eskimo everywhere for this purpose. These are, however, more generally used for scraping snow off their clothing, etc., at

FIG. 305.—Ivory snow knife.

present. We brought home two of these knives, which do not differ in any important respect from the many specimens collected by other explorers in Alaska.

No. 89478 [759], Fig. 305, is one of these—saviu'ra, "like a knife." It is of walrus ivory (following the natural outline of the tusk), 16½ inches

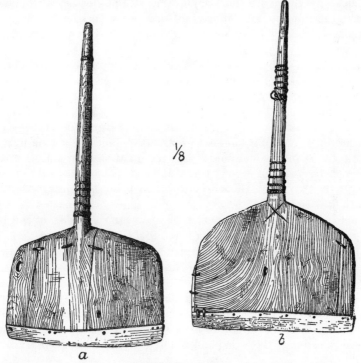

FIG. 306.—Snow shovels.

long. The blade is double-edged, the haft rounded on the edges and laced along the lower edge for 3¼ inches with a double piece of sinew braid. The object of this is to give the hand a firmer grip on the haft. These knives are also used for cutting the blocks of snow to supply the house with water.

Snow shovels.—The broad, short-handled snow shovel of wood with a

9 ETH——20

sharp edge of ivory is the tool universally employed whenever snow is to be shoveled, either to clear it away or for excavating houses or pit-falls in the snowdrifts, or " chinking " up the crevices in the walls of the snow house, and is an indispensable part of the traveler's outfit in winter. The shovels (pĭ′ksun) are all made on essentially the same pattern, which is well shown by Fig. 306a, No. 56739 [30]. The blade is 14 inches broad and 11 long. The whole upper surface of the shovel is flat. The handle is beveled off on the side to a rounded edge below, and is quite thick where it joins the blade, tapering off to the tip. The blade is thick and abruptly rounded off on the upper edge below and gradually thinned down to the edge. The edge of the wood is fitted with a tongue into a grove in the top of the ivory edge, which is 1½ inches deep. It is fastened on by wooden tree-nails at irregular intervals, and at one end, where the edge of the groove has been broken, by a stitch of black whalebone. The wooden part of the shovel is made of four unequal pieces of spruce, neatly fitted and doweled together and held by the ivory edge and three stitches of black whalebone close to the upper edge, and countersunk below the flat surface. The whippings of sinew braid on the handle are to give a firm grip for the hands.

No. 56738 [27], Fig. 306b, is a similar shovel of the same material and almost exactly the same dimensions, figured to show the way it has been pieced together and mended. The maker of this shovel was able to procure a broad piece of wood which only had to be pieced out with a narrow strip on the left side, which is fastened on as before. It was, however, not long enough to make the whole of the handle, which has a piece 8½ inches long, neatly scarfed on at the end and secured by six stout treenails of wood; three at each end of the joint, passing through the thin part of the scarf into the thick, but not through the latter. Nearly the whole handle was seized with sinew braid put on as before, but much of this seizing is broken off. At the right side of the blade the grain takes a twist, bringing it parallel to the ivory edge, and rendering it liable to split, as has happened from the warping of the ivory since the shovel has been in the Museum. The owner sought to prevent this by fastening to the edge a stout " strap " of walrus ivory 4½ inches, which appears to be an old bird spear point. The lower end of this fitted into the groove of the ivory edge, and it was held on by three equidistant lashings of narrow whalebone, each running through a hole in the edge of the wood and round the ivory in a deep transverse groove.

This pattern of snow shovel is very like that from Iglulik, figured by Capt. Lyon,[1] but the handle of the latter is so much shorter in proportion to the blade that there is an additional handle like that of a pot lid near the head of the blade on the upper surface. The ivory edge also appears to be fastened on wholly with stitches.

---

[1] Parry's Second Voy., pl. opposite p. 548, Fig. 5.

Fig. 307 (No. 89775 [1250] from Utkiavwĩñ) is a peculiar implement, the only one of the kind that we saw. It is a shovel, 17 inches long, made of a whale's scapula, with the anterior and posterior borders cut off straight so as to make it 13¼ inches broad, and the superior margin beveled off to an edge. The handle is made by flattening the neck of the scapula and cutting through it a large horizontal elliptical slot, below which the end of the scapula is worked into a rounded bar 1 inch in diameter. The cutting around this slot appears new, and red ocher has been rubbed into the crevices. On the other hand, the beveling of the digging edge appeared to be old. Though colored with red ocher, the edge is

gapped as if from use, and there are fragments of tundra moss sticking to it. It is probably an old implement "touched up" for sale. We did not learn whether such tools were now gener-

FIG. 307.—Snow shovel made of a whale's scapula.

ally used. This may have been a makeshift or an individual fancy.

Fig. 308 (No. 89521 [1249] from Utkiavwĩñ) is another peculiar tool of which we saw no other specimen. It appears to be really an old implement and was said to have been used for digging or picking in the snow. It is a stout sharp-pointed piece of bone, 3 inches long, inserted in the end of a piece of a long bone of some animal, 4·7 inches long and about 1½ wide, which serves as a haft.

Ice picks—The ivory ice pick (tu'u) always attached to the seal-harpoon has been already described. This differs from the *tôk* of the Greenlanders and other eastern Eskimo in having a sharp bayonet point, while the latter is often chisel-pointed. All the men now have iron ice picks which they use for cutting the holes for fishing, setting seal nets, and such purposes. These are made of some white man's tool which has a socket, like a harpoon iron, a whale lance,

½

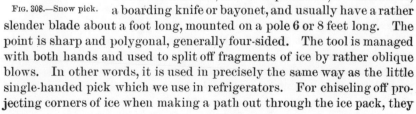

FIG. 308.—Snow pick.

a boarding knife or bayonet, and usually have a rather slender blade about a foot long, mounted on a pole 6 or 8 feet long. The point is sharp and polygonal, generally four-sided. The tool is managed with both hands and used to split off fragments of ice by rather oblique blows. In other words, it is used in precisely the same way as the little single-handed pick which we use in refrigerators. For chiseling off projecting corners of ice when making a path out through the ice pack, they often use whale spades, of which they have obtained a great many from wrecks.

No. 89483 [1313] from Utkiavwĭñ, is a very old pick made of a piece of reindeer antler, 11¼ inches long, split lengthwise, and tapered to a sharp curved point. The butt is cut into a sort of tang with a low shoulder. The split face is concave, the soft interior tissue having been removed by decay and perhaps also intentionally. Another peculiar tool is shown in Fig. 309 (No. 89479 [1064] from Utkiavwĭñ). This was called kăkaiyaxion, and is a rounded piece of antler 10·4 inches long, tapering from the butt where there is a low shoulder and the broken remains of a rounded tang to be fitted to a shaft. One side is cut off flat from the shoulder to the tip, gradually becoming concave. The concavity is deepest near the middle. The tip is slightly expanded, rounded, and somewhat bent toward the convex side. The specimen is smoothly and neatly made and dark brown from age. No other specimens were seen. We were told that this tool was mounted on a long pole and used for drilling holes in the ice by making the pole revolve with the hands.

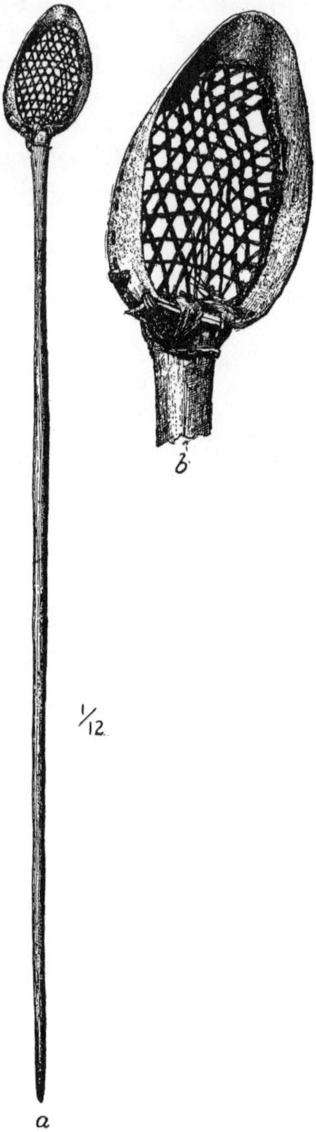

FIG. 309.—Snow drill.

Ice scoops.—When picking a hole through the ice they use a long-handled scoop, made of a piece of antler bent round into a hoop, and netted across the bottom with strips of whalebone, so that the water may drain off in dipping pieces of ice out of the water. We brought home one specimen of this universal implement (No. 89903 [1696], Fig. 310). The handle is of oak, 5 feet 1¾ inches long and elliptical in section. The rim of the bowl is a long thin strip of antler, apparently from the "palm," bent round into a pointed oval, 8½ inches long and 5¾ wide,

FIG. 310.—Ice scoop.

with the ends of the strip overlapping about 3 inches at the broader end. The ends are sewed together with two vertical stitches of whalebone. The left end has been broken across obliquely near the joint and mended with whalebone stitches. Round the lower edge of the rim runs a row of twenty-seven pairs of small holes 0·2 inch from the edge. The holes of each pair are connected by a deep channel, and a narrow shallow groove, probably for ornament, joins the pairs. On the left side are eight extra holes between the pairs, which are not used. Through these holes, omitting the first two pairs in the right-hand end, is laced a piece of seal thong, thus: Starting at the point of the oval, the two ends of the thong are passed through the pair of holes there from the outside and the bight drawn home into the channel; the ends are crossed, the left end going to the right, and vice versa, and passed out through the farther hole of the next pair and in through the nearer, and so on till the ends meet at the broad end of the oval where they are tied together, thus making twenty-five loops on the inside of the rim into which the netting is fastened. This is made of strips of thin whalebone, interwoven, over and under each other, passing up through one loop and down through the next. There are eleven longitudinal strands passing obliquely from right to left, the same number from left to right, and eleven transverse strands, making a network with elongated hexagonal apertures. The strips are not one continuous piece. The bowl thus made is fastened to the handle by three pieces of stout seal thong. The whole lashing was put on wet, and allowed to shrink.

Nordenskiöld mentions and figures a scoop of almost identically the same pattern, but smaller, in general use for the same purposes at Pitlekaj.[1] A smaller scoop or skimmer (ĕlauatĭn) is also universally used. We inadvertently neglected to preserve a specimen of this very common implement, though we had two or three about the station for our own use. I shall therefore have to describe it from memory. The handle is a flat, straight stick with rounded edges, about 18 inches or 2 feet long, 1½ inches broad, and three-fourths inch thick. The bowl is made of two pieces of antler "palm" of such a shape that when they are fastened together on the end of the stick they make a shallow cup about 3½ inches long by 3 wide, with a longitudinal crevice along the middle which allows the water to drain off. The tip of the handle is beveled off on both sides so as to fit into the inside of this cup, along the junction of the two pieces, each of which is fastened to it by one or two neat stitches of whalebone. The two pieces are fastened together in front of the handle with a stitch.

In addition to the use of these scoops for skimming the fishing holes, and reeling up the line, as already described, they also serve as scrapers to remove snow and hoar frost from the clothing. In the winter most of the men and boys, epecially the latter, carry these skimmers whenever they go out doors, partly for the sake of having something in their hands, as we carry sticks, and partly for use. The boys are very fond of using them to pick up and sling snowballs, bits of ice, or frozen dirt, which they do with considerable force and accuracy.

---

[1] Vega, vol. 1, p. 493.

IMPLEMENTS FOR PROCURING AND PREPARING FOOD.

Blubberhooks (nĭ′ksĭgû).—For catching hold of pieces of blubber or flesh when "cutting in" a whale or walrus, or dragging them round on shore or on the ice, or in the blubber rooms, they use hooks made by fastening a backward-pointing prong of ivory on the end of a wooden handle, which is bent into a crook at the other end. Those specially intended for use in the boats have handles 7 or 8 feet long, while those for shore use are only 2 or 3 feet long. These implements, which are common all along the Alaskan coast, may sometimes be used as boathooks, as appears to be the case farther south, though I never saw them so employed. We brought home two short hooks and one long one, No. 56766 [126], Fig. 311. This has a prong of walrus ivory fastened to a spruce pole, 7 feet 7¾ inches long, to the other end of which is fastened a short crook of antler. The pole is elliptical in section. The crook is a nearly straight "branch" of an antler with a transverse arm at the base made by cutting out a piece of the "beam" to fit against the pole, and is held on by three neat lashings of whalebone of the usual pattern. The upper two of these are transverse lashings passing through corresponding holes in the pole and crook. The lowest, which is at the tip of the arm, is at right angles to these, passing through wood and antler. The lashing of whalebone close to the tip of the crook, passing through a hole and round the under side of the latter, is to keep the hand from slipping off. The prong is held on by two lashings of small seal thong, each passing through a large transverse hole in the prong and a corresponding one in the pole. The upper pair of holes do not exactly match. There are also two unused holes, one in the pole below the upper hole and one above the upper hole in the prong. These holes and the new appearance of the lashings indicate that the prong is part of another hook recently fitted to this pole. The two lashings are made by a single piece of thong.

FIG. 311.—Long blubber hook.

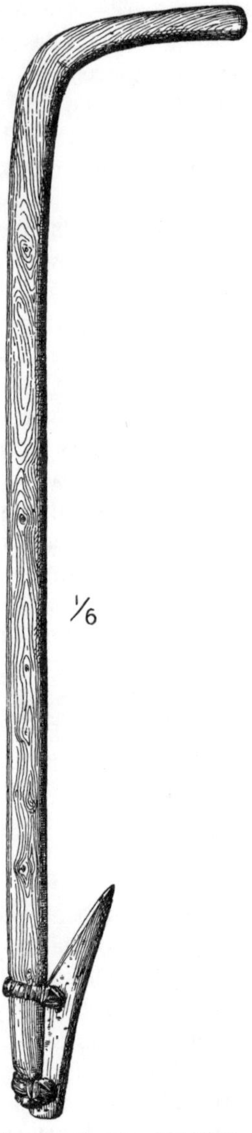

⅙

FIG. 312.—Short-handled blubber hook.

¹⁄₃₀

The whole is old and weathered and rather greasy about the prong and the tip of the pole.

Fig. 312 (No. 89836 [1203] from Utkiavwĭñ) is a similar hook with a short handle, 34 inches long, for use on land. The crook is made by bending the handle. The prong, of walrus ivory as before, is 7 inches long, and held on by two stout lashings of whalebone, which pass round the end of the handle instead of through it. The prong and tip of the handle are very greasy.

No. 89837 [1353], from the same village, is a similar hook rather rudely made. The crook is bent only at an angle of about 45°, and there is somewhat of a twist to the whole handle. The prong, which is of antler, is 7¾ inches long and shouldered at the butt like that of the long hook described. It is fastened on by two thick lashings of stout seal thong passing around prong and handle and kept from slipping by notches in the latter, and on the butt end of the former and by a large flat-headed brass stud driven into the prong below the upper lashing.

Fish scaler.—Fig. 313 (No. 89461 [1279] from Utkiavwĭñ) represents a little implement which we never saw in use, but which we were told was intended for scraping the scales off a fish. The specimen does not appear to be newly made. It is a piece of hollow "long" bone, 8 inches long, cut into the shape of the blade of a case knife, flat on one face with a broad, shallow, longitudinal groove on the other.

½

FIG. 313.—
Fish scaler.

MAKING AND WORKING FIBER.

Twisting and braiding—We had no opportunity of seeing the process of twisting the sinew twine, which is sometimes used in place of the braid so often mentioned but more generally when an extra strong thread is desired, as in sewing on boot soles. Fig. 314 (No. 89431 [1332] from Utkiavwĭñ) is a little shuttle of walrus ivory, 3 inches long and 1⅛ broad, which we were told was used in this process. The body of this shuttle is reduced to a narrow crosspiece, and the prongs at one end are twice as long as those at the other. The tips of the long prongs are about ¼ inch apart, while those of the short ones nearly meet. There is a small round hole in one side of the body. This specimen was made for sale. As well as I could understand the seller, the ends of several strands of fine sinew were fastened into the hole in the shuttle and twisted by twisting it with one hand, while the other end was held perhaps by the other hand. The part twisted was then wound on the shuttle and a fresh length twisted. This would be a very simple form of spinning with a spindle.

½

FIG. 314.—Ivory shuttle.

No special implements for twisting have been described among other

Eskimo. Mr. E. W. Nelson (in a letter to the writer) says that the natives of Norton Sound informed him that the cable twisters (kaputa—kĭbuʹtûk at Norton Sound) were also used for making twisted cord. He describes their use as follows: "The ends of the sinew cord are tied to the center holes in the two ivory pieces, one of the latter at each end of the cord, and then they are twisted in opposite directions, thus getting the hard-laid sinew cord used on the bows."

The sinew twine used at Point Barrow is generally braided, almost

⅓

FIG. 315.—Netting needle.

always in a three-ply braid, usually about the size of stout packthread, such as is found on many Eskimo implements from all localities represented in the Museum collections. That they also know how to braid with four strands is shown by the hair line already described (No. 56545 [410]). They also have a special word (which I can not recall) for braiding with four strands in distinction from braiding with three (pidrá).

Netting.—Two implements are used as usual in netting, a needle or long flat shuttle for carrying the twine (Fig. 315, No. 56570 [101]), and a mesh stick for gauging the length of the mesh. The knot is the universal "fisherman's knot" or becket hitch made in the usual manner. The method of using the mesh stick, however, is rather peculiar, and somewhat clumsy compared with that used by civilized net-makers, as it serves only to measure the mesh and not also to hold the successive meshes as they are made. It is a long flat piece of bone or antler, shaped like a case knife, with a blade square at heel and point. There is often also a little blunt hook (as in Fig. 316, No. 56581 [1021]) at the point, bending upward or toward the back of the blade. The blade is the part of the stick which measures the mesh, and its length from heel to point is always precisely half the length of the mesh to be made. It is used as follows: The workman, holding the mesh stick by the handle in his left hand, with the blade downward, catches the mesh into which the knot is to be made with the hook, and holds it while the twine is carried down the left side of the blade, round the heel and through the mesh as usual, and drawn up till the preceding knot comes just to the point of the blade. This makes a loop of the proper length for a mesh round the stick. The point where the next knot is to be made is now caught between the thumb and finger of the right hand and the mesh stick taken out of the loop. The left thumb and finger, while the other fingers of this hand still hold the

¼

FIG. 316.— Mesh stick.

handle of the stick, relieve the fingers of the right hand, which goes on to make the knot in the usual manner.[1]

We collected thirteen needles of different patterns and sizes. No. 56570 [101], Fig. 315, has been selected as the type (ĭ'nmuvwĭñ, mû'kutĭn.) It is of walrus ivory, 11·9 inches long. The small hole near the tip of one prong is for a lanyard to hang it up by when not in use. This needle could be used only for making a large meshed net, perhaps a seal net.

We collected seven needles of almost the same pattern as this, varying a little in proportions. The faces are usually more deeply hollowed out and the ends usually sinuate instead of being straight. Three of these are of reindeer antler and the rest of ivory. The longest is 9·9 inches long and the shortest 4½. This needle (No. 56574 [24], from Utkiavwĭñ) is rather broad in proportion, being nearly 1 inch wide. It is of walrus ivory. No. 89433 [942] is better suited for netting a small mesh, being only 0·7 inch broad at the widest part. It is made of reindeer antler and

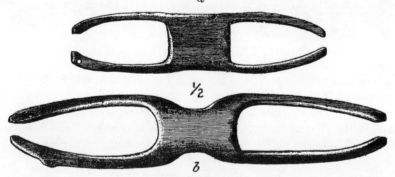

FIG. 317.—Netting needles.

is 7·3 inches long. These needles sometimes have a small hole through one end of the body for fastening the end of the twine, and most have some arrangement for fastening on a lanyard, either a hole as in the type or a groove round the tip of one prong as in No. 56574 [24].

No. 89427 [1283], from Utkiavwĭñ, is a needle of a slightly different pattern, being rather thick and not narrowed at the middle. It is of reindeer antler, 8·7 inches long and 1 wide. No. 89430 [1286], Fig. 317a, from Utkiavwĭñ, is a very broad needle, with short body and long prongs, one of which is expanded at the tip and perforated for a lanyard. It is a piece of the outside hard tissue of a reindeer antler, 5·4 inches long and 1·2 broad. It is but slightly narrowed at the middle, while No. 89428 [1381], Fig. 317b, from Utkiavwĭñ, a somewhat similar broad needle of the same material is deeply notched on each side of the body. This is made from antler of smaller diameter than the preceding, and conse-

---

[1] We had no special opportunities for watching the natives at work netting, as but few nets happened to be made at the village during our stay. It was, however, observed that the mesh stick was taken out every time a knot was tied. Since my return, after a careful study of the different mesh sticks in our collection, I have convinced myself by experiment that the above method of using the tool is the only one which will account for the shape of the different parts.

quently is not flat, but strongly convex, on one face and correspondingly concave on the other. It is 8·2 inches long and 1½ wide.

For making the seal nets a very large needle is used. The one in the collection, No. 56581 [102], Fig. 318, from Utkiavwĭñ, is 20½ inches long and only 1½ wide. It is made of two nearly equal pieces of antler, which are nearly flat, and lap over each other about 3¾ inches near the middle.

FIG. 318.—Netting needle for seal net.

They are strongly fastened together by five whalebone stitches, one at each corner of the splice and one in the middle. The corner stitches run round the edge of the two parts, and through a hole through both parts. The prongs are stout and curved, nearly meeting at the tips. They are about 3 inches long. The lateral distortion appears to be due to warping.

FIG. 319.—Netting needle.

A peculiar netting needle is shown in Fig. 319 (No. 89429 [1333], from Utkiavwĭñ), which is new and rather carelessly made from very coarse walrus ivory. The tips of the prongs, after nearly meeting, diverge again in the form of the letter U. This needle, which is 9½ inches long, was said by the maker to be of the pattern used by the "Kûñmû'd'lĭñ."

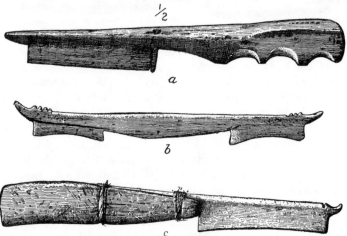

FIG. 320. —Mesh sticks.

There are no specimens resembling it in the museum collections, though it curiously suggests certain implements from Norton Sound, labeled "reels for holding fine cord," consisting of slender rods of antler, terminating at each end in similar shallow U-shaped forks.

The mesh stick (kú′brĭn) belonging to the large netting needle, No. 56581 [102], may be taken as the type of this implement. It is a piece of the hard outside tissue of a reindeer antler. The three notches on the lower edge of the haft are for the fingers. The incised line along one face of the blade is probably a mark to which the twine is to be drawn in making a mesh. The blade is just the proper length, 7½ inches, for the large mesh of the seal net. The remaining four mesh sticks are all small, and intended for making fish nets. Three are of reindeer antler and the fourth of hard bone, with a wooden haft.

Fig. 320a (No. 89436 [1284], from Utkiavwĭñ) is of antler, 7·2 inches long, with a blade of 2·7 inches, protected from splitting by a stout round peg of hard bone, driven through the handle so as to lie against the heel of the blade. It terminates in a blunt point instead of a hook, and has three finger notches in the haft. No. 89437 [942], also from Utkiavwĭñ, is of the same material, 5·2 inches long, without a hook and with a blade only 1 inch long. There are two finger notches in the haft. The last of the antler mesh sticks (No. 89439 [983], from Utkiavwĭñ, Fig. 320b) is double ended, having a hook and a short blade at each end. The blades are respectively 1·5 and 1·6 inches long, and the total length is 6·6 inches. Fig. 320c (No. 89435 [1019], also from Utkiavwĭñ) has a blade, with a small hook, of white compact bone, and what would be the handle lashed to one side of a haft of soft wood, which is shouldered to receive it. The haft is 4·3 inches long, and the two parts are held together by two lashings of fine sinew, kept from slipping by notches. The total length is 7·3 inches, that of the blade 2·7. Netting needles and mesh sticks of essentially the same type as those just described, but varying in material and dimensions, are in general use from the Anderson River to Bristol Bay, as is shown by the Museum collections.

Netting weights.—We collected 16 little ivory implements, each, when complete, consisting of the image of a fish about 3½ to 4 inches long, suspended by a string about 4 inches long to a little ivory spring hook. We never happened to see these implements in use, but we were told that they were used in netting to keep the meshes in proper shape. They generally were made in pairs. The only way of using them that I can think of is first to hook one into the bight of the first mesh made in starting the net. This would make the successive meshes, as they were netted, hang down out of the way. On starting the next row in the opposite direction, the second weight hooked into the first mesh of this row would draw the successive meshes down on the left-hand side of the stick, while the other weight would keep the meshes of the first row stretched so that one could be easily caught at a time. On beginning the third row the first weight would be transferred to the first mesh of this, and so on. Fig. 321a is one of a pair of these nĕpĭtaúra (No. 56596 [207]) which has been selected as the type. It is a rather rude figure of a salmon or trout 4 inches long, neatly carved out of walrus ivory. The string is of braided sinew and the hook of walrus ivory.

Fig. 321*b* (No. 89442 [899] from Nuwŭk) is a weight without the hook and made of compact whale's bone. It is 4·1 inches long, and very neatly carved, having all the fins in relief, the gill openings, mouth, and

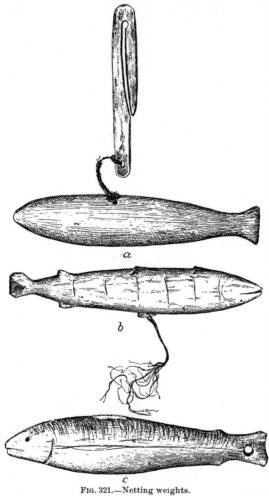

eyes incised. No. 56582 [173] from Utkiavwĭñ is one of a pair very rudely carved out of a piece of snow-shovel edge. The mouth and gill openings are indicated by incised and blackened lines, the latter fringed with short lines, each ending in a dot, perhaps to represent the gill filaments. It is 4·2 inches long, and hastily made for sale. Fig. 321*c* (No. 56578 [201] from Ut-kiavwĭñ) seems to be intended for a polar cod, and has the hole drilled through the root of the tail. The lateral line is marked by a scratch, colored with black lead, and the dark color of the back is represented by curved, transverse scratches also colored with black lead. When the carving is sufficiently good to show what sort of a fish is meant, it ıs generally a salmon or trout. Only 3 out of the 16 are of any-

FIG. 321.—Netting weights.

thing but walrus ivory. These 3 are of compact whale's bone, and one had small blue glass beads inlaid for eyes, of which one still remains.

$\frac{1}{2}$

FIG. 322.—Shuttle belonging to set of feather tools.

The shortest is 3·4 inches long, and the longest 4·3, but most of them are almost exactly 4 inches long.

Weaving.—A set of little tools made of bone and reindeer antler were brought over for sale, which were said to be those used in weaving the

feather belts.   I had no opportunity of seeing a belt made, but the work
evidently does not require all three of these tools.   The little netting
needle or shuttle of bone (Fig. 322, No. 89434 [1338]) can not be used in
feather weaving, because, as already mentioned, the strips of feather are

½

FIG. 323.—Mesh stick.

not fastened together into a continuous cord which could be carried on
a shuttle.   It is 5·9 inches long and 0·7 wide.   There is also a little mesh
stick of antler (Fig. 323, No. 89438 [1338]) 6·7 inches long, with a blade 1·9
inches in length, and a little hook, which appears to
be fitted for nothing except netting a small net.   The
lower edge of the handle, however, is cut into 10 deep
rounded notches, which perhaps serve the purpose of
a rude "frame" for keeping apart the strands of the
warp, while the woof of feather is passed through
with the fingers.   It would be held with this edge
up, and the beginning of the belt being fastened to
the wall, the warp strands would be stretched over
this, as over a violin bridge, each resting in one of the
notches.   The last tool of the set (Fig. 324, No. 89462
[1338]) is undoubtedly a "sword" for pushing home
the woof, and probably also serves to separate the
strands of the warp into a "shed."   It is a flat, thin
piece of antler, 9 inches long and three-fourths wide,
of which about 6½ inches forms a straight blade 6½
inches long, and the rest is bent round to one side and
slightly down, forming a handle.   When the strands
of the warp are stretched over the bridge as above described, pushing this horizontally through them alternately over and under the successive strands, would
make a "shed" through which the end of the woof
could be thrust with one motion, and pushed up
against the preceding strand of the woof by sliding
the sword forward.   It would then be withdrawn and
passed through again, going over the strands it went
under before and vice versa, so as to open a "shed"
for the next strand of the woof.

½

FIG. 324.—"Sword" for
feather weaving.

Sewing.—For sewing furs and leather they always
use thread made by stripping off thin fibers from a
piece of dried sinew of the reindeer, as is usual with
Eskimo.   Cotton or linen thread of civilized manufacture is now often
used for sewing the cotton frocks, etc., and sometimes for making an or-

namental seam on the waterproof gut shirts. The stitches employed have already been described under the head of clothing (which see). They hold the needle between the thumb and middle finger, with the thimble on the forefinger (both are called by the same name, tĭ′kyə) and sew toward them. This appears to be the regular Eskimo method of sewing.[1]

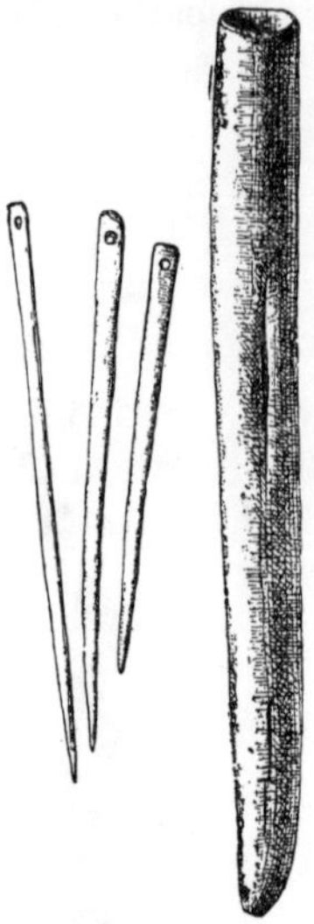

At the present day they are well supplied with steel needles (miksun) of all sizes and patterns, but formerly they used bone needles made from the fibula (amĭlyĕrûñ) of the reindeer. We collected sixty of these needles, eighteen of which appear to be old and genuine. The rest were more or less carefully made for sale. Nĭka-wáalu told us that once when he and a young man were out deer hunting a long distance from camp their boots gave out. Having killed a deer he made thread from the sinew, a needle from the bone, and with pieces of the skin repaired their boots, so that they got home in comfort.

No. 89389 [1191], Fig. 325 will serve as the type of these needles. This is a case 3½ inches long, made of

FIG. 325.—Quill case of the butt of a large quill, closed with a plug of walrus
bone needles. hide, and contains 6 needles. One is 1·8 inches long, stout, and round-pointed, with a large eye. It is much discolored from age. The second is also round-pointed but more slender, 1·9 inches long, and flattened and expanded at the butt. The third is 2·4 inches long, and has a four-sided point like a glover's needle. All three of these are very neatly made and appear old. The other three are stout, roughly made, and flat, respectively 2·1, 2·2, and 2·5 inches long. Two of them look suspiciously new. This set was said to have been the property of the wife of Puka, Nĭkawáalu's father.

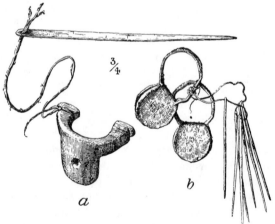

FIG. 326.—Needles and thimbles: (a) large bone needle and peculiar thimble; (b) leather thimbles with bone needles.

Fig. 326a is a peculiarly large and flat needle (No. 89392 [1195] from Utkiavwĭñ) 3·2 inches long, with a round, sharp point and a large eye, with little grooves running to the butt on each side for the thread to lie in. This needle was perhaps specially

---

[1] See Parry, Second Voy., p. 537; Lyon, Journal, p. 93; Kumlien, Contributions, p. 25.

meant for sewing boat skins. With this needle belongs a peculiar large bone or ivory thimble. The remaining needles are all very much alike, though some are more roughly made than the others. Three of them have the butt square instead of rounded, and half of them, including some which are undoubtedly old, are four-sided at the point like a glover's needle. The longest is 3 inches long and the shortest 1·4 inches, but the commonest length is about 2 or 2½ inches. Similar bone needles are mentioned by various authors.[1]

Nearly all the women now use ordinary metal thimbles, obtained in trade, but they wear them in the old-fashioned way, on the tip of the forefinger. Some of the older women, however, still prefer the ancient leather thimble. There are two patterns of these: one intended for the fore-finger only, and the other of such a shape that it may also be worn on the other fingers as a guard against chafing in pulling stout thread through thick leather. It is often so used at the present day.

We collected three of the first-mentioned pattern, which is represented by Fig. 326*b* (No. 89396 [1202, 1246]). It is made by cutting out a narrow ring of raw sealskin 0·7 inch in diameter, with a circular flap 0·5 inch in diameter on the outside of the ring and a corresponding one on the inside of the same size, cut out of the middle of the ring. The flaps are doubled over so as to make a pad on the inside of the forefinger when the tip of the latter is inserted into the ring. The butt of the needle presses against this pad.

The third thimble, which belongs with the needlecase (No. 89371 [1276]), is of precisely the same form and dimensions.

There appeared to be little if any variation among those which we saw. Capt. Lyon[2] figures two similar thimbles from Iglulik, which are described on page 537 of the same work as being made of leather. The flaps, however, seem to be only semicircular and not folded over, so that the shield consists of only one thickness of leather.

A similar thimble with the flap also not folded is used at Cumberland Gulf.[3]

The other pattern, of which we brought home nine specimens, is represented by No. 89389 [1191], which belongs with the set of bone needles of the same number. It is a tube, open at both ends, one of which is larger than the other, made by bending round a strip of split walrus hide and sewing the ends together. It is 0·4 inch long and 2·1 in circumference at the larger end. It is worn smooth with handling, and impregnated with grease and dirt and marked with small pits where it has been pressed against the butt of the needle in use.

Four other old thimbles (No. 89393 [1194], from Utkiavwĭñ, are made

---

[1] Formerly they used the bones of fishes or the very fine bones of birds instead of needles. Crantz, vol. 1, p. 136.

"Their own clumsy needles of bone," Parry, Second Voy., p. 537 and pl. opposite p. 548, Fig. 11. Kumlien also speaks of "steel needles or bone ones made after the same pattern" at Cumberland Gulf (Contributions, p. 25).

[2] Parry, Second Voy., pl. opposite p. 550, Fig. 25.

[3] Boas, Central Eskimo, p. 524, Fig. 473 and Kumlien, Contributions, p. 25.

in the same way, but are a trifle larger. As they show no needle-marks, they were probably used only as finger guards. The remaining four are similar to the above, but newly made, for sale.

A most peculiar thimble, the only one of the kind seen, is shown in Fig. 326a (No. 89392 [1195] from Utkiavwiñ, belonging with the large bone needle of the same number already described and figured). This is made of a single piece of walrus ivory, browned with age, and the round shallow socket is for the butt of the needle. The ends of the half ring are slightly expanded and notched on the outside to receive a string to complete the ring so that it can be fitted round the finger, with the flange in the same position as the pad of a leather thimble.

Needles are kept in a case (ujyami), consisting of a tube of bone or ivory about 5 or 6 inches long, through which is drawn a broad strap of leather furnished with a knot at one end to keep it from slipping wholly through. Into one side of this strap the needles are thrust obliquely, so that when the strap is pulled in they are covered by the tube. To the other end of the strap is usually attached an ivory snap hook for fastening the needle case to the girdle of the pantaloons. These needle cases are made of two slightly different patterns, of which the first is represented by No. 89365 [1277], Fig. 327a. It is of white walrus ivory, 4½ inches long, and the strap is of seal thong about 11 inches long and 0·3 inch wide. At one end of this is a pear-shaped knob of walrus ivory, which is shouldered off at the small end and worked into a short flattened shank perforated with a large eye, through which the end of the strap, which is cut narrow, is thrust. It is fastened by doubling it back and sewing it to the standing part. A sky-blue transparent glass bead is inlaid in the large end of the knob. The other end of the strap is fastened in the same way into a tranverse slot in the end of the belt hook (tǐ'tkǐbwǐñ) of ivory, 4·7 inches long.

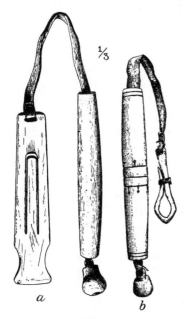

FIG. 327.—Needle cases with belt hooks.

This pattern appears to be usually made of walrus ivory. Only one of the six brought home is of bone, and this is an unusually small one, only 3·6 inches long, made for sale. The usual length is 4½ to 5 inches. No. 89363 [1105], Fig. 327b, from Utkiavwiñ, is a tube very-much like the one described, but is ornamented with an incised pattern colored with red ocher, and has a differently shaped belt hook. When the latter is hooked over the girdle the ring is pushed up the shank over the point of the hook till it fits tight, and thus keeps the hook from slipping off the belt.

Fig. 328*a* (No. 89364 [1243] from Utkiavwɪñ) is another ivory needle case, 4·7 inches long. The tube was once ornamented with incised patterns, but these are almost wholly worn off by constant handling. The knob is carved into an ornamental shape, having a circle of six round knobs round the middle. It has been suggested that this is meant to represent a cloud-berry (Rubus chamæmorus), a fruit known to the "Nunatañmiun" though not at Point Barrow. The hook is a snap hook very much like those described in connection with the netting weights, but larger (3 inches long) and very broad at the upper end, which is made into a broad ring. The point of a steel needle still sticking in the flesh side of the strap shows how the needles are carried with the points toward the knob.

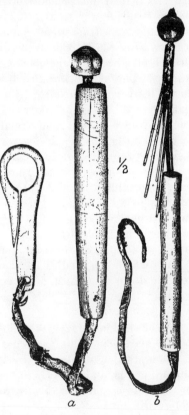

No. 89370 [1033], also from Utkiavwɪñ, has no knob, but the end of the strap is kept from slipping through by rolling it up transversely and catching it with a stitch of sinew. It has a broad flat snap hook similar to the last, but cut on the edges into ornamental scallops. The tube is ornamented with an incised pattern colored red with ocher, and is 5·2 long. No. 56575 [7] is an old tube of brown walrus ivory, enlarged into a knob at one end. It has no knob or hook, but a new strap of white seal skin, in the lower end of which is tied a large knot. The other pattern has the cylinder made of a hollow "long" bone, in its natural shape. This bone appears to be almost always the humerus of some large bird, probably a swan. The strap has usually no knob, but is kept from slipping

FIG. 328.—Needle cases: (*a*) case with belt hook; (*b*) case open, showing bone needles.

through by knotting the end or tying on a large bead or a bear's toe, or some such object too large to go through the tube. None of these have belt hooks except one new and roughly made specimen.

These bone tubes are apparently older than the neat ivory cylinders, and it is not unlikely that the belt hook was not invented till the former was mostly out of fashion. No. 89361 [1239], Fig. 328*b* from Utkiavwɪñ, is one of these which has for knob one of the large dark blue glass beads which used to bring such enormous prices in the early days of Arctic trading, and which are still the kind most highly prized. The end of the strap is cut narrow, passed through the bead, and knotted on the end.   This case carries a half-dozen of the old-fashioned bone needles, which appear to be genuine.   It is 3·7 inches long and, roughly speaking, 0·4 in diameter.   No. 89369 [1201], also from Utkiavwĭñ, resembles the above, but has a wolverine's toe sewed to the end of the strap.   No. 89371 [1276], from Utkiavwĭñ, also has the toe of a wolverine for a knob, and has a belt hook with two tongues made of reindeer antler.   No. 89366 [1137], from Utkiavwĭñ, is a highly ornamented case of this pattern, which has a short cylindrical knob, also ornamented.   No. 89368 [1089], from Utkiavwĭñ, is not made of bird's bone, but is a piece of a long bone from some mammal, and has a brown bear's toe for a knob.   No. 89367 [1339], from the same village, is roughly made of a branch of antler, 3·9 inches long and 0·8 wide, hollowed out.   It has a knob of whale's bone, but no belt hook, the end of the strap being knotted into a leather thimble of the first pattern.   Of the six specimens of this pattern in the collection only the first is a genuine old implement.   All the others are merely commercial imitations rather carelessly made.

This kind of needle case is very commonly used throughout Alaska, as is shown by the enormous collections in the National Museum brought home by various explorers, Nelson, Turner, Dall and others.   The needle case from Iglulik, figured by Capt. Lyon,[1] resembles the second or older pattern, being of bone, not tapered at the ends, and having neither knob nor belt hook.   To the ends of the strap are hung thimbles "and other small articles liable to be lost."[2]   Dr. Simpson[3] speaks of the needle case in use at Point Barrow, but merely describes it as "a narrow strip of skin in which the needles are stuck, with a tube of bone, ivory, or iron to slide down over them, and kept from slipping off the lower end by a knob or large bead."   This appears to refer only to the second or older pattern.

The old-fashioned ring thimbles were usually carried on the belt hook of the needlecase, but modern thimbles require a box.   These boxes (kigiune), which are usually small and cylindrical, also serve for holding thread, beads, and all sorts of little trinkets or knickknacks, and many of them are so old that they were evidently used for this purpose long before the introduction of metal thimbles.   Little tin canisters, spice boxes, etc., are also used for the same purpose nowadays.   We brought home thirteen of these boxes, of which No. 89407 [1158] Fig. 329a has been chosen as the type.   It is a piece of the beam of a stout antler, 4·3 inches long, cut off square on the ends and hollowed out.   Into the large end is fitted a flat bottom of thin pine, fastened in by four little treenails of wood.   The cover is of the same material.   It is held on by a string of sinew braid about 11 inches long, which passes out through the lower of the two little holes on one side of the box, being held by a knot at

---

[1] Parry's Second Voyage, pl. opposite p. 550, Fig. 25.
[2] Ibid., p. 537.
[3] Op. cit, p. 245.

the end, in through the upper, then out and in through two similar holes in the middle of the cover, and out through a hole on the other side of the box. Pulling the end of this string draws the cover down snugly into its place.

Some of the remaining boxes are made of antler, and vary in length from 4·7 to 8 inches. The last is, however, unusually large, most of the others being about 5 inches long. The covers are generally held on by strings much in the manner described, and the ends are both usually of wood, though two old boxes have both ends made of antler, and one has a top of hard bone. The last is a specimen newly made for sale. These boxes are sometimes ornamented on the outside with incised lines, colored red or blackened, either conventional patterns as in Fig. 329b

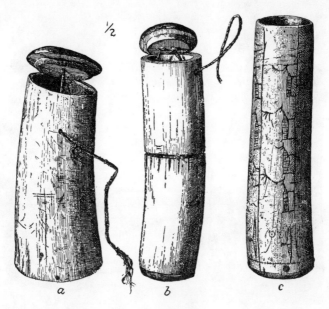

Fig. 329.—Trinket boxes.

(No. 89405 [1335], from Utkiavwĭñ) or figures of men and animals as in Fig. 329c (No. 56615 [41] from the same village). The former is a new box, 4·7 inches long, and has the wooden ends both shouldered to fit tightly. The cover is worked with a string.

No. 56615 [41] on the other hand is very old, and has lost its cover. The wooden bottom is shouldered and held in with treenails. The surface is elaborately ornamented with incised and blackened figures. It is divided by longitudinal lines into four nearly equal panels, on which the figures are disposed as follows (the animals all being represented as standing on the longitudinal lines, and facing toward the right, that is, toward the open end of the box): On the first panel are 4 reindeer, alternately a buck and a doe, followed by a man in a kaiak, and over his head two small "circles and dots," one above the other.

All the deer on this box are represented strictly in profile, so as to show only two legs and one antler each. On the second panel are 4 deer, all does, followed by a man with a bow slung across his back. On the third, a man in the middle appears to be calling 2 dogs, who, at the left of the panel, are drawing a railed sled. Reversed, and on the upper border of the panel, is a man pushing behind a similar sled drawn by 3 dogs. The head dog has stopped and is sitting down on his haunches. The dogs, like the reindeer, are all strictly in profile and rather conventionalized. In the fourth panel are 3 reindeer followed by a man in his kaiak, and upside down, above, a deer without legs,

FIG. 330.—Trinket boxes.

supposed to be swimming in the water, and a very rude figure of a man in his kaiak. These figures probably represent actual occurrences, forming a sort of record.

Fig. 330a (No. 89408 [1371] from Sidaru) is a piece of stout antler, 4·7 inches long, which has the bottom of pine fitted tightly in without fastenings. The cover is of wood, covered, to make it fit tight, with parchment, apparently shrunk on and puckered on the upper surface. A thick hank of untwisted sinew is fastened as a handle through the middle of the cover. This box is old and dirty, and contains an unfinished flint arrow-head. No. 56505 [59] from Utkiavwïñ, is a new box, closed at the ends with thick shouldered plugs of pine wood. The tube is 8 inches long and ornamented with a conventional pattern of incised lines colored with red ocher.

Fig. 330*b* (No. 89402 [1359] also from Utkiavwĭñ), is peculiar from the material of which it is made. It is of about the same pattern as the common antler boxes, but is made of the butt end of the *os penis* of a large walrus, cut off square and hollowed out, and has ends of hard whale's bone. Its length is 4·2 inches. No. 89403 [1425] Fig. 331 from Sidaru, is made of the hollow butt of a good-sized walrus tusk, 3·2 inches long. It has a neatly fitted wooden bottom, held in with 6 treenails, two of ivory and four of wood. The box has been cracked and split and mended with stitches of sinew and whalebone. Peculiar conventional patterns are incised on the box and

FIG. 331.—Ivory box.

cover. A peculiar box is shown in Fig. 332 (No. 56583 [37] from Utkiavwĭñ). This is of compact white bone, with a flat wooden bottom. I do not recollect seeing any other boxes of the same sort.

Fig. 333 (No. 89409 [1372]) is the tip of a walrus tusk

FIG. 332.—Bone box.

cut off and hollowed out into a sort of flask, 3·8 inches long, closed at the large end by a flat wooden bottom, fastened in with treenails and at the small end by a stopper of soft wood.

The most peculiar box of all, however, is shown in Fig. 334 (No. 56512 [2] from Utkiavwĭñ), the only specimen of the kind seen. It is 5·5 inches long, made of reindeer antler, and very neatly carved into a most excellent image of a reindeer lying on its left side, with the head, which has no antlers, turned down and to the left. The legs are folded up against the belly, the forelegs with the hoofs pointing backward, the hind hoofs pointing forward. The eyes are represented by small sky-blue glass beads, and the mouth, nostrils, and navel neatly incised, the last being particularly well-marked. The tips of the hoofs are rounded off, which, taken in connec-

FIG. 333.—Little flask of ivory.

FIG. 334.—Box in shape of deer.

tion with the attitude and the well marked navel, lead me to believe that the image is meant to represent an unborn fetus. The whole of the body is hollowed, the aperture taking up the whole of the buttocks, and closed by a flat, thick plug of soft wood. A round peg of wood is driven in to close an accidental hole just above the left shoulder. The box is old and discolored, and worn smooth with much handling.

Rarely these little workboxes are made of basketwork. We obtained four specimens of these small baskets, of which No. 56564 [88] Fig. 335, workbasket (águma, áma, ipiáru), will serve as the type. The neck is of black tanned sealskin, 2½ inches long, and has 1 vertical seam, to the middle of which is sewed the middle of a piece of fine seal thong, a foot long, which serves to tie up the mouth. The basket appears to be made of fine twigs or roots of the willow, with the bark removed, and is made by winding an osier spirally into the shape of the basket, and wrapping a narrow splint spirally around the two adjacent parts of this, each turn of the splint being separated from the next by a turn of the succeeding tier. The other basket from Utkiavwiñ (No. 56565 [135]) is almost exactly like this, but larger (3·5 inches in diameter and 2·2 high), and has holes round the top of the neck for the drawstring.

FIG. 335.—Small basket.

Two baskets from Sidaru are of the same material and workmanship, but somewhat larger and of a different shape, as shown in Fig. 336, No. 89801 [1366], and Fig. 337, No. 89802 [1427]. This was the only species of basketwork seen among these people and is probably not of native manufacture.

Prof. O. T. Mason, of the National Museum, has called my attention to the fact that the

FIG. 336.—Small basket.

method of weaving employed in making these baskets is the same as that used by the Apaches and Navajos, who have been shown to be linguistically of the same stock as the Athabascan or Tinné group of Indians of the North. The first basket collected, No. 56564 [88], was said by the owner to have come from the "great river" in the south. Now, the name Kuwûk or Kowak, applied to the western stream flowing into Hotham Inlet, means simply "great river," and this is the region where the Eskimo come into very intimate commercial relations with Indians of Tinné stock.[1] Therefore, in consideration of the Indian

---

[1] Dall, American Association, Address, 1885, p. 13.

workmanship of these baskets, and the statement that one of them came from the "great river, south," I am well convinced that they were made by the Indians of the region between the Koyukuk and Silawĭk Rivers, and sold by them to the Kuwûñmiun, whence they could easily find their way to Point Barrow through the hands of the "Nunatañ-miun" traders.

The Eskimo of Alaska south of Bering Strait make and use baskets of many patterns, but east of Point Barrow baskets are exceed-ingly rare. The only mention of anything of the kind will be found in Lyon's Journal.[1] He mentions seeing at Iglulik a "small round bas-ket composed of grass in precisely the same manner as those constructed by the Tibboo, in the southern part of Fezzan, and agreeing with them also in its shape." Now, these Africans make baskets of precisely the same "coiled" work (as Prof. Mason calls it) as the Tinné, so that in all probability what Lyon saw was one of these same baskets, carried east in trade, like other western objects already referred to. The name áma applied to these baskets at Point Barrow (the other two names appear to be simply "bag" or receptacle) corresponds to the Greenlandic amât, the long thin runners from the root of a tree, "at present used in the plural also for a basket of European basketwork," (because they had no idea that twigs could be so small)—Grønlandske Ordbog.

⅓

FIG. 337.—Small basket.

No. 89799 [1329] from Utkiavwĭñ, is a peculiar bag, the only one of the kind seen, used for the same purpose as the boxes and baskets just described. It is the stomach of a polar bear, with the muscular and glandular layers removed, dried and carefully worked down with a skin scraper into something like goldbeater's skin. This makes a large, nearly spherical bag 7½ inches in diameter, of a pale brownish color, soft and wrinkled, with a mouth 6 inches wide. A small hole has been mended by drawing the skin together and winding it round tightly on the inside with sinew.

---

[1] P. 172.

MEANS OF LOCOMOTION AND TRANSPORTATION.

TRAVELING BY WATER.

Kaiaks and paddles.—Like all the rest of the Eskimo race, the natives of Point Barrow use the kaiak, or narrow, light, skin-covered canoe, completely decked over except at the middle, where there is a hole or cockpit in which the man sits. Although nearly every male above the age of boyhood owns and can manage one of these canoes, they are much less generally employed than by any other Eskimo whose habits have been described, except the "Arctic highlanders," who have no boats, and perhaps those of Siberia and their Chuckche companions. The kaiak is used only during the season of open water, and then but little in the sea in the neighborhood of the villages. Those who remain near the villages in the summer use the kaiak chiefly for making the short excursions to the lakes and streams inland, already described, after reindeer, and for making short trips from camp to camp along the coast. At Pernyû they are used in setting the stake-nets and also for retrieving fowl which have fallen in the water when shot.

According to Dr. Simpson[1] the men of the parties which go east in the summer travel in their kaiaks after reaching the open water "to make room in the large boat for the oil-skins." We obtained no information regarding this. It is at this time, probably, that the kaiak comes specially in play for spearing molting fowl and "flappers", and for catching seals with the kúkiga. They manage the kaiak with great skill and confidence, but we never knew them to go out in rough weather, nor did we ever see the practice, so frequently described elsewhere, of tying the skirts of the waterproof jacket round the coaming of the cockpit so as to exclude the water.

It should, however, be borne in mind that from the reasons above stated our opportunities for observing the use of the kaiak were very limited. At all events it is certain that the people depend mainly on the umiak, not only for traveling, but for hunting and fishing as well, which places them in strong contrast with the Greenlanders, who are essentially a race of kaiakers and have consequently developed the boat and its appendages to a high state of perfection.

We brought home one complete full-sized kaiak, with its paddle, No. 57773 [539], Fig. 338a and b, which is a very fair representative of the canoes used at Point Barrow. This is 19 feet long and 18 inches wide amidships. The gunwales are straight, except for a very slight sheer at the bow, and the cockpit is 21 inches long and 18½ inches wide. It has a frame of wood, which appears to be all of spruce, held together by treenails and whalebone lashings, and is covered with white-tanned seal-skins with the grain side out. The stoutest part of the frame is the two gunwales, each 3¼ inches broad and ½-inch thick, flat, and rounded off on the upper edge inside, running the whole length of the boat and meet-

---

[1] Op. cit. p. 264.

ing at the stem and stern, gradually tapered up on the lower edge at
each end. The ribs, of which there are at least forty-three, are bent into
nearly a half-circle, thus making a U-shaped midship section, and are
¾-inch wide by ⅓-inch thick, flat on the outer side and round on the inner.
Their ends are mortised into the lower edge of the gunwale and fastened with wooden treenails. They are set in about 3 inches apart and
decrease gradually in size fore and aft. Outside of these are seven
equidistant streaks running fore and aft, ¾ inch to 1 inch wide and ¼ inch

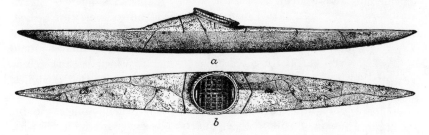

FIG. 338.—Kaiak.

thick, of which the upper on each side reaches neither stem nor stern.
These are lashed to the ribs with a strip of whalebone, which makes a
round turn about one rib, above the streak, going under the rib first,
and a similar turn round the next rib below the streak (Fig. 339).

There is a stout keelson, hemi-elliptical in section, under the cockpit
only. This is 4½ feet long, about 2 inches deep, and 1½ inches wide, and
is fastened in the middle and about 1 foot
from each end by a strip of whalebone, which
passes through a transverse hole in the keelson, round the rib on one side, back through
the keelson, and round the rib on the other
side twice. The end is wrapped spirally
round the turns on one side and tucked into
the hole in the keelson. The deck beams

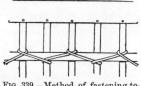

FIG. 339.—Method of fastening together frame of kaiak.

are not quite so stout as the ribs and are mortised into the upper edge
of the gunwales a little below the level of the deck. The ends are
secured by lashings or stitches of some material which are concealed
by the skin cover. They are about as far apart as the ribs, but neither
exactly correspond nor break joints with the latter.

At the after end of the cockpit is an extra stout beam or thwart to
support the back, 1¾ inches wide and three-quarters inch thick, with
rounded edges, the ends of which are apparently lashed with thong.
The first beam forward of the cockpit is rounded, and appears to be
a natural crook forming a U-shaped arch, and is followed by seven
V-shaped knees, thickest in the middle and enlarged a little at the
ends, successively decreasing in height to the seventh, which is almost
straight. This makes the rise in the deck forward of the cockpit.

Every alternate deck beam is braced to the gunwale at each end by an oblique lashing of whalebone, running from a transverse hole in the beam about 1 inch from the gunwale to a corresponding hole in the gunwale, three-quarters inch from the lower edge. The lashing makes three or four turns through these holes and around the lower edge of the gunwale, and the end is wrapped spirally round these turns for their whole length. Above these beams a narrow batten runs fore and aft amidships from cockpit to stem and stern, mortised into the two beams at the cockpit, and lashed to the others with whalebone. The coaming of the cockpit is made of a single flat piece of wood, 1¾ inches broad and one-quarter inch thick, bent into a hoop with the ends lapping about 6 inches and "sewed" together with stitches of whalebone. Round the upper edge of this, on the outside, is fitted a "half-round" hoop, which appears to be made of willow, three-quarters by one-third inch, with its ends lapped about 4 inches, this lap coming over the joint of the larger hoop. It is fastened on by short stitches of whalebone about 5 or 6 inches apart, leaving room enough between the two hoops to allow a lacing of fine whalebone to pass through. The coaming is put on over the edge of the skin cover, which is drawn up tight inside of the coaming and over its upper edge and fastened by a lacing of whalebone, which runs spirally round the outer hoop and through holes about one-half inch apart in the edge of the cover.

½12

The coaming fits over the crown of the arch of the forward deck beam and rests on the middle of the thwart aft, and is secured by lashings of whalebone, which pass through holes in the coaming and over its upper edge. The forward lashing makes three turns, which pass round the beam with the end wrapped spirally round the parts between beam and coaming; the after lashing, four similar turns, which pass through a hole in the thwart and around its forward edge. On each side is a stout vertical brace of wood 3¼ inches long, 1 inch wide, and one-half inch thick, with rounded edges and corners. The ends are cut out parallel to the breadth, so that one end fits on to the upper edge of the gunwale, while the other receives the lower edge of the coaming, protruding on the outside through a hole in the cover.

The cover is of six sealskins, put together heads to tails, so that there is only one longitudinal seam, which runs irregularly along the deck. The transverse seams, which run obliquely across the bottom are double and sewed

FIG. 340.—Double kayak paddle.

with a blind stitch, like the seams already described on the waterproof boots, from the inside. These seams are nearly 2 inches wide. The longitudinal seam is sewed in the same way from the outside, but not so broadly lapped, with the edge turned over into a roll. There are two pieces of stout thong stretched across the deck, one forward of the cockpit and the other aft, which serve to fasten articles to the deck. The thong passes out through a hole in the gunwale, one-half inch from the upper edge and 6 inches from the cockpit, on the starboard side forward and on the port side aft, and is secured by a knot in the end inboard. The other end passes in through a corresponding hole in the other gunwale and is loosely knotted to the deck beams, so that the line can be slackened off or tautened up at pleasure. Three feet from the bow is a becket for holding spears, etc., fastened into two little holes bored diagonally outward through the edge of the gunwales. It is of two parts of seal thong, one part twisted round the other, but is broken in the middle, so that only one-half of it is left. The weight of this kaiak in its present dry condition is 32 pounds.

This is about the ordinary pattern of kaiak used at Point Barrow, and is a medium-sized one. These boats are made to fit the size of the owner, a youth or small man using a much smaller and lighter kaiak than a heavy adult. They are never made to carry more than one person, and I have never heard of their being used by the women. In carrying the kaiak across the land from lake to lake, it is held horizontally against the side with the bow pointing forward, by thrusting the forearm into the cockpit. We never saw them carried on the head, in the manner practised at Fury and Hecla Straits.[1]

In entering the canoe the man takes great care to wipe his feet clean of sand and gravel, which would work down under the timbers and chafe the skin. The canoe is launched in shoal water, preferably alongside of a little bank, and the man steadies it by sticking down his paddle on the outer side and holding it with his left hand, while he balances himself on his right foot, and with his free hand carefully wipes his left foot. He then steps with his left foot into the kaiak, and still balancing himself with the help of the paddle, lifts and wipes his right foot before he steps in with that. He then pushes his feet and legs forward under the raised deck, settles himself in a proper position for trimming the boat, and shoves off. As elsewhere, the kaiak is always propelled with a paddle.

No. 89246 [539], Fig. 340, is the paddle which belongs to the kaiak just described. It is 7 feet long. The shaft joining the blades is elliptical in section, with its greatest width at right angles to the plane of the blades so to present the greatest resistance to the strain of paddling. The shape of the blade, with rounded tip and thin rounded edges is admirably adapted to give the blade a clean entry into the

---

[1] Lyon, Journal, p. 233. See also Capt. Lyon's figure in Parry's 2d Voy., pl. opposite p. 274.

water. The whole is very neatly and smoothly made, and the blades are painted with red ocher. This is a much more effective paddle than those used by the Greenlanders and other eastern Eskimo, the blades of which, probably from the scarcity of wood[1] are very narrow, not exceeding 4 inches in width. In Greenland and Labrador, also, the blades are square at the ends like those of ordinary oars, and are usually edged with bone to prevent them from splitting. The absence of this bone edging on the paddles from Point Barrow perhaps indicates that they are meant for summer use only and not for working among the ice. In accordance with the general custom in northwestern America, the double-bladed paddle (páutïñ) is used only when great speed is desired, as in chasing game. It is handled in the usual way, being grasped with both hands near the middle, and dipped alternately on opposite sides. For ordinary traveling they use a single-bladed paddle (áñun), of the same shape as those used in the umiak but usually somewhat smaller, of which we neglected to procure a specimen. With this they make a few strokes on one side, till the boat begins to sheer, then shift it over and make a few strokes on the other side. They do this with very great skill, getting considerable speed, and making a remarkably straight wake. The use of this single paddle appears to be universal along the coast of Alaska, from Point Barrow southward, and it is also used at the Mackenzie and Anderson rivers, as shown by the models collected by MacFarlane in that region. It is, however, unknown among the eastern Eskimo about whom we have any definite information on the subject, namely, the Greenlanders, the people of Baffin Land, Hudson Strait, and Labrador.[2]

Curiously enough the Greenlanders had a superstition of a sort of malevolent spirits called kajariak, who were "kayakmen of an extraordinary size, who always seem to be met with at a distance from land beyond the usual hunting grounds. They were skilled in the arts of sorcery, particularly in the way of raising storms and bringing bad weather. Like the umiarissat [other fabulous beings], *they use one-bladed paddles*, like those of the Indians."[3] This tradition either refers back to a time when the ancestors of the Greenlanders used the single paddle or to occasional and perhaps hostile meetings between eastern and western Eskimo.

Though the kaiak is essentially the same wherever used, it differs considerably in size and external appearance in different localties. The kaiak of the Greenlanders is perhaps the best-known model, as it has

---

[1] It is a curious fact, however, that the narrowest kaiak paddles I have ever seen belonged to some Eskimo that I saw in 1876, at Rigolette, Labrador, who lived in a region sufficiently well wooded to furnish them with lumber for a small schooner, which they had built.

[2] For information concerning the last two regions I am indebted to Mr. L. M. Turner; for the others to the standard authorities.

[3] Rink, Tales and Traditions, p. 47. See also p. 374 for a story of the meeting of a Greenlander with one of these beings.

been figured and described by many authors. It is quite as light and sharp as the Point Barrow model, but has a flat floor, the bilge being angular instead of rounded, and it has considerably more sheer to the deck, the stem and stern being prolonged into long curved points, which project above the water, and are often shod with bone or ivory. The coaming of the cockpit also is level, or only slightly raised forward. The kaiaks used in Baffin Land, Hudson Straits, and Labrador are of a very similar model, but larger and heavier, having the projecting points at the bow and stern rather shorter and less sharp, and the coaming of the cockpit somewhat more raised forward. Both of these forms are represented by specimens and numerous models in the museum collections. I have seen one flat-floored kaiak at Point Barrow. It belonged to a youth and was very narrow and light.

The kaiak in use at Fury and Hecla Straits, as described by Capt. Lyon[1] and Capt. Parry[2] is of a somewhat different model, approaching that used at the Anderson River. It is a large kaiak 25 feet long, with the bow and stern sharp and considerably more bent up than in the Greenland kaiaks, but round-bottomed, like the western kaiaks. The deck is flat, with the cockpit coaming somewhat raised forward.[3]

In the kaiaks used at the Anderson and Mackenzie rivers, as shown by the models in the National Museum, the bending up of the stem and stern posts is carried to an extreme, so that they make an angle of about 130° with the level of the deck. The bottom is round and the cockpit nearly level, but sufficient room for the knees and feet is obtained by arching not only the deck beams just forward of the cockpit, but all of them from stem to stern, so that the deck slopes away to each side like the roof of a house. At Point Barrow, as already described, the deck beams are arched only just forward of the cockpit, and the stem and stern are not prolonged. This appears to be the prevailing form of canoe at least as far south as Kotzebue Sound and is sometimes used by the Malemiut of Norton Sound. At Port Clarence the heavy, large kaiak, so common from Norton Sound southward, appears to be in use from Nordenskiöld's description, as he speaks of the kaiaks holding two persons, sitting back to back in the cockpit.[4] The kaiaks of the southwestern Eskimo are, as far as I have been able to learn, large and heavy, with level coamings, with the deck quite steeply arched fore and aft, and with bow and stern usually of some peculiar shape, as shown by models in the Museum. See also Dall's figure (Alaska, p. 15.)[5]

---

[1] Journal, p. 233.

[2] Second voyage, p. 506, and pls. opposite pp. 274 and 508.

[3] There is quite a discrepancy in regard to this between Capt. Lyon's description referred to above and the two plates drawn by him in Parry's second voyage. In his journal he speaks of the coaming of the cockpit being about 9 inches higher forward than it is aft, while from his figures the difference does not appear to be more than 3 or 4 inches.

[4] Vega, vol. 2, p. 228.

[5] I have confined myself in the above comparison simply to the kaiaks used by undoubted Eskimo. I find merely casual references to the kaiaks used on the Siberian coast by the Asiatic Eskimo and their companions the Sedentary Chuckchis, while a discussion of the canoes of the Aleuts would carry me beyond the limits of the present work.

While the kaiak, however, differs so much in external appearance in different localities, it is probable that in structure it is everywhere essentially the same. Only two writers have given a detailed description of the frame of a kaiak, and these are from widely distant localities, Iglulik and western Greenland, both still more widely distant from Point Barrow, and yet both give essentially the same component parts as are to be found at Point Barrow, namely, two comparatively stout gunwales running from stem to stern, braced with transverse deck-beams,[1] seven streaks running fore and aft along the bottom, knees, or ribs in the form of hoops, and a hoop for the coaming, bound together with whalebone or sinew.[2]

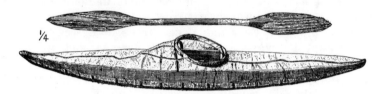

FIG. 341.—Model kaiak and paddle.

The double-bladed paddle is almost exclusively an Eskimo contrivance. The only other hyperborean race, besides the Aleuts, who use it, are the Yukagirs, who employ it in their narrow dugout canoes on the River Kolyma in Siberia.[3] Double-bladed paddles have also been observed in the Malay Archipelago.

Fig. 341, (No. 56561 [224] from Utkiavwiñ) is a very neatly made model of a kaiak, 13·3 inches long. It is quite accurate in all its details, but has only five streaks on the bottom, and its width and depth are about twice what they should be in proportion to the length. The frame is lashed together with fine sinew and covered with seal entrail. The paddle is also out of proportion. Many similar neatly fin-

---

[1] Since the above was written Boas has published a detailed description of the central kaiaks. in which he says there are only four streaks besides the keel (Central Eskimo, p. 486).

[2] Dr. Kane's description, though the best that we have of the flat-bottomed Greenland kaiak and accompanied by diagrams, is unfortunately vague in some important respects. It is in brief as follows: "The skeleton consists of three longitudinal strips of wood on each side * * * stretching from end to end. * * * The upper of these, the gunwale * * * is somewhat stouter than the others. The bottom is framed by three similar longitudinal strips. These are crossed by other strips or hoops, which perform the office of knees and ribs. They are placed at a distance of not more than 8 to 10 inches from one another. Wherever the parts of this framework meet or cross they are bound together with reindeer tendon very artistically. * * * The *pah* or manhole * * * has a rim or lip secured upon the gunwale and rising a couple of inches above the deck." (First Grinnell Exp., p. 477.) It will be seen that he does not mention any deck beams, which would be very necessary to keep the gunwales spread apart. They are shown, however, in Crantz's crude section of a kaiak frame. (History of Greenland, vol. 1, pl. vii), and are evidently mortised into the gunwale, as at Point Barrow. Crantz also (op. cit., p. 150) speaks of the use of whalebone for fastening the frame together.

Capt. Lyon's description of the round-bottomed kaiak used at Fury and Hecla Straits (Journal, p. 233) is much more explicit. He describes the frame as consisting of a gunwale on each side 4 or 5 inches wide in the middle and three-fourths inch thick, tapering at each end, sixty-four hoop-shaped ribs (on a canoe 25 feet long), seven slight rods outside of the ribs, twenty-two deck-beams, and a batten running fore and aft, and a hoop round the cockpit. These large kaiaks weigh 50 or 60 pounds. There is a very good figure of the Point Barrow kaiak. paddled with a single paddle. in Smyth's view of Nuwŭk (Beechey's Voyage, pl. opposite p. 307).

[3] Wrangell, Narrative of an Expedition, etc., p. 161, footnote.

ished models were made for sale. The natives are so skillful in making them that it is possible that they are in the habit of making them for the children to play with. I do not, however, recollect ever seeing a child with one.

Umiaks and fittings.—The large skin-covered open boat, essentially the same in model as that employed by almost all Eskimo, as well as the Aleuts and some Siberian races, is the chief means of conveyance by water, for traveling, hunting, and fishing. Though the women do a great share of the work of navigating the boat when a single family or a small party is making a journey, it is by no means considered as a woman's boat, as appears to be the case among the Greenlanders and eastern Eskimo generally.[1] On the contrary, women are not admitted into the regularly organized whaling crews, unless the umialik can not procure men enough, and in the "scratch" crews assembled for walrus hunting or sealing there are usually at least as many men as women, and the men work as hard as the women. I do not, however, recollect that I ever saw a man pull an oar in the umiak. They appear always to use paddles alone. This is interesting in connection with the Greenland custom mentioned by Egede in the continuation of the passage just quoted: "And when they first set out for the whale fishing, the men sit in a very negligent posture, with their faces turned towards the prow, pulling with their little ordinary paddle; but the women sit in the ordinary way, with their faces towards the stern, rowing with long oars."

We were unable to bring home any specimen of these boats on account of their size, but Fig. 342, from a photograph by Lieut. Ray, will give a good idea of the framework. These boats vary considerably in size, but are usually very nearly the dimensions of an ordinary whaleboat—that is, about 30 feet in length, with a beam of 5 or 6 feet and a depth of about 2½ feet. The boat resembles very much in model the American fisherman's dory, having a narrow flat bottom, sharp at both ends, with flaring sides, and considerable rake at stem and stern. Both floor and rail have a strong sheer, fore and aft, and the gunwales extend beyond the stem so as to meet at the bow. Both stem and stern are sharp nearly to the rail, where they flare out and are cut off square. These boats are exceedingly light and buoyant, and capable of considerable speed when fully manned. They are very "quick" in their motion and quite crank till they get down to their bearings, but beyond that appear to be very stiff.

I never heard of one being capsized, though the natives move about aboard of them with perfect freedom. The frame is neatly made of pieces of driftwood, which it usually takes a considerable time to accumulate.[2]

---

[1] For example: "For they think it unbecoming a man to row such a boat, unless great necessity requires it." Egede, Greenland, p. 111. "It would be a scandal for a man to meddle, except the greatest necessity compels him to lend a hand." Crantz, vol. 1, p. 149.

[2] Part of the description of the umiak frame is taken from the model (No. 56563 [225]), as the writer not only had few opportunities for careful examination of these canoes, but unfortunately did not realize at the time the importance of detail.

A stout square timber, of perhaps 3 inches scantling, runs along the middle of the bottom forming a keel or keelson. This of necessity is usually made of several pieces of wood scarfed together and fastened with treenails and whalebone lashings. At each end it is fastened in the same way to the stem and sternpost, which are both of the same shape, broad and flat above or inside, but beveled off to a keel outside, and curving up in a knee, at the same time tapering off to the point where the bow (or stern) begins to flare. Here it is mortised into the under side of a trapezoidal block of wood, widest and thickest on the inboard end, and concaved off on the under face, to a thin edge outboard. It is held on by a transverse lashing passing through holes in the end of the post and the thickest part of the block. Along each side of the bottom, at what would be the bilge of a round-bottom boat, runs a stout streak,

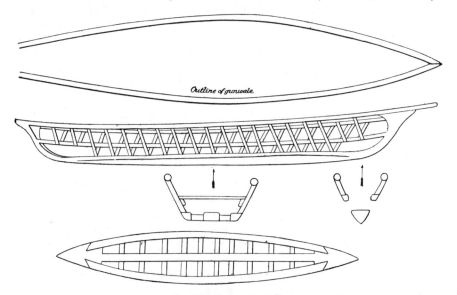

FIG. 342.—Frame of umiak.

thinner and wider than the keelson and set up edgewise. These are spread apart amidships, but bent together fore and aft so as to be scarfed into the stem and sternpost (see diagram, Fig. 343a).

On the model they are fastened here with treenails, and this is probably also the case on the large canoes. They are spread apart by cross pieces or floor timbers, flat rather broad boards laid across the keelson with their ends mortised into the bilge streaks. These are longest amidships and decrease regularly in length fore and aft. There were fifteen of them on Nikawáalu's umiak. On the model they are pegged to the keelson and bilge streaks. The ribs are straight, slender, square timbers, eighteen on each side (on Nikawáalu's umiak; the canoe photographed has fifteen). These are all of the same length, but fitted obliquely to the outer edge of the bilge-streaks in such a way (see diagram, Fig.

343b) that those amidships slant considerably outward while the others become gradually more and more erect fore and aft, thus producing the sheer in the lines. To these ribs, inside, a little below the middle of each, is fastened a streak on each side, of about the dimensions of the bilge streak, running from stem to stern, and the gunwales are fitted into the notched ends of the ribs, where they are secured by lashings of whalebone. These on Nikawáalu's umiak were each a single round pole about 2 inches in diameter. Such long pieces of wood as this were probably obtained by trade from the Nunatañmeun. These extend about 2½ or 3 feet beyond the stem, to which they are fastened on each side by whalebone lashings, and meet at a sharp angle, being lashed together with whalebone. On the model, this lashing passes through holes in both gunwales and round underneath. The gunwales are fastened to the sternpost in the same way as to the stem, in both cases resting on the upper surface of the block so as to form a low rail, but project only 5 or 6 inches.

Between the post and the last pair of long ribs at each end are two pairs of short ribs running only from the gunwale to the inside streak. The frame is still further strengthened by an outside streak between the bilge streak and the inside streak, and Nikawáalu's canoe had an extra streak of "half-round" willow out-

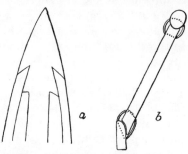

FIG. 343.—Construction of umiak: (*a*) method of fastening bilge streaks to stem; (*b*) method of framing rib to gunwale, etc.

side of the latter. The thwarts rest on the inside streak and are secured by whalebone lashings. The block or head of the stern-post serves as a high seat for the steersman. Crantz's[1] description and diagram show that the frame of the Greenland umiak consists of essentially the same timbers, lacking only the two outside streaks.

The cover is made of the skins of the larger marine animals. Walrus hide is often used and sometimes the skin of the polar bear, which makes a beautifully white cover, but the skin of the bearded seal is preferred, the people from Point Barrow sometimes making journeys to Wainwright Inlet in search of such skins, which are dressed with their oil in them in the manner already referred to. We were informed that six of these skins were required to cover one umiak. They are put together in the same way as the skins for the kaiak and sewed with the same seam. The edges of the cover are stretched over the gunwale, and laced to the inside streak with a stout thong, which passes through holes in the edge of the cover. At stem and stern the cover is laced with a separate thong to a stout transverse lashing of thong running from gunwale to gunwale close to the edge of the posthead.

History of Greenland, vol. 1, p. 148, and pl. vi.

The cover is removed in the winter and stowed away on the cache frame or some other safe place (Mûñialu, when preparing to start for the spring deer hunt in 1883, carefully buried his boat cover in a snow-bank) out of reach of the dogs, and the frame is placed bottom upwards on a staging 4 or 5 feet from the ground.

When they are ready to refit the canoe for the spring whaling, a hole is cut in the sea ice close to the shore, and the cover immersed in the sea water for several days to soften it, the hole being covered with slabs of snow to keep it from freezing up. Crantz [1] mentions a similar custom in Greenland. After removing the hair from the boat-skins "they lay them in salt water for some days to soften them again, and so cover the women's boats and kajaks with them." When not in use, the umiak is drawn up on the beach and usually laid bottom upward with the gear, spears, etc., underneath it, but sometimes propped up on one gunwale to make a shelter against the wind. This is a common practice in the camp at Pernyû, where there is usually at least one boat set up edgewise, sheltered by which the men sit to whittle and gossip.

In the whaling camp at Imêkpûñ in 1883, the boats which were not ready to go out to the open water were laid up bottom up with one end resting on a sled set up on its side and the other supported by a block of snow. They do not appear to be in the habit of using the canoe for a tent, as is said to be the custom among the more southern natives,[2] as they always carry a tent with them on their journeys. The umiak is propelled by paddles, oars, and a sail, and in smooth weather when the shore is clear of ice by "tracking" along the beach with men and dogs, one person at least always remaining on board to steer with a paddle at the stern.

The sail, which they are only able to use with a free wind, is square, narrow, and rather high, and is nowadays always made of drilling. Dark blue drilling appeared to be the most popular sort at the time of our visit. The head of the sail is laced to a light yard, and hoisted to the masthead by a halyard through a hole in the latter. The mast is a stout square pole 10 or 12 feet long and is set up well forward of amidships, without a step, the square butt resting against a bottom board, and held up by two forestays and two backstays, running from the masthead to the inside streak. All the rigging, stays, halyards, towing line, etc., are made of stout thong. The Greenlanders set up the mast in the bow of the umiak—as a sailor would say, "in the very eyes of her,"[3] but as far as I can learn the Western Eskimo all set it up as at Point Barrow.

The oars are very clumsily made with very narrow blades not over 3 inches broad. They are about 7 feet long and somewhat enlarged at the loom. Instead of resting in rowlocks, they are secured by two long

---

[1] Vol. 1, p. 167.

[2] See Kotzebue's Voyage, etc., vol. 1, p. 216.

[3] This is also the custom among the Central Eskimo. (See Boas "Central Eskimo," p. 528, Fig. 481.)

loops of thong as in the diagram Fig. 344. To keep the oar from chafing the skin on the gunwale, they lash to the latter a long plate of bone. No. 89696 [1197] from Utkiavwĭñ is one of these plates. Two of these oars are commonly used in an umiak, one forward and one aft, and the women row with great vigor, swinging well from the hips, but do not keep stroke. The use of oars is so unusual among savages that it would be natural to suppose that these people had adopted the custom from the whites. If this be the case, the custom reached them long ago, and through very indirect channels.

When Thomas Simpson, in 1837, bought an umiak from some Point Barrow natives at Dease Inlet, he bought with it "four of their slender oars, which they used as tent poles, besides a couple of paddles; fitted the oars with lashings, and arranged our strange vessel so well that the ladies were in raptures, declaring us to be genuine Esquimaux, and not poor white men."[1] The custom, moreover, appears to be widespread since Lyon speaks of seeing in 1821, "two very clumsy oars with flat blades, pulled by women," in the umiaks at Hudson Strait.[2] It was practiced at a still earlier date in Greenland.[3]

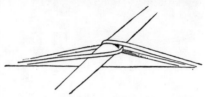

FIG. 344.—Method of slinging the oar of umiak.

While at Point Barrow the oars have very narrow blades and the double paddles very broad ones, the reverse seemed to be the case in Greenland, where the double paddle, as already noticed, has blades not over 3 or 4 inches broad. Crantz describes the oars as "short and broad before, pretty much like a shovel, but only longer, and * * confined to their places on the gunnel with a strap of seal's leather." (Vol. 2, p. 149 and pl. VI) Although both oars and sails are undoubtedly quite ancient inventions (Frobisher in his description of Meta Incognita in Hakluyt's Voyages (1589) pp. 621 and 628, speaks of skin boats with sails of entrail),[4] I am strongly inclined to believe that they are both considerably more recent than the paddles, not only on general principles, but from the fact that the whaling umiaks ᵗt Point Barrow use only paddles. There is no practical reason againɛt using either oars or sails, and in fact the latter would often be of great advantage in silently approaching a whale, as the American whalemen have long

[1] Narrative, p. 148.

[2] Journal, p. 30. Compare also Chappell, "Hudson Bay," p. 57.

[3] See Egede, Greenland, p. 111.

[4] These passages being, as far as I know. the earliest description of the umiak and kaiak are worth quotation: "Their boats are made all of Seale skins, with a keel of wood within the skinne; the proportion of them is like a Spanish shallop, saue only they be flat in the bottome, and sharp at both endes" (p. 621, 1576). Again: "They haue two sorts of boats made of leather, set out on the inner side with quarters of wood, artificially tyed with thongs of the same; the greater sort are not much unlike our wherries, wherein sixteene or twenty men may sitte; they have for a sayle, drest the guttes of such beasts as they kill, very fine and thinne, which they sewe together; the other boate is but for one man to sitte and rowe in, with one oare" (p. 628, 1577).

ago discovered. It seems to me that this is merely another case of adhering to an obsolete custom on semireligious grounds. The paddles are usually about 4 or 5 feet long, made of one piece of driftwood, with slender round shafts, and lanceolate blades about 6 inches broad, and a short rounded cross handle at the upper end. (Fig. 345 shows two of the paddles belonging to the model.) The steersman uses a longer paddle, and stands in the stern or sits up on the head of the sternpost.

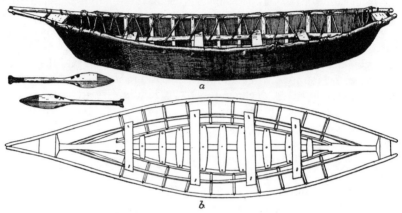

FIG. 345.—Model of umiak and paddles: (*a*) side view; (*b*) inside plan.

Fig. 345*a* represents the model (No. 56563 [225] from Utkiavwĭñ), which gives a very good idea of the shape of one of these boats. It is quite correct in all its parts, though the timbers are rather too heavy, and there are not so many ribs and floor timbers as in a full-sized canoe. The breadth of beam, 6·2 inches, is at least 1 inch too great in proportion to the length, 25 inches. The cover is one piece of seal skin which has been partially tanned by the "white-tanning" process, and put on wet. In drying it has turned almost exactly the color of a genuine

FIG. 346.—Ivory bailer for umiak.

boat cover. The frame, as is often the case with a full-sized boat, is painted all over with red ocher. (See Fig. 345*b*, inside plan.)

For bailing these boats a long narrow dipper of ivory or bone is used, of such a shape as to be especially well suited for working in between the floor timbers. Fig. 346 represents one of these (No. 56536 [40] from Utkiavwĭñ). It is a piece of walrus tusk 16·3 inches long. The cavity is 1·1 inches deep and was excavated by drilling vertical holes and cutting away the substance between them. Some of the holes have not been completely worked out. A similar bailer (No. 89835 [1010] also from Utkiavwĭñ) is made of reindeer antler, a substance much more easily worked than the ivory, as the soft interior tissue exposed by cutting the upper side flat is readily carved out. As with the walrus tusk, the natural curve of the material gives the proper inclination to the handle. It is 18·3 inches long.

When the umiak is fitted out for whaling a stout U-shaped crotch of ivory or bone, about 7 inches long and 5 wide, is lashed between the gunwales where they meet at the bow. In this the heavy harpoon rests when they are approaching a whale. It is only used when whaling. The Museum collection contains specimens of this sort from as far south as the Diomede Islands.

We brought home five specimens of these kû′nnɐ, of which No. 56510 [117] Fig. 347 has been selected as the type. This is made of two bilaterally symmetrical pieces of white walrus ivory, each piece consisting of one arm of the crotch and half the shank. Its total length is 7·8 inches. The two pieces are held together by a stout wooden tree-nail, and above this a lashing of sinew-braid, lodged in two deep vertical channels one on each side of the shank just below the arms, and wedged above and below on both sides with slips of wood. A hole is drilled through each side of the butt close to the end, and through these a lashing is stretched across the reentering angle of the butt consisting of four turns of sinew braid with the end

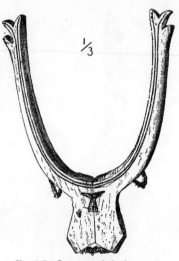

FIG. 347.—Ivory crotch for harpoon.

closely wrapped round the parts between the holes, and neatly tucked in.

Just at the bend of each arm is a small round becket hole, running obliquely from the back to the outer side. In each of these is a neat becket, about ¾ inches long, made of several turns of sinew braid, with the end neatly wrapped around them. These beckets serve to receive the lashings for attaching the crotch to the gunwales. All the ornamental figures are incised and blackened.

Three of the remaining four specimens are of walrus-ivory, and of essentially the same pattern, differing only in ornamentation and other minor details. No. 56511 [116], from Utkiavwĭñ, is almost exactly like the type and of very nearly the same size. It is fastened together with a lashing only, but no treenail, and the beckets have been removed from the becket holes. The border is colored with red ocher, and there are two whales' tails instead of one on the shank. The other two have the tips of the arms carved into the shape of whales' heads. No. 89418 [1224], Fig. 348, from Utkiavwĭñ, is otherwise of the same shape as those already described, but is lashed together with stout seal thong, and has four beckets of the same material, two in the usual position and two at the widest part of the shank. These take the place of the loop running across the butt. On the middle of the back of each arm is a small cross incised and blackened with a small blue glass bead inlaid in the center, and there are two whale's tails on the opposite face of the shank. It is 8 inches long.

No. 89419 [926], from Nuwŭk, has a nearly straight shank with a flange on each side at the butt. It is lashed together with whalebone and has also a treenail, like the type. The upper beckets are of sinew-braid. A large becket at the butt is made by looping and knotting the ends of a bit of thong into a hole in each flange. There is one whale's tail engraved on the front of the shank. When lashed in posi-

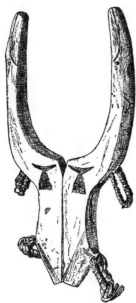

FIG. 348.—Ivory crotch for harpoon.

FIG. 349.—Crotch for hapoon made of walrus jaw.

tion the front or ornamental side faces inboard, as is indicated by the shape of the shank, which is slightly narrower behind than in front, so as to fit between the converging gunwales. No. 8917 [1104], Fig. 349, from Nuwuk, the only one of the kind seen, is a very interesting form. It is made by cutting a horizontal slice out of the lower jaw of a walrus, so that it form the arms of the crotch, while the thick symphysis is cut into a shank of the usual shape, with the two upper beckets in the usual place and a large one at the butt, passing through a transverse hole. These beckets are roughly made of thong. Its total length is 6·6 inches.

This specimen from its soiled condition is undoubtedly quite ancient, and probably of an older type than the highly ornamented ivory crotches of the present day. The latter are evidently only copies of the jaw-bone crotch in a material susceptible of a higher finish than the coarse bone. The only reason for making them in two pieces is that it is impossible to get a single piece of walrus ivory large enough for a whole one. It seems to me highly probable that the crotch was suggested by the natural shape of the walrus jaw, since these are frequently used for crotches to receive the cross pieces of the cache frames. Perhaps, for a while, the whole jaw was simply lashed to the bow of the boat. The next step would obviously be to cut out the shank and reduce the weight of the crotch by trimming off the superfluous material. The reason for making the crotch of ivory is perhaps purely esthetic; but more likely connected with the notions already referred to which lead them to clean up their boats and gear and adorn themselves and paint their faces when they go to the whale fishery.

Although, as I have already stated, there appears to be no essential difference in the general plan of the frame of the Greenland umiaks and those used at Point Barrow, there seems to be considerable difference in the size and outward appearance. As well as can be judged from the brief descriptions and rude figures of various authors[1] and various models in the National Museum (the correctness of which, however, I can not be sure of, without having seen the originals) the umiak not only in Greenland, but among the Eskimo generally as far west as the Mackenzie, is a much more wall sided square ended boat than at Point Barrow, having less sheer to the gunwales with the stem and stern-post nearly vertical.[2] Mr. L. M. Turner informs me that this is the case at Ungava Bay. It was also a larger boat. Egede says that they "are large and open * * * some of them 20 yards long;"[3] Crantz gives their length as "commonly 6, nay 8 or 9 fathoms long;"[4] Kumlien says that it required "about fifteen skins of Phoca barbata" to cover an umiak at Cumberland Gulf,[5] and Mr. Turner informs me that eight are used at Ungava. Capt. Parry found no umiaks at Fury and Hecla straits[6] and Kumlien says that they are becoming rare at Cumberland Gulf. The so-called Arctic Highlanders of Smith Sound have no boats of any kind. The model used at Point Barrow probably prevails as far south as Kotzebue Sound. The boats that boarded us off Wainwright Inlet in the autumn of 1883, and those of the Nunatañmiun who visited Point Barrow, seemed not to differ from those with which we were familiar, except that the latter were rather light and low sided, nor do I remember anything peculiar about the boats which we saw at Plover Bay in 1881.

---

[1] Compare for instance Kane's figure 1st Grinnell Exp. p. 422, and Lyon, Journal, p. 30.

[2] See Beechey Voyage, p. 252. In describing the umiaks at Hotham Inlet he says: "The model differs from that of the umiak of the Hudson Bay in being sharp at both ends." Smyth gives a good figure of the Hotham Inlet craft in the plate opposite p. 250.

[3] Greenland, p. 111.

[4] Vol. 1, p. 148.

[5] Contributions, p. 43. Boas, however, says three to five skins. (Central E. kimo, p. 528.)

[6] 2d Voy., p. 507.

There is very little accessible detailed informtion regarding the umiaks used in the rest of Alaska. From Dall's figure[1] and a few models in the Museum, the Norton Sound umiak appears to have the gunwales united at both stem and stern. Those that we saw at St. Michael's in 1883, were so much modified by Russian ideas as to be wholly out of the line of comparison. The same is true of the Aleutian "baidara," if, indeed, the latter be an umiak at all.

TRAVELING ON FOOT.

Snowshoes (*túglu.*)—Snowshoes of a very efficient pattern and very well made are now universally employed at Point Barrow. Although the snow never lies very deep on the ground, and is apt to pile up in hard drifts, it is sufficiently deep and soft in many places, especially on the grassy parts of the tundra, to make walking without snowshoes very inconvenient and fatiguing. I have even seen them used on the sea ice for crossing level spaces when a few inches of snow had fallen. Practically, every man in the two villages, and many of the women and boys, have each their own pair of snowshoes, fitted to their size. Each shoe consists of a rim of light wood, bent into the shape of a pointed oval, about five times as long as the greatest breadth, and much bent up at the rounded end, which is the toe. The sides are braced apart by two stout cross-bars (*toe* and *heel bar*) a little farther apart than the length of the wearer's foot. The space between these two bars is netted in large meshes (*foot netting*) with stout thong for the foot to rest upon, and the spaces at the ends are closely netted with fine deerskin "babiche"[2] (*toe* and *heel netting*). The straps for the foot are fastened to the foot netting in such a way that while the strap is firmly fastened round the ankle the snowshoe is slung to the toe. The wearer walks with long swinging strides, lifting the toe of the shoe at each step, while the tail or heel drags in the snow. The straps are so contrived that the foot can be slipped in and out of them without touching them with the fingers, a great advantage in cold weather. When deer hunting, according to Lieut. Ray, they take a long piece of thong and knot each end of it to the toe of one snowshoe. The bight is then looped into the belt behind so that the snowshoes drag out of the way of the heels. When they wish to put on the shoes they draw them up, insert their feet in the straps, and fasten the slack of the lines into the belt in front with a slip knot. When, however, they come to a piece of ground where snowshoes are not needed, they kick them off, slip the knots, and let them " drop astern."

We brought home three pairs of snowshoes, which represent very well the form in general use. No. 89912 [1736], Fig. 350, has been selected as the type. The rim is of willow, 51 inches long and 10½ inches

<hr>

[1] Alaska, p. 15.

[2] Twisted sinew is sometimes used. A pair of snowshoes from Point Barrow, owned by the writer, are netted with this material.

wide at the broadest part, and is made of two strips about 1 inch thick and ¾ wide, joined at the toe by a long lap-splice, held together by four short horizontal or slightly oblique stitches of thong.   Each strip is elliptical in section, with the long axis vertical, and keeled on the inner face, except between the bars.   Each is tapered off considerably from the toe bar to the toe, and slightly tapered toward the heel.   The two points are fastened together by a short horizontal stitch of whalebone.   The tip is produced into a slight "tail," and the inner side of each shoe is slightly straighter than the outer—that is to say, they are "rights and lefts."

The bars are elliptical in section, flattened, and have their ends mortised into the rim.   They are about a foot apart, and of oak, the toe bar 9·2 inches long and the heel bar 8·5.   Both are of the same breadth and thickness, 1 by ½ inch.   There is also an extra bar for strengthening the back part of the shoe 10 inches from the point.   It is also of oak, 4·8 inches long, 0·5 wide, and 0·3 thick.   The toe and heel nettings are put on first.   Small equidistant vertical holes run round the inside of each space.   Those in the rim are drilled through the keel already mentioned, and joined by a shallow groove above and below; those in the bars are about ½ inch from the edge and joined by a groove on the under side of the toe bar only.   Into these holes is laced a piece of babiche, which is knotted once into each hole, making a series of beckets about ¾ inch wide round the inside of the space.   There are no lacing holes in the parts spliced at the toe, but the lacing passes through a bight of each stitch.   At the toe bar the lacing is carried straight across from rim to rim about three times, the last part being wound round the others.

On the left shoe the end is brought back on the left-hand side, passed through the first hole in the bar from above, carried along in the groove on the underside to the next hole, up through this and round the lacing, and back through the same hole, the two parts being twisted together between the bar and lacing.   This is continued, "stopping" the lacing in festoons to the bar, to the last hole on the right,

⅛

FIG. 350.—Snowshoe.

where it is finished off by knotting the end round the last "stop." The stops are made, apparently, by a separate piece on the right shoe. The lacing on the heel bar is also double or triple, but the last part, which is wound round the others, is knotted into each hole as on the rim. The lacings on the rim of the heel space are knotted with a single knot round each end of the extra bar.

In describing the nettings it will always be understood that the upper surface of the shoe is toward the workman, with the point upward, if describing the heel nettings, and vice versa for the toe. To begin with the heel netting, which is the simpler: This is in two parts, one from the heel bar to the extra bar (heel netting proper) and one from the latter to the point (point netting). The netting is invariably fastened to the lacing by passing the end through the becket from above and bringing it back over itself. In making the point netting the end of the babiche is knotted round the bar at the right-hand lower corner with a single knot. The other end goes up to the lacing at the point and comes down to the left-hand lower corner, where it is

FIG. 351.—Knot in snowshoe.

hitched round the bar, as in Fig. 351, then goes up to the lowest becket on the left side, crosses to the corresponding one on the right, and comes down and is hitched as before round the bar inside of the starting point. This makes a series of strands round the outside of the space, two running obliquely from right to left, a long one on the right side and a short one on the left side; two similar strands from left to right, the long one on the left and the short one on the right, and one transverse strand at the base of the triangle (see diagram, Fig. 352a). The next round goes up to the first becket at the top on the left hand, crosses to the corresponding one on the right, and then makes the same strands as the first round, running parallel to them and about half an inch nearer the center of the space (see diagram, Fig. 352b). Each successive round follows the last, coming each time about ½ inch nearer the center, till the space is all filled in, which brings the end of the last round to the middle of the bar, round which it is knotted with a single knot. This makes three sets of strands, two obliquely longitudinal, one set from right to left and one from left to right, and one transverse, all of each set parallel and equidistant, or nearly so, and each interwoven alternately over and under each successive strand it meets.

The right shoe has fourteen longitudinal strands in each set and thirteen transverse; the left, one less in each set. On the left shoe the end is carried up from the last knot to the lacing at the point, and then comes back to the bar, fastening the other part to the netting with six equidistant half-hitches. The heel netting proper is put on in a slightly different fashion, as the space to be filled is no longer triangular. It starts as before in the right hand lower corner, where it is knotted into the becket, running across from the rim to the heel-bar; goes up to the middle of the extra bar, round which it is hitched as already described, then down to the left hand lower corner; up to the first becket on the left rim, across to the corresponding one on the right, and down to the first becket on the heel bar. This completes the first round (see diagram, Fig. 353a). The second round goes up to the hind bar at the left of the first, comes down only to the transverse strand of the first round on the left, goes up to the becket on the rim above the first, crosses to the right, and comes back to the transverse turn of the first rounds. All these strands except the transverse one are on the left of the first round. The third round follows the first, which brings all its strands except the transverse one to the right of the first round (see diagram,

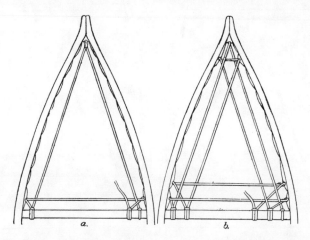

Fig. 352.—Point netting of snowshoe heel: (a) first round; (b) first and second rounds.

Fig. 353b). The successive odd rounds follow the first and the even rounds the second, bringing the longitudinal strands alternately to the right and left of the first round, until the ends of the hind bar are reached—that is to say, till the space *outside* of the first round is filled— each transverse strand coming above the preceding. This is done regularly on the left shoe, the tenth round coming to the left end of the bar, and the eleventh to the right. The twelfth round comes to the becket in the left hand upper corner, and crosses to the corresponding becket on the other side. It then follows the odd rounds, thus making six strands, four longitudinal and two transverse, as in the point nettings. All the remaining rounds follow this till the whole space is filled in, which brings the end of the last round to the middle of the heel bar, where it is knotted do the becket.

On the right shoe the maker seems to have made a mistake at the eighth round, which obliged him to alter the order of the other strands and finish with half a round. Instead of taking the end of the eighth round down to the preceding transverse strand only, he has brought it down to the heel bar, which brings the ninth round to the left, following the even rounds, and coming to the end of the hind bar, the tenth to the right end of the bar, so that it is the eleventh which makes the first transverse turn at the top. The pattern is the same as in the point nettings. The right shoe has 25, 24, and 19 strands in the three sets respectively, and the left, 25, 25, and 19. The toe nettings are put on in the same way, the first round going to the middle becket at the toe, and crossing to the first becket on the right hand, the second going to the first becket on the left hand and crossing on the right to the first round, and the third going to the first round at the toe and crossing on the right to the becket.

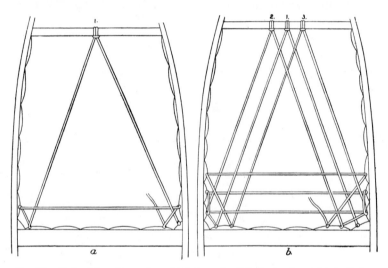

Fig. 353.—Heel netting of snow shoe; (a) first round; (b) first, second, and third rounds.

All the even rounds go to the becket at the toe and cross to the preceding even round, and all the odd rounds go to the preceding odd round at the toe and cross to the becket, until the space outside of the first round is filled with longitudinal strands, when they begin to make descending transverse turns across the toe, going from the becket on the left to the corresponding one on the right and thus following the odd rounds. The fourteenth round on the right shoe begins this, the twelfth on the left. This brings the end of the last round to the middle of the toe bar. It is then carried up to the becket at the toe, brought down and up again, and the end is used to fasten these three parts to the netting with equidistant half hitches—fourteen on the right shoe and thirteen on the left. The pattern, of course, is the same as before, with 33, 33, and 26 strands on the right shoe, and 31, 3r, and 25 on the left, in each set respectively.

The foot-netting is of a very different pattern, and consists of seven transverse and thirteen longitudinal strands, of which six, in the middle, do not reach the toe bar, leaving an oblong transverse hole, through which the toe presses against the snow at the beginning of the step. The cross strands are a piece of stout thong (the skin of the walrus or bearded seal), to the end of which is spliced with double slits a long piece of thinner seal thong, which makes the longitudinal ones. The seven transverse strands pass in and out through holes in the rim, while the longitudinal strands pass over the bars, except the middle three pairs, which pass round the horizontal strand behind the toe hole, drawing it down to the next strand. The end of the thirteenth strand wattles these two firmly together, as it does also the two pairs of longitudinal strands on each side of the toe hole, and finishes off the netting by whipping the two sets of strands together with a "birdcage stitch."

The object of the complicated wattling round the toe hole is, first, to strengthen the hind border against which the toe presses in walking, and second to give a firm attachment for the straps, which are fastened at the junction of the doubled and twisted longitudinal strands with the first and second transverse ones. Each strap is a single piece of stout seal thong fastened to the shoe with two loops as follows: At the inner side of the shoe the end is passed into the toe hole and makes a round turn about the doubled longitudinal strands, and then goes under the two cross strands, coming out behind them and between the twelfth and thirteenth longitudinal strands. It is then spliced into the standing part with two slits, making a becket about 3 inches in diameter. The other end, leaving a loop large enough to go round the wearer's heel, is passed through the becket just made, wound in the same way as before round the strands at the other corner of the toe hole, and made into a similar becket by knotting the end to the standing part with a marlinghitch with the bight left in. On the right shoe this hitch is made in a slit in the standing part. The end is probably left long for the purpose of adjusting the length of the strap to the wearer's foot.

In putting on the shoe, the toe is thrust sideways through the loop till the bight comes well up over the heel, and then turned round and stuck under the two beckets, which together form a strap to fasten the toe down to the shoe, leaving the latter free to swing when the heel is raised. By reversing the process the shoe is easily kicked off. These straps must be fitted very nicely or else the shoe is apt to come off. This is a very neatly made pair of shoes, and the woodwork is all painted red above.

No. 89913 [1737] is a pair of similar shoes also from Utkiavwĭñ. The frame is made in the same way and is wholly of willow except the extra hind bar, which is of walrus ivory. These shoes are shorter and somewhat broader than the preceding and not so well made. They are 48·5 inches long and 11 broad. The two shoes are not perceptibly different in shape. The lacing, which is of sinew braid, is put on in the same way as on the preceding pair, except that it is fastened directly into the holes on the toe bars. The whole of the heel netting is in one piece, and made precisely in the same way as the point nettings of the first pair, the end being carried up the middle to the point of the heel and brought down again to the bar as on the toe nettings, but fastened with marling hitches. The number of strands is the same in each shoe, twenty-three in each set. The toe nettings follow quite regularly the pattern of the preceding pair.

FIG. 354.—Small snowshoe.

The shoes are not quite the same size, as the right has 35, 35, and 28 strands, and the left 33, 33, and 25, in each set respectively. There is no regular rule about the number of strands in any part of the netting, the object being simply to make the meshes always about the same size. The foot netting is made of stout and very white thong from the bearded seal. These shoes have no strings.

No. 89914 [1738] is a pair of rather small shoes from Utkiavwiñ, one of which is shown in Fig. 354. They are rights and lefts, and are 42 inches long by 10 broad. The frame is wholly of oak, and differs from the type only in having no extra hind bar, and having the heel and toe bars about equal in length. The points are fastened together with a treenail, as well as with a whalebone stitch. The heel-nettings are put on with perfect regularity, as on the pair last described, but the toe-nettings, though they start in the usual way, do not follow any regular rule of sucession, the rounds being put on sometimes inside and sometimes outside of the preceding, till the whole space is filled. The foot-nettings are somewhat clumsily made, especially on the right shoe, which appears to have been broken in several places, and "cobbled" by an unskillful workman. There are only five transverse strands which are double on the left shoe, and the longitudinal strands are not whipped to these, but interwoven, and each pair twisted together between the transverse strands. There is no wattling back of the toe hole, and one pair of longitudinal strands at the side of the latter is not doubled on the left shoe. The strings are put on as on the type except that the ends are knotted instead of being spliced. This pair of shoes was used by the writer on many short excursions around the station during the winters of 1881-'82 and 1882-'83. They were old when purchased.

I had but one opportunity of seeing the process of making the frames of the snowshoes. Ilûbw'ga, the "inland" native frequently mentioned, a particularly skillful workman, undertook to make a pair of snowshoes for Lieut. Ray at our quarters, but did not succeed in finishing them, as the ash lumber which we brought from San Francisco proved too brittle for the purpose. Having a long piece of wood, he "got out" the whole rim in one piece. Ordinarily the splice at the toe must be made, at least temporarily, before the frame can be bent into shape. He softened up the wood by wrapping it in rags wet with hot water. Some of the other natives, however, recommended that the wood should be immersed in the salt water for a day or two, from which I infer that this is a common practice. After slowly bending the toe, with great care, nearly into shape, he inserted into the bend a flat block of wood of the proper shape for the toe and lashed the frame to this. A pointed block was also used to give the proper shape to the heel; the bars being inserted in the mortises before the ends were brought together. The temporary lashings are kept on till the wood dries into shape. The toes are turned up by tying the shoes together, sole to sole, and inserting a transverse stick between the tips of the toes.

The use of finely finished snowshoes of this pattern is of comparatively recent date at Point Barrow. Dr. Simpson[1] is explicit concerning the use of snowshoes in his time (1853–'55). He says: "Snowshoes are so seldom used in the north where the drifted snow presents a hard frozen surface to walk upon, that certainly not half a dozen pairs were in existence at Point Barrow at the time of our arrival, and those were of an inferior sort." I have already mentioned the universal employment of these snowshoes at the present day, so that the custom must have arisen in the last thirty years. The pattern of shoe now used is identical with those of the Tinné or Athabascan Indians (as is plainly shown by the National Museum collections), and I am inclined to believe that the Point Barrow natives have learned to use them from the "Nunatañmiun," from whom, indeed, they purchase ready-made snowshoes at the present day, as we ourselves observed. The "Nunatañmiun," or the closely related people of the Kuwûk River, are known to have intimate trading relations with the Indians, and even in Simpson's time[2] used the Indian shoe, sometimes at least. The fact that in recent times families of the "Nunatañmiun" have established the habit of spending the winter with the people of Point Barrow and associating with them in the winter deer-hunt, would explain how the latter came to recognize the superior excellence of the Indian shoe.

This is more likely than that they learned to use them from the eastern natives, whom they only meet for a short time in summer, though

---

[1] Op. cit., p. 243.   [2] Op. cit., p. 244.

the latter used the Indian style of snowshoes at least as early as 1826. Franklin [1] speaks of seeing, at Demarcation Point, a pair of snowshoes netted with cords of deerskin and shaped like those of the Indians of the Mackenzie.

Most of the other Eskimo of Alaska, who need to use snowshoes at all, use a style of shoe very much less efficient and more roughly made, the rim being of heavy, rather crooked pieces of willow or alder. Simpson's description will apply very well to this form, which is used even as far north as Icy Cape, whence Mr. Nelson brought home a pair. It also appears to be the prevailing, if not the only, form on the Siberian coast and St. Lawrence Island, judging from Nordinskiöld's figure [2] and Mr. Nelson's collections.

Simpson says: [3] "The most common one is two pieces of alder, about two feet and a half long, curved towards each other at the ends, where they are bound together, and kept apart in the middle by two cross-pieces, each end of which is held in a mortise. Between the crosspieces is stretched a stout thong, lengthwise and across, for the foot to rest upon, with another which first forms a loop to allow the toes to pass beneath; this is carried round the back of the ankle to the opposite side of the foot, so as to sling the snowshoe under the joint of the great toe."

When there are toe and heel nettings, they are of seal thong with a large open mesh. The snowshoe from Norton Sound, figured by Dall, [4] is a rather neatly made variety of this form. South of the Yukon, the use of the snowshoe appears to be confined to the Indians. As shown by the Museum collections, the strings are always of the pattern described throughout the whole northwestern region. [5]

Snowshoes appear to be rarely used among the eastern Eskimo. The only writer who mentions them is Kumlien. [6] He says: "When traveling over the frozen wastes in winter, they [i. e., the natives of Cumberland Gulf] use snowshoes. These are half-moon shaped, of whalebone, with sealskin thongs tightly drawn across. They are about 16 inches long. Another pattern is merely a frame of wood, about the same length and 8 or 10 inches wide, with sealskin thongs for the foot to rest on."

The latter is apparently quite like the western snowshoes described by Simpson.

Staff.—The only staff used by the young and vigorous is the shaft of the spear, when one is carried. The aged and feeble, however, support their steps with one or two staffs about 5 feet long, often shod with bone or ivory. (The old man whom Franklin met on the Copper-mine River walked with the help of two sticks. [7]) Fig. 355 from a photograph represents old Yûksĭña from Nuwŭk, with his two staffs, without which he was hardly able to walk.

---

[1] 2d Exped., p. 142.
[2] Vega, vol. 2, p. 102 a.
[3] Op. cit., p. 243.
[4] Alaska, p. 190, Fig. A.
[5] See, also, Dall, Alaska, p. 190, and Figs. A and C.
[6] Contributions, p. 42.
[7] 1st Exp., vol. 2, p. 180.

LAND CONVEYANCES.

Sledges.—The only land conveyance employed at Point Barrow is the universal sledge of the Eskimo, of which there are two forms in general use, one, kă′motĭ, with a high rail on each side, and especially intended for carrying loads of the smaller articles, clothing, camp equipage, etc., and the other (unia) low and flat, without rail or "upstander," for carrying bulky objects, like whole carcasses of deer, frozen seals, rough dried deerskins, etc., and especially used for carrying the umiak across the land or solid ice. Both kinds are made without nails, but are fastened together by mortises and lashings and stitches of thong and whalebone. I have, however, seen one unia, which was made in 1883, fastened together with nails, a rather inferior substitute for the lashings, as they not only would not hold so firmly, but would also be liable to break in cold weather.

FIG. 355.—Old "Chief" with staffs.

Both kinds of sledge are made of driftwood and shod with strips of whale's jaw, about three-fourths of an inch thick, fastened on with bone treenails. These bone runners, which are about 2 inches wide, run sufficiently well over ice, hard snow, the frozen gravel of the beach or even on the bare tundra, but for carrying a heavy load over the softer snow of the interior they are shod with ice in a manner peculiar to this region.

It is well known that not only the Eskimo generally, but other hyperborean people coat the runners of their sleds with ice to make them run more smoothly, but this is usually only a comparatively thin crust, produced by pouring water on the runners or applying a mixture of snow or mud and water.[1] Mr. Turner informs me that at Ungava they are particular to use fine black vegetable mold for this purpose.

The method at Point Barrow is quite different from this. To each

---

[1] For example, Lyon says that at Fury and Hecla Straits the runners are coated with ice by mixing snow and fresh water (Journal, p. 235); (See also Parry, 2d Voyage, p. 515). At Cumberland Gulf "they pour warmed blood on the under surface of the bone shoeing; some use water, but this does not last nearly so long as the blood and is more apt to chip off." Kumlien, Contributions, p. 42; (See also Hall, Arctic Researches, p. 582). Around Repulse Bay they ice the runners by squirting over them water which has been warmed in the mouth, putting on successive layers till they get a smooth surface. This is renewed the first thing every morning. Gilder, Schwatka's Search, p. 66. A native of the eastern shore of Labrador, according to Sir John Richardson (Searching Expedition, vol. 2, p. 82), applied to the runners coat after coat of earth or clay tempered with hot water, and then washed the runners with water, polishing the ice with his naked hand. MacFarlane in his MS. notes speaks of covering the sled runners with "earth, water, and ice" in the Mackenzie region. Petitot (Monographie, etc., p. XVII) says the runners in the Mackenzie and Anderson district are shod with "un bourrelet de limon et de glace," which has to be often renewed. Nordenskiöld says that at Pitlekaj "the runners, before the start, are carefully covered with a layer of ice from two to three millimeters in thickness by repeatedly pouring water over them," (Vega, vol. 2, p. 94), and according to Wrangell (Narrative, etc., p. 101, footnote) it is the common custom in northern Siberia to pour water over the runners every evening to produce a thin crust of ice.

runner is fitted a heavy shoe of clear ice, as long as the runner, and fully 1 foot high by 6 inches thick. The sledge with these ice runners is estimated to weigh, even when unloaded, upwards of 200 or 300 pounds, but it appears that the smoothness of running more than counterbalances the extra weight. At any rate these shoes are almost universally employed on the sleds which make the long journey from the rivers in the spring with heavy loads of meat, fish, and skins. One native, in 1883, shod his sledges with salt-water ice in this way before starting for the hunting grounds. As these ice shoes are usually put on at the rivers, I had no opportunity of seeing the process, though I have seen the sledges thus shod after their return to the village. Lieut. Ray, who saw the process, describes it as follows:

"From the ice on a pond that is free from fracture they cut the pieces the length of a sled runner, 8 inches thick and 10 inches wide; into these they cut a groove deep enough to receive the sled runner up to the beam; the sled is carefully fitted into the groove, and secured by pouring in water, a little at a time and allowing it to freeze. Great care is taken in this part of the operation, for should the workman apply more than a few drops at a time, the slab of ice would be split and the work all to do over again; after the ice is firmly secured the sled is turned bottom up and the ice-shoe is carefully rounded with a knife, and then smoothed by wetting the naked hand and passing it over the surface until it becomes perfectly glazed."[1]

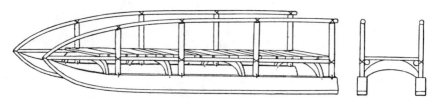

FIG. 356.—Railed sledge, diagrammatic (from photograph).

In traveling they take great care of these runners, keeping them smooth and polished, and mending all cracks by pouring in fresh water. They are also careful to shade them from the noonday sun, which at this season of the year is warm enough to loosen the shoes, for this purpose hanging a cloth or skin over the sunny side of the sled.[2]

We were unfortunately not able to bring home specimens of either style of large sled. The rail sled (kămotĭ) is usually about 8 or 9 feet long, and 2½ to 3 feet wide, and the rail at the back not over 2½ feet high. The thick curved runners, about 5 or 6 inches wide (see diagram, Fig. 356,

[1] Rep. Point Barrow Exp., p. 27.

[2] Schwatka, in "Nimrod in the North," (p. 159) describes a practice among the "Netschillik," of King William's Land, which appears very much like this, though his description is somewhat obscure in details. It is as follows: "We found the runners shod with pure ice. Trenches the length of the sledge are dug in the ice, and into these the runners are lowered some two or three inches, yet not touching the bottom of the trench by fully the same distance. Water is then poured in and allowed to freeze, and when the sledge is lifted out it is shod with shoes of perfectly pure and transparent ice." Strangely enough, these curious ice shoes are not mentioned by Schwatka's companions, Gilder and Klutschak, nor by Schwatka himself in his paper on the "Netschillik" in *Science*, although Klutschak describes and figures a sledge made wholly of ice among the Netsillingmiu.. ("Als Eskimo, etc." p. 76). Also referred to by Boas ("Central Eskimo," p. 533).

made from a small photograph) meet the curved slender rails (which are usually round) in front, but are separated from them behind by four stout vertical posts on each side, increasing in length toward the other end and mortised into the runners and rails. An equal number of stout wooden arches half the height of the posts are mortised into the runners, each arch a little in front of each pair of posts. A longitudinal strip runs along the middle of each side, and slats are laid across these, supported by the arches. The sledge is rather heavy and clumsy, but usually carefully made and often painted with red ocher.

FIG. 357.—Flat sledge.

Of the unia or flat sledge we have, fortunately a good photograph, Fig. 357. To the thick straight wooden runners are fastened directly seven cross slats, which project about 2 inches at each end beyond the runner, to which they are fastened by two stitches of whalebone each. A longitudinal strip runs along above the slats on each side. These sledges are generally made on the same pattern, varying somewhat in

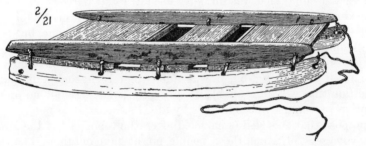

FIG. 358.—Small sledge with ivory runners.

size. A common size is about 6 feet long, about 2½ feet wide, and 9 or 10 inches high. Very small sledges of this pattern are sometimes made, especially for the purpose, as we were told, of carrying provisions, perhaps when one or two persons desire to make a rapid journey of some length, or for carrying a small share of meat from camp to camp.

One of these (Fig. 358, No. 89889 [1140], from Utkiavwĭñ), which shows signs of long use, was brought home. It is 20·7 inches long and 13 broad, and has ivory runners, with three wooden slats across them, held down

[1] The word used was "kau-kau." Perhaps it referred to a seal for food, as the sledge appears very like one described by Hooper (Corwin Report, p. 105) as used on the "Arctic Coast." "When sealing on solid ice a small sled is sometimes used, the runners of which are made of walrus tusks. It is perhaps 16 inches long by 14 inches wide and 3 inches high. It is used in dragging the carcass of the seal over the ice."

We, however, never saw such sleds used for dragging seals. This one may have been imported from farther south. See also, Beechey, Voyage, etc., p. 251, where he speaks of seeing at Kotzebue Sound, a drawing on ivory of "a seal dragged home on a small sledge."

by a low wooden rail on each side. Each runner is a slice from a single large walrus tusk, with the butt at the back of the sled. The slats, which are pieces of a ship's paneling, are lashed to the upper edge of the runners so as to project about one-half inch on each side. The rails flare slightly outward. The whole is fastened together by lashings of rather broad whalebone, passing through a hole near the upper edge of the runner, a notch in the end of the slat and a hole in the slat inside of the rail. There are two lashings at each end of each broad slat and one in the middle, at each end of the narrow one. The last and the ones at each end of the sled also secure the rail by passing through a hole near its edge, in which are cut square notches to make room for the other lashings. The trace is a strip of seal thong about 5 feet long and one-fourth inch wide, split at one end for about 1 foot into two parts. The other end is slit in two for about 3 inches. This is probably a broken loop, which served for fastening the trace to a dog's harness.

I do not recollect ever seeing so small a sled in actual use, though Lieut. Ray says he has frequently seen them drawn by one dog. The people who came down from Nuwŭk with a small load of things for trade sometimes used a small unía about 3 feet long, with one dog, and the same was often used by the girls for bringing in firewood from the beach.

A very peculiar sled was formerly used at Point Barrow, but we have no means of knowing how common it was. It was a sort of toboggan, made by lashing together lengthwise slabs of whalebone, but is now wholly obsolete, since whalebone has too high a market value to permit of its being used for any such purpose. We obtained one specimen about 10 feet long, but it was unfortunately in such a dilapidated condition that we were unable to bring it home. I find no previous mention of the use of such sleds by any Eskimo. It is not necessary to suppose that this sled is modeled after the toboggan of the Hudson Bay voyagers, of which these people might have obtained knowledge through the eastern natives, since the simple act of dragging home a "slab" of whalebone would naturally suggest this contrivance.

We did bring home one small sled of this kind (No. 89875 [772], Fig. 359, from Utkiavwĭñ), which from its size was probably a child's toy, though from its greasy condition it seems to have been used for dragging pieces of blubber. It is made of the tips of 6 small "slabs" of black whalebone, each about 2 inches wide at the broad end, and put together side by side so as to form a triangle 19¼ inches long and 9¾ wide, the apex being the front of the sled, and the left-hand edge of each slab slightly overlapping the edge of the preceding. They are fastened together by three transverse bands, passing through loops in the upper surface of each slot, made by cutting two parallel longitudinal slits about one-half inch long and one-fourth inch apart part way through, and raising up the surface between them. The hindmost band is a strip of whalebone nearly one-half inch wide, passing through these loops, and wound closely in a spiral around a straight rod of whalebone, 0·4 inch wide and 0·1 inch thick, as long as the band. The ends of the band are knotted into rings or beckets about $2\frac{1}{4}$ inches in diameter. The other two bands are simple, narrow strips of whalebone, running straight across through the loops and knotted at the ends into similar beckets. These beckets were obviously for tying on the load.

The sled with side rails does not appear to be used east of the Mackenzie region, but is found only slightly modified at least as far south as Norton Sound.[1] The sledge used on the Asiatic coast, however, as shown in Nordenskiöld's figure,[2] belongs to a totally different family, being undoubtedly borrowed from the reindeer Chukches.[3] The sleds of the eastern Eskimo vary somewhat in pattern and material, but may be described in general terms as essentially the same as the unía, but usually provided with what is called an "upstander," namely, two upright posts at each side of the back of the sled, often connected by a

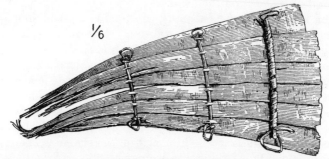

FIG. 359.—Small toboggan of whalebone.

cross rail, which serve to guide the sled from behind. Many descriptions and figures of these sleds will be found in the various descriptions of the eastern Eskimo.

Dogs and harness.—These sledges are drawn by dogs, which, as far as I am able to judge, are of the same breed as those used by the eastern Eskimo. They are, as a rule, rather large and stout. A number of the dogs at Utkiavwĭñ would compare favorably in size with the average Newfoundland dogs, and they appear to be capable of well sustained exertion. The commonest color is the regular "brindle" of the wolf, though white, brindle-and-white, and black-and-white dogs are not uncommon. There was, however, but one wholly black dog in the two villages. This was a very handsome animal known by the name of Allúa ("coal").

Every dog has his name and knows it. Their disposition is rather quarrelsome, especially among themselves, but they are not particularly ferocious, seldom doing more than howl and yelp at a stranger, and it is not difficult usually to make friends with them. There was

[1] See Dall's figure, Alaska, p. 165.
[2] Vega, vol. 1, p. 498.
[3] Compare also the various illustrations in Hooper's "Tents of the Tuski."

very little difficulty in petting the half dozen dogs which we had at the station, and they grew to be very much attached to the laborer who used to feed them. The natives treat their dogs well as a rule, seldom beating them wantonly or severely. Though they do not allow them to come into the houses, the dogs seem to have considerable attachment to their masters. Considerable care is bestowed on the puppies. Those born in winter are frequently reared in the iglu, and the women often carry a young puppy around in the jacket as they would a child.

We saw no traces of the disease resembling hydrophobia, which has wrought such havoc in Greenland and Baffin Land. I once, however, saw a puppy apparently suffering from fits of some kind, running wildly round and round, yelping furiously, and occasionally rolling over and kicking. The natives said, "Mŭlukŭ'lĭrua, asi'rua", ("He is howling [?];[1] he is bad"), and some of the boys finally took it out on the tundra and knocked it on the head.

The dog harness, ánun (Gr. anut), consists of a broad strip of stout rawhide (from the bearded seal or walrus), with three parallel loops at one end, frequently made by simply cutting long slits side by side in the thong and bending it into shape. The head is passed through the middle loop and a foreleg through each of the side-loops, bringing the main part of the thong over the back. This serves as a trace, and is furnished at the end with a toggle of bone or wood, by which it is fastened to beckets in a long line of thong, the end of which is usually made fast to the middle of the first slat of the sledge. The dogs are attached in a long line, alternately on opposite sides of this trace, just so far apart that one dog can not reach his leader when both are pulling.

The most spirited dog is usually put at the head of the line as leader, and the natives sometimes select a bitch in heat for this position, as the dogs are sure to follow her. The same custom has been observed by Kumlien at Cumberland Gulf.[2] Ten dogs are considered a large team, and few of the natives can muster so many. When the sledge is heavily loaded men and women frequently help to drag it. The dogs are never *driven*, and except over a well known trail, like that between Utkiavwĭñ and the whaling camp in 1883, will not travel unless a woman trots along in front, encouraging them with cries of "Añ! añ! tû'lla! tû'lla! (Come! come on!), while the man or woman who runs be-hind the sled to guide it and keep it from capsizing, urges them on with cries of "Kŭ! kŭ! (Get on! get on!), occasionally reproving an individual dog by name. After they are well started, they go on without much urg-ing if nothing distracts their attention. It is not easy to stop a dog team when the destination is reached. Commands and shouts of " Lie down!" are seldom sufficient, and the people generally have to pull

---

[1] I failed to get the translation of this word, but it seems to be connected with the Greenlandic mâlavok, he howls (a dog—).

[2] Contributions, p. 51.

back on the sled and drag back on the harness till the team comes to a halt.

The leader, who is usually a woman or child sometimes guides the team by a line attached to the trace, and Lieut. Ray says he has seen them, when traveling in the interior, tie a piece of blubber or meat on the end of a string and drag it on the snow just ahead of the leader. The natives seldom ride on the sledge except with a light load on a smooth road. A few old and decrepit people like Yû′ksĭña always traveled on sledges between the villages, and the people who came down with empty sledges for provisions from the whaling camp, always rode on the well beaten trail where the dogs would run without leading.[1] The dog whip so universally employed by the eastern Eskimo, is not used at Point Barrow, but when Lieut. Ray made a whip for driving his team, the natives called it ĭpirau′ta, a name essentially identical with that used in the east. They especially distinguished ĭpirau′ta, a whip with a lash, from a cudgel, anau′ta. The latter word has also the same meaning in the eastern dialects.

We saw nothing of the custom of protecting the dogs' feet with sealskin shoes, so prevalent on the Siberian coast.[2] Curiously enough the only other localities in which the use of this contrivance is mentioned are in the extreme east.[3] During the first warm weather in the spring, before the dogs have shed their heavy winter coats, they suffer a great deal from the heat and can go only a short distance without lying down to rest.

The method of harnessing and driving the dogs varies considerably in different localities. Among the eastern natives the dogs are usually harnessed abreast, each with a separate trace running to the sledge. and the driver generally rides, guiding the dogs with a whip. The leader usually has a longer trace than the rest. The harness used at Fury and Hecla Straits is precisely the same as that at Point Barrow, but in Greenland, according to Dr. Kane, it consists of a "simple breast-strap," with a single trace. The illustration, however, in Rink's Tales and Traditions, opposite p. 232, which was drawn by a native Greenlander, shows a pattern of harness similar to that used in Siberia and described by Nordenskiöld[4] as "made of inch-wide straps of skin, forming a neck or shoulder band, united on both sides by a strap to a girth, to one side of which the draft strap is fastened." It is a curious fact that the two extremes of the Eskimo race (for even if the people of Pitlekaj be Chukchi in blood, they are Eskimo in culture) should use the same pattern of harness, while a different form prevails between them. The Siberians also habitually ride upon the sledges, and use a whip, and on some parts of the coast, at least, harness the dogs abreast. In

---

[1] Compare Dall. Alaska, p. 25.
[2] See Hooper, Tents, etc., p. 195, and Nordenskiöld, Vega, vol. 2, p. 96, where one of these shoes is figured.
[3] See Kumlien. Contributions, p. 42.
[4] Vega, vol. 2, p. 95.

the region about Pitlekaj, however, the dogs are harnessed "tandem" in pairs, as is the case at Norton Sound, where a more efficient harness is also used, which is probably not Eskimo, but learned from the whites.[1] Nordenskiöld[2] expresses the opinion that the Eskimo method of harnessing the dogs abreast indicates that the Eskimos have lived longer than the Chukchis north of the limit of trees; in other words, that the method of harnessing the dogs tandem is the older one, and that the Eskimo have learned to harness them abreast since they left the woodland regions. I can hardly agree with these conclusions, for it seems to me that the easiest and most natural method of attaching the dogs would be to fasten each directly to the sled by its own trace. Now, when many dogs are attached to the sled in this way, the outer dogs can not apply their strength in a direct line but must pull obliquely, and, moreover, as we know to be the case, so many long traces are constantly becoming entangled, and each individual dog has to be kept straight by the driver. If, however, the dogs be made fast to a long line, one behind the other, not only does each pull straight ahead, but if the leader be kept to the track he pulls the other dogs after him, relieving the driver of the greater part of the care of them.

It seems to me therefore, that the tandem method is an improvement in dog harnessing, which has been adopted only by the natives of northeastern Siberia, and northwestern America, and has no connection with the wooded or unwooded state of the country.[3]

HUNTING SCORES.

The only thing that we saw of the nature of numerical records were the series of animals engraved upon ivory, already alluded to. In most cases we were unable to learn whether the figures really represented an actual record or not, though the bag handle, No. 89424 [890] already figured, was said to contain the actual score of whales killed by old Yû'ksĭña. The custom does not appear to be so prevalent as at Norton Sound (see above, p. 117). Many of these possible scores being engraved on ivory implements have already been described. With one exception they only record the capture of whales or reindeer. The exception (No. 89425 [1732], Fig. 153b) presents a series of ten bearded seals. The reindeer are usually depicted in a natural attitude, and some of the circumstances of the hunt are usually represented. For instance, a man is figured aiming with a bow and arrow toward a a line of reindeer, indicating that such a number were taken by shooting, while a string of deer, represented without legs as they would ap-

---

[1] See Dall, Alaska, pp. 163 and 166.

[2] Vega, vol. 2, p. 95, foot note.

[3] For descriptions of the sledges and methods of harnessing used by the eastern Eskimo, see Bessel's Naturalist, vol. 18, pt. 9, p. 868, figs. 4 and 5 (Smith Sound); Kane, 2d Grinnell Exp., vol. 1, p. 205 (Smith Sound) and first Grinnell Exp., p. 443 (Greenland); Kumlien, Contributions, p. 42, and Boas, "Central Eskimo," pp. 529-538 (Cumberland Gulf); Parry, 2d voyage, p. 514, and Lyon, Journal, p. 235 (Iglulik); Gilder, Schwatka's Search, pp. 50, 52, and 66, and Schwatka's "Nimrod in the North," pp. 152, 153 (NW. shore of Hudson Bay and King Williams Land).

pear swimming, followed by a rude figure of a man in a kaiak, means that so many were lanced in the water. Other incidents of the excursion are also sometimes represented. On these records the whale is always represented by a rude figure of the tail cut off at the " small," and often represented as hanging from a horizontal line.

We also brought home four engraved pieces of ivory, which are nothing else than records of real or imaginary scenes. I have figured all of these. Fig. 360 (No. 89487 [1026] from Nuwŭk) is a narrow flat tablet of ivory, 4·8 inches long and 1 inch wide, with a string at one end to hang it up by. On each face is an ornamental border inclosing a number of incised figures, which probably represent actual scenes, as the tablet is not new.

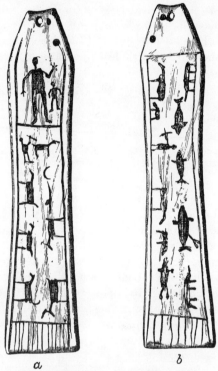

The figures on the obverse face are colored with red ocher. At the upper end, standing on a cross line, with his head toward the end, is a rudely drawn man, holding his right hand up and his left down, with the fingers outspread. At his left stands a boy with both hands down. These figures probably represent the hunter and his son. Just below the cross line is a man raising a

FIG. 360.—Hunting score engraved on ivory.

spear to strike an animal which is perhaps meant for a reindeer without horns. Three deer, also without horns, stand with their feet on one border with their heads toward the upper end, and on the other border near the other end are two bucks with large antlers heading the other way, and behind them a man in a kaiak. Between him and the animal which the first man is spearing is an object which may represent the crescent moon. The story may perhaps be freely translated as follows: " When the moon was young the man and his son killed six reindeer, two of them bucks with large antlers. One they speared on land, the rest they chased with the kaiak."

On the reverse the figures and border are colored black with soot. In the left-hand lower corner is a she bear and her cub heading to the left, followed by a man who is about to shoot an arrow at them. Then come two more bears heading toward the right, and in the right-hand lower corner is a whale with two floats attached to him by a harpoon line. Above this is an umiak with four men in it approaching another whale which has already received one harpoon with its two floats. The harpoon which is to be thrust at him may be seen sticking out over the bow of the boat. Then come two whales in a line, one heading to the left and one to the right. In the left-hand upper corner is a figure which may represent a boat, bottom up, on the staging of four posts. We did not learn the actual history of this tablet, which was brought down for sale with a number of other things.

Fig. 361 (No. 89473 [1349] from Utkiavwĭñ) is a piece of an old snow-shovel edge with freshly incised figures on both faces, which the artist

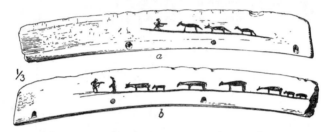

FIG. 361.—Hunting score engraved on ivory, obverse and reverse.

said represented his own record. The figures are all colored with red ocher. On the obverse the figures all stand on a roughly drawn ground line. At the left is a man pointing his rifle at a bear, which stands on its hind legs facing him. Then comes a she bear walking toward the left followed by a cub, then two large bears also walking to the left, and a she bear in the same attitude, followed by two cubs, one behind the other. This was explained by the artist as follows: "These are all the bears I have killed. This one alone (pointing to the 'rampant'

FIG. 362.—Hunting score engraved on ivory.

one) was bad. All the others were good." We heard at the time of his giving the death shot to the last bear as it was charging his comrade, who had wounded it with his muzzle-loader. On the reverse, the figures are in the same position. The same man points his rifle at a string of three wolves. His explanation was: "These are the wolves I have killed."

Fig. 362 (No. 89474 [1334] from Utkiavwĭñ) is newly made, but was said to be the record of a man of our acquaintance named Mûñĭñolu. It is a flat piece of the outside of a walrus tusk 9·7 inches long and 1·8 wide at the broader end. The figures are incised on one face only, and colored with red ocher.   The face is divided lengthwise into two panels by a horizontal line.   In the upper panel, at the left, is a man facing to the right and pointing a gun at a line of three standing deer, facing toward the left.   Two are bucks and one a doe.   Then come two bucks, represented without legs, as if swimming in the water, followed by a rude figure of a man in a kaiak.   Below the line at the left is an umiak with five men, and then a row of twelve conventionalized whales' tails, of which all but the first, second, and fifth are joined to the horizontal line by a short straight line.   The record may be freely translated as follows: "I went out with my gun and killed three large reindeer, two bucks and a doe.   I also speared two large bucks in the water.   My whaling crew have taken twelve whales."   The number of whales is open to suspicion, as they just fill up the board.

Fig. 363.—Hunting score engraved on ivory, obverse and reverse.

Fig. 363 (No. 56517 [121] from Utkiavwĭñ) is a piece of an old snow-shovel edge 4·2 inches long, with a loop of thong at the upper side to hang it up by.   It is covered on both faces with freshly incised figures, colored with red ocher, representing some real or imaginary occurrence.

The obverse is bordered with a single narrow line.   At the left is a man standing with arms outstretched supporting himself by two slender staffs as long as he is.   In the middle are three rude figures of tents, very high and slender.   At the right is a hornless reindeer heading to the left, with a man standing on its back with his legs straddled

apart and his arms uplifted.   On the reverse, there is no border, but
a single dog and a man who supports himself with a long staff are dragging an empty rail sledge toward the left.

I find no mention of the use of any such scores among the eastern
Eskimo, but they are very common among those of the west, as shown
by the Museum collections.   They record in this way, not only hunting
exploits but all sorts of trivial occurrences.

GAMES AND PASTIMES.

Gambling.—These people have only one game which appears to be of
the nature of gambling.   It is played with the twisters and marline
spikes used for backing the bow, and already described, though Lieut.
Ray says he has seen it played with any bits of stick or bone.   I never
had an opportunity of watching a game of this sort played, as it is not
often played at the village.   It is a very popular amusement at the
deer-hunting camps, where Lieut. Ray often saw it played.   According
to him the players are divided into sides, who sit on the ground about
3 yards apart, each side sticking up one of the marline spikes for a
mark to throw the twisters at.   Six of the latter, he believes, make a
full set.   One side tosses the whole set one at a time at the opposite
stake, and the points which they make are counted up by their opponents from the position of the twisters as they fall.   He did not learn
how the points were reckoned, except that twisters with a mark on them
counted differently from the plain ones, or how long the game lasted,
each side taking its turn of casting at the opposite stake.   He, however,
got the impression that the winning side kept the twisters belonging
to their opponents.   Mr. Nelson informs me in a letter that a similar
game is played with the same implements at Norton Sound.

No. 56532 [9], from Utkiavwĭñ, is a bag full of these tools as used
for playing this game.   It contains 18 twisters, of different patterns,
and 7 marline spikes.   The bag is of membrane, perhaps a bladder.   It
is ovoid in shape, all in one piece, with a long opening in one side,
which is closed by a piece of sinew braid about 40 inches long.   This is
knotted by one end round a fold of membrane at one end of the mouth,
and when the bag is shut up is wrapped round the middle of it.

Some of these people have learned what cards are from the Nunatañmiun, though they do not know how to use them.   They described how
they were used by the "Nunatañmiun," however, going through the
motions of dealing cards.   They told us that the latter played a great
deal, and "gave much."   This "giving much" evidently referred to
gambling, for they told Capt. Herendeen how two of the "Nunatañmiun" would sit down to play, one with a big pile of furs and one with
out any, and when they got up the furs would all belong to the other man.

Fig. 364 (No. 56531 [21]) represents some of a bunch of 25 little ivory
images which were strung on a bit of seal thong.   One is a neatly
carved fox, 2·7 inches long, and the rest are ducks or geese, rather

roughly carved, with flat bellies. The largest of these is 1·3 inches long and the smallest 0·8 inch. These were purchased at Plover Bay, eastern Siberia, during our brief visit in August, 1881, and were sup-

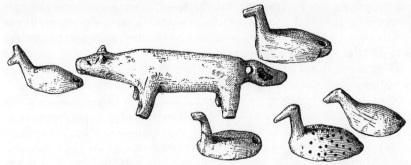

FIG. 364.—Game of fox and geese, from Plover Bay.

posed to be merely works of art. I was, however, very much interested on my return to Washington to find that Dr. Franz Boas had brought from Cumberland Gulf a number of precisely similar images, which are there used for playing a game of the nature of "jackstones." The player tosses up a handful of these images, and scores points for the number that sit upright when they fall.[1] It is therefore quite likely that they are used for a similar purpose at Plover Bay. If this be so, it is a remarkable point of similarity between these widely separated Eskimo, for I can learn nothing of a similar custom at any intermediate point.

Festivals.—The most important festivals are apparently semireligious in character and partake strongly of the nature of dramatic representations. At these festivals they make use of many articles of dress and adornment, not worn on other occasions, and even some "properties" and mechanical contrivances to add to the dramatic effect. All festivals are accompanied by singing, drumming, and dancing.

At the formal festivals, in the early winter, the performers are dressed in new deerskin clothing, with the snow-white flesh side outward, and in certain parts of the perform-

¼

FIG. 365.—Dancing cap.

ance wear on their heads tall conical caps covered with rows of mountain sheep teeth which rattle as the wearer dances.

We brought home one of these dancing caps (kă′brû, käluka′) (No. 89820 [863] Fig. 365), made of deerskin with the hair inward and

---

[1] This game is briefly referred to by Hall, Arctic Researches, p. 570.

clipped close. The outside is painted all over with red ocher. The front is nearly all in one piece, but the back is irregularly pieced and gored. It is surmounted by a thick tuft of brown and white wolverine fur about 5 inches long, sewed into the apex. To the middle of one side at the edge is sewed a narrow strip of deerskin with the hair clipped close, which is long enough to go under the wearer's chin and be knotted into a slit close to the edge of the other side of the cap. On the front edge is sewed a row of thirty-five incisor teeth of the mountain sheep by a thread running through a hole drilled through the root of each.

The series is regularly graduated, having the largest teeth in the middle and the smallest on the ends. Above this is a narrow strip of brown deerskin running two-thirds round the cap and sewed on flesh side out so that the hair projects as a fringe below. Above this are three ornamental bands about 2 inches apart running two-thirds round the cap, each fringed on the lower edge with sheep teeth strung as on the edge of the cap. The lower row contains 54 teeth, the middle 29, and the upper 31. The lowest band is made of 2 strips of mountain sheepskin with a narrow strip of black sealskin between them, and a narrow strip of brown deerskin with the hair out; the next is of coarse gray deerskin with the hair

FIG. 366.—Wooden mask.

out; and the uppermost of brown deerskin with the flesh side out The cap is old and dirty, and has been long in use.

The custom of wearing this style of cap appears to be peculiar to the northwestern Eskimo, as I find no mention for it elsewhere. It is perhaps derived indirectly from the northern Indians, some of whom are represented as wearing a similar headdress.

In certain parts of the same ceremony as witnessed by Lieut. Ray the dancers also wore rattle mittens, which were shaken in time to the music. A pair of these were offered for sale once, but Lieut. Ray did not consider them sufficiently of pure Eskimo manufacture to be worth the price asked for them. They were made of sealskin and covered all over the back with empty Winchester cartridge shells loosely attached by a string through a hole in the bottom, so as to strike against each other when the mitten was shaken. The five men who wore these mittens wore on their heads the stuffed skins of various animals, the wolf, bear, fox, lynx, and dog, which they were supposed to represent. These articles were never offered for sale, as they were probably too highly valued.

We collected twelve wooden masks, which we were told were worn in some of these ceremonies, though none of our party ever witnessed any performance in which they were used.   Some of them are of undoubted age.   No. 56499 [6] (Fig. 366) has been selected as the type of these masks. (ki'nau, from ki'na, face).   This is a rather good representation of a male human face, 8·8 inches long and 5·8 wide.   It is quite smoothly carved out of cottonwood, and the back is neatly hollowed out, being more deeply excavated round the eyes and mouth and inside of the nose.   The mouth is represented as wide open, showing the tip of the tongue attached to the underlip, and has six small teeth which look like dog's incisors inserted in a row in the middle of the upper lip.   The eyebrows and moustache are marked out with blacklead, and there are traces of red ocher on the cheeks.   The holes for the strings are in the edge about on a level with the eyes.   One end of a string of seal thong long enough to go around the wearer's head is passed out through the hole on the right side, slit close to the tip, and the other end passed through this.   The other end is passed out through the hole on the left

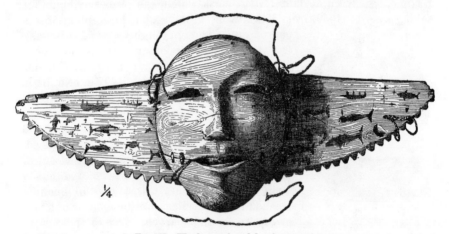

FIG. 367.—Wooden mask and dancing gorget.

and made fast with two half hitches.   A row of small holes round the edge of the mask shows where a hood has been tacked on.   This mask is rather old and somewhat soiled.

A very old weathered mask (No. 56497 [235] from Utkiavwïñ), 7·8 inches long, and made of soft wood, apparently pine, is similar to the preceding, but has no tongue, and the teeth in both jaws are represented as a continuous ridge.   It has an "imperial" as well as a moustache, marked with blacklead like the eyebrows.   The cheeks are colored with red ocher.   The edge is much gapped and broken, but shows the remains of a deep narrow groove running round on the outside about ¼ inch from the edge, and pierced with small holes for fastening on a hood.

Figure 367 (No. 89817 [856] also from Utkiavwïñ) is a mask much like the preceding, 7·5 inches long, and made of spruce.   It is peculiar in having the outer corners of the eyes rather depressed, and in addition to the moustache and imperial has a broad "whaleman's mark" drawn with black lead across the eyes. It is grooved round the edge for fastening on a hood. The lower part of the face has been split off at the corners of the mouth and mended on with two stitches of whalebone, and a piece which was broken out at the left-hand corner of the mouth is secured by a wooden peg at the inner edge and a stitch of whalebcne on the lower side. This mask has been for a long time fastened to an ornamented wooden gorget, and appeared to have been exposed to the weather, perhaps at the cemetery. The string is made of unusually stout sinew braid.

The remaining four ancient human masks are all masculine, and only one has any indication of labrets. On this mask, No. 89812 [1063], there are two small holes in the position of the labrets. It is probable that the wearers of these masks are supposed to represent the ancient Eskimo, who wore no labrets. A mask which was carelessly made for sale (No. 89814 [1056] from Utkiavwĭñ), however, has large plug-labrets

¼

FIG. 368.—Old grotesque mask.

carved out. Though roughly carved this mask is a very characteristic Eskimo face, and would almost pass as the portrait of a man of our acquaintance in Utkiavwĭñ. The two little roughly carved human faces on the top of this mask are probably merely for ornament. No such things are to be seen on any of the old masks which have been actually used. This mask seems to have been whittled out of the bottom of an old meat tray, and has a string of whalebone. Most of the genuine masks are of excellent workmanship, but two are quite roughly carved. One of these especially is such a bungling piece of work that it would be set down as commercial were it not weathered and evidently old. The painting never goes farther than marking out the beard and eyebrows with soot or black lead, and sometimes reddening the cheeks with ocher. Fig. 368 (No. 89816 [1583] from Utkiavwĭñ) is a very old mask of cottonwood, blackened with age and so rudely carved that the work was probably done with a stone tool. It is grooved around the edge for fastening on a hood and is 6·8 inches long.

The only female human masks seen are new and made for sale. One of these (No. 89819 [1057], Fig. 369, from Utkiavwĭñ) is roughly whittled from the bottom of an old meat tray, and has the hair, eyebrows, and a single line of tattooing on the chin painted with soot. It is 8·7 inches long and has strings of whalebone.

Another (No. 56498 [73] from Utkiavwĭñ) is about the size of the common masks and tolerably well made. It has the hair and eyebrows marked with black lead. The last is a foot long, and like the one figured is roughly whittled out of the bottom of an old meat tray. It has the hair, eyebrows, and a single stripe of tattooing on the chin marked with black lead. This came from Utkiavwĭñ (No. 89811 [1037]).

Another "commercial" mask (No. 89813) [1074] from Utkiavwĭñ) is very elaborate, but roughly and carelessly made. It is almost flat, with the features hardly raised in relief. In each corner of the mouth is inserted a slender ivory tusk about 1 inch long, and besides the eyebrows, moustache, and imperial, there is a broad "whaleman's mark" running obliquely across the right cheek from the bridge of the nose. Six long feathers are stuck in the edge of the forehead. Curiously enough these are the feathers of the South American ostrich, and came from the feather duster in use at our station.

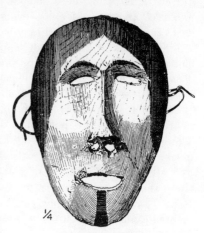

¼

FIG. 369.—Rude mask of wood.

Fig. 370 (No. 56496 [258] from Utkiavwĭñ) represents, rather rudely, a wolf's face and ears, and is the only animal mask we obtained or saw. It is of cottonwood, old and weathered, and is 4·7 inches long and 6·5 wide. It is painted on the edge with red ocher and has a streak of the same color down the ridge of the nose. The string is of whalebone and unbraided sinew pieced together.

Fig. 371 (No. 89815 [1050] from Utkiavwĭñ) is a mask that seems almost too small to have been worn, being only 6·1 inches long and 4·7 wide. It is very old, made of blackened cot-

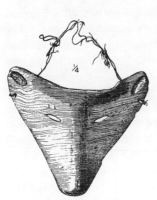

¼

FIG. 370.—Wolf mask of wood.

¼

FIG. 371.—Very ancient small mask.

tonwood, and is the rudest representation of the human face which we saw. It is simply an oval disk, concavo-convex, with holes cut for the eyes, nostrils, and mouth. The rough cutting about the chin appears to have been done with a stone tool, and the mouth seems to be smeared with blood. The string passed through the holes in the forehead to hang it up by is much newer than the mask, being braided from cotton twine and fastened to a common galvanized boat nail.

The more southern Eskimo of Alaska are in the habit of using in their dances very elaborate and highly ornamented and painted masks, of which the National Museum possesses a very large collection. The ancient Aleuts also used masks.[1] On the other hand, no other Eskimo, save those of Alaska, ever use masks in their performances, as far as I can learn, with the solitary exception of the people of Baffin Land, where a mask of the hide of the bearded seal is worn on certain occasions.[2] Nordenskiöld saw one wooden mask among the people near the *Vega's* winter quarters, but learned that this had been brought from Bering Strait, and probably from America.[3]

The masks appear to become more numerous and more elaborate the nearer we get to the part of Alaska inhabited by the Indians of the T'linket stock, who, as is well known employ, in their ceremonies remarkably elaborate wooden masks and headdresses. It may be suggested that this custom of using masks came from the influence of these Indians, reaching in the simple form already described as far as Point Barrow, but not beyond.[4] With these masks was worn a gorget or breast-plate, consisting of a half-moon shaped piece of board about 18 inches long, painted with rude figures of men and animals, and slung about the neck. We brought home three of these gorgets. all old and weathered.

No. 89818 [1132], Fig. 372a, has been selected as the type of the gorget (sŭkĭmûñ). It is made of spruce, is 18·5 inches long, and has two beckets of stout sinew braid, one to go round the neck and the other round the body under the wearer's arms. The figures are all painted on the front face. In the middle is a man painted with red ocher; all the rest of the figures are black and probably painted with soot. The man with his arms outstretched stands on a large whale, represented as spouting. He holds a small whale in each hand. At his right is a small cross-shaped object which perhaps represents a bird, then a man facing toward the left and darting a harpoon with both hands, and a bear facing to the left. On the left of the red man are two umiaks with five men in each, a whale nearly effaced, and three of the cross-shaped objects already mentioned. Below them, also, freshly drawn with a hard, blunt lead pencil or the point of a bullet, are a whale, an umiak, and a three-cornered object the nature of which I can not make out.

Fig. 372b (No. 56493 [266] from Utkiavwĭñ) is a similar gorget, which has evidently been long exposed to the weather, perhaps at the cemetery, as the figures are all effaced except in the middle, where it was probably covered by a mask as in Fig. 367 (No. 89817 [855] from the same village). There seems to have been a red border on the serrated edge. In the middle is the same red man as before standing on the

---

[1] See Dall, Alaska, p. 389, and contributions to N. A. Ethn., vol. 1, p. 90.
[2] See Kumlien, Contributions, p. 43. Kumlien says merely "a mask of skins." Dr. Boas is my authority for the statement that the skin of the bearded seal is used.
[3] Vega, vol. 2, p. 21.
[4] See also Dall's paper in the Third Annual Report of the Bureau of Ethnology, pp. 67-203, where the subject of mask-wearing is very thoroughly discussed in its most important relations.

black whale and holding a whale in each hand.   At his right is a black
umiak with five men in it, and at his left a partially effaced figure which
is perhaps another boat.   The strings are put on as before, except that
the two beckets are separate.   The upper is made of sinew braid, and
the lower, which is now broken, of seal thong.   This gorget is 15·5 inches
long and 4·7 wide.   No. 89817 [855] (Fig. 367 already referred to) has a
mask tied over the middle by means of the beckets, so that the figures
in the middle are much fresher than those on the ends.   The edges are

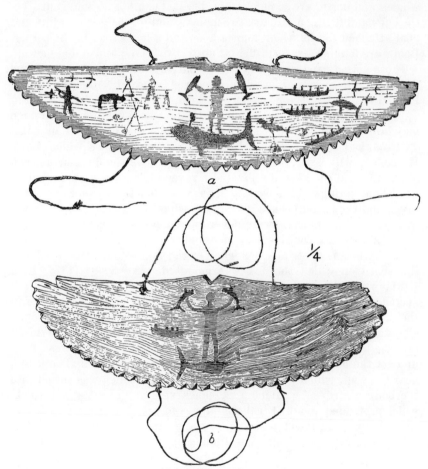

FIG. 372.—Dancing gorgets of wood.

painted red.   In the middle is the same red man or giant holding the
whale.   The other figures are painted with soot.

   This man or giant, able to hold out a whale, appears to be a legendary character, as we have his image carved in ivory.   We unfortunately
did not succeed in learning anything more about him, except that his
name (apparently) was "kikámigo."   Hanging by the head to each elbow
of this figure is a seal, and opposite its thighs two of the usual conventional

whale's tails, one on each side, with the flukes turned from him. The one on his left is attached to his waist by a straight line from its upper corner. At its right hand are a number of objects irregularly grouped. At the top an umiak with five men towing at a three-cornered object, which probably represents a dead whale; then a smaller umiak containing five men and apparently "fast" to a whale, which is spouting. A figure above this, almost obliterated, appears to be a small whale. Below are a large seal, three of the cross-shaped figures, four small whales, and one figure so much effaced that it can not be made out. On the left hand of the figure are two umiaks, and a whale with a line and float attached to him, then four crosses and a large seal in the corner. Below are four whales of different sizes, two bears, and a dog or wolf.

These gorgets appear to have gone out of fashion, as we saw none which were not very old, or which appeared to have been used recently. From the nature of the figures upon them, they were probably used in some of the ceremonies connected with the whale fishing. Kika'mĭgo may be the "divinity" who controls the whales and other sea animals.[1]

Mechanical contrivances.—In one of the performances which Capt. Herendeen witnessed, there stood in the middle of the floor facing each other, the stuffed skins of a fox and a raven. These were mounted on whalebone springs and moved by strings, so that the fox sprang at the raven and the raven pecked at the fox, while the singing and dancing went on. These animals were never offered for sale, but they brought over a stuffed fox very cleverly mounted so as to spring at a lemming, which by means of strings was made to run in and out of two holes in the board on which the fox was mounted. (No 89893 [1378] from Utkiavwĭñ.) We unfortunately did not learn the story or myth connected with this representation.[2] It was the skin of an Arctic fox in the summer pelage, with the paws and all the bones removed, and clumsily stuffed with rope yarn, not filling out the legs. A stick was thrust into the tail to within about two inches of the tip, so that it was curled up over the back. The skin was taken off whole by a single opening near the vent, which was left open, and through which was thrust into the body a strip of whalebone 2 inches wide and about $\frac{1}{8}$ inch thick, which protruded about $4\frac{1}{4}$ inches and was fastened to the front edge of the hole by tying the flap of skin to the whalebone with three or four turns of sinew braid, kept from slipping by a notch in each edge of the whalebone.

The fox was attached to a piece of the paneling of a ship's bulkhead, 29 inches long and 7·5 wide, by bending forward $2\frac{3}{4}$ inches of the end of the whalebone, and lashing it down parallel to the length of the board with four turns of stout thong, kept from slipping by a notch in each edge of the whalebone and running through holes in the board.

---

[1] Cf. Crantz, vol. 1, p. 206.

[2] This very interesting specimen was unfortunately destroyed by moths at the National Museum after the description was written, but before it could be figured.

The fox was thus held up by the spring parallel to the length of the board with its head and forelegs raised. A string of sinew braid 10 feet long was passed through a hole in the septum of the fox's nose and knotted once so as to leave two equal ends. These ends were carried down through two holes, one in each edge of the board 9½ inches from the forward end, and each was tied to a roughly-rounded bit of pine stick round which it was reeled when not in use. By pulling these strings together, the fox was made to dart down his head, which was raised by the spring as soon as the string was slackened. By pulling one or the other string the fox could be made to dart to one or the other side of the board.

One man manipulated the fox, pulling a string with each hand. The lemming's holes were about 1¼ inches in diameter, one in each edge of the board and at such a distance from the end that when the string, which was 7 feet 4 inches long, was drawn through them, it crossed the board just where the fox's nose struck, when it was pulled down. The ends of the string were reeled round bits of stick. The lemming was a narrow strip of wolf's fur, about 3 inches long, doubled in the middle, with the middle of the string hitched into the bight. By pulling the ends of the string alternately, the lemming was made to jump out of the hole on one side, run across the board and into the other, very much as a live lemming runs from one tunnel to another on the tundra. It took two persons, one on each side, to handle the lemming. The fox-skin and spring appeared to be older than the rest of the machine. The board was originally 10 inches or 1 foot longer at each end, but had to be cut off to pack it.

Petroff mentions a similar custom among the " Nushegagmute " of Bristol Bay, of introducing stuffed animals moved with hidden strings in their performances;[1] and Dall[2] describes a festival at Norton Sound, where a dead seal was brought in and moved about with strings.

Description of festivals.—It is greatly to be regretted that we had not established such intimate relations with the natives, as afterwards was the case, in the winter of 1881–'82, since this was the only one of the two seasons that the great winter festival was held at Utkiavwĩñ. In the winter of. 1882–'83 there had been so many deaths in the village that the natives did not feel like celebrating any regular festival, and only indulged in a few impromptu dances late in the season. These were unfortunately held in the evening when the writer's tour of duty at the station prevented his witnessing them. Those of the party who did go over brought back only fragmentary and rather vague accounts of the performance. The confining nature of the work at the station prevented our witnessing any of the celebrations at Nuwŭk or at Pernyû, when the "Nunatañmiun" visitors were entertained.

The best accounts we have of any performance is given by Lieut.

---

[1] Report, p. 135.　　　　　　　[2] Alaska, p. 156.

Ray. He and Capt. Herendeen went over to Utkiavwĭñ by special invitation on December 3, 1881, and witnessed one scene of the " wood," or " tree dance." Many visitors were present from Nuwŭk on the occasion of this dance, which lasted for two days and nights. On arriving at the village they found a crowd of upwards of 200 people assembled round the entrance of the kŭ'dyĭgĭ. In front of the entrance were drawn up in line five men and two women dancing to the music of a drum and two singers.

They were all dressed in new deerskin clothes, with the snow-white flesh side turned out, and wore conical dance caps like that already described. They kept time to the music with their feet, moving their bodies to right and left with spasmodic jerks. To quote from Lieut. Ray's MS. notes:

Each dancer in turn sprang to the front and in extravagant gestures went through the motions of killing seal, walrus, and deer, and the pursuit of the whale. Each, as he finished, took his place in the line, was cheered by the crowd, then added his voice to the monotonous chant of the singers.

After all had finished as many as could get in entered the "dance house." At one end of this a small space was partitioned off with a piece of an old sail, and from the roof in the middle hung an object intended to represent a tree. This was made of two oblong boxes about 6 inches in diameter, open at both ends, the lower about 2½ feet long and the upper about 1½, hinged together with seal thong. At one side hung a wolf's skull, and on the other a dried raven. Two performers sat in the middle of the floor with their legs extended one between the other's legs, with his nose touching the tree. A row of old men beat drums and sang, while the performers chanted a monotonous song, in which could be heard the words "rum, tobacco, seal, deer, and whale."

Presently the bottom of the curtain was lifted and out crawled five men on all fours, wearing on their heads the stuffed skins of the heads of different animals—the wolf, bear, fox, lynx, and dog. They swung their heads from side to side in unison, keeping time to the music, uttering a low growl at each swing and shaking their rattle mittens. This they kept up for fifteen or twenty minutes, while the chant still went on, and the chief performer, with excited gestures, embraced the tree and rubbed his nose against it from time to time. At last all "sprang to their feet with a howl, and ended the dance with wild gestures." Similar scenes, with new performers, which our party did not stay to witness, succeeded this, with feasting in the different houses.

Capt. Herendeen also witnessed a small dance, lasting only one evening, which bore a curious resemblance to some of the so-called "favor figures" performed in the "German cotillon" of civilized dancers. This kind of dance was performed purely for pleasure, and had nothing religious or dramatic about it. The music was furnished by the usual orchestra of old men, who beat drums and sang a monotonous song. Each person who intended to take part in the dance came provided with some small article to be given away as a "favor," and rising in his turn, danced a few minutes, and then called out the name of the partner he wished to give it to. The latter then rose, and having received the "favor," danced a while with him, and then both resumed their places among the spectators.

We never heard of any such elaborate "donation parties" as are described at Norton Sound and the Yukon region, where a man "saves up his property for years" to distribute it among his guests.[1] A festival, however, was held at Nuwŭk in June, 1883, which apparently resembled the second kind described by Dall.[2] Two men came down from Nuwŭk to invite Lieut. Ray and Capt. Herendeen, telling them what presents they were expected to bring. Unfortunately it was considered that too much was asked and the invitation was declined. The messengers carried "notched sticks."[3]

Dances in which the children only take part, entirely for amusement, sometimes take place in the kŭ′dyĭgĭ, and people occasionally amuse themselves by dancing in the iglu. I have often seen the natives, especially the children and young people, dancing in the open air, and the dancing was always of very much the same character. The feet were but slightly moved, keeping time to the music, while the body swayed gracefully and the arms were waved from side to side. All the dancing which I saw was rather quiet and graceful, but they told us that when they got warmed up at a great dance they went at it with tremendous vigor, throwing off their garments to the waist. The dance which accompanies the song sung by the children to the aurora, however, is more violent. The dancer clenches his fists and, bending his elbows, strikes them against the sides of his body, keeping time to the song and stamping vigorously with the right foot, springing up and down with the left knee (see Fig. 373, from a sketch by the writer).

FIG. 373.—Youth dancing to the aurora.

We never heard of any of the licentious festivals or orgies described by Egede[4] and Kumlien.[5]

---

[1] See Dall, Alaska, p. 151.

[2] Ibid, p. 154.

[3] Compare the wand "curiously ornamented and carved" carried by the messenger who was sent out to invite the guests to the festival at Norton Sound, Alaska, p. 154.

[4] Greenland, p. 139.

[5] Contributions, p. 43.

The festivals of the eastern Eskimo appear to be less formal and elaborate than those in the west, consisting simply of singing and dancing.[1]

TOYS AND SPORTS FOR CHILDREN AND OTHERS.

Playthings.—Though the children amuse themselves with a great many sports and plays, we saw very few toys or playthings in use. We brought home six objects which appear to have no use except as playthings.

Fig. 374*a* (No. 89806 [1189] from Nuwŭk) is a whirligig in principle very like that made for civilized children. It is a block of spruce, fitted with a shaft of narwhal ivory. This fits loosely in the straight tubular handle, which is a section of the branch of an antler, with the soft inside tissue cut out. A string of seal thong passes through a hole in the middle of the handle and is fastened to the shaft. This string is about 8 feet long, and about half of it is tied up into the hank to make a handle for pulling it. It works very much like a civilized child's whirligig. The string is wound around the shaft and a smart pull on the handle unwinds it, making the block spin round rapidly. The reaction, spinning it in the opposite direction, winds up the string again. A couple of loose hawk's feathers are stuck into the tip of the block, which is painted with red ocher for about an inch. Four equidistant stripes of the same color run down the sides to a border of the same width round the base. This was made for sale and appears to be an unusual toy. I do not recollect ever seeing the children play with such a toy. It is called kai'psa (Gr. kâvsâk, "a whirligig or similar toy").

Fig. 374*b* is a similar whirligig from Utkiavwĭñ (No. 89807 [1356]). The block, which is 4·2 inches long, is made of the solid tip of a mountain sheep's horn, and is elaborately ornamented with a conventional pattern of lines and "circles and dots," incised and colored red with ocher. The shaft is of hard bone, and the line has a little wooden handle at the end. The block is so heavy that it will hardly spin.

Fig. 375 (No. 56491 [46] from Utkiavwĭñ) is a teetotum (also called kaipsa). The shaft is of pine and the disk of spruce and is ornamented with black lead marks, forming a border about one-quarter inch broad

---

[1]Descriptions of Eskimo festivals are to be found in Egede's Greenland, p. 152, and Crantz, History of Greenland, vol. 1, p. 175, where he mentions the sun feast held at the winter solstice. This very likely corresponds to the December festival at Point Barrow. If the latter be really a rite instituted by the ancestors of the present Eskimo when they lived in lower latitudes to celebrate the winter solstice, it is easy to understand why it should be held at about the same time by the people of Kotzebue Sound, as stated by Dr. Simpson, op. cit., p. 262, where, as he says, the reindeer might be successfully pursued throughout the winter. It is much more likely, considering the custom in Greenland, that this is the reason for having the festival at this season than that the time should be selected by the people at Point Barrow as a season when "hunting or fishing can not well be attended to," as Simpson thinks. We should remember that this is the very time of the year that the seal netting is at its height at Point Barrow. See also Parry, Second Voyage, p. 538; Kumlien, Contributions, p. 43; Gilder, Schwatka's Search, p. 43; Beechey, Voyage, p. 288 (Kotzebue Sound); Dall, Alaska, p. 149 (very full and detailed); Petroff, Report, etc., pp. 125, 126, 129, 131 (quoted from Zagoskin), 135, 137 (quoted from Shelikhof), and 144 (quoted from Davidof); Hooper, Tents, etc., pp. 85, 136; and Nordenskiöld, Vega, vol. 2, pp. 22, 131.

on each face.   The upper face is divided into quadrants by four narrow
lines radiating from the hole, and each quadrant is divided into two by
bands one-quarter inch broad.   The order of these lines is reversed on

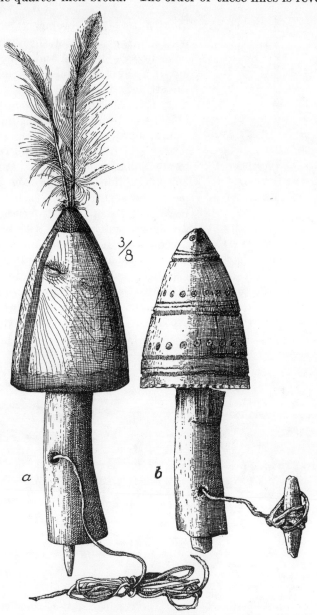

$\frac{3}{8}$

a   *b*

FIG. 374.—Whirligigs.

the under face.   This is spun, like a common teetotum, with the fingers,
and does not seem to be common.   I do not recollect ever seeing anyone except the maker of this toy spinning one.

The same is true of No. 89722 [1087] (Fig. 376, from Utkiavwĭñ) which is what American boys would call a "buzz" toy. It is of pine wood, and through two round holes in the middle are passed the ends of a

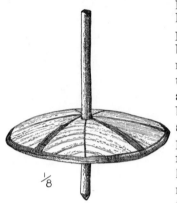

FIG. 375.—Teetotum.

piece of stout sinew braid, which are knotted together. When the board is placed in the middle of the string it can be made to spin round and whiz by alternately pulling and relaxing the ends of the string. The board is rather elaborately painted. One end has a border of black lead on both faces, the other a similar border of red paint, which appears to be red lead. Broad red bands form a square 1 inch across around the holes, with lines radiating from each corner to the corners of the board, on both faces. On the spaces between these lines are figures rudely drawn with black lead. On one face, in the first space, is a goose; in the second, a man with a staff; in the third, the conventional figure of a whale's tail; and in the fourth, a whale with line and float attached to him, pursued by a whaling umiak. On the other side, the first space contains a dog or wolf walking; the second, two of these animals, sitting on their haunches, facing each other; the third, another walking; and the fourth, a reindeer in the same attitude.

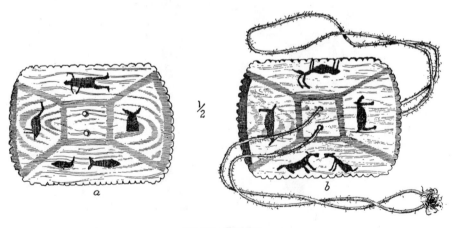

FIG. 376.—Buzz toy.

Fig. 377 (No. 89800 [1331] from Utkiavwĭñ), on the other hand, is a toy which the children often play with. It is the well known "whizzing-stick" found among savages in so many widely distant parts of the world, and often used in religious ceremonies. The Eskimo name is ĭmĭglúta. It consists of a thin board of pine wood, fastened by a string of sinew braid about 1 foot long to the end of a slender rod, which serves as a handle. When swung rapidly round by the handle it makes a loud, whizzing sound. It is very neatly made, and painted with black lead and red ocher. The tips of the board are black for about one-half inch and the rest is red, and the upper half of the handle marked with five rings about one-half inch wide and 1 inch apart, alternately black and red. This appears to be purely a child's toy and has no mystical signification. I never saw one in the hands of an adult. This specimen was made and brought over for sale by a lad about thirteen or fourteen years old.

Fig. 378 (No. 56687 [181] from Utkiavwïñ) is another plaything rather common with the boys, which takes the place of the American boy's "bean snapper." It is known by the name of mĭtĭ'-glĭgaun, and is a rod of whalebone, stiff and black, 4·8 inches long and 0·5 wide, narrowed and bent sharply up for about an inch at one end. On the upper side of this end, close to the

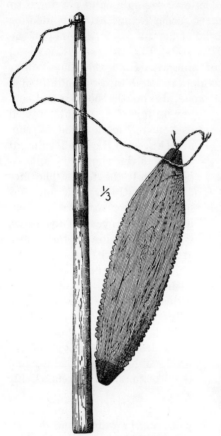

FIG. 377.—Whizzing stick.

tip, is a little hollow, large enough to hold a small pebble, and the other is cut into sharp teeth. This is purely an instrument of mischief and is used for shooting tiny pebbles at people when they are looking the other way. Mûñialu showed us, with great glee, in an expressive pantomime, how a boy would hit a person in the eye with a little pebble, and, when the man turned round angrily, would have the snapper slipped up his sleeve and be ooking earnestly in another direction. The toothed end, he said, was for mischievously scratching hairs out of a man's coat when he was looking another way. The "snapper" is used as follows: It is held in the left hand, a little pebble is set in the socket, and the tip of the whalebone bent back with the right hand. When this end is let go the elasticity of the whalebone drives the pebble at the mark with considerable force. As far as I can learn this mischievous toy is peculiar to the Northwest.

FIG. 378.— Pebble snapper.

Dolls.—Though several dolls and various suits of miniature clothing were made and brought over for sale, they do not appear to be popular with the little girls. I do not recollect ever seeing a child playing with a doll. Those in the collection, indeed, seem rather less intended for playthings than as, so to speak, works of art to catch the fancy of the strangers. Such an object is No. 89728 [1304] (Fig. 379 from Utkiavwïñ.) This is a human head carved out of pine wood, and shouldered off at the neck into a stout round peg, which is fitted into the middle of a thick elliptical pedestal of the same wood, flat on the bottom and convex on top. The head is dressed in a neatly made hood of thin deerskin with the flesh side cut off round the shoulders and exposing only the face. The face is very neatly carved, and has bits of green oxidized copper inlaid for the eyes. The cheeks, gums, and inside of the mouth are colored with red ocher, and the hair, eyebrows, and beard with black lead. The top of the pedestal is painted red and divided into eight equal parts by shallow grooves colored with black lead. The height of the whole object is 4½ inches, and the workmanship is remarkably good.

FIG. 379.—Carving of human head.

No. 89827 [1138] (from Utkiavwïñ), on the other hand, is very roughly and carelessly made. It is 18·2 inches long, roughly whittled out of a flat piece of redwood board into the shape of a man with his legs wide apart and holding up his hands on each side of his head. The arms are very short and broad, with five fingers all nearly of the same length, and the legs are simply two straight four-sided pegs rounded on the edges. It is dressed in a hooded frock of seal gut reaching to the knees and leaving only the face and hands uncovered, and has sealskin knee boots on the legs. The face is rudely in relief, with two narrow bits of ivory inlaid for eyes, and a long canine tusk of the same material inserted in each corner of the mouth. Three small round bits of wood are inlaid in the forehead, one in the middle and one over each eye, and one in the right cheek above the corner of the mouth. The gut frock is carelessly made of irregular pieces. It is trimmed round the bottom and the edge of the hood with a strip of dogskin, but is left with a raw edge round the wrists. The boots are rather well made models of the regular waterproof boots, with soles of white sealskin and a band round the top 1 inch wide of the same material. A short peg projects from the top of the forehead. A string of stout sinew braid about 2 feet long is passed through a hole in the middle of the body and a knot tied in the end in front. Though the design is elaborate the workmanship is very rude, and the clothes seem to be made of odds and ends. The maker perhaps had in mind a fabulous man with teeth like a walrus, about whom we heard some fragmentary traditions.

Fig. 380 (No. 89826 [1358] from Utkiavwĭñ) is a clever, though somewhat roughly

¼

FIG. 380.—Mechanical doll: drum player.

made, mechanical doll. It represents a man dressed in deerskins sitting with his legs outstretched and holding in his extended left hand a drum and in his right a stick, as if beating the drum. The arms are of whalebone, and by pressing them he can be made to beat the drum. The doll is made of a single piece of wood—a knot with two branches, which make the legs. (I learned this from Capt. Herendeen, who saw this doll at the village before it was finished.) The height of the sitting figure is 11½ inches.

FIG. 381.—Mechanical toy: kaiak paddler.

A still more ingenious mechanical toy which, however, like the preceding, was made for sale, is shown in Fig. 381 (No. 89855 [1351] from Utkiavwĭñ). This is a man sitting in a kaiak in the attitude of paddling on the left side with a single-bladed paddle. His arms are of whale-bone, and by means of strings he can be made to paddle and turn his head from side to side. The kaiak is 29 inches long, very neatly carved from a single block of wood, and solid except at the cockpit. The bottom is flat, to allow it to stand on the floor, but it is otherwise precisely of the model of the kaiaks in the Museum from the Mackenzie and Anderson region. The nation who made it called it a "Kûñmû'd'lĭñ" kaiak. It is painted all over with red ocher, except on the bottom. The figure has no legs and fits into the cockpit, which is without any coaming. The head is separate and mounted on a long, slender pivot, which is fitted into a hole in the neck just loosely enough to allow it to turn easily. It is dressed in a hood of seal gut. The face is very natural, though rather rudely carved, and is lightly colored all over with red ocher, with the mouth painted deeply red, and the eyebrows, eyes, nostrils, and beard marked with black lead. The arms are narrow strips of whalebone, the ends of which protrude at the wrists, and are tied to the paddle by the ends of the strings which work it. The body is covered with a gut shirt.

The paddle is of the common shape, and has the blade and the lower end of the shaft painted red. The strings for working this contrivance are of fine sinew braid. One string is tied into a little hole in the edge of the hood, where the left ear would be, the other passes round the

⅛

FIG. 382.—Kaiak carved from a block of wood.

edge of the hood, and is tied at the right ear. These strings cross back of the head, and pass through two neat little ivory eyebolts inserted in the deck, 1 inch abaft the cockpit, and 1 inch apart. The strings from the hands are not crossed, but pass through two similar eyebolts, one at each edge of the deck, 2·5 inches from the cockpit. The ends of each set of strings are tied together. When the right pair and left pair of strings are pulled alternately, the man makes a stroke and looks to the right, then "recovers" and looks to the left. Both stroke and "recovery" are aided by the elasticity of the arms. This specimen shows a great deal of mechanical ingenuity, and was the only finished object of the kind seen.

Fig. 382 (No. 89856 [783] from Utkiavwĭñ) is a kaiak intended for a similar toy, which, when brought over for sale, had an unfinished armless doll in the cockpit. This was, unfortunately, lost in unpacking. The kaiak, which is 27·6 inches long, is not new, but has been freshly scraped and painted on deck. It is also a foreign kaiak, being precisely like a model brought by Mr. Nelson from Norton Sound. It is not unlikely that this boat itself came from that region through the "Nunatañmiun," unless, possibly, a southern kaiak had passed through the hands of enough people to reach a point where some Point Barrow native might see it. As far as we know no Point Barrow natives visit the regions where this form is used, and the model seems too accurate to have been made from a description.

Juvenile implements.—We sometimes saw the children playing with little models of the implements and utensils used by their parents. Perhaps the commonest thing of this sort is the boy's bow. As soon as a boy is able to walk his father makes him a little bow suited to his strength, with blunt arrows, with which he plays with the other boys, shooting at marks—for instance, the fetal reindeer brought home from the spring hunt—till he is old enough to shoot small birds and lemmings. We also saw children playing with little drums, and one man made his little boy an elaborate kă′moti about 4 feet long. In the collection are a number of miniature implements, spears, etc., some of which have been already described, which were perhaps intended as playthings for the children. As, however, they were all newly made, it is possible that they were merely intended to catch the fancy of the strangers.

No. 89451 [1113], from Nuwŭk, is a little snow shovel 4·5 inches long, with a blade 2·1 inches wide, rather roughly carved from a piece of walrus ivory.

No. 89695 [1280] from Utkiavwĭñ, is a similar model of a deer lance, 7 inches long, all in one piece and made of reindeer antler.

No. 89797 [1186] from Utkiavwĭñ, is a quite well made model of the drum used for accompanying singing and dancing, and is almost large enough to have been used for a plaything. The stick is entirely out of proportion, being merely a roughly whittled bit of lath, 13 inches long.

Games and sports.—The men have very few sports, though I have sometimes known them to amuse themselves by shooting at a mark with their rifles, and I once heard of a number of them wrestling. As far as I could learn, they wrestle " catch-as-catch-can " without any particular system. We never heard of anything like the athletic sports mentioned by Egede[1] and Crantz[2] or the pugilism described by Schwatka among the people of King William's Land, when two men stand up to each other and exchange buffets till one or the other gives in.[3] The women are very fond of playing " cat's cradle " whenever they have leisure, and make a number of complicated figures with the string, many of which represent various animals. One favorite figure is a very clever representation of a reindeer, which is made by moving the fingers to run down hill from one hand to the other.[4] Another favorite amusement with the women and children is tossing three bullets or small pebbles with the right hand, after the manner of a juggler,

---

[1] Greenland, p. 162.

[2] Vol. 1, p. 177.

[3] Science, vol. 4, No. 98, p. 545.

[4] Hall (Arctic Researches, p. 129) says the " cat's cradle " is a favorite amusement in Baffin Land, where they make many figures, including representations of the deer, whale, seal, and walrus.

keeping one ball constantly in the air. Some of the women are very skillful at this, keeping the balls up for a long time. This play is accompanied by a chant sung to a monotonous tune with very little air, but strongly marked time. I never succeeded in catching the words of this chant, which are uttered with considerable rapidity, and do not appear to be ordinary words. It begins "yú ̨ yú ̨ yuká, yú ̨ yú ̨ yuká;" and some of the words are certainly indelicate to judge from the unequivocal gestures by which I once saw them accompanied.

In the winter the young women and girls are often to be seen tossing a snowball with their feet. A girl wets some snow and makes a ball about as big as her two fists, which of course immediately becomes a lump of ice. This she balances on the toe of one foot and with a kick and a jump tosses it over to the other foot which catches it and tosses it back. Some women will keep this up for a number of strokes.

The young people of both sexes also sometimes play football, kicking about an old mitten or boot stuffed with rags or bits of waste skin. I never saw them set up goals and play a regular game as they did in Greenland.[1]

The little girls also play with the skipping rope. I once watched three little girls jumping. Two swung the rope and the other stood in the middle and jumped. First they swung the rope under her feet to the right, then back under her feet to the left, and then once or twice wholly round under her feet and over her head, and then began again.[2] They also play at housekeeping, laying sticks round to represent the sides of the house, or outlining the house by pressing up ridges of snow between their feet. Sometimes they mark out a complicated labyrinth on the snow in this way, and the game appears to be that one shall guard this and try to catch the others if they come in, as in many of the games of civilized children.

I have already spoken of the formal children's dances. They often also dance by themselves, beating on old tin cans for drums. One night I saw a party of children having quite an elaborate performance near our station. The snow at the time was drifted up close under the eaves of the house. On the edge of the roof sat three little boys, each beating vigorously on an empty tomato can and singing at the top of his lungs, while another boy and a little girl were dancing on the snow waving their arms and singing as usual, and at the same time trying to avoid another girl about thirteen years old, who represented a demon. She was stooping forward, and moving slowly round in time with the music, turning from side to side and rolling her eyes fiercely, while she licked the blade of an open clasp knife, drawing it slowly across her lips. They seemed intensely in earnest, and were enjoying themselves hugely. After dancing a while at the station they went over to the village, and as they told me the next day spent the whole night singing in a vacant snow-house.

---

[1] See Egede, p. 161, and Crantz, vol. 1, p. 177.
[2] Compare Parry's Second Voyage, p. 541.

They also amuse themselves in the winter by sliding on their knees down the steepest snowdrifts under the cliffs. A good deal of the time, however, they are following their parents or other grown people, catching little fish or fetching twigs for firewood or helping drive the dogs, though as a rule they are not made to do any regular work until they are pretty well grown.

MUSIC.

Musical instruments.—The only musical instrument in use among these people is the universal drum[1] or tambourine (kĕlyau), consisting of a membrane stretched over a hoop with a handle on one side, and used from Greenland to Siberia. It is always accompanied by the voice singing or chanting. The player holds the handle in his left hand with the membrane away from him, and strikes alternately on each side of the rim with a short heavy piece of ivory, or a long slender wand, ro-
tating the drum slightly at the same time to meet the stroke. This produces a loud, resonant, and somewhat musical note. There appears, however, to be no system of tuning these drums, the pitch of the note depending entirely on accident.

FIG. 383.—Drum.

We collected four of these drums, of which every household possesses at least one. They are all of essentially the same construction, but vary in size. No. 56741 [79], Fig. 383, has been selected as the type. The frame is a flat strip of willow 67 inches long, 1 inch wide, and 0·3 inch thick, bent till the two ends meet, thus making a hoop 22·2 inches long and 19 inches wide. The ends are fastened together by a strap of walrus ivory on the inside of the hoop, secured to the wood by neat stitches of black whalebone. The handle is of walrus ivory 5·2 inches long. The larger end is rather rudely carved into a human face. Back of this head and 1 inch from the large end of the handle is a square transverse notch, deep and sufficiently wide to fit over both rim and strap at the joint. It is held on by a lashing of sinew braid passing through holes in rim and strap, one on each side of the handle, and a large transverse hole in the latter, below and a little in front of the notch. The membrane, which appears to be a sheet of the peritoneum of a seal, is stretched over the other side of the hoop, which is beveled on the outside edge, and its edge is brought down to a deep

---

[1] Nordenskiöld calls this "the drum, or more correctly, tambourine, so common among most of the Polar peoples, European, Asiatic, and American; among the Lapps, the Samoyeds, the Tunguses, and the Eskimo." (Vega, vol. 2, p. 128).

groove 0·2 inch from the edge of the hoop and 0.3 inch wide, running round the hoop, where it is secured by three or four turns of sinew braid. The end of this string is crossed back and forth four or five times round the handle, where it is fitted to the hoop and then wrapped around it and finished off with a knot.

No. 56742 [514], from Utkiavwĭñ, is a similar drum, but somewhat larger, the hoop being 24·6 inches long and 22 inches wide. It is of the same materials, except that the strap at the joint is of reindeer antler. Opposite the joint the hoop appears to have shown signs of weakness, as it has been strengthened with two straps of walrus ivory, one on the inside and one on the outside of the hoop, fastened together

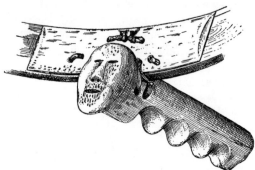

by stitches of sinew which pass through the wood and through both straps. The inside strap is 4·7 inches long, the outer 3·5 inches long, and only half the width of the rim, and is let into the latter. This strap appears to have been put on first, as at each end there is a stitch which only runs through the

FIG. 384.—Handle of drum secured to rim.

wood. The handle is fastened on as before, but has two transverse holes instead of one, and has four deep rounded notches for the fingers. (See Fig. 384.) The joint is tightened by driving a thin sliver of wood in at the bottom of the notch.

No. 56743 [31], from U tkiavwĭñ, closely resembles the type, but has a notch for the thumb as well as for the forefinger on the handle. The hoop is 23·5 inches long and 21 wide. No. 56740 [80] from the same village is rather smaller than the ordinary drums, having a hoop 16·2 inches long and 14·7 wide. The handle is of antler, but has the usual face on the large end.

We also brought home eight handles for these drums, which exhibit but slight variations. The commonest material for the handle is walrus ivory. Only two out of the twelve are of antler. They are usually about 5 inches long (the longest is 5·4 inches and the shortest 4·6). Handles with grooves for the fingers and sometimes for the thumb seem to be quite as common as the plain handles. Fig. 385a represents an ivory handle from Nuwŭk (No. 89267 [898]), which has a groove for each finger and a shallow one on the right side for the thumb. It is 5 inches long.

With one exception all these handles have the large end more or less neatly carved into a human face, with the mouth open as if singing, probably from an idea similar to that which makes the decorative artists of civilized countries ornament the pipes of a great organ with singing faces. This face is usually in the position shown in the specimens figured, but No. 89266 [784] (Fig. 385b), a handle of antler from Utkiavwĩñ, has the axis of the face parallel to that of the handle. Nos. 89269 [975] and 56515 [76], both from Utkiavwĩñ, are peculiar in their ornamentation. They are both of walrus ivory. The former has a well-carved face at the large end with small blue beads inlaid for eyes. In addition to this the small end has been rather freshly carved into a rather rude seal's head, and an ornamental pattern has been incised round the middle. This specimen exhibits the grooves for the fingers very well. The latter is a plain handle, but has a little sharp tusk

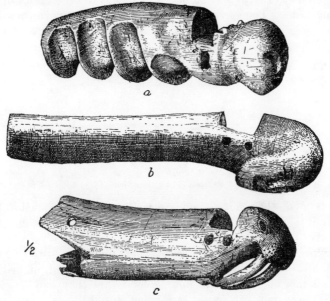

FIG. 385.—Drum handles.

inserted at each corner of the mouth. The only handle without a human face on the large end (No. 56514 [65] Fig. 385c, from Utkíavwĩñ) is peculiar in many respects. It is the butt end of a small walrus tusk, with a large pulp cavity, the edges of which are much notched and irregularly broken. The notch for fitting it to the handle is at the smaller end, which is neatly carved into a very good figure of a walrus head, with the tusks bent back to the under side of the handle. The head has oval bits of wood inlaid for eyes. None of the drums or handles in the collection are newly made.

The stick employed for beating these drums is commonly a slender elastic wand about 2½ feet long, but they also sometimes use a short thick stick of ivory resembling that used by the eastern Eskimo.[1] We brought home two of these sticks, both of which belong with the drum No. 56743 [31]. Fig. 386a (No. 56540 [31]) is a roughly cylindrical rod of ivory with a hole for a lanyard. The larger end is ornamented by rudely incised and darkened lines which represent the eyes and outline of the mouth of a "bow-head" whale. Fig. 386b (No. 56540 [31a]) is a plain round stick of ivory 9·4 inches long. It is rather roughly made and somewhat warped. The use of the long stick is perhaps derived from Siberia, where the short thick stick does not appear to be used.[2]

Holes in the membrane of the drum are sometimes mended with pieces of the crop of the ptarmigan. At any rate, this is what I was told by a native, who begged from me the crops of two of these birds that I was skinning, saying that he wanted them to mend his drum. These drums are always beaten as an accompaniment to invocations of spirits or incantations. This practice is so common that some authors are in the habit of always speaking of them as "shaman drums". As I have

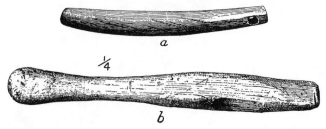

FIG. 386.—Ivory drumsticks.

already stated, their most common use is purely as a musical instrument, and they are used not only by the so-called "shamans" but by everybody.

Character and frequency of music.—Their music consists of monotonous chants, usually with very little perceptible air, and pitched generally in a minor key. I could not perceive that they had any idea of "tune," in the musical sense, but when several sang together each pitched the tune to suit himself. They, however, keep excellent time. The ordinary songs are in "common" or $\frac{4}{4}$ time.[3] The words are often extemporaneous, and at tolerably regular intervals comes the refrain, "A yáña yáña, a yáña ya," which takes the place of the "ámna aja" of the eastern Eskimo. Sometimes, when they are humming or singing to themselves, the words are nothing but this refrain. Their voices, as a general thing, are musical.

Like all Eskimo, they are very fond of music, and are constantly

---

[1] See, for example, Bessell's Naturalist, vol. 18, pt. 9, p. 881. (The people of Smith Sound use the femur of a walrus or seal. Cf. Capt. Lyon's picture, Parry's 2d Voyage, pl. opposite p. 530, and Gilder, Schwatka's Search, p. 43, where the people of the west shore of Hudson Bay are described as using a "wooden drumstick shaped like a potato-masher.")

[2] See Hooper, Tents, etc., p. 51, and Nordenskiöld, Vega, vol. 2, pp. 23 and 128; figure on p. 24.

[3] Compare Crantz, vol. 1, p. 176.

singing and humming to themselves, sometimes, according to Capt. Herendeen, waking up in the night to sing. Besides their regular festivals they often amuse themselves in their houses by singing to the drum. They are fond of civilized music, and, having usually very quick and rather acute ears, readily catch the tunes, which they sing with curiously mutilated words. We found "Shoo Fly" and "Little Brown Jug" great favorites at the time of our arrival, and one old woman from Nuwŭk, told us with great glee, how Magwa (Maguire) used to sing "Tolderolderol." Our two violins, the doctor's and the cook's, were a constant source of delight to them.

Capt. Parry[1] gives an excellent account of the music of the people of Fury and Hecla Straits.[2]

I regret extremely that I was not enough of a musician to write down on the spot the different tunes sung by these people. The ordinary monotonous chant is so devoid of air that I can not possibly recollect it, and the same is true of the chant which accompanies the game of pebble-tossing. I was able, however, to catch by ear the song sung by the children when they dance to the aurora. I never had the whole of this song, which we were told had a large number of stanzas. The first three are as follows:

> 1. Kióya ke, kióya ke,
>   A, yáñɐ, yáñɐ, ya,
>   Hwi, hwi, hwi, hwi!
> 2. Túdlĭmaná, túdlĭmaná,
>   A yáñɐ, yáñɐ, ya,
>   Hwi, hwi, hwi, hwi!
> 3. Kálutaná, kalutaná,
>   A yáñɐ, yáñɐ, ya,
>   Hwi, hwi, hwi, hwi!

We did not succeed in learning the meaning of these words, except, of course, that the first word, kióya, is aurora. When there is a bright aurora, the children often keep on dancing and singing this song till late into the night. A tune was introduced in the spring of 1883 by a party of men from Kĭlauwĭtáwĭñ, who came up to take part in the whale-fishing at Utkiavwĭñ. It became at once exceedingly popular, and everybody was singing or humming it. It is peculiar in being in waltz or $\frac{3}{4}$ time, and has considerably more air than the ordinary tunes. I heard no words sung to it except: "O hai hai yáña, O hai yáña, O haíja he, haíja he." Mr. Dall informs me that he recognizes this tune as one sung by the Indians on the Yukon.

ART.

The artistic sense appears to be much more highly developed among the western Eskimo than among those of the east. Among the latter,

---

[1] 2d Voyage, p. 541.
[2] See also the passage from Crantz, quoted above; Dall, Alaska, p. 16; and Nordenskiöld, Vega, vol. 2, pp. 23 and 130.

decoration appears to be applied almost solely to the clothing, while tools and utensils are usually left plain, and if ornamented are only adorned with carving or incised lines.[1] West of the Mackenzie River, and especially south of Bering Strait, Eskimo decorative art reaches its highest development, as shown by the collections in the National Museum. Not only is everything finished with the most extreme care, but all wooden objects are gaily painted with various pigments, and all articles of bone and ivory are covered with ornamental carvings and incised lines forming conventional patterns.

There are in the collections also many objects that appear to have been made simply for the pleasure of exercising the ingenuity in representing natural or fanciful objects, and are thus purely works of art. Want of space forbids any further discussion of these interesting objects. There is in the Museum sufficient material for a large monograph on Eskimo art. As would naturally be expected, art at Point Barrow occupies a somewhat intermediate position between the highly developed art of the southwest and the simple art of the east. I have given sufficient figures in my description of their clothing and various implements to illustrate the condition of purely decorative art. A few words may be added by way of résumé. It will be noticed that whenever the bone or ivory parts of weapons are decorated the ornamentation is usually in the form of incised lines colored with red ocher or soot. These lines rarely represent any natural objects, but generally form rather elegant conventional patterns, most commonly double or single borders, often joined by oblique cross lines or fringed with short, pointed parallel lines.

A common ornament is the incised "circle and dot," so often referred to in the foregoing descriptions. This is a circle about one-quarter inch in diameter, described as accurately as if done with compasses, with a deeply incised dot exactly in the center. This ornament is much more common south of Bering Strait, where, as Mr. L. M. Turner informs me, it is a conventionalized representation of a flower. Some of the older implements in our collection, ornamented with this figure, may have been obtained by trade from the southern natives, but the Point Barrow people certainly know how to make it, as there are a number of newly made articles in the collection thus ornamented. Unfortunately, we saw none of these objects in the process of manufacture, as they were made by the natives during odd moments of leisure, and at the time I did not realize the importance of finding out the process. No tool by which these figures could be made so accurately was ever offered for sale.

Neither Mr. Turner nor Mr. Dall, both of whom, as is well known, spent long periods among the natives of the Yukon region, ever observed the process of making this ornament. The latter, however, suggests that it is perhaps done with an improvised centerbit, made by sticking

---

[1] See the various accounts of the eastern Eskimo already referredto.

two iron points close together in the end of a handle. While weapons are decorated only with conventional patterns, other implements of bone or ivory, especially those pertaining to the chase, like the seal drags, etc., already mentioned, are frequently carved into the shape of animals, as well as being ornamented with conventional patterns. Carvings of animals' heads usually have the mouth, nostrils, etc., indicated by blackened incisions, and often have small, colored beads, bits of wood, or ivory inlaid for the eyes. When beads are used, the perforation of the bead is generally made to represent the pupil of the eye. Beads were also used for ornamenting dishes and other wooden objects.

The harpoon blade boxes of wood carved into the shape of the animal to be pursued have been already described. Other wooden objects, like the shafts of lances, and arrows, paddles, boxes, dishes, the woodwork of snowshoes, sledges, umiaks, etc., are frequently painted either all over, or in stripes or bands. The pigment generally used is red ocher, sometimes set off with stripes of black lead. The only case in which a different pigment is used is that of some arrows from Sidaru, which, in addition to the usual black or red rings, have a rather dingy green ring round the shaft. This green looks as if it might have been derived from the "green fungus or *peziza*," mentioned by Dall as in use among the ancient Aleuts.[1] The red ocher is applied smoothly in a rather thin coat which looks as if it were always put on in the manner observed by Capt. Herendeen, who saw a man painting a new sled at Utkiavwĭñ. He licked the freshly scraped wood with his tongue, so as to moisten it with saliva and then rubbed it with a lump of red ocher. The custom of painting wooden objects with red ocher seemed to be rather more common among the "Nunatañmiun," from whom perhaps the Point Barrow people borrowed the fashion, which is not mentioned among the eastern Eskimo. Nordenskiöld states that red is the favorite color among the natives of Pitlekaj.[2]

The painting of the arrow shafts in many cases curiously resembles the marks used by modern archers to distinguish the ownership of their shafts, and may have formerly served the same purpose. We made no inquiries about the matter on the spot, and there is no certain evidence in the series of arrows collected that these are or are not marks of ownership. Some arrows, apparently the property of the same man, have different marks, while arrows from different villages are similarly marked. On examining our series of fifty arrows from the three villages (fourteeen from Nuwŭk, twenty from Utkiavwĭñ, and sixteen from Sidaru) it will be seen that the commonest style of painting is to have the shaft painted red from the beginning or middle of the feathering to about one-fifth of its length from the head. Twenty arrows are marked in this way—eleven from Nuwŭk, belonging to at least two distinct sets, and nine from Utkiavwĭñ, belonging to three sets. Nine have

---

[1] Contributions to N. A. Ethn., vol. 1, p. 86.   [2] Vega, vol. 2, p. 135.

about 8 inches of the middle of the shaft painted red, with a black ring at the middle of the feathering. Seven of these are from Sidaru, one from Nuwŭk, aḣd one from Utkiavwĭñ. Five from Sidaru have a red ring round the middle, and a green one about the middle of the feathering, and four of the same set have also a red ring in front of the green one. Three from Utkiavwĭñ, belonging to different sets, have the shaft painted red from the middle to the beginning of the feathering, and three red rings 2 inches from the nock. Seven belonging to these sets from the two northern villages are unpainted.

A set of two small arrows which belong with the boy's bow No. 89904 [786] are peculiar in their marking. About 5½ inches of the middle of the shaft is painted red, there is a black ring round the middle, and a black spiral running the whole length of the feathering.

The only decorative work in metal is to be seen in the pipes and their accompanying picks and fire steel which have already been described.

In addition to these illustrations of decorative art, we brought home a series of seventy-nine objects which may be considered as purely works of art without reference to decoration. Some of the older objects in this series perhaps also served the purpose of amulets or charms,[1] but a number of the new ones were made simply as works of fancy for sale to us. These objects are all carvings of various materials, sometimes very rude and sometimes very neatly finished, but in most cases even when rudely made highly characteristic of the object represented.[2] Walrus ivory, usually from the tusks, but sometimes from the teeth, is the commonest material for these carvings. Thirty-six of the series are made of this material, which is very well suited for the purpose, being worked with tolerable ease, and capable of receiving a high finish. Soapstone, from the ease with which it can be cut, is also rather a favorite material. Seventeen of these carvings are made of soapstone, in many cases evidently pieces of an old lamp or kettle. Other mineral substances appear to be rarely used. Three images, all made for sale and by the same hand, are of soft white gypsum and one tiny image of a bear is rudely flaked out of gray flint. (There are in the collection a number of rude images of whales, made by flaking from flint, jasper, and glass, but as these were ascertained without doubt to be amulets, they will be described under that head.) Eleven are made of wood, nine of bone, one of antler, and one of the tooth of the polar bear. Twenty-three of these carvings represent human beings, sometimes intentionally grotesque anɑ caricatured; twenty-one, bowhead whales; fourteen, polar bears; five, seals; three, walruses; one, a beluga; one, a fish; and seven, fanciful monsters. Four are ornamented objects made for sale; not, strictly speaking, images.

Six of the representations of the human face or figure are of wood,

---

[1] Compare Nordenskiöld, Vega, vol. 2, p. 126 and Rink, Tales, etc., p. 52.

[2] Compare Bessels, Naturalist, vol. 18, No. 9, p. 880, where he speaks of finding among the people of Smith Sound ivory carvings representing animals and human figures "exceedingly characteristic." (See also Fig. 21 of the same paper.)

and with one exception were all freshly made for sale. Fig. 387 represents the only antique specimen of this kind (No. 56496 [655]). This
was found among the débris in one of the old ruined houses in Utkiavwiñ by Lieut. Ray, and is very old, blackened, and dirty. The carving was evidently done with a blunt instrument, probably a stone tool.
This specimen, which was perhaps the head of a doll, is 7·1 inches in
total length, with a head 3·4 inches long. We saw no similar object of
modern construction.

Figs. 388a and 388b (Nos. 89726 [1192] and 89727 [1193], from Utkiavwiñ) are a pair of rather roughly whittled human figures, a man
and woman, respectively, both without clothes (except that the woman
has a black-lead mark round the calf of each leg to indicate the tops of

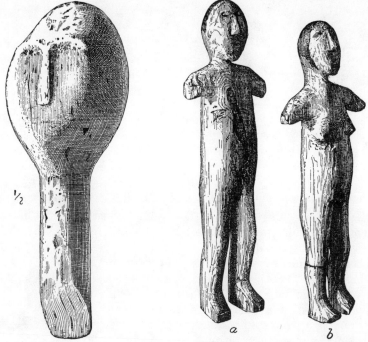

FIG. 387.—Ancient carving, human head.   FIG. 388.—Wooden figures.

the boots). They were made for sale, and are perhaps unfinished dolls.
The man (No. 89726 [1192]) is 11 inches long and tolerably well proportioned, except about the feet, which are very clumsily made. The
eyes and mouth are incised and the hair colored with black-lead. The
woman (No. 89727 [1193]) is a very similar figure, but only 9·2 inches
long. She has prominent breasts, and her legs are shorter in proportion than the man's.

No. 89725 [1185], from Utkiavwiñ, is a clumsy image of a man, rudely
whittled out of a flat, hard-wood stick, 7¼ inches long. The body and
legs are long, the latter somewhat straddling, with clumsy feet. The
outstretched arms are very short and stumpy. It has been painted all

over with a thin coat of red ocher, and the legs and feet have a coat of black lead over this. The hair also is marked out with black lead, and a small opaque white bead is fastened with a peg to the middle of the breast. This image was made for the market.

No. 56495a [203], from Utkiavwĭñ, is of a pair of very rude images, also made solely for the market. Each is 8 inches long, and is merely

an oblong piece of board, flat and rough on the back, roughly beveled f r o m t h e middle to each side in front. One end is surmounted by a rather rudely carved human head, with the features in relief and the eyes and mouth i n c i s e d. The eyebrows are marked out with black lead, and there is a longitudinal line of black lead down the middle o f t h e front.

FIG. 389.—Carving, face of Eskimo man.

Fig. 389 (No. 89724 [1123] from Nuwŭk) is the face of a male Eskimo, 3·2 inches long, carved out of a flat piece of some coniferous wood weathered to a dark, reddish brown. The labrets are represented by two small, red glass beads with white centers, fastened on in the proper position with wooden pegs. There is a deep groove around the edge of the face into which is fastened a strip of yellowish wolfskin with long fur to represent the trimming around the hood of the jacket. This specimen was made for sale, and the carving is well executed. It is a characteristic Eskimo face, and would pass for a portrait of Apaidyáo, a well known young Eskimo, who was employed by Lieut. Ray as a guide and hunter.

We collected only two soap-stone carvings representing men, both of which were newly made. One of these, Fig. 390 (No. 89569 [1095] from Nuwŭk), is a grotesque image 2·9 inches long, roughly carved from a flat piece of an old

FIG. 390.—Grotesque soapstone image, "walrus man."

lamp or pot. This is almost exactly the form in which the Eskimo, especially the children, usually draw a man. The writer's *portrait* has been drawn in very much the same shape. The features are very rudely indicated, and a long projecting tusk of bone is inserted at each corner of the mouth and glued in with refuse oil. This figure is probably meant to represent the "man with tusks," before referred to, who figures in several of the legendary fragments which we obtained.

No. 89568 [1108], from Utkiavwĭñ, probably represents the same being. It is a mask of soapstone, a piece of an old lamp, 2·8 inches long, with very characteristic features in low relief, and a pair of sharp, projecting, decurved tusks, about 1 inch long, which appear to be made of the vibrissæ of the walrus. The back of the mask is roughly hollowed out. No. 89575 [1014], from Nuwŭk, is a clumsy and carelessly made image of a man, 3·4 inches long, whittled out of a flat, rough piece of soft, white gypsum. The arms are short and clumsy and the legs straddling, and there is a large elliptical hole through the middle of the body. The features are indicated only by digging little cavities for the eyes, nostrils, and mouth. This and two other images of the same material, a bear equally rude, and a very well carved and characteristic beluga, were made by the ingenious young native, Yöksa, previously mentioned.

FIG. 391.—Bone image of dancer.

The best bone figure of a man is shown in Fig. 391 (No. 89353 [1025], from Nuwŭk), also newly made. This is an image, 5 inches long, of the giant "Kikámigo," previously mentioned, and is a very excellent piece of workmanship. The material is rather vascular compact bone. On the head is a conical dancing cap, 1·4 inches high, made of deerskin, with the flesh side out, and colored with red ocher, with a tuft of wolf hairs, 3 inches long, protruding from the apex. Around the middle of the cap is a narrow strip of the same material fringed on the lower edge with fifteen flat, narrow pendants of ivory, made to represent mountain-sheep teeth. To the back of this strip is fastened a half-downy feather nearly 4 inches long. A slender wooden stick is stuck into the strip behind, so that the tip reaches just above the apex of the cap. To a notch in the end of this is tied a bit of dressed deerskin, 1¼ inches long, cut into three strips.

Fig. 392 (No. 89348 [1127], from Utkiavwĭñ) is an image neatly carved from whale's bone, which may have been meant for an amulet, or possibly the handle of a drill cord, as it is not new, and has two oblique holes in the middle of the back, which meet so as to form a longitudinal channel for a string. The eyes, mouth, and labret holes are incised and filled with black dirt. The total length is 3·3 inches.

Fig. 393 (No. 89344 [1272], from Utkiavwiñ) is a very grotesque image of a naked man, rudely carved from compact, rather porous bone, impregnated with oil, but scraped smooth.

It is 5 inches long. The mouth and eyes are incised and blackened, and the nostrils simply bored out.

The ivory carvings representing human figures are all of rather rude workmanship. No. 89352 [1100], Fig. 394, from Nuwŭk, is a tolerably good figure, 3·3 inches long, of a sitting man holding up his hands before his face. This specimen is old and is made of walrus ivory yellow from age and oil. No. 89351 [1085] from Nuwŭk, is a similar

FIG. 392.—Bone image of man.

image, 3·8 inches long, newly made, with the arms at the sides, roughly carved from coarse walrus ivory. The eyes and mouth are incised and filled with dark colored dirt. Fig. 395 (No. 89349 [980], from Nuwŭk) is an old image made of yellow walrus ivory and closely resembling the bone image (No. 89348 [1127]) already figured, but with the hands by the sides. It is 2·7 inches long and has a string 4 inches long tied into the channel in the back.

Nos. 89346 and 89347 [990], from Nuwŭk, are a pair of little men, standing erect, about 2 inches high, rather roughly carved, of slightly yellow walrus ivory. Both have large, clumsy feet and legs, and the eyes, nostrils, and mouth incised

FIG. 393. — Grotesque bone image.

and filled in as usual with dark colored dirt. The arms are in high relief. No. 89346 [990b] has his hands clasped in front of him, while No. 89347 [990a] has them clasped behind his back. The legs of the latter are excavated on the inside as if to fit it upon the end of some object. It is more probable, however, that this image was carved from the foreshaft of a seal-dart, and that the excavation is merely the slot in the end of the latter. These two images are evidently modern, but do not appear freshly made. No. 89345 [1273] from Utkiavwiñ is a very rude image, 2·6 inches long, having a very small head and no arms. It is somewhat discolored walrus ivory and quite dirty, and though evidently modern, from the appearance of the ivory, does not appear to

FIG. 394.— Ivory image, sitting man.

FIG. 395.—Human figure carved from walrus ivory.

be freshly made. This figure is even ruder in design than those from Siberia figured by Nordenskiöld.[1]

The best of our human figures from Point Barrow show much greater art, both in workmanship and design, than those just mentioned, but can not compare with the elegant figures in the museum from the more southern parts of Alaska. The four remaining ivory carvings represent the human face alone. No. 89342 [989], Fig. 396, from Nuwŭk, is a thick piece of walrus ivory 3·3 inches long and 1·6 wide, carved into three human

FIG. 396.—Ivory carving, three human heads.

faces, a man in the middle and a woman on each side, joined together at the side of the head. Though the workmanship is rough, the faces are characteristic. The man has labrets and a curved line of tattooing at each corner of the mouth, indicating the successful whaleman, and the women, the usual tattooing on the chin. The eyes, nostrils, mouths, labrets, and tattooing are incised and blackened as usual. This specimen, though apparently modern, does not seem fresh enough to have been made for sale. The seller called it "a man and his two wives" without giving them any names. It may be intended as a portrait of some celebrated whaleman.

Fig. 397 is one of a pair of very rude faces (No. 56523 [52] from Utkiavwĭñ), 1½ inches long, which were made for sale. It is simply a walrus-tooth cut off square on the ends and on one side rudely carved into

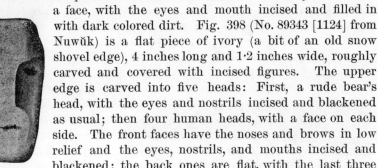

a face, with the eyes and mouth incised and filled in with dark colored dirt. Fig. 398 (No. 89343 [1124] from Nuwŭk) is a flat piece of ivory (a bit of an old snow shovel edge), 4 inches long and 1·2 inches wide, roughly carved and covered with incised figures. The upper edge is carved into five heads: First, a rude bear's head, with the eyes and nostrils incised and blackened as usual; then four human heads, with a face on each side. The front faces have the noses and brows in low relief and the eyes, nostrils, and mouths incised and blackened; the back ones are flat, with the last three features indicated as before. At the end is a rude figure of a bear, heading toward the right, with the ears in relief, the eyes and mouth roughly incised and blackened, and

FIG. 397.—Human head carved from a walrus tooth.

the legs indicated by roughly incised and blackened lines on the obverse face. Both faces are covered with rudely incised and blackened lines.

On the obverse there is a single vertical line between each pair of heads. Below the bear's head is a bear heading toward the right;

under the first human head, an umiak with four men; under the second, a "killer" (Orca) heading toward the right; under the third, two of the usual conventionalized whales' tails suspended from a cross-line; and under the last, a "killer" with very large "flukes" heading toward the left.

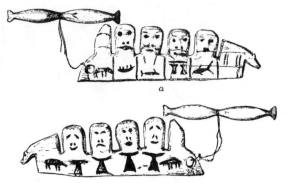

FIG. 398.—Elaborate ivory carving.

On the reverse there are, below the bear, a bear heading toward the right, below each of the human heads a whale's tail with the flukes up, and under the bear's head a bear heading toward the right. This end is perforated with a large round hole, into which is knotted a bit of deer sinew about 3 inches long, the other end of which is tied round the junction of two little bowhead whales, each about 1 inch long and carved out of a single piece of ivory, head to head. They are rather rudely carved and have the spiracles incised and blackened. This object appears freshly made, but perhaps commemorates the exploits of some four hunters. It was purchased along with other objects and its history was not learned at the time.

Perhaps the best image of a polar bear is No. 89566 [1252], Fig. 399,

FIG. 399.—Bear carved of soapstone.

from Utkiavwĭñ, which is quite characteristic. It represents the bear standing and was carved out of soft, gray soapstone with a knife, and finished off smoothly with a file. It is 4 inches long. No. 89571 [116b], from Nuwŭk, is a very rude flat soapstone bear, 1·9 inches long, in profile, showing only one fore and one hind leg. It was made for sale, but No. 89576 [966], from the same village, which is almost exactly like this, though smaller, is old. No. 89574 [1027], from Nuwŭk, is the gypsum carving of a bear, above referred to, which is very like the preceding two specimens. It is 2·5 inches long and has a large tail and large clumsy legs.

No. 89578 [1051], Fig. 400, from Utkiavwïñ, is a thin profile figure of a polar bear, made by flaking from dark gray flint. It is 1·4 inches long, and the tail is disproportionately long. The specimen does not appear to be new, and was perhaps intended for an amulet, like the flint whales already mentioned.

FIG. 400.—Bear flaker from flint.

The only bone figure of a bear in the collection, No. 89335 [1275], Fig. 401a, from Utkiavwïñ, is very crude. It has a very long, slim body and neck, and short, slender legs. The mouth, eyes, and nostrils are incised and are blackened as usual. The carving is rudely done, but the specimen, which was made for sale, has been scraped smooth. It is 5.5 inches long, and made of whale's bone, soaked in oil to make it appear old.

Fig. 401b (No. 89471 [997], from Utkiavwïñ) is the end of some old implement, 6 inches long, one end of which is carved into a rather rude

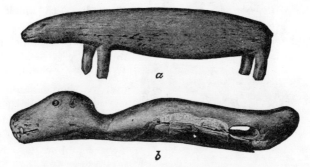

FIG. 401 —Bone figures: (a) bear; (b) bear's head.

bear's head, with the ears, nostrils, outline of the mouth, and the vibrissæ incised and blackened. Sky-blue glass beads are inlaid for the eyes and bits of tooth for the canine tusks. On the throat is a a conventional figure with two "circles and dots," all incised and blackened. The carving is freshly done, but soiled, to make it look old.

The three newly made ivory bears are all represented standing and are quite characteristic. All have the eyes, nostrils, and mouth incised and blackened. Fig. 402a (No. 89337 [1274], from Utkiavwïñ) is the best in execution. It is made of white ivory and is 3·3 inches long. No. 56524, [92], from Nuwŭk, is a small bear, 1·7 inches long, not quite so well carved, and disproportionally long-legged. The left hind leg has been broken off close to the body and doweled on with a wooden peg. Another little bear from Nuwŭk (No. 89841 [992]) is still more rudely carved, but closely resembles the preceding.

A larger carving, rather roughly executed (No. 89338 [1098], from Nuwŭk), represents a standing bear 3·2 inches long, holding a whale crosswise in his mouth. The whale is a separate piece, held in by a wooden peg driven through the bear's lower jaw. This specimen is newly made from rather coarse walrus ivory.

Fig. 402b (No. 89340 [953], from Utkiavwĭñ) is a very ancient ivory image of a bear, 3·4 inches long, which was evidently intended for an amulet, as there is a stout lug on the belly, into which are bored two oblique holes, so as to make a longitudinal channel for a string. Into this is knotted a stout cord of loosely twisted sinew. The execution of the image is particularly good, but the design is very rude. The specimen is so ancient that the ivory of which it is made has become almost black.

No. 56528a [56a] from Utkiavwĭñ is a walrus tooth, 1·6 inches long, carved into the shape of a bear's head. Both design and execution are

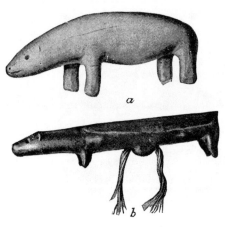

FIG. 402.—Ivory figures of bears.

very rude. Light blue glass beads are inlaid for the eyes, and the nostrils and outline of the mouth are incised and filled in with black dirt. It was made for sale. A still more rude carving, also made for sale, is No. 56528, from Utkiavwĭñ, which is an old and weathered canine tooth of the polar bear, with the point freshly whittled so as to look something like a bear's head. Two sky-blue glass beads are inlaid to represent the eyes and one for the nose, and the mouth is incised and blackened.

The walrus does not appear to be a favorite subject for representation. The part of the collection already described shows that it occurs very seldom as a decoration, and we obtained only three images of this animal, one in soapstone and two in ivory, all small and very rude, both in design and execution. They are all newly made. The best image is shown in Fig. 403a (No. 89333 [1384] from Utkiavwĭñ). This is 2·3 inches long and made of coarse walrus ivory. The head is rather good, but the body simply tapers to a broken point. A bit of wood is inlaid for the left eye, but the right is merely represented by a hole.

Fig. 403b (No. 89334 [1067], from Utkiavwĭñ) is exceedingly rude. The eyes, nostrils, and mouth are incised and blackened as usual, and the vibrissæ ("whiskers") are represented by rather large round pits on the snout, also filled in with black dirt. It is 2·9 inches long, and appears

to have been dipped in the oil-bucket to make it look old.   Both the
images bear a strong re-
semblance to the rude
carvings of walruses
from Siberia figured by
Nordenskiöld.[1]   No.
89570 [1271] from Nu-
wŭk is of soapstone, 2
inches long, with tusks
rudely carved from wal-
rus ivory.   The head is
but roughly indicated,
while the body is shaped
like a slug, and is bifid
at the pointed end to
represent the hind flip-
pers.   The eyes and nos-
trils are roughly incised.

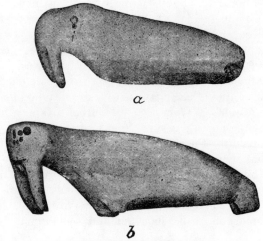

FIG. 403.—Rude ivory figures of walrus.

The seal, on the other hand, is a favorite object for artistic representation. It is seen often, as already described, as a decoration on various implements, especially the drag lines, generally in a very characteristic shape, and the five seal images in the collection are excellent in
design and execution.   Almost all are decidedly superior to those from

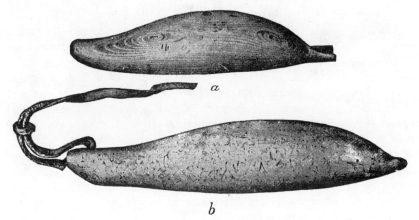

FIG. 404.—Images of seal—wood and bone.

Pitlekaj, figured by Nordenskiöld.[1]   All are newly made except No.
89737 [857a].   Fig. 404a, from Utkiavwĭñ, which is 4·2 inches long, and
made of spruce, very old, weathered, and discolored with dirt and grease.
It is nicely carved and scraped smooth, and is very good in its general
proportions, though the details are not represented as in the other
images.

[1] Vega, vol. 2, p. 142.

The best figure (No. 89330 [999] figured in the Point Barrow Rept. Ethnol., Pl. v, Fig.6, from Utkiavwĭñ) is carved from walrus ivory and is 4·3 inches long. It represents a male rough seal, and is exceedingly accurate and highly finished. The lower jaw is perforated and a bit of sinew thread tied in to represent the drag line. Small red glass beads with white centers are inlaid for the eyes. The other three are all of bone and represent dead male seals stretched on their backs with the drag line in their jaw as they are dragged home.

No. 56579 [75], Fig. 404b, from Utkiavwĭñ, is 5·7 inches long, and very smoothly carved from walrus jaw bone, with round bits of wood inlaid for the eyes. The proportions are excellent, but the details are not strongly brought out. This specimen is a little older than the rest, and may have been an amulet for good luck in seal catching. The other two are of compact white bone, perhaps that of the reindeer.

No. 89331 [1143], from Utkiavwĭñ, is 3·4 inches long, and has the breast and back flattened and the flippers in high relief. The anus,

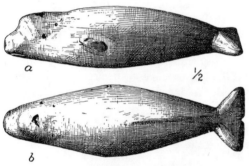

genital opening, and eyes are incised, the latter two filled in, as usual, with black dirt. The drag line is of sinew braid and has an ivory cylinder slipped over it.

No. 89328 [1167], from Utkiavwĭñ, is the poorest in design. It is 5·6 inches long and has the neck bent up as in dragging. The back of a freshly caught

FIG. 405.—White whale carved from gypsum.

seal is always somewhat flattened by dragging it over the ice, and this flattening is very much exaggerated in this carving by the natural shape of the bone. The fore flippers are in high relief, with three toes to each flipper, colored round the edge with red ocher. The tips of the hind flippers are joined together, and each has only two toes. The eyes, genital opening, and the spots on the back and belly are indicated by shallow round pits colored with red ocher. The drag line is a double bit of sinew braid, which has on it two ivory cylinders, one ornamented with an incised pattern.

We found but a single figure of the beluga, which is such a favorite subject for Eskimo artists farther south. This is the gypsum carving already mentioned (No. 89573 [1015], Fig. 405, from Nuwŭk). It is 3·5 inches long and is very characteristic, though rather short in proportion to its girth. It was neatly carved with a knife.

The "bow-head" whale (Balæna mysticetus), is a very favorite subject, appearing often as a decoration and represented by 21 carvings. Three of these are of wood, very much resembling in design and execution the harpoon boxes already described. They are all very old, and perhaps were charms to be carried in the boat to secure good luck in whaling. No. 89736 [857*b*], Fig. 406, from Utkiavwĭñ, is perhaps the best proportioned of these figures, though the only details represented are the flukes (which are broken), and the incised spiracles. It is 5·4

inches long and made of spruce or hemlock, stained almost black by dirt, grease, and weathering. A long string of sinew braid is tied round the "small."

No. 89735 [1036] from Utkiavwĭñ, is also a rather well proportioned figure, rude in execution, with no details carved out except

FIG. 406.—Wooden carving—whale.

the flukes, one of which is broken. An angular bit of iron pyrites is inlaid to represent the left eye, and a similar piece appears to have been lost from the right eye. The anus is represented by a light blue glass bead inlaid in the belly. It is 8·8 inches long and made of soft wood, probably cottonwood, weathered and stained to a dark brown. It is very old and much chipped and cracked. Two small oblique holes in the middle of the back make a transverse channel for a string. This specimen was said by the man who sold it to have been dug up among the ruins of one of the old houses in the village.

No. 89734 [987] from Nuwŭk, is 12 inches long, very broad in proportion to its length, and rather rude in design, with a flat belly, though

FIG. 407.—Whale carved from soapstone.

neatly carved and scraped smooth. The spiracles and the outline of the mouth are incised and little angular bits of brown quartz are inlaid for the eyes. Both flukes have been split off and part of the right fluke has been fastened on again with a single wooden treenail. It is of spruce or hemlock and has weathered to a brown color.

Fig. 407 (No. 89561 [1253] from Utkiavwĭñ) represents the best image of a whale in the collection. It is very well proportioned, though perhaps a little clumsy about the flukes, with the external details correctly represented. It is 4·5 inches long, neatly carved from soapstone, scraped smooth and oiled. It was made for sale. There are five other round soapstone carvings of whales in the collection, but none so good as this except a little one from Nuwŭk, (No. 89563 [986]) 2 inches long, which is almost an exact miniature of the preceding. This specimen is not new. Fig. 408 (No. 89557 [1267] from Utkiavwĭñ) is a rude *flat* representation of a whale seen from above. It is 5·2 inches long and

FIG. 408.—Rude flat image of whale.

roughly whittled out of the bottom of an old stone pot. The flippers are large and clumsy, and the spiracles slightly incised. The specimen appears to be old, as does a similar one from Nuwŭk (No. 89559 [1188a]).

No. 89558 [1266] from Utkiavwĭñ, and No. 89572 from Nuwŭk, both

FIG. 409.—Ivory image of whale.

flat images, are carelessly made for sale. The latter is simply a representation in soapstone of the conventional "whale's tail" with the "small" cut off to an angular point. No. 89325 [1160] from Utkiavwĭñ is a clumsy, broad whale with a flat belly, 4·1 inches long, freshly carved from whale's bone, and soaked in oil to make it look old. The eyes, spiracles, and outline of the mouth are incised and filled in with dark oil lees.

None of the ivory carvings of whales have any special artistic merit. Fig. 409 (No. 89323 [1024a] from Nuwŭk) is the best of these. It is a little better in design and execution than the preceding, which it resembles considerably. It is the female of a pair of little whales made of old brown walrus ivory, which is much cracked. The male differs from the female only in the shape of the external sexual organs, the male having a little round pit and the female a long sulcus. This, as well as the eyes, spiracles, and outline of the mouth, is incised and filled in with dark colored dirt. The female is 3·1 inches long, the male (No. 89324 [1024b]) 0·1 inch longer. These specimens appear to be quite ancient.

FIG. 410.—Ivory image of whale.

Fig. 410 (No. 89326 [1086] from Nuwŭk) is very long and slender— 4·3 inches long and only 0·7 inch wide—with the belly perfectly flat, but otherwise a very good representation, neatly carved. The flukes in particular are especially well done, and the flippers are in high relief. The eyes, the spiracles, and the outline of the mouth are incised and the first blackened. The material is a rather poor quality of walrus ivory, about half "core." The specimen was made for sale. No. 89327 [991] from Nuwŭk was also made for sale. It is a little whale 1·6 inches long, rudely carved in walrus ivory.

FIG. 411.—Pair of little ivory whales.

Fig. 411 (No. 56619 [66] from Utkiavwĭñ) represents a pair of little whales, each carved from a walrus tooth, which probably served for buttons or toggles of some sort, though I do not recollect ever seeing such objects in use. The belly of each is flat and has in the middle a

FIG. 412.—Soapstone image of imaginary animal.

stout lug perforated with a transverse eye, and they are tied together by a piece of thong about 14 inches long. They are quite well designed and executed, but rather "stumpy" in outline, with the outline of the mouth and the spiracles incised and blackened, and little round bits of tooth inlaid for eyes. In the middle of the back of each was inlaid a small blue glass bead, which still remains in one of them. They are old and dirty and somewhat chipped about the flukes.

Fig. 412 (No. 89567 [904] from Nuwŭk) represents an imaginary quadruped 2·5 inches long, with a short, thick body and legs, no neck, and a human head, with the eyes and mouth incised. It is roughly carved from light gray soapstone, and ground pretty smooth. This figure is not new, and has probably connected

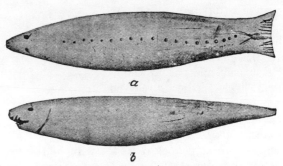

a

b

FIG. 413.—Ivory carving, seal with fish's head.

with it some story which we did not succeed in learning. The seller called it an "old man." No. 89332 [994] from Nuwŭk, is a fanciful monster, 4·2 inches long, carved in ivory. It has a human head with the tusks of a walrus, the body, tail, and flippers of a seal, with human arms. The hands, each of which has four fingers, clasp some round object against the belly. It is not old, but apparently was not made for the market. It was called a "walrus man;" but we did not learn whether it was simply a fancy figure or whether there was any story connected with it.

Fig. 413 (No. 89329 [1101] from Nuwŭk) is another monster, 3·9 inches long, carved in ivory. It has a fish's head with large canine teeth,

and a seal's body, tail, and hind flippers. The eyes, nostrils, gill slits, the outlines of the tail, and the toes, of which there are six on each flipper, are incised and blackened. A row of

FIG. 414.—Ivory carving, ten-legged bear.

nineteen small round pits, filled with dark colored dirt runs nearly straight from the nape to the tail.

Fig. 414 (No. 89339 [1099] from Nuwŭk) is a newly made ivory figure, which is interesting from its resemblance to one of the fabulous animals which figure in the Greenland legends. It is 4 inches long and represents a long-necked bear with ten legs, an animal which the maker gave us to understand had once been seen at Point Barrow. The resemblance of this animal to the "kiliopak" or "kilifvak" of the Greenland stories, which is described as "an animal with six or even ten feet"[1] is quite striking.

Fig. 415 (No. 89723 [1084] from Nuwŭk) is another representation of the giant who holds a whale in each hand. He was called in this instance "Kaióasu," and not "Kikámigo." This image is carved from very old pale brown walrus ivory, and is 2·3 inches high. A transverse incised

FIG. 415.—Ivory carving, giant holding whales.

line across each cheek from the wing of the nose, indicates the whaleman's tattoo mark of the Eastern fashion. The image is ancient, but is mounted in a socket in the middle of a newly made wooden stand, which has a broad border of red ocher and a broad streak of the same paint along each diameter.

Fig. 416 (No. 89336 [1369]) is a curious piece of carving, which Nĭkawdalu said he found in one of the ruined houses on the river Kulugrua.

---

[1] Rink, Tales, etc., p. 48. See also same work, passim, among the stories.

The carving is well executed and really seems to be old, although it has evidently been retouched in a good many places. It is made from an irregularly flattened bit of reindeer antler, 3·6 inches long, blackened by the weather on the flat surfaces, and represents an animal with four legs, which appear to be dog's legs, and at each end what appears to be a dog's head. One of these is smaller than the other and both have the ears in relief, and the eyes, nostrils, and outlines of the mouth incised.

FIG. 416.—Double-headed animal, carved from antler.

Fig. 417 (No. 56520 [85] from Nuwŭk) is a fanciful object made solely for the market. It consists of the rudely carved head of some carnivorous animal, made of ivory, and 2·6 inches long, fitted to the broad end of a flat-pointed wooden handle, painted red. The head was called a "dog", but it looks more like a bear. Small bits of wood are inlaid for the eyes, and the outline of the mouth is deeply incised and colored with red ocher, having bits of white ivory inlaid to represent the canine teeth. The ears, nostrils, vibrissæ, and hairs on the muzzle are indicated by blackened incisions. There is an ornamented collar round

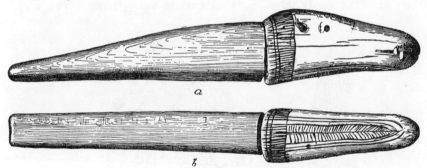

FIG. 417.—Ivory carving, dog.

the neck, to which is joined a conventional pattern of triangular form on the throat, and a somewhat similar pattern on the top of the head between the ears.

One of the natives at Utkiavwĭñ, in May, 1882, conceived the fancy of smoothing off the tip of a walrus tusk into the shape of a pyramid, surmounted by a little conical cap and ornamenting it with incised figures, which he colored with red ocher. It appears to have been purely an individual fancy, as it has no utility, nor are such objects made by the Eskimo elsewhere, as far as I know. Having succeeded in finding a sale for this object, either he or one of his friends, I do not now recollect which, made another, which was brought over for sale about ten days later. We saw no others afterwards.

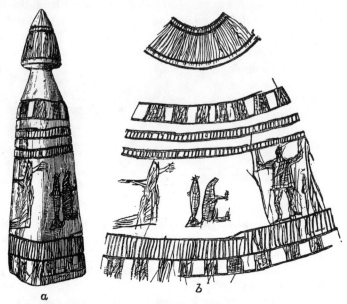

FIG. 418.—Engraved ivory: (*a*) piece engraved with figures; (*b*) development of pattern.

Fig. 418*a* (pattern developed in Fig. 418*b*, No. 56530 [220]) represents the first of these. It is made of solid white walrus ivory. The work-

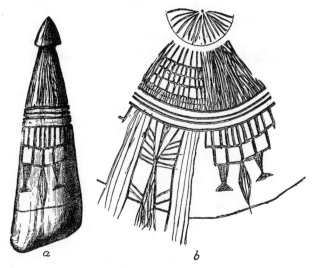

FIG, 419.—Engraved ivory: (*a*) piece with engraving; (*b*) development of pattern.

manship is quite rude, and the cap has been broken off and neatly fastened on with a wooden dowel. The other, Fig. 419*a*, 419*b* (No. 56529 [254]) is 3·7 inches long.

Fig. 420 (No. 89741 [1012] from Nuwŭk) is an ivory cross 15·5 inches long. The cross is ornamented by incised rings and dots colored with red ocher. The shaft of the cross is surmounted by a female human head neatly carved from soapstone, fastened on by a lashing of sinew braid, which passes through a transverse hole in the head and round the crosspiece. No. 89742 [1091], also from Nuwŭk, closely resembles the preceding, but is slightly shorter and has a four-sided shaft. The head, moreover, which is made of bone, represents a man, as is shown by the little pits, which indicate the labrets. The cheeks and crown of the head are colored slightly red with red ocher.

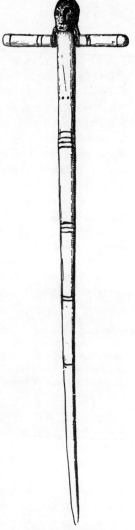

The ingenious Yöksa, so often mentioned, made the first image and brought it down for sale. All he could or would tell us about it was that it was "tună′ktûp kuni′a," "A kuni′a (jargon for woman) of soapstone." The successful sale of this first cross encouraged him to make the second, but we saw no others before or after. Other natives who saw these objects only laughed. The whole may be simply a fanciful doll, perhaps meant for a caricature, the shaft representing the body, and the crosspiece the outstretched arms. The object is very suggestive of a crucifix, and there is a bare possibility that the maker may have seen something of the sort in the possession of some of the eastern natives who have been visited by a missionary of the Roman Catholic Church (Father Petitot).

Under the head of works of art may properly be included No. 89823 [1130], from Utkiavwĭñ. This is the skeleton of the jaws of a polar bear, cut off just back of the nose, neatly sewed up in a piece of sealskin with the hair out, so as to leave uncovered only the tips of the jawbones and the canine teeth. This specimen was put up by the same quick-witted young native after his removal from Nuwŭk to Utkiavwĭñ, evidently in imitation of the work of preparing specimens of natural history, which he had seen done at the station. For the same

FIG. 420.—Ivory doll.

reason he dried and carefully preserved in a little box whittled out of a block of wood and tied up with sinew a little fresh-water sculpin (Cottus quadricornis), which he had caught at Kulugrua (No. 89536 [1145]).

I regret much that we did not save and bring home any of the pencil drawings made by these people. The children especially were anxious to get lead pencils, and made themselves rather a nuisance by covering the painted walls of the observatory with scrawls of ships and various other objects, perhaps rather more accurately done than they would have been by white children of the same age. The style of the figures on the hunting scores already described, however, is very like that of the pencil drawings.[1]

DOMESTIC LIFE.

Marriage.—As far as we could learn, the marriage relation was entered upon generally from reasons of interest or convenience, with very little regard for affection, as we understand it, though there often appeared to be a warm attachment between married people. A man desires to obtain a wife who will perform her household duties well and faithfully, and will be at the same time an agreeable companion, while he often plans to marry into a rich or influential family. The woman, on the other hand, appears to desire a husband who is industrious and a good hunter. There were, nevertheless, some indications that real love matches sometimes took place. Marriages are usually arranged by the parents of the contracting parties, sometimes when the principals are mere children. We knew of one case when a young man of about twenty-two offered himself as the prospective husband of a girl of eight or ten, when she should reach a marriageable age. This practice of child betrothal seems to be practically universal among the Eskimo everywhere.[2]

Dr. Simpson, in describing the marriage customs at Point Barrow, says:

The usual case is, that as soon as the young man desires a partner and is able to support one, his mother selects a girl according to her judgment or fancy, and invites her to the hut, where she first takes the part of a "kivgak" or servant, having all the cooking and other kitchen duties to perform during the day, and returns to her home at night. If her conduct proves satisfactory, she is further invited to become a member of the family.[3]

We only knew this to be done on one occasion; and on the contrary knew of several cases where the bridegroom became a member of the wife's family.

One youth, who had had his lips pierced for the labrets just previously to our arrival, was, we soon learned, betrothed to a young girl at Nuwŭk. This girl frequently came down from Nuwŭk and visited her lover's family, staying several days at a time, but we could not

---

[1] Compare these with Nordenskiöld's figures of "Chukch" drawings, Vega, vol. 2, pp. 132, 133. The latter are completely Eskimo in character.

[2] Compare Crantz, vol. 1, p. 159 (Greenland); Kumlien, Contributions, p. 164 (Cumberland Gulf); Hall, Arctic Researches, p. 567 (Baffin Land); Parry, 2nd Voyage, p. 528 (Fury and Hecla Straits); Schwatka, Science, vol. 4, No. 98, p. 544 (King William's Land); Gilder, Schwatka's Search, p. 250 (Hudson's Bay); Franklin, First Exp., vol. 2, p. 41 (Chesterfield Inlet); Hooper, Tents, etc., p. 209 (Plover Bay); Nordenskiöld, Vega, vol. 2, p. 26 (Pitlekaj).

[3] Op. cit., p. 252.

discover that she was treated as a servant. She went with them to the spring deer hunt, but we were distinctly given to understand that the young couple would not be married till after the return from this hunt, and that no intercourse would take place between them before that time. When the season came for catching reindeer fawns, the couple started off together, with sled and dogs and camp equipage in pursuit of them, and always afterwards were considered as man and wife.

Most of the marriages took place before we heard of them, so that we had no opportunity for learning what ceremony, if any, occurred at the time. Some of the party, however, who went over to make a visit at Utkiavwĭñ one evening, found the house full of people, who were singing and dancing, and were told that this was to celebrate the marriage of the daughter of the house. Marriage ceremonies appear to be rare among the Eskimo. A pretended abduction, with the consent of the parents, is spoken of by Bessels at Smith Sound[1] and Egede in Greenland (p. 142), and Kumlien was informed that certain ceremonies were sometimes practiced at Cumberland Gulf.[2] Elsewhere I have not been able to find any reference to the subject. A man usually selects a wife of about his own age, but reasons of interest sometimes lead to a great disparity of age between the two. I do not recollect any case where an old man had a wife very much younger than himself, but we knew of several men who had married widows or divorced women old enough to be their mothers,[3] and in one remarkable case the bride was a girl of sixteen or seventeen, and the husband a lad apparently not over thirteen, who could barely have reached the age of puberty.

This couple were married late in the winter of 1882–'83, and immediately started off to the rivers, deer hunting, where the young husband was very successful. This union, however, appeared to have been dissolved in the summer, as I believe the girl was living with another and older man when we left the station. In this case, the husband came to live with the wife's family.

As is the case with most Eskimo, most of the men content themselves with one wife, though a few of the wealthy men have two each. I do not recollect over half a dozen men in the two villages who had more than one wife each, and one of these dismissed his younger wife during our stay. We never heard of a case of more than two wives. As well as we could judge, the marriage bond was regarded simply as a contract entered into by the agreement of the contracting parties and, without any formal ceremony of divorce, easily dissolved in the same way, on account of incompatibility of temper, or even on account of temporary disagreements.

We knew of one or two cases where wives left their husbands on

<hr>

[1] Naturalist, vol. 18, pt. 9, p. 877.
[2] Contributions, p. 16.
[3] Compare Holm's observations in East Greenland—"idet et ganske ungt Menneske kan være gift med en Kone, som kunde være hans Moder." Geografisk Tidskrift, vol. 8, p. 91.

account of ill treatment. One of these cases resulted in a permanent separation, each of the couple finally marrying again, though the husband for a long time tried his best to get his wife to come back to him. In another case, where the wife after receiving a beating ran away to Nuwŭk, and, as we were told, married another man, her first husband followed her in a day or two and either by violence or persuasion made her come back with him. They afterwards appeared to live together on perfectly good terms.

On the other hand, we know of several cases where men discarded wives who were unsatisfactory or made themselves disagreeable. For instance, the younger Tuñazu, when we first made his acquaintance, was married to a widow very much his senior, who seemed to have a disagreeable and querulous temper, so that we were not surprised to hear in the spring of 1882 that they were separated and Tuñazu married to a young girl. His second matrimonial venture was no more successful than his first, for his young wife proved to be a great talker. As he told us: "She talked all the time, so that he could not eat and could not sleep." So he discarded her, and when we left the station he had been for some time married to another old widow.

In the case above mentioned, where the man with two wives discarded the younger of them, the reason he assigned was that she was lazy, would not make her own clothes, and was disobedient to the older wife, to whom he was much attached. As he said, Kakaguna (the older wife) told her, "Give me a drink of water," and she said, "No!" so Kakaguna said, "Go!" and she went. He did not show any particular concern about it.

Dr. Simpson says, "A great many changes take place before a permanent choice is made;" and again, "A union once apparently settled between parties grown up is rarely dissolved."[1] And this agrees with our experience. The same appears to have been the case in Greenland. Crantz[2] says, "Such quarrels and separations only happen between people in their younger years, who have married without due forethought. The older they grow, the more they love one another."

Easy and unceremonious divorce appears to be the usual custom among Eskimo generally, and the divorced parties are always free to marry again.[3] The only writer who mentions any ceremony of divorce is Bessels, who witnessed such among the so-called "Arctic Highlanders" of Smith Sound (Naturalist, vol. 18, pt. 9, p. 877). Dr. Simp-

---

[1] Op. cit., p. 253.
[2] Vol. 1, p. 160.
[3] "They often repudiate and put away their wives, if either they do not suit their humors, or else if they are barren, * * * and marry others." Egede, Greenland, p. 143. Compare also Crantz, vol. 1, p. 160; Parry, Second Voyage, p. 528 (Fury and Hecla Straits); Kumlien, Contributions, p. 17 (Cumberland Gulf); and Hooper, Tents, etc., p. 100—"repudiation is perfectly recognized, and in instances of misconduct and sometimes of dislike, put in force without scruple or censure. * * * The rejected wife * * * does not generally wait long for another husband;" (Plover Bay.) Compare also Holm, Geografisk Tidskrift, vol. 8, pp. 91–92, where he gives an account of marriage and divorce in east Greenland, remarkably like what we observed at Point Barrow.

son, in the paragraph referred to above, says that "A man of mature age chooses a wife for himself and fetches her home, frequently, to all appearance, much against her will." The only case of the kind which came to our notice was in 1883, when one of the Kĭlauwitawĭñmeun attempted by blows to coerce Adwû'na, an Utkiavwĭñ girl, to live with him, but was unsuccessful.

A curious custom, not peculiar to these people, is the habit of exchanging wives temporarily. For instance, one man of our acquaintance planned to go to the rivers deer hunting in the summer of 1882, and borrowed his cousin's wife for the expedition, as she was a good shot and a good hand at deer hunting, while his own wife went with his cousin on the trading expedition to the eastward. On their return the wives went back to their respective husbands.

The couples sometimes find themselves better pleased with their new mates than with the former association, in which case the exchange is made permanent. This happened once in Utkiavwĭñ to our certain knowledge. This custom has been observed at Fury and Hecla Straits,[1] Cumberland Gulf,[2] and in the region around Repulse Bay, where it seems to be carried to an extreme.

According to Gilder[3] it is a usual thing among friends in that region to exchange wives for a week or two about every two months. Among the Greenlanders the only custom of the kind mentioned is the temporary exchange of wives at certain festivals described by Egede.[4]

Holm also describes "the game of putting out the lamps," or "changing wives," as a common winter sport in East Greenland. He also, however, speaks of the temporary exchange of wives among these people much as described elsewhere.[5]

I am informed by some of the whalemen who winter in the neighborhood of Repulse Bay, that at certain times there is a general exchange of wives throughout the village, each woman passing from man to man till she has been through the hands of all, and finally returns to her husband. All these cases seem to me to indicate that the Eskimo have not wholly emerged from the state called communal marriage, in which each woman is considered as the wife of every man in the community.

Standing and treatment of women.—The women appear to stand on a footing of perfect equality with the men both in the family and in the community. The wife is the constant and trusted companion of the man in everything except the hunt, and her opinion is sought in every bargain or other important undertaking.[6]

---

[1] Parry, 2nd Voyage, p. 528.
[2] Kumlien, Contributions, p. 16.
[3] Schwatka's Search, p. 197.
[4] Greenland, p. 139.
[5] Geogr., Tids., vol. 8, p. 92.
[6] Compare Parry, 2d Voyage, pp. 526-528, Nordenskiöld (Vega, vol. 1, p. 449): The women are "treated as the equals of the men, and the wife was always consulted by the husband when a more important bargain than usual was to be made." (Pitlekaj.) This statement is applicable, word for word, to the women of Point Barrow.

Dr. Simpson's description[1] of the standing of the women at Point Barrow in his time is so true at the present day that I may be pardoned for quoting the whole of it:

A man seems to have unlimited authority in his own hut, but, as with few exceptions his rule is mild, the domestic and social position of the women is one of comfort and enjoyment. As there is no affected dignity or importance in the men, they do not make mere slaves and drudges of the women; on the contrary, they endure their full share of fatigue and hardship in the coldest season of the year, only calling in the assistance of the women if too wearied themselves to bring in the fruits of their own industry and patience; and at other seasons the women appear to think it a privation not to share the labors of the men. A woman's ordinary occupations are sewing, the preparation of skins for making and mending, cooking, and the general care of the supplies of provisions. Occasionally in the winter she is sent out on the ice for a seal which her husband has taken, to which she is guided by his footmarks; and in spring and summer she takes her place in the boat if required.

The statement in the first sentence that the husband's rule is mild is hardly consistent with that on the following page that " obedience seems to be the great virtue required, and is enforced by blows when necessary, until the man's authority is established." According to our experience the first statement is nearer the truth. We heard of few cases of wife-beating, and those chiefly among the younger men. Two brothers, who habitually ill-treated their wives, were looked upon with disfavor, by some of our friends at least. We heard of one case where a stalwart wife turned the tables on her husband who attempted to abuse her, giving him a thorough beating and then leaving his house.

Wife-beating was not uncommon among the Greenlanders.[2] We did not learn whether a woman brought anything like a dowry, but Simpson[3] says: " The woman's property, consisting of her beads and other ornaments, her needlecase, knife, etc., are considered her own; and if a separation takes place the clothes and presents are returned and she merely takes away with her whatever she brought." According to Crantz[4] a widow in Greenland had no share of her husband's property, but owns only what she brought with her, and I am inclined to believe that this is the case at Point Barrow.

One widow of my acquaintance, who appeared to have no relatives in the village, was reduced almost to beggary, though her husband had been quite well-to-do. All his property and even his boy were taken from her by some of the other natives. Widows who have well-to-do relatives, especially grown-up sons, are well taken care of and often marry again. According to Captain Parry,[5] unprotected widows were robbed at Iglulik.

Children.—From the small number of births which occurred during our stay at Point Barrow, we were able to ascertain little in regard to this subject. When a woman is about to be confined, she is isolated in

[1] Op. cit., p 252.
[2] See Egede, p. 144, " for according to them it signifies nothing that a man beats his wife."
[3] Op. cit., p 253.
[4] Vol. 1, p. 165.
[5] Second Voyage, p. 522.

a little snow hut in winter or a little tent in summer, in which she remains for some time—just how long we were unable to learn. Captain Herendeen saw a pregnant woman in Utkiavwĭñ engaged, on March 31, in building a little snow house, which she told him was meant for her confinement, but she had evidently somehow miscalculated her time, as her child was not born till much later, when the people had moved into the tents. She and her child lived in a little tent on the beach close to her husband's tent, evidently in a sitting position, as the tent was not large enough for her to lie down in. Her husband was desirous of going off on the summer deer hunt, but, under the circumstances, custom forbade his leaving the neighborhood of the village till the ice at sea broke up. The same custom of isolating the women during childbirth has been observed by Kumlien and Boas at Cumberland Gulf[1], and in Greenland the mother was not allowed to eat or drink in the open air.[2] Lisiansky describes a similar practice in Kadiak in 1805,[3] and Klutschak also notes it among the Aivillirnŭiut.[4]

The custom of shutting up the mother and child in a snow house in winter must be very dangerous to the infant, and, in fact, the only child that was born in winter during our stay lived but a short time. Capt. Herendeen visited this family at Nuwŭk shortly after the death of the child, and saw the snow house in which the woman had been confined. He was about to take a drink of water from a dipper which he saw in the iglu, but was prevented by the other people, who told him that this belonged to the mother and that it was "bad" for anyone else to use it. In Greenland the mother had a separate water pail.[5] For a time, our visitors from Utkiavwĭñ were very much afraid to drink out of the tin pannikin in our washroom, for fear it had been used by Nĭăksăra, a woman who had recently suffered a miscarriage. One man told us that a sore on his face was caused by his having inadvertently done so. This same woman was forbidden to go out among the broken ice of the land floe, during the spring succeeding her miscarriage, though she might go out on the smooth shore ice. Her husband also was forbidden to work with a hammer or adz or to go seal-catching for some time after the mishap.

Children are nursed until they are 3 or 4 years old, according to what appears to be the universal habit among Eskimo, and which is probably due, as generally supposed, to the fact that the animal food on which the parents subsist is not fit for the nourishment of young children. The child is carried naked on the mother's back under her clothes, and held up by the girdle, tied higher than usual. When she wishes to nurse it, she loosens her girdle and slips it round to the breast

---

[1] Contributions, p. 28, and "Central Eskimo," p. 610.

[2] Egede, p. 192; Crantz, vol. 1, p. 215, and Rink, Tales, etc., p. 54.

[3] Voyage, p, 200.

[4] "Als Eskimo, etc.," p. 199.

[5] Egede, p. 192; Crantz, vol. 1, p. 215, "no one else must drink out of their cup;" and Rink, Tales and Traditions, p. 54

without bringing it out into the air. Children are carried in this way until they are able to walk and often later.

A large child sits astride of his mother's back, with one leg under each of her arms, and has a little suit of clothes in which he is dressed when the mother wishes to set him down. When the child is awake, this hood is thrown back and the child raised quite high so that he looks over his mother's shoulder, who then covers her head with a cloth or something of the sort. The woman appears to be very little inconvenienced by her burden, and goes about her work as usual, and the child does not seem to be disturbed by her movements. The little girls often act as nurses and carry the infants around on their backs, in the same way. It is no unusual sight to see a little girl of ten or twelve carrying a well grown, heavy child in this way.

This custom or a very similar one seems to prevail among the Eskimo generally. In Greenland, the nurse wears a garment especially designed for carrying the child, an amaut, i. e., a garment that is so wide in the back as to hold a child, which generally tumbles in it quite naked and is accommodated with no other swaddling clothes or cradle.[1] In East Greenland, according to Capt. Holm, "Saa længe Børnene ere smaa, bæres de i det fri paa Moderens Ryg."[2]

Petitot's description of the method of carrying the children in the Mackenzie district is so naïve that it deserves to be quoted entire.[3]

> Les mères qui allaitent portent une jaquette ample et serrée autour des reins par une ceinture. Elles y enferment leur chère progéniture qu'elles peuvent, par ce moyen, allaiter sans l'exposer à un froid qui lui serait mortel. Ces jeunes enfants sont sans aucun vêtement jusqu'à l'âge d'environ deux ans. Quant aux incongruités que ces petites créatures peuvent se permettre sur le dos de leur mère, qui leur sert de calorifère, l'amour maternel, le même chez tous les peuples, les endure patiemment et avec indifférence.

At Fury and Hecla Straits, according to Parry[4], the children are carried in the hood, which is made specially large on purpose, but sometimes also on the back, as at Point Barrow. The enormous hoods of the Eskimo women in Labrador also served to hold the child. The same custom prevails at Cumberland Gulf.[5] In some localities, for instance the north shore of Hudson's Straits, where the woman wear very long and loose boots, the children are said to be carried in these.[6] Franklin[7] refers to the same custom "east of the Mackenzie River." The Siberian children, however, are dressed in regular swaddling clothes of deerskin, with a sort of diaper of dried moss.[8]

We never heard of a single case of infanticide, and, indeed, children

---

[1] Crantz, vol. 1, p. 138. See also Egede, p. 131, and the picture in Rink's Tales, etc., opposite p. 8.
[2] Geografisk Tidskrift, vol. 8, p. 91.
[3] Monographie, etc., p. xv.
[4] Second Voyage, p. 495.
[5] Kumlien, Contributions, p. 24.
[6] See Ellis, Voyage, etc., p. 136, and plate opposite p. 132.
[7] Second Ex., p. 226.
[8] Nordenskiöld, Vega, vol. 2, p. 101.

were so scarce and seemed so highly prized that we never even thought of inquiring if infanticide was ever practiced. Nevertheless, Simpson speaks of the occurrence of a case during the Plover's visit; "but a child, they say, is destroyed only when afflicted with disease of a fatal tendency, or, in scarce seasons, when one or both parents die.[1]" Infanticide, according to Bessels, is frequently practiced among the Eskimo of Smith Sound, without regard of sex,[2] and Schwatka speaks of female infanticide to a limited extent among the people of King William's Land.[3]

The affection of parents for their children is extreme, and the children seem to be thoroughly worthy of it. They show hardly a trace of the fretfulness and petulance so common among civilized children, and though indulged to an extreme extent are remarkably obedient. Corporal punishment appears to be absolutely unknown and the children are rarely chidden or punished in any way. Indeed, they seldom deserve it, for, in spite of the freedom which they are allowed, they do not often get into any mischief, especially of a malicious sort, but attend quietly to their own affairs and their own amusements.

The older children take very good care of the smaller ones. It is an amusing sight to see a little boy of six or seven patronizing and protecting a little toddler of two or three. Children rarely cry except from actual pain or terror, and even then little ones are remarkably patient and plucky. The young children appear to receive little or no instruction except what they pick up in their play or from watching their elders.

Boys of six or seven begin to shoot small birds and animals and to hunt for birds' eggs, and when they reach the age of twelve or fourteen are usually intrusted with a gun and seal spear and accompany their fathers to the hunt. Some of them soon learn to be very skillful hunters. We know one boy not over thirteen years old who, during the winter of 1881–'82, had his seal nets set like the men and used to visit them regularly, even in the roughest weather. Lads of fourteen or fifteen are sometimes regular members of the whaling crews. In the meantime the little girls are learning to sew, in imitation of their mothers, and by the time they are twelve years old they take their share of the cooking and other housework and assist in making the clothes for the family. They still, however, have plenty of leisure to play with the other children until they are old enough to be married.

Affection for their children seems a universal trait among the Eskimo and there is scarcely an author who does not speak in terms of commendation of the behavior and disposition of the Eskimo children. Some of these passages are so applicable to the people of Point Barrow that I can not forbear quoting them. Egede says:[4]

They have a very tender Love for their Children, and the Mother always carries the infant Child about with her upon her back. * * * They suck them till they are

---

[1] Op. cit., p. 250.　　　　　　　　[2] Naturalist, vol. 18, pt. 9, p. 874.
[3] Science, vol. 4, p. 544.　　　　　[4] Greenland, p. 146.

three or four years old or more, because, in their tender Infancy, they cannot digest the strong Victuals that the rest must live upon. The Education of their Children is what they seem little concerned about, for they never make use of whipping or hard words to correct them when they do anything amiss, but leave them to their own Discretion. Notwithstanding which, when they are grown, they never seem inclined to Vice or Roguery, which is to be admired. It is true, they show no great Respect to their Parents in any outward Forms, but always are very willing to do what they order them, though sometimes they will bid their Parents do it themselves.

According to Capt. Holm,[1] in East Greenland, "De opvoxe i den mest ubundne Frihed. Forældrene nære en ubeskrivelig Kjærlighed til dem og straffe dem derfor aldrig, selv om de ere nok saa gjenstridige. Man maa imidlertid beundre, hvor velopdragne de smaa alligevel ere."

Parry speaks still more strongly:[2]

The affection of parents for their children was frequently displayed by these people, not only in the mere passive indulgence and abstinence from corporal punishment for which Esquimaux have been before remarked, but by a thousand playful endearments also, such as parents and nurses practice in our own country. Nothing, indeed, can well exceed the kindness with which they treat their children. * * * It must be confessed, indeed, that the gentleness and docility of the children are such as to occasion their parents little trouble and to render severity towards them quite unnecessary. Even from their earliest infancy, they possess that quiet disposition, gentleness of demeanor, and uncommon evenness of temper, for which in more mature age they are for the most part distinguished. Disobedience is scarcely ever known; a word or even a look from a parent is enough; and I never saw a single instance of that frowardness and disposition to mischief which, in our youth, so often requires the whole attention of a parent to watch over and to correct. They never cry from trifling accidents, and sometimes not even from very severe hurts, at which an English child would sob for an hour. It is, indeed, astonishing to see the indifference with which, even as tender infants, they bear the numerous blows they accidentally receive when carried at their mothers' backs.

I should be willing to allow this passage to stand as a description of the Point Barrow children. It is interesting to compare with these passages Nordenskiöld's account[3] of the children at Pitlekaj, who, if not as he and other writers believe, of pure Chukch blood, are at any rate of mixed Chukch and Eskimo descent:

The children are neither chastised nor scolded. They are, however, the best behaved I have ever seen. Their behavior in the tent is equal to that of the best brought up European children in the parlor. They are not perhaps so wild as ours, but are addicted to games which closely resemble those common among us in the country. Playthings are also in use. * * * If the parents get any delicacy they always give each of their children a bit, and there is never any quarrel as to the size of each child's portion. If a piece of sugar is given to one of the children in a crowd it goes from mouth to mouth round the whole company. In the same way the child offers its father and mother a taste of the bit of sugar or piece of bread it has got. Even in childhood the Chukchs are exceedingly patient. A girl who fell down from the ship's stairs head foremost and thus got so violent a blow that she was almost deprived of hearing scarcely uttered a cry. A boy three or four years of age, much rolled up in furs, who fell down into a ditch cut in the ice on the ship's deck, and in consequence of his inconvenient dress could not get up, lay quietly still until he was observed and helped up by one of the crew.

---

[1] Geografisk Tidskrift, vol 8, p. 91.
[2] Second Voyage, p. 529.
[3] Vega, vol. 2, p. 140.

The only extraordinary thing about the Chukch children is their large number, mentioned by the same author.[1] This looks as if the infusion of new blood had increased the fertility of the race. All authors who have described Eskimo of unmixed descent agree in regard to the generally small number of their offspring. Other accounts of Eskimo children are to be found in the writings of Bessels,[2] Crantz,[3] Schwatka,[4] Gilder,[5] J. Simpson,[6] and Hooper.[7]

The custom of adoption is as universal at Point Barrow as it appears to be among the Eskimo generally, and the adopted children are treated by the parents precisely as if they were their own flesh and blood. Orphans are readily provided for, as there are always plenty of families ready and willing to take them, and women who have several children frequently give away one or more of them. Families that have nothing but boys often adopt a girl, and, of course, vice versa, and we know of one case where a woman who had lost a young infant had another given her by one of her friends.

This very general custom of giving away children, as well as the habit already mentioned of temporarily exchanging wives, rendered it quite difficult to ascertain the parentage of any person, especially as it seems to be the custom with them to speak of first cousins as "mĭlu ataúzĭk" ("one breast," that is, brothers and sisters). While a boy is desired in the family, since he will be the support of his father when the latter grows too old to hunt, a girl is almost as highly prized, for not only will she help her mother with the cares of housekeeping when she grows up, but she is likely to obtain a good husband who may be induced to become a member of his father-in-law's family.[8]

RIGHTS AND WRONGS.

I have already spoken of the feelings of these people in regard to offenses against property and crimes of violence. As to the relations between the sexes there seems to be the most complete absence of what we consider moral feelings. Promiscuous sexual intercourse between married or unmarried people, or even among children, appears to be looked upon simply as a matter for amusement. As far as we could learn unchastity in a girl was considered nothing against her, and in fact one girl who was a most abandoned and shameless prostitute among the sailors, and who, we were told, had had improper relations with some of her own race, had no difficulty in obtaining an excellent husband.

Remarks of the most indecent character are freely bandied back and forth between the sexes in public, and are received with shouts of laughter by the bystanders. Nevertheless, some of the women, espe

---

[1] Vega, vol. 1, p. 449.
[2] Naturalist, vol. 18, pt. 9, p. 874.
[3] History of Greenland, vol. 1, p. 162.
[7] Tents, etc., pp. 24, 201.

[4] Science, vol. 4, No. 98, p. 544.
[5] Schwatka's Search, p. 287.
[6] Op. cit., p. 250.

[8] Accounts of this custom of adoption are to be found in Crantz, vol. 1, p. 165; Parry, Second Voyage, p. 531; Kumlien, Contributions, p. 17; Gilder, Schwatka's Search, p. 247, and the passage concerning children quoted above, from Dr. Simpson.

cially those of the wealthier class, preserve a very tolerable degree of conjugal fidelity and certainly do not prostitute themselves to the sailors. I believe that prostitution for gain is unknown among themselves, but it is carried to a most shameless extent with the sailors of the whaling fleet by many of the women, and is even considered a laudable thing by the husbands and fathers, who are perfectly willing to receive the price of their wives' or daughters' frailty, especially if it takes the form of liquor. Dr. Simpson[1] says: "It is said by themselves that the women are very continent before marriage, as well as faithful afterward to their husbands; and this seems to a certain extent true." But he goes on to add: "In their conduct toward strangers the elderly women frequently exhibit a shameless want of modesty, and the men an equally shameless indifference, except for the reward of their partner's frailty." It seems to me that he must have been deceived by the natives concerning the first statement, since the immorality of these people among themselves, as we witnessed it, seems too purely animal and natural to be of recent growth or the result of foreign influence. Moreover, a similar state of affairs has been observed among Eskimo elsewhere, notably at Iglulik at the time of Parry's visit.[2]

SOCIAL LIFE AND CUSTOMS.

Personal habits, cleanliness, etc.—Though the idea of cleanliness among these people differs considerably from our ideas, they are as a rule far from being as filthy as they appear at first sight. Considering the difficulty of obtaining water, even for purposes of drinking, in the winter season, the iglu, unless dirty work, like the dressing of skins, etc., is going on, is kept remarkably clean. The floor and walls are scrupulously scraped and all dirt is immediately wiped up. They are particularly careful not to bring in any snow or dirt on their feet, and the snow and hoar frost is carefully brushed off from the outer garment, which is often removed before entering the room and left in the passage. They are also careful not to spit on the floor or in the passage, but use for this purpose the large urine tub. This is practically the only offensive object in the house, as it is freely used by both sexes in the presence of the rest. This is done, however, with less exposure and immodesty than one would suppose.[3]

---

[1] Op. cit., p. 252.

[2] Second Voyage, p. 529.

[3] Compare Nordenskiöld's account of the comparative cleanliness of the Chukch dwellings at Pitlekaj: "On the other hand it may be stated that in order not to make a stay in the confined tent chamber too uncomfortable certain rules are strictly observed. Thus, for instance, it is not permitted in the interior of the tent to spit on the floor, but this must be done into a vessel which, in case of necessity, is used as a night utensil. In every outer tent there lies a specially curved reindeer horn, with which snow is removed from the clothes; the outer *pesk* is usually put off before one goes into the inner tent, and the shoes are carefully freed from snow. The carpet of walrus skins which covers the floor of the inner tent is accordingly dry and clean. Even the outer tent is swept clean and free from loose snow, and the snow is daily shoveled away from the tent doors with a spade of whalebone. Every article, both in the outer and inner tent, is laid in its proper place, and so on." (Vega, vol. 2, p. 104.)

The contents of this vessel, being mixed with feces, is not fit for tanning skins, etc., and is consequently thrown out doors. The men use a small tub (kuovwĭñ) as a urinal, and the contents of this is carefully saved. Though the interior of the house is thus kept clean, as much can not be said for its surroundings. All manner of rubbish and filth is simply thrown out upon the ground, without regard to decency or comfort, and this becomes exceedingly offensive when the snow melts in summer. The only scavengers are the dogs, who greedily devour old pieces of skin, refuse meat, and even feces. In regard to personal cleanliness, there is considerable difference between individuals. Some people, especially the poorer women and children, are not only careless about their clothes, going about dressed in ragged, greasy, filthy garments, but seldom wash even their faces and hands, much less their whole persons. One of these women, indeed, was described by her grown-up daughter as "That woman with the black on her nose."

On the other hand most of the wealthier people appear to take pride in being neatly clad, and, except when actually engaged in some dirty work, always have their faces and hands, at least, scrupulously clean and their hair neatly combed. Even the whole person is sometimes washed in spite of the scarcity of water. Many are glad to get soap (íɐkăkun) and use it freely. Lieut. Ray says that his two guides, Mû′ñialu and Apaidyào, at the end of a day's march would never sit down to supper without washing their faces and hands with soap and water, and combing their hair, and I recollect that once, when I went over to the village to get a young man to start with Lieut. Ray on a boat journey, he would not start until he had hunted up a piece of soap and washed his face and hands. These people, of course, practice the usual Eskimo habit of washing themselves with freshly passed urine. This custom arises not only from the scarcity of water and the difficulty of heating it, but from the fact that the ammonia of the urine is an excellent substitute for soap in removing the grease with which the skin necessarily becomes soiled.[1] This fact is well known to our whalemen, who are in the habit of saving their urine to wash the oily clothes with. The same habit is practiced by the "Chukches" of eastern Siberia.[2] All, however, get more or less shabby and dirty in the summer, when they are living in tents and boats. All are more or less infested with lice, and they are in the habit of searching each others' heads for these, which they eat, after the fashion of so many other savages. They have also another filthy habit—that of eating the mucus from the nostrils. A similar practice was noticed in Greenland by Egede,[3] who goes on quaintly to say: "Thus they make good the old proverb, 'What drips from the nose falls into the mouth, that nothing may be lost.'"

---

[1] Compare Dall. Alaska, p. 20.
[2] See Nordenskiöld, Vega, vol. 2, p. 104.
[3] Greenland, p. 127.

Salutation.—We had no opportunity of witnessing any meeting between these people and strange Eskimo, so that it is impossible to tell whether they practice any particular form of salutation on such occasions. We saw nothing of the kind among themselves. White men are saluted with shouts of "Nakurúk!" (good), and some Eskimo have learned to shake hands. They no longer practice the common Eskimo salutation of rubbing noses, but say that they once did. Sergt. Middleton Smith, of our party, informs me that he once saw a couple of natives in Capt. Herendeen's trading store give an exhibition of the way this salutation was formerly practiced.

This custom was perhaps falling into disuse as early as 1837, since Thomas Simpson,[1] in describing his reception at Point Barrow, says: "We were not, however, either upon this or any other occasion, favored with the kooniks or nose-rubbing salutations that have so annoyed other travelers." Mr. Elson, however, expressly states that the people, probably Utkiavwĩñmiun, whom he met at Refuge Inlet eleven years before, rubbed noses and cheeks with him[2] and Maguire[3] narrates how the head of the party of visitors from Point Hope saluted him. He says: "He fixed his forehead against mine and used it as a fulcrum to rub noses several times."

Healing.—As is the case with Eskimo generally, these people rely for curing disease chiefly upon the efforts of certain persons who have the power of exorcising the supernatural beings by whom the disease is caused. A large number of men and, I believe, some women were supposed to have this power and exercise it in cases of sickness, in some instances, at least, upon the payment of a fee. These people correspond closely to the angekut of the Greenlanders and Eastern Eskimo, and the so-called "shamans" of southern Alaska, but, as far as we could see, do not possess the power and influence usually elsewhere ascribed to this class.

It was exceedingly difficult to obtain any definite information concerning these people, and we only discovered casually that such and such a person was a "doctor" by hearing that he had been employed in a certain case of sickness, or to perform some ceremony of incantation. We did not even succeed in learning the name of this class of people, who, in talking with us, would call themselves "tûktĕ," as they did our surgeon. On one occasion some of the party happened to visit the house of a sick man where one of these "doctors" was at work. He sat facing the entrance of the house, beating his drum at intervals, and making a babbling noise with his lips, followed by long speeches addressed to something down the trapdoor, bidding it "go!" We were given to understand that these speeches were addressed to a tuᴙña or supernatural being.[4] Their only idea of direct treatment of disease is

---

[1] Narrative, p. 155.

[2] Beechy's Voyage p. 312.

[3] N. W. Passage, p. 385.

[4] Dr. Simpson says (op. cit., p. 275): "Diseases are also considered to be turn'gaks."

apparently to apply a counterirritant by scarification of the surface of the part affected.

We know of one case where a sufferer from some liver complaint had inflicted on himself, or had had inflicted upon him, quite a considerable cut on the right side with a view of relieving the pain. We also know of several cases where the patients had themselves cut on the scalp or back to relieve headache or rheumatism, and one case where the latter disorder, I believe, had been treated by a severe cut on the side of the knee. A similar practice has been observed at Plover Bay, Siberia, by Hooper,[1] who also mentions the use of a kind of seton for the relief of headache.

They also practice a sort of rough-and-ready surgery, as in the case of the man already mentioned, whose feet had both been amputated. One of the men who lost the tip of his forefinger by the explosion of a cartridge was left with a stump of bone protruding at the end of the finger. Our surgeon attempted to treat this, but after two unsuccessful trials to etherize the patient he was obliged to give it up. When, however, the young man's father-in-law, who was a noted "doctor," came home he said at once that the stump must come off, and the patient had to submit to the operation without ether. The "doctor" tried to borrow Dr. Oldmixon's bone forceps, and when these were refused him cut the bone off, I believe, with a chisel. They appear to have no cure for blindness. We heard nothing of the curious process of "couching" described by Egede in Greenland, p. 121. We had no opportunity of observing their methods of treating wounds or other external injuries. Sufferers were very glad to be treated by our surgeon, and eagerly accepted his medicines, though he had considerable difficulty in making them obey his directions about taking care of themselves.

After they had been in the habit of receiving the surgeon's medicine for some time, one of the Utkiavwiñ natives gave Capt. Herendeen what he said was their own medicine. It is a tiny bit of turf which they called nuna kiñmölq, and which, therefore, probably came from the highland of the upper Meade River, which region bears the name of Kiñmölq. We were able to get very little information about this substance, but my impression is that it was said to be administered internally, and I believe was specially recommended for bleeding at the lungs. Possibly this is the same as "the black moss that grows on the mountain," which, according to Crantz[2] was eaten by the Greenlanders to stop blood-spitting.

CUSTOMS CONCERNING THE DEAD.

Abstentions.—From the fact that we did not hear of any of the deaths until after their occurrence, we were able to learn very few of their

[1] Tents, etc., p. 185.
[2] Vol. 1, p. 235

customs concerning the dead. The few observations we were able to make agree in the main with those made elsewhere. For instance, we learned with tolerable certainty that the relatives of the dead, at least, must abstain from working on wood with an ax or hammer for a certain period—I believe, four or five days. According to Dall,[1] in the region about Norton Sound the men can not cut wood with an ax for five days after a death has occurred. In Greenland the household of the deceased were obliged to abstain for a while from certain kinds of food and work.[2]

A woman from Utkiavwĭñ, who came over to the station one day in the autumn of 1881, declined to sew on clothing, even at our house, because, as she told Lieut. Ray, there was a dead man in the village who had not yet been carried out to the cemetery and "he would see her." After consulting with her husband, however, she concluded she could protect herself from him by tracing a circle about her on the floor with a snow-knife. In this circle she did the sewing required, and was careful to keep all her work inside of it.

One of the natives informed me that when a man died his labrets were taken out and thrown away. I remember, however, seeing a young man wearing a plug labret of syenite, which he said had belonged to an old man who died early in the winter of 1881–'82. It was perhaps removed before he actually died.

Manner of disposing of the dead.—The corpse is wrapped up in a piece of sailcloth (deerskin was formerly used), laid upon a flat sled, and dragged out by a small party of people—perhaps the immediate relatives of the deceased, though we never happened to see one of these funeral processions except from a distance—to the cemetery, the place where "they sleep on the ground." This place at Utkiavwĭñ is a rising ground about a mile and a half east of the village, near the head of the southwest branch of the Isûtkwa lagoon. At Nuwŭk the main cemetery is at "Nexeurá," between the village and Pernyû. The bodies are laid out upon the ground without any regular arrangement apparently, though it is difficult to be sure of this, as most of the remains have been broken up and scattered by dogs and foxes. With a freshly wrapped body it is almost impossible to tell which is the head and which the feet. We unfortunately never noticed whether the heads were laid toward any particular point of the compass, as has been observed in other localities. Dr. Simpson says that the head is laid to the east at Point Barrow.

Various implements belonging to the deceased are broken and laid beside the corpse, and the sled is sometimes broken and laid over it. Sometimes, however, the latter is withdrawn a short distance from the cemetery and left on the tundra for one moon, after which it is brought back to the village. Most people do not seem to be troubled at having the

---

[1] Alaska, p. 146.
[2] Egede, Greenland, p. 150.

bodies of their relatives disturbed by the dogs or other animals,[1] but we know of one case where the parents of two children who died very nearly at the same time, finding that the dogs were getting at the bodies, raised them on stages of driftwood about 4 or 5 feet high. Similar stages were observed by Hooper at Plover Bay;[2] but this method of disposing of the dead appears to have gone out of use at the present day, since Dall[3] describes the ordinary Siberian method of laying out the dead in ovals of stone as in use at Plover Bay at the time of his visit.

The cemetery at Utkiavwĭñ is not confined to the spot I have mentioned, though most of the bodies are exposed there. A few bodies are also exposed on the other side of the lagoon, and one body, that of a man, was laid out at the edge of the higher tundra, about a mile due east from the station. The body was covered with canvas, staked down all round with broken paddles, and over it was laid a flat sledge with one runner broken.[4] At one end of the body lay a wooden dish, and under the edge of the canvas were broken seal-darts and other spears. The body lay in an east and west line, but we could not tell which end was the head. All sorts of objects were scattered round the cemetery—tools, dishes, and even a few guns—though we saw none that appeared to have been serviceable when exposed, except one Snider rifle. If, as is the case among Eskimo in a good many other places, all the personal property of the deceased is supposed to become unclean and must be exposed with him, it is probable that his friends manage to remove the more valuable articles before he is actually dead.[5]

The method of disposing of the dead varies slightly among the Eskimo in different localities, but the weapons or other implements belonging to the deceased are always laid beside the corpse. The custom at Smith Sound, as described by Bessels,[6] is remarkably like that at Point Barrow. The corpse was wrapped in furs, placed on a sledge, and dragged out and buried in the snow with the face to the west. The sledge was laid over the body and the weapons of the deceased were deposited beside it. Unlike the Point Barrow natives, however, they usually cover the body with stones. In the same passage Dr. Bessels describes a peculiar symbol of mourning, not employed, so far as I can learn, elsewhere. The male mourners plugged up the right nostril with hay and the females the left, and these plugs were worn for several days.

---

[1] Compare Lyon, Journal, p. 269.

[2] Tents, etc., p. 88.

[3] Alaska, p. 382.

[4] Compare Samoyed grave described and figured by Nordenskiöld (Vega, vol. 1, p. 98), where a broken sledge was laid upside down by the grave.

[5] Compare Holm, Geografisk Tidskrift, vol. 8, p. 98: "kun Kostbarheder, saasom Knive eller lignende Jærnsager beholde den afdødes efterladte."—East Greenland.

[6] Naturalist, vol. 18, pt. 9, p. 877.

The custom of covering the body with stones appears to be universally prevalent east of the Mackenzie region.[1]

The bodies seen by Dr. Richardson in the delta of the Mackenzie were wrapped in skins and loosely covered with driftwood,[2] and a similar arrangement was noticed at Kotzebue Sound by Beechey, who figures[3] a sort of little wigwam of driftwood built over the dead man. At Port Clarence Nordenskiöld[4] saw two corpses "laid on the ground, fully clothed, without protection of any coffin, but surrounded by a close fence consisting of a number of tent-poles driven crosswise into the ground. Alongside one of the corpses lay a *kayak* with oars, a loaded double-barreled gun with locks at half-cock and caps on, various other weapons, clothes, tinder-box, snowshoes, drinking-vessels, two masks, * * * and strangely shaped animal figures." On the Siberian coast the dead are sometimes burned.[5]

Nordenskiöld believes that the coast Chukches have perhaps begun to abandon the custom of burning the dead, but I am rather inclined to think that is a custom of the "deermen," which the people of the coast of pure or mixed Eskimo blood never fully adopted. Dall, indeed, was explicitly informed that the custom was only used with the bodies of "good" men, and at the time of Nordenskiöld's visit he found it "at least certain that the people of Pitlekaj exclusively bury their dead by laying them out on the tundra." The body is surrounded by an oval of stones, but apparently not covered with them as in the east.[6] The Krause brothers observed by the bodies, besides "die erwähnten Geräthschaften" [Lanzen, Bogen und Pfeile für die Männer, Koch- und Hausgeräthe für die Weiber], "unter einen kleinen Steinhaufen ein Hunde-, Renthier-, Bären- oder Walross-Schädel." This custom shows a little Children die and are buried, they put the Head of a Dog near the curious resemblance to that described by Egede[7] in Greenland : "When Grave, fancying that Children, having no Understanding, they can not

---

[1] See the passage quoted from Bessels, for Smith Sound; Egede, Greenland, p. 148; Crantz's History of Greenland, vol. 1; p. 237; East Greenland, Holm, Geografisk Tidskrift, vol. 8, p. 98, and Scoresby, Voyage to Northern Whalefishery, p. 213 (where he speaks of finding on the east coast of Greenland graves *dug* and covered with slabs of stone. *Digging* graves is very unusual among the Eskimo, as the nature of the ground on which they live usually forbids it. Parry mentions something similar at Iglulik : "The body was laid in a regular, but shallow grave, * * * covered with flat pieces of limestone" (Second Voyage, p. 551) ; Lyon, Journal, p. 268 (Iglulik) ; Kumlien, Contribution, p. 44 (Cumberland Gulf) ; Hall, Arctic Researches, p. 124 (Baffin Land) ; Rae Narrative, pp. 22 and 187 (northwest shore of Hudson Bay), and Ellis, Voyage to Hudson's Bay, p. 148 (Marble Island). I myself have noticed the same custom at the old Eskimo cemetery near the Hudson Bay post of Rigolette, Hamilton Inlet, on the Labrador coast. Chappel, however, saw a body "closely wrapt in skins and laid in a sort of a gully," Hudson's Bay, p. 113 (north shore Hudson Strait), and Davis's account of what he saw in Greenland is as follows: "We found on shore three dead people, and two of them had their staues lying by them and their olde skins wrapped about them." Hakluyt , Voyages, 1589, p. 788.

[2] Franklin, Second Expedition, p. 192.

[3] Voyage, pl. opposite p. 332.

[4] Vega, vol. 2, p. 238, and figure of grave on p. 239.

[5] See Nordenskiöld, Vega, vol. 2, p. 88, and Dall, Alaska, p. 382.

[6] See Nordenskiöld, Vega, vol. 2, pp. 88-9 (Pitlekaj), and 225 (St. Lawrence Bay) ; Krause Bros., Geographische Blätter, vol. 5, p. 18 (St. Lawrence Bay, East Cape, Indian Point, and Plover Bay) and Dall, Alaska, p. 382.

[7] Greenland, p. 151. See also Crantz, vol. 1, p. 237.

by themselves find the Way, but the Dog must guide them to the Land
of the Souls." The body is usually laid out at full length upon the
ground. Among the ancient Greenlanders,[1] however, and in the Yukon
region the body was doubled up. In the latter region the body was laid
on its side in a box of planks four feet long and raised on four supports[2] or wrapped up in mats and covered with rocks or driftwood.[3]
The custom of inclosing the dead in a short coffin, to judge from the
figures given by the latter writer in Pl. VI. of his report, appears also
to prevail at the mouth of the Kuskokwim. In the island of Kadiak,
according to Dall and Lisiansky,[4] the dead were buried.

GOVERNMENT.

In the family.—I can hardly do better than quote Dr. Simpson's
words, already referred to (op. cit. page 252), on this subject: "A man
seems to have unlimited authority in his own hut." Nevertheless, his
rule seems to be founded on respect and mutual agreement, rather than
on despotic authority. The wife appears to be consulted, as already
stated, on all important occasions, and, to quote Dr. Simpson again
(ibid.): "Seniority gives precedence when there are several women in
one hut, and the sway of the elder in the direction of everything connected with her duties seems never disputed." When more than one
family inhabit the same house the head of each family appears to have
authority over his own relatives, while the relations between the two
are governed solely by mutual agreement.

In the village.—These people have no established form of government
nor any chiefs in the ordinary sense of the word, but appear to be
ruled by a strong public opinion, combined with a certain amount of
respect for the opinions of the elder people, both men and women, and
by a large number of traditional observances like those concerning the
whale fishery, the deceased, etc., already described. In the ordinary
relations of life a person, as a rule, avoids doing anything to his neighbor which he would not wish to have done to himself, and affairs
which concern the community as a whole, as for instance their relations
with us at the station, are settled by a general and apparently informal discussion, when the opinion of the majority carries the day. The
majority appears to have no means, short of individual violence, of en-
forcing obedience to its decisions, but, as far as we could see, the matter is left to the good sense of the parties concerned. Respect for the
opinions of elders is so great that the people may be said to be practically under what is called "simple elder rule."[5] Public opinion has

---

[1] Egede, Greenland, p. 149, and Crantz, vol. 1, p. 237.
[2] Dall, Alaska, pp. 19, 145, and 227.
[3] Petroff, Report, p. 127.
[4] Alaska, p. 403, and Voyage, p. 200.
[5] Compare, among other instances, Capt. Holm's observations in East Greenland: "Som Overhoved i
Huset [which is the village] fungerer den ældeste Mand, naar han er en god Fanger, etc." (Geogr.
Tids., vol. 8, p. 90.)

formulated certain rules in regard to some kinds of property and the division of game, which are remarkably like those noticed among Eskimo elsewhere, and which may be supposed to have grown up among the ancestors of the Eskimo, before their separation.

For instance, in Greenland,[1] "Anyone picking up pieces of driftwood or goods lost at sea or on land was considered the rightful owner of them; and to make good his possession he had only to carry them up above high-water mark and put stones upon them, no matter where his homestead might be." Now, at Point Barrow we often saw the natives dragging driftwood up to the high-water mark, and the owner seemed perfectly able to prove his claim. Lieut. Ray informs me that he has seen men mark such sticks of timber by cutting them with their adzes and that sticks so marked were respected by the other natives. On one occasion, when he was about to have a large piece of drift-timber dragged up to the station, a woman came up and proved that the timber belonged to her by pointing out the freshly cut mark. I have myself seen a native claim a barrel which had been washed ashore, by setting it up on end.

As far as we could learn, the smaller animals, as for instance, birds, the smaller seals, reindeer, etc., are the property of the hunter, instead of being divided as in some other localities, for example at Smith Sound.[2] The larger seals and walruses appeared to be divided among the boat's crew, the owner of the boat apparently keeping the tusks of the walrus and perhaps the skin. A bear, however, both flesh and skin, is equally divided among all who in any way had a hand in the killing. We learned this with certainty from having to purchase the skin of a bear killed at the village, where a number of men had been engaged in the hunt. When a whale is taken, as I have already said, the whalebone is equally divided among the crews of all the boats in sight at the time of killing. All comers, however, have a right to all the flesh, blubber, and blackskin that they can cut off.[3]

Dr. Rink, in describing the social order of the ancient Greenlanders,[4] says: " Looking at what has been said regarding the rights of property and the division of the people into certain communities, in connection with the division of property into the classes just given, we are led to the conclusion that the right of any individual to hold more than a certain amount of property was, if not regulated by law, at least jealously watched by the rest of the community, and that virtually

---

[1] Rink, Tales and Traditions, p. 28. Compare also Crantz, vol. 1. p. 181.

[2] Bessels, Naturalist, vol. 23, pt. p. 873.

[3] Compare Rink, Tales, etc., p. 29: " But if an animal of the largest size, more especially a whale, was captured, it was considered common property, and as indiscriminately belonging to every one who might come and assist in flensing it, whatever place he belonged to and whether he had any share in capturing the animal or not." (Greenland). Gilder (Schwatka's Search, p. 190) says that on the northwest shore of Hudson Bay all who arrive while a walrus is being cut up are entitled to a share of it, though the man who struck it has the first choice of pieces. At East Cape, Siberia, the Krause Brothers learned: " Wird nämlich ein Walfisch gefangen, so hat jeder Ortsbewohner das Recht, so viel Fleisch zu nehmen, als er abzuschneiden vermag." (Geographische Blätter, vol. 5, pt. 2, p. 120).

[4] Tales, etc., p. 29.

the surplus of any individual or community, fixed by the arbitrary rate which tradition or custom had assigned, was made over to those who had less." At Point Barrow, however, the idea of individual ownership appears to be much more strongly developed. As far as we could learn, there is no limit to the amount of property which an individual, at least the head of a family, may accumulate. Even though the whalebone be, as already described, divided among all the boats' crews " in at the death," no objection is made to one man buying it all up, if he has the means, for his own private use.

This has given rise to a regular wealthy and aristocratic class, who, however, are not yet sufficiently differentiated from the poorer people to refuse to associate on any terms but those of social equality. The men of this class are the umialiks, a word which appears in many corrupted forms on the coast of Western America and is often supposed to mean " chief." Dr. Simpson[1] says: "The chief men are called O-méliks (wealthy)," but " wealthy " is an explanation of the position of these men, and not a translation of the title, which, as we obtained it, is precisely the same as the Greenland word for *owner of a boat*, umialik (from umia(k), and the termination lĭk or lĭ-ñ. This is one of the few cases in which the final k is sounded at Point Barrow as in Greenland).

Dr. Rink has already observed[2] that the word used by Simpson "no doubt must be the same as the Greenlandish umialik, signifying owner of a boat," and as I heard the title more than once carefully pronounced at Point Barrow it was the identical word. The umialiks, as Simpson says,[3] " have acquired their position by being more thrifty and intelligent, better traders, and usually better hunters, as well as physically stronger and more daring."[4] They have acquired a certain amount of influence and respect from these reasons, as well as from their wealth, which enables them to purchase the services of others to man their boats, but appear to have absolutely no authority outside of their own families.[5] Petroff[6] considers them as a sort of " middlemen or spokesmen," who make themselves " prominent by superintending all intercourse and traffic with visitors."

This sort of prominence, however, appears to have been conferred upon them by the traders, who, ignorant of the very democratic state of Eskimo society, naturally look for " chiefs" to deal with. They pick out the best looking and best dressed man in the village and endeavor to win his favor by giving him presents, receiving him into the cabin, and conducting all their dealings with the natives through him. The chief,

[1] Op. cit , p. 272.
[2] Tales, etc., p. 25.
[3] Op. cit.
[4] Compare what the Krause Brothers say of the "chiefs" on the Siberian coast (Geographische Blätter, vol. 5, pt. 1, p. 29): " Die Autorität, welche die obenerwähnten Männer augenscheinlich ausüben, ist wohl auf Rechnung ihres grösseren Besitzes zu setzen. Der "Chief" is jedes Mal der reichste Mann, ein 'big man.' "
[5] See, also, Dr. Simpson, op. cit., p. 273.
[6] Report, etc., p. 125.

thus selected, is generally shrewd enough to make the most of the greatness thrust upon him, and no doubt often pretends to more influence and power than he actually possesses.[1]

As to the story of the whalemen, that the "chieftainship" is the reward of the best fighter, who holds it like a "challenge cup," subject to being called out at any time to defend his rank in a duel, as far as concerns Point Barrow, this is a sheer fable, perhaps invented by the Eskimo to impose upon the strangers, but more likely the result of misunderstanding and a vivid imagination on the part of the whites. Among umialiks, one or two appear to have more wealth and influence than the rest. Tcuñaura in Utkiavwĭñ and the late Katiga at Nuwŭk were said, according to Captain Herendeen, to be "great umialiks" and Tcuñaura was always spoken of as the foremost man in Utkiavwĭñ. We knew of one party coming up from Sidaru with presents for Tcuñaura, and were informed that the other Eskimo never sold to him, but only gave him presents. It was also said that Katiga's infant son would one day be a "great umialik."

All these men are or have been captains of whaling umiaks, and the title umialiks appears to be applied to them in this capacity, since many of the poorer men, who, as far as we could learn, were not considered umialiks, own umiaks which they do not fit out for whaling, but use only to transport their families from place to place in the summer.

RELIGION.

General ideas.—It was exceedingly difficult to get any idea of the religious belief of the people, partly from our inability to make ourselves understood in regard to abstract ideas and partly from ignorance on our part of the proper method of conducting such inquiries. For instance, in trying to get at their ideas of a future life, we could only ask "Where does a man go when he dies?" to which we, of course, received the obvious answer, "To the cemetery!" Moreover, such a multitude of other and easier lines of investigation presented themselves for our attention that we were naturally inclined to neglect the difficult field of religion, and besides under the circumstances of our intercourse it was almost impossible to get the attention of the natives when their minds were not full of other subjects.

Nevertheless, many of the fragments of superstition and tradition that we were able to collect agree remarkably with what has been observed among the Eskimo elsewhere, so that it is highly probable that their religion is of the same general character as that of the Greenlanders, namely, a belief in a multitude of supernatural beings, who are to be exorcised or propitiated by various observances, especially by the performances of certain specially gifted people, who are something of the nature of wizards. So much has been written by many authors

[1] Compare the case of the alleged "chiefs" of the Chukches, in Nordenskiöld's Vega, vol. 1, pp. 449 and 495.

about these wizards or " doctors," the angekut of the eastern Eskimo, the so-called " shamans " of Alaska and Siberia, that I need make no special reference to their writings except where they happen to throw light on our own observations. Dr. Simpson succeeded in obtaining more information concerning the religious belief of these people than our party was able to do, and his observations,[1] to which ours are in some degree supplementary, tend to corroborate the conclusion at which I have arrived.

Our information in regard to the special class of wizards was rather vague. We learned that many men in the village, distinguishable from the rest by no visible characteristics, were able to heal the sick, procure good weather, favorable winds, plenty of game, and do other things by "talking" and beating the drum. We did not learn the number of these men in either village, but we heard of very many different men doing one or the other of these things, while others of our acquaintance never attempted them. Neither did we learn that any one of these men was considered superior to the rest, as appears to be the case in some regions, nor how a man could attain this power. Some of these men, who appeared to give particular attention to curing the sick, called themselves " tû′ktĕ" ("doctor"), but, probably for want of properly directed inquiries, we did not learn the Eskimo name of these people. We were definitely informed, however, that their " talk," when treating disease or trying to obtain fair weather, etc., was addressed to " tu′ʁña," or a supernatural being. This name, of course, differs only in dialectic form from that applied in other places to the universal familiar spirits of Eskimo superstition.

We at first supposed that "tuʁña" meant some particular individual demon, but Dr. Simpson is probably right in saying that the Point Barrow natives, like the rest of the Eskimo, recognize a host of tuʁñain, since " tuʁña" was described to us under a variety of forms. Most of the natives whom we asked if they had seen tuʁña, said that they had not, but that other men, mentioning certain " doctors," had seen him. One man, however, said that he had seen tuʁña in the kûdyĭgĭ, when the people "talked" sitting in the dark, with their heads bowed and faces covered, and tuʁña came with a noise like a great bird.[2] He had raised his head and saw tuʁña, like a man with bloodless cheeks.[3] Tuʁña again was called "a bad man, dead" (appar-

---

[1] Op. cit., p. 273 et seq.

[2] Compare Graah's account of the ceremony of summoning a *torngak* in East Greenland (Narrative, p. 123). "Come he did, however, at last, and his approach was announced by a strange rushing sound, very like the sound of a *large bird* flying beneath the roof." (The italics are my own.) The *angekut* evidently have some juggling contrivance, carefully concealed from laymen, perhaps of the nature of a "whizzing-stick."

[3] Compare Rink's description of the ceremony of summoning a tornak to ask his advice, in Greenland (Tales, etc., p. 60). This was performed before a company in a darkened house. The angekok lay on the floor, beside a suspended skin and drum, with his hands tied behind his back and his head between his legs. A song was sung by the audience, and the angekok invoked his tornak, beating on the skin and the drum. The spirit announced his arrival by a peculiar sound and the appearance of a light or fire.

ently a ghost), sometimes as large as a man and sometimes dwarfish, sometimes a fleshless skeleton, while one man, to describe him, made the same grimace that a white man would use to indicate a hobgoblin, with staring eyes, gaping mouth, and hands outstretched like claws. Apparently "tuɐña" in conversation with us was used to designate all the various supernatural objects of their belief, ghosts as well as familiar spirits. For instance, in Greenland, according to Rink,[1] a ghost "manifests himself by whistling or singing in the ears." Now, Lieut. Ray was walking rapidly one day in the winter with an Eskimo and his wife, and the woman suddenly stopped and said she "heard tuɐña"—that he made a noise like *singing in the ears.*

The people generally have a great dread of "tuɐña," who they say would kill them, and are very averse to going out alone in the dark. One of each party that came over from the village in the evening usually carried a drawn knife, preferably one of the large double-edged knives, supposed to be Siberian and already described, in his hand as defense against tuɐña, and a drawn knife was sometimes even carried in the daylight "nanumunlu tuɐñamunlu," "for bear and demon." Notwithstanding their apparently genuine dread of "tuɐña," they are by no means averse to talking or even joking about him.

The knife also serves as a protection against the aurora, which most of them agree is bad, and when bright likely to kill a person by striking him in the back of the neck. However, brandishing the knife at it will keep it off. Besides, as a woman told me one night, you can drive off a "bad" aurora by throwing at it dog's excrement and urine.[2]

Lieut. Ray saw in one of the houses in Utkaiwiñ, a contrivance for frightening away a "tuɐña" from the entrance to a house should he try to get in. The man had hung in the trapdoor the handle of a seal-drag by means of a thong spiked to the wall with a large knife, and told Lieut. Ray that if "tuɐña" tried to get into the house he would undoubtedly catch hold of the handle to help himself up, which would pull down the knife upon his head and frighten him off. We never had an opportunity of witnessing the ceremony of summoning "tuɐña," nor did we ever hear of the ceremony taking place during our stay at the station, but we were fortunate enough to observe several other performances, though they do not appear to be frequent. The ceremony of healing the sick and the ceremonies connected with the whale-fishery have already been described.

On the 21st of February, 1883, Lieut. Ray and Capt. Herendeen happened to be at the village on time to see the tuɐña, who had been causing the bad weather, expelled from the village. Some of the natives said the next day that they had *killed* the tuɐña, but they said at the same time he had gone "a long way off." When Lieut. Ray reached

---

[1] Tales, etc., p. 14.

[2] Compare Rink (Tales, etc. p. 56): "Several fetid and stinking matters, such as old urine, are excellent means for keeping away all kinds of evil-intentioned spirits and ghosts."

the village, women were standing at the doors of the houses armed
with snow-knives and clubs with which they made passes over the entrance when the people inside called out. He entered one house and
found a woman vigorously driving the tuɐña out of every corner with
a knife. They then repaired to the kûdyĭgi, where there were ten or
twelve people, each of whom, to quote from Lieut. Ray's note book,
"made a charge against the evil spirit, telling what injuries they had
received from it." Then they went into the open air, where a fire had
been built in front of the entrance, and formed a half circle around the
fire. Each then went up and made a speech, bending over the fire
(according to Simpson, who describes a similar ceremony at Nuwŭk on p.
274 of his paper, coaxing the tuɐña to come under the fire to warm himself). Then they brought out a large tub full of urine, to which, Simpson says, each man present had contributed, and held it ready near the
fire, while two men stood with their rifles in readiness, and a boy stood
near the fire with a large stone in his hands, bracing himself firmly
with his feet spread apart for a vigorous throw. Then they chanted as
follows (the words of this chant were obtained afterward by the
writer):

> Tâk tâk tâk tohâ!
> Nìju'a hâ!
> He! he! he!
> Haiyahe!
> Yaiyahe!
> Hwı!

And instantly the contents of the tub were dashed on the fire, the
stone thrown into the embers, and both men discharged their rifles, one
into the embers, and one into the cloud of steam as it rose. Then all
brushed their clothes violently and shouted, and the tuɐña was killed.
By a fortunate coincidence, the next day was the finest we had had
for a long time.

Sacrifices are also occasionally made to these supernatural beings as
in Greenland "gifts were offered to the inue of certain rocks, capes and
ice firths, principally when traveling and passing those places."[1]

Capt. Herendeen, in the fall of 1882, went to the rivers in company
with one of the "doctors." When they arrived at the river Kuaru,
where the latter intended to stay for the fishing, he got out his drum and
"talked" for a long time, and breaking off very small pieces of tobacco
threw them into the air, crying out, "Tuɐña, tuɐña, I give you tobacco!
give me plenty of fish." When they passed the dead men at the
cemetery, he gave them tobacco in the same way, asking them also for
fish.[2] We noticed but few other superstitious observances which have
not been already described. As in Greenland and elsewhere, superstition requires certain persons to abstain from certain kinds of food.
For instance, Mûñialu, and apparently many others, were not permitted

---

[1] Rink, Tales, etc., p. 56.

[2] "When an Innuit passes the place where a relative has died, he pauses and deposits a piece of meat
near by." Baffin Land, Hall, Artic Researches, p. 574.

to eat the burbot, another man was denied ptarmigan, and a woman[1] at Nuwŭk was not allowed to eat "earth food," that is, anything which grew upon the ground. Lieut. Ray also mentions a man who was forbidden bear's flesh.[2]

We observed some traces of the superstition concerning the heads of seals and other marine animals taken in the chase, which has been noticed elsewhere. Crantz says:[3] "The heads of seals must not be fractured, nor must they be thrown into the sea, but be piled in a heap before the door,[4] that the souls of the seals may not be enraged and scare their brethren from the coast." And Capt. Parry found that at Winter Island they carefully preserved the heads of all the animals killed during the winter, except two or three of the walrus which he obtained with great difficulty. The natives told him that they were to be thrown into the sea in the summer, but at Iglulik they readily sold them before the summer arrived.[5]

I tried very hard to get a full series of skulls from the seals taken at Utkiavwĭñ in the winter of 1882–'83, but though I frequently asked the natives to bring them over for sale, they never did so, till at last one young woman promised to bring me all I wanted at the price of half a pound of gunpowder.a skull. Nevertheless, she brought over only two or three at that price. We did not observe what was done with the skulls, but frequently observed quantities of the smaller bones of the seals carefully tucked away in the crevices of the ice at some distance from the shore. We had comparatively little difficulty in obtaining skulls of the walrus, but I observed that the bottom of Tûseráru, the little pond at the edge of the village, was covered with old walrus skulls, as if they had been deposited there for years. The superstition appears to be in full force among the Chukches, who live near the place where the *Vega* wintered. Nordenskjöld was unable to purchase a pair of fresh walrus heads at the first village he visited, though the tusks were offered for sale the next day[6] and at Pitlekaj.[7] "Some prejudice * * * prevented the Chukches from parting with the heads of the seal, though * * * we offered a high price for them. 'Irgatti' (to-morrow) was the usual answer. But the promise was never kept."

Amulets.—Like the Greenlanders[8] and other Eskimos, they place great reliance on amulets or talismans, which are carried on the person, in the boat, or even inserted in weapons, each apparently with some

[1] Report Point Barrow Expedition, p. 46.

[2] Compare Rink, Tales, etc., p. 64; Crantz, vol. 1, p. 215, and Parry, 2d voyage, p. 548: "Seal's flesh is forbidden, for instance, in one disease, that of the walrus in the other; the heart is denied to some, and the liver to others."

[3] Vol. 1, p. 216.

[4] Beechey saw the skulls of seals and other animals kept in piles round the houses at Hotham Inlet (Voyage, p. 259).

[5] Second Voyage, p. 510.

[6] Vega, vol. 1, p. 435.

[7] Vega, vol. 2, p. 137.

[8] John Davis describes the Greenlanders in 1586 as follows: "They are idolaters, and have images great store, which they wore about them, and in their boats, which we suppose they worship." (Hakluyt, Voyages, etc., 1589, p. 782.)

specific purpose, which indeed we learned in the case of some of those in the collection. Like the amulets of the Greenlanders, they appear to be [1] "certain animals or things which had belonged to or been in contact with certain persons (e. g., the people of ancient times, or fortunate hunters) or supernatural beings," and "objects which merely by their appearance recalled the effect expected from the amulet, such as figures of various objects." To the latter class belong the rudely flaked flint images of whales, already mentioned, and probably many of the other small images of men and animals already described, especially those fitted with holes for strings to hang them up by.

FIG. 421.—Whale flaked from glass.

The flint whale is a very common amulet, intended, as we understood, to give good luck in whaling, and is worn habitually by many of the men and boys under the clothes, suspended around the neck by a string. The captain and harpooner of a whaling crew also wear them as pendants on the fillets already described, and on the breast of the jacket. We obtained five of these objects, all of very nearly the same shape, but of different materials and varying somewhat in size. Fig. 421 represents one of these (No. 56703 [208] from Utkiavwiñ) made of a piece of hard colorless glass, probably a fragment of a ship's "deadlight." It is rather roughly flaked into a figure of a "bowhead" whale, 3·4 inches long, as seen from above and very much flattened with exaggerated flukes. The flippers were rudely indicated in the outline, but the left one is broken off.

No. 89613 [771] from Utkiavwiñ is a very similar image, 2·4 inches long, which perhaps is of the same material, though it may be made of

FIG. 422.—Whale flaked from red jasper.

rock crystal. No. 56707 [159] from Utkiavwiñ is a very small whale (1·4 inches long), chipped in large flakes out of a water-worn pebble of smoky quartz, while No. 89577 [939] Fig. 422, from the same village, which is a trifle larger (2 inches long), is made of dark crimson jasper. The large black flint whale, No. 56683 [61], also from Utkiavwiñ, which is 3·9 inches long, is the rudest of all the figures of the whales. It is precisely the shape of the blade of a skin scraper, except for the roughly indicated flukes.

Fig. 423 (No. 89524 [1299] from Utkiavwiñ) is a rude wooden image of the same animal, 3½ inches long, very broad and flat-bellied. It is

---

[1] Rink, Tales, etc., p. 52.

smoothly carved and has a fragment of sky-blue glass inlaid to represent the left eye and a bit of iron pyrites for the right. The flukes have been split wholly off and fastened on with a lashing of narrow whalebone passing through a vertical hole in the "small" and round the edge of the flukes. The flukes themselves have been split across and appear to have been doweled together. This shows that the owner attached considerable value to the object, or he would not have taken the trouble to mend it when another could have been so easily whittled out. In the middle of the belly is an oblong cavity, containing something which probably adds greater power to the charm. What this is can not be seen, as a band of sealskin with the hair shaved off has been shrunk on round the hinder half of the body and secured by a seam on the right side. A double turn of sinew braid is knotted round the middle of the body, leaving two ends which are tied together in a loop, showing that this object was meant to be attached somewhere about the person.

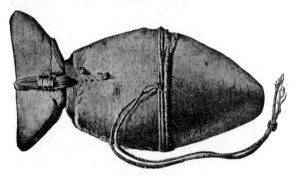

Fig. 423.—Ancient whale amulet, of wood.

To this class also probably belong the skins or pieces of animals worn as amulets, probably with a view of obtaining the powers of the particular animal, as in so many cases in the stories related in Rink's Tales and Traditions. We frequently saw men wearing at the belt bunches of the claws of the bear or wolverine, or the metacarpal bones of the wolf.[1] The head or beak of the gull or raven[2] is also a common personal amulet, and one man wore a small dried flounder.[3]

We collected a number of these animal amulets to be worn on the person, but only succeeded in learning the special purpose of one of them, No. 89532 [1307], from Utkiavwĭñ, which was said to be intended to give good luck in deer hunting. It is a young unbranched antler of a reindeer, 6 inches long, and apparently separated from the skull at the "bur," with the "velvet" skin still adhering, though most of the hair is worn off except at the tip. A bit of sinew is tied round the base.

No. 89522 [1573], from Utkiavwĭñ, is an amulet consisting of the last

[1] Parry mentions bones of the wolverine worn as amulets at Fury and Hecla's Strait (second voyage, p. 497).

[2] Compare the Greenland story told by Rink (Tales, etc., p. 195), when the man who has a gull for his amulet is able to fly home from sea because the gull seeks his prey far out at sea, while the one whose amulet is a raven can not, because this bird seeks his prey landward. Such an amulet as the latter would probably be chosen with a view to making a man a successful deer hunter.

[3] Compare the Greenland story, where a salmon amulet makes a man too slippery to be caught by his pursuers. (Rink Tales, etc., p. 182.)

three joints of the foot of a reindeer fawn, with the skin and hoof and about 1½ inches of tendon attached behind, through a hole in the end of which is knotted about 3 inches of seal thong. No. 89525 [1314] from the same village, is a precisely similar charm. No. 89699 [779] from Utkavwĭñ, is the subfossil incisor tooth of some ruminant with a hole drilled through the root for a string to hang it up by. It was said to be the tooth of the " ug'ru'nû," a large animal, long extinct. As the natives said, " Here on the land are none, only the bones remain." No. 89743 [1110], from Utkiavwĭñ, is a molar tooth of the same animal, probably, weathered and old, with a hole freshly drilled through one root and a long piece of sinew braid with the ends knotted together looped into it. There are also in the collection two very old teeth which probably were inclosed in little sacks of skin and worn as amulets.

No. 89698 [1580], from Utkiavwĭñ, is the tusk of a very young walrus, only 2½ inches long, and No. 89452 [1148] from Utkiavwĭñ, is the canine tooth of a polar bear. No. 56547 [656], from the same village, is a similar tooth.[1]

The only amulet attached to a weapon, which we collected, is the tern's bill, already alluded to, placed under the whalebone lashing on the seal-spear, No. 89910 [1694]. Perhaps the idea of this charm is that the spear should plunge down upon the seal with as sure an aim as the tern does upon its prey.[2]

A number of amulets of this class are always carried in the whaling-umiak. I have already mentioned the wolf-skulls, stuffed ravens and eagles, fox-tails[3] and bunches of feathers used for this purpose. Most of these charms are parts of some rapacious animal or bird, but parts of other animals seem to have some virtue on these occasions.

For instance, I noticed the axis vertebra of a seal in one whaling-umiak, and we collected a rudely stuffed skin of a godwit (Limosa lapponica baueri), which, we were informed, was "for whales." This specimen (No. 89526 [1328], Fig. 424, from Utkiavwĭñ) is soiled and ragged, and has a stick thrust through the neck to hold it out. The neck is wrapped around with a narrow strip of whalebone and some coarse thread, part of which serves to lash on a slip of wood, apparently to splice the stick inside. A bit of white man's string is passed around the body and tied in a loop to hang it up by. This charm is perhaps to keep the boat from capsizing, since Crantz says that the Greenlanders "like to fasten to their kajak a model of it * * * or only a dead

---

[1] Compare Kumlien, Contributions, p. 45. "Another charm of great value to the mother who has a young babe is the canine tooth of the polar bear. This is used as a kind of clasp to a seal-skin string, which passes round the body and keeps the breasts up. Her milk supply cannot fail while she wears this. (Cumberland Gulf.)

[2] Compare the story in Rink's Tales and Traditions (p. 445), where the kaiak, which had a piece of sheldrake fastened into the bow for an amulet, went faster than the sheldrake flies.

[3] Compare Crantz, vol. 1, p. 216. "The boat [for whaling] must have a fox's head in front, and the harpoon be furnished with an eagle's beak." The latter statement is interesting in connection with the tern's bill on the seal harpoon, from Point Barrow, already referred to.

sparrow or snipe, or a bit of wood, stone, some feathers or hair, that they may not overset" (vol. 1, p. 216), and perhaps the bone of a marine animal, like the seal, is to protect the crew from drowning should the boat upset, after all.

No. 89529 [1150] from Utkiavwĭñ is a bunch of feathers to be carried in the boat. It consists of nine wing feathers of the golden eagle, four tied in a bunch with a bit of sinew round the quills, four tied up with one end of the short bit of seal thong which serves to tie the whole bundle together, one of which has all the light-colored parts of the feather stained with red ocher, and a single feather shaft carefully wrapped up in a piece of entrail and wound spirally with a piece of sinew braid.

No. 89527–8 [1327] from Utkiavwĭñ is the charm which will secure good success in deerhunting if it is hung up outside of the snow house in which the family is encamped. It consists of two roughly stuffed skins of the black bellied plover (Charadrius squatarola), each with a

⅓

FIG. 424.—Amulet of whaling; stuffed godwit.

stick run through the body so that one end supports the neck and the other the tail, and the necks wound with sinew. One has no head. A string of sinew braid is tied around the body of each, so as to leave a free end at the back, to which is fastened a little cross piece of bone, by which it may be secured to a becket. Like the rest of the amulets in the collection this has evidently seen service, being very old, worn, and faded.

The other class of amulets, namely objects which have belonged to or been in contact with certain persons or supernatural beings, or I may

FIG. 425.—Amulet consisting of ancient jade adz.

add apparently certain localities, is represented by a number of specimens. To the custom of using such things as amulets, we undoubtedly owe the preservation of most of the ancient weapons and other implements, especially those made of wood, bone, or other perishable substances, like the ancient harpoon heads already described, one of which, No. 89544 [1419], is still attached to the belt on which it was worn.

Fig. 425, No. 56668 [308], from Utkiavwĭñ is one of the ancient black

jade adzes 5·1 inches, slung with thong and whalebone, making a becket
by which it can be hung up. We did not learn the history of this
amulet, which at the time of collecting it was supposed to be a net
sinker. There would, however, be no reason for using so valuable an
object for such a purpose, when a common beach pebble would do just
as well, unless it was intended as a charm to insure success in fishing.
It may even have been carried as a charm on the person, since we
afterwards saw a still more bulky object used for such a purpose.

Such an object seems rather heavy to be carried on the person, but
a well known man in Utkiavwĭñ always carried with him when he went
sealing a large pear-shaped stone, which must
have weighed upwards of two pounds, suspended
somewhere about his person. It is not unlikely
that this stone acquired its virtue as an amulet
from having been a sinker used by some lucky
fisherman in former time or in a distant country. Mr. H. W. Henshaw has already referred to
the resemblance of this amulet to the plummet-
like "medicine stones" of some of our Indians.[1]

FIG. 426.—Little box containing
amulet for whaling.

Fig. 426, (No. 89534 [1306] from Utkiavwĭñ) is an amulet for success
in whaling. It consists of three little irregular water-worn fragments
of amber carefully wrapped in a bit of parchment and inclosed in a little wooden box 1½ inches long, made of two semicylindrical bits of cottonwood, with the flat faces hollowed out and put together and fastened up by three turns of sinew braid round the middle, tied in a loose
knot. The box is old and brown from age and handling. We heard
of other pieces of amber and earth ("nuna") worn as amulets, wrapped
up in bits of leather and hung on the belt.

No. 89533 [1247], from Utkiavwĭñ, is simply a nearly square pebble, 1·4 inches long, of dark red jasper, slung in a bit of sinew braid
so that it can be hung on the belt. Fig. 427
(No. 89525 [1308] from Utkiavwĭñ) is some small
object, placed in the center of the grain side of a
square bit of white sealskin, the edges of which
are folded up around it and tied tightly round
with deer sinew, so as to make a little round
knob. I collected this amulet, and was particularly informed how it was to be used. If it be
fastened on the right shoulder it will insure success in taking ducks with the "bolas." Fig. 428
(No. 89535 [1244] from Utkiavwĭñ) is an amulet
whose history we did not learn. It is a little ob-

FIG. 427.—Amulet for
catching fowl with bolas.

long box 3·3 inches long, carved from a block of cottonwood, with a
flat cover tied on with nine turns of sinew braid, and contains twenty-
one dried humble-bees, which it was said came from the river Kulu-

grua. The natives have a great dread, apparently superstitious, of these bees and the large gadflies (Œstens tarandi), one of which I have seen scatter half a dozen people. A man one day caught one of these, and whittled out a little box of wood, in which he shut the insect up and tied it up with a shred of sinew, telling Capt. Herendeen that it was "tueñamun," for "tueña."

FIG. 428.—Box of dried bees—amulet.

A small lump of indurated gravel (No. 56725) [273] was one day brought over from Utkiavwĭñ, with the story that it was a "medicine" for driving away the ice. The man who uses this charm stands on the high bank at the village, and breaking off grains of the gravel throws them seaward. This will cause the ice to move off from the shore.

The essential identity of the amulets of the Point Barrow natives with those used by the Eskimo elsewhere is shown by the following passages from other writers. Egede says:[1]

A Superstition very common among them is to load themselves with Amulets or Pomanders, dangling about their Necks and Arms, which consist in some Pieces of old Wood, Stones or Bones, Bills and Claws of Birds, or Anything else which their Fancy suggests to them.

Crantz says:[2]

They are so different in the amulets or charms they hang on people, that one laughs at another's. These powerful preventives consist in a bit of old wood hung around their necks, or a stone, or a bone, or a beak or claw of a bird, or else a leather strap tied round their forehead, breast, or arm.

Parry speaks[3] of what he supposes were amulets at Iglulik, consisting of teeth of the fox, wolf, and musk-ox, bones of the "kablĕĕarioo" (supposed to be the wolverine), and foxes' noses. Kumlien says[4] that at Cumberland Gulf, "among the many superstitious notions, the wearing of charms about the person is one of the most curious. These are called *angoouk or amusit*, and may be nothing but pieces of bone or wood, birds' bills or claws, or an animal's teeth or skin." A little girl "had a small envelope of sealskin that was worn on the back of her inside jacket" containing two small stones.

Such little pockets of skin sewed to the inner jacket are very common at Point Barrow, but we did not succeed in any case in learning their contents. At Kotzebue Sound, Beechey saw ravens' skins on which the natives set a high value, while the beaks and claws of these birds were attached to their belts and headbands.[5] Petitot describes[6] the amulets used in the Mackenzie district, in the passage already quoted, as "défroques empaillées de corbeau, de faucon ou d'hermine." It is

[1] Greenland, p. 194.
[2] History of Greenland, vol. 1, p. 216.
[3] Second voyage, p. 497.
[4] Contributions, p. 45.
[5] Voyage, p. 333.
[6] Monographie, etc., p. xv.

not likely that the use of these is confined to the women, as his words, "Elles y portent," would seem to imply. Among the sedentary Chukches of Siberia amulets were seen consisting of wooden forks and wood or ivory carvings.[1] A wolf's skull, hung up by a thong; the skin, together with the whole cartilaginous portion of a wolf's nose, and a flat stone, are also mentioned.[2] Capt. Holm also found wonderfully similar customs among the East Greenlanders. He says,[3] "bære alle Folk Amuletter af de mest forskjelligartede Ting" to guard against sickness and to insure long life, and also for specific purposes. The men wear them slung round the neck or tied round the upper arm, the women in their knot of hair or "i Snippen foran paa Pelsen."

---

[1] Nordenskiöld, Vega, vol. 2, p. 126.
[2] Vega, vol. 1, p. 503.
[3] Geografisk Tidskrift, vol. 8, p. 94.